THE
Time Out
PARIS
GUIDE

The *Time Out Paris Guide* is more than a book for tourists. It's lively and informative and includes information that covers all of Paris, not just the city-centre attractions. We have listed the places to see (and be seen in) and the places to avoid. Unlike the majority of guides around, we are not afraid of giving honest and opinionated reviews of the sights, the nightclubs and every other aspect of Parisian life. We aim to ensure that by the time you've used the guide, you'll know Paris like a Parisian.

For eight years, *Paris Passion*, the sister company to London's *Time Out*, has been documenting all aspects of life in Paris, from museums, cabaret and shopping to the theatre, bars and restaurants. If something is worth seeing (or staying away from) in the city, we know about it. It must be stressed that the information we give you is impartial. No organization or enterprise is listed in this guide because its owner or manager has advertised in our publications. That's why our guides are so successful and well respected. If you disagree with our opinions, we want to know. Write to us and let us know what you think about the places you have visited. Make your views count: we take readers' comments very seriously. Welcome to *Time Out's* Paris.

THE Time Out PARIS GUIDE

Penguin Books

PENGUIN BOOKS

Published by the Penguin Group
27 Wrights Lane, London W8 5TZ, England
Viking Penguin Inc., 40 West 23rd Street, New York, New York 10010, USA
Penguin Books Australia Ltd, Ringwood, Victoria, Australia
Penguin Books Canada Ltd, 2801 John Street, Markham, Ontario, Canada L3R
1B4
Penguin Books (NZ) Ltd, 182–190 Wairau Road, Auckland 10, New Zealand

Penguin Books Ltd, Registered Offices: Harmondsworth, Middlesex, England

First published 1990
10 9 8 7 6 5 4 3 2 1

Made and printed in Great Britain by
Richard Clay Ltd, Bungay, Suffolk

Contents

Editor
Katja Faber

Consultant Editor
Robert Sarner

Edited and designed by
Time Out Publications Limited,
134-146 Curtain Road, London
EC2A 3AR
(729 5959).

Publisher
Tony Elliott
Managing Director
Adele Carmichael
Financial Director
Kevin Ellis
Managing Editor
Hayden Williams

Art Director
Paul Carpenter
Art Editor
Ashleigh Vinall

Advertisement Director
Lesley Gill
Sales Director
Mark Phillips

Cover Illustration
Lo Cole

Introduction

This is a **Paris Guide** for *all* visitors to the French capital: sightseers, weekend trippers, people over on business, shoppers, clubbers, gourmands and art and music lovers. Residents will also find it invaluable for steering them around the parts of Paris they never knew existed, or never dared to investigate. This Guide is a follow-up to our successful *Guide to Paris*, published in Filofax format; and it has been produced with help and advice from the staff and editors of *Paris Passion*, Paris's English-language listings magazine.

The Guide has been written by people who live and work in Paris. Naturally, we've covered all of Paris's famous attractions, but we take a critical look at them. Where other guides simply list, we explain and offer new perspectives on the familiar sights. We're honest about both the sights worth seeing and the ones that are living on hype and reputation.

The 2,000-plus detailed reviews are based on our recent experiences of Paris's attractions, restaurants, shops and places of entertainment. In addition, we review hundreds of lesser-known, unusual and local places in the centre of town and out in the suburbs. Whenever you visit Paris, you'll be grateful for our chapter listing the major events, exhibitions and festivals that happen every year in the capital. And, if the city ever gets you down, we suggest a few of the best day trips out of town.

WHO ARE WE?

For over 20 years, *Time Out* has been London's main listings magazine. We also produce guides to all aspects of life in London. In producing the **Paris Guide**, we've drawn on this experience and the expertise we gained from producing the best-selling *Time Out London Guide*. This **Paris Guide** is the latest addition to a series, published by Penguin, that also includes the *Time Out New York Guide*.

The **Paris Guide** will be revised and updated biennially. Most guide books are only re-edited once every few years. As well as being a good read, we've tried to make this book as useful as possible. Addresses, telephone numbers, opening times, admission prices and discounts are all printed in full; details of credit cards that are accepted are given. And, as far as possible, we've given details of facilities, services and events.

All the information we list was checked and correct at time of writing – but please bear in mind that owners and managers can change their arrangements at any time. We urge you to phone, before you set out, to check opening times, the dates of exhibitions, admission fees and other important details.

PRICES

The prices we've listed throughout the Guide should be used as guidelines. Fluctuating exchange rates and inflation can cause prices, in shops especially, to change rapidly. Occasionally, you may encounter a rip-off, so if prices or services somewhere vary greatly from those we've quoted, ask whether there's a good reason. If not, go elsewhere. Then, please let us know. We try to give the best and most up-to-date advice, so we always want to hear if you've been overcharged or badly treated.

CREDIT CARDS

In the listing entries marked **Credit**, we've used the following abbreviations: **Airplus; AmEx:** American Express; **CB:** Carte Bleue (linked to MasterCard); **DC:** Diners Club; **EC:** Eurocheque/card; **JCB/JCT:** Japanese credit cards; **MC:** MasterCard (linked to Access); **TC:** Travellers' Cheques in any currency accepted; **£TC, $TC, FTC** and so on means that Travellers' Cheques in sterling, US dollars, French francs, or other specified currencies are accepted; **V:** Visa/Barclaycard.

Sightseeing

The insider's guide to the sights, monuments and tourist traps that every visitor to Paris needs to see.

All of the following – the Pompidou Centre, the Eiffel Tower, the Arc de Triomphe – are the buildings, museums and monuments that every visitor associates with the city. You'll find them covered in greater depth in other chapters of the Guide; so use this section as a quick reference to the places you really should see. Experienced tourists will know that there's no point in trying to see or do too much in one trip; console yourself with the thought that you'll just have to come back to Paris another time.

Central Tourist Information Office

127 avenue des Champs-Elysées, 75008 Paris (47.23.61.72). Metro Etoile or George V. **Open** 9am-8pm Mon-Sat; 9am-6pm Sun. Here you will find brochures, maps and information on the sights and events in Paris, the suburbs, and the rest of France.

Arc de Triomphe

place Charles de Gaulle (access via undergorund passage), 75008 Paris (43.80.31.31). Metro Etoile/bus 22, 30, 31, 52, 92. **Open** 10am-5.30pm (5pm in winter) daily; closed public holidays. **Admission** *to panorama platform:* 22F adults; 5F under-17s; 12F OAPs, students.
A potent symbol of Paris, the Arc (*see picture and caption*) was commissioned by Napoleon in 1806 as a homage to (his own) martial victories. A modest 50m (164ft) tall, 45m (148ft) wide and surrounded by a vast frieze, it cost 10 million francs and was only finished in 1836 (*see chapter* **Empires & Rebellions**). In 1920 the body of an unknown soldier and an eternal flame (kindled daily at 6pm) were installed to commemorate the dead of World War I. Since 1923 this has been the site for national events, such as the celebrations for the 1944 liberation, Bastille Day (*see* **Paris by Season**) and the 1989 bicentennial of the Revolution. After passing through the subway – don't tempt the manic traffic – you can reach the top of the arch and the panoramic view by lift or steps via a long queue. *See also chapter* **The War.**

Place de la Bastille

75012 Paris. Metro Bastille.
Nothing remains of the infamous Bastille prison which, in July 1789, was stormed by the assembled forces of plebeian revolt. Though its reputation was largely unwarranted, it provided the rebels with gunpowder and gave the insurrection momentum, still remaining for most people the historical catalyst for the Terror and overthrow of the monarchy. (La Conciergerie, *see below,* was actually the more important of revolutionary prisons and the one where people such as Marie Antoinette and Danton would have paced before facing the Black Widow, or guillotine.) The prison was demolished within a week of the Revolution and today the July column, with a statue of *Liberté* (*see chapter* **Empires & Rebellions**) on top of it, is all that stands in the middle of the square, commemorating the Parisians killed during the riots of July 1830. *See also chapter* **The Revolution.**

Bastille Opera

Place de la Bastille, 75012 Paris (40.01.19.70). Metro Bastille. **Open** several tours daily, phone 11am-3am Mon-Sat for details.
The recently built Bastille Opera (*see* **picture and caption**) has been dogged by controversy from the start. Some say it's a stroke of socialist genius to locate an opera in a traditionally working class *quartier,* others suggest that it's a typical bit of Mitterrandish skulduggery, an extravagant piece of diversionary propaganda. Although the area undoubtedly needed a face-lift, the very modern, glass-encased structure has little in common with the surrounding architecture. It's been called the world's largest public toilet; you'll have to make up your own mind. *See also chapter* **Music: Classical & Opera.**

Bois de Boulogne

75016 Paris. Metro Porte d'Auteuil, Porte Dauphine, Porte Maillot. **Open** dawn-dusk daily.
The Bois was a private royal park for many centuries until Louis XIV flung the gates open to the public. But the place didn't become fashionable until the nineteenth century, when Baron Haussmann (who created many of Paris's boulevards and squares, *see chapter* **Empires & Rebellions**) landscaped the area. It's now immensely popular with Parisians. Attractions include restaurants and cafés, Le Jardin d'Acclimatation (a great play-area for children, *see chapter* **Children**), the Musée National des Arts et Traditions Populaires (a museum about industry and the industrial revolution, *see chapter* **Museums**), plus the Longchamp and

There's a museum about the monument at the top of the **Arc de Triomphe,** *but people come for the view over the 12 avenues radiating from place Charles de Gaulle, known as l'Etoile (the star). A map pinpoints the city's sights.*

Auteuil racecourses. There's also mini-golf, bowling and biking, as well as boating on the Lac Inférieur (*see* **picture and caption**). And, for those who prefer their sport sitting down, the Roland Garros tennis stadium is home to the French Open; *see chapter* **Sport & Fitness** for all. Go at the right time of year, and you'll find beautiful floral displays in the Parc de Bagatelle, famed for its rose gardens and glass-houses. There's also the less well-known Jardin Albert Kahn, near Pont de Saint Cloud. This garden is actually private, but the owner opens it to the public in spring and summer. If you're still lingering in the Bois when darkness falls, you'll find that the place has been taken over by prostitutes and transvestites.

Boating lake. Car park (south-east corner). Horse-racing. Restaurants and cafés. Tennis courts.

Bois de Vincennes

75020 Paris. Metro Chateau de Vincennes, Porte-Dorée/bus 46, 56, 86. **Open** dawn-dusk daily.

The Royal Forest of Vincennes was designed during the Second Empire by architects Alphand and Barillet Deschamps. Laid out in the style of an English park, the Bois is famous for its racecourse and for the Château de Vincennes. The Château was

An island of greenery, the **Jardin des Plantes** *also houses museums and a zoo.*

built in the twelfth century and has been, variously, a residence of Louis XIV, a prison and an army barracks. There are numerous other attractions, including: a zoo; a fine hot-house; Lake Daumesnil, where you can hire boats and bikes (*see chapters* **Children; Sport & Fitness**); and the Buddhist Temple of Paris, which contains a nine metre (30ft) high statue of Buddha and an Indo-Chinese memorial (*see chapter* **Survival**). The zoo has an exhaustive menagerie of exotic animals, all placed in settings which re-create their original habitats. If you feel like something more relaxing, head for the Paris Floral Garden, which is close to the Château and covers 70 acres.

Arboretum. Boating lakes. Boules. Cafés. Riding school. Zoo.

Champs Elysées

75008 Paris. Metro Concorde, Champs Elysées-Clémenceau, Franklin D Roosevelt, George V, Charles de Gaulle-Etoile.

The avenue of the Champs Elysées is still – just – fixed in French hearts and minds as the symbolic centre of the nation. So don't be surprised when you hear a great deal of grumbling about its run-down, shabby state and the fact that it's just a sordid shadow of its former self. Colonized by fast-food emporiums, retailing chains and anything processed, the famous thoroughfare linking the Arc de Triomphe with the place de la Concorde is now exclusively targeted at the hordes of tourists who flood the area. Eager businessmen linger at the entrance to the Lido (*see chapter* **Cabaret**), but the street has clung onto a tarnished grandeur that no amount of cut-price capitalism can entirely pollute. In the first half of this century it was the scene of Republican demonstrations and parades, the Victor Hugo funeral parade and the World War I departure parade. Hitler's army got a silently hostile reception in 1940, marching along the same route the Prussian invaders had taken in the previous century.

Planned as one of the many Grands Projets *by* Mitterrand *to celebrate the Bicentennial, the* **Bastille Opera** *echoes the President's love of the monumental translated into his own futuristic style.*

But the Champs Elysées was also a scene of joy in two world war victory parades. The English Gardens at the bottom, the Grand Palais (*see chapter* **Art Galleries**), the Petit Palais (with the Museum of Fine Arts), the Palais de la Découverte with the planetarium (*see chapter* **Museums** for both) and the Arc de Triomphe (*above*) are some of the Champs Elysées' major highlights. Better still, just amble around, ignore the hustlers and explore the many squares and parks which flank the lower half of the avenue. *See also chapter* **The Right Bank.**

La Conciergerie
Quai de l'Horloge, 750001 Paris (43.54.30.06). Metro Cité. **Open** *summer.* 9.30am-6pm daily; *winter.* 10am-4.30pm daily. **Admission** 22F adults; 12F children. **No credit cards.**
Viewed from the Right Bank, La Conciergerie (in what is now the Palais de Justice *below*) looks just like the forbidding medieval fortress and prison which it once

was. In fact, much of the gloomy façade was added later by nineteenth-century, neo-Gothic restorers. Major figures who sweated here before facing the chop include Marie Antoinette, Danton and Robespierre. The Chapelle des Girondins contains some grim souvenirs of the Terror, such as Marie Antoinette's crucifix and a guillotine blade, ready to replace its blunted predecessor, but apart from these, the Conciergerie doesn't hold a great deal for tourists. If you're interested in architecture you'll like the Salle des Gens d'Arme, an impressive example of late-Gothic style; otherwise gaze at the clock of the Tour de l'Horloge from the outside. Built in 1370 and carefully restored, it's the oldest clock in Paris. *See* **picture and caption.**
See also chapters **The Middle Ages & Renaissance; The Revolution.**

L'Ecole Militaire
avenue de la Motte-Picquet, 75007 Paris. Metro Ecole Militaire.
The façade is the only part of this fine eigh-

teenth-century building that you'll be able to see, unless you're planning on joining the French military. Napoleon was a cadet here at the age of 15 and passed out as a 'lieutenant with promise'. Today, the building is home to the School of Advanced War Studies and the Institute of Advanced National Defence Studies. Behind the Military College are the buildings housing the Ministry of Health and UNESCO.

Eiffel Tower
Quai Branly, 75007 Paris. Metro Trocadéro and walk across Pont d'Ilena/RER Champs de Mars. **Open** 10am-midnight Mon-Fri; 10am-11pm Sat, Sun. **Admission** *by lift:* 45F adults; 23F under-16s.
When this iron tower was built in 1889 for the World Fair on the centenary of the Revolution, it was the tallest building in the world at 300m (984ft). It's now 321m (1,053ft) with its aerial. The view of it from the Trocadéro is monumental, but the distorted aspect from its base dramatically

The spot for many a Parisian's Sunday outing, the **Bois de Boulogne** *provides numerous opportunities for unwinding. An afternoon's boating on the Lac Inferieur will rest the weariest of legs.*

shows off the graceful ironwork of Gustave Eiffel (*see* **picture and caption**). After a tediously long wait (it gets four million visitors a year), the climb up to the first platform is a killer. But the panoramas from the platforms are progressively more amazing: from the top you can see for 67km (42 miles) on a good day. The queue is not as long at night, when the city lights against the River Seine live up to their romantic image. Several restaurants on the tower get progressively better – and more expensive. *See also chapters* **The Left Bank; The Third Republic.**

Le Forum des Halles

rue Rambuteau, 75001 Paris (40.39.98.74). *Metro Les Halles.* **Open** shops usually open 10.30am-7.30pm Mon-Sat.

Designed by architects Vasconi and Penchreach, Le Forum des Halles is the largest urban development in Paris since the Second Empire, transforming what was the Parisian wholesale fruit and veg market into a huge, four-level, underground city: about 200 stores, cafés and restaurants, cinemas (*see chapter* **Film**) and sports centres (*see chapter* **Sport & Fitness**). There are some great shops – Londoners will be reminded of Covent Garden, although this complex replaces the demolished iron market arcades. The architects were forced to build downwards, because the RER station was so deep and so as to not clash with the surrounding area; but there's a glass dome which lets in some natural light. Despite these original features, the development has drawn criticism for being unimaginative. Les Halles contains various works of art and you should at least try to see the pink marble statue, 'Pygmalion'. *See* **picture and caption.** *See also chapter* **The Right Bank.**

Le Grand Palais

1-3 Avenue Général Eisenhower, 75008 Paris (42.89.54.10/recorded information 42.56.09.24). Metro Champs Elysées-Clémenceau. **Open** 10am-8pm Mon, Thur, Sun; 10am-10pm Wed. **Admission** 32F adults; 21F 13-25s, OAPs, students; free under-13s.

The **Champs Elysées** *have traditionally been used as the route for major military processions, including the one on Bastille Day. Despite overwhelming commercialism on the avenue itself, the surrounding area retains some of its former elegance.*

The Grand Palace was built for the Universal Exhibition of 1900 and covers a wide tract of land between the Champs Elysées and the Seine. You can't miss the immense glass, canopied roof – it's 43m

Medieval fortress and prison, **la Conciergerie** *retains its imposing façade.*

(141ft) high. The vast hall includes a lavish mosaic frieze and a central staircase spiralling underneath the glass canopy. The Palace is still used for exhibitions such as the National Automobile show or Household Equipment show; and it's also a cultural centre, hosting successful temporary art exhibitions (*see chapter* **Art Galleries**). Opposite the Grand Palais is the

*Many critics originally thought the **Eiffel Tower** vulgar, but there's no escaping its position as the popular symbol of Paris. Incredibly, though, only its telecommunications role saved it from demolition in 1909.*

Les Invalides

Esplanade des Invalides, 75007 Paris (45.55.37.67). Metro Invalides, Varenne, Latour-Maubourg. **Open** various buildings open different times, phone for information.

Made up of a collection of simply proportioned and classically styled buildings, Les Invalides exudes military tradition and atmosphere. The huge Hôtel des Invalides (constructed 1671-1676 by Louis XIV) was first built as a military hospital for the king's soldiers. He also built a retirement home for wounded soldiers that at one time housed 4,000 to 6,000 invalids (hence the name); *see also chapter* **Ancien Régime**. Other buildings on the site include the Army Museum, the Church of Saint Louis and the Church of the Dome. The Army Museum has a staggering display of weapons, maps and war-time paraphernalia from the Ancienne Monarchie to the two World Wars (*see chapter* **Museums**). The Church of the Dome is a typical, highly-decorated example of French architecture from Louis XIV's time (*see chapter* **The Left Bank**). It was re-gilded in 1989 and looks magnificent against a blue sky. Underneath the neo-classical Dome there's a circular crypt containing a small red porphyry sarcophagus of Napoleon. The Church of Saint-Louis is also known as the Church of the Soldiers. An austere, stone building, decorated with captured flags, it has a crypt filled with buried soldiers. On a more peaceful note, the organ is especially pleasing and attracts music lovers. A great deal to see in a small space – well worth a visit.

*Destroyed during the Commune uprising of 1871, the **Hôtel de Ville** was rebuilt in neo-Renaissance style.*

Musée du Petit-Palais, also built for the Exhibition, is now an art museum (*see chapter* **Museums**).

Hôtel de Ville

place de l'Hôtel de Ville (main public entrance at 3 Rue de Lobau), 75004 Paris (42.76.40.40/tour information 42.76.59.28)). Metro Hôtel de Ville. **Open** tours 10.30am Mon (phone to check).

The Hôtel de Ville is located on the Right Bank of the Seine, almost opposite Nôtre Dame cathedral. The fountains and plaza in front of its stately façade make it a pleasant place to stroll around. The Hôtel de Ville (town hall) dates back to 1260, but is best known for the part it played in the Revolution. King Louis XVI was received here with all due pomp and ceremony in 1789; but three years later, it was Danton, Marat and Robespierre who made the Hôtel de Ville its seat of government. Again, in early 1871 a revolutionary government made the Hôtel de Ville their base but, in May 1871, the place was recaptured and wrecked after savage fighting. In August 1871 the first municipal government of Paris was elected and the Hôtel de Ville was reconstructed in a neo-Renaissance style. Some find the ornate exterior rather overstated. Guided tours take visitors to view the seven types of wood on the dining-room floor, the 24 lavish chandeliers throughout the building and the statue on the roof symbolic of the city of Paris. The mayor's office is stacked with recent works of art. *See* **picture and caption**. *See also chapter* **The Third Republic**.

Jardin des Plantes
rue Cuvier, 75005 Paris (40.79.30.00).
Metro Gare d'Austerlitz, Jussieu, Mange/bus 24. **Open** dawn-dusk daily.
Founded in 1626, the Jardin des Plantes is the Parisian equivalent of London's Kew Gardens. About 10,000 species of plants flourish in the gardens and conservatories, including the oldest tree in the capital, which is apparently over 300 years old. The buildings and pavilions have been allowed to crumble over the years, although an effort has been made recently to restore and renovate some parts. The park also contains a zoo, an aquarium, a reptile house, a maze and a natural history museum (*see chapters* **Museums; Children**). *See* **picture and caption**. *See also chapter* **The Left Bank**.

Jardin du Luxembourg
main entrance on boulevard Saint Michel, 75006 Paris (42.34.20.00). Metro Saint Michel. **Open** dawn-dusk daily.
Frenzied Parisians, driven to distraction by the smog and traffic, pour into this formal garden on sunny days. It stretches out in front of the Luxembourg Palace (*see below*) and there are plenty of facilities for active enjoyment, as well as some leafy spots for relaxation. Adults and children can romp about on roller-skates, go-karts, donkeys and even compact cars. Children can enjoy sandpits, slides, roundabouts and they can sail boats on a large circular pond. In more sedate days, artists, poets and writers used to stroll about the park. Nowadays, the main artistic activity is provided by the Theatre des Marionettes, which plays to large crowds on Wednesdays, Saturdays and Sundays between 2.30pm and 3.30pm (*see chapter* **Children**).

The Louvre
rue de Rivoli, 75001 Paris (40.20.51.51). Metro Palais Royal, Louvre. **Open** 9am-9.45pm Mon, Wed; 9am-6pm Thur-Sun. **Admission** 25F adults; 13F 18-25s, students, OAPs; free under-18s.
Born in the library of Louis XIV, this is now the most prestigious art collection housed anywhere under one roof. The flagship of cultural France, the Louvre has assembled work ranging from the sculptured deities of many a lost civilization to a more contemporary range of icons including the *Mona Lisa*, the *Venus de Milo* and Delacroix's *Liberty Leading the People*. The underground approach to the Louvre passes the medieval foundations which are scratched with contemporary graffiti. The controversial glass pyramid by IM Pei, which was added in 1989 by Mitterrand to commemorate France's Bicentennial of the Revolution, now dominates the central courtyard. The new main entrance below makes it a lot easier to find your way around the galleries. Also in the central courtyard is the Arc de Triomphe du Carrousel, which was erected in 1806 and appeared under the guidance of one of the Louvre's great patrons, Napoleon Bonaparte; *see chapter* **Empires & Rebellions**. The palace itself is the largest in Europe and was the home to successive generations of French monarchs. *See* **picture and caption**. *See also chapter* **Museums**.

Luxembourg Palace
rue de Vaugirard, 75006 Paris (information 42.34.20.00). Metro Odéon. **Open** for visits Sun only, except when being used by the

Senate; phone for details.
Attracted by the perfectly proportioned symmetry of this place, Queen Marie de Medici, the Florentine wife of Henry IV, bought the Luxembourg Palace from François, Duke of Luxembourg, in 1612. The Palace and its grounds (*see above* **Jardins du Luxembourg**) were to remain in royal hands until the revolution of 1789 passed them over to the state. It would later house the French Senate. During World War II, the German High Command built a labyrinth of underground shelters to buffer them from the ire of Bomber Command. *See also chapter* **The Left Bank**.

La Madeleine
place de la Madeleine, 75008 Paris (42.65.52.17). Metro Madeleine. **Open** 7am-7pm Mon-Sat; 7.30am-1.30pm, 3.30-7pm, Sun.
In 1764, the architect Constant d'Ivry designed the church of La Madeleine as a small-scale version of Saint-Louis-des-Invalides (*see above* **Les Invalides**). In 1806,

Napoleon dedicated it to his Grand Army, but because it became a constant focus of revolutionary vandalism, its completion was put off until 1842. Despite the delays, La Madeleine remains both an undiluted tribute to the neo-classicism which fascinated Paris in the early nineteenth century and a favourite resting-point for tourists between the Gare Saint Lazarre and the Place de la Concorde. *See also chapters* **The Right Bank; Empires & Rebellions**.

Le Marais
75004 Paris. Metro Pont Marie, Saint Paul.
Careful restoration and renovation has ensured that this area north of the Ile Saint-Louis has retained much of its original ambience (*see chapter* **The Right Bank**). Buildings from the sixteenth, seventeenth and eighteenth centuries have largely survived speculation, modernization and the corrosive emissions of Parisian traffic. The Place des Vosges (*see* **picture and caption**), the earliest of Paris's planned squares, was completed

A controversial seventies' addition to a previously working class area, the **Forum des Halles** *is just one of the many changes in the quartier. The surrounding streets have been cleaned up and become trendy; many of them are for pedestrians only. Most of the crumbling buildings have undergone massive – and costly – renovation.*

under Louis XIV. It was originally known as the Place Royale and inspired royalty to build lavishly over Le Marais. Many of the hotels were once private mansions, such as the Hôtel Amelot de Bisseuil (*47 rue Vieille-du-Temple*), the Hôtel de Beauvais (*28 rue de Sévigné*) and the Hôtel de Rohan-Soubise (*60 rue des Francs-Bourgeois*). An exhausting but informative tour takes you from building to building explaining ornaments, façades, gardens and the architectural styles which dominate the district; phone the Tourist Office (*47.23.61.72*) for details.

Montmartre
75018 Paris. Metro Abesse, Lamarck-Caulaincourt.
In 250AD the martyred Saint Denis is said to have picked up his decapitated head and walked to the top of *La Butte* (the hill on which Montmartre is centred). The spirit of this indomitable and now canonized torso lives on, despite the influx of prostitutes, their exotic accessories and a less than subtle peddling of sex on many of the main squares. Nowhere else in Paris will you find a vineyard hidden among the neons and there's an annual festival to celebrate the harvest (*see chapter* **Paris by Season**). Although the Sacré Coeur (*see below*) is endlessly beseiged by tour buses discharging wave after wave of excited trippers, a walk

The Gothic masterpiece of **Nôtre Dame** *remains one of Paris's favourite landmarks.*

down one of the many cobbled streets leading away from the basilica exposes a network of unhurried cafés and quiet parks. Montmartre may have peaked artistically in the days of Lautrec and Modigliani, but there's still a current of precocious talent toiling away beyond the marketing of the place du Tertre (*see chapter* **Artistic Paris**). The emphasis may have overtly changed but the *quartier* retains all of its old charm away from the main attractions. *See also chapter* **Village Paris**.

Montmartre Cemetery
20 avenue Rachel, 75018 Paris (43.87.64.24). Metro Clichy, La Fourche, Abbesses. **Open** *winter:* 8am-5.15pm Mon-Sat; 9am-5.15pm Sun; *summer:* 7.30am-5.45pm Mon-Sat; 9am-5.45pm Sun.
First laid out in 1789, this cemetery covers a large area of La Butte with ornate headstones, raised tombs and marble icons. The graveyard's many celebrated residents include Degas, Offenbach and Jouvet.

It took a total of 660 years to build the **Louvre** *and there are now about 400,000 paintings in this massive building, which stretches endlessly along the right bank of the Seine. Try to plan in advance which period or painters you want to see, as the network of corridors, dripping with masterpieces, begins to blur after a couple of miles.*

Montparnasse

75014 and 75015 Paris. Metro Montparnasse-Bienvenue, Vavin.

Named after the Mount Parnassus of ancient Greece, which was the home of the Muses, this *quartier* originally evolved from a disused quarry. The district first began to develop an atmosphere of its own around the time of the Revolution and over the years artists were enticed away from the more celebrated hill of Montmartre. However, change has come to Montparnasse since the halcyon era of the *belle epoque* when Hemingway and Trotsky could be seen hovering around its many bistros and salons de thé (*see chapter* **Artistic Paris**). The rebuilding of the Montparnasse railway station and other nearby developments has eclipsed much of the area's architectural charm. Despite the recent upheaval, the area has more than a few reminders of its gilded past and its existing galleries, museums and thriving café society make a worthwhile diversion. *See also chapter* **The Right Bank.**

Montparnasse Cemetery

3 boulevard Edgar-Quinet, 75014 Paris. Metro Edgar Quinet. **Open** 8am-5.30pm Mon-Fri; 8.30am-5.30pm Sat; 9am-5.30pm Sun, public holidays.

You can view the tomb of many a famous person in this 44-acre cemetery. Look especially for the graves of the writers Baudelaire and Maupassant and the composers César Frank and Saint-Saens. Even if the occupant isn't of interest, many of the monuments and tombs are extraordinary. Brancusi's sculpture, *The Kiss*, is a prime example of some of the fine work in the cemetery. It's a tranquil place in which to while away some sweetly melancholic hours.

Musée d'Orsay

1 rue de Bellechasse, 75007 Paris (40.49.48.14/recorded information 45.49.11.11). Metro Solferino. **Open** 10am-

6pm Tue, Wed, Fri-Sun; 10am-9.15pm Thur. **Admission** 23F adults; 12F 18-25s, OAPs; free under-18s.

Opened in 1986, the Musée d'Orsay (which is on the left bank of the Seine, directly across from the Louvre) was originally a train station. The art dates from 1848 to early twentieth-century and is intended to span the gap between what's covered by the **Louvre** (*see above*) and the Musée National d'Art Moderne at the **Pompidou Centre** (*see below*). The main rooms are devoted to Courbet, Degas, Manet, Puvis, Cézanne, Van Gogh, Gaugin, Rodin and Guimard. Some grumble that the paintings are displayed too close together; certainly, the Impressionist gallery is tucked away on the top floor and is a bit crowded, but the light from the balcony windows provides good illumination. There's a small but interesting selection of sculptures, headlined by Rodin. The horribly expensive and crowded top floor restaurant looks over the Seine through a huge glass clock. There's also a photography gallery with exhibits dating from 1836, but it can only be reached by a different entrance and costs extra. *See also chapters* **De Gaulle to Mitterrand; Museums.**

Nôtre Dame

place du Parvis Nôtre Dame, 75004 Paris (43.26.07.39). Metro Cité. **Open** 8am-7pm daily.

It's said that all the roads of Paris lead to the Kilometre Zero square in front of Notre Dame cathedral. Catholics from all over the world come to pay homage to this Gothic masterpiece, which has been rebuilt several times since the foundations were laid by Pope Alexander III in AD1163. The cathedral staddles two architectural eras, echoing the great galleried churches of the twelfth century and looking forward to the buttressed cathedrals, such as Chartres, which were to follow. The evolution of the great Gothic milestone has not been without its setbacks. The structure had fallen into such a stage of

delapidation by the early nineteenth century that artists, politicians and writers (including Victor Hugo) petitioned the king, Louis Philippe, to restore the cathedral. During the Nazi occupation, every pane from the magnificent stained glass windows was removed, numbered and replaced with sandbags so that it wouldn't be destroyed. The nineteenth century spire is disliked by regular visitors, but provides a splendid view for anyone willing to scale the stairs. *See* **picture and caption.** *See also chapters* **The Seine; Roman Paris; The Middle Ages & Renaissance.**

L'Opéra de Paris

place de l'Opéra, 75009 Paris (47.42.57.50). Metro Opéra. **Open** for visits 11am-4.30pm daily; *museum:* 10am-5pm daily. **Admission** Opera visits 17F; museum 10F.

L'Opéra, the largest theatre in the world, was designed by Charles Garnier in a style which he obsequiously proclaimed as uniqe to Napoleon III. He stretched the neo-classicism which typified the architecture of the time to its extreme. Chagall painted a false ceiling with scenes from opera and ballet. The surrounding streets and squares were designed by the ubiquitous Baron Haussmann. It's possible to tour the library and the museum, the Grand Foyer, the Grand Staircase and the Principal Façade. *See* **picture and caption.** *See also chapters* **The Right Bank; Empires & Rebellions; Dance.**

Palais de Chaillot

place du Trocadéro, 75016 Paris. Metro Trocadéro.

Looming across the river from the Eiffel Tower (*see below*) and the Ecole Militaire (*see above*), the Palais de Chaillot in the place du Trocadero is home to several museums, including the Naval Museum, the Museum of Man and the Museum of French Monuments (*see chapter* **Museums**) and a theatre. It's an immense, intimidating, Romanesque-style building that was built for the international exhibition of 1937. During the daytime acrobats and other entertainers attract crowds on the terrace outside. The Gardens of Chaillot include a large pool with bronze and stone statues showered by powerful spraying fountains. At night, all lit up, the towering fountains give one of Paris's most spectacular displays. *See also chapter* **The Seine.**

Palais de Justice

boulevard du Palais, 75001 Paris (43.29.12.55). Metro Cité. **Open** 9am-6pm Mon-Fri.

This historical edifice was the seat of authority from Roman times until 1358. Today it's the focal point of justice in Paris. Visitors are free to walk the marble corridors and watch cases in both the civil and criminal courts (called *chambres correctionnelles*). Within the Palais gates beside the main edifice is the impressive Sainte-Chapelle, a church designed by Pierre de Montereau and built almost entirely of stained glass (*see* **picture and caption**). *See also above* **The Conciergerie;** *see also chapter* **The Middle Ages & Renaissance.**

The Panthéon

rue Clothilde, 75005 Paris. Metro Cardinal-Lemoine. **Open** *April-Sept:* 10am-6pm Mon, Wed-Sun; *Oct-March:* 10am-4pm Mon, Wed-Sun. **Admission** free.

Louis XV had the Panthéon built to thank Sainte Geneviève, patron saint of Paris, for helping him recover from an illness. It looks like a small, gloomy and windowless version

At the heart of seventeenth-century **Marais**, *the shop-lined* **place des Vosges** *is still the focus for the area's cosmopolitan residents.*

*The Grand Staircase alone is a reason to visit the **Opéra de Paris**. The Napoleon-commissioned opera house is a fury of ornate workmanship throughout.*

neutered by the head keeper who subsequently used the offending part as a paperweight. The cemetery wall, known as the 'Mur des Fédérés', got its name after 147 survivors of the Paris Commune of 1871 were shot against it (*see chapter* **The Third Republic**). *See also chapter* **Village Paris**.

Pompidou Centre (Beaubourg)

Rue du Renard, 75004 Paris (42.77.12.33/recorded information 42.77.11.12). Metro Châtelet, Hotel de Ville, Rambuteau/bus 29, 38, 47. **Open** noon-10pm Mon, Wed-Fri; 10am-10pm Sat, Sun. **Admission** *to NAAM:* 23F adults; 17F 18-25s, OAPs; free under-18s; *Galleries Contemporaines:* 16F adults; free under-13s; *CCI:* 15 F adults; free under-13s; *temporary exhibitions:* admission varies; *Day-pass to all exhibitions:* 50F adults; 45 F 13-25s, OAPs; free under-13s. **Credit** (bookshop only) DC, MC, V.

Twice as many people (eight million a year) visit this huge cultural centre as the Eiffel Tower (*see above*) – as much to see its boiler-house architecture as the art inside. Commissioned in 1968 by President Georges Pompidou, it was part of a redevelopment of a slum ironically called Beaubourg ('beautiful village'). Architects Richard Rogers and Renzo Piano won the competition to design it with their notorious 'inside-out' approach. The distinctive lift up the outside offers the best free panorama in Paris, but it's very crowded and the synthetic glass is grubby. The building's five sections are the Public Information Library,

*The once controversial **Pompidou Centre** now receives more visitors than any other building in Paris.*

of London's Saint Paul's Cathedral, although there are some fine views to be had from the top. Cracks were found in the walls after the dome was placed on top of the building. Following this embarrassing discovery, the architect, Soufflet, apparently died of shame. After the Revolution, the Panthéon was turned into a mausoleum for the rich and famous. If Gambetta's heart seems a little morbid, try the cenotaph of Jean Jacques Rousseau, a statue and monument to Voltaire, or the tomb of Victor Hugo. There's a great view from the top. The Sainte Geneviève library opposite on Panthéon square has one of the best manuscript and engraving collections in Paris. *See also chapters* **The Left Bank; The Dark Ages.**

Père Lachaise Cemetery

entry on the boulevard de Ménilmontant, 75020 Paris (43.70.70.33). Metro Père-Lachaise. **Open** *Mid March-5 Nov:* 7.30am-6pm Mon-Sat; 9.30am-6pm Sun and public holidays; *6 Nov-mid Jan:* 8.30am-5pm Mon-Sat; 9.30am-5pm Sun and public holidays.

This is supposedly the most visited cemetery in the world. Among the people to be buried in Père Lachaise's 116 acres are Balzac, Delacroix, Ingres, Chopin, Corot and Jim Morrison. Join the throng around Morrison's grave where the tributes include upturned bottles and joints. Jim's bust was stolen recently, to be replaced by a line reading, 'bring me back my head'. Also visit Oscar Wilde's tomb – the grave was carved by Epstein. It's a winged, naked, male angel which, because it was considered offensive when first erected (the *mot juste*), was

Founded in the thirteenth century, the **Sorbonne** *university is now well integrated in twentieth-century Paris. See chapters* **The Left Bank; Middle Ages & Renaissance.**

Industrial Creation Centre, Institute of Musical Acoustic Research & Coordination, National Museum of Modern Art (*see chapter* **Museums**) and a film library and cinema (*see chapter* **Film**). The plaza in front of the building is uncomfortable, but the attendant street performers attract huge crowds. *See* **picture and caption.** *See also chapters* **The Right Bank; De Gaulle to Mitterrand.**

Sacré Coeur
35 rue Chevalier de la Barre, 75018 Paris (42.51.17.02). Metro Abbesses, Anvers. **Open** *April-Sept:* 9.15am-1.30pm, 2-6.30pm, daily; *Oct-March:* 9am-noon, 1-5pm, daily. **Admission** to dome 10F; to museum 12F. Building was started on the Sacré Coeur as an act of penance after the nation's defeat by the Prussians in 1870. It wasn't finished until 1910. The mock Romano-Byzantine church dominates Montmartre's Butte and the pristine white towers can be seen from a great distance. A jumble of architects worked on the project, but its mixed style is held in affection by all but the most faddy purist. The lavishly adorned church, the crypt and the gallery in the dome are all open to visitors. Take a walk up the many (very steep) steps to Sacré Coeur for a stunning view – or hop into the available transport and get a ride to the top. *See also chapters* **Village Paris; The Third Republic.**

Sorbonne
rue des Ecoles, 75005 Paris. Metro Maubert-Mutualité. **Open** 9.45am-12.30pm, 2-5.15pm, Mon, Wed-Sun. **Admission** limited public access. *See* **picture and caption.**

Completed in 1248, the stained glass tableaux at the Sainte-Chapelle in the **Palais de Justice** *depict the major Bible scenes over a glass area of 1,500 square yards (1,254 square metres).*

Paris By Season

'I love Paris in the springtime, I love Paris in the fall' – whatever the season, France's capital has festivals and celebrations for you to indulge in to your heart's content.

The Paris calendar is peppered with impromptu street celebrations, local festivals and gastronomic jamborees. However, as the American-style show-time festivities of the Bicentennial of the Revolution showed, the French seem uncomfortable with the pomp and pageantry of such huge celebrations; the Bicentennial events got off to a slow start and hiccupped their way through the year. France is happier celebrating food and wine than regicide or the rights of man. This city takes the arrival of Beaujolais Nouveau seriously and does not ignore the *vendanges* (grape harvest) at Montmartre (*see below* **Autumn** for both events) or the *galette des rois* (traditional Epiphany cakes) in January (*see below* **Winter**). Not that Bastille day (*see below* **Summer**) is overlooked – there's plenty of music, dance and fireworks to celebrate the event, followed by a torrent of bad headaches the following morning.

So how does Paris mark the passing of the seasons ? Just keep the Three Cs firmly in mind – Culture, Couture and Cuisine – and you won't go far wrong. Much of Paris life take place on the streets. Each *quartier* has its own fête or festival with its own mix of culture and cuisine. However, all *arrondissements* have one thing in common: the bakeries. These celebrate all events with bread, proving that in Paris, at least, it is the stuff of life.

Paris today has a rich mix of people from all over the world. Emigrés from eastern Europe made up most of the minority groupings for many years. This changed, however, when immigrants began to arrive from what once had been French colonies. Although racial tension does still exist, most 'communities' have integrated to a certain degree and their festivals are well attended by Parisians from all walks of life.

What attracts many people to these events are the spicy food and abundance of drink that is available. The smell of grilled *merguez* (a spicy, North African sausage) dominates many a parade and street demonstration. More sedate but equally brilliant are the Russian Orthodox Christmas mass and the Buddhist festival (*see below* **Winter** and **Spring** respectively).

Although France is a Catholic country, it seems to pay little attention to religious dos and don'ts. Christmas mass at Nôtre Dame is an overplayed tourist event, while the royalist mass for poor beheaded Louis XVI offers a curious insight into another side of French society: what might have been if there had been no Bastille day. For details of both these events *see below* **Winter**.

Decide for yourselves if Paris is a city for all seasons. In our view, there's certainly something to keep you amused, whatever time of year you're here.

INFORMATION

Office du Tourisme
127 avenue des Champs-Elysées, 75008 Paris (47.23.61.72). Metro George V.
Open 9am-8pm daily.
The tourist office publishes a guide to events throughout Paris that covers even the most obscure of annual events. Staff are helpful and well informed.

SUMMER

Salon de Montrouge
Mairie de Montrouge, 43 rue de la République, 92000 Montrouge (43.38.52.67). RER Vanves-Malakoff, /bus 68, 125, 126, 128, 187. **Dates** whole month of May. **Admission** free.
The most important contemporary art exhibition for young up-and-coming artists. Painters, sculptors and photographers are invited to submit their work to the panel. Out of 2,000 applicants, 300 end up on show. For seekers of the avant-garde, it's worth the trek out to this otherwise unprepossessing suburb of Paris.

Les Semaines de la Marionette à Paris
Plateau Beaubourg, opposite the Pompidou Centre, 6 rue Quincampoix, 75004 Paris (46.60.05.64.). Metro Hôtel de Ville, Châtelet/bus 69, 67, 96. **Dates** second two weeks in May. **Admission** 70F.
Some very high-brow string jerking in a festival devoted to contemporary marionette works, including mime and animated film. Although most of the productions are performed in a theatre, spillage into the streets around Beaubourg is inevitable and, at times, even encouraged.

French Tennis Open
Stade Roland Garros, 2 avenue Gordon Bennett, 75016 Paris (47.43.48 00). Metro Porte d'Auteuil, Michel-Ange-Auteil/bus 22, 52, 62, 72. **Dates** 28 May-10 June 1990; usually last week in May, first week in June. **Admission** *advance tickets:* to outside courts & show courts, apply in writing from January onwards to above address; *in person:* on sale at Roland Garros one week before the Open. **Prices** *outside courts:* from 35F; *centre court & court No.1:* 300F; *after 6pm:* remaining seats in the two centre courts are sold for 10F on a ballot system at the door.
The French Open combines great tennis with glitzy show-biz. Movie stars rub shoulders with minor European royalty in the stands. Because it has not yet acquired the prestige of Wimbledon, tickets can still be bought on the day. We advise, nonetheless, to book in advance.

The Gay Parade
Starting point *place de La Bastille, 75011 Paris . Metro Bastille/bus 86, 87, 76, 69.*
Dates usually the last Sat in June.
Admission free.
This is the single largest gay and lesbian parade in France, complete with floats. It starts at the Place de la Bastille, that great symbol of *libération*, at 2pm come rain or shine. Consult *Gai Pied* magazine for details.

Paris Cricket Tournament
Terrain de Bagatelle, Bois de Boulogne, 75016 Paris (45.42.45.55). Metro Porte Maillot/bus 62, 63, 72. **Admission** free.
It may seem odd that such a British import would find favour in France but *le cricket* seems to have become *le must*, judging by the success of the last two tournaments. In 1990 Paris will host the third European cricket tournament, with teams from various neighbouring countries including one from Great Britain.

Garçons de Café
Starting point *at the Hôtel de Ville, place de lHôtel de Ville, 75004 Paris (organizer 40.20.00.38; this is a home phone number, please phone at reasonable times). Metro Hôtel de Ville/bus 70, 72, 74.* **Dates** second half of June (date to be announced).
Every year, some time in mid June, over 500 café waiters and waitresses race around the city holding a tray laden with a bottle and three glasses. It's a treat to

watch those long white aprons flapping like sails as runners trip and teeter to keep themselves from keeling over. Any spillage and breakage during the 8km (5mile) race disqualifies the participant. Non-French nationals can enter so long as he or she is a bona fide waiter or waitress. Participants start and finish at the Hôtel de Ville.

International Rose Competition at Bagatelle
The Rose Garden, Bagatelle, Bois de Boulogne, 75016 Paris (45.25.58.05). Metro Porte d'Auteuil/bus 43. **Date** 21 June every year; rose garden remains open until October.
Marie Antoinette once frolicked in this pretty English garden in the Bois de Boulogne, which nowadays hosts the International Rose Competition every year. Prizes for new blooms are awarded on 21 June and the public has access to the garden from 22 June until October.

SOS Racisme concert
Usually takes place in the Bois de Vincennes; venues for 1990 and 1991 yet to be confirmed (phone SOS Racisme for details: 48.06.40.00). **Date** 16 June 1990; usually third Sat in June. **Admission** free.
See **picture and caption.**

Tournoi International de Pétanque
Arenes de Lutece, Paris 75005 Paris (43.29.21.75). Metro Jussieu, Monge, Cardinal Lemoine/bus 63, 86, 87, 89. **Dates** five days in June; exact dates to be announced. **Admission** 30F.
For those who don't know, *pétanque*, France's favourite Sunday sport – which is played by men and women alike – consists of trying to hit a little wooden ball with a larger, heavy metal one. The Tournoi International de Pétanque (more commonly known as boules) takes place in Paris's Roman arena in the heart of the Latin Quarter. *See also chapter* **Roman Paris.**

Festival de la Butte Montmartre
In venues on the Butte Montmatre, 4bis rue Saint Isaure, 75018 Paris (Festival organizers 42.62.46.22). Metro Abesses, Lamarck-Caumartin/bus 64. **Dates** mid June to mid July.
The Butte has long been an artists' colony. The area continues to have a village atmosphere despite crowds of ice-cream slurping tourists. Theatre, dance and music dominate the distinctive local celebrations held every summer.

Fête de la Musique
All over Paris. **Date** 21 June every year.
This is the brainchild of dynamic socialist Minister of Culture, Jack Lang, who a few years ago set about encouraging the playing and enjoyment of music in all its forms. So pick up an instrument and head for the street corner. If you're more of a listener, there's free rock at the Bastille, chamber music in the Palais Royal or folk dancing at the Place du Caroussel. On the longest day of the year, Paris is a musical feast.

Chopin Festival at Bagatelle
Orangerie du Parc de Bagatelle, Bois de Boulogne, 75016 Paris (45.01.20.10). Metro Pont de Neuilly/bus 43. **Dates** last week in June-mid July. **Admission** 40F-100F.
For many, this is the most moving Parisian celebration: Chopin-dominated piano recitals, played by young musicians, in the elegant ambience of the Orangerie. A few candle-lit concerts complete the illusion of old-fashioned charm. For the romantically inclined.

Bastille Day
All over France: contact Office du Tourisme, 47.23.61.72, for details. **Date** 13 July (evening) and all day 14 July every year. **Admission** free.
See **picture and caption.**

The Tour de France
Finishing point *at the Champs-Elysées (Race organizers 40.93.20.20).* **Dates** third week in July. **Admission** free.
The most famous bicycle race in the world is as much a fixture of French life as a *café au lait* and a warm croissant. Every summer, crowds throng the Champs Elysées to catch a glimpse of the cyclists as they cross the finishing line. Cheering is loud for the winner, deafening if he is French. An electric atmosphere prevails.

Festival Estival
Contact Tourist Office for details. **Dates** throughout July, Aug, Sept. **Admission** 30F-150F.
Classical music concerts in churches and halls throughout Paris are the hallmark of the Festival Estival. The Festival is in its twenty fifth year and going strong.

Fête de L'Assomption
Nôtre Dame, place Nôtre Dame, 75004 Paris (43.26.07.39). Metro Cité, Saint Michel/bus 21, 38, 96. **Date** 15 Aug every year. **Admission** free.
The procession of the Feast of the Assumption that leaves Nôtre Dame is a sight to behold: jostling believers squeeze for space with people who just want to get a look in on this religious celebration. Mass is held inside the cathedral when it rains, outside when the weather's all right. Cathedral authorities are notoriously unhelpful when asked even the most straightforward of questions. Good luck.

Fête de L'Humanité
Parc de la Courneuve, Aubervilliers, 93000 Seine-Saint-Denis (49.22.72.72). Metro Porte de la Chapelle, Porte d'Aubervilliers, Porte de Paris/bus 65, 130, 134, 149, 150, 173. **Dates** second half of Sept. **Admission** free.
This left wing jamboree is organized by the French Communist Party and the staff of the Party's newspaper *l'Humanité*. The Fête combines music, dance and theatre with political party rhetoric, stands piled high with socialist literature, food and drink. Have a good time while retaining your social consciousness.

Festival de Musique de Chambre de Paris
in the Musée Carnavalet and other historical venues in Paris. Contact Festival organizers for details: 5bis rue Saint Gilles, 75003 Paris (42.77.44.58). **Dates** second half of Sept. **Admission** to be confirmed.

Harlem Désir and potes *(mates) founded* **SOS Racisme** *(listed under* **Summer***) a few years ago to protest against the growth of racism in France. Their slogan* touche pas à mon pote *(don't hurt my buddy) became a rallying cry for French people who were concerned about mounting tension. The yearly, free concert is a reminder of their message. It's also a good excuse for a party.*

THIS BOX CONTAINS EVERYTHING YOU WILL EVER NEED TO KNOW ABOUT GETTING TO PARIS.

With up to <u>thirty</u> flights every day, there's a good chance that one call to the team at Airtour France can answer your questions about getting to Paris.

Airtour France is part of the Holidaymaker Group Plc, that means more flights with more airlines at lower prices than any other tour operator.

Don't delay, call the Airtour France reservations department today on **071-706 3737**

ABTA   ATOL   IATA

157 Praed Street, London, W2 1RL

Holidaymaker Group plc

Even though not a year goes by without **Bastille Day** *(listed under* **Summer***) being celebrated with a bang and a ball, the Bicentennial celebrations of 1989 will prove to be a hard act to follow. Regular events include the night of the* bals populaires: *dancing in the streets, squares and fire stations to live bands (13 July). The liveliest areas are the place de la Bastille, place du Havre, place d'Italie, place Gambetta and the Jardin des Tuileries. Bastille Day itself (14 July) starts with an official military parade down the Champs Elysées, presided over by politicians and their guests. This is followed by superb fireworks at the Eiffel Tower that take place in the evening. Most* arrondissements *also stage local bonfires and pyrotechnics. Beware of too much champagne, which flows freely and leaves you wondering how the Revolution ever got started.*

The historical settings make this a very pleasant way to enjoy an all-French repertoire of chamber music.

Portes Ouvertes Monuments Historiques

In various historic houses and venues throughout Paris. To obtain a list check with Office du Tourisme de Paris (see above **Information***); Association Paris Historique: 44 rue François Miron, 75004 Paris (42.76.43.43); or Ministry of Culture (40.15.82.92).* **Date** *third Sun in Sept.* **Admission** varies.

One day each year, Parisians get a chance to visit private houses and *hôtels particuliers*, churches, archaeological digs and historic public buildings usually closed to the public. A must for the culturally minded.

AUTUMN

Festival d'Automne

In venues all over Paris. Contact Festival oganizers for details: 156 rue de Rivoli, 75001 Paris (42.96.12.27). **Dates** Oct-Dec. **Admission** 70F-250F.

A culture-feast *par excellence*, with top-notch performers putting on dance, music, theatre and folkloric productions. The repertoire is huge, so it's advisable to write in for a complete programme before making up your mind which events to attend. It's a festival with a very distinctive international flavour.

Festival d'Art Sacré

In various churches, synagogues and concert halls throughout Paris (Festival organizers 42.77.92.26) **Dates** Oct-Dec. **Admission** 75F-150F.

Traditional and contemporary works appear in Paris's festival of church music. A new grand organ has been installed in the magnificent seventeeth-century church of Saint Eustache and the effort in terms of both time and money was well worth it. Performances also include liturgies and church services of other denominations and a midnight mass on 24 December. *See also chapter* **Music: Classical & Opera**.

Fêtes des Vendanges à Montmartre

All over Montmartre and in the basement of the 18th arrondissement Mairie (45.62.84.58). Metro Abbesses, Lamarck-Caulaincourt/bus 64 **Date** first Sat in Oct. **Admission** free.

The only vineyard in Paris is the size of a pocket handkerchief, tucked away in the hills of Montmartre. Every year it produces 500 bottles of red wine simply called Clos Montmartre. The harvest fête goes back to the Middle Ages and offers ye olde worlde celebrations with a good splash of pageantry. The basement of the 18th *arrondissement Mairie* (town hall) is turned into a winery and parades and festivities fill the narrow streets of Montmartre. You probably won't get to taste the wine. It's auctioned off at 500F per bottle.

Le Mondial de l'Automobile

Parc de Versailles, Porte de Versailles, 75015 Paris (47.23.59.40). Metro Porte de Versailles/bus 39, 49, 80. **Dates** 4-14 Oct. **Admission** to be confirmed.

Car buffs will get a lot of mileage out of this huge international motor show, which is held every two years. It's got all the trimmings: the newest car models, beautiful hostesses – note, no males ones – and lots of glossy literature to tantalize you.

The Arc de Triomphe

Hippodrome de Longchamp, Jardin de Boulogne, 75016 Paris (42.66.92.02). **Dates** 7 Oct. **Admission** 45F.

The Arc opens the racing season and is a very social event. A million pounds' worth of horse flesh is watched desultorily by *le tout-Paris*, in Gucci shoes and Chanel suits, gloved hands clasping Baccarat glasses bubbling with flowing Veuve Clicquot. The nearest thing to royalty is the Agha Khan and the winner stands to get at least half a million pounds. *See also chapter* **Sport & Fitness**.

Les 20km de Paris Race

From Pont d'Iéna, 75007 Paris. Metro Champ de Mars/bus 42, 82. Contact Tourist Office for details. **Date** 14 Oct. **Admission** free.

Well over 21,000 participants will run this 20km (12 mile) race in the shadow of the Eiffel Tower. Not quite as taxing as the Paris Marathon, but a serious international event for the Nike brigade.

FIAC 90 (Foire Internationale d'Art Contemporain)

Grand Palais, Rond-Point des Champs Elysées, 75001 Paris (45.62.84.58). Metro Champs Elysées-Clemenceau/bus 28, 72, 73, 83. **Dates** 7 Oct-4 Nov. **Admission** 45F.

Galleries galore, both French and foreign, gather to show artists' work. Gaze, buy, or balk at avant-garde pieces. Each year a specific country is honoured; in 1990 it's the USA.

Génie de la Bastille

In artists' studios and venues around the Bastille area. Full details from 71 rue du Faubourg Saint Antoine, 75011 Paris (42.02.97.45). Metro Bastille, Ledru Rollin/bus 76, 86, 87. **Dates** coincide with week-end of the FIAC *(see above)* every other year; next Génie to be held in 1991. **Admission** free.

The Bastille area is beginning to resemble New York's SoHo, as artists scurry to take over abandoned *ateliers* (workshops) in this once traditional furniture-makers' enclave in the east of Paris. For four days every other year, resident artists open their doors to the public. A resolutely contemporary feast for the eyes; works by over 125 artists include drawings, paintings, sculpture, pottery and photography.

Festival de Jazz de Paris

In various concert halls around Paris. Full details from Festival de Jazz de Paris, 211 avenue Jean-Jaurès, 75019 Paris (40.56.07.17). **Dates** usually last two weeks of Oct. **Admission** 35F-120F.

Jazz has always found a home in Paris. Legendary figures – such as Miles Davis, Ray Charles, Dexter Gordon – and more recent newcomers Wynton Marsalis, Keith Jarrett and Dave Murray return like homing pigeons to set the beat straight. Although you can always hear good jazz in Paris, it's fun to have a festival and you can get a relatively cheap subscription ticket to all the concerts.

Beaujolais Nouveau
All over France. **Date** third Thur in Nov, barring any agricultural catastrophes.
Excitement builds to a pitch in the days preceding the arrival of the now oh-so-trendy Beaujolais Nouveau, the first wine of the Beaujolais vintage, which is pressed and drunk without any ageing process. On the night, wine bar, café and bistro owners polish glasses and look smug under posters that proclaim that the *Beaujolais Nouveau est arrivé.* Traditionally the tipple of coachmen, Beaujolais Nouveau is now required drinking for *le tout-Paris. Liberté, égalité, fraternité*, after you've had a few, of course.

Armistice Day Celebrations
at Arc de Triomphe, 75016 Paris. Metro Charles de Gaulle-Etoile/bus 22, 30, 73, 92. Contact Tourist Office for details.
Date 11 Nov. **Admission** free.
There's no fanfare and no military parade at this yearly remembrance ceremony for the dead of two World Wars. Wreaths are laid by the French President and various personalities at the Tomb of the Unknown Soldier under the Arc de Triomphe. Spectators can watch from the place de l'Etoile. *See also chapter* **The War.**

The Goncourt Prize
Awarded by the Académie Goncourt towards the end of Nov.
More than 1,000 literary awards are given in France every year, but out of that literary jungle, the Goncourt award for a work of prose emerges leonine. Not in monetary terms – the Goncourt is worth the paltry sum of 50F – but in the kinds of sky-rocketting sales the recipient of this most prestigious award can expect. Founded in 1903 by Edmond de Goncourt, the decision-making takes place comfortably over lunch at Paris's Drouant restaurant and the winner is announced immediately afterwards. *Grande Bouffe* equals *Grand Prix* and past winners have included Sacha Guitry, Louis Aragon and Michel Tournier.

The Femina Prize
Awarded last Mon in Nov.
This literary prize was founded in an attempt to encourage women writers. About 150 novels are selected and chewed over by a jury of 12 women. But they don't decide over lunch and they do award male writers. Femina winners – these include Marguerite Yourcenar, Antoine de Saint-Exupery and Zoé Oldenbourg – can expect terrific sales.

WINTER

Crèche sur le Parvis
On the main concourse in front of the Hôtel de Ville, place de l'Hôtel de Ville, 75004 Paris (42.76.40.40). Metro Hôtel de Ville/bus 70, 72, 74. **Dates** from the third week in Dec; exact date to be announced. **Admission** 25F.
Every year around the third week in December, the central *Mairie* of Paris organizes a large *crèche* with all the trimmings, under a tent at the place de l'Hôtel de Ville. If you're into life-size Nativity scenes, this is your big chance. Proceeds go to charity and judging by the queues, a lot of people still think of Christmas as not just being for consumers.

Christmas Mass at Nôtre Dame
Nôtre Dame Cathedral, place de Nôtre Dame, 75004 Paris (43.26.07.39). Metro Cité, Saint Michel/bus 21, 38, 96. **Date** 24 Dec.
'Tis the night before Christmas and there's no room to move, in this bastion of medieval Christendom (arrive by 11pm to hope to get a seat). Beware of camera-flashers; they really help to ruin what should be a memorable mass.

Russian Orthodox Christmas
Saint Alexandre Nievsky Cathedral, 12 rue Daru, 75008 Paris (42.27.37.34). Metro Ternes, Courcelles/bus 30, 43, 52, 83, 84, 94. **Dates** 6 Jan, 6pm Vespers; 7 Jan, 10am Christmas mass.
Smells, bells, processions and chants reminiscent of a Tolstoy novel. The old and young of Paris's large White Russian community gather here to listen to a majestic, solemn service. The church is bathed in a golden light from flickering candle-light and reflections from the icons on the walls. Afterwards, reel out to the Russian café next door for a shot of bison vodka and a hunk of black bread.

Epiphany
All over France. **Date** 6 Jan.
More popularly referred to as the Fête des Rois, this religious festival is, in true French style, an excuse for a gastronomic treat. The honour of this feast goes to the bakers who prepare the *galette des rois*, a round, buttery, almond paste cake in which a bean is hidden. Whoever finds the bean dons a crown and chooses a consort. This curious rite is performed in all self-respecting French homes to prove that in a Republic anyone can be king for a day.

Commemorative Mass for Louis XVI
At the Chapelle Expiatoire, 29 rue Pasquier, 75008 Paris (42.65.35.80). Metro Saint Lazare, Augustin/bus 21, 22, 26, 27, 29.
Date Sun closest to 21 Jan.
This is about as close as Royal-watchers can get to what remains of the noble House of Bourbon. Members of France's aristocracy and other fervent royalists gather to mourn the beheading of Louis XVI on 21 January 1793. This is a sombre occasion in a bleak setting. Reproach and anguish hang heavy in the oddly stifling atmosphere of the chapel and courtyard. If you're lucky, one of the pretenders to the French throne (there are currently three) may put in an appearance and you may cheer up at the sound of *Vive le Roi.* An interesting window on what's left of *la royauté française.*

The **Foire du Trône** *(listed under* **Spring***) is the largest funfair in France. Carousels, dodgems and French fries galore and a carnival, some time in May.*

Chinese New Year Festival
*Around Avenue d'Ivry and Avenue Choisy,
75013 Paris (details from Association
Culturelle Franco-Chinoise, 45.20.74.09).
Metro Porte de Choisy, Porte d'Ivry/bus 57,
61.* **Date** on a Sun around 15 Feb 1991,
phone for details. **Admission** free.
It's not easy to contain the festivities of this
New Year Festival, given the vast Chinese
and other Oriental population of Paris.
Everyone tumbles into the boulevards and
avenues of the 13th *arrondissement*, Paris's
unofficial Chinatown, to watch dragons,
lions and kung fu performers disport themselves outside shops and restaurants. Lots
of noise, colour and spicy food. The
imagery speaks for itself, but in case you
didn't know, 1990 is the Year of the Horse,
1991 the Year of the Ram.

Les Césars: French Film awards
*Shown on Antenne 2 television channel
(44.21.42.42).* **Date** some time in the
first quarter of 1990.
So-called because the statuette was
designed by the French sculptor César.
The French film awards have been going
for some 15 years and are now a certified
media event which keep television viewers glued to the box to watch luminaries
of the French screen do their thing.
Recently, Isabelle Adjani (best actress
award) lent a serious note to the ceremony by quoting Salman Rushdie, but
most years it's just a predictable carbon
copy of the American Oscars.

SPRING

Salon de l'Agriculture
*Parc de Versailles, Porte de Versailles, 75015
Paris (42.71.88.44).* *Metro Porte de
Versaille/bus 39, 49, 80.* **Dates** 4-11 March;
first full week in March. **Admission** 45F.
For a week in early March, wide-eyed farmers from Tuscany to Tulsa can be seen
riding the metro in search of the Paris of
their dreams. When not on the metro they
preside proudly over their beasts at the
'largest farm in the world'. With one million
visitors in 1989, the Salon de l'Agriculture is
a major Parisian event. Barbour-clad
trendies rub shoulders with French and foreign farmers inspecting cows, sheep, goats,
horses, pigs, chickens and all other farm animals imaginable, then repair to the food and
drink hall for some serious sampling of
regional food and wine. Try the British
stand for a warm pint and some soggy chips.

Jumping International de Paris
*Palais Omnisports de Bercy, 8 boulevard de
Bercy, 75012 Paris (43.46.12.21).* *Metro
Bercy/bus 63.* **Dates** usually early March.
Admission 55F-230F.
Forty of the world's finest show jumpers
gather to show off their skills and horses in
one of the media events of the year.

Foire du Trône
*Bois de Vincennes, 75012 Paris
(43.44.70.76).* *Metro Porte Dorée, Porte de
Charenton, Liberté/bus 46, 86, 87.* **Dates**
end March-end May. **Admission** free; rides vary.
See **picture and caption**.

French Trade Unions and left-wing political parties organize marches on
May Day *(listed under* **Spring***) every year to celebrate Labour Day.
Museums and public buildings are closed on this most public holiday in
France. Skip the sightseeing and enjoy the crowds. Remember to buy a posy of
muguet (lily of the valley), the traditional harbinger of Spring, sold by Boy
Scouts and gypsies on every street corner.*

Passion of Jesus Christ
*Théatre de Menilmontant, 15 rue du Retrait,
75020 Paris (46.36.98.60).* *Metro
Gambetta/bus 26, 96.* **Dates** March-April.
Admission 60F.
Since 1932, residents and actors from the
quartier of Ménilmontant have come
together every Easter season to put on this
Passion of Christ adapted from the
Gospels. Parts have been handed down
from generation to generation. An amateur
production lovingly performed.

April Fool's Day
All over France. **Date** 1 April.
In French it's called *Poisson d'Avril* (April's
Fish). Bakers do a roaring trade with
breads, cakes and chocolate in the shape of
fish, while you spend the day avoiding a
paper cut-out of a sea-beastie being stuck on
some part of your anatomy.

Buddhist New Year Fête
*Temple Bouddhiste, Route de la ceinture du
lac Daumesnil, Bois de Vincennes, 75012
Paris (43.41.54.48).* *Metro Porte Dorée,
Charenton Ecoles.* **Dates** second, third and
fourth Sun in April. **Admisson** free.
France's large Buddhist population
gather to say prayers and to party. Stands
selling food and products from the Far
East abound.

Shakespeare Garden Festival
*Shakespeare Garden, Pré Catelan, Bois de
Boulogne, 75016 Paris (42.76.45.09).*
Metro Porte Maillot/bus 224. **Dates** end
April-early Oct. **Admission** 30F-120F.
This small open-air theatre is set in a won-
derfully intimate garden in the Bois de
Boulogne devoted to much of the flora
described by Shakespeare. Plays are
mostly in French, by the likes of Molière,
Marivaux and Beaumarchais, but English
troupes do sometimes give English-lan-
guage performances.

Marathon de Paris
*Begins at place de la Concorde and ends at the
Hippodrome de Vincennes; details from
AMSP, 13 rue de Sevigné, 75004 Paris
(42.77.17.84).* **Date** usually late April.
Paris has jumped on the marathon band-
wagon, following in the footsteps of New
York and London. The run starts from
the Place de la Concorde, the square
where the guillotine once stood; there are
great views of the sweaty participants
along the Champs Elysées.

Foire de Paris
*Parc de Versailles, Porte de Versailles, 75015
Paris (49.09.60.00).* *Metro Porte de
Versailles/bus 39, 49, 80.* **Dates** usually late
April-early May. **Admission** 45F.
A treat for gadget lovers. All the latest inven-
tions for couch potatoes, amateur cooks and
wine bores. A real hotch-potch of stands and
lots to eat and drink.

May Day
All over France. **Date** 1 May.
See **picture and caption**.

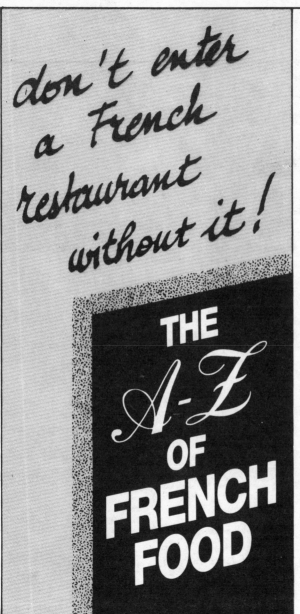

Essential Information

All you need to know to get started in Paris: from where to change your money to tipping etiquette.

VISAS

EEC nationals do not need a visa to enter France, though they will need a *carte de séjour* after a three-month period.

Americans do not require a visa either, unless they are planning to stay far more than three months. All other nationals should enquire at the French Consulate or Embassy before leaving home.

French Consulate
24 Rutland Gate, London SW7 (071 581 5292). Knightsbridge underground/9, 73 bus. **Open** phone for details.

INSURANCE

EEC nationals are entitled to French Health Services and Social Security Refunds (*see chapter* **Survival**). All other nationals should check whether their country has reciprocal arrangements with France. In any case, private travel insurance (available from any travel agency or in airports) is the simplest and safest solution, as it usually covers medical expenses as well as stolen (or even lost) cash, cameras, and other valuables.

MONEY

The currency in France is French francs (symbolized by 'F' after the amount). One franc equals 100 centimes. Five-centime, ten-centime and 20-centime coins are copper; 50-centime, one-franc, two-franc and five-franc coins are silver; ten-franc coins are either big copper coins or small, silver-centred coins with a copper outline. The size of notes increases according to their value (20F, 50F, 100F, 200F and 500F).

When getting your money changed at a bank or a *bureau de change*, avoid being given 500F notes as you will sometimes find it difficult to get change in small shops or in taxis.

FOREIGN EXCHANGE & BANKS

If you are planning to arrive in France late at night, make sure you have French francs on you. At **Roissy** and **Orly** airports, the bureaux de change are open from 7am to 11pm daily. At train stations, they are open from 8am to 9pm (daily at **Gare de Lyon** and **Gare du Nord**; closed Sunday at **Gare Saint Lazare** and **Austerlitz**).

Bureaux de change throughout Paris are generally open 9am to 6pm Monday to Saturday. The following agencies take no commission:

Europullman
10 rue d'Alger, 75001 Paris (42.60.55.58). Metro Tuileries. **Open** 9am-7pm Mon-Sat.

Société Générale de Change
112 rue de Richelieu, 75002 Paris (42.96.56.13). Metro Richelieu Drouot. **Open** 9am-6pm Mon-Fri.

Most banks also have foreign exchange counters. They are generally open from 9am to 4.30pm Monday to Friday; and 9am to noon on Saturdays. They are closed on public holidays (*see below* **Holidays**) and shut at noon the day before a national holiday.

The BNP (Banque Nationale de Paris) gives the best exchange rate and take the lowest commission. Branches are located throughout Paris. All banks, including foreign banks, are listed in the Yellow Pages under 'Banques'. Below we list some banks with extended hours:

Banque Régionale d'Escompte et de Dépots
66 avenue des Champs-Elysées, 75008 Paris (42.49.10.99). Metro George V. **Open** 24 hours daily.
The automatic exchange machine converts £10 and £20 notes as well as dollar, mark and lire notes into French francs.

CCF
103 avenue des Champs-Elysées, 75008 Paris (40.70.30.70). Metro George V. **Open** 9am-8pm Mon-Sat.

Société Financière de Change
11 rue Lincoln, 75008 Paris (42.25.21.97). Metro George V. **Open** 10am-midnight daily.

MAJOR BRITISH BANKS

Barclays
33 rue du Quatre-Septembre, 75002 Paris (42.66.65.31). Métro Opéra. **Open** phone for details.

Lloyds
43 boulevard des Capucines, 75002 Paris (42.61.51.25). Métro Opéra. **Open** phone for details.

Midland
6 rue Piccini, 75016 Paris (45.02.80.80). Metro Porte Maillot. **Open** phone for details.

National Westminster
18 place Vendôme, 75001 Paris (42.60.37.40). Métro Opéra. **Open** phone for details.

Thomas Cook
18 rue Toul, 75012 Paris (43.40.40.40). Metro Michel Bizot. **Open** phone for details.

American Express
11 rue Scribe, 75009 Paris (42.66.09.99). Métro Opéra. **Open** phone for details.

TOURIST INFORMATION

Central Tourist Information Office
127 avenue des Champs-Elysées, 75008 Paris (47.23.61.72). Metro Etoile or George V. **Open** 9am-8pm Mon-Sat; 9am-6pm Sun.
See picture and caption.

Gare du Nord Tourist Office
(45.26.94.82). **Open** *Nov-Easter:* 8am-8pm Mon-Sat; *Easter-Nov:* 8am-10pm Mon-Sat; 1-8pm Sun.

Gare de l'Est Tourist Office
(46.07.17.73). **Open** *Nov-Easter:* 8am-1pm, 5-8pm, Mon-Sat; *Easter-Oct:* 8am-10pm Mon-Sat.

Gare de Lyon Tourist Office
(43.43.33.24). **Open** *Nov-Easter:* 8am-1pm, 5-8pm Mon-Sat; *Easter-Oct:* 8am-10pm Mon-Sat.

Gare d'Austerlitz Tourist Office
(45.84.91.70). **Open** *Nov-March:* 8am-3pm Mon-Sat; *April-Oct:* 8am-10pm Mon-Sat.

Eiffel Tower Tourist Office
(45.51.22.15). **Open** *May-Sept only:* 11am-6pm only.

Recorded Information
(47.20.88.98). **Open** 24 hours daily.

A recorded tourist information service in English, detailing things to see and do in Paris.

Free maps are given out on request in metro stations; both large fold-out maps with bus and metro routes, and pocket-size maps are available. For details of recommended city maps and how to use the public transport system, *see chapter* **Travelling Around Paris.**

HOLIDAYS

In France, national holidays are known as 'Jours Feriés'.

New Year's Day 1January; **Easter Sunday** (15 April 1990); **Easter Monday** 16 April 1990); **Fête du Travail (May Day)** 1 May; **1945 Victory Day** 8 May; **Ascension** (24 May 1990); **Pentecost** 3-4 June 1990; **Bastille Day** 14 July; **Assumption** 15 August; **All Saints' Day** 1 November; **1918 Armistice Day** 11 November; **Christmas Day** 25 December.

On these days of celebration, you will find it difficult to get anything done: buses do not run, banks, museums and most stores are shut.

FRENCH TIME

France is one hour ahead of Greenwich Mean Time (GMT), except between the end of September and the end of October (when it's the same). For example, when it's 5pm in Paris, it's 4pm in London and 11am in New York. In France 'am' and 'pm' are not used; instead, time is based on the 24-hour system. Thus, 8am is *8 heures*, noon is *12 heures*, 5pm is *17 heures* and midnight is *24 heures*.

OPENING HOURS

Standard opening hours for shops are from 9am or 10am to 7pm or 8pm, Tuesdays to Saturdays. Usual closing days are Sundays and, occasionally, Mondays. Shops and businesses very often close for lunch for at least an hour, sometimes more, usually between 1pm and 3pm.

Everything you need to start discovering Paris can be found at the various **Tourist Offices** *(listed under* **Tourist Information***): brochures, maps and information on what's happening in Paris, the suburbs, and the rest of France. Staff can also help find a hotel room. Most languages are spoken; there is also an English-language recorded information service.*

THE SEASONS

Paris is beautiful all year round; visitors come at all seasons, but mostly during the Christmas period, and from April to the end of October.

Winter: In spite of the cold (temperatures sometimes drop below freezing point) and the rain (especially in February and March), there are more cultural events during the winter than during the other seasons.

Spring: Paris in the spring is magical, but also crowded with tourists. The weather is usually fine, with some rain.

Summer: A great time to visit; Parisians have fled the city (especially in July and August) and those who are left are less stressed. For those of you with a car, you'll find traffic smooth and parking possible. Unfortunately cultural life is slow. It can get quite hot and muggy during the day, but evenings are just right.

Autumn: The weather is usually good, but September and October are peak months for tourism, and finding a hotel room can be quite difficult.

Average Temperatures
January 7.5ºC (45.5ºF); **February** 7.1ºC (44.8ºF); **March** 10.2ºC (50.4ºF); **April** 15.7ºC (60.3ºF); **May** 16.6ºC (61.9ºF); **June** 23.4ºC (74.1ºF); **July** 25.1ºC (7.2ºF); **August**

25.6ºC (78.1ºF); **September** 20.9ºC (69.6ºF); **October** 16.5˚C (61.7˚F); **November** 11.7ºC (53.1ºF); **December** 7.8ºC (46ºF).

SAVOIR-FAIRE

Driving: Always keep your seatbelts fastened. At intersections when no signposts indicate the right of way, the car coming from the right has priority. Parisians are aggressive drivers, don't be put off by their honks, snorts or other vulgarities.
In the metro: Don't stand in the turnstiles while you're searching for your ticket, and don't block the passageway while trying to find your direction: this really annoys Parisians, who are always in a rush and hate to be delayed even for a second. For full details of how to use the metro and buses, *see chapter* **Travelling Around Paris.**
In restaurants: Don't call the waiter *garçon*, or click your fingers to attract his attention. A slight wave of your index and a polite *Monsieur* should suffice.

Tipping:
Restaurants and cafés: 15 per cent is already added to your bill when you receive it, but as this sum is not always given to the waiter, you could leave an extra tip (50 centimes to 2F in a café, 5F to 15F in a restaurant, or more for a very fancy meal).

Hotels: there is no real need for tipping in a hotel, except in fancier ones, where a coin to the porter will ensure good service.

Taxis: between 2F and 5F.

Travelling Around Paris

We give you the low-down on the Paris public transport system and how to survive it.

Finding your way around Paris can seem a nightmare, particularly on arrival. Don't despair. The public transport system is comparatively easy to understand; there's the **metro** (underground), a large number of **bus** routes and the suburban railways (called **RER**). If you're lost, ask a Parisian; they're often more helpful than the staff at tourist offices, who are fond of the axiom 'C'est pas possible', accompanied by a Gallic shrug. The shrug seems to go with the uniform. You're usually better off asking someone on the street or metro for quicker results.

ARRIVING IN PARIS

The first thing you should do is ask for a **map**. Staff at stations and airports give out free maps of the Paris metro, bus and RER system. They're extremely useful because they show how the different transport systems fit together. *Paris Patchwork*, a pocket-sized notebook filled with maps and phone numbers, is worth looking out for; it's printed by RATP and is available free from metro stations.

FROM CHARLES DE GAULLE

By taxi
Depending on when you arrive, getting a taxi can be by far the most convenient and fastest way to reach your final destination. It can take as little as 40 minutes, though add 30 minutes if you're travelling during rush hour. If there are no taxis in sight outside the arrivals area, press the small button at the front of the taxi rank. This will call up a cab from the subterranean car park below. Expect to pay around 130F to 200F plus a fee for the luggage if travelling into the centre of town.

By train (RER)
A quick and reliable way of travelling. Catch the courtesy (free) bus which stops outside Exit 7; there's one every five minutes. You can't miss it – it's a yellow single-decker and goes to **Roissy Aeroport**, the RER station. Train tickets to the centre of Paris can be bought once inside the station and cost 24F one way. Trains run every 15 to 20 minutes to central Paris. The journey takes about 45 minutes although it can take as long as one hour.

By bus
An **Air France Bus** leaves every 15 to 20 minutes from both terminals and stops at **Porte Maillot** and **Etoile** (the Arc de Triomphe). A one way ticket, bought as you board the bus, costs 36F. Alternatively, the **Charles de Gaulle/RATP Buses** also travel into central Paris: **No. 350** to **Gare de L'Est** leaves the airport every 15 minutes; **No. 351** to **Nation** leaves every 30 minutes. You can pay cash on the bus, but it's cheaper to use bus tickets. These are available from ticket machines in the airport halls; you'll need six bus tickets to pay for the journey.

Information
Charles de Gaulle Airport Information (48.62.22.80). **Open** 24-hours daily.

FROM ORLY AIRPORT

By Taxi
Travelling by taxi into town takes 30 to 40 minutes and costs approximately 100F. You'll need to pay a supplement for luggage, usually 5F per piece. As with other cities, allow more time if catching a taxi during the rush hour.

By train
Catch the courtesy bus to the RER station **Pont de Rungis**, where you can get a train to Paris. The most central stop to make for is **Châtelet/Les Halles**. Trains run every 15 to 20 minutes and a one way ticket costs 25F.

By bus
An **Air France Bus** leaves from both terminals every 12 to 15 minutes. It costs 29F (tickets are available from the Air France Terminus) and stops at **Les Invalides**. There are also **Orly/RATP Buses** which run every 15 minutes: **No. 215** goes to **Denfert Rochereau** and you need six bus tickets. There's also the **Orlybus** which costs 17.50F (or six bus tickets) which also stops at Denfert Rochereau and leaves every 15 minutes. Bus tickets are available from machines in the airport hall. The journey by bus takes 40 to 50 minutes.

Information
Orly Airport Information (48.84.52.52). **Open** 6am-11.30pm daily.

FROM TRAIN STATIONS

Taxi ranks
It's a strange phenomenon, but in Paris most journeys by taxi cost about 30F, no matter where you're going. During the rush hour or at night (when rates increase) expect to pay more. There are taxi ranks outside main-line stations.

Metro
If you feel up to it, and aren't lugging big bags around, catch the metro. *See below* **Metro**.

TRAVELLING AROUND

Paris is a compact city; from any given point it's rarely more than 10km (6 miles) across. It's circular in shape and cut across the middle by the River Seine which runs east to west separating the *rive droite* (the right bank) from the *rive gauche* (the left bank). The city is hemmed in by the *Boulevard Périphérique*, a giant ringroad which divides central Paris from the suburbs and industrial areas. The Périphérique carries all the heavy traffic in, out and round Paris; its intersections – which lead onto other main motorways – are called *portes* (gates). Driving on the Périphérique isn't as hair-raising as you might expect, and although congested at times, the traffic jams are small fry when compared to the tail-backs on London's M25.

Paris is divided into 20 *arrondissements* (local areas) which are numbered 1er (1st) to 20ème (20th) and spiral out clockwise, like a swiss roll. Each arrondissement is sandwiched between its numerical neighbours. For example, the 2nd arrondissement has the 1st arrondissement to the west and the 3rd to the east. Street signs are blue and indicate which arrondissement you're in.

MAPS

A map of Paris is a must if you want to minimise the hassle involved in getting around. The **RATP** and **tourist maps** available from train and metro stations provide basic information, though if you want detailed breakdowns, we recommend the following, available from most newsagents and bookshops:

Plan de Paris. A notebook-sized publication with a city map and maps of each arrondissement. Editions Leconte, price 32F.

The metro is quick, efficient and easy to use. It's clearly sign-posted, relatively safe and clean. An army of cleaners – dressed in bright yellow overalls and armed with brushes and rubbish bags – scrub away throughout the day making sure it stays that way.

Paris par Arrondissement. Filofax-size, this contains a fold-out map as well as more detailed maps of each arrondissement. L'Indispensable Editions, price 38F.

TICKETS AND TRAVEL PASSES

Paris and its surrounding area is divided into travel zones. Zones 1, 2 and 3 go as far as the Périphérique; beyond are zones 4 and 5 and the airports. The metro, buses and RER lines are all run by **RATP** (Régie Autonome des Transports Parisiens). RATP produces maps and issues tickets covering all the services, in addition to running their own tours and day trips.

Tickets issued by RATP are valid on the metro, on buses and on central Paris RER trains. They can be bought at RAPT offices and at all metro stations. You have the choice of first or second class travel and several types of ticket or pass to choose from. Second class travel is fine, although a bit cramped during the rush hour. Make sure you don't travel first class if you have a second class ticket; the police can be vicious if you're caught (*see below* **Metro**). Keep the ticket on you at all times as officials do spot-checks on trains and buses. Paris Visite, Coupon Jaune

and Carte Orange travel passes (*see below*) are the same size as metro tickets. You will receive a plastic wallet in which to keep your pass. Copy the number on the wallet on to the actual ticket.

Individual single tickets: buying tickets one at a time is an expensive way of getting around. They cost 5F (second class) and are valid for one journey only. A better idea is to buy them in blocks of ten (*see below*).

Block of tickets: called a *carnet*, this wadge of ten tickets costs 31.20F (second class). It's relatively good value for money if you're staying in Paris for a few days and have a tendency to catch taxis when pressed for time.

Paris Visite: a tourist pass which lasts three or five days, available for zones either 1, 2 and 3 or zones 1 to 4 plus the airports. It costs 70F for a three-zone, three-day pass or 115F for a three-zone, five-day pass. Travel is by first class only (which accounts for the high price) and the pass gives you discounts on admission to various tourist attractions, such as Canauxrama (*see below* **Tours: Boat Trips**).

Coupon Jaune: a weekly travel pass that is valid from Monday to Sunday inclusive, irrespective of when you buy it. You'll need a passport photo.

Carte Orange: a monthly season pass which is valid from the first day of the month

irrespective of when you buy it. Again, you'll need a passport photo.

RATP Offices
53 Quai des Grands Augustins, 75006 Paris (40.46.44.50/40.46.43.60). Metro St Michel. **Open** 8.30am-12noon, 1-5.15pm, Mon-Fri; 8am-12noon, 2-4pm, Sat.

Kiosk near Marché aux Fleurs, Place de la Madeleine, 75008 Paris (40.06.71.45). Metro Madeleine. **Open** May-Sept only: 7am-7pm Mon-Fri; 6.30am-6pm Sat, Sun.

RATP Information Phoneline
(43.46.14.14). **Open** 24 hours daily.
Phone for information (in French only) on the best way to get from A to B and details of tickets and passes.

METRO

Plans for a metro system in Paris existed as early as 1845, although it wasn't until 1900 that the first line (Line 1) was completed. Today, the metro boasts 13 lines, a total of 199km (123 miles) of tunnels. Lines 1, 4, 6 and 11 tend to be noisy because the trains still run on a pneumatic system. The remaining lines are electrified and are much quieter. Most lines end at a Porte, although there have been a couple of recent extensions beyond the Périphérique. There are plans to extend Line 1 to La Défense, the new commerce and shopping centre north-west of the city; the expected completion date is 1992 or 1993.

Some metro stations are worth a visit in their own right. **Liège** station (Line 13) has tiled panels on the platform walls; **Abbesses** (Line 12) has murals running alongside the spiral staircase which leads up to the surface; **Varenne** (Line 13) has exhibits from the nearby Rodin Museum; and at **Louvre** station (Line 1) there are replicas and exhibits from the Louvre.

The metro is marked by red and white signs at street level. Some lines run overground for short periods; **Line 6** near La Motte-Picquet allows for a good view of the Seine, the Eiffel Tower and the Trocadéro. **Line 7** near Pont-Marie looks across the Ile de la Cité, an especially striking view at night when Nôtre Dame is lit up. Metro stations are short distances apart; platforms and passages are wide, tiled and well lit. Interconnecting passages (*correspondances*), though clearly signposted, can be tiresomely long. Châtelet has the longest *correspondance*; there is a moving walkway 182m (600ft) long, not to mention

eUROLineS
TO
P·A·R·I·S

above the driver will light up.

Use the buses to get to know Paris: **Route 24** starts at Gare Saint Lazare and runs alongside the Seine; **Route 47** passes close to Les Halles and runs across the Ile de la Cité to the Sorbonne; **Route 82** starts at l'Etoile (Arc de Triomphe) and goes to the Eiffel Tower. In addition, you can catch the **Petite Ceinture** (small belt) from Porte Dorée (in the south east) to Porte d'Asnières (in the north west) which goes around the Périphérique.

RER

First opened in 1969, the Réseau Express Régional underground system is modern with up-to-date trains. Services start at 5.30am and stop at 12.30am daily, with trains running every 15 minutes. The three main RER lines (A, B and C) get very busy during the rush hours. Metro tickets are valid on RER journeys within Paris; for journeys to outlying districts and airports, purchase a separate ticket, unless you hold a travel pass card that covers the airport zones. Line C2 goes to **Orly**, **Line C5** to **Versailles** and **Line B3** to **Charles de Gaulle airport**.

TAXIS

Sometimes the challenge of finding an empty taxi defeats even the Parisians. Because there aren't enough taxis to go around, your chances of hailing one in the street are pretty slim. You're far better off making for one of the many taxi ranks dotted about town, and waiting for a taxi to pull up. What's more taxi ranks take precedence; if you hail a taxi in the street the driver is not obliged to stop if you're within 50m (165ft) of a taxi rank.

Taxi charges

These are based on area and time of day. Beneath the taxi light are three lights, **a**, **b** and **c**. One of these will light up according to what tariff applies. The tariff is also shown on the meter display inside the taxi. Most drivers will take only three people. It is normal to tip, and extra charges apply for heavy or awkward packages. The tariffs for journeys are as follows:

a – 6.30am to 8pm weekdays and Saturdays for journeys up to the Périphérique.

b – 8pm to 6.30am Monday to Saturday and all day Sundays for journeys up to the Périphérique.

c – beyond the Périphérique and to the airports at all times.

Commuters travel into Paris using the Réseau Express Régional (RER), an underground network which serves the airports and suburbs around Paris and stops at major stations within the city. An eastward bound extension to Line A is planned, in order to connect Paris with Euro Disneyland which is due to open in 1992. Whether either project makes the completion date remains to be seen.

nearly 2km (more than one mile) of underground passages.

The metro runs daily, from 5am until well after midnight, usually stopping at 1am. The morning rush hour on the metro is between 7.30am and 9am; the evening rush hour lasts longer, from 5pm till 8pm. Old trains have silver doorhandles which open the door when pushed upwards; newer carriages have push-button operated doors. One single tone sounds before the doors close.

Each train has a first class carriage, situated in the middle and painted yellow. Between 9am and 5pm these carriages are for first class passengers only, and ticket inspectors can fine you on the spot if you are caught in a first class compartment during this period without a first class ticket.

Use the indicator boards by ticket offices to map out your route; if you press the button for your desired stop the relevant metro lines will light up. Above the buttons, the direction of the first line you must take will come up in a square marked *première direction à prendre*. This is because lines,

instead of travelling due west or due east, are labelled by their final station at either end of the city. So Line 4 running to the north of Paris will be indicated as going in direction Porte de Clignancourt, while the same line travelling south will be going in direction Porte d'Orléans.

BUS

Buses run from 6am and continue until 12.30am daily, running every 12 to 15 minutes; there is a reduced service after 8.30pm and on Sundays. Bus shelters usually have a map outlining zones. If a journey takes you from one zone to another, you must use two bus tickets. These should be slotted into and punched by the machine next to the driver. **Do not** put your *Paris Visite*, *Coupon Jaune* or *Carte Orange* (*see above* **Tickets and Travel Passes**) into this machine, because it will destroy the metallic strip and render it useless. Just show the driver your card when you get on the bus. When you want to get off, press the request button near the exit and the *arrêt demandé* (stop requested) sign

Le jour où Alfonso a vu
comment cet étranger buvait sa Mariachi,
il s'est dit qu'il avait
enfin trouvé un mari pour sa fille.

Ogilvy & Mather

TEQUILA MARIACHI

CE QU'IL Y A DE PLUS MEXICAIN APRÈS UN MEXICAIN

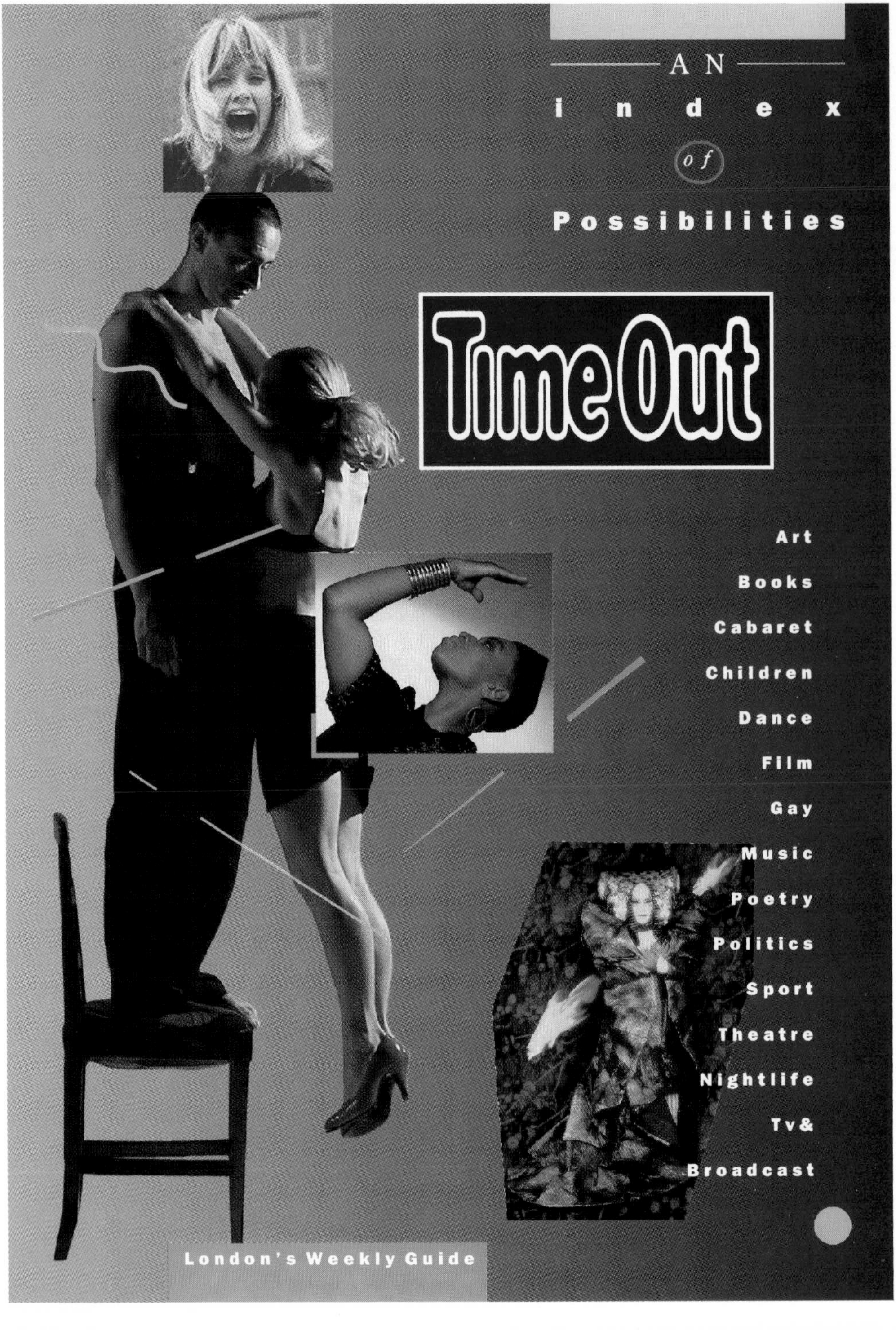

AN

index

of

Possibilities

Time Out

Art

Books

Cabaret

Children

Dance

Film

Gay

Music

Poetry

Politics

Sport

Theatre

Nightlife

Tv&

Broadcast

London's Weekly Guide

20/20

IT'S MORE THAN
FILM.
IT'S MORE THAN
THEATRE.
IT'S MORE THAN
MUSIC.
IT'S MORE THAN THE
ARTS.
IT'S MORE THAN
ENTERTAINMENT.

IT'S IN ON EVERY ACT.

20/20, Britain's arts and entertainment magazine - features, news, reviews, interviews and comment - every month from newsagents and bookshops across the land.

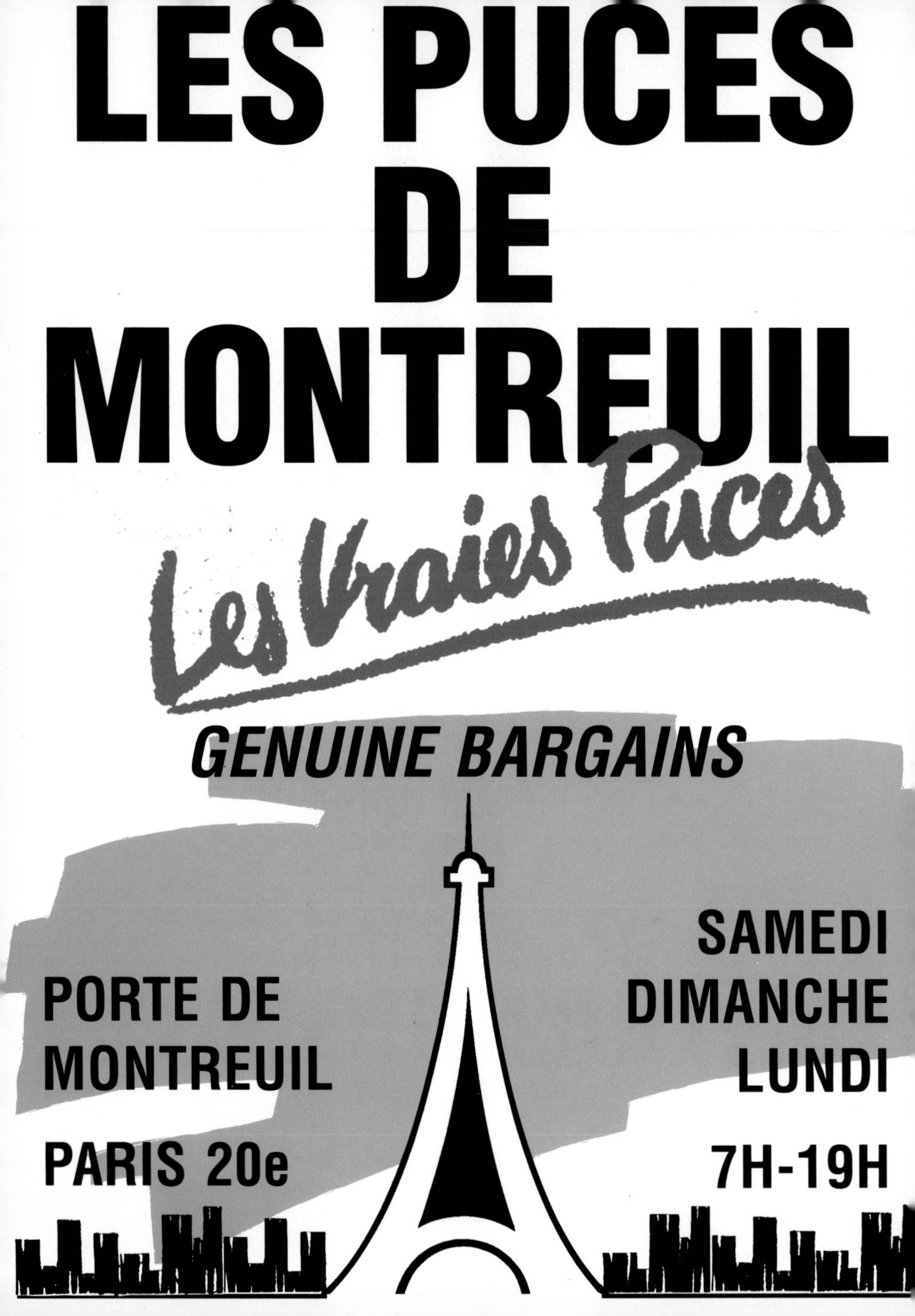

LES PUCES DE MONTREUIL

Les Vraies Puces

GENUINE BARGAINS

PORTE DE
MONTREUIL

PARIS 20e

SAMEDI
DIMANCHE
LUNDI

7H-19H

Taxi firms

The following taxi firms accept telephone bookings:

Alpha – 24-hour service *(45.85.85.85)*.
Taxi bleu – 24-hour service *(49.36.10.10)*.
Specialists in transporting the disabled – 24-hour service *(48.37.85.85)*.

RIVER BUS

At present Paris doesn't have a riverbus service. However, there has been talk of starting up a commuter service, leaving from Bercy (the sports and conference centre) near the Gare d'Austerlitz. Until then, Parisians and visitors alike will have to make the most of the **Batobus**, a boat service which runs from May until the end of September. Services operate between 10am and 8pm daily. The circuit lasts 56 minutes and has five stops; boats call at each stop approximately every 45 minutes. **Pick-up points** are at: **Port de la Bourdonnais** (near Eiffel Tower); **Porte de Solferino** (near Musée d'Orsay); **Quai Malaquais** (opposite the Louvre); **Quai de Montebello** (near Nôtre Dame); **Quai de l'Hôtel de Ville** (near Hôtel de Ville). One trip costs 30F; a day pass 70F; a three-day pass 160F; a seven-day pass 220F. Children travel half price.

CYCLING

Cycling in Paris can be dangerous. Even people who are used to cycling in cities should take extra care and wear protective head gear and reflective arm-bands and belts. Some metro and RER stations rent out bicycles: metros Château de Vincennes, Bobigny-Pantin and Raymond-Queneau; RER stations Saint-Germain-en-Laye and Courcelle sur Yvette. In addition, there are a number of bicycle rental firms within Paris. All will require a deposit and will ask you to pay a fee towards the insurance cover (usually about 30F per day).

Paris Vélo

2 rue du fer a Moulin (43.37.59.22). Metro Censier Daubenton/bus 47. **Open** 10am-12.30pm, 2-6.30pm, Mon-Sat. **Cost** 20F per hour; 80F-140F per day; 140F-200F per weekend.

Bicyclub de Paris

Chateau de Vincennes, near Floral Park (47.66.55.92). Metro Chateau de Vincennes/bus 75. **Open** 9am-7pm Wed, Sat, Sun. **Cost** 15F per hour; 60F per day.

It's a strong man or woman who chooses to travel by taxi in Paris. Spotting a cab is no problem; the trick is finding one that is empty. Just a note of warning; even when you spot a taxi rank complete with taxis, you might find that the drivers are nowhere to be seen.

TRAVELLING AT NIGHT

The metro and bus services operate until approximately 1am daily. If you want to travel after that hour, catch a **Noctambus** night bus. All services start from Châtelet; stops are arranged in two neat lines on Avenue Victoria and Rue Saint Martin. Look out for the logo – an owl perched on a branch. There are ten routes which cross Paris, all of them following metro routes. Buses run every 30 minutes from 1.30am to 5.30am daily and three bus tickets are required for each journey. Night bus maps are available from metro stations.

TRAVEL FOR THE DISABLED

Neither the metro nor the bus system is suitable for wheelchair use. However, **RER lines A and B** have wheelchair access. If travelling on **SNCF trains**, check with the information desk at the mainline station as some trains are equipped for wheelchairs. **Taxis** are obliged to take passengers in wheelchairs. Specially adapted taxis are available on *48.37.85.85*; book a day in advance. There is also a free service called **Voyage Accompagné** run by RATP, between 8am and 7pm Monday to Friday. Ring the day before you travel *(46.70.88.74)* to arrange for someone to accompany you on your journey. The service is available on metro Lines 1 to 13, bus routes in double figures and the Petite Ceinture, RER Line A and RER Line B south of Gare du Nord.

For further information on travelling in Paris if you're disabled get the leaflet entitled *Touriste quand même Paris*, from CNFLRH, 38 Boulevard Raspail, 75007 Paris.

TOURS

COACH TOURS

All guided coach tours listed below start in the centre of Paris and last approximately two hours. They either have a guide or use pre-recorded commentaries. Tours pass the major sights, but do not stop at all of them. There are various tours to choose from: a general tour; an artistic tour (including Nôtre Dame and the Louvre), Paris Panoramique (a bus ride that includes a trip on the Seine), and night tours. All coaches are non-smoking.

Cityrama
Depart from Cityrama bus stop, 4 Place des Pyramides, 75001 (42.60.30.14). Metro Palais Royal/bus 39, 48, 67, 72. **Trips** 9.30am, 10.30am, 1.30pm, 2.30pm, Mon, Wed-Sun. **Cost** 110F adults; 55F children; under-6s free. **Credit** AmEx, CB, MC, V.
Tours take visitors to the major sites, including Nôtre Dame and the Eiffel Tower. Individual cassettes with pre-recorded commentary are available in different languages. A hostess (not guide) accompanies the tour.

Paris Vision
Office: 3 rue d'Alger, 75001 Paris (42.60.31.25)/coaches depart from 214 rue de Rivoli, 75001 Paris. Metro Opera. **Trips** 9.30am, 10.30am, 11.30am, 1.30pm, 2pm, daily. **Cost** 110F adults; 55F under-12s. **Credit** AmEx, CB, MC, V.
Paris Vision coaches have pre-recorded commentaries only. Tickets are available from the main office or from the departure point 15 minutes before the trip.

Paris à la carte
9 place de la Madeleine, 75001 Paris (47.42.31.63). Metro Madeleine. **Trips** April-Sept, phone for details. **Cost** 70F per day; 100F for two consecutive days. **Credit**

AmEx, CB, MC, V.
Most major sights are covered on this tour; there are 25 stops (a map of stops is provided with the ticket), and you can get on and off as many times as you wish. Hostesses are English-speaking. Buses run every 2 hours; tickets can be bought at RATP Madeleine, Champs Elysées and Eiffel Tower.

WALKING TOURS
Walking tours of central Paris are a good idea if you prefer to see the city at first hand, instead of from the restricted comfort of a bus.

Caisse Nationale
62 rue Saint Antoine, 75004 Paris (42.74.22.22). Metro Bastille, Saint Paul. **Tours** phone for details.
Tours of monuments, museums, and – mainly during summer – of old *quartiers* (areas). English-speaking guides can be arranged.

Paris Secret
50 rue du Four, 75006 Paris (40.16.07.44). Metro Saint-Germain-des-Prés. **Tours** March-Oct: from 2.30pm daily.
Small groups (maximum 20 people) are taken on walking tours of 'unknown' Paris, such as Gustave Eiffel's private laboratory. English is spoken. Reservations required.

CANAL TRIPS
Canauxrama run canal trips from Bastille to La Villette, the new

Science park. Trips last about three hours and leave at 9.30am and 2.30pm from **Port de l'Arsenal**, opposite 50 boulevard de la Bastille. Return trips leave from **Bassin de la Villette**, 5 bis Quai de la Loire. Tickets cost 70F adults one way; 13F for under-12s. Phone reservations can be made on *42.39.15.00.*

BOAT TRIPS
A trip on the Seine is a marvellous way of seeing the spread of Paris. All companies listed below operate cruises which go from one end of Paris to the other and back again, passing major sites such as the Louvre, the Eiffel Tower, Nôtre Dame and the Mint. Most cruises last an hour and have commentaries in different languages.

Bateaux Mouches
Depart from Pont de l'Alma, 75005 Paris (42.25.96.10). Metro Alma Marceau/42, 63, 72, 80, 92. **Trips** *April-mid Nov:* every 30 minutes, 10am-9pm, daily; *mid Nov-March:* 11am, 2.30pm, 9pm, daily. **Cost** 30F.

Bateaux Parisiens
Depart from Pont d'Iena, 75015 Paris (47.05.50.00). Metro Trocadero/bus 82. **Trips** every 30 minutes, 9.30am-10.30pm, daily. **Cost** 30F.

Vedettes de Paris/Ile de France
Leave from Pont d'Iena, 75015 Paris (47.05.71.29). Metro Bir Hakeim/82. **Trips** every 30 minutes, 10am-11pm, daily. **Cost** 30F.

UNUSUAL TRIPS
Funiculaire de Montmartre
Leaves from rue Tardieu, 75018 Paris. Metro Abbesses, Anvers. **Open** 6am-midnight daily. **Cost** 5F.
A cable car which goes up the steep hill from rue Tardieu to the base of the Sacré Coeur (*see chapter* **Sightseeing**). Metro and bus tickets can be used on this service.

Le Petit Train de Montmartre
Leaves from Place Blanche, 75018. Metro Blanche/bus 2. **Open** *summer:* 9am-8pm Mon-Fri; 9am-midnight Sat, Sun; *winter:* 9am-8pm Mon-Fri; 10.30am-6.30pm Sat, Sun. **Trips** trains leave every 40 minutes. **Cost** 25F adults; 10F under-12s.
A miniature sightseeing train which takes a route (full of hairpin bends) around the crowded streets of Montmartre. You can get off at the place du Tertre to visit the artists' square and the Sacré Coeur and get another train back. Large groups are advised to book on 42.62.24.00.

Hélifrance
Heliport, 4 avenue de la Porte de Sevres, 75015 Paris (45.54.95.11). Metro Pont de Sevres/bus 136. **Open** *office:* 9am-5pm daily. **Cost** varies. **Credit** AmEx, CB, DC, V.

Pedestrians in Paris are second class citizens. Forget the niceties of courteous driving; here the motorist is boss and pedestrians do not have the right of way as they do in Britain. Pedestrian crossings are safe only when the traffic has been stopped either by lights or a traffic warden (gendarme). The 'cross now' symbol is, if nothing else, indicative of Parisians' attitudes; a little green man sprinting across the road, holding on to his hat for dear life.

Never underestimate the ruthlessness or rudeness of some French drivers. One apocryphal tale has it that a woman missed a change of lights and the motorist behind her got out of his car, went up to hers, opened the door and slapped her round the face. And she was French.

Fancy an expensive tour of Paris? You can book a helicopter tour to fly over the centre of Paris, and further out if you wish. Because of noise made by the propellers, there is no commentary. A 20-minute flight over Paris costs 560F per person; a 30-minute flight over Paris, La Défense and Versailles costs 840F per person; flights to La Defense only and Versailles only cost between 225F and 340F per person.

DRIVING

To drive in France you will need a green card (available from any insurance company), a first aid kit and red warning triangles. Headlights must be capped; you can buy yellow headlight covers from AA shops and most garages in Britain. When driving in France, carry some loose change, because a number of major routes go over toll bridges or form part of a *péage* (toll) motorway. Map out your route carefully as you approach Paris, or you may end up going round the périphérique several times. *See also chapter* **Survival**.

Driving etiquette and rules are generally the same as in Britain. However, *priorité à droite* (giving way to traffic that comes from the right), is a common occurrence and might take you by surprise, particularly on roundabouts.

If in doubt about routes or if travelling during peak holiday times (July and August), join the AA or RAC. You can then write for a recommended route map; allow up to 28 days for delivery.

If you're hitch-hiking around France **Allôstop** *(42.46.00.66)* matches hitchers to drivers, charging a small fee. Apart from this, hitching is not recommended.

ROUTES TO PARIS

Routes from Calais:
N43 then A26 then A1 or N1.
Routes from Boulogne:
N42 then A26 then A1 or N1.
Routes from Dunkerque:
A25 then A1 or N1.
Routes from Dieppe:
N27 then N138 then A13 or N915.
Routes from Le Havre: N182 then A13.

TRAINS

The Société Nationale des Chemins de Fer – **SNCF** – runs all train services in France. There are six major stations in Paris: Gare du Nord, Gare Saint Lazare, Gare de L'Est, Gare de Lyon, Gare d'Austerlitz, and Gare Montparnasse. There is a metro station at or very near to each terminal. Different platforms are used for trains for the *banlieux* (sub-

urban services) and *grandes lignes* (long distance and international services). Consequently there are many more *voies* (platforms) than in a British Rail station, often as many as 30. SNCF tickets are the size of a large cheque, and must be 'validated' by inserting them into the orange machine at the platform entrance. This punches a hole in the ticket and ensures it cannot be used for another journey. Theoretically, inspectors on trains are authorized to charge the full rate for the journey if tickets are not validated. Annoying if you already have paid at the station..

SNCF Information
(45.82.50.50). **Open** 6am-midnight daily.
Telephone rail information service, covering all national and international destinations.

GETTING TO PARIS

BY PLANE
Air France
London *(499 9511)*; Paris *(42.99.23.64)*.
Open 9am-5pm daily. **Credit** A, AmEx, DC, V.

British Airways
London *(897 4000)*; Paris *(47.78.14.14)*.
Open 7am-10.30pm daily. **Credit** A, AmEx, DC, V.

British Midland
London *(589 5599)*; Paris *(represented by Sabena Airways, 42.66.30.14)*. **Open** 6am-10pm daily. **Credit** A, AmEx, DC, V.

Charters: there are also many special offers from travel agents and charter flight companies. For more information read the *Time Out* small ads, or telephone the **Air Travel Advisory Bureau** *(636 5000)* for names of reputable agents.

BY TRAIN
British Rail International
(834 2345). **Open** 24 hours daily.
Credit A, V.
All trains to Paris leave from Victoria station and arrive at Gare du Nord. Crossings by boat or Hovercraft are available. Rail-boat journeys take about 11 hours. Rail-Hovercraft journeys take just under six hours, but Hovercraft crossings are prone to cancellation in rough weather and passengers are put on the next available ferry.

BY COACH
Eurolines
Victoria Coach Station, 52 Grosvenor Gardens, London SW1 (730 0202/730 8235). **Open** 9am-10pm daily. **Credit** A, V.
Eurolines operate several daily services to Paris (including a night coach), all arriving at Porte de la Villette.

Accommodation

Single rooms and lavish, sumptuous suites – whatever your budget we list the hotels to meet your needs.

There are some 1,400 hotels in Paris, so finding a place to crash out is relatively easy. What's more, most hotels – irrespective of price category – are located in the centre of town. If you're travelling to Paris in high season, finding the right place at the right price may pose a problem, so booking a room from home before you leave is advisable. Advance reservations should be made in June, September and October.

Hotel classification in Paris is based on a star system. At the very top are the four-star luxe (****l) establishments, justly called 'Palace Hotels'. A stay in one of these hotels will always be memorable: 24-hour hot and cold running service and concierges who will open almost any Parisian door you want to enter. Palace Hotels fall into the luxury tax category, so count on paying an additional 18.6 per cent on your room rates.

Regular four-star hotels usually have a more utilitarian, less glamorous aura. They tend to have in-house restaurants and bars. Three- and two-star hotels offer good accommodation at low rates, though count on a reduction in the number of private bathrooms, languages spoken at the front desk and services that are generally available. It's not uncommon for a well-managed two-star hotel to cost more than a run-down three-star hotel. At the bottom of the chain are the one-star and no-star hotels, where you often often share toilet and bath facilities with other guests. Since hotel rates rise regularly and renovations can cause a hotel to move up a grade, it's always sensible to ring in advance to check prices.

BOOKING AGENCIES

The Paris Tourist Office's information counters make same-day hotel reservations; they charge a small fee for this service. For example, expect to pay 35F for a reservation in a three-star hotel, 20F for a reservation in a two-star hotel.

Central Welcome Service
127 avenue des Champs-Elysées, 75008 Paris (47.23.61.72). Metro Georges V/bus 73. **Open** 9am-8pm daily (closed Christmas day, New Year's day).

Gare du Nord
18 rue de Dunquerque, 75010 Paris (45.26.94.82). Metro Gare du Nord (near International Arrivals)/bus 42, 43, 46, 47, 48, 49. **Open** May-Oct: 8am-10pm Mon–Sat; 1-8pm Sun; Nov-April: 8am-8pm Mon-Sat.

Gare de L'Est
Arrival Hall, 75010 Paris (46.07.17.73). Metro Gare de L'Est/bus 30, 31, 32, 33, 38, 39, 350. **Open** May-Oct: 8am-10pm Mon-Sat; Nov-April: 8am-8pm Mon-Sat.

Gare de Lyon
Exit Grandes Lignes, 75012 Paris (43.43.33.24). Metro Gare de Lyon/bus 20, 57, 63. **Open** May-Oct: 8am-10pm Mon-Sat; Nov-April: 8am-8pm Mon-Sat.

Gare d'Austerlitz
Arrivals Grandes Lignes, 75011 Paris (45.84.91.70). Metro Gare d'Austerlitz/bus 65, 89. **Open** May-Oct: 8am-10pm Mon-Sat; Nov-April: 8am-3pm Mon-Sat.

Bureau Tour Eiffel
Champs de Mars, 75007 Paris (45.51.22.15). Metro Ecole Militaire, Iéna/bus 69, 82, 90. **Open** May-Sept: 11am-6pm daily.

See also **AJF** *listed under* **Youth Accommodation** *below.*

'A great hotel is like a fine champagne', says Thierry Tattinger, whose family acquired **Le Crillon** *(listed under* **Palace Hotels**) *in 1979, thereby making it the only Palace Hotel in Paris to remain entirely French-owned. Though the high-profile clientele is eclectic – Michael Jackson, Madonna, Yassar Arafat, Richard Nixon – the hotel continues to stand on gilt-edged tradition. The eighteenth-century façade designed by Jacques-Ange Gabriel, the butterscotch marble lobby, the blue-draped restaurant styled by fashion designer Sonia Rykiel and the magnificent royal suites that look over the Place de la Concorde, ooze prestige.*

HOTELS

The hotels listed below have been classified according to average room price. Palace Hotels (1,500F and above); De Luxe (700F and above); Moderate (350F and above);

and Budget (less than 350F). All the Palace Hotels are located on the Right Bank. Unless otherwise indicated, the smaller hotels are located in the central and desirable neighbourhoods of Saint Germain, the Latin Quarter, Bastille and Marais.

PALACE HOTELS

Le Bristol
112 rue du Faubourg Saint-Honoré, 75008 Paris (42.66.91.45). Metro Miromesnil/bus 49, 80. **Rates** (breakfast not included) *single:* from 1,735F; *double:* from 2,400F. **Credit** Air Plus, AmEx, CB, DC, MC, EC, En Route, TC, V.
Built in 1924, the Bristol hotel, along with La Résidence – the new wing that was added in 1975 – is outrageously luxurious. The glittering lobby is lit by 23 Baccarat crystal chandeliers and the walls are hung with nineteenth-century Savonnerie tapestries. Both the summer restaurant, which overlooks the 1,200 square metre garden, and the winter restaurant – an oak-panelled, eighteenth-century-style oval room – are stunning. Rooms in the Bristol proper are furnished traditionally; rooms in La Résidence have Italian marble bathrooms that cost £17,000 each to build. Furthermore, all the rooms in La Residence overlook the gardens. Namedroppers will be delighted to know that the roof-top indoor pool was built to the specifications of Aristotle Onassis's yacht designer.
Hotel services: *Bar, restaurant. Business services. Hairdresser. Laundry/dry-cleaning. Private parking. Swimming pool, sauna and solarium.* **Room services:** *Air-conditioning. Minibar. Room service (24-hour). Television.*

Le Crillon
10 place de la Concorde, 75008 Paris (42.65.24.24). Metro Concorde/bus 24, 52, 84, 94. **Rates** (breakfast not included) *single:* 1,600F; *double:* from 2,000F. **Credit** AmEx, CB, DC, JCB, MC, TC, V.
See picture and caption.
Hotel services: *Baby-sitting. Bar, restaurants. Boutique. Business services. Conference rooms. Ticket agency.* **Room services:** *Air-conditioning. Minibar. Room service (24-hour). Television.*

The Georges V
31 avenue Georges V, 75008 Paris (47.23.54.00/Fax 47.20.40.00). Metro Georges V/bus 73. **Rates** *single:* from 1,729F; *double:* from 2,350F. **Credit** Air Plus, AmEx, CB, DC, EC, JCB, THF Gold Card, V.
The ornate and exclusive Georges V – now part of the Trust House Forte chain – continues to dazzle its guests with its opulence and high standards of service. Although it's

often compared to a museum because of the numerous antiques – human and otherwise

The **Plaza Athénée** *(listed under* **Palace Hotels***) is a sumptuous hotel, renowned for its lavish and elegant decor. In keeping with its image, it boasts a monthly flower bill that's larger than its electricity bill. Guests here expect to be pampered; there's a staff of 400 that look after the 200 silk and satin guestrooms. The in-house Relais Plaza restaurant, located just one block from the salons of Dior, Nina Ricci, Valentino, Chanel and Céline, is a major meeting place for the couture crowd.*

– that cram the lounges and guest-rooms, the management has recently made an effort to freshen up the ambience. They're even marketing a Georges V perfume. Rooms in this lavish hotel are huge and the suites (often with a real Boulle desk) are spectacular. Names in the guest register have included General Patton, General Peron, Greta Garbo, Duke Ellington and the Rolling Stones.
Hotel services: *Baby-sitting. Bar, restaurants. Boutiques. Bureau de change. Business services. Car rental. Chauffeurs. Hairdresser. Laundry/dry-cleaning. Ticket agency.* **Room services:** *Air-conditioning. Minibar. Room service (24-hour). Television.*

The Intercontinental
3 rue Castiglione, 75008 Paris (42.60.37.80/Fax 42.61.14.03). Metro Tuileries/bus 72. **Rates** *single:* from 1,700F; *double:* from 2,000F. **Credit** Air Plus, AmEx, CB, DC, En Route, EC, JCB, MC, Saison/SAS, TC, V.
This immense hotel, containing 500 rooms, seven courtyards and ten kilometres of hallways, straddles one whole city block between the Tuileries and the rue Mont-Thabor. The imperial ballrooms are declared national monuments and are so heavily gilded that you almost have to wear sunscreen when the chandeliers are lit. Twice a year, Yves Saint Laurent holds his *Haute Couture* showings here.

Hotel services: *Air-conditioning. Baby-sitting. Bar, restaurants. Business services. Conference rooms. Express checkout. Ticket agencies.* **Room services:** *Hair-dryers. Minibar. Room service (24-hour). Television.*

Plaza Athénée
25 avenue Montaigne, 75008 Paris (47.23.78.33/Fax 47.20.20.70). Metro Franklin D Roosevelt/bus 32, 73. **Rates** *single:* from 1,830F; *double:* from 2,470F. **Credit** AmEx, CB, DC, EC, TC, V.
See picture and caption.
Hotel services: *Baby-sitting. Business services. Garage. Hairdressing. Laundry/dry-cleaning. News-stand. Perfume/cosmetics boutique. Ticket agencies. Stockmarket information (Dow Jones teletype).* **Room services:** *Air-conditioning. Minibar. Radio, television. Room service (24-hour).*

Prince des Galles
33 avenue Georges V, 75008 Paris (47.23.55.11/FAX 47.20.96.92). Metro Georges V, Alma Marceau/bus 72, 73. **Rates** *single:* from 1,500F; *double:* from 1,700F. **Credit** AmEx, Air Plus, CB, DC, EC, MC, V.
Although part of the mammoth US hotel/motel chain Marriott since 1984, this hotel's management has proved to be both sensitive and imaginative regarding renovation. Many of the art deco mosaics in the original 1928 bathrooms have been painstakingly preserved, and London's Richmond

A DYNAMIC CONCEPT
3 STARS COMFORT HOTEL
EACH ROOM OFFERS A WHIRLPOOL AND STEAM BATH

THE TONIC HOTEL IN PARIS :
TONIC HOTEL TARANNE

153 Bd Saint-Germain PARIS 6
Tel. : (1) 42.22.21.65 Tx 205 340
Fax : (1) 45.48.22.25

TONIC HOTEL LES HALLES

12/14 rue du Roule PARIS 1
Tel. : (1) 42.33.00.71 Tx 205 340
Fax : (1) 40.26.06.86

TONIC HOTEL GARE DE LYON

19 rue d'Austerlitz PARIS 12
Tel. : (1) 40.19.04.05 Tx 205 340
Fax : (1) 40.19.09.08

TONIC HOTEL ODEON
19 rue Monsieur Le Prince PARIS 6
Tel. : (1) 46.33.31.69 Tx 205 340
Fax : (1) 45.48.22.25

THE TONIC HOTEL IN THE PROVINCE :
TONIC HOTEL DU GOLF

Carrefour de la Trache
Chateaubernard - 16100 COGNAC
Tel. : (16) 45.35.42.00 Tx 790 615
Fax : (16) 45.35.45.02

TONIC HOTEL DES THERMES

Village du Vallon des Sources
04000 DIGNE LES BAINS
OPEN JUNE 90
Reservations : Tel. : (1) 40.19.04.05 Tx 205 340
Fax : (1) 40.19.09.08

MAIN RESERVATION OFFICE : 19 rue d'Austerlitz - 75012 PARIS
Tel. : (1) 40.19.04.05 Telex : 205 340 Fax : (1) 40.19.09.08

Design Group has supervised much of the decoration of the public rooms. Of special interest are the *trompe-l'oeil* wall in the restaurant and the columned interior patio. Ask about the package *Gourmet weekends* that the hotel runs year-round on various gastronomic themes.
Hotel services: *Air-conditioning. Babysitting. Bar, restaurant. Conference rooms. Ticket agency.* **Room services:** *Hair-dryers. Room service (24 hour).Television.*

The Ritz
15 place Vendôme, 75001 Paris (42.60.38.30/Fax 42.86.00.91). Metro Tuileries/bus 42, 52, 72. **Rates** *single:* from 1,995F; *double:* from 2,460F. **Credit** AmEx, CB, DC, En Route, EC, JCB, MC, TC; telephone reservations by AmEx only.
Although Coco Chanel, the Duke of Windsor and Marcel Proust all lived here, the name most often associated with the Ritz is that of Ernest Hemingway, who reputedly 'liberated' the bar as the Germans left Paris. Hemingway is also claimed to have said that he hoped heaven would be as good as the Ritz. This hotel is, however, seemingly far more exclusive than heaven. It doesn't even have a lobby (no loitering for papparazzi) and the security is the tops; the windows overlooking the place Vendôme are not only sound-proof, they're bullet-proof. The good news for guests is, that following recent renovation, the Ritz is in better, Ritzier shape than ever. It now boasts a swanky new spa and a gorgeous, tiled swimming pool. Hotel guests have privileges at the new Ritz club – a late-night club that opened in 1988 – and are entitled to attend classes at the Ecole Gastronomique Française Ritz-Escoffier.
Hotel services: *Bars, restaurant. Baby-sitting. Business services. Conference rooms. Cookery school. Hairdressers. Health spa. Nightclub. Swimming pool. Ticket agency.* **Room services:** *Jacuzzi. Minibar. Room service (24-hour). Stereo, television, video.*

Royal Monceau
37 avenue Hoche, 75008 Paris (45.61.98.00/Fax 45.63.28.93). Metro Etoile/bus 30, 31, 73, 92. **Rates** *single:* from 1,450F; *double:* from 1,950F. **Credit** AmEx, CB, DC, EC, MC, V.
The Royal Monceau, occasionally overlooked by luxury travellers, has a lot of significant pluses in its favour. For example, there's a heated swimming pool, gym rooms and beauty treatments, in addition to the varied restaurants: Italian cuisine (the Carpaccio), French cuisine (the Jardin) and dietetic specialities in the restaurant by the pool (the Thermes). The guest rooms are pastel-tinted, large and traditionally decorated. This hotel concentrates more than most on the business traveller; the giveaway is the VIP Business Centre – equipped with office machines and teletypes – right on the main floor.
Hotel services: *Air-conditioning. Babysitting. Business services. Bar, restaurants. Conference rooms. Hairdressers. Health club/gymnasium. Swimming pool. Ticket agency.* **Room services:** *Room service (24 hour). TV, video.*

DE LUXE

L'Hôtel
13 rue des Beaux Arts, 75006 Paris (43.25.27.22). Metro Mabillon/bus 63, 70,

*A masterpiece of early art deco architecture, the **Hôtel Lutetia** (listed under De Luxe) is in the 'Grand Hotel' style typical of such buildings on the Left Bank. Both in-house restaurants – the fashionable Brasserie Lutetia that stays open till 1am and the gourmet Le Paris – are renowned as excellent eating venues. Under the supervision of Sonia Rykiel, the guest-rooms were given a thorough sprucing-up in 1989, and are now even more luxurious.*

86, 96. **Rates** *single:* from 750F; *double:* from 850F. **Credit** AmEx, CB, EC, MC, TC, V.
In 1968, Guy-Louis Duboucheron restored the Directoire-style Hôtel d'Alsace, which many literary fans know as the place where Oscar Wilde camped out until his death in 1900 claiming he was dying 'beyond his means'. The small-scale, ravishingly romantic L'Hôtel has arguably the kinkiest honeymoon suite in Paris, decorated with legendary showgirl Mistinguett's mirrored bedroom set.
Hotel services: *Baby-sitting. Massage. Piano bar, restaurant. Ticket agency.* **Room services:** *Air-conditioning. Minibar. Radio, television.*

Hôtel Cayre
4 boulevard Raspail, 75007 Paris (45.44.38.88/Fax 45.44.98.13). Metro Rue du Bac/bus 24, 83, 84, 94. **Rates** *single:* from 870F; *double:* from 900F. **Credit** AmEx, CB, DC, MC, TC, V.
Its central location (close to the Musée d'Orsay, the Louvre and Saint-Germain boutiques) makes the comfortable though rather bland Cayre a good bet.
Hotel services: *Private vaults.* **Room services:** *Television.*

Hôtel Lutetia
45 boulevard Raspail, 75007 Paris (45.44.38.10/Fax 45.44.50.50). Metro Sèvres-Babylone/bus 68, 94. **Rates** *single:* from 900F; *double:* from 950F. **Credit** A, Air Plus, AmEx, Carte Blanche, CB, DC, EC, En Route, JCB, MC, TC, V.
See **picture and caption.**

Hotel services: *Bar, restaurants. Parking.* **Room services:** *Air-conditioning. Minibar. Radio, television. Sound-proofing in rooms on boulevard Raspail and rue de Sèvres).*

Left Bank Hotel
9 rue de L'Ancienne Comédie, 75006 Paris (43.54.01.70/Fax 43.26.17.14). Metro Odéon/bus 58. **Rates** *single:* from 700F; *double:* from 800F. **Credit** AmEx, CB, DC, EC, MC, TC, V.
Antique-style furniture, a wood-panelled lobby and a perfect location near the Flore, les Deux Magots and the Saint-Germain shops are the main attractions of this three-star hotel. It opened in February 1989 in a seventeenth-century building next to the Café Procope where Voltaire used to hang out. Because the area is lively at night, the hotel's street-side windows are sound-proof.
Room services: *Air-conditioning. Built-in hairdryer. Laundry service. Minibar. Private safe. Television.*

Montana Tuileries
12 rue Saint Roch, 75001 Paris (42.60.35.10). Metro Tuileries, Pyramides/bus 24, 68, 69, 72. **Rates** *single:* from 500F; *double:* from 550F. **Credit** Amex, CB, DC, EC, MC, V.
A clean modern hotel, across from the Tuileries gardens, and within five minutes walk from the Louvre and Musée d'Orsay.
Room services: *Television.*

Pavillon de la Reine
28 place des Vosges, 75004 Paris (42.77.96.40/Fax 42.77.63.06). Metro Saint

Paul/bus 29, 69, 76, 96. **Rates** *single and double:* from 850F. **Credit** AmEx, CB, DC, MC, TC, V.

To reach the Pavillon de la Reine guests must walk through a seventeenth-century archway in the Royal Square that was commissioned by Henri IV. Once past the tiny courtyard, you'll find a thoroughly modern hotel. The inside is decorated in *ancien régime*-style, with reproduction baldachin beds, stone fireplaces and beamed ceilings. Though it has a slightly cloying, Disneyland air about it, it's nonetheless the plushest hotel in the popular Marais/Bastille district. **Hotel services:** *Private garage.* **Room services:** *Air-conditioning. Minibar. Television.*

Le Raphael
17 avenue Kléber, 75016 Paris (45.02.16.00/Fax 45.01.21.50). Metro Kléber/bus 22, 30. **Rates** *single and double:* from 1,400F. **Credit** AmEx, CB, DC, EC, MC, TC, V.

The Raphael is by far the most intimate four-star hotel on the Right Bank. It's because of this that groupies of the fashion and art worlds patronise it. How many other hotels have a Turner in the lobby? Rooms are decorated in traditional splendour: gilt fixtures, deep burnished wood panelling, sumptuous oriental rugs, and velvet cushions. **Hotel services:** *Baby-sitting. Bar, restaurant. Business services. Conference rooms. Laundry/dry cleaning service. Ticket agency.* **Room services:** *Minibar. Room service (24-hour). Television.*

Hotel Roblin
6 rue Chaveau-Lagarde, 75008 Paris (42.65.57.00/FAX 42.65.19.49). Metro Medeleine/bus 52. **Rates** *single:* from 520F; *double:* from 610F. **Credit** AmEx, CB, DC, EC, MC, V.

The best bets in this hotel are the romantic, oval-shaped rooms (nos. 12, 32, 52, 72) that have preserved their old-fashioned charm. The newly modernized rooms are rather plain and uninteresting, but the location – near the Madeleine, Fauchon's Gourmet market and the Concorde – and the pleasant art-decoish restaurant make up for this shortcoming. The rooms on the streetside can get noisy, when vans deliver to the flower market in the morning. **Hotel services:** *Bar, restaurant. Conference rooms.* **Room services:** *Minibar. Radio, television.*

La Villa
29 rue Jacob, 75006 Paris (43.266.60.00). Metro Saint-Germain-des-Prés/bus 48, 95. **Rates** *single:* from 700F; *double:* from 1,000F. **Credit** AmEx, CB, ED, MC, TC, V.

The top choice for the chic set since this post-modernist inn opened in 1989. The décor, by Marie-Christine Dorner, features a purple and orange ground-floor bar and impressive marble, glass and chrome bathrooms. The hotel is in a good location on a quiet street one block away from the Deux Magots café. **Hotel services:** *Piano bar.* **Room services:** *Air-conditioning. Minibar. Television..*

Villa Maillot
143 avenue de Malakoff, 75016 Paris (45.01.25.22). Metro Porte Maillot/bus 82. **Rates** *single:* from 1,300F; *double:* from 1,500F. **Credit** AmEx, CB, DC, EC, MC, TC, V. *See* **picture and caption.**

Hotel services: *Bar, restaurant. Conference room.* **Room services:** *Air-conditioning. Kitchenettes. Minibar. Room service. Television. Trouser press.*

MODERATE
Bac Saint Germain
66 rue du Bac, 75007 Paris (42.22.20.03). Metro Rue du Bac/bus 69. **Rates** *single:* from 350F; *double:* from 400F. **Credit** AmEx, CB, DC, MC, TC, V.

Rooms aren't terribly large, but the great location – near fashion shops, clubs, museums, antique stores and banks – and a spotless décor make this hotel a winner. After a £1 million renovation in 1989, many bathrooms have built-in hairdryers and marble walls. Breakfast is served in the glassed-in seventh-floor terrace. **Hotel services:** *Elevator. Upstairs lobby.* **Room servies:** *Radio/alarm. Television.*

Bastille Speria
1 rue de la Bastille, 75004 Paris (42.72.04.01). Metro Bastille/bus 69, 76. **Rates** *single:* from 380F; *double:* from 430F. **Credit** AmEx, CB, DC, MC, FTC, V. *See* **picture and caption.** **Room services:** *Built-in hairdryer. Minibar. Television.*

Brittanique
20 avenue Victoria, 75001 Paris (42.33.74.59/Telex 230 600). Metro Châtelet/bus 21, 72. **Rates** *single:* from 440F; *double:* from 520F. **Credit** AmEx, CB, DC, EC, MC, FTC, V.

An understated hotel in a central location, the Brittanique served as a Quaker mission throughout World War I. It has recently been refurbished. **Hotel services:** *Elevator.* **Room services:** *Built-in hairdryer. Minibar. Television.*

Hôtel des Celestins
1 rue Charles V, 75004 Paris (48.87.87.04). Metro Sully-Morland. **Rates** *single:* from 340F; *double:* from 360F. **Credit** CB, MC, V.

In the eighteenth century, the Hôtel des Celestins building belonged to the Celestins Convent. Many of the fourteen (very small) rooms still have their original dark wood walls and beamed-ceilings. The tiny Marais street is quiet at night, but does get noisy during early morning traffic jams. Note that the five-storey hotel's status as a landmark has prevented the owners from installing an elevator.

Hôtel de la Louisiane
60 rue de Seine, 75006 Paris (43.29.59.30/Fax 46.34.23.87). Metro Odéon/bus 87, 96. **Rates** *single:* from 350F; *double:* from 450F. **Credit** CB, DC, MC, V.

Because many of the people who check in as guests stay on as permanent residents, it can be hard to get a room at this hotel. The Louisiane, overlooking the colourful and noisy rue de Buci vegetable and flower markets, attracts artists and insomniacs. Simone de Beauvoir occupied one of the hotel's prized oval rooms for years.

Hôtel de l'Orchidée
65 rue de l'Ouest, 75014 Paris (43.22.70.50/Telex 203 026 ORCHID). Metro Pernet/bus 28, 58. **Rates** *single:* from

A stone's throw from the Etoile is the **Villa Maillot** *(listed under* De Luxe*), a splendid art deco hotel that was renovated in 1988. At one time it was the Embassy of Sierra Leone. Bleached wood, polished pink marble and thirties-style fixtures are the main decorative features in the rooms and public areas. For anyone needing access to the Palais des Congrès convention centre, this is a blissful alternative to the tower hotels that blot the Porte Maillot district.*

The seventeenth-century presbytery that adjoins the sixteenth-century Church of Saint Merry has a very chequered past. Before Christian Crabbe, the current owner,

The **Bastille Speria** (listed under **Moderate**) is the perfect Bastille location: right next door to the Brasserie Bofinger and only steps away from the new Opéra, the place des Vosges and the rue de Lappe nightspots. The interior of this hotel, which was renovated from top to bottom in 1988, is muted, uncluttered bayberry green. Rooms on the street side have been soundproofed.

350F; _double:_ from 380F. **Credit** AmEx, CB, DC, EC, MC, TC, V.
A brand-new three-star hotel in the heart of the new Montparnasse, the Orchidée was inaugurated in 1989. It's across the street from Ricardo Bofill's enormous neo-classical _Place de Seoul_ apartment complex. Its location makes this hotel convenient for Montparnasse train station, nightclubs and theatres.
Hotel services: _Conference rooms. Private garden. Sauna. Jacuzzi._ **Room services:** _Television._

Hôtel Places des Vosges
12 rue de Birargue, 75004 Paris (42.72.60.46/Fax 42.72.02.64). Metro Saint Paul. **Rates** _single:_ from 277F; _double:_ from 394F. **Credit** AmEx, CB, DC, MC, TC, V.
Though rooms here are quite small and spartan – reminiscent of a spa or dormitory – the hotel is in a good location and room prices are low. If you have a car, parking is not easy in this neighbourhood.
Hotel services: _Elevator._

Hôtel de Saint-Germain
50 rue du Four, 75006 Paris (45.48.91.64/Fax 45.48.46.22). Metro Saint Sulpice/bus 39, 63, 70, 87. **Rates** _single:_ from 480F; _double:_ from 520F. **Credit** AmEx, CB, DC, En Route, MC, TC, V.
The cosy, comfortable rooms are decked out in English pine furniture and Laura Ashley prints giving a real home-from-home atmosphere in a prime Left Bank location.

Hotel services: _Baby-sitting. Business services. Laundry. Small room service menu. Ticket agency. Tourist buses for hire._ **Room services:** _Minibar. Television._

Hôtel de Verneuil Saint-Germain
8 rue de Verneuil, 75007 Paris (42.60.82.14/42.60.24.16/Telex 211 608F HOT VERN). Metro Rue du Bac/bus 68, 69. **Rates** _single:_ from 580F. _double:_ from 610F. **Credit** AmEx, CB, DC, JCB, MC, TC, V.
The Verneuil is located in the heart of the Left Bank antiques shop district, but the management went ahead and decorated the hotel's parlour with life-size plaster casts of Roman goddesses anyway. The rooms here are small and could do with some dusting, but the overall effect is cosy.
Hotel services: _Large lobby._ **Room services:** _Television._

Saint-Merry
78 rue de la Verrerie, 75004 Paris (42.78.14.15). Metro Hotel de Ville/bus 69, 76, 96. **Rates** _single:_ from 370F; _double:_ from 600F. **Credit** TC.

turned it into a hotel, it was a very merry, down-at-heel whorehouse. The décor is fascinating: room No. 9 is built right into the church buttresses. All rooms have bits and pieces of authentic, flamboyant Gothic bric-à-brac, painstakingly restored by Mr Crabbe. The hotel is centrally located, on a lively – and noisy – pedestrian street one block south of the Pompidou Centre and three blocks north of Notre Dame.
Hotel services: _Elevator._

Welcome Hotel
66 rue de Seine, 75006 Paris (46.43.24.80). Metro Odéon/bus 87, 96. **Rates** _single:_ from 250F; _double:_ from 380F. **No credit cards.**
A charming hotel with double-glazed windows overlooking the Buci flower market. Many of the 30 rooms have beamed ceilings. The bathrooms tend to be very small, crammed into whatever available space the carpenter could find. The rooms on the top floor get very hot during the summer.
Hotel services: _Elevator._ **Room services:** _Television._

BUDGET

Bellevue et Chariot d'Or
39 rue de Turbigo, 75003 Paris (48.87.45.60). Metro Etienne Marcel/bus 29. **Rates** _single:_ from 280F; _double:_ from 300F. **Credit** AmEx, CB, DC, EC, MC, TC, V.
The rooms here are imaginatively decorated, and the prices are very low: there are six rooms that sleep four for 400F per night. The location is convenient for Les Halles, the Pompidou Centre and the fashion shops on rue Etienne Marcel and the place des Victoires.
Hotel services: _Bar. Elevator._

Castex
5 rue Castex, 75004 Paris (42.72.31.52). Metro Bastille/bus 67, 69, 76, 86, 87. **Rates** _single:_ from 175F; _double:_ from 235F. **Credit** CB, MC, FTC, V.
A simple, family-run establishment, which was entirely renovated in 1989, located in the Bastille/Marais area. The entrance door is locked at midnight so make sure you've got a special passkey to get in. The hotel is so lovingly cared for you may decide to stay on after winning the national lottery.

Esmerelda
4 rue Saint Julien le Pauvre, 75005 Paris (43.54.19.20). Metro Saint Michel, Maubert/bus 21, 38, 85, 96. **Rates** _single:_ from 100F; _double:_ from 250F
No credit cards.
See **picture and caption.**

HOTEL DU CONTINENT
* * *
N.N

Tel: 42.60.75.32
Telex: 213 249
Fax: 42.61.52.22

30, rue du Mont-Thabor
75001 PARIS
Metro: Concorde

In the heart of Paris- between Concorde, Opera and the Louvre Museum. 28 bedrooms

---

HOTEL DE BRETAGNE
* * *
N.N

Main reservation office:
Hotel du Continent.
See above for tel. & fax

33, rue R. Losserand
75014 PARIS
Metro: Montparnasse

Close to the new Montparnasse Station, 10 min. walk from St Germain des Prés. Equipped conference room.

HOTEL ST ROMAIN
* * *
N.N

Tel: 42.60.31.70
Telex: 217 511
Fax: 42.60.10.69

5-7 Rue St Roch
75001 PARIS
Metro: Tuileries

Recently renovated. Close to the Louvre Museum and the rue St Honoré where all the famous designer boutiques are. 33 bedrooms . 2 duplex apartments .

Henry IV
*25 place Dauphine, 75001 Paris
(43.54.44.53). Metro Pont Neuf/bus 24, 27.*
Rates *single:* from 100F; *double:* from 120F;
triple from 160F. **Credit** TC.
A well-loved, ultra-modest hotel overlooking the gorgeous place Dauphine on the
Ile de la Cité. Don't expect the Ritz treatment – or even a private bath – here.
However, do expect that the no-frills rooms
will be booked up months in advance, so
book well ahead.

Hôtel Floridor
*28 place Denfert-Rochereau, 75014 Paris
(43.21.35.53). Metro Denfert-Rochereau/bus
216.* **Rates** *single:* from 194F; *double:* from
213F. **No credit cards.**
The Floridor is excellent value: the rooms
are newly wallpapered, the bathrooms have
all been recently renovated, and there's
even a tiny elevator to carry one thin person, and a small suitcase, up to the top
floors. Rooms overlooking the square – a
pretty view – are currently being equipped
with sound-proof windows.

Hôtel du Marais
*2bis rue des Commines, 75003 Paris
(48.87.78.27). Metro Filles du Calvaire/bus
20, 65 96.* **Rates** *single:* from 220F; *double:*
from 280F. **Credit** CB, MC, TC, V.
The Marais has clean and simple rooms
with small private bathrooms and lots of
'luxury' extras, in addition to its good
Marais location.
Hotel services: *Elevator.* **Room services:**
Minibar. Radio, television.

Prima Lepic
*29 rue Lepic, 75018 Paris (46.06.44.64).
Metro Abbesses.* **Rates** *single:* from 220F; *double:* from 300F. **Credit** CB, MC, FTC, V.
This six-storey hotel, on the winding market
street that leads down from the Moulin
Rouge, represents bohemian Montmartre at
its best. The rooms have pretty Sanderson
floral wallpaper and there is a delightful
trompe-l'oeil garden breakfast salon.
Hotel services: *Elevator.*

Saint-André-des-Arts
*66 rue Saint-André-des-Arts, 75006 Paris
(43.26.96.16). Metro Odéon/bus 87, 96.*
Rates *single:* from 240F; *double:* from 330F.
No credit cards.
The hotel was built in the seventeenth century and many of the rooms look as though
they've hardly changed since the
Mousquetaires (Musketeers) du Roi – the
building's first residents – moved out.
However, this is one of the liveliest hotels in
Paris, with the tiny breakfast room packed
late each morning with models, photographers and artists. 'People stay here *before*
they get famous and boring', confides the
owner. If you plan on sleeping, bring
earplugs or prepare to be deafened by the
street-life and strolling musicians on the rue
Saint-André-des-Arts.

BED &
BREAKFAST

Bed and Breakfast 1
*73 rue Nôtre-Dame-des-Champs, 75006 Paris
(43.25.43.97). Metro Vavin, Nôtre-Dame-des-*

Champs/bus 91. **Rates** (including breakfast)
single: from 190F; *double:* from 240F. **Open**
9am-1pm, 2-6pm, daily.
B&B is not a likely option in this capital, as
hotels in every price range are plentiful and
Parisians tend to be more reserved than
many Britons about inviting strangers into
their home. Bed and Breakfast 1 has 300 par-
ticipating hosts in Paris and the staff does its
best to match preferences, such as smoking
and allergy to animals. Phone or write for
brochures and reservation forms. There is a
two-night minimum stay. The association's
annual membership card (50F per person) is
included in the reservation fee. Visitors to
Paris without reservations or membership
may call or stop by the office to see if last-
minute accommodation is available.

RESIDENCE
HOTELS

Residence hotels, with studios and
one- or two-bedroom flats equipped
with kitchenettes, are generally
leased by the week. Maid service is
once a week or once every three
days (extra charge for daily service). Towels, sheets and kitchenware are provided. A refundable
deposit (1,000F to 2,000F) is payable
on arrival.

Le Claridge
*74 avenue des Champs-Elysées, 75008 Paris
(43.59.67.97/Fax 42.25.04.88). Metro
Franklin D Roosevelt, Georges V/bus 73.*
Rates *studios* from 5,500F per week; *one-bed
flats* from 9,000F per week; *two-bed flats* from
14,000F per week. **Credit** AmEx, CB, DC,
EC, MC, V.
Clean-cut, rather standardized apartments
above the Claridge mall, in what was once
one of the grandest mansions on the
Champs-Elysées.

Home Plazza
*74 rue Amelot, 75011 Paris
(40.21.20.00/Fax 47.00.82.40). Metro St
Sebastien Froissart.* **Rates** *studios 1-2 persons*
400F per night; *3 persons* 500F per night; *4
persons* 600F per night; discounts for longer
stays. **Credit** AmEx, CB, DC, EC, En Route,
JCB, MC, Plus, TC, V.

Rooms are available by the day, week or
month in this 270-unit three-star residence
which opened in April 1989. Rooms are bright
and attractive, with cheerful flowered chintz

*Stay at the **Jardin des Plantes** (listed under **Moderate**) and you'll be able
to make use of the sunny fifth-floor terrace for breakfast and sunbathing.
Brightly decorated with floral wallpaper and white furniture, many rooms in
this Left Bank hotel offer splendid views of the Botanical Gardens.*

curtains that match the sofabed covers.
Hotel services: *Bar, restaurant. Baby-sitting. Business services and conference rooms. Health spa, sauna, Jacuzzi. Private garden.*
Room services: *Television.*

Pierre et Vacances Montmartre
10 place Charles Dullin, 75018 Paris (42.57.14.55/Telex 290 532). Metro Anvers/bus 39, 48, 80. **Rates** *apartments* 480F-1,060F per night; discounts for longer stays. **Credit** AmEx, CB, EC, MC, TC, V.
A 76-unit residence, close to the Sacré Coeur and the place du Tertre, with apartments that sleep from one to six people.
Room services: *Television.*

Pierre et Vacances Porte de Versailles
20 rue Oradour-sur-Clane, 75015 Paris (45.54.97.43/Telex 201 344). Metro Porte de Versailles/bus 39, 48, 80. **Rates** *2-room apartments for 4 persons* 570F-690F per night; discounts for longer stays. **Credit** AmEx, CB, EC, MC, TC, V.
A 188-unit complex, near the Porte de Versailles trade centre on the southern edge of Paris.
Hotel services: *Bar. Garden. Salon. Sauna.*
Room services: *Television.*

APARTMENT RENTALS

Rothray
10 rue Nicolas-Flamel, 75004 Paris (48.87.13.37/Fax 40.26.34.33). Metro Châtelet/bus 38, 47. **Credit** TC.
Ray Lampard, an Englishman in Paris, offers a unique and personalized accommodation service: fully furnished Parisian apartments for lease by the week (seven-day minimum). All apartments are centrally located – Marais, Châtelet, Ile Saint-Louis, Les Halles – and include a weekly cleaning service. Mr Lampard arranges for you to have fresh flowers on arrival and stocks the kitchen with breakfast tea, coffee, milk, sugar and other sundries. The price of a studio flat averages 350F per night; larger multi-roomed apartments average 1,100F per night.

YOUTH ACCOMMODATION

Acceuil des Jeunes en France
12 rue des Barres, 75004 Paris (42.72.72.09/Telex 240 909). Metro Pont Marie/bus 69, 76, 96. **Office open** 9.30am-7pm Mon-Sat.
The AJF maintain 5,550 clean, safe and cheap beds in youth centres throughout the Paris area, and can book an additional 8,000 beds in one- to three-star hotels in Paris for travellers aged 18 to 30. Groups of eight or more may book in advance through the above office. Individuals and smaller groups must apply in person at one of the four AJF centres listed *below*. The Youth Centres in the Marais area, namely Maubuisson, Fauconnier, François Miron and Fourcy – 450 beds in total, open all year round – are the most desirable. They are located in seventeenth-century mansions and house one to eight people per room for 77F to 90F per person per night, including breakfast. In order to secure a room in one of these, the AJF suggests getting to the office by 8am.

The **Esmeralda** *(listed under* **Budget***) is an arty, charming, cheap hotel located in the noisiest sector of the Latin Quarter. Each of the nineteen rooms is decorated differently with real flea-market flair. Not all the rooms have complete toilet facilities.*

The AJF Bastille (150 beds, open all year) is also centrally located, as are the AJF Coubertin and Luxembourg that have 670 beds in total. Both are open in the summer only and have fine Left Bank locations. Many other centres are on the periphery of the city. The 30 hotels booked through the AJF cost from 85F to 350F per night and most are located on the Right Bank.

AJF Beaubourg
(opposite Pompidou Centre) 119 rue Saint-Martin, 75004 Paris (42.77.87.80). Metro Rambuteau/bus 38, 47, 75. **Office open** 9.30am-7pm Mon-Sat.

AJF Gare du Nord
(inside the Gare Banlieu, new suburban station) rue de Dunkerque, 75009 Paris (42.85.86.19). Metro Gare du Nord/bus 42, 43, 46, 47, 48, 49. **Office open** *May-Sept:* 9.30am-7pm Mon-Fri.

AJF Marais
16 rue Pont Louis-Philippe, 75004 Paris (42.78.04.82). Métro Hotel de Ville/bus 67. **Office open** all enquiries through AJF Beaubourg office *(see above).*

AJF Saint Michel
139 boulevard Saint Michel, 75005 Paris (43.54.95.86). Metro Port Royal/bus 21, 27, 38, 85. **Office open** 10am-6.45pm Mon-Fri.

CAMPING

Camping d'Ile de France
allée du Bord de l'Eau, in the Bois de Boulogne, 75016 Paris (45.24.30.00). Metro Porte Maillot (connected during the summer by a free shuttle-bus to camp grounds)/bus 43. **Open** all year. **Credit** TC.
There's a no-reservations policy at the only major campsite in the Paris area: there is no demand in the winter and huge queues every morning during the summer months.

The cost for a one- to four-person *emplacement* with electricity and water for either tent or caravan is 135F per night, or 55F per night for a pitch without electricity. For large groups, advance reservations are occasionally accepted.

Paris by Area

You've defied vertigo up the Eiffel Tower, wandered through miles of art housed in the Louvre, explored the tubing of the Pompidou Centre. Take a break from the better-known tourist attractions to stroll along the *quais* of the Seine, raunch it up in Pigalle, work up an artistic sweat in the galleried alleys of Montparnasse or simply linger over a *café crème* in one of the many bistros scattered around Montmartre. We take you through the areas that make up Paris and chart the more recent trends that have shaped each district, so that when you arrive in a *quartier*, you'll have some insider knowledge to get the most from your visit.

CONTENTS:

Setting the Scene

From the bright lights of the Champs Elysées, to the elegant tranquillity of the Marais; we outline the main characteristics of the Parisian areas you're most likely to visit.

BASTILLE

Forever branded with the notoriety of the French Revolution, this area became a focus of plebeian insurrection and the catalyst from which anarchy spread throughout the capital in 1789 (*see chapter* **Revolution**). Until the Bastille was stormed, the peasants were impotent in their attempts to loosen the aristocratic stranglehold which had stood unchallenged for centuries. Once the prison had been taken, the Revolution gained both momentum and, more importantly, gunpowder.

The Bastille previously consisted of a rather uninspiring collection of shops and craftsmen's studios but has recently been colonized by artists' studios and galleries. It's well-served by a variety of restaurants, cafés and *de rigueur* nightspots where you can indulge in whatever social delicacy takes your fancy (*see chapter* **Nightlife**).

CHAMPS ELYSEES

Originally a serene, tree-lined avenue commissioned by Marie de Medicis in 1616, it was designed as a continuation of the Tuileries and to provide a vista running from the Louvre, at that time a royal palace. The avenue starts at the Place de la Concorde with its obelisk from the temple of Luxor (a gift from the Viceroy of Egypt in 1829) and ends at the Arc de Triomphe (*see chapter* **Sightseeing**).

Once popular with the rich as a catwalk on which to parade their bouffant finery, the Champs Elysées (*see chapter* **The Right Bank**) is now a blaze of gaudy neon and fast-food joints, geared towards snaring unwary tourists as they make their way up towards the Arc de Triomphe. Despite the contrived and painfully familiar nature of some of these more recent additions, there are still many picturesque squares and parks that border the lower half of the avenue, providing a much-needed haven away from the frenzied consumerism of the main avenue.

ILE DE LA CITE & ILE SAINT-LOUIS

The Ile de la Cité is the geographical and historical heart of Paris. It was here, in the first century AD, that the Romans founded Lutecia, as it was then called, and Paris fanned out from this imperial settlement (*see chapter* **Roman Paris**). Its tree-lined quays now surround some of the city's oldest monuments, including Notre Dame, the Palais de Justice – the King's palace during the Middle Ages – the Sainte Chapelle, built in 1248, and the Conciergerie or residence of the King's Guard (*see chapter* **Sightseeing**). Cross the bridge to the Ile Saint-Louis and gaze at the aristocratic seventeenth-century residences, or enjoy the main street's fashionable boutiques, exclusive shops and gourmet restaurants.

LES HALLES

Up until 1970, Les Halles was the wholesale market centre of Paris, but after a series of face-lifts it has been transformed into an area packed with fashionable cafés, restaurants and shops (*see chapter* **The Right Bank**). The glass and steel exterior of the Centre Pompidou, for some an innovative triumph, and for others an unrivalled eye-sore (*see chapter* **Museums & Galleries**), sits uncomfortably beside the Gothic façade of the Saint Merri church. The *parvis*, or square, with its buskers, impromptu cabaret artists and vendors is a throw-back to the street entertainers of the Middle Ages and adds to the informality of the area. You can spend an unhurried afternoon outside one of the many cafés which encircle the square, surrounded by fire-eating, sword-swallowing bohemia.

LE MARAIS

Originally set in outlying farmland, Le Marais remained officially outside Paris until Henry IV abandoned his medieval palace on the Ile de la Cité in 1612 and took up residence in the Place des Vosges, one of Paris's most idyllic squares (*see chapter* **The Right Bank**). Despite the auspices of the royal presence, the area was later abandoned and fell into neglect until, in 1962 the then Minister of Culture, André Malraux, began restoring it to its former beauty. In addition to the stately private residences, there's also a fair sprinkling of young designer shops and trendy galleries, as well as some popular nightclubs.

MONTMARTRE

Perched high above Paris on the Buttes, this once-peaceful village is where Picasso painted his *Demoiselles d'Avignon* at the turn of the century, and together with Van Dongen, Braque and Juan Gris introduced the world to cubism. Much has changed since then, and the area has now become a strange hybrid of old and new. Picturesque winding streets collide with crowded modern boulevards and prostitutes exchange glances with milling hordes of tourists who flock here. The area is spoilt for attractions, all within easy access of each other. Once you've indulged in a little licensed debauchery around the Moulin Rouge (*see chapter* **The Right Bank**), you can stroll towards the Sacré Coeur for some reflective atonement. Unfortunately, you may have to share the moment with a few thousand others, as this is one of the most visited sights in Paris (*see chapter* **Sightseeing**).

QUARTIER LATIN

This has been the home of students and academics since the Sorbonne, or University of Paris, was founded in 1215. Latin was the official language of the University until the eighteenth century and the area still retains its scholarly tradition with an abundance of book and art shops (*see chapter* **The Left Bank**). Its popularity among the budding bohemians of the capital is guaranteed by a concentration of night clubs and cafés *au fait* with the latest tastes and trends.

The Seine

An artery flowing through the heart of the city, the Seine provides seven miles of celebrated embankments from which to catch the best views of Paris.

Stretching along 776 slow-moving kilometres (480 miles), the Seine is the fourth-longest river in France, giving life-blood to the capital which it dominates. It was Julius Caesar who named the river Sequana, at a time when Lutecia was only a medium-sized town, in perpetual competition with its neighbour Rotomagus (now Rouen). The central location and its two islands eventually ensured the supremacy of Paris over its rival, and so the Seine carries the most important river traffic. From the heart of the old city, using the Pont Neuf as a starting-point, we follow the embankments and tow-paths of the river upstream and downstream, as far as the outskirts of the city.

RIVER CRUISES

Today, a trip on the Seine is a relaxing way of seeing Paris pass before your eyes, away from the frenetic traffic of the boulevards. All the companies listed below operate cruises which go from one end of the city to the other, taking in most of the major sites en route, such as the Louvre, the Eiffel Tower, Nôtre Dame and the Mint. Most of the tours last an hour and have multi-lingual commentaries. Especially rec-

ommended for incurable romantics are the dinner cruises – enquire at the boat office for more information.

Batobus
May-Sept 10am-8pm daily. **Cost** 30F one trip; 70F day pass; 160F 3-day pass; 220F 7-day pass; half-price for children.
The circuit of this boat service lasts 56 minutes and covers five stops; boats call at each stop approximately every 45 minutes. The pick-up points are at: **Port de la Bourdonnais** (near Eiffel Tower); **Porte de Solferino** (near Musée d'Orsay); **Quai Malaquais** (opposite the Louvre); **Quai de Montebello** (near Nôtre Dame); **Quai de l'Hôtel de Ville** (near Hôtel de Ville).

Bateaux Mouches
From Pont de l'Alma, 75005 Paris (42.25.96.10). Metro Alma Marceau/bus 42, 63, 72, 80, 92. **Trips** *April-mid Nov:* every 30 minutes, 10am-9pm, daily; *mid Nov-March:* 11am, 2.30pm, 9pm, daily. **Cost** 30F.

Bateaux Parisiens
From Pont d'Iéna, 75015 Paris (47.05.50.00). Metro Trocadéro/bus 82. **Trips** every 30 minutes, 9.30am-10.30pm, daily. **Cost** 30F.

Vedettes de Paris/Ile de France
From Pont d'Iéna, 75015 Paris (47.05.71.29). Metro Bir Hakeim/bus 82. **Trips** every 30 minutes, 10am-11pm, daily. **Cost** 30F.

THE OLD CITY

The Pont Neuf on the **Ile de la Cité** is a good place to start your walk along the Seine. In the square du Vert Galant on the island's western tip, 'Good King Henri' on his bronze horse points the way to the sea. Behind him, what was once the heart of closely-packed medieval Paris has mostly given way to Haussmann's mid-nineteenth-century replacements in the form of monumental administrative buildings (*see chapter* **Empires & Rebellions**). Only **Nôtre Dame** and the little area north of the cathedral were left untouched. One of the more unexpected sights on this island is the animal market, held every day on the Quais de la Mégisserie and de Corse. Here you will find anything from chickens and rabbits to exotic birds.

For a taste of the old Paris, cross the Pont Saint Louis into the **Ile Saint-Louis**. Still mostly residential, with small, meandering streets filled with restaurants and small shops, the Ile Saint-Louis is one of the capital's

An arduous 386-step climb to the viewing platform 69 metres (228 feet) above **Nôtre Dame**'s *portals (listed under* **The Old City***) will be rewarded by an unequalled view of the Seine and Paris.*

most romantic areas for a stroll. It's easy to limit your exploration of the river to the *quais* of these two islands, and join the crowds relaxing by the river. But for those of a more energetic disposition, the embankments can be followed from one end of Paris to the other. Once the main arteries of communication and trade, most of Paris's monuments can now be inspected from these *quais*.

Nôtre Dame Cathedral
place du Parvis Nôtre Dame, 75004 Paris (43.26.07.39/crypt 43.29.83.51). Metro Cité. **Open** 8am-7pm daily. **Archaeological crypt open** *July, Aug*: 9.30am-6.30pm daily; *Sept, April-June*: 10am-5.30pm daily; *Oct-March*: 10am-4.30pm daily. **Admission** 22F. **Towers open** (entrance at foot of the Norther tower) 10am-5.30pm (4.30pm in winter) daily. **Admission** 22F.
See **picture and caption**. *See also chapter* **Sightseeing**.

UPSTREAM

Once again taking the Pont Neuf as a starting point, walk eastwards along the Left Bank, passing the cathedral to your left across the river. The Quais Malaquais, de Conti, des Grands Augustins and Montebello are lined with booksellers, now the only traders remaining along the river, apart from the bird-sellers on the Quai de la Mégisserie, on the other side of the Ile de la Cité. These outdoor stalls bear a jumble of second-hand and rare books, as well as prints and postcards old and new. A gentle stroll to the Quai Saint Bernard (opposite the eastern tip of the Ile Saint-Louis) will take you past the Jardin Tino Rossi, the **Open-air Sculpture Museum**, and the **Jardin des Plantes**.

From here to the Pont National, the river-bed is one huge building site, heralding the Paris of the future. The old warehouses, which were once used to unload goods coming from the river, are now being destroyed or converted to more modern use. The **Quai de la Gare**, for instance, has been taken over by painters, musicians and theatre companies. The warehouses at **Bercy**, an almost village-like area once devoted to the wine trade, were condemned and a completely new neighbourhood is being built next to the Palais Omnisport de Paris-Bercy. The new **Ministry of Finance**, a glass and steel ramp overlooking the river, is attracting myriad businesses. With a bit of luck, you might catch the Finance Minister arriving here in his personal boat. *See also chapter* **Village Paris**.

Jardin des Plantes
main entrance on rue Cuvier, 75005 Paris. Metro Monge, Jussieu. **Open** dawn-dusk daily.
This eighteenth-century and Second

Empire park includes a zoo, a botanical gardin, tropical greenhouses and the Museum of Natural History. The Crêperie Bretonne, an open-air restaurant next to the bear pit, is open from noon to 6pm. *See also chapter* **Sightseeing; Children**.

Quai de la Gare
Entrepots Frigorifiques, Quai de la Gare, 75013 Paris. Metro Quai de la Gare.
Among the desert of abandoned warehouses lining this stretch of the river is a warren of young artists' studios. Most will be pleased to welcome visitors.

Palais Ominisport Paris-Bercy
8 boulevard Bercy, 75012 Paris (43.46.12.21). Metro Gare de Lyon/bus 24, 87.
In an act of architectural delirium, the lawns at POPB were set at a 45º angle. It is one of France's biggest multi-function buildings (*see also chapter* **Sport**), part of a massive re-development project in a previously run-down area which is bringing new life to the *quartier*. There are many *petits bistros sympas* where the weary can rest their feet and have a drink.

Pavillon de l'Arsenal
21 boulevard Morland, 75004 Paris (42.76.63.46). Metro Gare d'Austerlitz, Sully-Morland. **Open** 10.30am-6.30pm Tue-Sat; 11am-7pm Sun.
The temporary exhibitions at the Pavillon concentrate on themes of contemporary urbanization. The neighbouring Marina de la Bastille is full of houseboats and is a pleasant spot to relax. City noise is so muffled that on a sunny day you can imagine yourself on the Côte d'Azur.

The embankments around the old city were once packed with market stalls. Strollers along the tree-shaded quais *now content themselves with browsing through the book and print stalls lining the river opposite the Ile de la Cité and Ile Saint-Louis.*

DOWNSTREAM

Back at the Ile de la Cité, but this time on the Right Bank, a leisurely day's walk takes us from the Hôtel de Ville (the administrative headquarters of Paris) to the Pont d'Iéna.

Hôtel de Ville
main entrance by rue Lobeau, 75004 Paris. Metro Hôtel de Ville. **Open** for exhibitions 11am-7pm Tue-Sun.
Burnt down by the *communards* in 1871 (*see chapter* **The Third Republic**), the present structure was completed in 1882. There are several imposing exhibition rooms which often show contemporary art. *See also* **picture and caption.**

Place du Châtelet
75001 Paris. Metro Châtelet.
The strategic centre of Paris, the *place* is crowned by the Tour Saint Jacques, one of the best demonstrations of the Flamboyant Gothic style (*see also* **Middle Ages & Renaissance**). It's surrounded by restaurants and brasseries, and Les Halles and the Beaubourg Centre are a short stroll away, along the boulevard de Sébastopol.

Hotel des Monnaies
11 Quai de Conti, 75006 Paris (40.46.66.66). Metro Pont Neuf, Saint Michel, Odéon. **Open** for visits 12.15pm Tue, Fri; other days by arrangement.
Built in 1771, the Mint now contains a museum covering the history of coins and medals.

Pont des Arts
off Quais de Conti or Quai du Louvre, 75001 Paris. Metro Pont Neuf.
Presenting an archetypical picture of romantic Paris, this footbridge was first opened in 1803 and recently rebuilt to the old design. It links the Palais du Louvre to the Quai de Conti and offers a wonderful view of the city.

The Louvre Museum
rue de Rivoli, 75001 Paris (40.20.51.51). Metro Palais Royal, Louvre/bus 21, 24, 69, 72, 74, 76, 75. **Open** *permanent collection:* 9am-9.45pm Mon, Wed; 9am-6pm Thur-Sun; *temporary exhibitions:* noon-10pm Mon, Wed-Sun. **Admission** 25F adults; 13F 18-25s, OAPs; free under-18s.
Credit (bookshop only) A, V.
Separated from the river by the Cour Carrée, it's worth the detour to admire the new glass pyramidal entrance of the Louvre, if nothing else. *See also chapter* **Museums**.

Musée d'Orsay
1 rue de Bellechasse, 75007 Paris (40.49.48.14/recorded information 45.49.11.11). Metro Solferino/bus 24, 68, 69. **Open** 10am-6pm Tue, Wed, Fri-Sun; 10am-9.15pm Thur. **Admission** 23F adults; 12F 18-25s, OAPs; free under-18s,
Credit (bookshop only) AmEx, MC, V.
Once a railway station, and now an art museum covering the latter half of the nineteenth and early twentieth century, the exhibits here vie for attention with the architecture. *See also chapter* **Museums**.

For centuries one of Paris's biggest squares, the **place de l'Hôtel de Ville** *(listed under* **Downstream***) has suffered a turbulent history. Always a centre for local government, the present town hall is a typical example of Third Republic architecture, with its many statues on the outside and ornate decoration inside.*

Jardin des Tuileries
from the river, the park can be entered via the Pont Royal and avenue du Général Lemonnier, 75001 Paris. Metro Solferino.
One of the biggest areas of greenery in central Paris, Tuileries was landscaped in traditional French style by André Le Nôtre in 1664. It was originally the garden of Louis XIV's now demolished palace (*see chapter* **Ancien Régime**). The tree-lined paths are now peopled with shady cafés.

Place de la Concorde
75008 Paris.
Unfortunately designers and architects in the eighteenth century couldn't have predicted the invention of the car, and so the place de la Concorde, imposing as it is, is now a nightmare for pedestrians and drivers alike. It's always windswept, and almost impossible to cross in the face of constant traffic, so your best bet is to admire the view from the relative safety of the western side of the Tuileries. The statue of Louis XV (the square was originally a gift to him from the city of Paris) is surrounded by hundreds of street lamps, and by groups of statues representing the eight biggest cities in France. This is where the first guillotine was set up during the Revolution, and it was the site of Louis XVI's death (*see also chapter* **Revolution**).

Pont Alexandre III
between Cours de la Reine and Quai d'Orsay, 75008 Paris. Metro Invalides, Champs Elysées-Clémenceau, Concorde.
From this extravagantly decorated bridge

you can enjoy an uninterrupted view of the Invalides and the Grand and Petit Palais (*see chapters* **Art Galleries; Museums**). *See also* **picture and caption.**

A far cry from the picturesque *quais* of the Ile Saint-Louis, the Cours Albert Ier, is a long strip of greenery

framed by expressways. It takes you to the Pont de l'Alma, from which point the roads beside the river become a nightmare of roaring traffic. However, you can still walk along the embankment itself to the

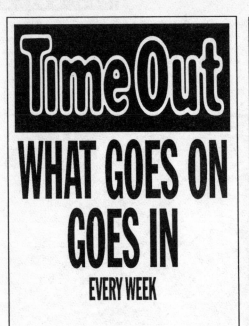

gardens of the Trocadéro, a last oasis on this side of the river. The view stretching from the place du Trocadéro to the Eiffel Tower seen from the other side of the Pont d'Iéna, reveals the splendour of early twentieth-century Paris.

Palais de Tokyo (Musée d'Art Moderne de la Ville de Paris)
11 avenue du Président Wilson, 75116 Paris (47.23.61.27). Metro Iéna/bus 63. **Open** 10am-5.30pm Tue, Thur-Sun; 10am-8.30pm Wed. **Open** 35F adults; 20F students; free under-7s, OAPs. **Credit** (bookshop only) A, DC, MC, FTC, V.
The palais dates, as does the Trocadéro *below*, from 1937. Home to the city's Museum of Modern Art, don't miss Dufy's *La Feé Electricité*. The temporary exhibitions are always superb, as is the cafeteria on the ground floor. *See also chapter* **Museums**.

Palais de Chaillot
main entrance place du Trocadéro, 75016 Paris. Metro Trocadéro.
Enormous (70,000 square metres/753,200 square feet) and unimpressive from the outside, the Palais de Chaillot houses a number of museums, as well as a repertory cinema, a 3,000-seat theatre, an aquarium, gardens, cafés, and a roller-skating track. Certainly enough to keep you amused for a day, if you're so inclined.

Eiffel Tower
Champs de Mars, 75007 Paris (45.50.34.56/recorded information 45.55.91.11). Metro Bir Hakeim, Ecole Militaire, Trocadéro/bus 82. **Open** *summer:* 9.30am-midnight daily; *winter:* 10am-11pm daily. **Admission** *by lift:* 14F-35F adults, depending on floor; 6F-20F under-12s; free under-4s; *by stairs to 2nd floor:* 7F adults; free under-4s; group discounts available.
No credit cards.
See chapter **Sightseeing.**

PARIS OUTSKIRTS

Modern developments take over as you carry on downstream from the Eiffel Tower. This part of the Seine is lined with futuristic buildings, controversial seventies' additions to the Parisian skyline. The city limits are marked by two monuments: a replica of the American Statue of Liberty and the Pont Mirabeau. Once again, though, the traffic deters anyone from continuing on foot. The only place where you can stand unscathed, is the Allée des Cygnes, a mid-river strip of land linking the Pont Bir Hakeim and the Pont de Grenelle. From here you can catch a last glimpse of Paris.

Statue of Liberty
Allée des Cygnes, 75015 Paris.
This is a replica of the New York landmark, offered to France by the United States in 1885. If you don't like the setting, there is yet another replica in the Luxembourg Gardens.

Maison de la Radio
116 avenue du President Kennedy, 75016 Paris (42.30.21.80). Metro Ranelagh, Passy. **Open** guided tours 10.30am, 11.30am, 2.30pm, 3.30pm, 4.30pm, Mon-Sat.
Admission 10F.
A pure product of the sixties, born at a time of great audio-visual developments, this is the headquarters of Radio France. The circular corridors with their thousands of identical doors are a nightmarish sight, but the quality of the acoustics in the auditorium is undeniable. *See chapter* **Music: Classical & Opera.**

We have reached the city limits; but if you dream of shaded and secluded river banks, there are many outlying areas which can be reached by public transport. Take the RER (line A to Joinville le Pont) to the Marne river, a tributary of the Seine, and enjoy lunch in a *guinguette* (tavern) while watching the ducks; or travel further out to Maison Lafitte, once the point of departure for Rouen. Information on day trips along the Seine and its many tributaries can be found at the Tourist Office (*see chapter* **Essential Information**).

Created for the 1900 World Exhibition, the **Pont Alexandre III** *(listed under* **Downstream***) is the loveliest and most ornate of the Seine's bridges and a good example of* belle époque *architecture.*

The Right Bank

Parisians will vouch for the difference between the Left and the Right Banks, but they cannot so easily analyse it: there is not so much a visible difference as a change in atmosphere and feel.

The larger of the two banks, the Right Bank also has the greater population. It was developed after the Left Bank, as it originally consisted of swampland. When space finally ran out on the Cité, the food market of the capital was the first to be forced to move to the Right Bank, which then continued to expand. In the Middle Ages, King Philippe Auguste built fortifications around the Louvre against the numerous invaders who were undeterred by the swamps. As more people from the outlying villages came to seek refuge within the city walls, the city expanded, eventually encompassing all the outlying villages and hamlets.

LES HALLES & BEAUBOURG

Les Halles is at the true centre of Paris, bordered by the Louvre to the west, and the Marais to the east. Like the Latin Quarter (*see chapter* **The Left Bank**), it has a rich history. It was the central market for Paris, not only selling food, but also wine, leather, and other goods. All sorts of articles changed hands here every day. The place was chaotic: a seething mass of people buying, selling, stealing, and begging, rubbing shoulders with pickpockets, jugglers and musicians. Dogs and pigs roamed about the area, scavenging for food that had been left to rot in the gutters. All this took place around the **Cemetery of the Innocents** which was in the middle of Les Halles on the site of the present-day **place des Innocents**. This was the only cemetery for what was then the largest parish in Paris, and it was literally overflowing. Corpses were stacked on top of each other with only a thin layer of dirt separating them. Eventually, in the eighteenth century, the corpses were moved to the **Catacombs** (*see chapter* **The Left Bank/Montparnasse**). It took three years to transport over two million skeletons.

In the nineteenth century, Napoleon III ordered the cleaning up of the area, and the architect Baltard was hired to design the *Halles* or halls. Ten of these huge buildings were constructed in glass and steel to house the market, hence the name 'Les Halles'. This form of simple, bright and spacious construction became a model for numerous other large public places. The only surviving hall, the 'Pavillon Baltard' has been removed to Nogent-sur-Marne.

The market became a wholesale market, through which all the food for Paris passed before being redistributed, and in 1969 it was moved out to Rungis in the southern suburbs.

Life went out of the area with the departure of the market, and the locals were left trying to fill the gaping hole, which was all that remained of eight centuries of market life. Eventually the idea of the **Forum** was accepted. However, a few streets still retain their former glory: those around the church of **Saint Eustache** and the **rues Montorgueil** and **du Jour** at the bottom of the **rue Montmartre**. There are small butchers, grocers and wine shops which open at dawn for deliveries, to be followed by a glass of white wine over the counter of one of the small bars, in true Parisian style. Other traditions have also remained. The brasserie **Au Pied de Cochon**, and the **Alsace aux Halles** are open 24 hours a day, so you can still enjoy some onion soup at 5am.

Nowadays Les Halles is the trendy place to be. The café terraces are bigger than the cafés themselves, and offer ample opportunity for watching the world go by – and ensuring the world is watching you. The most famous is the **Café Costes**, which lives up to its name – nothing costs under 20F. It was designed by Philip Starck, and although we can't recommend the uncomfortable chairs, the loos are definitely worth a visit. The café has proved so successful, that another (almost identical) version – the **Café Beaubourg** – has opened opposite the **Pompidou Centre**.

The area is not simply the playground of the rich and beautiful. The diversity of the shops and restaurants, from designer-wear to second-hand bargain basements, fast food joints to pricey bistros, ensures a steady stream of cosmopolitan visitors who come to spend time and money in Les Halles and Beaubourg.

Les Halles-Beaubourg is an area where the juxtaposition of old and new architecture is particularly apparent. The Forum and the Pompidou Centre stand out against the creamy lead-roofed buildings and the medieval churches. Much of the quarter is for pedestrians only, and the old buildings remain relatively free from pollution and therefore clean. By wandering round the area, you can see how it is finally beginning to find its new feet.

NIGHTLIFE

Once the day-time commercialism has finished by 7pm, the Halles nightlife takes over. At night, it positively teems with bars, restaurants, jazz clubs, and the odd porn show. To sample some Parisian rock or jazz, stroll down the **rue des Lombards**, where you'll find **Le Baiser Salé**, **Le Sunset**, **Les Trottoirs de Buenos Aires** – the last a must for all tango nostalgics. Have a drink and listen to the music until dawn, and if you're lucky you may catch a band on its way to stardom. The **rue Berger**, opposite the Halles garden, houses **L'Eustache** – a jazz bar with a hot, crowded atmosphere that, for once, is not too expensive. Further down the street is the **Distrito**, which is expensive, but *very* trendy. The upstairs bar closes at 2am, but if you look the part, or know the boss, you can go downstairs and listen to the band until 4am.

If you can't bear the thought of being separated from a pub for too long, there's always the **Guinness Tavern** in the rue des Lombards or the **James Joyce** in the rue du Jour. Watch out, though: a pint will set you back 30F or more. For those who are more into the Manhattan scene, try **The Front Page** or **Conways**, both in the **rue Saint Denis**. These cocktail bars dispense American food and beer to a largely American clientele. Of course, for those who come to Paris to eat French food, there are numerous opportunities; *see chapter* **Restaurants**.

Forum des Halles
75001 Paris. Main entries: Porte Lescot, Porte Berger, Porte Rambuteau and from the RER Les Halles station.
This is the project which filled the hole left after the departure of the market for the suburbs. The Forum sinks to four levels underground, and is the largest commercial centre in France. The shops here mainly sell clothes, and include the outlets of many young French designers. After indulging in a spending spree, you can recover in the cinema: the Forum Horizon is one of the best in Paris. There's also a museum and a swimming pool in the complex. Like all adventurous projects, the success of the Forum is constantly being called into question. Many would still prefer that the proposed marina, linked to the Seine, had been built in its place. But although people condemn the place, they still turn up in their thousands every day to take advantage of its services. The revenue of the shops in the Forum is twice the national average. *See also* **picture and caption**.

Musée Grévin
Niveau 1, Grand Balcon, rue Pierre Lescot (40.26.28.50). **Open** 10am-6.45pm Mon-Sat; 1pm-7.15pm Sun and holidays. **Admission** 40F adults; 28F 6-14s; free under-6s. **No credit cards**.
The Halles branch of the waxworks museum presents figures from the *belle époque* – Balzac, Victor Hugo, Verlaine – in historical tableaux. There are also reproductions of whole areas of Paris, like Montmartre, and of course Les Halles, seen as they were during the same period, with every possible historical detail accounted for. The main museum is at 10 boulevard Montmartre (47.70.85.05); *see chapter* **Museums**.

Holography Museum
Level -1, Forum des Halles, 75001 Paris (40.39.96.83). Metro Châtelet, Les Halles/bus 67, 69, 70, 72, 76, 85. **Open** 10am-7.30pm Mon-Sat; 1-7pm Sun. **Admission** 28F adults; 22F students, OAPs; under-18s free. **Credit** (shop only) V.

The **Forum des Halles** *(listed under* **Les Halles & Beaubourg***) is made up of seven hectares of corridors that all have street names; some covered with brightly coloured murals. The complex is so vast that it is possible to live a subterranean life from it, rarely surfacing for air. Luc Besson's film* Subway *was inspired by this idea, and was filmed on location at Les Halles RER station.*

This museum displays some of the most remarkable examples of the holography process, invented by Dennis Gabor in 1947, which produces striking 3D images. *See also chapter* **Museums**.

Cousteau Oceanic Centre
Forum des Halles, 75001 Paris (40.28.98.98/99). Metro Châtelet, Les Halles/bus 38, 47. **Open** noon-7pm Tue-Sun (last ticket 5.30pm). **Admission** 75F adults; 52.50F 5-14s; free under-5s; group discounts available. **No credit cards**.
Fans of Jacques Cousteau can dive into his underwater world here with the help of a few videos and various other visual aids. You can even make a Jonah-like journey into the belly of a whale. *See also chapter* **Children**.

The Paris Videothèque
2 Grande Galerie du Forum (40.26.34.30). **Open** 10.30am-9pm Tue-Fri, Sun; 10am-9pm Sat. **Admission** 18F. **No credit cards**.
Have Paris at your fingertips for a minimal sum: the Videothèque is a mammoth library of film and video documentation on the city. From factual documentaries or films shot in Paris on location, to films on people who lived here, everything remotely connected with Paris can be found in this library. Choose what you want to see from the carefully-documented files. From time to time special showings of films on a specific topic are organized, phone for details.

Saint Eustache
2 rue du Jour, 75002 Paris (42.36.31.05). RER Châtelet-les-Halles/bus 39, 48, 63, 65, 70, 86, 87, 95, 96.

The construction of the parish church of Les Halles began in 1532. Living as they did in the biggest parish, the market people saw no reason why they shouldn't have a big church, so they modelled theirs on Nôtre Dame. Saint Eustache is one of the most beautiful churches in Paris, and, like Nôtre Dame, it took over 100 years to complete. The church was a fundamental part of life around the market. Inside, there's a modern fresco painted in the sixties, called *The Departure of the Fruit and Vegetables from the Heart of Paris*, a vivid work which shows what a wrench it must have been for the market people to move to Rungis. The church now overlooks the Forum and the Jardin des Halles, a welcome slice of greenery amongst the modern architecture. *See also chapter* **Music: Classical & Opera**.

rue Saint Denis
75001 Paris. Metro Etienne-Marcel, Réaumur-Sébastopol.
One of the oldest streets in Paris, the rue Saint Denis runs as far as the Basilique Saint Denis (hence the name), where the kings of France were once crowned, and later, buried. The Right Bank developed outwards from this important thoroughfare, which was also the path taken to the scaffold by those condemned to be hanged. Now essentially a 'street of shame', the end towards Les Halles has been cleaned up a bit by the arrival of the trend-setters, but the street reverts to its true character the nearer you get to the Sentier *(see below* **Sentier***)*.

rue Saint Honoré

75008 Paris. Metro Miromesnil, Saint Philipppe-du-Roule, Ternes.
See **picture and caption.**

rue de la Ferronnerie

75001 Paris. Metro Châtelet.
Henri IV was assassinated in this street. He was knifed in front of No.11, an inn coincidentally called *Au Coeur Couronné, percé d'une flêche* (the crossed heart, pierced by an arrow). The name of the street itself harks back to the Middle Ages when it was an iron-making centre.

Beaubourg/Pompidou Centre

Plateau Beaubourg, 75004 Paris (42.77.12.33/recorded information 42.77.11.12). Metro Châtelet, Hotel de Ville, Rambuteau/bus 29, 38, 47. **Open** noon-10pm Mon, Wed-Sun; 10am-10pm Sat, Sun.
Admission *to MNAM:* 23F adults; 17F 18-25s, OAPs; free under-18s; *Galeries Contemporaines:* 16F adults; free under-13s; *CCI:* 15F adults; free under-13s; *temporary exhibitions:* admission varies; *Day pass to all exhibitions:* 50F adults; 45F 13-25s, OAPs; free under-13s.
Credit (bookshop only) DC, MC, V.
In the beginning there was a Car Park. Then came Georges Pompidou, President of France, who gave his people a Cultural Centre of Contemporary Art. From the 600 proposed designs, an Anglo-Italian one was chosen. The architects were Ronzo Piano and Richard Rogers, who adopted the now-famous 'inside-out' technique as a means of liberating as much space as possible inside – hence the visible plumbing on the outside. The colours of these pipes, which are more evident on the rue Beaubourg side, each represent a specific function: white for fresh air ducts, blue for air conditioning, yellow for electricity, and so on. It took eight years for the Centre to be completed and it is now visited by some seven and a half million people a year – twice the number who visit the Eiffel Tower. There is also a superb view from the fifth floor. There is no doubt that the Centre fulfils it original purpose as a window on contemporary culture. The Parvis in front of the centre is always a lively place. A sort of unofficial Speaker's Corner, it's always packed with street entertainers, buskers, and poets, who enjoy a large audience of tourists.

HORLOGE QUARTER

Between the rues Saint Martin, Rambuteau, Beaubourg and Grenier Saint Lazare, this quarter has been subjected to one of the less-successful renovation schemes in old Paris. Tarted up and made into a shopping gallery, it has become rather characterless, and in comparison to the bustle of Beaubourg, it remains surprisingly empty of people. At night it's even worse, to the point of being depressing. The huge clock is nonetheless worth seeing. Overlooking the rue Bernard de Clairvaux, it houses the 'Defender of Time', who, armed with a spear, fights a daily battle with a crab, a bird and a dragon, at noon and again at 6pm.

THE MARAIS

The name *marais* in French means swamp, which is what this area was originally. It is one of the few quarters in Paris that has almost entirely retained its original pre-Revolution architecture. This consists mainly of private town houses, or *hôtels particuliers*. These beautiful buildings, usually constructed around a private courtyard and garden, were at the height of fashion during the seventeenth century. The place Royale (now the **place des Vosges**), built under the auspices of Henri IV, was the heart of the quarter. One part of the Marais is predominantly a Jewish area – as it has been since the twelfth century – centred around the **rue des Ecouffes**, the **rue des Rosier** and the **rue Saint Antoine**. It is also one of the main gay areas in Paris (*see chapter* **Gay & Lesbian**). The *hôtels particuliers* still exist, and make up the intellectual character of the Marais, as many have been turned into museums of art history.

The Marais, as elsewhere, has had its fair share of modern development. During the fifties, when it was a run-down, working-class area, a far cry from its halcyon days, any of the old mansions in need of restoration were simply torn down. More than half of the area was considered hazardous and ripe for demolition. Property speculators flocked in to snap up bargains at knock-down prices and the resulting mixture of cheap new and splendid old buildings is still all too evident. The **rue Barbetie**, which contains the **Swedish Cultural Centre** in a beautiful mansion at the bottom of it, is a typically schizophrenic street, with one side modern and the other old. Behind many of the mansions loom characterless square concrete bunkers.

In 1962 André Malraux, then the Minister of Culture, declared the whole area a historical monument, and no demolition has been

*Running from the Palais Royal to the rue des Halles, the **rue Saint Honoré** (listed under **Les Halles & Beaubourg**) used to be jammed with shops wanting to be as near to the market of Les Halles as possible. Some of these old houses and shops remain. During the Terror, it was one of the principal routes taken by the tumbrels that took people to their death at the guillotine. At No. 43 is the Press Museum, which houses all the newspapers and magazines that have been published in France since the beginning of the century.*

allowed since. He attacked the extensions and alterations to historic monuments as 'parasitic constructions' and 'pustules' and the speculators therefore turned their attention to other areas, like Montparnasse and the 13th *arrondissement*. But with the 'historic monument' label, came high rent and property values, and while demolition is no longer allowed, construction has not stopped: a new project in the **rue François-Miron** threatens to obscure the **Eglise Saint Gervais**.

Saint Paul Village

Between the quai des Célestins, the rue Saint Paul and the rue Charlemagne, 75004 Paris. Metro Sully-Morland. **Open** 11am-7pm Mon, Thur-Sun.
As one of the many controversial development projects in the quarter, this area of old antique shops has been restored and hyped up. It's still a nice place for a stroll, but now where once stood little second-hand stalls selling all manner of goods stacked at random on tables, there now stand chic little shops selling all manner of goods carefully presented and at twice the price. Twice a year a slice of the old tradition can still be found, when the *Grande fête de l'occasion*, a large festival of the second-hand, with temporary stalls selling bric-à-brac, takes place. For more details on when this happens, phone (48.08.85.20).

Place des Vosges

75003 Paris.
See **picture and caption.**

Maison de Victor Hugo

6 place des Vosges,75003 Paris (42.72.16.65). Metro Bastille, Saint Paul. **Open** 10am-5.40pm Tue-Sun. **Admission** 16F; free on Sun. **No credit cards.**
Also known as the Hôtel Rohan-Guéménée, this is where the great writer lived from 1832 to 1845, and where he penned such classics as *Les Misérables*.The museum documents his life and some of the rooms preserve their original decorations.

Hôtel Sully

62 rue Saint Antoine, 75012 Paris (42.72.22.22). Metro Ledru-Rollin. **Open** 10am-6pm daily.
Wander through the Hôtel – it's used as a short-cut by pedestrians making their way to the place des Vosges. The courtyard is Louis XIII-style, discreetly lit, and in the evening, very romantic.

Memorial to the Unknown Jewish Martyr

17 rue Geoffroy l'Asnier 75004 Paris (42.77.44.72). Metro Saint-Paul. **Open** 10am-noon, 2-5pm, Mon-Fri; also 10am-noon, 2-5pm, Sun in July and Aug. Closed on Jewish holidays and 1 May. **Admission** 12F.
A testament to the strong Jewish presence in the Marais for the last eight centuries, the Memorial documents Jewish history.

Hôtel Carnavalet

23 rue de Sévigné, 75003 Paris (42.72.21.13). Metro Saint Paul/bus 29. **Open** 10am-5.40pm Tue-Sun. **Admission** 15F adults; 8.50F students, teachers; free under-7s. **Credit** (bookshop only) A, V.
One section of this museum contains souvenirs of the Marquise de Sévigné, and the rest is dedicated to the history of Paris from

François I to the *belle époque*. If this hasn't satisfied you, carry on through to the Hôtel Le Peletier Saint Pargeau, which is behind the Museum and covers history from the Revolution to the present day.

LES FETES DU MARAIS

This has replaced the Festival du Marais, which was considered too élitist. It is held throughout the Marais in October for a fortnight – check the press at the time for details. The partying now takes place out on the street and the accent is on commerce by day and culture by night. There's always something interesting going on.

PIGALLE

And now for something completely different. Had enough of the beautiful seventeenth-century architecture? Been up the Eiffel Tower? For all those who feel tempted to say 'been there, done that', Pigalle awaits. Or rather a certain slice of Pigalle: we are not talking about the pretty little winding streets that run through Montmartre, but about those running from the **place de Clichy**, through the **place Blanche** and ending up at the **place Pigalle** itself, with the odd diversion into dimly-lit streets on either side.

A conglomeration of famous Parisian revue bars, sex shops, porn shops, bars and cafés, Pigalle has a vibrant nightlife. It is Paris's 24-hour district *par excellence*. On Friday nights, by 9pm, the entire area is blocked with coaches and the streets are filled with visitors wondering which French Lover's joint to go to next. But the area has life, and not all of it sordid, which is why so many artists, writers, actors and directors have made it their home.

Nevertheless, there are a few things you should be aware of before you embark on your night out in Pigalle. Nowadays, sex for sale in France has moved up a VAT bracket, from the standard 18.5 per cent, to the 33 per cent 'luxury goods' slot. In this hooker's heaven, sex comes dear, and the pimps who drag you into their clubs are becoming more aggressive as a result. Along the boulevard de Clichy, the neon signs still beam out, advertising peep shows, 'live sex' and much more. At the top of the rues Pigalle, de Douai, Fontaine and Victor

*High rents bring a new kind of resident: in recent years, **the Marais** has become a focal point of interest for young designer shops, trendy art galleries and so on. The combination of beautiful historic setting and hot and cold running tourists has proved too much to resist, and much to the annoyance of the locals, mansions are being restored and turned into offices or luxury apartments. Pessimistic locals will tell you that the area is fast losing its character, if not architecturally, then spiritually, and that you must hurry to visit the Marais before it dies.*

Masse lie the plush velveteen bars with ultraviolet lights silhouetting the girls propped up against the counters. Business is not good, and these are not places for 'just looking'. The side streets which wind up to the Sacré Coeur are peopled with transvestites and transsexuals.

The darlings of Les Halles have decided to grace Pigalle with their presence. Shabby old night-time dives have recently become very popular. The **Locomotive**, once an original place to go to, has undergone a radical image-change. The **Bus Palladium**, **La Cigale**, and the **Elysée Montmartre** – a venue with good music – have followed suit, but the Elysée still manages to provide a varied clientele. Bright young things from *arrondissements* such as the 16th, which are dead at night, head for Pigalle. They stick together and stick out, but Pigalle is a tolerant area – it has to be.

An increase in 'safe' 24-hour cafés and bars, like the **Dépanneur**, has also given a new aspect to the area. You can sip beer or tequilas at prices that are not too exorbitant, in a leather-jacketed environment and not even notice the clock hands creeping towards dawn. Such places are a happy complement to the traditional all-night and late-night brasseries of the boulevard de Clichy, such as **L'Omnibus**, **Le Pigalle**, and the **Café Blanche**. Alternatively, if it's a warm evening, you could buy something from the Arab corner stores which stay open all night.

If you want to blend in and not get hassled in Pigalle, don't hang about outside the Bus or Locomotive looking lost or speaking English loudly. This way no one will try to lure you into an over-priced meat show, and you may even get taken for a local. You can then enjoy the less-obvious sites fully, like **Le Chat Noir**, or the **Cloche d'Or**, although the latter is somewhat daunting. Pigalle locals are a distinct advantage, as the so-called 'gentrification' of the area will never take place while they're still around. This is an area which saves the fun for those who know how to find it. You have been warned.

SEX SHOPS & LIVE SHOWS

A word of warning before you run amok in Pigalle: although the prices marked outside a venue might seem pretty low for watching a sex show, there's more to it than that. Whilst inside, you will be prevailed upon to buy drinks for the girls employed by the establishment. These can be very expensive and you may get faced with a daunting bill at the end. Also, if the show didn't impress you, don't try going next door to see another – performers tend to do the rounds each night, moving tiredly from one joint to the next.

Bruno Maitre Tatooist
4 rue Germain-Pilon, 75018 Paris (42.64.35.59). Metro Pigalle. **Open** 10am-7pm Mon, Tue, Thur-Sat. **No credit cards.**
This is one of the better-known tatooists. You can check out some of Bruno's designs in the window beforehand if you're undecided about what you want. Bruno is an officer of the Order of Artistic Merit, and promises body art without scarring. He only uses new needles and disposable ink cartridges.

Rue des Martyrs
75009 Paris. Metro Saint Georges.
A lively, commercial street which proves that there is day-time life in this area. It's not strictly Pigalle as we've defined it, but we wanted to show you the other side of the coin. At the bottom of the street there's a good market.

Moulin Rouge
82 boulevard de Clichy, 75011 Paris (46.06.00.19). Metro Blanche/bus 30, 54. **Open** 8pm-2am daily. **Show** 8pm, 10pm & midnight daily. **Admission** *dinner & dance:* at 8pm from 530F per person (includes tourist menu and half bottle champagne); *show only:* at 10pm or midnight, from 365F per person (includes half bottle champagne). **Credit** AmEx, DC, MC, V.
We hate to disillusion you, but the girls up there doing those sexy French numbers are mainly English. This place was probably amusing in Toulouse Lautrec's day. *See also chapter* **Cabaret & Chanson.**

Webler Cinema
place de Clichy, 75009 Paris. Metro Clichy.
Now a rather average cinema, the Webler stands on the site of what was once the Gaumont Palace – the largest auditorium in Paris. This in turn was built on the site of the Hippodrome, built for the World Exhibition of 1900, which did much to establish the place de Clichy as a fun spot.

Gustave Moreau Museum
14 rue la Rochefaucault, 75009 Paris (48.74.38.50). Metro Saint George. **Open** 10am-12.45pm, 2pm-5.15pm Mon, Wed-Sun. **Admission** 15F Mon-Sat; 8F Sun.
Once the residence of the painter, this is now a museum and houses 11,000 paintings and drawings by Moreau. A well-kept Pigalle secret, in an area where you would be forgiven for thinking that there was no culture.

The **Place des Vosges** (listed under **The Marais**) was the first square to be built in Paris. Once established as the place to go to for amusement during the seventeenth century, the Marais took off in its wake as an area popular among the élite. It was also the first coherent construction running all the way around in a continuous square. At ground level you can rummage about in the antique shops, which display their wares on the pavement under the arches. Many a famous person lived here – including Victor Hugo and Madame de Sevigné who wrote her infamous Lettres here.

Le Dépanneur
Corner of rue Fontaine and rue de Dousi, 75009 Paris. Metro Blanche.
Open 24 hours daily.
A 24-hour café-bar done up like an American diner, the prices go up a little at night and the food is basic sandwich fare. There is loud music, a pool table upstairs, and Miss Tequila, who wanders around sinuously, trying to persuade you to buy another drink. She does pretty well, too. What's particularly nice about this place is that you don't get stared at or approached if you're on your own or waiting for someone.

La Locomotive
90 boulevard de Clichy, 75018 Paris. (42.57.37.37). Metro Blanche. **Open** 10pm-dawn daily. **Admission** 50F, includes one beer; subsequent beers 30F. **Credit** MC, V.
Not as fun as it used to be, but then you have to get used to that in Paris these days. Now a be-bop club, and still good for a laugh. In fact it's considered one of *the* places to go. *See also chapters* **Music: Rock, Folk & Jazz** and **Nightlife.**

Elysée Montmartre
72 boulevard de Rochechouart, 75018 Paris (42.76.22.60). Metro Pigalle. **Open** average 100F; phone for details.
This is a large venue in the style of the Brixton Academy in London. It has a lot of character and attracts a variety of people. Recent bands have included The Waterboys and the Dead Cats from Washington. Once a month there's a free concert that features new and unknown groups. Check with them

for details of what's on. After a day or two listening to French FM radio, it's a relief to know the Elysée exists.

Le Pigalle
22 boulevard de Clichy, 75018 Paris (45.06.72.92). Metro Pigalle or Blanche.
The enormous yellow neon sign ensures that even in a drunken stupor you can't miss Le Pigalle, although you may wish you had. The new management has given this bar a face-lift, optimistically hoping that the area really is on the up and up. It's a great place from which to watch the activities of the square. Open all night.

Marché Aux Puces
Porte de Clignancourt/Saint Ouen, 75018 Paris. Metro Porte de Clignancourt. **Open** 9.30am-6.30pm Sat, Sun, Mon. **Credit** Stalls have individual policies, but most only accept cash and French cheques.
Moving further north from Pigalle, in the 18th *arrondissement*, is one of the many Parisian **Marché aux Puces** or flea markets. Just under the *Périphérique* overpass which surrounds Paris, it consists of a collection of street markets, selling everything from second-hand clothes, old Johnny Halliday records, and leather jackets, to a random assortment of pharaphernalia. Alternatively, you can track down your trash or treasure in one of the several massive buildings teeming with stalls. The **Marché Vernaison** is the largest of these, selling furniture from the Second Empire, antique dolls and games, baubles and estate silver. The **Marché Paul-Bert** specializes in art

deco and early twentieth-century furnishings, including glass and chandeliers. Sift through turn-of-the-century *objets d'art* at the **Marché Jules-Valles**, or the assortment of vintage men and women's clothing and accessories, mostly dating from the forties and fifties, to be found at the **Marché Malik**. For those that have gone overboard on their shopping, **Camard**, a reputable shipping agent inside the Marché Paul-Bart, is open on Saturdays only and will arrange shipment and containers for your booty. Addresses for the indoor markets are listed below.

Marché Vernaison
99 rue des Rosiers, 75018 Paris.

Marché Paul-Bert
16 rue Paul-Bert, 75018 Paris.

Marché Jules-Valles
5 rue Jules-Valles, 75018 Paris.

Marché Malik
60 rue Jules-Valles, 75018 Paris.

SENTIER

Just above Les Halles, surrounded by the Grands Boulevards (*see below*) is Sentier, an area devoted to selling – whether it be it goods, high finance or sex. On the whole the commercial and wholesale activities are devoted to the clothing industry. A strange place, Sentier is very active during the day. There are an impressive number of wholesale warehouses and sweat shops crammed into often very narrow streets, which can get positively claustrophobic – certainly not the area for a quiet stroll. Delivery trucks block the streets, all honking loudly – typical Parisian behaviour, which helps no one, annoys everyone, but gives the driver a sense of power.

To get away from the crowds, slip down one of the passages. Many of these were built during the nineteenth century, when they were particularly popular. Shops for rent in these passages were always in demand. In this area alone, 130 were constructed. Today the traffic on the roads and pavements of the Grands Boulevards is making the passageways popular again. Apart from anything else, they are covered over, warm and calm. If you're particularly after the sinister, sneak into the **Passage Beauregard** which is level with No.57 rue de Clery. It's narrow, sinuous, black and full of little staircases

La Bourse
place de la Bourse, 75002 Paris (42.33.99.83). Metro Bourse. **Open** Tours lasting 1½ hours

*The old passages in the **Sentier** area are charming from an architectural point of view. However, those that spill out onto the rue Saint Denis tend to be the haunt of prostitutes, and marching into one with a camera could provoke an angry reaction. Try exploring the **Passage de la Trinité** (pictured above). It runs into the rue Saint Denis and forms a striking contrast to the hectic streets. The Passage Basfroi is a thirteenth-century side street with some fine gabled houses, and the Passage du Caire also has some typical examples of this style of architecture.*

du lundi au vendredi en soiree

Fiesta Mexicana!

DEL RIO Café
MEXICAN GRILL & CANTINA

15 rue du cygne
75001 PARIS
reservations:
42.21.10.77

12 rue Princess
75006 PARIS
reservations:
43.26.79.95

avec Rodrigo et ses Mariachis

every half hour from 11am-1pm Mon-Fri; *1 July-15 Sept:* one tour at 12pm. **Admission** 8F (form of identification required).

The tour of France's stock exchange lasts 1½ hours. It hasn't undergone the Big Bang yet, and the brokers still run around like ants in the pit. A gallery has been built so you can look down and get an idea of how the whole process works. The best time to be in the gallery is from 12.30pm to 2.30pm, at quotation time. There are also audio-visual aids, which explain the importance of the Bourse to the French economy.

rue de Réaumur
75002 Paris. Metro Réaumur-Sebastopol.
If you pass this street during the day, you're more than likely to get caught in a frantic traffic jam. This will give you the time to admire the superb iron and glass façades of the art nouveau buildings, created as a result of a competition between the various architects.

rue Saint Denis
75002 Paris. Metro Saint Denis.
See **picture and caption.**

LES GRANDS BOULEVARDS

From the Bastille to the Madeleine, the Grands Boulevards have long been a favourite promenade for Parisians. Up until the fifties, they were also places of high fashion, but when they lost their exclusivity, the bourgeoisie migrated towards Saint-Honoré and the Champs Elysées. Like the large boutiques, the large boulevards have lost their charm of old, but they neverthless give Paris a feeling of spaciousness. Most of them were created by Haussmann in the nineteenth century as part of his urbanization plan, and are now commercial areas, with the usual range of brasseries, cinemas, restaurants and shops.

Around the **rue du Faubourg Montmartre** the nightlife is lively, centred around theatres, clubs and the **Palace** nightclub. While it attracts the trendies, the area is not too dominated by the Les Halles clan. During the day, these are the streets to hit for your serious shopping sprees. The **boulevard Haussmann** is the home of the department store, with the **Galeries Lafayette, Au Printemps,** a huge **Monoprix** and even **Marks and Spencer.** Surprisingly, in this centre of culinary excellence, the food hall of the latter is always packed, so watch out for the mad rush on tea cakes, sliced bread, crumpets and the like.

There are more good passages to explore near the Grands Boulevards. The **Passage des Panoramas** (11 boulevard Montmartre, Metro Richelieu-Drouot) is where the first gas lamps were used in Paris, and was therefore very popular because it was bright and warm. The **Passage Jouffroy** (Metro Richelieu-Drouot) has a market-town atmosphere, with lots of craft shops selling photos and old postcards. If you're into pipe smoking you should visit the nearby **Passage des Princes** where the pipe makers hang out.

The Opéra Palais Garnier
Place de l'Opéra, 75002 Paris (42.66.50.22/Fax 47.42.57.50). Metro Opéra. **Open** *Tours:* 11am-4.30pm not every day, call for exact days; *box office:* 11am-7pm daily.
One of the most beautiful buildings of the Second Empire, built between 1860 and 1875. Today l'Opéra is the scene of grand soirées, and since the construction of the Bastille Opera, presents mainly dance. The grandiose architecture, sumptuous main staircase and general decoration shouldn't be missed, particularly the ceiling painted by Chagall inside the auditorium. *See also chapter* **Dance.**

Galeries Lafayette
40 boulevard Haussmann, 75009 Paris (42.82.34.56). Metro Chausée d'Antin, Opéra/RER Auber/buses 20, 21, 22, 27, 42, 53, 68, 81, 95. **Open** 9.30am-6.30pm Mon-Sat. **Credit** AmEx, CB, DC, EC, JCB, MC, V, F$DMYen£TC, all currencies.
This department store has over 75,000 brand names, including the high fashion, in-house boutiques of Christian Lacroix, Claude Montana, Thierry Mugler and Yohji Yamamoto. There's also a vast array of housewares and an entire floor devoted to lingerie.

Printemps
64 boulevard Haussmann, 75009 Paris (42.82.50.00). Metro Havre-Caumartin, St-Lazare, Opéra/RER Auber. **Open** 9.35am-6.30pm Mon-Sat.
Credit A/c, AmEx, CB, DC, EC, MC, Takashiyama, V, all TC and all currencies.
During the Christmas period this has got to be the busiest area in Paris. The queues at the cash desks are unbelievable, and some departments in the shops still use the old system of queueing separately to collect and to pay for your goods. These department stores are big business: you will find the biggest stock turnover per square metre here, as well as the biggest perfume departments in the world.

Musée Grevin
10 boulevard Montmartre, 75009 Paris (47.70.85.05). Metro Montmartre.
Open 1-7pm daily. **Admission** 40F.
This is the original Parisian waxworks museum, founded at the end of the last century. It has all the same sort of stuff as

The **rue Saint Denis** *(listed under* **Sentier***) is not as saintly as its name implies: the street has been a traditional pick-up spot since the Middle Ages. The street also contains many sex shops and porn theatres. There are often massive traffic jams, particularly on Saturday nights when there is an influx of suburbanites. There are some picturesque passages that cut across the rue Saint Denis, many of which are very old, but if you're easily scared, don't wander into them at night.*

In an attempt to retain the original beauty of the broad, sweeping **Champs Elysées,** *there is a rule that shop signs that stick out onto the avenue must be in black and white, whatever the company logo, but this doesn't seem to have made an enormous difference. Designed in the early 1600s as a continuation of the Tuileries Gardens to provide a vista from the Louvre, it is now a mixture of exclusive shops and fast-food joints.*

London's Madame Tussaud's, as well as a section on the Revolution for added gore. Kids' stuff.

The Museum of Romantic Life
16 rue Chaptal, 75009 Paris (48.74.95.38).
Metro Saint Georges. **Open** 10am-5.40pm Tue-Sun. **Admission** 12F adults; 6.50F students; free under-16s.
This small museum, housed in a pretty building, is devoted to the life of Georges Sand. Good for a peaceful visit.

CHAMPS ELYSEES

Often cited as the most beautiful avenue in the world, you'll have to make up your own mind about the Champs Elysées. It certainly looks very beautiful from above, but from close up, the view is very different (*see* **picture and caption**). Don't stop off for a snack if you're hard up: the only places that don't cost an arm and a leg are the numerous fast-foods chains. The avenue is certainly never dull, filled with numerous office workers, tourists, cinemagoers, and shoppers, all on the go at once. It's also *the* place to be (if you're into that sort of thing) on New Year's Eve, but be warned that in France you have to kiss everyone at least twice on each cheek, so you come away with a rough face.

Once you've strolled along the Champs, there are numerous other things to see in the area.

Museum of French Monuments
place du Trocadéro, 75016 Paris (42.27.35.74). Metro Trocadéro/B22, 30, 32, 63, 72, 82. **Open** 10am-6pm Mon, Wed-Sun. **Admission** 15F Mon, Wed-Sat; 8F Sun.
A museum that follows the history of French monuments from Roman times to the present day. There are copies of sculptures and paintings, as well as reconstructions of many of the famous monuments, which makes close-up viewing of them a lot easier than in the great outdoors.

Henri Langlois Cinema Museum
Entry via the Trocadéro Garden 75016 Paris (45.53.21.86). **Open** Guided tours at 10am, 11am, 2pm, 3pm and 4pm Mon, Wed-Sun. **Admission** 20F. Cinémathèque (47.04.24.24).
Here you can follow the evolution of film from its earliest days at the end of the last century to the present. Learn about the techniques involved, the creation of costume and scenery, and see the sets from some celebrated films. The cinémathèque here was

much talked about during the new wave film explosion, and is still a meeting place for all cinephiles who can see films here not shown anywhere else, and might even get a chance to buttonhole the director afterwards.

The Wine Museum
rue des Eaux, 75016 Paris (45.25.63.26). Metro Passy. **Open** 12-6pm Tue-Sat. **Admission** 25F (includes wine-tasting).
A succession of wine cellars built during the Middle Ages, this 'museum' can be a treat for the palate. You can also eat here at lunchtime, and line your stomach before embarking on some serious tasting.

Palais de la Découverte
avenue Franklin D Roosevelt, 75008 Paris (43.59.16.65). Metro Franklin D Roosevelt. **Open** 10am-6pm Tue-Sat. *Seances:* 2pm, 3.15pm, 4.30pm. **Admission** 20F adults; 10F students and under-18s. *Planetarium:* 13F supplement; 9F students and under 18s.
An educational centre which presents science and scientific history in a form made palatable for the general public. Each of the 56 rooms, which make up the palace, contains games and demonstrations that you can take part in, covering physics, mechanics, electronics, biology, astronomy and other sciences, all made easy and fun. Stop off at the planetarium and spend 45 minutes with your head above the clouds.

La Madeleine
place de la Madeleine, 75008 Paris. Metro Madeleine. **Open** 7.30am-7pm Mon-Sat; 8am-1pm, 4-7pm Sun.
It took 80 years to finish this church. Built between 1764 and 1842 in classical temple mode, it survived the Monarchy, the Revolution and the Empire. With each new regime came a new function for the Madeleine, but it finally wound up as a church and is today the setting for several national ceremonies. *See also chapter* **Sightseeing.**

Fauchon
26 place de la Madeleine, 75008 Paris (47.42.60.11). Metro Madeleine. **Open** 9.40am-7pm Mon-Sat.
Credit AmEx, DC, MC, V.
This is a truly luxurious foodstore where the posh come to buy their dinner. Fauchon sell all kinds of fruit – whatever the season – and has a *traiteur*-cum-delicatessen, a patisserie whose tantalizing smells can draw you in from sixty paces, and generally sells all the most expensive products you can imagine. The answer to all your gift quandaries.

Hédiard
21 place de la Madeleine, 75008 Paris (42.66.44.36). Metro Madeleine/bus 42, 52. **Open** 9.15am-11pm Mon-Sat.
Credit AmEx, DC, V.
The other luxury foodstore in the square, Hédiard was responsible for starting a craze for tropical fruit in France. The shop sells excellent cakes, as well as pre-cooked meals that are irresistible.

AVENUE MONTAIGNE

All the big *couturiers* are amassed together in this peaceful avenue. None of the shops open until the respectable hour of 10am, and it's usually about

*The **Buren Columns** (listed under **Palais Royal**) look rather out of place, but this doesn't seem to bother the visitors who dutifully flock to them and try to toss coins onto the top of each column.*

midday before the clients turn up, in between coffee on the Champs, and lunch in a little bistro somewhere. It's another world. Listed below are some of the famous addresses.

Celine
38 avenue Montaigne, 75008 Paris (47.23.74.12). Metro Franklin D Roosevelt, Alma Marceau.

Guy Laroche
29 avenue Montaigne, 75008 Paris (47.23.78.72). Metro Franklin D Roosevelt, Alma Marceau.

Chanel
42 avenue Montaigne, 75008 Paris (47.23.74.12). Metro Franklin D Roosevelt, Alma Marceau.

Scherrer
51 avenue Montaigne, 75008 Paris (43.59.55.39). Metro Franklin D Roosevelt, Alma Marceau.

Thierry Mugler
49 avenue Montaigne, 75008 Paris (47.23.37.62). Metro Franklin D Roosevelt, Alma Marceau.

Torrente
60 avenue Montaigne, 75008 Paris (42.56.14.14). Metro Franklin D Roosevelt, Alma Marceau.

Christian Dior
11 avenue Montaigne (corner of the rue François 1er), 75008 Paris (40.73.54.44).

Metro Franklin D Roosevelt, Alma Marceau. Last, but not least, is the largest *haute couture* shop in the world – all 1,400 square metres (15,070 square feet) of it. It was the first to be revamped and be modernized, and the whole of the Avenue Montaigne and the rue François 1er are gradually following suit.

Marine Museum
Palais de Chaillot, place du Trocadéro, 75016 Paris (45.54.31.70). Metro Trocadéro. **Open** 10am-6pm Mon, Wed-Sun. **Admission** 18F.
An impressive collection of model ships, from the antique to the modern, are displayed here. There is an exhaustive collection of exhibits – over 20,000 of them – on anything to do with the sea, whether historical or scientific.

Museum of Man
place du Trocadéro, 75016 Paris (45.54.70.60). Metro Trocadéro. **Open** 9.45am-5.45pm Mon, Wed-Sun. **Admission** 15F.
The history of Man is traced at this museum, from a prehistorical, anthropological and ethnological angle. There's also a section on palaeontology that has some fossils worth taking a peek at.

PALAIS ROYAL

During the eighteenth and nineteenth centuries the Palais Royal was filled with gambling houses located in the Palace Arcades and encircling the gardens. They were beyond the jurisdiction of the police, and by the end of the nineteenth century the area had got completely out of hand. Suicides of those who had lost everything in the gambling joints increased to such an extent that finally the houses had to close down, bringing an end to a hectic era.

Today, the Palais Royal couldn't be more different. Savour the peace and quiet in the gardens or have a browse in the antique shops. Nearer the **avenue de l'Opéra** the area becomes increasingly commercial and busy. Make sure you explore some of the passages around here.

Place Vendôme
75001 Paris. Metro Concorde, Tuileries.
This classical square is incredibly chic and preserves a stately calm in contrast to the hassle of the rue de Rivoli, from which you can approach it. The column in the centre has an eccentric history. The square originally had a statue of Louis XIV in the centre, but this was removed during the Revolution, and replaced by the Vendôme column which Napoleon had run up from some captured Russian and Austrian cannon. When the Empire fell, so did the statue of Napoleon which was on top, only to be reinstated in a fit of nostalgia several years later. In the square itself, you'll find the jet-setters browsing in Cartier's and other expensive jewellery, fur and fashion shops. It also houses the principal offices of several banks, including a branch of Nat West Bank in an abnormally luxurious setting.

The National Library
58 rue de Richelieu, 75001 Paris (47.03.81.26). Metro Palais-Royal, Bourse. **Open** noon-6pm daily. Phone for details of guided tours.
Several million books and papers accumulated over the centuries are housed here. There's an incredible collection of original editions by authors such as Rabelais and François Villon, as well as the original manuscripts of Victor Hugo, Proust and many others. Intellectual snobbery rules, though, as only graduates are let loose in some areas. There's also a medal and sword museum, a music library and a lot of leather-bound gold-leafed rare books, heavily guarded. The tranquil library atmosphere should be appreciated by all bibliophiles.

Passage Choiseul
23 rue Saint Augustin to 40 rue des Petits Champs, 75002 Paris. Metro Palais-Royal.
Harrowingly described in Céline's *Mort à Crédit* under a different name, the real passage today is utterly different – active, lively and popular, with an enormous range of boutiques worth investigating.

The Buren Columns
Palais Royal, 75001 Paris.
See **picture and caption.**

The Left Bank

The smaller of the two banks contains only six of the Parisian arrondissements. Many Parisians profess to being incurable Left Bankers, who only cross the Seine when it's absolutely necessary.

THE LATIN QUARTER

The Romans founded the Latin Quarter in 50BC when they built a city on the **Montagne Sainte Genevieve**, but very few traces of their occupation remain, with the exception of the **Musée de Cluny** and the **Arènes de Lutèce**. The quarter did not really come to life until the twelfth century, when some clergymen emigrated from the Cité (*see chapters* **The Right Bank; Roman; Middle Ages & Renaissance**) in order to found France's first University there. The most famous, and oldest, university still in existence is the **Sorbonne**, created by Robert de Sorbon in 1253. Started as a theological school, students came from all over the world to study here, creating the atmosphere in the surrounding area which to some extent still remains.

In those days, the students ruled the roost, and the University was an independent power. The quarter became an infamous area, full of gambling houses, bordellos and drunken students, and much-loved by the great medieval poet, intellectual and criminal François Villon. The area was called the Latin Quarter because the students all spoke Latin – even outside classes – until the time of the Revolution, when the University was closed down for a time. Today the area holds the largest concentration of colleges and *lycées* (secondary schools) in France.

The Latin Quarter belongs to students and young people. The **boulevard Saint Michel** (otherwise known as the boul' Mich) is packed with large terrace cafés, bookshops, stationers and cheap clothes stores. It's one of the few areas to have escaped Haussmann's bulldozing (*see chapter* **Empires & Revolution**), so that the small crowded streets remain, such as the **rue Descartes, rue Champollion,**

and the **rue de la Harpe**, complete with more than their fair share of bars, cafés and little restaurants. There are also several small cinemas here, such as the **Action Écoles** and the **Studio Galande**. These show films in rep, old classics and cult movies, and sometimes hold all-night screenings. There is no shortage of places in which to burn the midnight oil.

Take a walk down the cobbled alleys behind the **Panthéon**, where several medieval doorways and façades still exist and you can imagine the rich past of this area.

The Panthéon
place du Panthéon, 75005 Paris (43.54.69.57). Metro Cardinal Lemoine. **Open** *Oct-May:* 10am-4pm Mon, Wed-Sun; *April-Sept:* 10am-6pm Mon, Wed-Sun. **Admission** free.
See picture and caption.

Musée de Cluny
6 place Paul Painlevé, 75005 Paris (43.25.62.00). Metro Saint Michel. **Open** 9.45am-12.30pm, 2-5.15pm, Mon, Wed-Sun. **Admission** 18F adults; 8F 18-25s, OAPs; free under-18s. **No credit cards.**
The Hôtel de Cluny is one of the oldest residences in Paris. Dating from the fifteenth century, it was built on the site of the old Roman baths, a few remnants of which can still be seen. In the museum there's an impressive number of statues from Nôtre Dame cathedral, as well as a large number of medieval tapestries. The most famous of these is the superb *Lady and the Unicorn*.

The Sorbonne
rue des Ecoles, 75005 Paris. Metro Maubert-Mutualité. **Open** 9.45am-12.30pm, 2pm-5.15pm, Mon, Wed-Sun. **Admission** limited public access.
Rebuilt in the nineteenth century in rather dubious taste, the oldest remaining part of this ancient university is the seventeenth-century chapel, which is now open to the public only during temporary exhibitions. The Sorbonne has been a seat of political and educational power for centuries, and has always operated under its own laws. It was during the student uprising of May 1968, in which the Sorbonne played a major part, that police dared for the first time to enter its walls and arrest demonstrators. Go in and wander round the inner courtyard: there are some interesting sculptures to be seen. Some lecture theatres (not open to the public) are covered in wall-to-wall paintings, which must provide a welcome distraction for the students.

Saint Étienne du Mont
rue Clovis, 75005 Paris (no phone). Metro Cardinal Lemoine. **Open** 7.30-11.45am, 2.15-7.15pm, Mon-Sat; closed July, Aug. **Admission** free.
Saint Etienne is an unusual fifteenth-century church – an amalgamation of Italian, Gothic and classical architectural styles. The tombs of Racine and Pascal can be found inside.

MAUBERT & SAINT SEVERIN

Running alongside the Latin Quarter, this area is also a traditional haunt of students. In the Middle Ages lessons were held in the open air in the **place Maubert.** It has managed to retain a certain charm from the past, with narrow streets such as the **rue Saint Séverin** and the **rue de la Huchette**. Many of the streets run the same course as they did in the Middle Ages and the area is one of the capital's rare pedestrian quarters.

There's no shortage of restaurants crammed into the narrow streets; for some reason most of them are Greek. You can eat cheaply here, a three-course meal with wine costing between 60F and 70F, although the quality of the food is not always guaranteed. It's hard to choose between the many restaurants offering the same menu, but they all stay open late and won't kick you out as soon a you've finished your coffee.

Although it's pleasant to be able to wander around without fear of being flattened by a 2CV, on a summer's evening it is almost impossible to squeeze your way past the tourists packing the pedestrian streets. If you want some peace and quiet, try turning down the smaller side streets, or head deeper into the Latin Quarter.

Saint Séverin
rue Saint Séverin, 75005 Paris. Metro Saint Michel/bus 21, 24, 27, 38, 47, 63, 81, 85, 86, 87, 96. **Open** 11am-1pm, 3-7.30pm, Tue-Fri. **Admission** free.
In the twelfth century Foulques de Neuilly launched the Fourth Crusade from this church. It underwent many changes until the seventeenth century, but has retained its Romanesque tower. The porch is thirteenth-century, the spire sixteenth, and the ambulatory and façade are fine examples of Flamboyant Gothic.

Saint Julien le Pauvre
rue Saint Julien le Pauvre, 75005 Paris. Metro Maubert-Mutualité, Saint Michel/bus 21, 24, 27, 38, 47.

This small, picturesque church was built at the same time as Nôtre Dame. Student assemblies and elections were held here from the thirteenth to the sixteenth centuries, but in 1524 it was decided that these assemblies had become too raucous and the church was closed to student meetings forever. There is a marvellous view of old Paris from the square in front of the church, down the rues Saint Séverin and Galande.

The Arènes de Lutèce
Entry in rue de Navarre and rue Monge, 75005 Paris. Metro Cardinal-Lemoine, Jussieu, Monge/bus 47, 89. **Open** visible any time.
Situated in what is now a public park, the remains of the Arènes were discovered in 1869. Together with the baths at Cluny (*see above*), they are the oldest Roman ruins in Paris. Although restored at the beginning of this century, the arena isn't recognizable as such, and is now favoured only by *boules* players and children. Paris (or Lutèce as it was then called) was not a major city in Roman times, which is obvious when you compare the size and quantity of ruins with what remains of Roman civilization in the south of France.

RUE MOUFFETARD

Once you've visited the Panthéon, you could walk past the **Lycée Henri IV**, in the rue Clothilde just behind.

One of the most famous *lycées* in Paris, its list of past students includes Molière and Racine. Much later, Sartre taught here. Once here, you're ideally placed for a wander down the **rue Mouffetard**. This narrow, winding street has an ancient feel to it, despite the presence of a few fast-food joints and yet more Greek restaurants. The adjacent roads, like the **rue du Pot-de-Fer** and the **rue Tournefort**, with their tiny shops and restaurants, are also worth a visit. Get a feel of real Parisian life by visiting the market here. Situated right at the bottom of the rue Mouffetard, just before the place Saint Médard, it's one of the most picturesque of Parisian markets. You have to get there early, though, as everything is shut by 1.30pm.

Saint Médard
41 rue Mouffetard, 75005 Paris. Metro Censier-Daubenton. **Open** irregular hours; always closed Mon.
This church dates from the fifteenth century, but wasn't completed until the seventeenth century. Interesting from a historical as well as an architectural point of view, during the eighteenth century it was at the centre of a controversial cult. It was believed that miraculous cures came to

those who prayed by the tomb of a Jansenist deacon who was buried there. News of this spread, and the church became the scene of mass hysteria. In the end Louis XV intervened. He closed the cemetery where the tomb lay, and decreed that by his order God could no longer perform miracles there.

The Jardin des Plantes
57 rue Cuvier, 75005 Paris (40.79.30.00). Metro Jussieu, Monge, Gare d'Austerlitz/bus 24. **Open** dawn-dusk daily. Includes the following: **The Menagerie: open** *winter.* 9am-5pm Mon-Sat; *summer.* 9am-6pm Mon-Sat; 9am-6.30pm Sun. **The Winter Garden: open** 1-5pm Mon, Wed-Sun. **The Botany School: open** 8-11am Mon-Fri; closed on public holidays. **The Alpine Garden: open** April-Sept; see programme for details. **Minerology Gallery: open** 10am-5pm Mon, Wed-Fri; closed on public holidays. **Entomology Gallery: open** 2-4.50pm Mon, Wed-Sun; closed on public holidays. **Anatomy & Palaeontology Gallery: open** 10am-5pm Mon, Wed-Fri, Sun; 11am-6pm Sat; closed on public holidays. **Zoological Gallery: open** closed for restoration at time of going to press.
Even if you're not interested in science or the natural history of the world, the Jardin des Plantes contains a memorable collection of plants and flowers, and is worth visiting in the spring when it's at its most colourful. Until the seventeenth century, the gardens contained every conceivable species of medicinal plant. All of the great French naturalists, including Buffon and Lamarck, worked here, bringing back innumerable insects, plants and minerals from their expeditions around the world. These are now housed in the park's various museums which contain exhaustive collections of the strange, rare and beautiful, and extinct. The winter garden has a large hothouse of various tropical plants. The gardens also contain the only inner-Paris zoo. *See also chapters* **Sightseeing, Children.**

The Mosque
place du Puits de l'Ermite, 75005 Paris (45.35.97.33). Metro Monge/24, 47, 57, 61, 63, 67, 89 bus **Open** guided tours 9am-noon, 2pm-6pm, Mon-Thur, Sat, Sun; closed to visitors during Muslim holidays.
Opposite the Jardin des Plantes, the architecture of the green-and-white Mosque comes as a surprise against the Parisian surroundings. The interior is sumptuously decorated with ancient carpets, Arabian art and huge sculpted wooden doors. There's also a beautiful courtyard and inner garden. Apart from its religious functions, the mosque also houses a library, Turkish baths, a restaurant and a *salon de thé*. Relax on a couch by one of the brass tables, sip a cup of mint tea, and admire the fabulous decorations. If you really feel like treating yourself, set aside some time to visit the Hammam (Turkish baths). They're the best in Paris; *see chapter* **Services**, listed under **Health & Beauty**, for details.

The Institute of the Arab World
23 quai Saint Bernard, 75005 Paris (40.51.38.38). Metro Jussieu, Cardinal Lemoine. **Open** 1-8pm Tue-Sun. **Admission** to exhibitions varies.
Commissioned by the French Government and 20 Arab counties, the building is one of the great architectural and cultural successes of the eighties. Designed to represent Arab culture of the past and present, it

The **Panthéon** (*listed under* **The Latin Quarter**) *dominates the summit of the Montagne Sainte Geneviève. Construction began during the reign of Louis XV to replace a ruined church, since when its function has often changed. Today it houses the ashes of some of France's most illustrious countrymen, including Victor Hugo, Voltaire, Rousseau, Zola, Louis Braille (inventor of the writing system) and Jean Moulin, the leader of the French Resistance.*

Quite the biggest event in **Montparnasse**'*s recent history has been the construction of the Montparnasse Tower* (pictured above) *and the railway station. This involved the razing of the old parts of the quarter, and the destruction of its artistic soul. Of course, the view from the top of the tower is magnificent – especially as it's the only place from which you can't see the Montparnasse Tower.*

houses permanent and temporary exhibitions on the art, literature and other cultural forms of the Arab world. There is also a library, a *mediathèque*, a museum and a restaurant, which surprisingly serves French rather than Arab dishes.

The Police Museum
1bis rue des Carmes, 75005 Paris (43.29.21.57, ext 336). Metro Maubert-Mutualité. **Open** 9am-5pm Mon-Thur; 9am-4.30pm Fri. **Admission** free.
To get to the museum you have to pass through the whole *commissariat* (police station), so make sure you've got a clear conscience. On display is a macabre collection of objects linked to infamous crimes of the past and present. There is an interesting showcase explaining the system of anthropology developed by Bartillon.

ODEON

Having discovered the joys of the Latin Quarter, and before heading off in search of echoes of the *belle époque* in Saint Germain (*see chapter* **Village Paris**), cross the boulevard Saint Michel to the **Odéon** quarter. Although on the face of it similar to the Latin Quarter, after a few minutes and several beers you can feel the difference, especially at night.

This area is steeped in Revolutionary history. Danton lived here, in the **place de l'Odéon**, at a spot now marked by his statue. Unappreciative of its historical significance, Haussmann had the original building demolished as part of his rebuilding programme under Napoléon III. Danton also founded the famous Club des Cordeliers in what is now the **rue de l'Ecole de Médecine**. Stroll down the narrow, almost medieval streets, and spot the numerous commemorative plaques on the buildings. Pascal lived at No.54 **rue Monsieur-le-Prince**, now a good street for alternative nightlife (*see chapters* **Music: Rock, Folk & Jazz; Nightlife**).

The **rue Saint André des Arts**, and the neighbouring rue Séguiers, rue Christine and passage de l'Hirondelle, as well as the oddly-named rue Git-le-Coeur (literally, Lies-the-Heart), all hold a great deal of old-fashioned charm. The effect is most striking if you approach them from the broad panorama of the Seine and the quai de Grands Augustins. Off the rue Saint André des Arts, the courtyard of the Commerce Saint André with its old low houses, is also worth a visit. It was outside No. 9 that the first guillotine was constructed.

The **passage Commandant Saint André** is a delightful cobbled pedestrian passageway which shelters a very good tea room, usually blissfully free from crowds. During the day the area bustles with people shopping in the numerous boutiques, and at night it is one of Paris' most animated quarters, full of busy bars, cafés, and restaurants of every nationality. As in the Latin Quarter, many of these close late, if at all. For those suffering late-night hunger pangs, there's always the 24-hour *boulangerie*, at 10 rue de l'Ancienne Comédie. There are also several small cinemas showing an eclectic range of new and old films.

Théatre National de l'Odéon
Place de l'Odéon, 75006 Paris (43.25.70.32). RER Luxembourg. **Open** 11am-6.30pm daily; no show Mon.
This theatre was opened in 1908. It's always worth checking the programme to see if anything takes your fancy. The marvellous seventeenth- and eighteenth-century houses in the surrounding square have all been listed as historic monuments. Camille Desmoulins, heroine of the Revolution, lived at No.1. The famous Café Voltaire was at No.2, favoured haunt of literary Americans, such as Scott Fitzgerald and Hemingway.

The Luxembourg Palace and Gardens
Rue de Vaugirard, 75006 Paris. RER Luxembourg/21, 27, 38, 58, 82, 84, 85, 89. **Open** *gardens:* 10-11am, 2.30-3.30pm, Mon-Sat.
The palace was built under the orders of Marie de Medici by Simon de le Brosse, who drew his inspiration from the Pitti Palace in Florence. It remained a royal residence until the Revolution. Access is limited, but there are guided tours on Sundays. The gardens are typically French and have traditionally been a favourite spot for poets. Baudelaire, Gerard de Nerval and Verlaine have all strolled here.

AROUND MONTPARNASSE

The area of Montparnasse and the 14th *arrondissement* is defined by the long boulevard which takes its name, and which runs from the borders with the 15th *arrondissement* to Port Royal. The rest of the 14th *arrondissement* is divided into smaller areas, such as Pernéty and Montsouris.

In the eighteenth century this area consisted of nothing but quar-

BOULEVARD DE LA BELLE EPOQUE

Fondé en 1854, l'un des plus vieux cafés de Paris rouvre grand ses portes.
Dans un décor moderne et chaud où se fond l'âme de la Grande époque du XIXe, là où Baudelaire, poètes, ministres et tribuns refaisaient le monde , régalez-vous d'huîtres et de coquillages, de grillades et de poissons, ou tout simplement sur fond de cocktail ou

CAFÉ LE MADRID

6-8, Bd Montmartre
75009 PARIS
Tél. : 48 24 97 22/23/24

d'apéritif, laissez-vous rêver à la Belle Epoque ...

Formule MADRID pour les déjeuners d'affaires ou les diners entre amis.
10 entrées, 10 plats, 10 desserts au choix. Vin, café, et service compris 150 FR

de 8 heures à 2 heures du matin
tous les jours et sans interruption.
Carte, menu et formule de 12h à 1h

PARIS' ONLY AUTHENTIC ENGLISH-LANGUAGE MAGAZINE

Art, music, theatre, fashion, eating out...everything that's
making waves in the French capital is in PARIS PASSION every month.
PARIS PASSION is on sale in newsstands and bookshops
in Paris, the U.K. and around the world.
Or send £18 for 10 information-packed issues to:

PARIS PASSION - 23 Rue Yves Toudic - 75010 Paris

Coca-Cola light

Just for the taste of it.
Less than one Calorie per glass*

*Less than 4 KJ or less than one Calorie per 20 cl glass.

Featured above are clothes from: CHANEL, ALAIA, MONTANA, VALENTINO, FERAUD, LANVIN. (Except long, tiered evening gown and silver fox coat)

⋩ RECIPROQUE ⋩
Nicole Morel

HIGH FASHION
CLOTHING
Women
Men

CONSIGNMENT SHOP
600 m2 Retail Space

TRINKETS-GIFTS
ACCESSORIES
Jewelry
Furs

The best and biggest second-hand boutique in Paris.
Ladies and mens clothing by famous fashion designers,
all in perfect condition.
Housewares and gifts.

95, 101, 123 rue de la Pompe • 75116 Paris • Metro: Pompe
Telephone: 47.04.82.24/47.04.30.28

ries. On a hill which had been created from the rubble, students used to congregate and declaim verses. They named the hill Mont Parnasse after Mount Parnassus, the mythological home of Apollo and the Muses. The hill was eventually destroyed when the boulevard Montparnasse was laid down, but the name stuck.

After the Revolution, Montparnasse became the festive quarter of Paris, packed with cafés, bistros and theatres. It attracted the intellectuals and artists of Paris – and the rest of the world – to its thriving streets. The bistro La Closerie des Lilas, the oldest existing remainder of this era, was the site of many an agitated poetry evening. With the arrival of La Coupole, Le Dôme and the other cafés which line the **boulevard Montparnasse**, came an exciting era of artistic and intellectual movements. Café society was born, and was to continue until after World War II. Today artistic Montparnasse is a changed place: *see chapter* **Artistic Paris**.

The character of the quarter changes between day and night. In the daytime, there are endless shops to be found in the Commercial Centre underneath Montparnasse Tower (*see picture and caption*), which houses a small version of the **Galéries Lafayette**. The **rue de Rennes**, which runs towards Saint Germain, is a good place to find affordable clothes.

The boulevard Montparnasse comes into its own at night. Always lively, the many cafés, brasseries and restaurants provide sustenance until 2am. The other attractions are the cinemas, some of which show films in the original version.

Montparnasse station is the point of arrival from Brittany. The proliferation of crêperies, restaurants, and bistros in the **rues Odessa**, **Delambre** and **Montparnasse** (the latter not to be confused with the boulevard), give the area a distinctly Breton feel. Crêpe and cider lovers need look no further.

Montparnasse Cemetery
boulevard Edgar Quinet, 75014 Paris. Metro Edgar Quinet. **Open** 8am-5.30pm Mon-Fri; 8.30am-5.30pm Sat; 9am-5.30pm Sun and holidays. **Admission** free.
Built in 1824, this is the third largest Parisian cemetery. A small haven of peace among the busy boulevards, it's an ideal place to rest during your travels. Before you go in, ask the attendant for a map of the place and find the burial

The idea of exploiting the disused parts of the quarries of Montparnasse and Montrouge, by turning them into ossuaries, was first put forward in 1785. **The Catacombs** (listed under **Around Montparnasse/Alesia & Montsouris**) now boast a total of between five and six million skeletons, including those of La Fontaine and Madame de Pompadour. Inside, there are bones stacked right up to the vaulted ceilings.

place of your favourite celebrity: Baudelaire, Sartre, de Beauvoir, Maupassant and Saint-Saëns are all here. *See also chapter* **Sightseeing.**

Musée de la Poste
34 boulevard de Vaugirard, 75014 Paris. Metro Montparnasse-Bienvenue. **Open** 10am-5pm Mon-Sat; closed Sun and Bank Holidays.
A philatelist's dream, this newly-renovated museum follows the evolution of the postal service – the oldest international institution.

The Observatory
61 avenue de l'Observatoire, 75014 Paris (43.20.12.10). Metro Port Royal. **Open** first Sat of each month by appointment.
The Observatory is the oldest astronomical institution in Europe. Constructed by Colbert in 1668, its four sides are orientated towards the four compass points. The calculation of the true dimensions of the solar system was first made here, the planet Neptune was (mathematically) discovered, and the speed of light was calculated. You can visit the small museum on the first Saturday of each month, by applying to the Secretariat in writing, enclosing a stamped addressed envelope.

Rue de la Gaité
75014 Paris. Metro Gaité, Edgar Quinet.
A little street with a lively history, which used to live up to its name. Once thriving with life, atmosphere, popular theatres and bistros, property development and real-estate speculation have now turned the rue de la Gaité into a much less happy street. Much of the property on the street has been let to sex-shops, fast-food and take-away joints. However some of its former inhabitants

are still hanging on trying to preserve the old spirit of the street. The old theatres, the Gaité-Montparnasse and the Montparnasse are still alive, and sometimes, with a lot of effort and imagination, the former gaiety can be recaptured.

Plaisance-Pernéty
75014 Paris. Metro Pernéty or Plaisance.
Much the same story applies to Plaisance-Pernéty as to the rue de la Gaité. A walk down the rues Vercingetorix, Plaisance, and de l'Ouest once held many attractions, before the new urban developments erased most of the life from this once-popular area with its many bistros and little shops. However the modernization of the area has produced some interesting architecture.

ALESIA & MONTSOURIS

This area is in the extreme south of the 14th *arrondissement*, bordered by the **rue d'Alésia**, **avenue Général Leclerc**, and the **rue de l'Admiral Mouchez**, and is centred around the **Parc Montsouris**. This setting has attracted many artists, who have established studios in the area (*see chapter* **Artistic Paris**).

Parc Montsouris
75014 Paris. RER Cité Universitaire. **Open** dawn-dusk daily.
Parks are all too rare in Paris. This one is the second largest, after the Buttes Chaumont. On the top of the hill is the Bardo, which is a

*The interior of the **Church of the Dome** at the **Hôtel des Invalides** (listed under **The 7th Arrondissment**), realized by the greatest artists of the time, houses the tombs of some of France's famous men of arms, including, of course, Napoleon. The emperor's body lies within six successive coffins, the first in white iron. the second in mahogany, two in lead, the fifth in ebony and the last in rich oak. The sarcophagus stands on a thick base of green granite from Vosges.*

replica of the palace of the Beys in Tunisia. It was built for the Universal Exhibition in 1867, and then moved to the park. Now in ruins, it is being restored, and by 1990 should be ready to take on its new rôle as the Tunisian Cultural Centre. Le Pavillon Montsouris restaurant (noon-10pm daily), old haunt of Mata Hari, Lenin and Sartre, has a superb terrace where you can eat expensive but slightly disappointing food. A good place for a promenade, the park is full of tree-lined pathways, and also has a lake with swans and ducks on it.

Cité Universitaire
19-21 boulevard Jourdain, 75014 Paris (45.89.68.52). RER Cité Universitaire.
The university includes an impressive complex of halls of residence which houses 6,000 students of 120 nationalities. Each of the 40 halls represents a different country, and the buildings echo the architectural styles of that country – some with more success than others. The Swiss and Brazilian houses were designed by Le Corbusier. Part of the funding for each of the halls comes from its home government. Included in the complex are two theatres, a swimming pool, and the usual bars and cafés.

Lenin's House
4 rue Marie Rose, 75014 Paris (43.22.82.38). Metro Alésia. **Open** by appointment only.
When forced to leave Russia, Lenin came to Paris before the Revolution, accompanied by several fellow-revolutionaries, including Trotsky. Hours were spent discussing the politics of revolution in the neighbouring bars of the rue de la Gaité, and the café Denfert. Lenin moved to the house in the rue Marie Rose, after he was kicked out of No. 24 rue Beaunier by the concierge, who was fed up with the suspicious types who were constantly hanging around. The house in rue Marie Rose, where Lenin lived for four years, has been turned into a museum covering Lenin's Paris years.

The Catacombs
1 place Denfert Rochereau, 75014 Paris (43.22.47.63). Metro Denfert Rochereau. **Open** 2-4pm Tue-Fri; 9-11am, 2-4pm, Sat-Sun. Closed on public holidays. **Admission** 15F adults; 8.50F under-18s. Lecture every Wed at 2.45pm 20F + entry fee.
The catacombs are a popular, if macabre, tourist spot, especially in summer, when they provide a welcome escape from the heat of the streets. There are still 200-300km/124-186 miles of unused passages running underneath Paris, and at night they play host to various types of 'alternative' entertainment from concerts to meetings of obscure religious sects – all highly illegal, of course. *See also* **picture and caption.**

THE 15TH ARRONDISSEMENT

The largest and most populated *arrondissement* in Paris, the 15th doesn't offer much in the way of tourist attractions, which is precisely why it's worth exploring, to get a breath of real Parisian life. In the area around the **rue du Commerce** or the **rue des Morillons**, you'll find commercial activity that isn't geared towards fleecing tourists. Fans of urban modernism should visit the Fronts de Seine. This area, running alongside the Seine, is made up of modern buildings and walkways, which are best enjoyed by the pedestrian. It is a very exclusive address, but nevertheless not a particularly safe or interesting place at night.

La Ruche
Passage 52 rue de Danzig, 75015 Paris. Metro Convention.
Designed by Mr Eiffel, la Ruche, or the bee-hive, took over from the Bateau Lavoir in Montmartre as a lodging-place for impoverished artists. Modigliani, Chagall and Soutine all lived here (*see chapter* **Artistic Paris**). Now restored, it still houses artists, and is a good place for a walk.

Parc Georges Brassens
rue des Morillons, 75015 Paris. Metro Convention.
Situated on the site of the old Vaugirard abattoir, the recent development of this park in an otherwise not very 'green' *arrondissement* is a great success story. There is a mini vineyard with 700 feet of vine; you can also wander through the Garden of Scents, especially created for the blind.

Aquaboulevard
4 rue Louis Armand, 75015 Paris (40.60.10.00). Metro Balard. **Open** 8am-10pm Mon-Thur, Sun; 8am-midnight Fri, Sat. **Admission** 25F visitor's day pass. *Aquatic Park*: 60F for 4 hours, 10F per hour thereafter; 45F children under 12; free babies under 3.
This is the biggest recreational park in Paris, and, as you might have guessed, the emphasis is on water. You can sample the imitation tropical beaches, complete with palm trees and exotic vegetation, or the huge range of sporting activities, including tennis, squash, golf, bowling, billiards, bridge and more. There is a special section for 6 to 12 year-olds, the Archipel des Enfantaisies, that has video shows and a game park. There are also shops, bars, and restaurants.

THE 7TH ARRONDISSEMENT

When the Marais fell from fashion at the end of the eighteenth century, many of the great personalities of the time began to have their town houses built in the **Faubourg Saint Germain** and the 7th *arrondissement*. So many, in fact, that you will find the greatest concentration of town houses per square metre in Paris here. Still inhabited by the conservative bourgeoisie, the only real signs of life in this area come from the ministries and embassies which are housed in the most beautiful of the *hôtels particuliers*. The quarter is now bisected by the **boulevards Saint Germain** and **Raspail**, but certain streets, such as the **rues de Lille**, **Grenelle** and **Varenne** still evoke the *belle epoque* of the Faubourg.

LES INVALIDES

This is one of the most beautiful and most spacious of Parisian monuments. Construction of the Hôtel began in 1670 under the orders of Louis XIV, as a place for housing soldiers too old or too injured to serve. The Invalides consists of the Hôtel, the Army Museum, the Museum of Relief Maps and Plans, the Church of Saint Louis and the Church of the Dôme.

The Hôtel des Invalides
75007 Paris. Metro Invalides, Varenne, Latour-Maubourg/RER Invalides/28, 49, 63, 69, 82, 83, 92 bus. **Open** *7am-7pm daily.*
This building, with its superb 196m/643ft façade, once housed 5,000 old soldiers. Today there are no more than 33, and the rest of the building is used for administration. In the complex are:
The Army Museum *(45.55.37.70).* **Open** *Apr-Sept:* 10am-6pm; *Oct-Mar:* 10am-5pm.
The museum houses thousands of military relics, such as the sword of François I, and has a huge collection of arms and armour from all over the world. There are also many emotive relics from World War II. One of the richest military museums in the world.
The Museum of Relief Maps and Plans *Access through the Army Museum with the same ticket.*
This houses a collection of maps and plans from the time of the strongholds of Vauban up to the present day.
Church of Saint Louis *2 rue de Tourville, 75007 Paris (45.55.92.30).* **Open** *Apr-Sept:* 10am-6pm daily; *Oct-Mar:* 10am-5pm daily.
Also known as the Church of Soldiers, the church of Saint Louis is decorated with captured enemy flags. The bones of many famous military leaders are interred here.
The Church of the Dôme *Access through the Army museum with the same ticket.*
The Dôme was added to the Hôtel between 1679 and 1706 by the architect Hardouin-Mansart and is one of the high points of French classical style. The exterior of the cupola has just been regilded in honour of the Bicentennial celebrations and can now be seen in all its glory. *See also* **picture and caption**. *See chapter* **Sightseeing**.

The Eiffel Tower
Champs de Mars, 75007 Paris (45.50.34.56/recorded information 45.55.91.11). Metro Bir Hakeim, Ecole Militaire, Trocadéro/bus 82. **Open** *summer:* 9.30am-midnight daily; *winter:* 10am-11pm daily. **Admission** *by lift:* 14F-35F adults, depending on floor; 6F-20F under-12s; free under-4s; *by stairs to 2nd floor:* 7F adults; free under-4s; group discounts available.
The most famous landmark in Paris caused uproar when it was first built by Mr Eiffel for the Centenary of the Revolution. A remarkable feat of construction for its day, and even today, when standing directly beneath it, it is hard to take in the stupendous structure and latticework. *See also* **picture and caption**. For more information on the tower, *see chapter* **Sightseeing**.

Musée Rodin
77 rue Varenne, 75007 Paris (47.05.01.34). Metro Varenne. **Open** *summer:* 10am-5.45pm Mon, Wed-Sun; *winter:* 10am-4.30pm Mon, Wed-Sun. **Admission** 16F Mon, Wed-Sat; 8F Sun.
A delightful museum occupying the house and gardens where the sculptor once lived. Rodin left all his works to the State and you'll see all the old favourites – *The Kiss*, *The Thinker*, *The Burghers of Calais*.

Palais Bourbon
126 rue de l'Université, 75007 Paris (42.97.64.08). Metro Assemblée Nationale.

Entry at 33 Quai d'Orsay. Visit on application to the Office of Administrative Affairs, 33 Quai D'Orsay, in person.
Built in 1722, the Palace now houses the National Assembly. It's worth visiting the library, which is decorated with frescoes by Delacroix, charting the history of civilization. Apply in writing if you want to attend an Assembly debate.

Au Bon Marché
Corner of rue de Sèvres and the rue du Bac, 75007 Paris (45.49.21.22). Metro Sèvres-Babylone. **Open** *9.30am-6.45pm Mon-Sat.*
This was the first department store in Paris, and its name literally means 'the good bargain'. The metallic structure was designed by Eiffel. As is the case with all Parisian department stores, it's easy to get lost inside, but in doing so you may find a good bargain.

Hôtel Lutétia
45 boulevard Raspail, 75007 Paris (45.44.39.10).
The façade of this superb hotel sports various statues by Paul Belmondo (father of Jean-Paul). The hotel has a chequered history: many famous names have stayed here, including de Gaulle who chose it for his wedding night. It also spent several less festive years as Gestapo headquarters during the Occupation, but has since regained all its splendour.

The **Eiffel Tower** *(listed under* **The 7th Arrondissement***) was in danger of being demolished in 1909, when it was claimed that there was no more use for it, so a use was quickly found, as a transmission tower for radio and later television. Today, over four million visitors find a use for it every year and it is one of Paris's biggest tourist attractions.*

USA Food & Bar
EST. 1981

Chili, Guacamole, Nachos
Burgers, T-Bones, Salads
Cocktails - Alive & Kickin'
Sunday Brunch
Happy Hour Sunday - Thursday
18h00-19h00
7 days a week - Noon till late
68, rue de Ponthieu, 75008 PARIS • 45.62.01.77

Artistic Paris

Although Paris is no longer the centre of the art world, it's still possible to get a sense of past glories and to experience today's thriving art scene.

Despite the *bidonvilles* (ugly estates which ring the capital), congested streets, and roads stacked with honking Renaults, Paris remains one of the most aesthetically pleasing capitals in the world. However, the great names of the late nineteenth and early twentieth centuries who immortalized 'gay Paris' now exist only in memory. Property speculation, yuppification and a lack of space have meant that life as a *bohème* has become increasingly difficult. Garrets, where the likes of Picasso and Utrillo might have burned a masterpiece to stave off hypothermia, now mean countless *sous* to the estate agents of Paris.

For the visitor though, Paris is unequivocally beautiful. Nôtre Dame still commands the city's skyline, the Sacré Coeur still eclipses the gaudy tourist traps which surround it and the capital still embraces the arts in a way that few other cities have ever done. Its galleries offer everything from the traditional to an unceasing flow of unknowns (*see chapter* **Art Galleries**). Whatever your mood and whatever your tastes in art, you'll find what you're looking for.

MONTMARTRE

Undoubtedly the *quartier* which, more than any other, has fired the imagination of many a budding genius. Once the unquestioned Mecca for artists, it reached its prime in the latter half of the nineteenth century and remained a favourite until the beginning of World War I. The man held most responsible for bringing Montmartre to the world is **Toulouse Lautrec**. Intrigued by the human form and a passionate fan of dance, his paintings were the ideal vehicle for conveying the mood of the great French cabarets which captivated Paris: the **Moulin Rouge**, the Folies Bergères, and Les Ambassadeurs. He immortalized the acts in his publicity posters for the forthcoming cabarets. Perhaps his most famous is the image of Aristide

Bruant in black coat, hat and red scarf slung casually around his neck.

Other artists were also inspired by these great music halls. The Moulin de la Galette was painted by Renoir, Van Gogh and Picasso, among others. Likewise, the Moulin Rouge was immortalized by Picasso and Bonnard, Les Ambassadeurs by Degas and the Folies Bergères by Manet. Even now, if you stand at the bottom of the rue Norvins and look up towards the Butte and the rue Saint Rustique, you'll see the Consulat bar, immortalized by Manet and still looking just as it did. Try to visit the area at off-peak times to avoid the tourist stampede.

Painters were not the only artistic inhabitants of Montmartre. Poetry circles appeared during this period and clubs such as the Chat Noir sprang up. Here Aristide Bruant performed satiric songs, mocking the bourgeois, the tourists and the snobs. The name on the café door, sited on the boulevard Rochechouart, is the only link with its vitriolic predecessor, but the café remains popular with the locals.

The last twenty years of the nineteenth century were known as the *Années Folles* in Montmartre. Of 58 houses on the rue des Martyrs, 25 were cabaret venues. The Moulin Rouge and the Elysées Montmartre battled it out in the popularity stakes. Within a few square kilometres, artists, writers, poets and egos of all description mingled to enjoy the bordellos, revues and exotic sideshows which gave the *quartier* its notoriety.

Le Bateau Lavoir
13 place Emile Goudeau, 75018 Paris. Metro Abbesses/bus 31, 80, 85.
Created to house impoverished artists, one of the first tenants was Picasso, who painted the *Demoiselles d'Avignon* here. Threatened with destruction, it was classified a Historical Monument in 1970 only to be gutted by fire a few weeks later. The house was then rebuilt in 1978 following the original plans by Claude Charpentier. Today, it fulfils its original role and houses 25 artists.

Le Lapin Agile
22 rue des Saules, 75018 Paris (46.06.85.87). Metro Lamarck Caulincourt/bus 74, 81, 95. **Open** 9-2am daily. **Admission** (incl one drink) 90F

adults; 70F students. Average price of a drink: 22F beer, 25F spirit.
An institution, this cabaret has been around since 1860. A down-to-earth place, its customers (Verlaine, Renoir and so on) would lay the tables themselves and Picasso once paid for a meal with one of his Harlequin paintings, today worth several million pounds. *See also* **picture and caption.**

The Moulin Rouge
82 boulevard de Clichy, 75011 Paris (46.06.00.19). Metro Blanche/bus 30, 54. **Open** 8pm-2am daily. **Admission** *dinner & dance*: from 530F; *show only*: from 365F. **Credit** AmEx, DC, MC, V.
This revue has a vast supply of anecdotes to justify its notoriety. In 1896 the 'Bal des Quat'z'Arts' got a little out of hand. Various artists' models participated in a striptease contest to establish the first 'integral nude'. The matter was investigated, reached the courts and one 'model' was imprisoned for three months. The students of the Latin Quarter, ever-ready for a dust-up with the authorities, set up barricades and goaded the government for three days. During the unrest, the windows of the the Saint Germain Church were smashed and two students were killed by the police. The War of the Artistic Nude dominated the headlines and the right of every self-respecting 'model' to strip at will had been defended, if not written into the constitution.

Montmartre Cemetery
Entry Avenue Rachel, 75018 Paris. Metro Lamarck Caulincourt/bus 74, 81, 95. **Open** 8am-5.30pm Mon-Fri; 8.30am-5.30pm Sat; 9am-5.30pm Sun.
The great and illustrious are buried in Montmartre cemerty. Louis Jouvet, Alexandre Dumas Jnr, Degas, Stendhal, Offenbach, Nijinsky, the Goncourt brothers, Alfred de Vigny and Alphonsine Plessis (the Dame aux Camélias) are among the many legends who rest here.

MONTPARNASSE

When the artists moved out of Montmartre around the beginning of the twentieth century, they moved to Montparnasse which became the new epicentre of artistic Paris. Modigliani, Utrillo, Max Jacob, Apollinaire, and, after World War II, Hemingway, Chagall, Picasso and Klee frequented the many cafés that litter its streets. Artists' studios sprang up on the little dead-end streets and a new atmosphere was created. However, the demands made on a small city experiencing an influx of wealth and people sparked off an era of property speculation. The rebuilding of the Montparnasse station and the arrival of the Commercial Centre and Tower meant the virtual destruction of the old streets and the character of the area behind the station.

Roads which housed the studios of famous artists, such as rue de l'Ouest, rue Vercingétorix and avenue du Maine have been completely renovated. However, in the general area of the 14th *arrondissement*, comprising Montparnasse, Pernety, Plaisance and Alésia, you'll stumble across some marvellous studios which survived the Blitz. In Montparnasse, wander down the **boulevard Raspail** where the studio Raspail is to be found at No. 216, or the **rue Froidevaux** (opposite the Montparnasse Cemetery). Around Pernety and Plaisance you'll find less of these lofts, but there are some hidden villas, plus the Impasse Florimond, where Brassens lived in the Maison de Jeanne. **Alésia** has a limited number of famed artistic stake-outs around **Montsouris Park**, such as 83 rue de la Tombe Issoire and the aptly named rue des Artistes (off the rue de l'Aude).

Café society thrived in Montparnasse: eating and drinking interspersed with late-night discussions and poetry readings. Still firm favourites among the Parisian intelligentsia, these Montparnasse cafés retain much of their original charm.

La Closerie des Lilas
171 boulevard Montparnasse, 75005 Paris (43.26.70.50). Metro Vavin/bus 58, 68. **Open** 11-2am daily.
The most famous of them all, frequented by the likes of Verlaine, Mallarmé and Baudelaire. La Closerie has seen all the artistic movements of the twentieth century in addition to surviving a few political ones. Max Jacob, André Breton, Modigliani, Lenin, and Strindberg all came here in their time. It remains the favourite haunt of many a Parisian journalist, writer and artist.

La Coupole
102 boulevard Montparnasse, 75006 Paris (43.20.14.20). Metro Vavin/bus 58, 68. **Open** 7.30-10.30am (for breakfast); noon-2am (for the café and brasserie).
Another renowned favourite and the largest restaurant in France, La Coupole has been restored to its original art deco style, complete with columns, frescos and tiles. It's as popular with today's arty types as it was with Man Ray and Kiki de Montparnasse. Tea dances are held during the week.

The Academy of the Grande Chaumière
Rue de la Grande Chaumière, 75005 Paris (43.26.13.72). Metro Vavin/bus 58, 68. **Open** 9am-noon, 2-6pm, Mon-Sat. **Admission** 50F.
This is where the true painting was done, where the teachers were (and are) as famous as the students. The entire street was inhabited by some of the greatest painters ever known. Commemorative plaques highlight this unique concentration of talent. Teachers like Gleizes (Cubism), Grosz (Dadaism) and Brayer (Traditional) all lived and worked here. Modigliani kept turning up to keep himself warm after a night in his draughty garret. This street also plays host to some of the best paint shops in Paris, where nothing is on display and where they make up their own colours.

Musée Zadkine
100bis, rue d'Assas, 75005 Paris (42.26.91.90). Metro Vavin/bus 58, 68. **Open** 10am-7.30pm daily. **Admission** phone for details; free Sun.
This tiny little museum is in the house of the great sculptor. It holds a great many sculptures and some drawings: ideal for spending a comtemplative and informative hour or two.

Montparnasse Cemetery
boulevard Edgar Quinet, 75014 Paris. Metro Quinet/bus 68. **Open** 8am-5.30pm Mon-Fri; 8.30am-5.30pm Sat; 9am-5.30pm Sun.
A haven of quiet around the Montparnasse Tower, this cemetery has some distinguished residents: Saint-Saens, Hachette, Baudelaire, Dreyfuss, Zadkine, de Beauvoir and Sartre (buried next to each other in the cemetery opposite where they lived). A sculpture of Baudelaire glares down from the east wall of the Large Cemetery.

SAINT GERMAIN

Starting at the **boulevard Saint Germain**, this tiny little area disappears into the Seine after a short walk. For all its brief duration, it is a worthy diversion and plays host to a variety of galleries (most representing the more exclusive and elitist end of the market). The Saint Germain church typifies most peoples' stereotype of a chapel set deep in the heart of an unambiguously artistic area. Picasso lived here for twenty years in the rue des Grands Augustins, just a short stroll from the two most celebrated cafés in Paris, **Les Deux Magots** and the **Café Flore**. Needless to say, *le tout Paris* hung around there too. Besides the artistic heritage, the *quartier* offers all the charm of nineteenth-century Paris with cobbled alleys and quiet shops. The names on every café and street bear witness to the heritage of the district: rue des Beaux Arts, rue Visconti, La Palette and L'Aquarelle. The plaques on the houses testify to the astonishing amount of celebrities who lived in such a small area and it retains such an idiosyncratic ambience that it's impossible to stray into the nearby Latin Quartier without noticing an immediate change.

The walls of the **Lapin Agile** *(listed under* **Montmartre***) are plastered with souvenirs from its rich past: poems by Bruant, newspaper cuttings and the like. At the weekend you have to arrive early to secure a good seat at the cabaret show and to browse through the memorabilia.*

Les Deux Magots
*6 place Saint Germain des Prés, 75006
(45.48.55.25). Metro Saint Germain des
Prés.* **Open** 8-2am daily.
Originally the celebrated haunt of Verlaine,
Rimbaud and Mallarmé. Now the world of
art and literature rubs shoulders with that of
fashion and politics and it has become the
favourite for name-droppers and the
paparazzi; it also serves a very good hot
chocolate. The Café has lost none of its literary appeal and even lent its name to the 'Prix
des Deux Magots', created in 1933, which
has in the past paid homage to the work of
Raymond Queneau and Simenon.

Café Flore
*174 boulevard Saint Germain, 75006
(45.48.55.26). Metro Saint Germain des
Prés.* **Open** 7-1.30am daily.
The hot chocolate's not as good here but the
clientele has been and is just as famous.

La Palette
*43 rue de Seine, 75006 Paris (43.26.68.15).
Metro Mabillon.* **Open** 8-2am daily.
This café has a great terrace, ideal for balmy
summers, great *jambon de pays* sandwiches
and an undiluted Parisian ambience.

Galerie Loft
*3 bis rue des Beaux Arts, 75006 Paris
(46.33.18.90). Metro Saint Germain des
Prés.* **Open** 10am-6pm Tue-Sun.
A two-year-old gallery. The owners take more
risks than their neighbours and show innovative work by artists under the age of thirty.

Isy Brachot
*Corner of rue Mazarine and rue Guénégaud,
75006 Paris (43.54.22.40). Metro Odéon.*
Open 11am-12.30pm, 2-7pm, Tue-Sat.
Essentially figurative in emphasis, the
gallery is both spacious and established. If
you haven't been to a preview here, you
haven't tasted Parisian life.

Galerie Adrien Maeght
*42-46 rue du Bac, 75007 Paris
(45.48.45.15). Metro rue du Bac.* **Open**
10.30am-1pm, 2-6.30pm, Mon-Sat.
A talent scout extraordinaire, Maeght was
responsible for discovering Miro, Calder
and Giacometti. The gallery also produces
its own in-house publications.

Galerie Samy Kinge
*54 rue de Verneuil, 75007 Paris
(42.61.19.07). Metro rue du Bac.* **Open**
10.30am-1pm, 2.30-7pm, Tue-Sat.
Gallery specializing in painters from the
Middle East.

BASTILLE

Today, the Bastille has become the
breeding ground for innovative talent in the capital. Hidden behind
what looks like a normal Parisian
front door you'll find whole cobbled
streets with houses made up of two
floors of immense studios. In keeping with the influx of talent, the area
has responded with an outbreak of
galleries and accompanying shops.

The choice of galleries and styles
is exhaustive so it's advisable to
select in advance a venue most likely
to appeal (*see chapter* **Art Galleries**).
The principal roads are the **rue de
Charonne, rue de Lappe, rue de
la Roquette**, and **rue Keller**. Very
few tend to specialize; most exhibit a
variety of work.

Le Génie de la Bastille
Metro Bastille, Ledru-Rollin. Every year,
around September/October. Dates change
so check press for details, or contact the
Tourist Office, *see chapter* **Essential
Information**.
Each year all the members of the Artistic
Association (that is, the painters who live
in the area), hold five open days. Their studios are opened to anyone who cares to
visit, so it's an ideal time to see behind the
scenes, as well as to view their work.
Arrows are pinned up indicating which

doorways you should slip through. Rogue
artists not belonging to the Association
also put up arrows. In total you can see
over a hundred studios and the event
shouldn't be missed by either window-
shoppers or bargain hunters.

La FIAC – Foire
Internationale d'Art
Contemporain
*Grand Palais, 1-3 Avenue du Général
Eisenhower, 75008 Paris (42. 89.32.13).
Metro Champs Elysées Clémenceau.* Annual
event taking place in October. Dates vary so
check press for details, or contact the
Tourist Office, *see above.*
The culmination of months of mutual back-
slapping and the massaging of egos. Despite
the elitism, at least one hundred galleries
from all over the world set up stalls here and
exhibit a selection of works. The FIAC is also
sure to have a couple of big names on show;
in 1989 it was Warhol. Huge and crowded
but a must if you're interested in art.

*Even now, despite the recent property speculation, the large and commercial
boulevard Montparnasse (listed under* **Montparnasse***) has its surprises: at
No.126 (above), if you go through the main door and pass through to the second
courtyard you'll come across some incredible artists' studios.*

Village Paris

From the vineyards of Montmartre to the gambling houses of Chinatown, we give an overview of those last bastions of village life still thriving in the heart of the metropolis.

MONTMARTRE

While other areas may cling to their village status by a whisker, Montmartre is the only quarter in Paris still truly deserving the title. It has managed to remain an unsullied and self-contained throwback

to a bygone era, with plunging narrow staircases, cloistered streets, houses with gardens, and artists' studios remaining just as you imagine they always were. The area, however, is not without its eyesores. One such blemish is the **place du Tertre** above. As Ronald Searle, expatriate-turned-Parisian, despondently remarked: 'The Place du Tertre, more fraud, more phoneys and more wide-eyed children per square metre than anywhere in the world...and two born every minute to keep it going'. The square is almost unavoidable in a visit to the area, so be prepared for this much-publicized aberration.

Stretched over a hill, Montmartre, or *La Butte*, offers an enticing choice of directions at every corner. Coming to a crossroads poses a serious dilemma, as verdant avenues, cobbled alleyways and secluded squares vie for your attention. One consolation is that it's almost impossible to take a wrong turn: with few exceptions, the area is so uniformly

beautiful and accessible that you should be able to see everything of interest in a single visit.

The inspirational ambience of the area is borne out by the long list of celebrated *bohèmes* who have resided here. These artists have left their imprint on Montmartre in a variety of ways. Not only will you recognize streets immortalized by Utrillo or Lautrec, you can also relax in one of their favoured watering-holes or visit an old studio (*see chapter* **Artistic Paris**). However, the area is not exclusively inhabited by young artists, flirting with insolvency and keen to make their mark. It also plays host to designers, musicians, writers, actors and ordinary people who all live here, giving the hill its village feel.

One of the principal roads in Montmartre is the **rue Lepic** (*see picture and caption*). The **avenue Junot** is another main thoroughfare which has been colonized by the very rich, giving it an exclusive feel. Look twice, though, and you'll find the spirit of Montmartre peeping through these polished exteriors. What at first sight might appear a gateway or flight of stairs leading up to a private house and garden, after a little tentative exploration may reveal a tiny square ringed by magnificent town houses with a collection of artistic accessories poking out from behind studio blinds.

The large boulevard-type brasseries which typify other parts of Paris have made little impression on Montmartre. The area is a warren of small, intimate cafés, free from the hurried formality of the city. The timelessness of some of these places is more characteristic of the countryside than a

*Winding its way through the heart of the area and ending at the boulevard de Clichy, **rue Lepic** (listed under **Montmartre**) is a long-established market street where a variety of traditional delicacies is on offer. In the old days, it was a constant scene of mayhem as stall-holders pushed their overflowing barrows up the cobbled hill, cursing with Gallic flair as their merchandise tumbled onto the filthy street.*

quartier deep in the centre of the French metropolis. Small enclosed parks flourish throughout the district, self-contained green spots which have little in common with the other large, stylized gardens dotting the capital.

Don't linger around the more obvious attractions, particularly the three or four streets which border the **Sacré Coeur**. They tend to be mobbed by hordes of foreigners, lining up to pay homage to one of the capital's most over-worked tourist attractions. Despite the crowds, however, it's worth a peek, and probably the least painful approach is to take the metro to Abesses (one of the few remaining Guimard-style stations) and follow the rue Yves Le Tac until the Sacré Coeur comes into view at the top of the hill.

Those more energetic can climb the stairs, but a lift is at hand to take you to the top of the basilica

itself, from which you can enjoy some of the finest views of Paris. If you get swept up by the current of tourists, normally heading off to the place du Tertre, don't be tempted by the swarm of expectant artists willing to trace your image in charcoal. Talent is particularly thin on the ground here and the prices range from brazenly overpriced to exploitational.

Montmartre is more suited to someone who'd rather wander unhurriedly through its leafy alleyways than stick regimentally to a prearranged timetable of sightseeing. Try to spend time in the **Allée des Brouillards**, visit **7bis rue Girardon** which is actually a park with a *boules* area, or stop off at **No.11 avenue Junot** (*see picture and caption*)

Try not to be intimidated by the lack of obvious signposting throughout **Montmartre** *and explore the many unlocked gates which you'll discover. If you wander into a private residence by mistake, the worst that can happen is a little remonstration from the owner. Typical of the area's many beautiful houses in tranquil squares and private gardens,* **No.11 avenue Junot** *(pictured above) was home to Poulbot, famed for his images of street urchins.*

where you'll encounter the entrance to one of those idyllic little squares mentioned above.

The village atmosphere is further bolstered by the **Montmartre Vineyard**, located near the **Montmartre Museum** which keeps exhaustive records of the *quartier* and its more celebrated residents. If you're no good at keeping your bearings, then start off your journey in the **Montmartrobus**: in true village style the area has its own bus. Its small proportions allow it to negotiate the narrow streets and dodge the day-dreaming pedestrians who wander out in front of it. You can pick it up anywhere but its starting points are the Place Pigalle

and the *Mairie* (town hall). The bus and the **Montmartre train** are spurned by the locals and don't give you access to anything that can't be discovered with a little intuitive exploration. But they are ideal for those who might find the winding slopes of the quarter exhausting.

The **Bateau Lavoir** in the Place Emile Goudeau is Montmartre's most famous artistic residence (*see chapter* **Artistic Paris**). The square contains the most untainted and pleasant cafés in the area, free from the chatter of tourists unwinding over a *café au lait*. Montmartrians regard this as the centre of their flamboyant past and flock here to chat about their art, their culture

Montmartre has a long-standing history of wine production. During the sixteenth century, it was known for its windmills and vines, and the inhabitants were mainly grapepickers. **Montmartre Vineyard** *(the last remaining commercial vineyard in Paris) has been pressing wine since 1933: the process takes place in the eighteenth-century town hall and any profits gained from its sale help to finance* la Butte's *programme of social reform.*

and the issues that have moulded their unique past.

History throws some light on why Montmartrians share a sense of common identity. When it was a separate village in the nineteenth century, the Montmartrians formed a Commune, and repelled the invading Prussians with the help of 170 cannons (*see chapter* **Third Republic**). The Commune only officially lasted for two months, but the spirit which kindled its original formation still exists today. There is still a Montmartre Commune which organizes parties, festivals and a variety of events throughout the year (*see*

chapter **Paris by Season**). This community spirit is matched by a spirit of democracy – hence the existence of the Republic of Montmartre. All republics need a president and each year one is duly elected from among the locals. General Assemblies are held in one of the many nearby cafés.

Le Petit Train de Montmartre
Leaves from Place Blanche, 75018. Metro Blanche, bus 2. **Open** *summer:* 9am-8pm Mon-Fri; 9am-midnight Sat, Sun; *winter:* 9am-8pm Mon-Fri; 10.30am-6.30pm Sat, Sun. **Trips** trains leave every 40 minutes. **Cost** 25F adults; 10F under-12s.
A miniature sightseeing train which takes a route (full of hairpin bends) around the

crowded streets of Montmartre. You can get off at the place du Tertre to visit the artists' square and the Sacré Coeur and get another train back. Large groups are advised to book on *42.62.24.00.*

Montmartre Museum
12 rue Cortot, 75018 Paris (46.06.61.11). Metro Lamarck Caulincourt/bus 74, 81. **Open** 2.30pm-6pm Tue-Sat; 11am-5.30pm Sun. **Admission** 20F adults; 10F under-18s and students.
An eighteenth-century manor house, overlooking the Montmartre Vineyard (*see below*), which was founded in 1886 by a group of collectors committed to the preservation of the arts in Montmartre. These individuals were also responsible for setting up the Montmartre Society of Art and Archaeology. The museum traces the history of Montmartre as village, Commune and artistic haunt. Rooms have been reconstructed true to their original design, including an old bar from the rue de l'Abreuvoir, Lautrec's original posters which once enticed the glamourous and amorous to the Moulin Rouge, and a vast array of trivia from the *belle époque.* The office of composer Gustave Charpentier, pictures of Montmartre through the ages and the salvaged jottings of past residents such as Zola and Colette are all on display. The house itself is of considerable significance and interest, having played host to Renoir, Dufy and Utrillo, whose studio is in the courtyard. The Old Montmartre Society looks after the museum and organizes soirées when everything under the Montmartrian sun is discussed at length. Every Saturday at 5.30pm there's an open evening for all. Contact the Society at the museum for details of their address and a programme of events. Temporary exhibitions are also organized throughout the year.

The Montmartre Vineyard
Corner of rue De Saules and rue Saint Vincent, 75018 Paris. Metro Lamarck Caulincourt/bus 74, 81.
The 'Wine Harvest Festival' takes place after the grapepicking towards the end of September (anyone can take part) and includes traditional parades and colourful festivities peculiar to the area (*see chapter* **Paris by Season**). Montmartre wine is famous for its diuretic qualities, as aptly expressed in a seventeenth-century proverb: *'C'est du vin de Montmartre. Qui en boit pinte en pisse quarte'* (With wine from Montmartre, drink a pint and you piss a quart). *See also* **picture and caption.**

Moulin de la Galette
Corner of the rues Girardon and Lepic, 75018 Paris (45.58.50.71). Metro Abbesses, Lamarck Caulincourt/bus 31, 80, 85.
See **picture and caption.**

Le Bateau Lavoir
Place Emile Goudeau 75018 Paris. Metro Abbesses/bus 31, 80, 85.
This building functions as a haven for impoverished, but promising artists who lack the financial encouragement to continue their work. It was here that Picasso painted *Les Demoiselles d'Avignon* and later, in 1970, the building was designated a historical monument. Burnt down a few weeks after it achieved this status, it was rebuilt in 1978 and continues to offer studio space to young artists.

Its hallowed portals are generally closed to the public, but it's still possible to sneak through and glimpse a few precocious talents coming to terms with their art. *See also chapter* **Artistic Paris.**

Sacré Coeur
35 rue Chevalier de la Barre, 75018 Paris (42.51.17.02). Metro Abesses. **Open** *April-Sept:* 9.15am-1.30pm, 2-6.30pm, daily; *Oct-March:* 9am-noon, 1-5pm, daily. **Admission** to dome 10F; to museum 12F. *See* **picture and caption.** *See also chapters* **Sight seeing; Third Republic.**

Chez Camille
Bottom of the place Emile, 75018 Paris. Metro Lamarck Caulincourt, Abbesses/bus 31, 80, 85. A *pastis*-swilling haunt for garrulous Parisians (the life expectancy of a bottle of *pastis* here is 30 minutes) where you can experience the relaxed debauchery of a café noted for its informality and limitless supply of exotic spirits and conversation. The bar counter wouldn't look out of place in the Montmartre Museum (*see above*). This is not surprising when you discover that it's 100 years old and has featured as backdrop in several films.

The original wooden windmill of the **Moulin de la Galette** *(listed under* **Montmartre***) is still accessible to the public but the gardens which Renoir so vividly painted are now zealously guarded by Alsatian dogs, laser beams and video cameras tucked behind every rhododendron. The people that live in the area tend to be very rich but, despite the elitism, the nearby restaurant of the same name offers an appetizing set menu for around 60F.*

LA BUTTE AUX CAILLES

With the exception of the people who live there, hardly anybody goes to the 13th *arrondissement*. It's true that the area hasn't been particularly fortunate when it comes to architecture or exciting nightlife. It was always a working-class area, with a liveliness that the recent construction of tower blocks hasn't yet completely destroyed. The people of the Butte aux Cailles have fought to preserve their surroundings, and the narrow paved streets and low houses built in various styles, from art deco to 'futuristic', retain their old-world charm. Everyone seems to knows everyone else here, greeting each other in shops and gossiping over a drink in the local bar. People appear oblivious of the tower blocks rising on the avenue d'Italie a few metres away. No other *arrondissement* has been subjected to such brutal changes, and it's almost unbelievable to find a village surviving in the middle of property-development mayhem.

The historical centre of the Butte (not to be confused with Montmartre) is the **rue de la Butte** which starts from the **rue Bobillot** (just past the enormous and insipid Galaxy Commercial Centre in the place d'Italie). Here you'll find little narrow roads branching out; the rues Buot, Michal and Alphand are particularly rustic, with their cobbles and their little houses. Further on in the rue Daviel, at No.10, live some of the most privileged tenants in Paris. This *cité*, or estate (built and maintained by the local government), is made up of forty or so villas built around a square.

La Manufacture des Gobelins
42 avenue des Gobelins, 75013 Paris (42.74.44.50). Metro Gobelins. **Open** guided tours 2pm, 2.45pm, Tue, Wed, Thur. **Admission** 22F.
Tapestries have been made here using traditional methods since the seventeenth century, and vivid pictorial designs are the speciality. A visit to the workshop and museum includes the Savonnerie carpet workshop, the Gobelins and Beauvois workshops which produce wall coverings in 17,000 different colours, and the National Furniture section, where the furniture for ambassadors and ministers is made.

and Choisy, forming a Parisian Chinatown. The community now accounts for more than ten per cent of the population of the *arrondissement*. Living in a close-knit group, and carefully preserving their own customs, the inhabitants seem oblivious to the Parisian life around them. Little by little, in an area dominated by monumental buildings, flats and shops have changed hands and begun to acquire distinctively oriental characteristics. Shop-fronts like pagodas, with windows crammed full of curiosities from another world, and luminous signs in Chinese all contribute to the un-Parisian atmosphere.

Although off the tourist track, this is an absorbing area to take in. But the community is a very closed one, and although you can explore the colourful shops and sample exotic delicacies in the restaurants, the clubs and numerous gambling houses remain closed to outsiders. This is just as well – extraordinary sums of money and whole livelihoods are said to be lost or won in the gambling dens.

Chinese New Year Festival
Around Avenue d'Ivry and Avenue Choisy, 75013 Paris (details from Association Culturelle Franco-Chinoise 45.20.74.09). Metro Porte de Choisy, Porte d'Ivry/bus 57, 61. **Dates** usually end Jan-early Feb, phone for details.
Not just local residents, but people from all over Paris come to watch and participate in the Chinese New Year festivities: lots of noise, colour and spicy food.

BELLEVILLE & MENILMONTANT

Belleville in the 20th *arrondissement*, like so many other areas in Paris, is in the throes of an identity crisis. Inevitably, but sadly, the charm of this old village is disappearing in the face of modern development.

Built on the second highest hill in Paris (after Montmartre), Belleville was originally an agricultural area – an aspect of its past now only visible in street names such as the rue des Grands-Champs, rue des Champeaux, rue de la Plaine, rue des Amandiers, and rue des Pruniers. After the Revolution it became a working-class area, in which many refugees sought asylum. The Auvergnats were the first to colonize Belleville,

The inevitable symbol of Montmartre, most Parisians advise admiring the bee-hive domes of this **Basilica of the Sacré Coeur** *(listed under* **Montmartre***) from a distance. Originally constructed as a place where the sins of the Commune could be purged, there is still a 24-hour vigil of atonement, held on a rota system, which has continued for 110 years without interruption. Despite the hordes of gawping tourists, the Sacré Coeur deserves a detour from the more subtle neighbourhood it inhabits.*

La Cité Fleurie
65 boulevard Arago, 75013. Metro Glacière.
The *cité*, which has so far managed to escape demolition, houses about 30 studios, and is filled with rose bushes and 100 year-old trees. Past prestigious occupants have included Gaugin, Modigliani and Rodin.

La Cité Verte
147 rue Léon-Maurice—Nordmann, 75013 Paris. Metro Glacière.
A neighbour of the above, this *cité* had a close brush with death, but the occupants fought to keep it alive and it has recently been classed as a historical

monument. People do still live in these *cités*, and so hordes of tourists are not welcome: discretion is therefore *de rigueur* when visiting them.

CHINATOWN

During the past few years a new area has been developing in the 13th *arrondissement*. The Far Eastern community has installed itself around the avenues d'Italie, d'Ivry

Couronnes, and Julien Lacroix where there are still little shops selling spices and all kinds of bizarre paraphernalia. Parts of the area are reminiscent of Montmartre – from the rue Jouye-Rouve there's a superb view over Paris. There are still some art deco cinemas left on the rue Belleville, showing karate films or old American B movies. There's also a colourful street market here with an tropical flavour, as well as an impressive number of lively bistros.

Belleville, like the 13th *arrondissement*, is fast losing its village atmosphere. It seems impossible that it can retain animation and individuality in the face of demolition and modern development, but while it does, this glimpse of 'real' Paris is essential viewing.

Père-Lachaise Cemetery
entry on the boulevard de Ménilmontant, 75020 Paris (43.70.70.33). Metro Père-Lachaise. **Open** *Mid March-5 Nov:* 7.30am-6pm Mon-Sat; 9.30am-6pm Sun and public holidays; *6 Nov-mid Jan:* 8.30am-5pm Mon-Sat; 9.30am-5pm Sun and public holidays.
Far from being a desolate place, the Père-Lachaise Cemetery is a popular spot for outings. If you search for long enough you're bound to discover an idol: one of the most

Popular with a huge variety of people, the **Père-Lachaise Cemetery** *(listed under* **Belleville & Ménilmontant***) attracts lovers who roam among the tombstones, mystics who come to celebrate black masses, mothers with children who come to stroll in the park, perverts and peeping Toms – the list is endless. The list of famous incumbents is equally lengthy.*

and there has followed a steady stream of immigrants ever since: Russian Jews, Poles, North Africans, Spanish Republicans, Armenians and Greeks.

The immigrant population gave the area a cosmopolitan character, and it was filled with the workshops of leatherworkers, furriers, shoemakers and other craftsmen. Also famous for its lively nightlife and the subject of count-

less popular songs, this was where Edith Piaf was born: a memorial plaque can be found at No.12 rue de Belleville.

Despite recent changes to the area, pockets of the past still exist. The rues Deroyez and Ramponeau are the heart of Belleville. On all sides you'll find passages falling into ruin, earmarked for demolition, but these streets still retain their identity. Take a look at the rues Palikao,

sought-after is Jim Morrison whose grave is always crowded with flowers, fans and graffiti. Graves of other notables include those of Proust, Oscar Wilde, Sarah Bernhardt, Chopin, Musset, Molière, La Fontaine, Balzac, Edith Piaf, and Apollinaire. For the list of Père-Lachaise's stars, ask for a map at the entrance. *See also* **picture and caption.**

Saint Germain de Charonne
4 place Saint Blaise, 75020 Paris. Metro Porte de Montreuil/bus 76.
The church of the old village of Charonne, this is one of the most original churches

in Paris, and one of the few that has its own cemetery. Little of the original twelfth-century structure remains, and the church has been modified several times over the centuries, but despite this it has managed to maintain an extraordinary symmetry.

La Villa Caltel
83 rue des Couronnes (at the end of the Passage Plantin), 75020 Paris. Metro Belleville.
This is one of the last surviving villas in Belleville. Go down the picturesque passage Plantin, with its large cobbles and central drain, and you'll come to a superb wrought-iron gate. On the other side you can see a voluptuous garden and some charming houses. François Truffaut filmed a few scenes of *Jules et Jim* here.

Ganachaud Bakery
150 rue de Ménilmontant, 75020 Paris (46.36.13.82). Metro Ménilmontant.
Open 2-8.30pm Tue; 7.30am-8pm Wed-Sat; 7.30am-1.30pm Sun; closed whole month of August.
Walking up the rue Ménilmontant, you'll be surprised by the long queues and the double-parked cars in front of this simple bakery. If you try the bread, you'll understand why it's worth waiting for. There's a choice of no less than 30 varieties, cooked in a wood-burning oven. *Real* French bread.

THE GOUTTE D'OR

A unique corner of Paris in the 18th *arrondissement* where families representing more than 30 different nationalities coexist within a small perimeter, each preserving their own customs and way of life, each with their own shops and restaurants. The first immigration wave hit the Goutte d'Or in the fifties when workers from North Africa came to join the expanding car manufacturing industry, and it now has the atmosphere of a very cosmopolitan village (*see picture and caption*).

Things aren't all that rosy, though. For a long time the prostitutes in this area were reputed to have as many as eighty clients a day. The ruined houses were full of squatters and it was one of the main drug-dealing areas in Paris. This image gave the renovators fuel for their campaign and some of the inhabitants have been literally chucked out, without rehousing promises, and buildings have been boarded up.

The Villa Doissoniere
42 rue de la Goutte d'or to 41 rue Polonceau, 75018 Paris. Metro Marcadet.

An oasis of calm in a busy area, this is a collection of Louis Philippe-style houses, some of which are covered in tiles.

Tati
4 boulevard de Rochechouart, 75018 Paris (42.55.13.09). Metro Anvers, Barbel. **Open** 10am-7pm Mon; 9.30am-7pm Tue-Fri; 9.15am-pm Sat.
You really won't believe your eyes: Tati sells everything you could possibly need (or not need) at prices which defy all competition. There are shirts costing 5F and jumpers for 50F – make up your own mind up about the quality. People come from miles around, all contributing to the frenetic atmosphere which is like the first day of a sale every day. Only for the hardened bargain hunter.

The Saint Pierre Market
2 rue Charles-Nodier, 75018 Paris (46.06.92.25). Metro Anvers. **Open** 9.30am-6.30pm Mon-Fri.
Although this market is full of bargains generally – and especially good for exotic foodstuffs – this is where you can find the best textile bargains in Paris.

The area of **La Goutte d'Or** *is a national, if not an international, centre of commerce. The shops and markets, like those in the rue de la Goutte d'Or, are brilliant, and the frantic rate at which bargains are driven and goods exchange hands is quite unreal. People come from all over Paris to shop here and take their pick from the huge choice, particularly of food, available. Tonnes of merchandise are sold every day and you won't find such a truly lively atmosphere anywhere else.*

History

If your knowledge of France has been gleaned from *Les Misérables, Dangerous Liaisons* and old black and white war movies, French history may seem to begin with Joan of Arc, progress to Marie Antoinette and *Vive la Revolution!* and end with the liberation of Paris during World War II. But once in France, you'll find that a lot more remains to be discovered beyond these stereotypes. We give a sweeping appraisal of the major events and personalities which have shaped Paris, from the taming of the 'city of the Parisii' by Rome around 50BC to contemporary France. Much of Paris has withstood the ravages of time, war and property speculation and we list many buildings, parks and other sites which give a visual perspective of the city's colourful past.

CONTENTS:

Roman Paris

From Asterix to Caesar, Paris was a hot-house of steaming baths and gladitorial arenas.

The Parisii were Celts who settled what is now the Ile de la Cité around 250BC, in the second Iron Age. Located on an ancient road linking Germania to Hispania, at the confluence of three important rivers – the Seine, the Marne and the Oise – Lucoticia was a natural commercial crossroads. Rich in agricultural land, stone quarries and gypsum (which was used as fertilizer) the new Parisii settlement flourished. The Celts also proved to be canny traders and their community grew wealthy. Remarkably beautiful gold coins minted in the first century BC are a measure of the city's prosperity. A collection of these can be seen at the **Musée des Antiquités Nationales** (*see below*).

Its strategic position also made this settlement a prime military target. Caesar in his *Gallic Wars*, made the first recorded reference to Lutetia (the latin name for Lucoticia), describing it succictly as the 'city of the Parisii, situated on an isle in the Seine'. In the spring of 52BC he sent his lieutenant, Labeinus, and four legions against the Parisii, who were crushed in a bloody encounter. Shortly after, at Alesia, Caesar defeated Gaul Vercingétorix – who had fought against the invader with the help of men from Lucoticia – and the conquest of Gaul was complete.

Lutetia throve under Roman rule. During the Augustun age (27BC-AD14) the town spread from the Cité to the Left Bank, fanning out from the Seine up the slopes of the Montagne Sainte-Genevieve, on either side of the *cardo* (main thoroughfare), the present day rue Saint Jacques. Indigenous Gallic habitations of freestone, masonry, brick and mortar (the latter was a Roman innovation), often embellished with carving, stucco and frescoes lined the streets. The increase in the number of inhabitants meant that the amount of water drawn from the Seine was insufficient to cope with demand. Therefore, three aqueducts were built to carry fresh water to the town. By this stage the Seine was so polluted that the Romans made it an offence to sweep the streets when it rained, as this Celtic habit only helped to further pollute the river. A model of the ancient city – along with architectural vestiges such as column capitals, fragments of murals and mosaics – is on view at the **Musée Carnavalet** (*see below*). Artefacts from pre-Roman Lutetia, as well as many Gallo-Roman finds, are displayed also in the Musée des Antiquités Nationales at Saint-Germain-en-Laye, 20 kilometres (12 miles) west of Paris.

Musée Carnavalet
23-29 rue de Sévigné, 75003 Paris (42.72.21.13). Metro Saint-Paul. **Open** 10am-5.30pm Tue-Sun. **Admission** 15F adults; 8F50 under-18s, OAPs; free on Sunday. **Credit** (shop only) V.
The recently renovated Musée Carnavalet aims to present 'the history of Paris through works of art'. The Gallo-Roman collection is small but selective, including architectural vestiges from Lutetia's principal monuments. Unfortunately, it is the exhibit most likely to be closed from lack of staff. It is currently being revamped, we are told, and the room will 'probably' reopen 'sometime in 1990'.

Musée des Antiquités Nationales
Château de Saint-Germain-en-Laye, place du Général de Gaulle, 78100 Saint-Germain-en-Laye (34.51.53.65). **Getting there** *by train:* RER line A1 to St-Germain-en-Laye. **Open** 9.45am-noon, 1.30-5.15pm, Mon, Wed-Sun. **Admission** 15F adults; 8F 18-25s, OAPs, everyone on Sun; free under-18s.
The imposing royal château dominates the centre of this pretty Parisian suburb and was mainly rebuilt by François I in the sixteenth century. Since 1867, it has been used as a museum and its exhibits date from prehistory to the Gallo-Roman civilization, with a passing nod at the Merovingian period. Admirers of Gallic and Gallo-Roman antiquities will be riveted by the exhibits in this archaeological treasure house, which contains the oldest artefacts found on French soil. Ornate weapons and jewels from princely tombs, finely wrought statues of Celtic deities and rare coins may be viewed along with the usual pottery shards and bits of silex. The star exhibit must be the oldest known representation of a woman's face, The Lady of Brassempouy, dating from 22,000BC. If you begin to feel a little

Old men now play boules in the **Arènes de Lutèce** *(listed under* **Steamy Empire***), once the Roman arena, where roaring beasts and wounded gladiators met their deaths. The site is artfully landscaped with rare trees and plants.*

**Cluny Baths
(Musée des Thermes et de
l'Hotel de Cluny)**
*6 place Paul-Painlevé, 75005 Paris
(43.25.62.00). Metro Cluny-La Sorbonne.*
Open 9.45am-12.30pm, 2-5.15pm Mon, Wed-
Sun. **Admission** 15F adults; 8F under-18s,
OAPs. **Credit** (shop only) V.
The water for the baths was supplied by an
aqueduct in Arcueil (south of Paris) and
heat for the *tepidarium* and *caldarium*
(warm and hot baths) came from a
hypocaust (a system of flues in the walls
and floor), fed by an underground furnace.
The *frigodarium* (cold bath) is well preserved and has impressive vaulted ceilings
which are almost 15m (50 feet) high. There
are also traces of the room's marble floor-
ing, fresco and mosaic décor and hand-
hewn masonry. In addition to the Gallo-
Roman baths, the Museum houses the
renowned Boatman's Pillar (*Pillar des
Nautes*), a tribute to the emperor Tiberius
that is interesting for its juxtaposition of
Celtic deities with gods from the Roman
pantheon. *See also* **picture and caption.**

BARBARIAN ANTICS

But, as all readers of Asterix and
Obelix books know, the days of
the Roman Empire were numbered. When Barbarian invasions
destroyed the Left Bank in the
mid-third century, most of
Lutetia's inhabitants dropped their
togas and ran for the cover of
their ancestral island in the Seine.
Now on the defensive, the Gauls
and Romans built a wall around
the Cité using stones from the
ruined monuments on the Left
Bank in the hope of retaining control of this military and trading
post. Lutetia was still strategically
important because of its proximity
to the Empire's threatened northern and eastern borders, which
were being attacked by Alamans,
Franks and Barbares. It was only
at the end of the Roman period
that Lutetia took the name of its
early Gallic settlers, and came to
be known as Paris.

Crypte Archéologique de Nôtre-Dame de Paris
*place du Parvis-Nôtre-Dame, 75004 Paris
(43.25.42.92) Metro Saint-Michel, Notre-
Dame, Cité.* **Open** phone for information.
During construction of an underground
parking lot, workmen came across part of
Lutetia's defensive wall, in addition to
other Gallo-Roman artefacts. These
reliefs, statues, inscriptions and grave-
stones are now on show in a gallery,
along with sections of the third-century
defensive wall.

*The **Cluny Baths** (listed under **Steamy Empire**), built around AD200, is
the best-preserved Gallo-Roman monument in Paris. It's rumoured that these
thermae were commissioned by the rich and powerful boatmen's guild, which
controlled all river traffic in and around Lutetia.*

hemmed in by the cloistered passages of
this austere mansion, try the castle terrace;
a return trip around it covers 5km (3 miles).
*Library. Shop. Temporary exhibitions.
Wheelchair access.*

STEAMY EMPIRE

The Romans revolutionized the
social scene in Gaul. They built hundreds of baths (*see below* **Cluny
Baths**) and amphitheatres from the
Urbs itself to the farthest reaches of
the Empire, on the principle that
nothing cemented the social bond –
and promoted the cause of
Romanization – like giving the people a chance to steam, sweat and
swim together in confraternal
nudity. In fact, such was their desire
to create a strong and united Gaul
that they brought a spot of ferocious
combat to entertainment-starved
Celts. Gladiators fighting to the
death and wild animals tearing each
other to bits immediately became
big attractions with the home
crowd. In order to cope with the
demand for pre-booked action, the

Romans built an amphitheatre in
Lutetia that could hold a capacity
crowd of 10,000; this made it the
second largest amphitheatre in
Gaul. In addition to an arena, it
boasted a stage where the more
refined aspects of entertainment –
mimes, dances, plays and acrobatics
– could be enjoyed.
   It was during the Golden Age
of Gallo-Roman architecture
(from about AD50 to AD200)
that Lutetia acquired its grandest
public buildings. In the compact
area that is now the heart of the
Latin Quarter, archaeologists
have uncovered the remains of a
forum (rue Soufflot, between the
boulevard Saint Michel and the
rue Monge) and a trio of bathing
establishments (rue des Écoles,
rue Gay Lussac and boulevard
Saint-Michel). Only the **Arènes
de Lutèce** (the amphitheatre)
and the **Cluny Baths** now
reflect anything approaching
their former glory.

Les Arènes de Lutèce
*between rues Monge and Navarre, 75005
Paris. Metro Jussieu.* **Open** visible any time.
See **picture and caption.**

The Dark Ages

Attila the Hun and the saintly Geneviève; the history of Paris is filled with legend, mystery and suspense.

MIRACLE CITY

It was in the third century that Saint Denis, first bishop of Lutetia, evangelised the Parisii. Legend has it that one day, seized with missionary zeal, he and two companions began to knock pagan statues off their pedestals. Such was their frenzy, that they failed to cover their tracks and were immediately arrested. The Roman governor decreed that Denis and his accomplices should be decapitated on mount Mercury, thereafter known as the Mount of Martyrs in Montmatre. Headless and bleeding, Saint Denis picked up his bonce and walked away, his lips chanting psalms. He eventually fell at a seemingly predestined site north of Paris where a pious Christian woman buried him. The magnificent Basilica of Saint Denis reputedly stands on the exact spot where his body lies, a Gothic marvel rising out of what is now a working-class suburb.

Basilique de Saint Denis
place de la Legion d'Honneur, 93200 Saint-Denis (48.20.15.57). Metro Saint Denis Basilique/bus 153, 154. **Open** 10am-5pm Mon-Sat; noon-5pm Sun; closed 1 Nov, 11 Nov, 25 Dec, 1 Jan, 1 March; *Guided tours:* 10.30am, 3pm daily. **Admission** 22F (includes headphones with commentary in French, English, or German).

Important Christian sanctuaries have occupied this site since the fifth century. The first may have been erected at the urging of Sainte Geneviève (*see below*). The church that visitors see today dates from the twelfth and thirteenth centuries, though Viollete-le-Duc carried out extensive restorations in the mid-nineteenth century. As the first large scale Gothic edifice, Saint Denis was widely copied; virtually all French kings, from Dagobert (monarch in the seventh century) to Louis XVIII, were entombed in the Basilica. At the time of the Revolution the bodies of kings were thrown into anonymous graves. The royal monuments make Saint Denis an exceptional museum of funerary sculpture.

Martyr's Chapel
11 rue Yvonne-le-Tac, 75018 Paris (no telephone). Metro Abbesses/bus montmartrobus. **Open** 2.30-5pm Sat, Sun. **Admission** free. This tiny chapel marks the spot where Saint Denis and his companions were martyred. This is also the place where Saint Ignatius Loyola and Saint Francis Xavier founded the Society of Jesus (Jesuits) in 1534.

SAINTLY GENEVIEVE

Gradually Christianity took root in Paris, although considerable numbers remained faithful to traditional Gallic gods. It was the exemplary life of Sainte Geneviève – and the threat of war – that helped win many new converts to the faith. In AD451, Attila's army, over half a million strong, was rumoured to be approaching Paris. The inhabitants panicked and prepared to flee. But Geneviève, a saintly Christian girl, urged the frightened populace to stay put. She told them that the Hun would spare their city so long as they repented of their sins and prayed with her. Sceptical, the Parisii men mocked and threatened her. She managed, however, to win over the womenfolk, who joined her in prayer. And miraculously, Attila did not attack but instead made a decidedly unstrategic detour around the city, avoiding it entirely. Geneviève was acclaimed as the saviour of Paris.

In AD512, Geneviève was buried on the hill that today bears her name, Montagne Sainte-Geneviève. Her body was later moved (*see below* **Towards the Millennium**). Relics of the patroness of Paris abound in this area: part of her tomb is enshrined in the splendid **Church**

It was Puvis de Chavannes who devoted his talents to painting the frescoes depicting the life of Sainte Geneviève in the **Pantheon** *(listed under* **Saintly Geneviève***). Other painters who decorated this national shrine include Sicard, Detaille, Bonnat, Cabanel and Laurens.*

of **Saint-Etienne-du-Mont** and in the **Pantheon** – formerly the Church of Sainte-Geneviève – a fresco cycle by symbolist painter Puvis de Chavannes commemorates her life and religious exploits.

Pantheon
rue Clotilde, 75005 Paris. Metro Cardinal-Lemoine/bus 21, 24, 38, 89. **Open** *April-Sept:* 10am-6pm Mon, Wed-Sun; *Oct-March:* 10am-4pm Mon, Wed-Sun. **Admission** free.
The Pantheon contains the remains of the great men of the Republic, from Rousseau to Jean Moulin, as well as the the shrine containing Gambetta's heart. *See also* **picture and caption.** For more information on the Pantheon *see chapter* **Sightseeing.**

Saint-Etienne-du-Mont
rue Clovis, 75005 Paris (no telephone). Metro Cardinal-Lemoine/bus 47, 89. **Open** 7.30-11.45am, 2.15-7.15pm, Mon-Sat; 4-7pm Sun. **Admission** free.
See **picture and caption.**

TOWARDS THE MILLENNIUM

Clovis, Christian leader of the Franks, cleared the Romans out of northern Gaul and the Alamans out of the east. So when Paris opened its gates to him in AD497, Clovis converted the inhabitants of the city to Christianity. He was baptized and anointed at Reims – as virtually all future kings of France would be – and in AD508 he made Paris, with its royal palace on the Ile de la Cité, the seat of his realm. Thus began the Merovingian dynasty .

On the vine-clad slopes of the Left Bank, Clovis founded an immense basilica and abbey where he, Queen Clotilde, and dear Sainte Geneviève – after whom the abbey came to be called – were eventually buried side by side. Clovis's son, Childeric, followed his father's example, and founded the equally renowned abbey of Saint Germain-des-Prés to enshrine relics extorted from the inhabitants of Saragossa in Spain, whom he had held under siege. The basilica of Saint Germain was a splendid church set in the countryside, with marble walls, mosaic floors and a gilded dome that glittered in the sunlight. Around the Left Bank abbey, small communities of farmers, vintners, artisans and soldiers sprang up, but they didn't have time to prosper. For in and around Paris, the Dark Ages were exactly that; gloomy.

The Merovingians proved to be a murderous lot and – with the exception of 'good King Dagobert' who reigned for just ten years – their fratricidal antics finally snuffed out the line in AD751.

The Carolingians who succeeded the Merovingians forsook the capital for Aix-La-Chapelle. Thereafter, Paris suffered from famine, floods and invading Normans: the latter sacked the city four times between AD840 and AD880, leaving not a stone unturned. Don't search Paris for 'Treasures of Merovingian Art' – there aren't any left

Parisians – well, those who could count – regarded the approaching millennium with apprehension. Was this the Day of Reckoning? The end of the world as they knew it? Surely not, for in AD987 the Count of Paris, Hugues Capet, was elected King of France by his peers at Senlis. Paris, now the capital of a mid-size royal domain, was to share and to shape the destiny of the Capetians for centuries to come.

Tour de Clovis
23 rue Clovis, 75005 Paris (no telephone). Metro Cardinal-Lemoine/bus 47, 89.
Along with the refectory and the kitchens, the Gothic-style Tour de Clovis and its Romanesque base, is all that remains of Sainte Geneviève's Abbey. The Lycée Henri IV, which now occupies the site, does not permit visitors on the grounds.

Church of Saint Germain-des-Prés
3 place Saint-Germain-des-Prés, 75006 Paris (no telephone). Metro Saint-Germain-des-Prés/bus 39, 48, 63, 95. **Open** 9am-6pm daily. **Admission** free.
The spectacular sixth-century basilica of Saint-Germain-des-Prés was totally demolished by the Normans. The present church was constructed in a considerably simpler style at the end of the ninth century. With a bell tower that dates from the year 1000, Saint Germain-des-Prés is the oldest standing church in the city.

Inside the church of **Saint-Etienne-du-Mont** *(listed under* **Saintly Genevieve***), to the right of the choir, is the Shrine of Sainte Geneviève. Visitors will note that the interior of the church is Italian in style; this is because the original edifice was pulled down and the new church – which you see today – was built in 1492.*

Middle Ages & Renaissance

The vile stench of putrid mud, bubonic plague, awe-inspiring Gothic buildings and scholastic fever: this idiosyncratic epoch in Paris's history is filled with more than just Quasimodo's tale.

SPIRIT OF LEARNING

Twelfth-century Paris was the centre of a spectacular renaissance, fuelled by peace, flourishing trade and a burgeoning population. The boom in commerce and construction quickly turned Paris into a political, economic, religious, and cultural capital – according to medieval writers it was both a students' and consumers' paradise.

By virtue of the stoical efforts of monks, the spirit of learning had been kept alive in Parisian abbeys during the darkest hours of the ninth and tenth centuries. Paris became the intellectual hub of France, abetted by peace, safe travel and the encouragement of both church and crown. Abélard, a brilliant logician and dialectician, left the cathedral school of Nôtre Dame in 1102 and set up a school of his own on the Montagne Sainte-Geneviève. Other masters soon followed his example and Parisian schools enjoyed prodigious success. Students and academics swarmed here from all over France. In 1215 the schools combined to form a 'university', under papal protection, with the right to organize curricula, conduct examinations and grant diplomas. The greatest and most influential medieval thinkers studied and taught in this 'New Athens'. The German theologian Albert the Great, the Italians Thomas Aquinas and Bonaventure, the Scots Duns Scotus and Englishman William of Ockham all flocked to Paris to improve their learning.

Sorbonne
place de la Sorbonne, 75005 Paris. Metro Luxembourg/bus 21, 27, 38, 85.
Named after Robert de Sorbon, chaplain of Saint Louis, who started a school for penniless theology students in 1257, the Sorbonne soon became one of the largest and most prestigious university colleges in Paris. The present building is a turn-of-the-century collection of classrooms and lecture halls and its warren of corridors is adorned with allegorical frescoes, some by Symbolist Puvis de Chavannes. The elegant dome that dominates the place de la Sorbonne belongs to the seventeenth-century chapel. It houses paintings by Philippe de Champaigne and the tomb of the infamous Cardinal Richelieu.

The Cathedral School Quarter
between rue du Cloître Nôtre-Dame, rue d'Arcole and the Seine, 75001 Paris.
The area of the Cité that lies between the rue du Cloître Nôtre-Dame, the rue d'Arcole and the Seine miraculously escaped Second Empire 'improvements'. Visitors can catch a glimpse of streets once walked on by eleventh and twelfth-century scholars who attended the cathedral school in the cloister of Nôtre-Dame. After being lectured to by academics such as Abélard or Saint Bonaventure, students would have returned to houses like those at numbers 22 and 24 rue Chanoinesse, where they boarded with cathedral canons. On the rue des Ursins, the courtyard of number 19 – the twelfth-century Chapelle Saint Aignan – once part of the Nôtre-Dame cloister, can still be admired.

THE GOTHIC AGE

Just as Aristotle's rediscovered writings inspired medieval philosophical scholasticism, so the invention of the ogival vault and flying buttress sent Gothic spires soaring over the Parisian skyline. The spires of the cathedral of Nôtre-Dame de Paris are the embodiment of this peculiarly French aesthetic, which first appeared in the Ile de France. Paris, however, remained an extremely congested city throughout the Middle Ages, hemmed in by ridiculously narrow streets. For example, rue de Venise – which no longer exists – was only one metre (just over a yard) wide. It is in this hotch-potch of street vendors, scurrying maids and sanctimonious priests that Victor Hugo placed his hunch-back, Quasimodo.

Cathedral of Nôtre-Dame
Place du Parvis Nôtre-Dame, 75004 Paris. Metro Cité/bus 21, 38, 85, 96. **Open** 10am-5.30pm daily (4.30pm in winter); closed 1 Jan, 1 May, 1 and 11 Nov, 25 Dec. **Admission** to bell tower 22F adults; 12F children. **No credit cards.**
Begun in 1163 and completed in the fourteenth century, Nôtre-Dame is indicative of every phase and form of the Gothic movement. This dominates the structure and ranges from the 'Transition' Gothic style of the choir (finished in 1182) to the 'Classic' Gothic sculptures of the cathedral's harmonious western façade (1200-1250). Maurice de Sully, bishop of Paris during the reigns of Louis VII and Philip Augustus, was the driving force behind the construction of Nôtre-Dame, but the names of the cathedral's first master-builders remain a mystery. Tours of the bell tower start at the foot of the northern tower. The view is superb, but remember you must walk up nearly 400 steps to the top. *See also* **picture and caption.** For more information on the cathedral, *see chapter* **Sightseeing.**

Sainte-Chapelle
in the Palais de Justice, boulevard du Palais, between Pont au Change and Pont Saint Michel, 75005 Paris. **Open** *April-Sept:* 10am-6pm daily; *Oct-March:* 10am-5pm daily. **Admission** free.
Architect Pierre de Montreuil, who completed Nôtre-Dame's transept, made his reputation with the Sainte-Chapelle. This was commissioned by Louis IX (called Saint Louis) to house the Crown of Thorns and other Christian relics, purchased for exorbitant sums from the Emperor of Constantinople. The Sainte-Chapelle is one of the city's most celebrated sights, though now obscured by the ungainly bulk of the Palais de Justice (the Law Courts). *See also* **picture and caption.**

Saint-Julien-le-Pauvre
Rue Saint-Julien-le-Pauvre, 75005 Paris. Metro Maubert-Mutualité, Saint-Michel/bus 24, 47.
Mid way between Romanesque and Gothic, this charming, rustic-looking church is set in one of the city's most picturesque squares and is a contemporary of Nôtre-Dame.

Saint-Martin-des-Champs
270 rue Saint-Martin, 75003 Paris (40.27.23.75). Metro Arts-et-Metiers, Temple/bus 38, 47, 75. **Open** 1-5.30pm Tue-Sat; 10am-5.15pm Sun. **Admission** 15F adults; 8F children; free for all Sun. **No credit cards.**
With its architecture on the cusp of the Romanesque and Gothic (the choir dates from 1130-40), Saint Martin-des-Champs is one of the most idiosyncratic churches in Paris. It is unique in incorporating a museum of technology within the building. The thirteenth-century Gothic refectory (in the courtyard), built by Pierre de Montreuil, is a splendid piece of period architecture. Unfortunately, prospective visitors to the refectory must apply in writing to the Museum Curator for a letter of authorization enabling them to enter the private area.

Saint-Pierre-de-Montmartre

Rue Saint Eleuthère, 75018 Paris. Metro Abbesses/Montmartrobus.
The origins of the Gothic style are still visible in this sombre church which was founded in 1133: admire the oldest ogival arches in Paris. It makes a striking contrast to the extravagance of the Sacré Coeur.

THE CLEAN-UP

A deep layer of putrid mud clogged the streets of medieval Paris. One day in 1186 King Philippe-Auguste decided the stench was more than he could bear and ordered the major roads of his capital to be paved. The following year he had the pestilent Cemetery of the Innocents (an environmental deathtrap responsible for several epidemics) sanitized and walled in. This energetic monarch was the first great builder Paris had known since Roman times. He enclosed the *faubourgs* (the settlements on the Left and Right bank of the Seine) within a great defensive wall, causing the value of the protected land to soar; he established permanent covered markets, *Les Halles*, in the neighbourhood they were to occupy until 1969; he also built the first version of the Louvre – a massive rectangular fortress – in 1202, to discourage invasions from the west.

Saint Louis, when not abroad fighting the infidel, put his stamp on Parisian architecture. In addition to the Sainte-Chapelle, he commissioned convents, hospices and even student housing. The Saint wasn't above making a few home improvements on his palace either, but it was his grandson, Philippe le Bel (who reigned from 1285 to 1314) who converted the inelegant fortress on the Cité into a palace fit for a king.

Philip's monumental Salle des Gens d'Armes – built for the lawyers and clients who thronged to the palace as plaintiffs – was reputed to be the most beautiful hall in the country. On the northern side of the palace, fringed by the Seine, until the Quai de l'Horloge was completed in the seventeenth century, Philip commissioned the magnificent Gothic façade of the Conciergerie, now heavily restored. Visitors and Parisians alike still admire its powerful towers with their 'pepper pot' roofs, which once concealed a prison.

Little is known of the first master builders of **Nôtre-Dame** *cathedral (listed under* **The Gothic Age***). We do know, however, that between 1265 and his death in 1267, architect Pierre de Montreuil completed Nôtre-Dame's magnificent transept and replaced the choir's double flying buttresses with dramatic new ones which extend 15 metres (50 feet) from the sides of the building. The cathedral is, however, still best known for its fictional resident, poor old Quasimodo.*

The Fortified Wall of Philip Augustus

Rue des Jardins-Saint-Paul, 75004 Paris. Metro Saint Paul/bus 69, 76.
The largest surviving section of the wall, complete with towers, extends along the rue des Jardins-Saint-Paul, between the rue Charlemagne and the rue l'Avé-Maria. Another large section of the wall can still be seen at 3 rue Clovis, in the Latin Quarter.

Palais de Justice

Boulevard du Palais (entrance by the Cour de Mai), 75001 Paris. Metro Cité/bus 21, 38, 85, 96. **Open** 9am-6pm Mon-Fri.
Just as Nôtre-Dame embodied the religious life of Paris, for centuries the palace on the Cité symbolized the royal presence in the capital. Roman governors and Merovingian monarchs resided there, and the first dozen Capetians made it their home. It later became the seat of Parliament and is now the home of the judiciary.

Conciergerie

Entrance at 1 quai de l'Horloge, 75001 Paris (43.54.30.06). Metro Cité/bus 21, 38, 85, 96. **Open** *summer:* 9.30-6pm daily; *winter:* 10am-4.30pm daily. **Admission** 22F adults; 12F children. **No credit cards.**
A guided tour takes visitors through the cells where Danton, Robespierre, Marie Antoinette and others were held prisoner before being escorted to the Black Widow of the revolution, the guillotine. But the most remarkable attractions here are the immense Gothic halls and kitchens. Outside, there is a fourteenth-century clock-tower worthy of your attention. *See also chapter* **Sightseeing**.

BLOODY TIMES

The fourteenth century signalled the start of troubled times for the French crown. Philippe le Bel died in 1314, the end of his reign marred by the bloody suppression of the Order of the Templars, the debasement of the currency, insurrection in Paris and riotous debauchery at Court. In suspiciously quick succession, his three sons ascended the throne. They all perished within fifteen years of their father's death and the last, Charles IV, left no male heir. It was the end of the direct Capetian line and the beginning of a bloody epoch.

Spotting an irresistible opportunity, the English swooped in and claimed the French crown for young Edward II, son of Philippe le Bel's daughter. The French, needless to say, failed to recognize the relevance of her lineage, pointing out that the male-made Salic law barred women from the throne of France. It therefore came as no surprise to the English to hear that Philip de Valois, the late king's cousin, had promptly claimed the crown for himself. Greed – and a desire to do battle, as was the fashion in those days – inevitably led to war; a state of conflict that was to last for over 100 years.

During this time, Paris became a capital of chaotic unrest. Recurrent outbreaks of bubonic plague alternated with bourgeois revolts, popular insurrections and bloody vendettas between aristocratic factions and their bands of hired bullies, adept with a cleaver and skilled in the art of wholesale butchery. Destruction, rather than construction, was the tenor of the times. One noteworthy addition was made by the astute Charles V, who – mistrusting both Parisians and English alike – had a stronghold built on the eastern edge of Paris as a counterpart to the Louvre in the west. Known as the Bastille, it was later to become a celebrated focus of plebeian outrage. He transformed the Louvre into a royal residence, where he installed both his library and works of art. For, despite the disorder that persisted throughout their realm, the

Valois kings were never able to resist the lure of beauty and luxury. In the late Middle Ages, Parisian artisans produced peerless miniatures, tapestries, illuminated manuscripts, and objects carved in ivory or wrought in silver and gold that the kings loved to collect.

The fighting continued on the battlefields of France. Joan of Arc came into her own, and fought with the best of the men. But all to no avail, for in 1431 Henry VI of England was crowned King of France in Nôtre-Dame. Paris was to remain under English rule until 1437 when Charles VII, the anointed King of France, entered his capital in triumph.

The following decades saw prosperity return to the capital, in the form of trade, printing and a variety of crafts. Masons began erecting churches in the flamboyant Gothic style, as well as an impressive array of hotels commissioned by nobles, prelates and the wealthy bourgeoisie.

Hôtel et Musée de Cluny
6 place Paul Painlevé, 75005 Paris (43.25.62.00). Metro Sainy Michel/bus 63, 86, 87. **Open** *9.45am-12.30pm, 2pm-5.15pm, Mon, Wed-Sun.* **Admission** *15F; 8F 18-25s; free under-18s.* **No credit cards.**
The beautiful, Flamboyant fifteenth-century residence of the Cluny abbots houses a well-displayed collection of medieval artifacts rang-

ing from high art to everyday objects. The celebrated tapestry *La Dame à la Licorne* is here, along with other superb examples of the *tapissier's* art. Admirers of medieval religious statuary can enjoy superbly restored sculptures taken from Parisian churches in the light, airy room next to the Gallo-Roman baths (*see also chapter* **Museums**).

Hôtel de Sens
1 rue du Figuier, 75004 Paris (42.78.14.60). Metro Saint-Paul/bus 67. **Open** *1.30-8.30pm Tue-Fri; 10am-8.30pm Sat.* **Admission** *15F adults; 10F students, OAPs.* **No credit cards.**
One of the oldest private residences in Paris (built in 1475), this extensively restored hotel belonged to the archbishops of Sens. The Guise brothers hatched many an anti-royalist intrigue within its walls during the Ligue (*see below*). The Bibliotheque Forney, which includes both a resident collection of decorative arts and temporary exhibitions, is located in the building.

Saint-Germain-L'Auxerrois
2 place du Louvre, 75001 Paris (42.60.13.96). Metro Louvre/bus 21, 67, 74, 81, 85. **Open** *9am-noon, 3-6pm, daily.* **Admission** *free.*
The parish church of the kings of France boasts the only original Flamboyant porch in Paris, built in 1435. It was from the Romanesque bell-tower of Saint-Germain that the signal rang out for the Saint Bartholomew's Day Massacre on 24 August 1572 (*see below*).

Saint-Séverin
Rue des Prêtres-Saint-Séverin, 75005 Paris. Metro Saint Michel/bus 21, 24, 27, 85, 96. **Open** *11am-1pm, 3.30pm-7.30pm, Mon-Fri.*
The Primitive and Flamboyant Gothic styles merge in this complex, composite church. Look out for the remarkable 'palm tree' vaulting of the ambulatory, then explore the nearby twisting, evocatively named medieval streets, which were once home to parchment shops, scribes and copyists.

Tour Saint Jacques
Place du Châtelet, 75001 Paris. Metro Châtelet, Hotel de Ville/bus 67, 69, 75, 76, 96.
Much-loved by the surrealists and complete with gargoyles, the Flamboyant bell-tower is all that remains of the church of Saint-Jacques-La-Boucherie, built for the powerful Butchers' Guild in the early sixteenth century. A weather station now crowns the tower, 52 metres (172ft) high. The tower can only be admired from outside.

RENAISSANCE MAN

Modern times purportedly arrived: slowly, the typical Parisian home benefited from Renaissance innovations. For example, glass replaced greased cloth and paper in windows. In rich households, forks appeared for the first time on tables and clocks on mantelpieces. Thanks to the printing press, books

Inside the **Sainte-Chapelle** *(listed under* **The Gothic Age***), visitors are dazzled by what seem to be walls of pure colour and light: 15 shimmering stained-glass windows, each over 15 metres (50 feet) high, illustrating Biblical allegories and the saga of the Crown of Thorns' transfer to the chapel. This is exposed for veneration on the main altar of Nôtre-Dame on Fridays in Lent.*

were no longer reserved for the learned and wealthy and 25,000 titles were published in Paris during the sixteenth century.

The golden boy of the Valois dynasty, François I was the epitome of a Renaissance monarch. In his sumptuous Loire Valley châteaux at Blois and Chambord, he gathered about him a glittering court of knights, poets and Italian painters. When he was imprisoned in Madrid after a humiliating defeat at the Battle of Pavia in 1525, the aldermen of Paris agreed to pay a hefty portion of their Cavalier King's ransom if he promised to reside in his capital in future. François agreed and set about making the Louvre livable. He demolished the castle keep, ordered architect Pierre Lescot to construct façades in the new Italianate style, and hung a few of his favourite pictures: a couple of Titians, some Raphaels, the *Mona Lisa* among others, to give the palace a more familiar feel.

Saint-Etienne-du-Mont
Place Saint-Geneviève, 75005 Paris (43.54.11.79). Metro Cardinal-Lemoine/bus 84, 89. **Open** 7.30am-noon, 2.30-7pm, Mon-Sat; 4-7pm Sun; closed every Mon in July and Aug. **Admission** free.
The tombs of Pascal and Racine can be found in this curious composite church, built over the sixteenth and seventeenth centuries. The tombs are located to the right of the delicately wrought rood screen (*jubé*) that surrounds the altar. Possibly the work of the brilliant Renaissance architect, Philibert Delorme, this dates from 1530 and is the only one of its type to be found in Paris.

Saint Eustache
Rue du Jour, 75001 Paris (40.26.47.99). Metro les Halles/bus 29, 67, 74, 85. **Open** 9am-7pm Mon-Sat; 9am-1pm, 3-7pm, Sun. This beautiful, cathedral-sized church dominates *Les Halles*. Though the structure is inherently Gothic, its decoration is just as distinctively Renaissance. A favourite with musicians and music-lovers, Saint-Eustache boasts a magnificent 8,000-pipe organ. There is one guided tour per week, at 3pm Sunday.

Palais du Louvre
Rue de Rivoli, 75001 Paris. Metro Palais Royal, Louvre/bus 21, 67, 69, 74, 76, 85.
The façade of the west wing of the Cour Carrée is one of the very few surviving masterpieces of French Renaissance architecture in Paris. The work of architect Pierre Lescot and sculptor Jean Goujon, it combines evenly balanced proportions with exuberantly Italianate decoration.

Fontaine des Innocents
Square des Innocents, 75001 Paris. Metro les Halles/bus 38, 47.
See **picture and caption.**

HERETICS

Paris watched uneasily as flames licked around the feet of the first Lutherans and Huguenots, burned at the stake for their unorthodox beliefs. Along with the heretics, the Renaissance and its carefree ambience also went up in smoke.

The realm was split by civil wars of religion. Tension, fuelled by ignorance and religious fervour, grew to uncontrollable proportions. Paris – unambiguously pro-Catholic – turned into a blood-bath. When the signal rang out on 24 August 1572, the residents willingly helped the King's men murder thousands of their Huguenot neighbours, in what later became known as the Saint Bartholomew's Day Massacre. Emotions were to run high for many a decade. Years later, when Henry III disavowed the slaughter and granted Protestants freedom of worship, Paris turned savagely on its sovereign, forcing him to flee the Louvre and a city banked with barricades.

Not to be out-done, the King – with the help of the protestant King of Navarre – laid siege to Paris. But Henry was never to have satisfaction. While on the loo, preparing his strategy, a fanatical monk stabbed him to death. The sordid murder was France's first recorded regicide.

Alone, but unabaited, Henry's ally from Navarre – also called Henri – carried on with the planned siege. To his annoyance, the siege dragged on for almost four years because Parisians refused to accept a protestant as their king. Conditions deteriorated inside the city barricades: residents ate cats, rats, horses, donkeys and even grass. Henri finally had to give in and renounced his faith in favour of catholicism saying 'Paris vaut bien une messe' (Paris is well worth a mass). Only then was he allowed to enter Paris.

Architect Lescot and sculptor Goujon are responsible for the **Fontaine des Innocents** *(listed under* **Renaissance Man***), a Renaissance masterpiece which has become one of the city's most popular meeting-points. The fountain's charming original bas-reliefs have been transferred to the Louvre (see chapter* **Museums***) for safe-keeping.*

Ancien Régime

Regicide marked the beginning and the end of the Ancien Régime: an era that saw the emergence of Paris as a monumental city.

URBAN RENEWAL

From the moment he was master of Paris, Henri IV set about changing the face of his ravaged capital, giving Paris some of its most familiar and enduring features. An equestrian bronze of the *Vert Galant* (as his subjects dubbed the lusty Henri) presided over the Pont-Neuf and the Place Dauphine, which he commissioned and named in honour of his heir, the future Louis XIII. Across the Seine Henri ordered the construction of an elegant neighbourhood – the Marais – with the city's first closed, geometrical square as its centrepiece. This square, called the Place Royale, is known to us as the Place des Vosges. Like the Place Dauphine, it is surrounded by symmetrical slate-roofed houses faced with a distinctive pattern of brick and stone. The central space was given over to festivities, equestrian exhibitions, bowlers and strollers. Henri also had his subjects' enjoyment in mind when he added to his own residence: the Louvre's Galerie du Bord de l'Eau was planned to please the eye of all who walked or sailed along the Seine.

Unfortunately, Henri never got round to improving the city's congested streets, habitually clogged with pedestrians, horses, donkeys and the latest innovation, the coach. On 14 May 1610, while caught in a bottleneck on the Rue de la Ferronnerie, the King was stabbed to death by a religious fanatic named Ravaillac. The *ancien régime* began as it would end: with regicide.

Place Dauphine
75004 Paris. Metro Cité, Saint Michel/bus 21, 35, 85, 90.
Only a few of the buildings on the Place look as they did in 1607 – No.14 is one.

Place des Vosges
75004 Paris. Metro Saint Paul, Bastille/bus 29, 69, 76.
Originally known as the Place Royale, this large and beautifully preserved square is the oldest in the city (begun in 1605) and retains much of its original splendour.

Statue of Henri IV
Pont-Neuf, 75004 Paris.
See **picture and caption**.

RICHELIEU ASCENDANT

Henri's widow, Marie de Medici, continued to live in the Louvre until Louis XIII came of age. For her remaining years, she asked Salomon de Brosse to build a retirement home reminiscent of the Pitti Palace in Florence, her birthplace. The resulting Palais du Luxembourg (now home to the Senate) is a fine example of how French architects domesticated the *furia* of Italian baroque. However, Marie had only just hung the 24 panels painted by Rubens to glorify her marriage and motherhood (and now in the Louvre), when the Royal offspring packed her off to exile in Cologne. Behind the plot was the Queen Mother's former protégé, Cardinal Richelieu.

Reason of State was the only reason Richelieu recognized. He won the confidence of anxious, tormented Louis XIII, who stuck by his minister through numerous plots hatched by his queen, Anne of Austria, assorted other Royals and disgruntled grandees. Richelieu returned the favour by creating a strong, centralized monarchy, effectively paving the way for the absolutism of Louis XIV.

RELIGIOUS ARCHITECTURE

Louis XIII did not share his father's enthusiasm for town planning. But the Counter-Reformation was in full swing, and architects were busy on projects for the Church and for Richelieu, Catholicism's champion. Scores of convents sprang up in Paris before the century was 40 years old, and the domes of churches inspired by Il Gesù (the baroque mother-church of the Jesuit order in Rome) mushroomed on the horizon, irrevocably altering the city's skyline.

Saint-Gervais-Saint-Protais
place Saint Gervais, 75004 Paris (48.87.32.02). Metro Pont-Marie/bus 67. **Open** 6am-9pm Tue-Sat; opening times on Sun vary.
The church owes much to Rome's Il Gesù, but the original triple-tiered façade (1616) with its Doric, Ionic and Corinthian columns was widely copied in the seventeenth and early eighteenth centuries.

Saint-Joseph-des-Carmes
21 rue d'Assas, 75006 Paris (45.48.05.16). Metro Rennes, Saint Placide/bus 83. **Guided tours** in French at 2.30pm and 3.30pm Tue-Sat; closed public holidays; 5 July-15 August. **Admission** 10F. **No credit cards.**
This Carmelite chapel marked the first appearance of the Jesuit style in Paris (1613). The marvellous wood-and-plaster dome depicts the prophet Elijah ascending to heaven in a fiery chariot. Ring to reserve a place on one of the tours.

Temple de la Visitation-Sainte-Marie
19 rue Saint Antoine, 75004 Paris. Metro Saint Paul, Bastille/bus 69, 76. **Open** 8am-noon Sun, or may be visited with tours organized by the *Caisse Nationale des Monuments Historiques (CNMH) (42.74.22.22)*.
François Mansart's circular design (1632) is accentuated by the absence of decoration inside this Protestant church. The huge but symmetrically proportioned dome soars to 33m (108ft).

Saint-Paul-Saint-Louis
rue Saint Antoine, 75004 Paris (42.72.30.32). Metro Saint Paul, Bastille/bus 69, 76. **Open** 8am-7.30pm daily; closed mornings July and Aug; closed 1, 8 May; Easter Mon and Whitsun Sun, 14 July.
Two Jesuit architects created this composite sanctuary. The façade conceals a Jesuit-style dome, best viewed from behind the church on the rue Charlemagne.

Val-de-Grâce
15 rue Val-de-Grâce, 75005 Paris. Metro Port-Royal/bus 83, 91.
See **picture and caption**.

MARAIS & ILE SAINT-LOUIS

Construction fever hit the Marais under Louis XIII. Since the days of Charles V the area had attracted aristocratic residents, and the noble Carnavalet and Lamoignon mansions date from the Renaissance. But it was the creation of the Place Royale that really launched the Marais as a desirable address. The Parisian *hôtel particulier*, an aristocratic dwelling set between a courtyard and a garden, here flowered into a highly distinctive architectural genre.

The literary lights of the *Grand Siècle* often found their patrons in the Marais. Salons hosted by lettered ladies (including celebrated authors like Mlle de Scudéry, Mme de la Fayette, Mme de Sévigné and the erudite courtesan, Ninon de l'Enclos) rang with saucy wit, pithy asides and political intrigue. By comparison, Richelieu's Académie Française (founded in 1634) was a fusty and rather pedantic reflection of the establishment.

Though it boasts fewer exceptional monuments than the Marais, the Ile-Saint-Louis offers a less sanitized picture of seventeenth-century Paris. The entire island was urbanized in just 20 years, and has remained virtually unchanged over the centuries. A cartel of property developers created the district out of two small islets in 1614, and built stone bridges to connect it to the Right and Left Banks. The Ile-Saint-Louis grew into a slightly less blue-blooded suburb of the Marais, home to high-level administrators, financiers and rich builders.

It would be impossible to list all the architectural riches of the Marais. French-speakers are urged to join the tours organized by the Caisse Nationale des Monuments Historiques (42.74.22.22). We list a few of the area's most renowned landmarks:

Hôtel de Lamoignon
24 rue Pavée, 75004 Paris (42.74.44.44).
Metro Saint Paul/bus 69, 76, 96. **Open** 9.30am-6pm Mon-Sat; closed public holidays and first two weeks of August. **Admission** free.
Built in 1585 for Diane de France, the legitimized daughter of Henri II, this austere, monumental *hôtel* heralds the seventeenth-century Classical style. It houses the Bibliothèque Historique de la Ville de Paris, a rich source of documents (particularly on the Revolution).

Hôtel de Sully
62 rue Saint-Antoine, 75004 Paris (48.87.24.14). Metro Saint Paul, Bastille/bus 69, 76, 96. **Tours** Sat, Sun at 3pm. **Admission** 28F. **No credit cards.**
Now perfectly restored, the Louis XIII-style

Hôtel de Sully was designed by Jean Androuet du Cerceau in 1624. The orangery in the garden is home to the Caisse Nationale des Monuments Historiques, which offers a vast array of guided tours (in French) to Paris. Telephone for a recorded message or call for brochures.

Hôtel Guénégaud
60 rue des Archives, 75004 Paris (42.72.86.43). Metro Hôtel de Ville/bus 75. **Open** 10am-12.30pm, 1.30pm-5.30pm, Mon, Wed-Sun; closed public holidays. **Admission** 10F. **No credit cards.**
One of the Marais' finest residences, designed in 1650 by François Mansart, the *hôtel* nearly fell victim to the developers. Inside, the Musée de la Chasse et de la Nature displays hunting weapons, trophies and a fine art collection, with works by Chardin, Oudry and Desportes (*see chapter* **Museums**).

Hôtel de Soubise
60 rue des Francs-Bourgeois, 75004 Paris (40.27.62.18). Metro Rambuteau/bus 29. **Open** 1.30-5.45pm Mon, Wed-Sun. **Admission** 12F adults; 8F students, OAPs, teachers; free under-18s. **No credit cards.**
The monumental façade and courtyard date from the early eighteenth century and the rococo interior is irresistible. It houses the Musée de l'Histoire de France and its collection of documents which date back to the seventh century (*see chapter* **Museums**).

CLASSICAL CITY

Pressured by the Fronde (an alliance of tax-weary Parisians, parliamentarians and rebellious princes, all united in their hatred of the prime minister Mazarin) ten-year-old Louis XIV and his mother, Anne of Austria, were forced to flee the capital in 1649. The incident left Louis with a lingering grudge against Paris. Some historians see in that episode the seed of his decision to quit Paris for Versailles, which became the seat of the Bourbon monarchy in 1678.

Louis XIV's architectural tastes were strictly monumental. Ruler of what was then Europe's mightiest nation, he scorned anything small-scale and was even known to have said, *L'état, c'est moi'*. Known as *le roi soleil*, he commemorated his early military successes with triumphal arches: the Porte Saint Denis (1672) and the Porte Saint Martin (1674), which stand at the heads of the boulevards that bear their names. But as various wars dragged on, they left a legacy of crippled veterans reduced to begging in the streets. The Invalides, one of the most impressive architectural ensembles in Paris, was built to house them. To

deal with another urban nuisance – the city's many vagabonds, delinquents, outlaws, women of easy virtue et al – Louis XIV appointed Paris's first Lieutenant of Police. It was his mission to clean up the infamous *Cours des Miracles* – blind alleys where nests of beggars, thieves and other undesirables hid out. 'Courts of Miracles' were so named for the apparently maimed mendicants who 'miraculously' recovered their limbs, sight and so forth when they gathered there at night. The police netted so many undesirables that existing facilities were swamped. The **Salpêtrière**, a veritable city within a city, was erected to shelter the women. Thus did the French administration try to camouflage the misery of its sordid underside – beneath grandiose domes and colonnaded façades.

Invalides
esplanade des Invalides, 75007 Paris (45.55.37.67). Metro Invalides, Varenne, Latour-Maubourg/bus 28, 49, 69, 93. **Church of the Dome. Open** *June-Aug:* 10am-7pm daily; *Jan-May, Sept-Dec:* 10am-6pm daily.
Powerful, severe yet undeniably elegant, the Invalides' 200-metre façade, a masterpiece of Classical architecture, was designed by Libéral Bruant. The impressive Dome Church is the work of Jules Hardouin-Mansart. Military history buffs will find an incredibly rich collection of art, armour, weapons, scale models and lots of Napoleonabilia. *See also chapter* **Museums**.

Salpêtrière
square Marie-Curie, boulevard de l'Hôpital, 75013 Paris. Metro Saint-Marcel. **Open** 8.30am-6.30pm daily.
Libéral Bruant's domed Chapelle Saint-Louis (1670) contains eight separate naves, designed to separate the sick from the insane and the poor from the debauched and so on.

MURMURS OF DISCONTENT

France had axes to grind with just about all of its neighbours in the final years of the Sun King's reign. Though financiers made wartime fortunes, famine and economic hardship embittered ordinary Parisians. Life at Versailles had soured as well, under the dour Mme de Maintenon, whom Louis had secretly wed in 1684. A pillar of sanctimonious piety, she threw the immensely popular Italian comedians out of the country, claiming they had caricatured her on stage. Nobles started to sneak away from

Versailles to build handsome *hôtels particuliers* in the fashionable new Faubourg Saint-Germain. Yet when Louis died in 1715, the courtiers and populace alike knew it was the end of an era.

Faubourg Saint-Germain

75007 Paris. Metro Assemblée Nationale, Varenne, Invalides/bus 63, 83.
The interiors of the splendid *hôtels particuliers* of this aristocratic district (which roughly corresponds to the 7th *arrondissement*) are mostly hidden behind grandiose and imposing doors. Still, the antique shops and galleries of the rues de Lille, de Bellechasse, Varenne and Grenelle offer a pleasant ramble. The **Hôtel Biron**, at *No. 77, rue de Varenne*, designed in 1728 by the elder Gabriel, houses the Musée Rodin (*see* chapter **Museums**).

A MODERN SODOM

Hardly had the Sun King disappeared over the horizon than the Regent, Philippe d'Orléans, kissed Versailles goodbye and moved the Court (along with the five-year-old Louis XV) back to Paris. The city was overjoyed to be at the centre of

things once more; Parisians were more than ready for a *bon viveur* after the deprivations of the recent past. The Regent had proved himself to be an able general and diplomat, but was better known as a reckless drinker, blasphemer and all-round rake. At home at the Palais-Royal, he regularly threw lavish dinners that degenerated into orgies. The palace precincts became the haunt of sycophants and prostitutes.

The existence led by pleasure-loving courtiers and the Parisians who assiduously aped them, spawned a sizeable service population of dressmakers, jewellers, hairdressers, decorators and domestics of every degree. True-life tales of country youths corrupted by the city where they came to seek their fortune inspired writers from Marivaux to Rousseau, Rétif de la Bretonne to the Marquis de Sade: Paris was the *nouvelle Babylone*, the modern Sodom.

For aristocrat, bourgeois and Bohemian alike, living any version of the Paris high life required considerable resources. The financial schemes of Scotsman John Law seduced Parisians from the Regent down to the lowest citizen with a few

spare sous to invest. The wheeling and dealing also drew a host of unsavoury hucksters and merchants: buying the last bit of jewellery or lace from insolvent punters; selling land, furnishings or sexual partners to the newly rich.

Predictably, the bubble burst. A run on Law's bank revealed that very little gold and silver was on hand to back up the paper bills. Panic ensued. There were suicides on the rue Quincampoix. Law himself was expelled from France, some financiers were pilloried and the episode left Parisians with an abiding animosity towards money merchants.

THE AGE OF ENLIGHTENMENT

As soon as he was his own man, Louis XV quit Paris for Versailles, which was once again the scene of sumptuous festivities and royal entertainments. But in the Age of Enlightenment, Paris was the real capital of Europe, the focus of intense artistic and intellectual activity. 'One lives in Paris; elsewhere, one simply vegetates,' wrote Casanova. The era's most brilliant minds met and matched wits in the salons of Mesdames Geoffrin, du Deffand and de Tencin. At such gatherings social distinctions counted for less than talent, conversation and *esprit*.

It was to this lettered milieu that the King's mistress, the beautiful and cultivated Marquise de Pompadour, belonged. Daughter of a financier and wife of a *fermier général* (tax collector), she was a friend and protectress of Diderot and the *encyclopédistes*, of Marivaux and of Montesquieu; she also corresponded with Voltaire. She encouraged Louis XV to embellish his capital with monuments like Jacques-Ange Gabriel's Ecole Militaire, where poor noblemen went to learn the gentle art of soldiering.

After cutting his teeth on L'Ecole Militaire, Gabriel was ready to design his Parisian masterpiece, the Place Louis XV (now the Place de la Concorde), one of the world's largest and most beautiful *places*. Its open plan marked a departure from the closed royal *places* of the previous century.

The equestrian bronze statue on the Pont Neuf depicts **Henri IV** *(listed under* **Urban Renewal**)*, town-planner and commissioner of some of Paris's most memorable features. This is a replica of the original, which was demolished by the mob in August 1792, and melted down.*

The reign of Louis XVI started out auspiciously enough. Admittedly, people grumbled at food shortages, but in Paris prosperity was in evidence everywhere. From as far as Washington and Moscow, people craved Parisian luxuries: furniture by Boulle, Sèvres porcelain, Gobelins and Savonnerie tapestries. Even then, fashionable ladies swore by Parisian modistes and *couturières*, such as Rose Bertin, who dressed the extravagant Marie Antoinette in her finery.

Paris looked sprucer than ever. The houses and shops that made the city's bridges a fire hazard were demolished; trees were planted on the Champs-Elysées. Roads were widened, lamps erected, and boulevards, gardens and promenades created. The disease-ridden Cemetery of the Innocents was finally closed, and the remains placed in catacombs. Overall, the city benefited from more space, more air and more light.

Paris offered a wide selection of distractions. Nobs indulged in horse racing (a taste acquired from the English) at tracks Louis XVI had built at Vincennes and on the edge of the Bois de Boulogne. On the boulevard du Temple, all classes rubbed shoulders to enjoy the performances of dancers, singers, acrobats and trained monkeys. The Tuileries, Palais-Royal and Jardin du Luxembourg were open to the public; art lovers could visit the royal picture collection exhibited in the Luxembourg Palace. And after a hard week, working-class Parisians headed for the *guinguettes* and cabarets of the city's *faubourgs*, where wine was untaxed and the entertainment uncensored.

On the eve of the Revolution, students of architecture could observe the neo-classical style making inroads in Paris. The Hôtel des Monnaies (the Mint), with its austere façade and uniform Ionic columns, went up in 1775; the Théâtre de l'Odéon in 1782. In 1790, ten years after his death, Soufflot's gigantic Greco-Roman church of Sainte-Geneviève (the Panthéon) was finally completed.

Catacombs

1 place Denfert-Rochereau, 75014 Paris (43.22.47.63). Metro Denfert-Rochereau/bus 38, 68. **Open** 2-6pm Tue-Fri; 9-11am, 2-4pm, Sat, Sun; closed public holidays. **Admission** 13.50F. **No credit cards.**
These former quarries, which date back to Roman times, are now home to the bones of 30 generations of Parisians, neatly arranged in sinister skull-and-crossbone formation. Bring a flashlight, a strong stomach and be prepared for lots of steps.

Hôtel des Monnaies

11 quai de Conti, 75006 Paris (40.46.56.66). Metro Pont Neuf, Odéon/bus 24, 27. **Open** 1-6pm Tue, Thur-Sun; 1-9pm Wed; closed public holidays. **Admission** 10F. **No credit cards.**
This building remains a splendid example of the architectural style of Louis XVI; the museum hosts temporary exhibits, as well as a resident collection of medals, coins and minting equipment.

A FISCAL WALL

In 1785 the Fermiers Général won authorization to build a fiscal wall around Paris; anyone passing through the toll-gates was subject to search by the customs officers, who collected duty on merchandise brought into the city. Inevitably, the wall, like the men who built it, was extremely unpopular. Hardly surprising then, that before the good people of Paris got into their stride at the Bastille, they mounted an attack on the wall.

Only four of the toll-houses (*barrières*) built by the visionary architect Ledoux survived the nineteenth century. Those that remain may be seen in the Parc Monceau, at La Villette, Place Denfert-Rocheareau and Place de la Nation. The Barrière de La Villette is now the Centre des Recherches Archéologiques de la Ville de Paris. All illustrate Ledoux's powerful, massive neo-classicism.

Val-de-Grâce *(listed under* **Religious Architecture***) was built by Mansart and Lemercier, in fulfilment of Anne of Austria's vow to erect 'a magnificent temple' if God blessed her with a son. He promptly presented her with two. Amazingly expensive and built over a 20-year period, the recently restored Val-de-Grâce is the most luxuriously baroque of the city's seventeenth-century domed churches. Referring to Mignard's dome fresco, Bernini said that it was 'the masterpiece of French art'. Its swirling colours and forms are meant to give the viewer a foretaste of heaven.*

The Revolution

As Louis dined imperiously on sweetmeats, his subjects starved and revolution brewed in eighteenth-century Paris. Reports reached Versailles of the insurrection. 'Is this a revolt?' asked Louis, aghast. 'No sire, it's a revolution' came the reply.

The spring of 1789 found Louis XVI increasingly isolated as civil unrest swept through France. The Crown's finances were spiralling towards insolvency: the royal balance sheet for that year would show a deficit of five billion *livres*. What's more, in Paris the people were restless after a disastrous harvest and a brutally cold winter. Recent riots had left hundreds dead or wounded in the Faubourg Saint-Antoine. Obliged to convene the Etats Généraux for the first time in nearly 200 years, the King was understandably apprehensive.

The elected members of the third estate (the commoners), aware that they outnumbered the nobility and the clergy, and conscious of representing ninety-five per cent of Frenchmen, declared themselves a National Assembly. On 20 June 1789, at the *Jeu de Paume* (tennis court) at Versailles, they pledged not to separate until the constitution of the realm was solidly established. The Crown's reaction could not have been less diplomatic. Louis ringed the capital with Swiss and German troops; he dismissed his minister, Jacques Necker, whom the commoners considered to be their sole ally in the government. Parisians gathered, thousands strong, to protest against these measures in the garden of the Palais Royal.

In the final years of the Ancien Régime, the Palais Royal had been the preferred rendezvous of the Parisian intelligentsia. Arcades surrounding the gardens housed hundreds of luxury shops alongside the cafés and print shops which became hotbeds of revolutionary ferment. In the galleries and gardens, polemicists and orators found a receptive public for their harangues, and rumour-mongers could rely on news spreading fast among scandal-loving Parisians.

This motley crew was unofficially protected by the King's cousin, Louis-Philippe d'Orléans (soon to be Philippe-Egalité), owner of the Palais-Royal and landlord of the arcades tenants. A sworn enemy of Marie Antoinette and her coterie, Louis-Philippe was not averse to sponsoring, albeit indirectly, the anti-monarchical sentiments that blossomed in his garden. On 12 July 1789, an obscure lawyer named Camille Desmoulins, miraculously cured of the stammer that had plagued him all his life, leapt up on a café table and likened Necker's dismissal to another Saint Bartholomew's Day (*see chapter* **Middle Ages & Renaissance**). 'Aux armes!' he exhorted the excited crowd: 'To arms! To arms!'

Palais Royal
avenue de l'Opéra, 75001 Paris. Metro Palais Royal.
Built by Richelieu, the Palais Royal came into its own in the eighteenth century as a popular society tryst when Louis-Philippe d'Orléans had the gardens enclosed within a three-storey peristyle of lodgings and shops. After the Revolution, establishments like Grand Véfour – one of the oldest, still one of the best and arguably the prettiest restaurant in town – and the celebrated Very made the Palais Royal a gastronomic Mecca for roving gourmets. Today, it's a tranquil spot for shopping or strolling. Try to take in Daniel Buren's controversial sculptural group of black and white striped columns in the main courtyard.

TO ARMS

Obtaining arms became a city-wide obsession. Parisians stormed the Invalides military hospital, carrying off thousands of guns. But what good were guns without powder? However, the Revolution was not without its fair share of ingenuity and someone remembered that the Bastille prison was the powder-keg of Paris. All the gun-powder and weaponry a militia might desire were stored behind moats, drawbridges, walls three metres (ten feet) thick and towers 24 metres (79 feet) high. The Marquis de Launay, governor of the Bastille, quickly realized that trouble was afoot. When the militia arrived at his door in the form of a municipal delegation, he coolly snubbed demands for arms, but nonchalantly invited the members in for lunch. Meanwhile, the baying hordes waiting outside were certain they had been betrayed and attacked. Inside the fortress, de Launay accused the delegates of having deceived him in order to gain time. He ordered his men to fire on the invaders and in a few minutes 87 rebels lay dead. The two sides were evenly matched until the arrival of several cannon-bearing revolutionaries who proved to be an irresistible addition to the plebeian ranks.

Worried that a real massacre might ensue, de Launay resolved to offer a conditional surrender. He warned the insurgents that the fortress was packed with gunpowder and that he was prepared to blow himself, his men, and the entire area to smithereens if his surrender was not accepted. It was, but in the end de Launay's prudence was ill-rewarded. Outside, the walls of the Bastille were surrounded by a frenzied crowd craving vengeance. Guards could not long protect him against the blood lust of the mob; de Launay was lynched, decapitated and his head, skewered on a pike, was paraded through Paris to the Palais Royal (*see above*).

The turbulent summer of 1789 produced an excellent harvest, but communications networks suffered from the unrest and delivery of wheat became more and more unreliable – the price of bread remained extortionate and malnutrition ravaged the populace. So when news reached Paris of a lavish banquet given by the Royal Guardsmen in the sumptuous Opéra de Versailles, at which the soldiers shouted anti-revolutionary slogans and drank the health of the King and Queen, the people were incensed. Thousands of angry Parisiennes, fishwives and bourgeoises alike, exasperated by long bread queues and empty bakeries, set off for Versailles, led by a *pasionaria* named Thérogine de Méricourt.

As they marched, their ranks swelled with the unbridled rage of revolutionary France; this furious throng invaded the royal apartments, brandishing the heads of guardsmen who had attempted to resist its onslaught. Believing that the King's presence in the capital would ensure a supply of bread, the women demanded that Louis, the Queen and the Dauphin return with them to Paris. On the way, the mob danced around the royal carriage chanting, 'Here comes the baker, his wife and the little baker boy!' To all intents and purposes, the monarchy was now imprisoned in the Tuileries.

At Easter 1791, the royal family prepared to travel to their château at Saint-Cloud, not far from Paris, to attend mass. But a crowd of demonstrators flooded the courtyard of the Tuileries and surrounded the King's carriage, haranguing the monarch and shouting 'We won't let him leave, he will not leave'. The episode dissipated Louis' reluctance to flee. On the night of 20 June, he and his family stole out of their quarters through an unguarded door, already two hours behind schedule. Aided by Axel de Fersen, a Swedish nobleman in love with the Queen, they headed east to rendezvous with royalist troops. Their slow, heavy coach proved an inappropriate vehicle for escape and they crawled towards freedom. A postmaster finally recognized the party, though they were simply dressed and equipped with false passports; they were arrested at Varennes. Paris, simultaneously stunned and indignant to learn of the royal flight, greeted their return with a terrible silence.

In 1792 the Prussian army was approaching the capital. From Koblenz, the Duke of Brunswick threatened to raze Paris if the King came to any harm. This ultimatum threw the city into an indignant frenzy; on 10 August, to cries of 'No more king!', a popular army, spearheaded by sans-culottes (revolutionaries; literally, without knee breeches) from the Faubourg Saint-Antoine, attacked the Tuileries. Louis had withdrawn from the palace moments before the first shots were fired. He was found and, under pressure, ordered his troops to cease fire. The Swiss Guard and many noblemen were cut down

without mercy. A mob turned on the Tuileries, ripping, slashing and hurling furniture out of the windows. France was now governed by the Commune de Paris, led by Danton, Herbert, Marat and Robespierre.

Arrested in short order, the royal family was imprisoned in the Donjon du Temple, the former Templar's stronghold. That same month, Paris pulled down and melted statues of Henry IV (Pont-Neuf) and Louis XIV (places Vendôme and des Victoires). In September, the bloodthirsty press spurred Paris on to 'purge' the prison of aristocrats, loyalist soldiers, counterfeiters (blamed for the economic crisis), and other 'criminals'. Vengeful mobs of sans-culottes soaked the city's prisons and hospices in blood, sparing neither women, children nor the old and infirm. All were slaughtered in the name of the Republic.

Quartered on the place de la Révolution (formerly place Louis XV, now place de la Concorde), the Black Widow – as the guillotine came to be called – claimed Louis XVI in January 1793. In October, Marie Antoinette, condemned by the Revolutionary Tribunal, was taken from the prison of the Conciergerie to suffer the same fate as her husband.

The royal couple might have taken solace in the knowledge that a similar fate awaited their executioners. In September 1793 the National Assembly put 'terror on the agenda'. An infernal machine was wound up that would claim victim after victim until its energy expired almost a year later. The Revolution devoured its children: Herbert and his allies; Philipe-Egalité, who had voted for the death of his cousin; Danton; Camille Desmoulins. Their partisans all travelled the same soulless road from the Conciergerie to the scaffold (Desmoulins shouting to the crowd 'People of Paris your friends are being murdered!').

After Danton's death the authorities thought it politic to transfer the increasingly unpopular guillotine to the place du Trone-Renversé (now place de la Nation), on the relatively remote eastern edge of Paris. There, during the Grande Terreur, 1,300 heads fell in just six weeks. But for the execution of Robespierre

and his party (105 in all), Saint Guillotine was trundled back to its original site.

The Bastille

place de la Bastille, 75012 Paris. Metro Bastille.
Although the Bastille no longer exists, visitors can view the square where it once stood. Today, it is the scene of much merriment and celebration on Bastille Day, 14 July (*see also chapter* **Paris by Season**). More a symbol than an actual instrument of repression, the Bastille held only a handful of prisoners; indeed, by the end of its career the Bastille had earned a reputation as a luxury prison for privileged inmates; good food, good books and other amusements were readily available to those who could pay. The Revolution would shortly breed prisons far more terrible. But the Bastille's symbolic value, reinforced by the events of 14 July, was not overlooked by the entrepreneurial elements of the revolution. An individual named Palloy, who secured the rights to demolish the fortress, turned patriotic fervour into hard cash by selling Bastille keys, balls and chains, bolts and bars; the prison archives were pleated into fans for fashionable ladies and stones of the razed fortress were carved into replicas of the Bastille (one is now on view in the Musée Carnavalet, *see chapter* **Museums**).

La Conciergerie

quai de L'Horloge, 75001 Paris (43.54.30.06). Metro Cité. **Open** 9.30am-5pm daily. **Admission** 22F adults; 12F children. **No credit cards.**
For years a name to strike fear into the heart of Parisians because of its appalling and inhumane conditions, La

Conciergerie became most notorious during the Revolution when it was filled with famous aristocrats and counter-revolutionaries. Danton, Robespierrre, Charlotte Corday, and the judges who a short while ago had been sitting in judgement on others, all found their way here. You can still see the cell where Marie Antoinette spent her last night before going to the guillotine. Once inside prisoners were likely to emerge only once. On the day of execution, the condemned were taken to a small, barred cell where their hair was cut and shirt-collars ripped off in preparation for the guillotine.

Empires & Rebellions

France's great Revolution failed to liberate the city from rebellion and monarchy. With more than one demagogue aiming to leave his architectural stamp on the capital, Paris soon became a speculator's paradise.

NAPOLEON'S ERA

After Bonaparte's successful invasion and subduing of the land of living gods and monumental architecture, a wave of Egyptomania swept Paris: enigmatic sphinxes suddenly sprouted on the arms and legs of chairs and fashionable women cast aside their transparent Greek draperies in favour of couture *à l'égyptienne*. A more enduring monument to Napoleon's conquests is the area of the place du Caire (Cairo Square), where street names commemorate the Nile, Aboukir and Alexandria. Paris is littered with remnants of this once-blossoming empire. On the rue de Sèvres, for example, a swarthy *fellah* carrying water amphorae adorns a fountain. Once the conquering Corsican had returned to Paris, he unceremoniously ejected the *Directoire* with a well-aimed *coup d'état* (in November 1799) and declared himself First Consul. Not known for his moderation, he was soon Consul for life and in 1804, **Napoleon I, Emperor of France**, was crowned at Nôtre Dame.

Napoleon had great ambitions for his imperial capital. He desired to be master of the 'most beautiful city in the world', complete with palaces, broad boulevards, colossal monuments and temples evoking the monumental splendour of Augustan Rome – such as the Greco-Roman **church of the Madeleine**, originally conceived as a temple of glory, or the **Bourse** with its Corinthian peristyle, a temple of money. The Emperor's taste can be simply summed up: big is beautiful ('*Ce qui est grand est toujours beau*'). The **rue de Rivoli** is an example of his aes-

thetic credo, with its grand, arcaded façade designed by Napoleon's official architects, Percier and Fontaine.

As the self-annointed successor of the kings of France, Napoleon inevitably showed great interest in the Louvre. Percier and Fontaine completed the Cour Carrée, which Louis XIV had left unfinished when he moved to Versailles. The Emperor crammed the palace museum with the fabulous booty his armies had 'liberated' in Italy. Antique sculptures such as the *Discus Thrower*, the *Apollo Belvedere*, the *Dying Gladiator* as well as hundreds of paintings and precious illuminated manuscripts, were paraded through the streets of Paris before going on display at the Louvre.

Arc de Triomphe
place Charles de Gaulle (access via underground passage), 75008 Paris (43.80.31.31). Metro Etoile/bus 22, 30, 31, 52, 92. **Open** 10am-5.30pm (5pm in winter) daily; closed public holidays. **Admission** *to panorama platform*: 22F adults; 5F under-17s; 12F OAPs, students.
Chalgrin's colossal arch was commissioned by Napoleon, but it was Louis-Philippe who inaugurated the monument in 1836. *See also chapter* **The War.**

Bourse
place de la Bourse, 75002 Paris (42.33.99.83). Metro Bourse/bus 67, 74, 85. **Tours** *mid Sept-June*: every half hour, 11am-1pm, Mon-Fri; *July-mid Sept*: noon Mon-Fri. **Admission** 8F; ID required.
The Paris stock exchange (designed by Brongniart in 1808, finished in 1827) is a sombre building devoted to finance. The four statues surrounding the building are Justice, Prudence, Abundance and Fortune, the cardinal virtues of nineteenth-century bourgeoisie. A tour includes audio-visual presentations, a short talk describing how the Bourse operates and time to gaze through the viewing gallery, which overlooks the trading floor.

Colonne d'Austerlitz
place Vendôme, 75001 Paris. Metro Tuileries/bus 42, 52, 72.
See **picture and caption.**

La Madeleine
place de la Madeleine, 75008 Paris (42.65.52.17). Metro Madeleine. **Open** 7am-7pm Mon-Sat; 7.30am-1.30pm, 3.30-7pm, Sun. **Admission** free.
Started by Vignon in 1806, this church wasn't finished until 1840. Napoleon wanted a 'monument like those of Athens, which Paris lacks'. Huge, heavy and severe, this temple was uncompromisingly fashioned in the neo-classical style and is now a parish church.

GALERIES

Some of the ambience of bygone days still lingers in the glass-roofed *galeries* that thread their way through the teeming boulevards. These picturesque passages were once crowded with restaurants and shops, where strollers could inspect the latest novelties, safe from the rain, mud, and equine traffic. The *galeries* still allow astute pedestrians to make their way, unmolested by weather or traffic, from the *grands boulevards* to Palais-Royal. Over 100 *galeries* existed in 1840; fewer than 20 remain today.

Galeries and *passages* are situated mainly in the 1st, 2nd and 9th *arrondissements*: Metro Bourse, Richelieu-Drouot or Rue Montmartre.

Galerie Véro-Dodat
75001 Paris. Metro Palais-Royal/bus 39, 48, 67.
A pair of prosperous *charcutiers* – Mr Véro and Mr Dodat – built this commercial arcade during the Restoration, equipping it with gaslights and more than recouping their investment by charging their tenants astronomical rents. The *galerie's* interesting decoration, with columns, capitals, arcades and curious old shops, are worth a tour.

Galerie Vivienne
75002 Paris. Metro Bourse/bus 29.
This bright and spacious *galerie* near the place des Victoires is decorated in the neo-classical manner, with bas-reliefs and a beautifully crafted mosaic pavement. Jean-Paul Gaultier's innovative couture, the highly coveted ornaments and home furnishings of Casa Lopez, Legrand's wines and a pretty tea-room (A Priori Thé) make it the ideal place for an afternoon browse.

Passage des Panoramas
75002 Paris. Metro Rue Montmartre/bus 20, 39, 48.
The evocative name is taken from the panoramas of Rome, Naples, Jerusalem, London, Athens and other celebrated capitals created by Robert Fulton – the American inventor of the steamship – and landscape painter Pierre Prévost. These drew large crowds (including the artist David) to this early nineteenth-century passage. Enticing shops and restaurants have recently given the place a new lease of life. For a glimpse of how things used to look, take in the superb premises of Stern (No. 47), a smart engraving firm founded in 1830.

Two more passages worth exploring, both in the 9th *arrondissement*, are the **passage Verdeau** *(Metro Richelieu-Drouot/bus 20, 39, 48)*, with its superb iron-and-glass roof, and the **passage Jouffroy** *(Metro Richelieu-Drouot/bus 20, 39, 48)*, a warren of lovely, old-fashioned shops.

BACK TO THE BARRICADES

Along with the often repressive regimes and conservative values that gripped nineteenth-century France, Paris nurtured a strong feeling of rebellion. This was fed by a progressive press, liberal intellectuals – including many Romantic artists and authors, such as Victor Hugo, Daumier, Delacroix and Lamartine – radical students and a growing, desperately poor and dangerously anarchic underclass. When provoked, this volatile coalition could explode into revolutionary violence. On several occasions Paris proved that she was prepared to do much more than merely vocalize such dissatisfaction.

In 1830 **Charles X** (yet another brother of the ill-fated Louis XVI) sensed a threat to the monarchy from the liberal opposition. His impolitic reaction was to dissolve the legislature, muzzle the press and control electoral procedures to suit his royal whim. Paris retorted with the Revolution of 1830, which brought an end to the Bourbons' come-back.

On 27 July 1830, government troops commanded by the 'traitor' Marmont (who had surrendered Paris to the Prussians and Austrians back in 1814) fired on a crowd of demonstrators. A young woman was shot in the head. Her corpse was carried by a butcher's boy to the place des Victoires where popular feeling was whipped up with an emotional plea for vengeance. There followed *les Trois Glorieuses*, three days and nights of insurrection which swept through the capital.

The outcome, however, was not a republic but another monarchy, although it was to prove the last. As Charles X set sail for England, never to return, yet another eccentric leftover of the Ancien Régime was winched onto the throne. **Louis-Philippe**, Duc d'Orléans, son of Philippe-Egalité, was known as the 'Citizen King'. A father of eight, who

Fountains were Bonaparte's passion. Like Rome, he wanted Paris to resound with the splash of flowing water. But though some 60 fountains were planned, only about a dozen were actually built (including the Palm Fountain of the Châtelet). Napoleon was also an indefatigable bridge builder: the Pont de la Cité, Pont d'Austerlitz and Pont d'Iéna all date from his reign, as does the 1804 **Pont des Arts** *(see above photo) – the city's first iron span, recently rebuilt in steel. It was as popular then as it is now as a place for a leisurely stroll while taking in some of the finest views in Paris.*

never went out without his umbrella and considered it his duty to carve the Sunday roast, he was eminently acceptable to the Parisian bourgeoisie. But the workers, who had spilled their blood in 1830 only to see their quality of life worsen, simmered with rancour and frustration throughout the July Monarchy.

Colonne de Juillet
place de la Bastille, 75004 Paris. Metro Bastille/bus 20, 29, 65, 86, 87, 91.
See **picture and caption.**

LES MISERABLES

At the time of the Restoration and the July Monarchy, Parisians rich and poor alike, inhabited the same streets, and sometimes the same buildings, with the well-heeled on the first floor (the *étage noble*) and the less privileged under the rafters, or in obscure alleys and culs-de-sac.

But between 1800 and 1860, the population of Paris doubled to over a million as railroad construction and a building boom flooded the capital with droves of workers from

the provinces. The overflow emptied into the poorest quarters, which were utterly unequipped to cope. Overcrowding brought a host of other evils: filth, disease, violence and crime. Contemporary novelists such as Balzac, Hugo and Eugène Sue penned hair-raising accounts (confirmed in their reality by historians) of dank, tomb-like hovels where the sun never shone, and of dismal, dangerous streets in central Paris, whose denizens subsisted on pauper's wages.

The well-fed, complacent bourgeoisie (mordantly caricatured in Daumier's drawings) regarded this populace with fear, loathing and even, perhaps a twinge of guilt. For while the bourgeoisie prospered after 1830 – when Rothschild's and other banks flourished, as did the Bourse, real-estate speculation and industry – workers under Louis-Philippe were still forbidden from forming unions or from striking. Gaslight, which made city streets so much more pleasant, also enabled the working day to be extended to 15 hours or more. Factory owners pruned salaries to the limit, exploited children and were unfettered by any legislation geared to protect their workforce. With no safety net, unemployed or disabled workers and their families were obliged to beg, steal or starve.

A cholera epidemic in 1832 claimed 19,000 victims in just three months and aggravated the already bitter class divisions. The rich blamed workers, beggars and immigrants for breeding disease; the poor hated the fortunate bourgeoisie who could afford to escape the city's fetid air, or move to the spacious new neighbourhoods developing in the 8th and 9th *arrondissements*. The stage was set for a battle and it was to have an even more ferocious edge than that of 1830.

BUILDING CONTINUES

Louis-Philippe's prefect, Rambuteau, was no Baron Haussmann, but he managed to keep busy by finishing several urban works in progress including the Arc de Triomphe, and the Madeleine, *see above* **Napoleon's Era**. He also initiated some projects of his own, the most notable of these being the **Louis-Philippe bridge**, *75004 Paris (Metro Pont Marie/bus 67)* and the **Carrousell bridge**, *75006 Paris (Metro Palais Royal/bus 27, 39, 48*. He was also responsible for some handsome public fountains which may still

be seen today. The **Fontaine Molière** (by Visconti and Pradier), erected near the great playwright's residence at *40 rue de Richelieu, 75001* and the monumental **Fontaine des Quatre-Evêques**, also by Visconti, on the *place Saint Sulpice, 75006* are well worth your attention.

REVOLUTION AGAIN

History repeated itself on 23 February 1848, when, in a tragic rerun of 1830, trigger-happy troops fired on a crowd massed along the boulevard des Capucines. Once again, the corpses were carried to the place des Victoires, where demonstrators demanded blood for blood. Paris earned its title of *capitale des révolutions*: once again barricades covered the city and citizens chanted 'Down with the King!'. The national guard – called out to put down the insurrection – defected to the rebels' side. In the Tuileries, Louis-Philippe abdicated, and then abandoned his palace, his capital, and his country, just as Charles X had done 18 years earlier.

The workers' revolution of 1848 made France a republic once again

– but not for long. In 1848 a progressive **provisional government**, which included the Romantic poet Lamartine and a mechanic – the first French proletarian to hold such a position – abolished slavery in the colonies and the death penalty for political crimes; it gave most French men (but only men) the vote and guaranteed jobs for all workers. Paris was euphoric. The capital, however, had not counted on the reaction of the provinces, which took a dim view of Parisian radicalism. In May 1848, general elections put a **conservative commission** at the head of the Republic. One of its first official acts was to liquidate the 'make work' scheme, as too costly and allied with socialism.

Desperate workers took to the streets in June. There were more barricades, more battles, and more blood. And this time the insurgents got the worst of it: thousands fell under government fire, and others were massacred in reprisals after the combat had ended. To justify this harsh repression, officials pointed to the rebels' responsibility for the deaths of two generals and the Archbishop of Paris.

A clean sweep was called for; new elections gave an overwhelming mandate to a new President of the Republic, the anti-republican **Louis-Napoléon Bonaparte**. After a couple of years consolidating his position as President, Napoléon's nephew decided that he didn't merely want to preside, he wanted to reign. The *coup d'état* on 2 December 1851 that gave Bonaparte dictatorial powers met with little resistance, for the memory of June 1848 was still fresh in people's minds. Still, Bonaparte's troops arranged to fire on an unarmed crowd and kill at least a hundred innocent people, just for good measure. A year later, in 1849, after further restricting the freedom of the press and of the Assembly, the *Prince Président* moved into the Tuileries Palace as Emperor of France: *Vive Napoléon III*.

HAUSSMANN

Like his illustrious uncle **Napoleon Bonaparte**, Napoleon III had grandiose plans for Paris which he quickly put into action. His far-

Napoleon, draped in Roman garb, stands on the 44-metre (145 feet) **Colonne d'Austerlitz** *(listed under* **Napoleon's Era***) is based on Trajan's column in Rome. The bronze relief that spirals up the column's sides comes from 1,250 melted-down cannons captured from the Russians and Austrians at the Battle of Austerlitz (1805).*

reaching urbanization programme included completing the Louvre, landscaping the Bois de Boulogne and constructing new, enclosed markets on the site of *Les Halles.*

The man appointed to carry out this daunting mission was an Alsatian Protestant named **Baron Haussmann,** an energetic, iron-fisted administrator. He hired a couple of engineers ('architects' would have given the impression of fanciful indulgence) to draw up plans. He imported teams of masons from the Limousin and for the next 17 years he expropriated, demolished, designed and built; so vast was the undertaking that many of the labourers turned entrepreneur and made a fortune.

It was on the Ile de la Cité that Haussmann won his reputation as an urban Jack the Ripper. He ousted the population and swept away the precious remnants of medieval and classical Paris. The ancient, teeming Cité was turned into a somber administrative desert. Only the island's western tip and the little quarter to the north of Nôtre-Dame were spared. As for the cathedral itself, Viollet-le-Duc carried on with his zealous restoration until 1864.

A project close to the Emperor's heart was the construction of an opera house worthy of his imperial capital. Charles Garnier won the competition for the most popular design and when asked by the Empress Eugénie what name could be applied to its novel architectural style, replied 'It is Napoleon III. Don't you like it?'. In fact quite a lot of people didn't, as a sizeable portion of Paris was razed to accommodate the pompous temple. The style never attained popularity and the Opéra remains the only bona fide Napoleon III monument in Paris.

On balance, Haussmann created more than he destroyed. In 15 years, 40,000 houses went up, and 20,000 were torn down. But among his victims were some of the finest *hôtels particuliers* of the Faubourg Saint Germain, sacrificed to make way for the rue de Rennes and the boulevard Saint Germain. Ancient vestiges of the Latin Quarter disappeared overnight, as did the much-loved *boulevard du crime,* its theatres and Ledoux's fine tollhouses. '*Le vieux Paris n'est plus*' (the old Paris is no more) lamented Baudelaire.

Haussmann's least controversial contribution to Paris was the gift of greenery. At the request of Napoleon III, who harboured fond memories of Hyde Park and verdant English gardens, the Baron commissioned 24 local squares, manicured the Bois de Boulogne and the Bois de Vincennes adding lakes, waterfalls and winding paths, and created three of the city's loveliest parks.

L'Opéra Garnier
1 place de l'Opéra, 75009 Paris (40.17.33.33, ext 3514). Metro Opéra/bus 27, 29, 42, 52, 68, 81. **Open** *for visits:* 11am-4.30pm daily (closed public holidays); *museum, entrance on rue Aubert side:* 10am-5pm daily.
Admission *Opera visits:* 17F; *museum:* 10F.
A few statistics worth mentioning about the opera house: it is 56m (185ft) high, 172m (568ft) long and 101m (333ft) wide. The main chandelier weighs in at six and a half tonnes; 19km (12 miles) of halls and corridors wind over several levels; and it took 13 painters, 73 sculptors and 14 plaster and stucco specialists to achieve the opulent décor. Yet because a large proportion of the space was devoted to the Opéra's public rooms, the auditorium only seats 2,156 spectators. The personalities on view in the foyer and on the sumptuous marble-and-onyx Grand Staircase are considered as important as the artists on stage singing *Faust, La Traviata* or *Lucia di Lammermoor.*

Parc des Buttes Chaumont
main access from rue Botzaris, 75019 Paris (42.41.19.19). Metro Buttes Chaumont, Botzaris/bus 60, 75. **Open** dawn-dusk daily.
On a bare hilltop haunted by the ghosts of those who perished on the old gallows of Montfaucon, Haussmann planted this highly picturesque 60-acre park. The little neo-classical temple atop the scraggy island which rises out of the lake was designed by the sculptor Davioud, who was also responsible for Michael and the Dragon on the Fontaine Saint Michel.

Parc Monceau
boulevard de Courcelles, 75017 Paris (42.94.08.08). Metro Monceau/bus 30.
Open dawn-dusk daily.
A luxurious, English-style park within a very chic area. Children enjoy the ponies and the play areas, while adults can enjoy the magnificent trees, rare plants, Ledoux's tollhouse (at the entrance gate) and the ruins of King Henri II's mausoleum.

Parc Montsouris
main access from boulevard Jourdan, 75014 Paris (45.45.67.14). Metro Porte d'Orléans/RER Cité Universitaire/bus 28, 38, 68. **Open** dawn-dusk daily.
On the park's opening day in 1878, the man-made lake suddenly and inexplicably emptied. The engineer responsible promptly committed suicide. Notwithstanding that tragic event, this attractive park is a favourite with children and with students from the nearby Cité Universitaire.

Victor Hugo called the **Colonne de Juillet** *(listed under* **Back to the Barricades***) a 'botched monument to an aborted revolution', but the* Génie de la Liberté, *poised on top of the column, brandishing broken chains and the flame of freedom, is one of the capital's best-loved landmarks. Regilded for the bicentennial of the French Revolution, the genie glitters 62 metres (205 feet) above the place de la Bastille. In the base of the column are entombed the remains of Parisians who died in the insurrections of 1830 and 1848.*

The Third Republic

From the Prussian war to the Fascist threat of the 1930s, Paris swung from Impressionism, through to riots and finally war.

PARIS COMMUNE

Just days after the Empire's defeat at Sedan, on 4 September 1870, Parisian rioters demanded and won a new Republic, proclaimed to much cheering at the **Hôtel de Ville** *(see below)*. A provisional government of National Defence was formed, yet within weeks Paris was under siege by the Prussians, cut off from the rest of the nation.

Beleaguered Parisians shivered and starved through the winter. In addition to horses, dogs, cats, and rats, the camel, bear, tiger, and hippo from the zoo ended up in the city's butcher shops. With no horses to pull their carriage, even the Rothschilds had to travel to the city on foot. Christmas dinner at the fashionable Restaurant Voisin featured an hors-d'oeuvre of stuffed ass's head, a *consommé d'éléphant* for the soup course, followed by *civet de kangourou* and *cuisson de loup sauce chevreuil*.

In January, Prussian artillery bombarded the city's southern *arrondissements*. The government negotiated a temporary armistice with Bismarck, then hastily arranged elections for a National Assembly mandated to make peace. Though Paris voted republican, the vast majority of successful candidates were conservative, pacifist monarchists. The peace terms to which they agreed – a five billion-franc indemnity, occupation and the concession of Alsace-Lorraine – disgusted Parisian patriots who protested vociferously. When the time came for the Assembly to reconvene, the representatives spurned the left-leaning, mutinous capital and chose Versailles instead. Paris understandably regarded this *décapitalisation* as an act of hostility.

Paris remained in a state of nervous agitation. The National Guard – a popular, fervently republican and patriotic corps – formed an illegal 'federation' and refused to lay down arms. On 1 March 1871 the *fédérés* hauled nearly 200 cannons to Montmartre; when government troops from Versailles attempted to confiscate them, the furious mob fought off the army and lynched two generals. **Adolphe Thiers**, provisional leader of the government, evacuated Paris in view of the siege; Paris was left in the hands of **radicals** who declared the city a free **Commune**. The fuse of civil war was lit.

SHOOTINGS

Late in May, the **Bloody Week** commenced, when 70,000 *versaillais* – government-backed troops – marched into Paris. The radical communards dug in and fought back street by street, but it was an unequal fight. Desperate insurgents torched the **Tuileries** *(see below)*, the Hôtel de Ville, the Finance Ministry, the Palais-Royal...the Louvre barely escaped destruction. The 'men of Versailles' summarily shot anyone suspected of belonging to the rebel federation; on their side, communards massacred priests and the archbishop of Paris. On Sunday evening, 20 May, as black smoke fogged the Paris sky, the last defenders of the Commune made their final stand in a ferocious battle among the graves of **Père-Lachaise cemetery** *(see below)*; at dawn, soldiers shot the 147 survivors against the *mur des fédérés*, and cast the bodies into a common grave. The tragic, traumatic *Semaine Sanglante* claimed at least 20,000 victims – more than the revolution of 1789.

Basilique du Sacré-Coeur
35 rue Chevailer-de-la-Barre, 75018 Paris (42.51.17.02). Metro Abbesses, Anvers. **Open** *1 April-30 Sept:* 9.15am-1.30pm, 2-6.30pm, daily; *1 Oct-31Mar:* 9am-noon, 1-5pm, daily. **Admission** *dome:* 10F; *museum:* 12F. *See* **picture and caption.**

Cemetery of Père-Lachaise
boulevard de Ménilmontant, 75020 Paris (43.70.70.33). Metro Gambetta, Père-Lachaise/bus 26, 61, 69, 76. **Open** *mid March-early Nov:* 7.30am-6pm Mon-Fri; 8.30am-6pm Sat; 9am-6pm Sun; *early Nov-mid March:* 8am-5.30pm Mon-Fri; 8.30am-5.30pm Sat; 9am-5.30pm Sun. *See* **picture and caption.**

Hôtel de Ville
place de l'Hôtel de Ville, 75004 Paris (42.76.43.43). Metro Hôtel de Ville/bus 38, 47, 58, 67, 69, 70, 72, 74, 75, 76, 96. **Open** *tour of public rooms:* 10.30am Mon, meet at Bureau d'Accueil, 29 rue de Rivoli, 75004 Paris.
Burned to the ground during the Commune, the Hôtel de Ville was reconstructed from 1874 to 1882. Architects Ballu and Deperthes respected Boccador's original Renaissance design (1533), but the present edifice is much larger, with an eclectic décor; the statues that look down from the façade represent figures from French history, art and science.

Les Tuileries
75001 Paris. Metro Concorde/bus 21, 24, 27, 39, 48, 68, 69, 72.
After its destruction at the hands of the communards, the Palais des Tuileries, which dated back to the sixteenth century, was not rebuilt. The Republic preferred to raze the remains of the palace, and replace it with an *espace libre* that symbolized the obliteration of the monarchy. The space is now punctuated by Maillol's serene, powerful bronzes.

IMPRESSIONISM

By the end of the Second Empire, Paris was on the verge of becoming the art world's centre of gravity. Around the same time, Paris itself appeared more and more as the model for modern artists' canvases. Manet, for example, painted contemporary urban idylls such as concerts in the Tuileries, horse races at Longchamp, the masked ball of the Opéra, Saint-Lazare station and the bar at the Folies-Bergères.

In 1873, after years of arguing and experimenting, Manet, Edgar Degas and Paul Cézanne adopted the clear, bright colours that were to characterize the 'new school' of painting; and Claude Monet, Berthe Morisot, Auguste Renoir and Camille Pissarro banished grey from their palettes. The next year, these artists (minus Manet) organized an independent exhibition of their work in the *atelier* (workshop) of photographer Félix Nadar.

Misunderstood by the public, mocked by the critics, the show was a disaster. Monet's *Impression, Sunrise* (origin of the epithet 'impressionist', not intended kindly by the critic who coined it) sold for 1,000F, a mere pittance compared to the 10,000F or 20,000F that works by established Academic painters commonly fetched. But the new school continued to exhibit annually well into the 1880s. The death of Manet in 1883 marked the end of Impressionism's heroic Parisian period. After that, the artists dispersed. Renoir, Monet, Sisley and Cézanne were all absent from the group's final exhibition in 1886 – they refused to have their pictures hung in the same room as works by Gauguin and Seurat.

Many of the Impressionists, as well as their models, art dealers and friends, lived in or around Montmartre. Long after Paris was Haussmannized, the Butte, with its wells, thatched cottages, farms and windmills, retained a rustic atmosphere that appealed to artists. Coachmen refused to force their horses up the area's steep inclines; to hail a cab, residents of the mount's upper reaches had to descend to the place des Abbesses; omnibuses didn't climb any higher than the boulevard de Rochechouart. So, though it was officially within the city limits, Montmartre seemed positively pastoral. Cézanne rented an *atelier* on the Butte, and Manet (who lived near Saint-Lazare station) frequented the neighbourhood's cafés. He painted *Au café* and *La serveuse de bocks* at the Brasserie Reichshoffen on the boulevard de Rochechouart, where fellow artist Gustave Caillebotte resided. And painters of all persuasions hired models at the 'market' on the place Pigalle, at the foot of Montmartre.

Renoir, who lived on the Butte for years, and Degas, who resided just south of place Pigalle, left vivid records of *la vie montmartroise*: *La chanson du chien, La chanteuse au gant, Le café-concert. See also* chapter **Artistic Paris.**

Musée Marmottan
2 rue Louis-Boilly, 75016 Paris (42.24.07.02). Metro Muette. **Open** 10am-5.30pm Tue-Sun. **Admission** 18F.
A major selection of pictures by Claude Monet is on view here, including his famous *Impression, Sunrise* to which the school owes its name. Also on display are some fine works by Sisley, Pissarro and Renoir.

The hulking Romano-Byzantine pastiche that crowns the Butte Montmartre, the **Basilique du Sacré-Coeur** *(listed under* **Shootings***) was born of a vow of penitence made by French Catholics after the nation's defeat in 1870. In 1873, the National Assembly declared the basilica a state project, and provided land and additional funds. The architect, Abadie, adapted a Syrian-style plan for the sanctuary, adding a hint of Byzantine flavour (à la San Marco) and a sprinkling of Gothic gargoyles. Easier to take in from afar than at close hand, the Sacré-Coeur is now regarded with affection even by those who doubt its aesthetic value.*

Musée de l'Orangerie
Jardin des Tuileries (Terrasse du Bord de l'Eau), 75001 Paris (42.97.48.16, ext 406). Metro Concorde or Tuileries. **Open** 9.45am-5.15pm Mon, Wed-Sun.
Admission 15F, 6F Sun.
Within this Second Empire pavilion is housed the Walter-Guillaume collection of late-nineteenth and early-twentieth-century paintings. Works by Soutine, Cézanne, Derain, Renoir, Matisse, Rousseau and others hang in the first-floor galleries; on the ground floor, two large, windowless rooms are given over to Monet's *Water Lilies.*

CAFE CONCERTS

From the 1870s, through the *belle époque* before World War II, glorified beer halls, thick with smoke and lit first with gas, later with garish electric lights, were immensely popular with all Parisians. High up in the cheap seats, hatless women – in those days a woman in public *sans* hat was no lady – and men in cloth caps, threw cherry pips and orange peel at the rest of the audience. But respectable families, gents in evening clothes and women glittering with jewels, were also a common sight at spots like the Alcazar, the Ba-ta-Clan or the Moulin-Rouge. On stage, colourful *artistes* (think of Toulouse-Lautrec's posters of *Jane Avril* or *La Goulue*) danced, clowned, trilled sentimental ditties or belted out patriotic anthems and bawdy drinking songs; the public chimed in with the chorus, and riotous applause.

Writers and bohemian intellectuals frequented Montmartre's cabarets, where poets and satirists provided popular entertainment a cut above *caf'conc'* fare. The celebrated **Lapin Agile** *(see below)*, a rustic cabaret set at the foot of the Butte's sole remaining vineyard, was one of these. Local artists knew that they could count on the bearded old *patron*, Frédé, to stand them drinks in exchange for a picture or a song. At the dawn of the twentieth century, Montmartre was the seed-bed of modern painting, and Frédé's customers included Fauves (Vlaminck, Derain, Dufy), Cubists (Picasso and Braque would come over from the **Bateau-Lavoir**, *see below*), along with the 'literary cubists', Apollinaire, Mac Orlan and Max Jacob, and Modigliani, before he emigrated to Montparnasse.

Au Lapin Agile
22 rue des Saules, 75018 Paris (46.06.85.87). Metro Lamarck-Caulaincourt. **Open** 9pm-2am Tue-Sun. **Admission** 90F adults, 70F students (includes free drink). **No credit cards**.
A variety of cabaret acts incorporating songs, comedy routines, and poetry, can still be seen here

Le Bateau-Lavoir
13 place Emile-Goudeau, 75018 Paris. Metro Abbesses.
The birthplace of Cubism, where Braque and Picasso invented a new aesthetic that changed the way we see the world, was nothing more than a dilapidated wooden building. Destroyed by fire in 1970, it has since been rebuilt to house artists' studios and apartments.

EXPOSITIONS UNIVERSELLES

France celebrated its faith in science, technology and progress at the World Exhibitions of 1889 and 1900. The Centennial of the Revolution was commemorated in Paris from 6 May to 6 December 1889 with festivities that combined elements of a trade fair and a patriotic paean to Republican values. That exhibition left few landmarks in its wake, but the ones that can be viewed today reflect the political tenor of the times: a replica of Bartholdi's Statue of Liberty at the *pont de Grenelle, 75015 Paris*, Dalou's **Triumph of the Republic** and, of course, the **Eiffel Tower** (*see below* for both).

On 1 April 1900, another World exhibition greeted the new century. On the banks of the Seine an imaginary city sprang up, where nations from all over the globe vied with each other in constructing luxurious, fantastic pavilions. Not satisfied with such ephemeral constructions, Paris launched an ambitious building programme, which produced the Grand and Petit Palais, as well as the Pont Alexandre-III, with its elegant arch of moulded steel and extravagant decoration. And in July 1900, thanks to the Herculean efforts of engineer Fulgence Bienvenüe, the first line of the Paris *Métro* ferried passengers from the Porte Maillot to Vincennes in the unheard of time of just 25 minutes (instead of an hour and a half by carriage).

The Exhibition drew well over 50 million visitors, who marvelled at the wonders of electricity, rode on the exciting new Ferris wheel, and drank in the heady atmosphere of Paris. Some of that drinking (and eating) went on at the **Ritz**, where Escoffier served *homard en bellevue* to toffs who could afford it. And then there was **Maxim's** (*see below* for both).

The last ten years of the *belle époque* were a time of prestigious artistic activity in Paris. When the Countess Greffulhe – Proust's model for the ethereal Princesse de Guermantes in *Remembrance of Things Past* – bestowed her patronage on Debussy, Caruso, Mussorgsky, Diaghilev and his Ballet Russe, high-society snobs discovered that it was chic to favour avant-garde artists and musicians.

Eiffel Tower
75007 Paris. Metro Trocadéro and walk across Pont d'Iéna. **Open** 10am-midnight Mon-Fri; 10am-11pm Sat, Sun. **Admission** 45F adults; 23F under-16s. *See* **picture and caption.**

Le Triomphe de la République
place de la Nation, 75012 Paris.
Dalou's bronze group is less stiff and pompous than the statue on the place de la République, for which Dalou's work was originally intended. It is also more radical, for here the Republic is shown advancing in triumph, accompanied by Labour – personified by a blacksmith – and Justice. Executed in plaster for the Centennial of the Revolution, the statue was officially inaugurated ten years later.

Maxim's
3 rue Royale, 75008 Paris (42.65.27.94). Metro Concorde. **Open** noon-2pm, 8-11.30pm, Mon-Fri; noon-2pm, 8pm-1.30am, Sat. **Credit** AmEx, DC, V.
Maxim's – 'where all the girls are dreams' – won worldwide fame during the 1990 Exhibition. On 22 September 1900, President Emile Loubet threw an epic luncheon party for the mayors of France. Waiters on bicycles served salmon, *filet de boeuf*, pheasant and numerous desserts, along with vintage claret, champagne, Cognac and rum (distilled in the colonies, of course) to 22,295 mayors, all assembled under twin marquees in the Tuileries gardens. 'Funny', remarked a wag, 'but I've noticed that every time we're more than 20,000 at table, one of us always dies within the year.' Later that day, several of these provincial notables staggered up the rue Royale to Maxim's and demanded more to drink. One thing led to another, and the evening ended with a riot. Don't go to Maxim's for the food, or even for the atmosphere (it doesn't bubble anymore) but do pop in for a glimpse of the incomparable décor.

The mur des fédérés *in the south-east corner of the* **Cemetery of Père-Lachaise** *(listed under* **Shootings***) still draws many pilgrims from leftist political organizations, for whom it remains a powerful symbol of struggle and courage. This vast, handsomely landscaped cemetery is also a veritable museum of nineteenth-century funerary sculpture. Colette, Chopin, Proust, Delacroix, Edith Piaf and rock-star Jim Morrison, among others, are buried here.*

THE GREAT WAR

On 2 August 1914, France learned
that the **Reich** had declared war on
Russia and that German patrols had
been detected on French soil. In the
streets of Paris, people sang the
Marseillaise, sacked German-
owned shops and beat up the proprietors. The next day, Germany
declared war on France, and the
Gare de l'Est became the busiest
site in Paris. Soldiers kissed their
sweethearts and jumped aboard
flower-laden trains bound for the
eastern front, confident that they
would be back from Berlin in a few
months, victorious…Flags flew all
over the city; butchers and bakers
hung out signs saying 'Closed temporarily; re-opening after victory'.

Victory proved elusive, and those
same shops soon put signs in their
windows announcing the rationing
of bread and meat.

On 2 September, **von Kluck**'s
army was just 15 miles from Paris.
The government took refuge in
Bordeaux, and the defence of the
capital was entrusted to **General
Galliéni**. Von Kluck crossed the
Marne south-east of Paris. The populace watched convoys of immigrants from the northern and eastern provinces roll into the city, while
they waited anxiously to learn the
outcome of the **battle of the
Marne**. By 13 September, the
Germans were pushed back to the
Dise, and Paris was safe. Until the
end of 1916, the war would rage in
the trenches of northern and eastern France. Paris industrialized to
produce weapons and chemicals.

By the autumn of 1917 a strong
current of defeatism infected the
government, the populace and even
the army. There was strong public
pressure for an immediate peace
settlement. But in November,
Georges Clémenceau, ex-mayor of
Montmartre and veteran of the

Commune, was made premier by
President Poincaré. 'The Tiger', as
Clémenceau was called, injected a
new fighting spirit into France. For
Parisians, it was not a moment too
soon. They needed a boost to survive a raging epidemic of Spanish flu
and the shells of Big Bertha – a
gigantic German cannon levelled at
the city from over 75 miles away.
The summer of 1918 saw the
Germans at the Marne once again,
but **Foch**'s counter-attack forced the
assailants to retreat. With the arrival
of American reinforcements, Foch
could launch a final, successful
counter-offensive.

On 11 November at 11am, the
shooting stopped. At 4pm Parisians
poured out onto the place de l'Opéra
and the Grands Boulevards in a
tumultuous show of joy and grati-
tude. The celebration in the streets
lasted for days.

MONTPARNASSE

With the return of peace, the
fabled post-war era of fun and
frivolity began in Montparnasse.
Throughout the twenties the area
was an international attraction.
As early as 1910, avant-garde
artists – Derain, Soutine, van
Dongen, Chagall, Kisling,
Modigliani and Picasso; the
entire *Ecole de Paris* – had abandoned Montmartre for
Montparnasse. Artists' colonies,
such as *La Ruche* (the hive)
where Expressionism reigned,
and cafés clustered around the
rue Vavin became the talking
point of Paris. Following the misery, terror and grief of the war,
bohemian Montparnasse became
the white-hot centre of jazz-age
nightlife: Le Jockey opened in
1923, its crowded dance floor and
bar attracting a cosmopolitan
crowd that included Cocteau,
Aragon, Hemingway and Man
Ray's model and paramour, Kiki
de Montparnasse. On the rue
Blomet, Le Bal Nègre – not to be
confused with Josephine Baker's
Revue Nègre, which performed
at the Théâtre des Champs-
Elysées in 1925 – brought a
mixed crowd of Antilleans, artists
and night owls together to dance
and get a kick from the powerful
rum cocktails.

*Hector Guimard's exuberant **Métro** entrances – Abbesses, Blanche, Porte
Dauphine and others – inspired by the fluid, flexible lines of flowers, vines and
dragonfly wings, epitomized the 'modern style' that triumphed in the decorative
arts, and to a lesser extent in architecture, around 1900.*

On 20 December 1927, a new chapter in the history of Montparnasse began, with the opening of **La Coupole** *(see chapter* **Restaurants***)*, then as now, one of the nerve centres of Montparnasse life. Inaugurated with one of the most fabulous parties in the annals of the *quartier*, attended by Foujita, Vlaminck, Cocteau and Blaise Cendrars, La Coupole was an immediate success. The Surrealists soon adopted it for their Left Bank HQ. On the brasserie's brown velvet benches poet Louis Aragon met his muse Elsa Triolet, and André Breton planned scandals with his band of bad-boy poets and painters (Eluard, Desnos, Max Ernst).

URBAN VIOLENCE

The Depression didn't hit France until after 1930. But when it arrived, its repercussions disrupted an already precarious social balance and unleashed a wave of urban violence. The Stavisky scandal, a monumental financial swindle mounted by a con-man with alleged government connections, lit the fuse of a crisis. On 6 February 1934, extreme right-wing groups, including avowed fascists, demonstrated in Paris against a corrupt regime. Thirty thousand rightists, at least half of them World War I veterans, shouted 'Down with the thieves' as they converged on the place de la Concorde, just across the Seine from Parliament. Through the afternoon, tensions mounted, nearly reaching the point of spontaneous revolution. Veterans tried repeatedly to break through police cordons and invade the *Chambre des Députées*. Fire hoses and bullets beat the protesters back. Fifteen were killed, and 1,500 wounded. Not since the Commune had so much blood been shed in Paris.

The events of 6 February caused intense emotion on the Left. Violent counter-demonstrations took place within the week. The seeds of the **Popular Front** were sown at this time; socialists and communists forgot their differences in the face of the Fascist threat and the worsening economic plight of the working class. The union of the Left was cemented at public events that rallied hundreds of thousands of supporters, such as the

The **Eiffel Tower** *(listed under* **Expositions Universelles***) is a bold engineering feat , the apotheosis of iron architecture. As the tower went up, gawkers followed its progress with interest; they were intrigued, fearful, enthusiastic or appalled. A posse of indignant artists – including Charles Garnier, architect of the Opéra – protested violently: 'Foreigners will mock us, and with reason, for the sublime city of the Gothic masters, of Jean Boujon and Germain Pilon will henceforth be known as the Paris of Monsieur Eiffel.' And in a way they were right, since today the Tour Eiffel is as much a symbol of Paris as Nôtre Dame or the Louvre.*

14 July rally parade of 1935, and the ceremony on 24 May 1936 at the *mur des fédérés* *(see above* **Shootings***)*, honouring those who died for commune.

Following the triumph of socialist **Léon Blum**'s Popular Front at the polls in 1936, France was paralyzed by massive sit-down strikes. In the Paris region, workers at over 1,200 companies sang, danced, ate and confabulated, while owners and managers looked on, terrified by this unprecedented job action. Workers wanted the government to know that they had no intention of waiting for reforms to be enacted. And indeed, their demands were met in the euphoric 'workers' spring' of 1936; they obtained the right to unionize, have higher salaries, a 40-hour week and, for the first time, paid holidays.

But the worm turned when the government reconvened in the autumn. Debate about the Spanish War divided the coalition; the bourgeoisie, which execrated the Popular Front, took their money out of the country; unem-

ployment soared and production dropped; the franc was devalued. Blum's one-year-old government fell in June 1937. France was within an inch of a revolution. The working class was disenchanted, seeing their hopes dashed once again; right-wing parties grew, feeding on people's visceral fear of communism, which to many seemed a far more immediate threat than Hitler.

Yet war was once again upon the horizon. In September 1938, upon his return to Paris from Munich, where he and Neville **Chamberlain** had sold Czechoslovakia down the river, Premier Edouard **Daladier** was astonished to hear himself acclaimed by a crowd of Parisians for having 'saved the peace'. Tragically – if understandably, having been traumatized by the losses of the Great War and preoccupied with grave social conflicts – each camp of a France that was divided into fascist and bolshevik, bourgeois and socialist, right and left, feared the enemy within far more than the real enemy that was waiting on its doostep: Hitler.

The War

Under occupation some Parisians continued to live as they always had done – by becoming collaborators. Others joined the Resistance.

England and France declared war on Germany in September 1939. The *drôle de guerre* (phoney war) lasted through the winter of 1939-40. It was characterized by false alarms of impending invasion, bitter squabbles between the French and the British and a frenzied attempt by France to update her existing forces in the hope of withstanding Hitler's offence. As the storm clouds gathered, life in the *City of Light* continued much as before, except that curfews and black-outs put a brake on the capital's usual *joie de vie*.

Domestic unrest resulted in a cabinet crisis in March 1940. A new prime minister brought a fresh mood of optimism but it was short-lived. On June 6, the Germans broke through French lines and marched on the capital. A shell-shocked government wrung its hands of the affair, requisitioned transport and left for Bordeaux. Archives and works of art such as the *Mona Lisa* were hurriedly hidden or bundled off to safety just in case they came under the covetous gaze of Field Marshal Goering. Thousands of ordinary Parisians threw belongings into cars, into carts, prams and bikes and began their own exodus south.

By mid June, the tread of Nazi jack-boots rang on the cobblestones, Panzer tanks rolled down the boulevards and the swastika of the Third Reich fluttered menacingly over ministries and palaces. The city had been occupied without a fight. As the invaders began to settle in, the French cabinet voted to request armistice terms and **Marshal Pétain** – a World War I octogenarian hero – took over the reins of government. He chose pro-Nazi Pierre Laval as his right-hand man. The Germans decided to occupy two-thirds of France and make their host pay for the pleasure of occupation. Unsurprisingly, the French army and navy were immobilized. The French government moved to **Vichy** – in the unoccupied southern part of France – and decided they had no choice but to collaborate with the Nazis. Disgusted by this turn of affairs, at least two dozen notable cabinet members left for North Africa to try and set up a government-in-exile. The brilliant and autocratic **Charles de Gaulle** – at 49 the youngest general in the French army – went to London where he founded **The Free French** movement which rejected both the Nazi domination and the Vichy peace-makers. Though wary at first, by the end of the war Churchill was giving him enormous support, as did the BBC who helped broadcast messages to his agents in France.

Arc de Triomphe
Place Charles-de-Gaulle, 75008 Paris. Métro Charles-de-Gaulle-Étoile.
See **picture and caption.**

Back in Paris, numbed inhabitants were waking up to the fact that there was a war on and war for most Parisians would mean going without a lot of the creature comforts they'd previously enjoyed. For the Nazis, Paris was the western headquarters of the *Werhmacht* (the German Armed Forces) and an attractive assignment compared to events on the eastern front. They lost no time in requisitioning food and wine, lapped up luxury goods and swamped Paris's best nightspots, restaurants and hotels. There was no shortage of Parisians who accepted them, *Parisiennes* who warmed to an enemy offering a champagne life style for collaborators. In the entertainment world, there were also those who spurned patriotism and continued to dance, sing and perform for their new masters. Crooner Maurice Chevalier and impresario Sacha Guitry were later accused of collaborating. At the end of the war, the actress Arletty was gaoled for striking up a less than professional liaison with a German. The famed couturier, Coco Chanel, received criticism of a similar nature. There was a prevailing mood that as long as Paris glittered – and for some it certainly did – then the fact that the capital was being exploited by an emsemble of soulless and committed fascists, was – to some – a secondary consideration to that of having a good time.

Occupied Paris had its share of pro-Vichy bureaucrats who preferred to work with the Germans and help oil their propaganda machine than embrace what many saw as a futile opposition. There were also *attentistes* (the wait and seers), and the *zazous* (black marketeers) who exploited the shortages to become rich on the back of Nazi rationing. No-one relished the thought of being hauled off to the torture chambers of the **Gestapo** at **Rue des Saussaies** in the 8th *arrondissement*, **Avenue Foch** or **Rue Lauriston**, both in the 16th, but many were willing to risk it. Treachery and heroism, submissiveness and resistance, co-existed in a city torn by allegiances.

Master-minded by de Gaulle in London, there was a large and very brave underground movement that harried the Nazis. By the summer of 1941, the first executions of the French by Germans had begun, in response to the activities of the patriots. Prisons filled up and train loads of Frenchmen were deported to work in German factories. Other, more sinister trains containing French Jews and those opposing the Third Reich, began to shuttle between the concentration camps and the capital. In its own way, Paris was beginning to be a thorn in the Third Reich's side.

Mémorial de la Déportation
square de l'Île de France, Île de la Cité, 75004 Paris. Métro Cité, Les Halles/bus 21, 96. **Open** every day. **Admission** free.
The Memorial is situated at the western end of the island, behind Nôtre Dame in a small public garden where the morgue once stood. Go down a few steps to the river level. The memorial is a stark yet moving reminder of the hundreds of thousands who were sent away under the German occupation of France. It was built by architect Henri Pinguisson and inaugurated by Général de Gaulle in 1960.

Musée de l'Armée

*Hôtel des Invalides, Esplanade des Invalides,
75007 Paris (45.55.37.67). Metro Varenne,
Latour-Maubourg/bus 28, 49, 69, 93.* **Open**
10am-5pm daily. **Admission** (valid for 2 consecutive days) 23F adults; 11.50F under-18s,
students, OAPs; free under-7s, soldiers in
uniform. **No credit cards.**
See **picture and caption.**

LIBERATION

June 1944: A beautiful summer
greeted an exhausted city. Four
years had taken their toll and a
great many had died. The resistance groups had dug themselves
even deeper underground into the
warren of sewers which snake
under Parisian streets. These
became their headquarters in the
final months before the Liberation.
For those determined to continue
as though nothing had happened,
fashion designer Jacques Fath had
just introduced his new *Mode
Martiale,* featuring broad shoulders,

wide belts and short skirts to save
on material. Much of it was made
out of wood fibres and Parisians
joked that when it rained termites
might appear in the hem of your
dress. For the *nouveaux riches* –
who maintained the black market –
the collaborators and their protec-
tors, there was still champagne and
caviar at Maxim's and the Lido. The
racing season continued at
Longchamp and Auteuil. Yves
Montand and Edith Piaf sang
together at the Moulin Rouge and
cinemas kept projectors going by
using bicycle pedals to generate a
current. Ballet, theatre and music
also survived the Nazi colonization.
While other cities burned, Paris
remained alive and largely intact.

Then came the Allied invasion on
the Normandy beaches (*see chapter*
**Trips Out of Town/Special
Interest**). The weakened German
troops began to retreat eastwards
and Parisians saw a real opportunity
to seize their city back from

German hands. First came strikes –
from 10 to 18 August – railway
workers, police and public servants
took action. Overnight, Parisians
were bereft of metro services, gas
and electricity. There was no radio
broadcasting and no news. Parisians
began to sense that liberation was
finally at hand, sweeping down
towards them from the north.

August 19: The lid was about to
blow. Early that morning the
Tricolore was hoisted over the Hôtel
de Ville. The **National Resistance
Council** called for insurrection.
Police troops occupied the
Préfecture which became the headquarters of the revolt. The **FFI**
(French Interior Forces) commanded by Colonel Rol occupied
official buildings and newspaper
offices. Resistance groups took over
several *Mairies,* whilst other militias
occupied **Les Halles** and the central Post Office in the **Rue du
Louvre.** Fighting broke out everywhere. That afternoon, the
Germans used tanks to attack the
Préfecture, but were forced to
retreat with 40 dead and 70
wounded. The Swedish consul general Raoul Nordling obtained a
truce from the German Governor-
General **Von Choltitz** who agreed
to stop pounding buildings taken
over by the Resistance. The truce
only lasted 48 hours amid sporadic
street-fighting. On August 22,
Colonel Rol sent up the cry:
'Everyone to the barricades!'. With
true revolutionary spirit, Parisians
once more took to the streets. The
fighting gained momentum;
German trucks, cars and tanks
were attacked and blown up.

August 23: An irate Hitler
ordered Von Choltitz to waste no
more time destroying the French
capital. Von Choltitz stalled. He had
orders to blow it sky-high, but
would he do it? Fighting had meanwhile spread to the Latin Quarter, to
the Ile de la Cité and around place
de la République and the Châtelet.
Meanwhile, the Allies were closing
in on the capital.

August 24: The Germans made
their final attack on the Préfecture
with Tiger tanks. By that afternoon,
free French troops led by **General
Leclerc** had arrived at Sceaux on
the outskirts of the city.

August 25: General Leclerc and
his Deuxieme Division Blindée (2nd
Armoured Division) entered Paris

A renowned symbol of France's power and influence, the **Arc de Triomphe**
(listed under **The Occupation***) has been used by invading armies to humiliate
the French in times of war: in 1871 the Prussians marched in triumph beneath the
arch, and from 1941 to 1944 (during the Nazi occupation), the edifice was almost
unrecognizable beneath swastika banners and flags. The architect, Soufflot, created
the Arc on a levelled hill for Napoleon in honour of the Grand Army. In 1920 a
body of an unknown soldier and an eternal flame were placed underneath the Arc.
This was to commemorate all who had fallen in the First Great War. Today, the
Tomb of the Unknown Soldier also honours those who died in World War II.*

On the second floor of Les Invalides is the **Musée de l'Armée** (listed under **Collaborators**). This huge military museum has a room that is devoted to World War II and to life in France under the occupation.

On the following day, a triumphant General de Gaulle made his way down the Champs Elysées to Nôtre Dame to hear a special mass of deliverance. On 2 April 1945, Paris was awarded the Croix de la Libération.

END OF WAR

Unlike London or Berlin, Paris rather than being at war had been under occupation. It lost many of its inhabitants but suffered little structural damage. There are no famous cabinet rooms, no war-time aerodromes or any other form of warlike construction. For that you must go to Normandy. In Paris, the most moving testimony to the occupation is the **Mémorial de la Déportation** (*see above* **Collaborators**). Plaques to Resistance members killed by the Nazis are scattered all over the city. However, traces of the Gestapo's sinister work have long been erased. In the courtyard of the Préfecture is a monument to the tragic losses during the closing days of the occupation and at the **Musée de l'Armée** (*see above* **Collaborators**) there is a room devoted to World War II. **The Musée de l'Ordre de la Libération** also houses exhibits relating to the French Resistance and you can visit the sewers which became the Resistance HQ during the occupation. The tomb of the unknown soldier under the Arc de Triomphe holds the remains of the dead of both world wars.

Musée de l'Ordre de la Libération
51bis boulevard de la Tour Maubourg, 75007 Paris (47.05.04.10). Metro Latour-Maubourg, Invalides, Varennes/bus 63, 93. **Open** 2pm-5pm Mon-Sat. **Admission** 5F.
Everything you always wanted to know about the French Resistance movement. Some of de Gaulle's manuscripts are also contained here.

Les Egouts de Paris (the sewers)
place de la Résistance (entrance at junction of pont de l'Alma), 75007 Paris (47.05.10.29). Metro Alma-Marceau/bus 42, 63, 80, 92. **Open** 3-7.30pm Wed-Sun. **Admission** 12F; free under-6s. **No credit cards.**
The Resistance HQ was based in the sewers of Paris. Today you can wander through these sinister tunnels and get an idea of how appalling it must have been to work from here.

and German resistance points surrendered one by one. That afternoon, General Von Choltitz was taken prisoner at the **Hôtel Meurice** (German HQ), met with General Leclerc and signed a capitulation. Again, thanks to the intervening diplomacy of Raoul Nordling, he had been dissuaded from giving the order to blow up Paris. In 1968, Von Choltitz would receive the Légion d'Honneur (the highest French military accolade) as thanks for not bowing to the genocidal orders he had received from Berlin. The German occupying forces had been routed and Paris returned to the French and, ultimately, to the free world.

With true Gallic exuberance, the city went wild. Paris was still a dangerous place, with snipers hidden on rooftops waiting to pick off soldiers or settle old scores. In the euphoria of the moment no one seemed to care. After General

Leclerc, the Americans arrived to a tumultuous heroes' welcome. And then, late in the afternoon, General de Gaulle arrived and was greeted and cheered by the Resistance leaders at the Hôtel de Ville. 'We are living minutes that go far beyond our paltry lives' he cried out to an ecstatic crowd.

On Liberation night, Parisians threw caution to the wind. On that balmy August evening, the streets were full of people dancing, drinking and eating supplies hidden away from the insatiable appetites of the Germans and saved 'for liberation day'. **Ernest Hemingway** – who had entered Paris with the American troops – dined at the Ritz and when he was handed his bill declared 'Millions to defend France, thousands to honour your nation but not one *sou* in tribute to Vichy' for at the bottom of his bill, the waiter had, unthinking, included the Vichy sales tax.

Post-war Paris

Freed at last of the Nazi yoke, Parisians began to look to the future and a new social consciousness.

NYLONS & G.I. JOES

Those who had led the fight against the Vichy government and the Germans felt that now was the time to build a new society and a new republic. The Vichy government's collaboration had vastly discredited the traditional right wing, which left the field clear for reformers. Resistance had created unity among very divergent political parties and, not surprisingly, de Gaulle was determined to capitalize on it. The National Resistance Council's postwar programme of reforms was uniformly approved by underground leaders and spokesmen of most prewar parties from left to right. Charles de Gaulle was proclaimed temporary President by popular demand and promptly moved back into his pre-war office in the Ministry of Defence. He began his first cabinet meeting with the words 'Well gentlemen, where were we?'

While the government of France tried to pick up the political pieces of a defunct system, Parisians resurrected their lives free of the Nazi yoke. The city had been spiritually shaken but was spared many of the physical atrocities seen elsewhere during World War II. For many, liberated Paris seemed like heaven on earth, an impossible dream that had miraculously survived the four years of occupation, to rise phoenix-like from the ashes.

The first tourists to arrive in Paris were members of the Allied armies, brash Americans who doled out nylons, chocolate, cigarettes and charm to anyone willing to entertain them. Life began to resemble normality, though there were ugly accounts to settle in those post-liberation days. Vigilante justice prevailed as neighbour turned against neighbour and accusations of collaboration began to fly. Mock trials were set up and severe punishments doled out to the *collabos*: women accused of sleeping with Germans, were often half-stripped, had their heads shaven and were made to walk down the middle of the street before the mocking jeers of fellow Parisians. Ironically, it was in 1945 that French women received the vote. Official records show that these special purge courts condemned 39,000 people to prison terms, 40,000 to a loss of civic rights for a determined period and 2,000 to death. Marshal Pétain was given life imprisonment but Pierre Laval was shown little mercy and met an ignominious end before a firing squad.

IDEALISTS

For a while, post-war Paris was a fairly grim place; shortages and rationing were in effect for many months. Nonetheless, the new-found freedom following the liberation was celebrated throughout Paris. On the Left Bank, Parisian intellectuals began to dust off their ideas and find voice once again. They gathered around Saint Germain des Prés in cafés – Deux Magots and the Café de Flore were favourites – or in bars such as the Montana and Tabou. New literature was born in Saint Germain together with a new life style. Not everyone was an existentialist, read Jean-Paul Sartre or craved a *raison d'être* but they rebelled on cue, clamouring for personal freedom and political expression. While Sartre wrestled with communist ideology and Simone de Beauvoir argued for the emancipation of the female psyche over a *café-crème* at the Deux Magots, Albert Camus stood for a new social consciousness. In his editorials in *Combat* – a post-liberation newspaper – Camus came to represent the anxieties of liberal consciences everywhere trying to come to terms with the horrifying revelations about concentration camps, the atomic bomb and the arrival of the Cold War.

Pre-war Paris had been the artistic capital of the world. Just after the war it still was. The doyens of the 'Paris School' – Picasso, Braque, Bonnard and Matisse – all lived in the south of France but painter Fernand Leger and sculptor Alberto Giacometti, another Saint Germain luminary, remained in Paris to work. Other new artists began to assert themselves in the late forties: Soulages, Manessier, Bazaine and Mathieu. It was soon clear that figurative painting was *passé* and abstraction had secured the interest of the art world. By the fifties there were so many exhibitions, painters and new galleries in Paris that it would be impossible to comprehensively list their work here. However, three painters dominated the period: Wols, an Austrian who patronized the Saint Germain cafés, Jean Dubuffet and Nicolas de Stael. By the time the latter died in 1955, New York was already replacing Paris as the art capital of the Western world.

The arts came through the Nazi occupation relatively unscathed. When Christian Dior introduced his *New Look*, the couturiers of the world still sat up and took note. However, the architecture of the fifties was marked by recurring ineptitude and lack of innovation. The US-sponsored Marshall Plan for the economic recovery of Europe enabled France to recoup economically from the crippling drain of the war years.

Post-war Paris became a magnet for thousands of French men and women for whom the capital represented a new and opportune dawn after the repression of occupation. The population rose dramatically: in 1946, there were 6.6 million inhabitants in Paris but by 1950 that number had increased by 700,000. In response to a housing crisis, which still remains unsolved, the state reacted by building several *Villes Nouvelles* (new towns) and low-income housing developments. These resulted in vast concrete monoliths, made possible by the post-war use of steel, reinforced concrete, glass and stainless steel. Land within the city, that would have once been used for industrial purposes, was given over to new residential blocks. Artistic flair and aesthetics played second fiddle to economics in the architecture of this time.

Café des Deux Magots
6 place Saint-Germain-des-Prés, 75008 Paris (45.48.55.25). Metro Saint-Germain-des-Prés/bus 39, 38, 63, 86, 95. **Open** 7am-1.30am daily; closed second week of January. **No credit cards.**
Still one of Saint Germain's trendiest places from which to watch *le monde*. Today there are few literary lions or even struggling artists sipping coffee – the prices are too high – but the new glitterati haunt the *terrasse* where the ghosts of Sartre and de Beauvoir hover disdainfully.

Café de Flore
172 boulevard Saint-Germain, 75006 Paris (45.48.55.26). Metro Saint-Germain-des-Prés/bus 39, 48, 63, 86, 95.
Open 7am-1.30am daily. **No credit cards.**
This place is a stone's throw from the Deux Magots. The Flore manages to seem less worldly. People in the know say you may trip over a philosopher or two at breakfast time. Movie stars come out at night.

Boulevard Saint Germain
75006 Paris.
Stroll along the boulevard or duck into side streets. Bookshops, art galleries and jazz bars in this recently smartened up *quartier* still remind one of how it must have been. A literary-artistic feel somehow prevails. There are more fur coats and Gucci loafers than corduroy jackets and blue berets, but earnest types do still stride down the Rue Jacob clutching tomes.

Musée d'Art Moderne
11 avenue du Président Wilson, 75016 Paris (47.23.61.27). Metro Iéna/bus 63.
Open 10am-5.30pm Tue, Thur-Sun; 10am-8.30pm Wed. **Admission** 35F adults; 20F students; free under-7s, OAPs.
Credit (bookshop only) A, DC, MC, FTC, V.
See **picture and caption**

COLONIAL WAR

De Gaulle relinquished office in 1946. Thereafter, French troops were constantly engaged in a doomed policy of saving France's Empire from disintegration. Algeria had no intention of remaining a colony, but the French government was adamant that it should and had no intention of abandoning the one million French *colons* living there. After the revolt in 1956, the socialist prime minister Guy Mollet sent in almost half a million French troops, the largest French expeditionary force since the Crusades. The army was understandably demoralized after capitulation to the Germans and then to the Vietnamese. (France's ill-fated involvement in Vietnam culminated in its defeat at Dien Bien Phu). They hadn't tasted victory since World War I. Moreover, many of the troops sent to Algeria were young conscripts and the reality of a war fought so far away from native soil was suddenly brought forcefully home to thousands of French families. The matter also gained a high profile in intellectual circles, and it was only a matter of time before the battle spread to Paris where plots were simmering against the regime.

During the winter of 1955-56, police troops prowled Paris trying to keep the peace. The nation, so jingoistic in the first bellicose flush of *après-guerre*, was becoming divided. The death knell of the Fourth Republic was to be rung in Algiers and not Paris. Mutinous army officers took over the government headquarters in Algiers and declared a revolutionary administration. The number of troops that might follow suit, and whether the country would erupt into total civil war, were questions which dogged the government. It was time, decided the Fourth Republic, to admit defeat and wheel the old demagogue out of retirement. De Gaulle came back with the understanding that he was to be allowed to rewrite the constitution and give France the republic she deserved.

There is no great monument, building, statue or museum which marks the post-war period in any way. Post-war Paris didn't need to rebuild since it had suffered no great war damage. Moreover, in France it is the state that builds and in the immediate post-war years, the French government was far too shaky to think about such niceties as embellishing its capital.

The **Musée d'Art Moderne** *(listed under* **Idealists***) contains the works of many post-war artists who live and work in Paris: Bazaine, Soulages, Esteve, Lapicque and Pignon.* See also chapter **Museums** *for more information on modern painters and sculptors.*

De Gaulle to Mitterrand

From the end of the Algerian war to the forth-right eighties; we examine the role of French politics and culture throughout those decades.

DE GAULLE VICTORIOUS

Ostensibly, De Gaulle was hauled out of village retirement to deal with the Algerian crisis. The wily General used time-honoured tactics: he appeared to promise one thing to the European settlers in Algeria, while negotiating with the Algerian rebel leaders for their country's independence. At the time, both Algiers and Paris were rocked by terrorist attacks, and the President escaped two assassination attempts, but in 1962 Algeria was proclaimed independent and some 700,000 embittered colonists came straggling back to France. Yet De Gaulle emerged once more into the political arena crowing victory, and the Gaullists were established as ruling the French roost.

France was at peace and economically prosperous. De Gaulle beamed down from his presidential throne like the monarch he wasn't. He commanded foreign policy, intervened in domestic policy when he felt like it, and reported to the nation at least twice a year, by means of carefully-orchestrated press conferences or using television, which had by now muscled its way into many French homes.

Spectacularly avant-garde and resolutely modern, the **Centre National d'Art et de Culture Georges Pompidou** *(listed under* **Pompidou's Paris***) is still a big draw for visitors – some six million a year come to see it. It's beginning to look a little frayed around the edges and could do with a new lick of paint. Time to call in the plumbers?*

PARISIAN SKYLINE

Television wasn't the only thing to invade Parisian homes: the consumer society was making its presence felt. The post-war baby boom, coupled with an increased prosperity, meant that the state was under pressure to provide new housing, or undertake the renovation of the old. For the burgeoning population – together with their dish-washers, TVs, radios, hi-fis and gadgets galore – was in dire need of more space. With this came the requirement for updating the metro and the need for new forms of transport, for example, the RER (*see chapter* **Travelling Around Paris**). Building new roads, highways and parking areas for a nation with an automobile fixation, also became a priority.

Between the years 1954 and 1962, the population of Paris swelled to 1.2 million inhabitants and in 1964 and 1965 urbanization plans were hastily drawn up to propel Paris into the twentieth century. Although historic areas were considered sacrosanct, at least a third of the city eventually succumbed to the demolishing ball and chain. New projects included several totally unsuitable high-rise constructions: the 'Manhattanization' of Paris was underway.

De Gaulle was no builder, and his monarchical tendencies stopped short of a desire to Haussmanize the capital. A hotchpotch of forgettable building styles emerged during his presidency, as architects flexed their muscles and tested the characteristics of new materials like reinforced concrete, steel and glass. The **UNESCO building** is worth taking a look at because of the contributions of Moore, Calder, Picasso and Miro, but the most spectacular skyline-breaker of the period is the **Tour Montparnasse**. This undistinguished office block soars into the skies above the 14th *arrondissement* in the centre of Paris; it vies with the Eiffel Tower for height. It is one of the only 'monuments' started during De Gaulle's presidency and is a building everyone loves to hate. The view from the top is spectacular.

The distinguished author André Malraux was de Gaulle's Minister of Culture. He took one look at the historic buildings in Paris and set

The old train station – Gare d'Orsay – was going to be turned into a hotel in the seventies. The idea was abandoned and it now houses the Louvre's nineteenth- and early twentieth-century collections in what is called the **Musée d'Orsay** *(listed under* **Last of the Gaullists***). The magnificent renovation job was masterminded by the Italian architect, Gae Aulenti.*

about their restoration. Off came the dirt of centuries and historic buildings took on a new lustre. He also legislated in order to protect certain historical areas, in particular the **Marais** (*see chapter* **Paris by Area**), which is choc-a-bloc with sixteenth- and seventeenth-century town houses. New conservation laws included legislation against putting up buildings which were out of context with or higher than those already in an area. Walk around the Marais and you will soon see that it is one of the few quarters left in Paris with something of a homogeneous architectural feel to it.

Tour Montparnasse
Place du 18 Juin, 75015 Paris. Metro Montparnasse. **Open** *April-Sept:* 9.30am-11.30pm Mon, Wed, Fri; 9.30am-6pm Tue, Thur; *Oct-March:* 10am-10pm Mon-Fri.
Paris's tribute to Manhattan, this steel and glass arrow is the tallest building in Europe, that is, until the Canary Wharf tower in London is completed. It's 200m/656ft high, and you can use it as a landmark if you get lost in central Paris. The view of the Left Bank from the top is terrific and the panoramic bar on the 56th floor will help keep you high. The tower mainly houses offices, but at the foot there is a shopping complex, a sports centre and an underground car park.

UNESCO Building
7 place de Fontenoy, 75007 Paris (45.68.03.59). Metro Ségur. **Open** 9am-6pm Mon-Fri. **Admission** free.
An American (Breuer), an Italian (Nervi) and a Frenchman (Zehrfuss) designed this building, which houses the United Nations' Education, Science and Culture Organization. It opened in 1958, and is made up of lots of concrete and glass. Stop by and see the huge Picasso composition on wood, a gigantic Calder mobile, a monumental Henry Moore and two large Miro compositions. A great treat.

NOUVEAU EVERYTHING

Political and economic stability affected the intellectual climate of Paris. The post-war mood of crisis was over and existentialism, with its overtones of gloom and doom, was also on the way out. Into the breach thundered a 'new wave' of cinema directors, novelists and critics, who breathed new life into Parisian culture. Michel Butor, Natalie Sarraute and Alain Robbe-Grillet industriously produced the 'new novel'; experimental 'anti-novels' devoid of storyline or distinguishable characters that baffled many readers. The novels worked better in cinematic form,

and among the more famous film versions are Alain Resnais's *Last Year at Marienbad* and *Hiroshima Mon Amour*. Saint Germain cafés were suddenly full of earnest young intellectuals, dropping Gauloises ash into their wine as they discussed the merits of new-wave film-makers such as Resnais, Jean-Luc Godard and François Truffaut.

All Parisians love a new *ism*, and they applauded happily when 'structuralism' made its literary début. Philosophers and critics borrowed the word and the concept from linguists, who were busy trying to analyse the form and function of language. Claude Levi-Strauss, France's leading ethnologist in the post-war years, tried to use structuralism as a way of understanding and comparing all human cultures from all periods. After 1960, he had a number of devotees who seized his ideas for their own purposes. These included psychologist Jacques Lacan, literary critic Roland Barthes and philosopher Jacques Derrida. Paris was holding fast to its claim to be the Western world's cradle for new ideas.

By 1968, 50 million people inhabited the Hexagon – the term by which the French describe France – which led one pundit to change a well-known slogan to *Liberté, Egalité, Maternité*. Whilst intellectuals thought great thoughts, youth chaffed against their yokes. Rock 'n' roll had given way to hard and acid rock, Elvis to the Stones and finally to Dylan, Joan Baez and the protest songs of the Vietnam war. The post-war babies had grown into their Levi's and their numbers were swelling the over-stretched French educational system. In fashionable Paris, as Yves Saint Laurent, Paco Rabanne and a 'new wave' of fashion designers stuck huge price-tags on *la mini-jupe*, in the student preserve of the Latin Quarter there thronged an ever-increasing crowd: long hair, frayed jeans, pot, easy sex and social unrest were its emblems. The time-bomb was about to explode.

MAY 1968

In May 1968 the students erupted. Angry at the appalling conditions in French universities, they took to the streets, burnt cars and chanted slo-

Some love it, some hate it, and it's certainly hard to keep clean; mountain climbers – a sight worth catching – are used to wipe off the mess left by persistent Parisian pigeons on the **Louvre Pyramid** *(listed under* **Grands Travaux***). This new edifice is flanked by three smaller pyramids that act as a hi-tech skylight and entrance. From the start the project had its opponents. What really makes French conservatives bristle is that Mitterrand, a socialist president, deliberately chose the Louvre, with its overwhelmingly monarchical associations, as the spot on which to leave his mark.*

gans. They occupied university buildings, and eventually the cops were called in. In keeping with long-standing Parisian tradition, the students prised up cobblestones and hurled them at police troops from behind hastily-erected barricades. Methods of police retaliation stopped just short of gunfire. The government wavered between repression and conciliation and the conflict spread to provincial universities like wildfire.

By mid-May workers and trade unions had joined in the protest. Strikes closed down one factory after another, and by 20 May, seven million French workers had stopped work. Public services broke down and transportation ground to a halt. Paris became a ghost city: the ministries were empty, the public buildings closed. Picket-lines stood before all major industrial buildings. Residential areas were deserted and an eerie quiet prevailed. People were glued to their radios for news as the acrid pall of tear gas hung over much of the city. In the Latin Quarter the battle raged on. Trees were uprooted, cars set alight and

slogans splashed across the walls. The chant 'Ten years, that's enough!' referring to De Gaulle's tenure in office, filled the streets.

Everyone knows the outcome. Disaster was avoided, but only just, and confidence in De Gaulle was sorely shaken. He continued to hold office for another ten months. Then, after losing a referendum – a vote of no confidence – he resigned and went back to his provincial retreat, where he died in 1970 at the age of 79. In the meantime, the cobblestones in Paris were replaced and paved over, so that they could never again serve as ammunition.

POMPIDOU'S PARIS

Pom-Pom – as De Gaulle's successor was often affectionately called – didn't preside over any earth-shattering political developments during his time in office. What he did do was begin the process that changed the architectural face of Paris radically, and which firmly afixed the

state's signature on some of the most monumental building schemes since those of Haussmann and the Third Republic.

It was Georges Pompidou, a right-wing conservative, who took the decision to implant an uncompromisingly avant-garde building into the heart of one of Paris's oldest neighbourhoods. At the time – this was 1969 – conservatives and socialists alike (with the notable exception of François Mitterrand), condemned the **Centres Georges Pompidou**. It was the brainchild of English architect, Richard Rogers, and Italian Renzo Piano, and critics accused it of looking like a bunch of sewerage pipes, which had no place in the historic Beaubourg area. Nowadays, this vast complex of tubes and glass draws six million visitors a year, and is one of France's most popular landmarks.

Pompidou also gave the go-ahead to the clearing of **Les Halles**, which housed the main Parisian market and was situated near the Pompidou Centre, as well as the plateau Beaubourg project in the same area.

Paris in the fifties and sixties owed its intellectual life essentially to its writers, thinkers and emerging filmmakers. May 1968 changed all that. Ideologies had been put to the test, taken out into the street and found wanting. A new, more materialistic, complacent generation was on its way, heavily subsidized by transatlantic exports. In the early seventies, fast food greased its way onto the Paris scene. A 'drugstore' opened on the Champs Elysées and more and more bright French graduates jetted off to the USA to get an MBA.

Le Quartier des Halles
75001 Paris. Metro Châtelet, Les Halles.
Punks, pickpockets and pleasure-seekers prowl around the old market-place of Paris, which was dismantled in 1969 and transported to Rungis. In its place is the large Forum des Halles, an underground complex devoted to consumer goodies. The Carreau des Halles is full of shops, fast food eateries, cafés and junk. *See also chapter* **Paris by Area.**

Centre National d'Art et de Culture Georges Pompidou
Plateau Beaubourg, 75004 Paris (42.77.12.33/recorded information 42.77.11.12). Metro Châtelet, Rambuteau/bus 29, 38, 47. **Open** noon-10pm Mon, Wed-Fri; 10am Sat, Sun. **Admission** *to* MNAM; 23F adults; 17F 18-25s, OAPs; free under-18s; *Galeries Contemporaines:* 16F adults; free under-13s; CCI: 15F adults; free under-13s; *temporary exhibitions: admission varies;*

Day-pass to all exhibitions: 50F adults; 45F 13-25s, OAPs; free under-13s. **Credit** (bookshop only) DC, MC, V. *See* **picture and caption.** *See also chapter* **Museums.**

LAST OF THE GAULLISTS

Valéry Giscard d'Estaing became president in 1974, on the sudden death of Georges Pompidou. His relative youth and informal style reminded many people of John F Kennedy, and he made clear his desire to transform France into an 'advanced liberal society'. In 1977 he inaugurated the Pompidou Centre and promptly embarked on some projects of his own. Notable among his decisions were those to transform the defunct but monumental **Gare d'Orsay** into a museum that would house the nineteenth- and early twentieth-century collections of the Louvre; and the creation at **La Villette** of a museum of science and technology in the vast sales hall of the old abattoirs in the north of Paris. Another of his projects was

the creation of an **Institut du Monde Arabe**. These building schemes were all successfully inaugurated by Giscard's successor, François Mitterrand.

Musée d'Orsay
1 rue de Bellechasse, 75007 Paris (40.49.48.14/recorded information 45.49.11.11). Metro Solferino/bus 24, 68, 69. **Open** 10am-6pm Tue, Wed, Fri-Sun; 10am-9.15pm Thur. **Admission** 23F adults; 12F 18-25s. OAPs; free under-18s. **Credit** (bookshop only) AmEx, MC, V. *See* **picture and caption.** *See also chapter* **Museums.**

La Villette
30 avenue Corentin Cariou, Cité des Sciences et Industrie, 75019 Paris (46.42.13.13). Metro Corentin Cariou, Porte de la Villette/bus PC. **Open** *Inventorium sessions:* 11am, 12.30pm, 2pm, 3.30pm, Tue, Thur, Fri; extra session 5pm Wed, Sat, Sun. **Admission** *day pass to Cité des Sciences:* 30F adults; 12F under-16s (extra charge for Discovery Space and Planetarium); *ticket for Inventorium only:* 15F per session. **Credit** A, MC, V.
Paris's principal cattle market and abattoir along the Ourcq canal was previously an insalubrious spot. Then it was transformed into the Parc de la Villette, complete with a science museum, a 'Géode' – a kind of geodesic dome – a grand hall and the Zenith musical auditorium. La Villette features Bernard Tschumi's deconstructivist architecture, which is great fun.

Institut du Monde Arabe
23 quai Saint Bernard, 75005 Paris (40.51.38.38). Metro Jussieu, Cardinal-Lemoine/bus 24, 63, 89. **Open** *museum:* 1-8pm Tue-Sun; *library:* 1-8pm Tue-Sun; *temporary exhibitions:* 10am-10pm Tue-Sun. **Admission** *museum:* 20F adults; 10F students, 18-25s, OAPs; free under-18s; *temporary exhibitions:* usually the same as museum; mixed tickets available. **No credit cards.**
A joint agreement between France and 19 Arab countries resulted in the decision to build an Institute of the Arab World in Paris. The architect, Jean Nouvel, won the Agha Khan prize for architecture in 1989 for the building, which is all glass and steel. It has a very complicated system of window shuttering which opens and closes against the light, reminiscent of traditional Arab *musharabia* or wooden screens. *See also chapter* **Museums.**

GRANDS TRAVAUX

France was getting tired of the Gaullist élite. In an abrupt political turn-around, the socialists, led by François Mitterrand, swept into power in 1981. The mood in Paris was electric. On election night, 75,000 people gathered at the Colonne de la Bastille draped in red flags and sang *Le roi Giscard est mort* (the king Giscard is dead) showing that France, even though a republic, is still haunted by its days under the Ancien Régime.

Socialist France is not wildly different from Gaullist France. After a few hiccups – nationalizing some banks and industries – the socialists dropped many of their hardline tactics and settled into a comfortable bourgeois rule. There was a wave of terrorist bombing and further student unrest in 1986, but on the whole life in France was pretty stable and prosperous during the eighties.

Right from the beginning of his presidency, François Mitterrand cherished ambitions of his own for transforming the landscape of Paris. His first operation was the most daring: open-heart surgery on the **Louvre**. This former royal palace had remained unchanged for 200 years: it was high time, said Mitterrand, to prop up its prestige. He called on I M Pei, the Chinese-American architect, to take charge. The result was a vast underground reception and ticket area, crowned by a glass pyramid which rises 22 metres (72 feet) into the Cour Napoleon.

Plagued by bureaucratic bloopers, six months after its opening the **Opéra Bastille** *(listed under* **Grands Travaux***) still had not announced its forthcoming musical programme. Its opponents call the style of the building lavatorial, while local residents try unsuccessfully to ignore the monster.*

*At the end of the sixties the decision was taken to build a high-rise city just outside Paris. La Défense was the result. About 100,000 people work here, but only 20,000 actually live in this futuristic Manhattan-style town, near the banks of the Seine. The recent addition of the **Grande Arche** (listed under **Grands Travaux**) has put La Défense on the tourist map, but only just.*

the great cube, so giving a new twist to the historic vista.

President Mitterrand's *Grands Projets* have not necessarily met with uniform acclaim. On the other hand, no one questions the right of the President or the state to devote huge sums to the contemporary embellishment of the French capital. Thanks to the tentacular nature of the French state, Paris has been able to apply strict zoning laws to building schemes, and so maintain its magnificent perspectives. But many Parisians agree with Mitterrand that to keep the urban fabric of Paris alive, new blood must be injected into it regularly. Paris offers tremendous scope for architects the world over, for chauvinism is conspicuously absent from the international competitions held to select candidates for projects of such magnitude.

By electing him to office for a second term in 1988, the French people have demonstrated their liking and respect for 'Ton-Ton', as Mitterrand is more commonly known. They are therefore prepared to indulge him in his most recent project: the Grande Bibliothèque de France, a new national library to replace the existing, heavily over-strained, Bibliothèque Nationale. This time a French architect has been chosen: he is 35-year-old Dominique Perrault and the chosen site is at Tolbiac close to the Seine.

Worse still for the conservatives who ran the coalition government of 1986-88, the Louvre project had a corollary. This was the transfer of the Ministry of Finance from the Rivoli wing of the palace to a new site at **Bercy** on the Seine. The Bercy office complex, designed by the French architect Paul Chemetov and his Chilean partner Borja Huidobro, is the largest of its kind in Europe. It's anchored in the Seine to the east of Paris and extends for 225,000 square metres (about two and a half million square feet) across a former industrial site behind the Gare de Lyon. Conservatives viewed the move as banishment to a Gulag.

Choice of the Bercy site was part of a vast programme for the urban renewal of eastern Paris. No one was surprised when Mitterrand decided on the historic place de la Bastille for his third big scheme: the new opera house. The cry went up: does Paris, home to Napoleon III's magnificent Palais Garnier, really need another opera house? Mitterrand appeared to think so, and called for an international competition of entries that

would be anonymous, to select an architect. The winner out of the ensuing 6,000 candidates, was the little-known Carlos Ott. But the French practice of giving unknown architects a chance can backfire. For many, the **Opera Bastille**, which opened in July 1989, is a hideous anomaly, totally dwarfing its environment. Moreover, bureaucratic squabbles held up its opening and the cost of construction was a staggering £250 million.

In monumental terms, Mitterrand's new triumphal arch at **La Défense**, stands head and shoulders above his other grand schemes. This 25-storey, 300,000-tonne hollow cube sits slightly askew at La Tête Défense, the conglomeration of Manhattan-like skyscrapers west of Paris. Public debate long centred on the suitable shape for a monument which would open or close the historic axis running between the Louvre, the Place de la Concorde and the Arc de Triomphe. The winning project was designed by the late Danish architect Johan Otto von Spreckelsen. His Triumphal Arch of Man ends the perspective without closing it, by angling

The Louvre
rue de Rivoli, 75001 Paris (40.20.51.51).
Metro Palais Royal, Louvre/bus 21, 24, 69, 72, 74, 76, 85. **Open** *permanent collection:* 9am-9.45pm Mon, Wed; 9am-6pm Thur-Sun; *temporary exhibitions:* noon-10pm Mon, Wed-Sun. **Admission** 25F adults; 13F 18-25s, OAPs; free under-18s. **Credit** (bookshop only) A, V.
See **picture and caption.**

Opéra Bastille
place de la Bastille,75004 Paris (43.12.55.02). Metro Bastille. (Not open to the public at time of going to press.)
See **picture and caption.**

Ministères des Finances
quai de Bercy, 75012 Paris. Metro Bercy. Welcome to the largest ministerial complex in Europe. It is not open to visitors, but you can get a good view of it if you stand on the Pont d'Austerlitz and look downriver.

Grande Arche
Tête Défense: 2km/1.2 miles from Paris. RER La Défense. For more information, contact EPAP, tour FIAT, La Défense, 6 place de la Coupole, Paris (47.96.24.24).
See **picture and caption.**

Paris Today

Today's Paris is a city that refuses to sit still. Or rather President Mitterrand refuses to see it become a museum, the privileged enclave of foreign tour operators.

Mitterand – the socialist President who wants to see Paris become the 'capital' of Europe – is at odds with Paris's mayor since 1977, Jacques Chirac, a right-wing conservative who was briefly Prime Minister under the ill-starred coalition years of 1986-88. Chirac, who rules his fief with an iron fist, is often accused of turning Paris into a city for the rich, and although the capital is surrounded by 'red-wing' communist-dominated outlying areas, most Parisians are right-wing when it comes to local elections. The mayor of Paris seems intent on snubbing government-inspired projects: witness his behaviour during the recent Bicentennial celebrations, when he refused to attend the government-sponsored Grand Parade down the Champs Elysées on 14 July.

Stroll around central, historic, Paris today and you can't help feeling it's comfortably complacent as it prepares to take its place in a unified Europe. There's no reason why it shouldn't be pleased with itself. It

certainly has a lot going for it, despite the problems – traffic, pollution, housing – that beset most capital cities today. Thanks to Mitterrand's building projects, a

strong streak of French arrogance and the determination to be number one, the city never slumbers. It is constantly renovating, shifting, changing. But Parisians themselves are equally responsible for making Paris what it is.

CHIC LIVING

Parisians have three great loves: haute cuisine, haute couture and haute culture – not necessarily in that order. Paris has become a foodie's Mecca, with its temples of great cuisine like Taillevent, Lucas Carton and the Tour d'Argent. There are also more humble bistros and cafés, to say nothing of its Burger Kings, and the myriad of ethnic joints which pop up all over the city. Fashion also runs rampant. The big *couturières* still hold sway in the avenue Marceau or the Faubourg Saint Honoré, but the new fashion gurus, like Thierry Mugler, Jean-Paul Gaultier and others, like to convert warehouses in more down-market districts or inhabit tiny Left Bank boutiques around Saint Germain, now *the* area for aspiring French yuppies. The staid 16th *arrondissement*, once the last word in chic living, has given way to the Left Bank, forcing out its last remaining cultural relics. The artists, writers and dilettantes have pushed off to the newly trendy east of Paris around the Bastille, where they have begun to take over artisans' lofts and workshops, so forcing the latter's departure to the suburbs. And so on...

PARISIAN TRAITS

Have you ever noticed how many pharmacies, patisseries and bookshops there are in Paris? The French are health-obsessed and will take any pill that is offered yet stubbornly refuse to admit the dangers of cholesterol, which lie in wait in the form of sweet, eggy delights greedily indulged in at *goûter* time. Guiltily, they repair to a bookshop to feed the intellect. The literary scene, however, is low-key, despite the fact

that more people watch *Apostrophes* – the book programme hosted by the popular Bernard Pivot – than any of the other dull offerings on French TV.

However, there are more art galleries today than there have ever been, mostly collected around Beaubourg, with strange names like Neotu or Waiting for the Barbarians; and Philippe Starc, whose Café Costes is definitely worth a visit – particularly the loos – is one of an increasing number of new designers beginning to make their mark on Paris. Cinema is also big in Paris now, though exciting new French directors are scarce, and American films are dominating the screens.

Parisians grumble about transport, about traffic (which is really bad) and about the cost of living – rents have sky-rocketed. Recently they grumbled about the celebrations for the Bicentennial of the French Revolution, which got off to a slow start and culminated in ad-man Jean-Paul Goude's glitzy parade in the dark on 14 July 1989.

POLITICAL GRIPES

When they're not actively grumbling, Parisians are worrying about racial integration and whether or not Moslem girls should be allowed to wear the veil in French state-run schoolrooms. More importantly, they worry about the rising star of the National Front, ultra-conservative Jean-Marie le Pen, whose racist tendencies would have met with Hitler's thorough approval. With President Mitterrand's re-election in 1988, the socialists have a narrow majority in Parliament and are having to prove they are fit for the the task of bringing France into a united Europe in 1992. The right-wing parties are in such disarray that they don't offer much of an alternative, and most people would like to avoid seeing another coalition government, with each side bent on sabotaging the other's moves. Recent worries also include a fear of German reunification and the possible threat that might pose to French supremacy in Europe. For above all, left-wing and right-wing supporters alike regard Paris as the capital of a united Europe. They may well be right.

Eating and Drinking

Whether you wish to treat your-self to the best haute cuisine that money can buy, or sample some simpler but equally irre-sistible local cooking, Paris offers a range of restaurants that few cities could match. On the following pages we list a selection of the best restaurants, bistros and brasseries, cafés, *salons de thé* and bars in the French capital. If the thought of navigating your way through a menu *en français* has you head-ing for the nearest fast-food chain, a browse through our A La Carte section will help you distinguish between *darne de saumon avec pommes dauphine* and fish and chips.

CONTENTS:

A la Carte

A quick look through this menu might help you avoid making a terrible *faux pas*.

THE MENU

Eating out should be a pleasurable experience. Yet menus are fraught with danger. Before embarking on a foodie expedition, brush up on restaurant terms and culinary jargon; it might make the difference between you eating what you wanted and what you actually ordered.

A

Aiguillettes (de canard): thin slices of duck breast.
Anchoïade: spicy paste containing anchovies and olives.
Andouillette: sausage made with pig's offal, served cold.
Assiette: plate.

B

Ballotine: literally a 'small bundle' – a piece of meat or fish boned, stuffed and rolled up.
Bavarois: moulded cream dessert, flavoured with vanilla and cooked.
Beignet: fritter or doughnut.
Bisque: any kind of shellfish soup.
Blanquette: a 'white' stew (with eggs and cream).
Bouché: miniature vol-au-vent.
Boudin noir/blanc: black or white pudding, served grilled.
Bourride: bouillabaisse-type soup containing no shellfish.
Brochette: a kind of kebab.
Brunoise: tiny, diced vegetables.

C

Campagne: country-style.
Canard: duck.
Carbonnade: a beef stew with onions and stout or beer.
Carré d'agneau: leg of lamb.
Cassis: blackcurrants, also blackcurrant liqueur used in kir.
Cassoulet: stew, often with haricot beans.
Cèpes: spongy dark brown mushrooms.
Cervelles: brains.
Charcuterie: cold meat hors d'oeuvres, such as saucisson.
Charlotte: moulded cream dessert with a biscuit edge; there are also baked versions with fruit.
Chateaubriand: thick fillet steak, usually served between two with a béarnaise sauce.
Chaud: hot.
Chaud-froid: a sauce thickened with gelatine or aspic, used to glaze cold dishes.
Chèvre: goat's cheese.
Clafoutis: thick batter tart filled with fruit, often cherries.
Confit (de canard): potted duck.
Coquille: scallop or scallop-shaped dish used to serve fish, shellfish or poultry.

Coquille Saint-Jacques; scallops, usually cooked with mushrooms in wine, lemon juice and butter.
Cornichon: tiny tart pickle.
Crème anglaise: custard sauce.
Crème brulée: cream custard or flan with caramel glaze.
Crème chantilly: sweetened whipped cream.
Crème fraîche: thick, sour mix of cream and buttermilk.
Crépinettes: small, flattish sausages, often grilled.
Croque-madame: snack sandwich of toasted cheese and ham topped with an egg.
Croque-monsieur: snack sandwich of toasted cheese and ham.
Croustade: case of bread or pastry, brushed with egg and deep-fried.
en croûte: in a pastry case.
Cru: raw.

D

Darne (de saumon): salmon steak.
Daube: meat braised in a red wine stock with herbs.
Dégustation: tasting or sampling.
Duxelles: mushrooms sautéd in butter with shallots.

E

Estouffade: a dish containing meat that has been marinated, fried and braised.

F

Farci: stuffed.
Feuilleté: literally, 'leaves' of (puff) pastry.
Fines de claire: crinkle-shelled oysters which are fattened in special beds.
Fines herbes: mixture of herbs, usually parsley, chervil, chives and tarragon.
Flambé cooking: food tossed into a pan in which brandy or other alcohol is burning.
Florentine: with spinach.
Foie gras: liver of force-fed goose or duck, usually served as pâté. The process, called *gavage* in France, involves stuffing up to 6lb of salted, fatty maize down the bird's throat every day.
Fraise: strawberry.
Fraise des bois: wild strawberry.
Framboise: raspberry.
Friandises: sweetmeats.
Fricadelle: meat ball.
Fricassé of veal: fried in butter, simmered in stock, and finished with cream and egg yolks.
Frisée: curly endive.
Froid: cold.
Fromage: cheese.
Fromage blanc: smooth low-fat cheese.
Fruits de mer: seafood.
Fumé: smoked.
Fumet: fish stock.

G

Galantine: boned meat or fish pressed together, usually with a stuffing.
Galette: case of flaky pastry.

Garni: garnished.
Gelée: aspic.
Gibier: game.
Gigot: leg of mutton; gigot d'agneau: leg of lamb.
Gingembre: ginger.
Girolle: delicate wild mushroom.
Goujon: small strips of white fish, coated with egg and breadcrumbs and fried.
Granité: water ice.
Gratiné: browned with breadcrumbs or cheese.
Greque (à la): vegetables served cold in the cooking liquid including oil and lemon juice.
Grenouille (cuisses de): frogs' legs

H

Homard: lobster.
Huître: oyster.

I

Infusion: herbal tea.

J

Jambon: ham.
Jambon cru: cured or smoked ham.
Julienne: vegetables cut into matchsticks.

K

Kir: aperitif made with crème de cassis and (usually) white wine.

L

Langoustine: Dublin Bay prawns.
Lapin: rabbit.
Lardon: small cube of bacon.
Lotte: monkfish.
Lyonnaise: served with onions.

M

Mâche: tiny green lettuce.
Magret: choice part of a duck's breast.
Maison (de la): of the house.
Mariné: marinated.
Marmite: small cooking pot.
Marquise: light mousse-like cake.
Médaillon: a small round of any foodstuff cut into the shape of a medallion.
Mélange: mixture.
Merguez: spicy sausage.
Mesclum: salad of many varieties of exclusively green leaves.
Meunière: coated with flour, sautéd (q.v.), served with lemon.
Mignon: small fillet of meat.
Mirepoix: small cubes of vegetables, cooked with meat to heighten its flavour.
Morille: wild morel mushroom.
Mouclade: creamy mussel stew.
Moules (à la) **marinière**: mussels served with a reduced reduction of white wine, shallots, parsley, thyme, butter, lemon juice and the cooking liquid.
Mousseline: mixture that has been lightened by the addition of whipped cream or egg white.
Mousseron: delicate wild mushroom.
Moutarde: mustard.

N

Nage: aromatic liquid used for poaching.
Navarin: lamb and vegetable stew.
Noisettes: small round portions, usually of meat. Also hazelnut.

Noix: walnut.
Nouilles: noodles.

O

Oeuf: egg.
Offert: free.
Oie: goose.
Onglet: cut of beef, similar to entrecôte.

P

Pain: bread.
Pamplemousse: grapefruit.
Panaché: mixture.
Pané: breaded.
en Papillote: usually fish, cooked in paper and opened at the table.
Parfait: mousse-like mixture, can be sweet or savoury.
Parisienne (pommes): potatoes fried and tossed in a meat glaze.
Parmentier: with potato.
Paupiette: a thin slice of meat, stuffed and rolled into a cork shape.
Pommes dauphine: mashed potatoes mixed with egg, brushed with egg and baked.

Q

Quenelles: poached dumplings; made with fish or meat, mixed with a panade (bread and milk, thickened with egg yolk) and beaten egg, and shaped into little sausages.

R

Ragoût: brown beef stew.
Rognons: kidneys.

S

Sauté: fried lightly and rapidly.
Suprême (de volaille): fillets of spring chicken seasoned, dipped in flour, sautéd in butter, and covered in a rich sauce, usually containing cream.

T

Tarte tatin: a cold apple tart.
Timbale: dome-shaped mould, or food cooked in one.
Terrine: a rectangular earthenware dish or a pâté cooked in one.
Tisane: infusion.
Tournedos: small slices taken from the heart of a fillet of beef, sautéd or grilled; tournedos **Rossini**: garnished with noodles, Parmesan, foie gras (q.v.) and truffles, coated with Marsala or Madeira sauce.
Tripes: tripe.
Truffes: famous (and expensive) underground fungus.

V

Vacherin: a cake of round meringue layers filled with cream, fruit and ice cream; or, a soft, cow's milk cheese, wrapped in pine bark.
Vichyssoise: cold leek and potato soup.
Volaille: poultry.

SAUCES

THE CLASSICS

Sauces are crucial to classic French cooking. With the exception of coulis (literally, the juices that come out of meat during cooking, but the term now means a flour-free sauce or purée, sometimes sweet) and fumet (a liquid used to flavour or thicken stocks and sauces), nearly all the sauces in a *chef saucier*'s considerable repertoire are based on five core sauces, as follows:

Béchamel: a white roux with milk, onion and nutmeg flavoured with bouquet garni.
Common derivations:
Albuféra: with sweet peppers.
Mornay: with Parmesan.
Soubise: with rice and cream.

Demi-glace: reduced brown stock strengthened with meat jelly or strong veal stock.
Common derivations:
Bordelaise: with wine, shallots, herbs and beef marrow.
Charcutière: with white wine, chopped onions and gherkins.
Chasseur: with mushrooms, shallots, white wine and a dash of tomato purée.
Diable: with cayenne pepper, shallot, white wine.
Poivrade: with carrot, onions, celery, game trimmings, vinegar and freshly-ground pepper.
Robert: with onions, white wine and mustard.

Hollandaise: a rich sauce of butter, egg yolks and lemon juice.
Common derivations:
Béarnaise: with tarragon, vinegar and shallots.
Mousseline: with whipped cream.
Valois: Béarnaise with meat jelly.
Choron: Béarnaise with tomato purée.
Paloise: Béarnaise with mint.

Mayonnaise: egg yolks, vinegar, lemon juice and olive oil. Served cold.
Common derivations:
Chantilly: with whipped cream.
Remoulade: with mustard, gherkins, capers and anchovy.
Tartare: with hard-boiled egg yolks, vinegar, capers and parsley.
Verte: with spinach, watercress, parsley and herbs.

Velouté: white sauce made with white roux and bouillon.
Common derivations:
Allemande: bound with egg yolks.
Suprême: with cream, mushroom trimmings and a little meat jelly.

NEW SAUCES

Modern French cooking has spawned a number of new sauces, the most famous of which is:

Beurre blanc: butter whisked into a reduction of white wine and chopped shallots to form a rich emulsion.
Common derivation:
Beurre rouge: substitute red wine for the white wine.

Dining out in one of Paris's better restaurants need not be as expensive as some would have you believe. Many restaurants carry fixed menus; these offer excellent value for money, while a moderately priced wine won't add dramatically to the price of the meal.

Restaurants

A host of superlative and exotic restaurants awaits you in Paris; choose from the vast selection of food emporia specializing in French, Asian, North African or American cuisine.

As well as being the bicentennial of the Revolution, 1989 was also the year in which Paris celebrated the 200th anniversary – give or take a generation – of the birth of the modern restaurant. Today, there are approximately 12,000 cafés and restaurants in Paris, and virtually every country's cuisine is represented. Paris tends to act as a magnet, attracting much of the country's top culinary talent to the city's restaurants. Consequently, the capital is currently enjoying a Golden Age of dining.

As far as the restaurants serving strictly French cuisine are concerned, anything goes. There is an outstanding choice, to suit every mood, budget and appetite. The chefs at the grand restaurants have abandoned labels such as *nouvelle cuisine* and now proudly prepare personalized dishes. Regional cuisine is 'in' and hearty country cooking has never been more popular. Brasseries also are enjoying a tremendous new popularity and provide the opportunity to eat as much or as little as is desired.

For a glossary of common dish names and culinary terms, *see chapter* **A la Carte**. Below we give a few tips to help you work your way through the Paris restaurant world.

RESERVATIONS

Except for the very simplest restaurants listed here, it is wise – if not imperative – to book ahead. For most places, this can be done the same morning or the day before. More time should be allowed for the *grands restaurants*, as a few of them require reservations weeks if not months in advance. You must reconfirm your booking the day before, if you're going to one of these exclusive restaurants.

ETIQUETTE

Dogs are almost always allowed in French restaurants; children *usually* are. Parisians tends to under-dress and except for one or two of the Michelin three-star restaurants, clients can wear pretty much anything.

TIPPING

All restaurants, cafés and bars in France are now obliged to include a service charge in the bill. Therefore, no additional tip is necessary, though if you are pleased with the service, a supplementary five per cent or thereabouts left on the table is always appreciated. It is no longer the practice to 'palm' *maîtres d'hotels* or *sommeliers* (wine stewards) in the fancier places. One, global tip is quite enough.

LICENSING LAWS

Paris restaurants all serve wine and other alcoholic beverages, but will normally only do so with food, or to those customers who are waiting to be seated. Alcohol is available during a restaurant's opening times, whether it's the afternoon or early evening.

Average prices listed below are based on the cost of a starter, main course and dessert, but do not include drink.

HAUTE CUISINE

L'Ambroisie
9 place des Vosges, 75004 Paris (42.78.51.45). Metro Bastille. **Open** noon-2pm, 8-10pm, Tue-Sat. **Average** 700F. **Credit** MC, FE$TC, V.
One of only five Michelin three-star restaurants in Paris, L'Ambroisie is also the newest and the smallest. The handsome, Italianate décor of its restored townhouse on the Place des Vosges, refined and reserved cuisine of chef-owner Bernard Pacaud and discreet service, make this a jewel among restaurants. Book about a month in advance.
Babies, children welcome.

L'Arpege
84 rue de Varenne, 75007 Paris (45.51.47.33/45.51.20.02). Metro Varenne. **Open** noon-2pm, 7.30-10pm, Mon-Fri; 7.30-10pm Sun. **Average** 450F. **Set menu** (lunch only) 200F. **Credit** AmEx, DC, MC, FE$TC, V.
Young chef Alain Passard exploded on to the Paris scene immediately on opening his tiny restaurant in 1986. His creative ways –

especially with fish and desserts – are surprising and compelling. The wine list is among the best in Paris. Energetic, slightly boisterous atmosphere.
Babies, children welcome. Vegetarian dishes on request.

Le Bristol
112 Faubourg Saint Honoré, 75008 Paris (42.66.91.45). Metro Champs-Elysées-Clemenceau. **Open** noon-2.30pm, 7-10pm, daily. **Average** 550F. **Set menus** 370F, 450F. **Credit** AmEx, DC, MC, FE$TC, V.
Le Bristol is one of Paris's premier hotel restaurants. In spring and summer, meals are served in the new marble and glass garden room; in the autumn and winter in the elegant, wood-panelled elliptical dining-room. Chef Emile Tabourdiau, who has won the MOF award of Best Worker, is also one of the top hotel restaurant chefs in France.
Babies, children welcome.

Le Carré des Feuillants
14 rue de Castiglione, 75001 Paris (42.86.82.82). Metro Tuileries, Opéra. **Open** noon-2.30pm, 7.30-10.30pm, Mon-Fri; 7.30-10.30pm Sat; closed Sat July, August. **Average** 450F. **Set menus** 250F (lunch only), 490F incl ½ bottle of wine. **Credit** AmEx, DC, MC, FTC, V.
See **picture and caption**.
Babies, children welcome. Pets admitted. Vegetarian dishes on request.

Le Clos Longchamp
in Hôtel Méridien, 81 boulevard Gouvion-Saint-Cyr, 75016 Paris (40.68.34.34). Metro Porte Maillot. **Open** 7.15am-noon, 12.30-4pm, 7.30pm-1am, Mon-Sat. **Average** 500F. **Set menu** 400F (menu dégustation). **Credit** AmEx, DC, FE$TC, V.
The excellent restaurant of the Hôtel Méridien boasts a former Louis Outhier three-star chef and an award-winning *sommelier* (wine steward). The restaurant's horsey clientele and hot-house décor is compensated by the outstanding cuisine and service.
Babies, children welcome. Pets admitted. Vegetarian dishes on request.

La Couronne
in Hôtel Warwick, 5 rue de Berri, 75008 Paris (45.63.14.11). Metro Georges V. **Open** noon-2.30pm, 8-10.30pm, Mon-Sat; 8-10.30pm Sun. **Average** 400F. **Set menu** 290F. **Credit** AmEx, DC , MC, FE$TC, V.
On the bustling rue de Berri just off the Champs-Elysées, La Couronne has built a fine reputation for itself and the Hôtel Warwick, thanks to the skill of Dutch chef Paul Van Gessel and an excellent wine list. Almost unique in Paris for its separate, low-calorie menu. Piano-bar in the evening.
Babies, children welcome.

L'Espadon
in the Ritz Hotel, 15 place Vendôme, 75001 Paris (42.60.38.30). Metro Concorde, Madeleine. **Open** noon-11.30pm daily. **Average** 800F. **Set menu** 310F. **Credit** AmEx, DC, MC, TC, V.
The elegant restaurant of the Hôtel Ritz is one of only two Paris hotel restaurants with two Michelin stars. The classical, yet modern cuisine of chef Guy Legay is inspired; the service is impeccable; and famous wine steward Georges Lepré masterminds an excellent list.

Babies, children welcome. Vegetarian dishes by arrangement.

Faugeron
*52 rue de Longchamp, 75016 Paris
(47.04.24.53). Metro Trocadéro.* **Open**
noon-2pm, 7.30-10pm, Mon-Fri. **Average**
600F. **Set menus** 300F (lunch only), 460F,
600F. **Credit** MC, F£$TC, V.
Chef-owner Henri Faugeron is one of
Paris's most respected chefs; his small
but opulent restaurant near the Trocadéro
is a kind of elegant laboratory for his creations and revivals of provincial classics.
The wine service is supervised by the
Best Sommelier in the World award-win-
ner, Jean-Claude Jambon.
Children over the age of 10 admitted.

Gérard Besson
*5 rue du Coq-Héron, 75001 Paris
(42.33.14.74). Metro Palais Royal, Louvre.*
Open noon-2.30pm, 7.30-10.30pm, Mon-Fri.
Average 500F. **Set menu** 250F.
Credit AmEx, DC, MC, F£$TC, V.
An archetypal fine chef-owned restaurant,
serving a limited number of customers in
comfortable, quiet surroundings. Mr Besson
is famous for his *foie gras*, fish and game –
prepared with a strong classic style that is
unusual today. The wine list is outstanding.
*Babies, children welcome. Vegetarian dishes
on request.*

Le Grand Véfour
*17 rue de Beaujolais, 75001 Paris
(42.96.56.27). Metro Palais Royal.* **Open**
12.30-2.15pm, 7.30-10.15pm, Mon-Fri; 7.30-
10.15pm Sat. **Average** 600F. **Set menu** (lunch
only) 310F. **Credit** AmEx, DC, MC, F£$TC, V.
*See picture and caption.
Babies, children welcome. Vegetarian dishes
on request.*

Guy Savoy
*18 rue Troyon, 75017 Paris (43.80.36.22).
Metro Charles de Gaulle-Etoile.* **Open** noon-
2pm, 7.30-10.30pm, Mon-Fri; also open 2-
4pm Sat, winter only. **Average** 700F. **Set
menu** 575F. **Credit** MC, F£$TC, V.
Guy Savoy is one of Paris's top young
chefs. His uncanny ways with contrasts
and combinations of flavours, textures and
colours are appealing and, together with
the contemporary, green-and-beige dining-
room, make this one of the very top
Michelin two-star restaurants in Paris.
Service is crisp and professional.
Babies, children welcome.

Jacques Cagna
*14 rue des Grands Augustins, 75006 Paris
(43.26.49.39). Metro Saint Michel.* **Open**
noon-2pm, 7.30-10.30pm, Mon-Fri. **Average**
300F lunch, 500F dinner. **Set menu** (lunch
only) 250F. **Credit** AmEx, DC, MC, F£$TC, V.
Affable chef Jacques Cagna is a master at combining new cuisine with classic dishes. The
restaurant is located in a lovely seventeenth-
century town house and the soft lighting, terra-
cotta-coloured walls and period paintings make
it one of the most attractive in Paris.
*Children admitted. Pets admitted. Vegetarian
dishes on request.*

Jamin/Robuchon
*32 rue de Longchamp, 75016 Paris
(47.27.12.27). Metro Trocadéro.* **Open**
12.30-2pm, 7.30-10pm, Mon-Fri. **Average**
900F. **Credit** AmEx, DC, MC, FTC, V.

Chef Alain Dutournier of **Le Carré des Feuillants** *(listed under* **Haute
Cuisine***) has created an original mix of French city and rustic chic, imaginative
and rural dishes, in this handsome restaurant specializing in the cuisine of south-west
France. There is an interesting food-and-wine-tasting menu. Dutournier also owns
the* Trou Gascon *(listed under* **Bistros***).*

Joël Robuchon is one of the greatest living
French chefs; his restaurant has three
Michelin stars. His cuisine is astoundingly
beautiful and rich in flavours and subtlety, and
leaves everyone quite amazed. Tables at the
small, pastel-coloured restaurant are highly
coveted; book at least two months ahead.
*Children admitted. Vegetarian dishes by
arrangement.*

Jules Verne
*second floor, Eiffel Tower, 75007 Paris
(45.55.61.44). Metro Champ de Mars.* **Open**
12.30-2.30pm, 7.30-10.15pm, daily. **Average**
600F. **Set menu** (lunch Mon-Fri only) 220F.
Credit AmEx, DC, MC, F£$TC, V.
An award-winning chef, Louis Grondard, a
private lift and top-notch dining-room have
made the Eiffel Tower's Jules Verne one of
the hardest dinner reservations to book in
Paris. Less difficult to reserve at lunch.

Lucas-Carton
*9 place de la Madeleine, 75008 Paris
(42.65.22.90). Metro Madeleine.* **Open**
12.30-2.30pm, 8-10.30pm, Mon-Fri. **Average**
900F. **Set menu** 780F. **Credit** MC, F£$TC, V.
This *belle époque* landmark is now, ironically,
home to chef Alain Senderens, one of the
most inventive modern cuisine chefs in
France. His sometimes unusual and provocative creations can be fabulous and are always
interesting, as is the wine list. Lucas-Carton
is one of the dressiest and most expensive
restaurants in Paris (three Michelin stars).
*Children admitted. Vegetarian dishes by
arrangement.*

Michel Rostang
*20 rue Rennequin, 75017 Paris
(47.63.40.77). Metro Ternes.* **Open** 12.30-
2pm, 7.30-10pm, Mon-Fri; 7.30-10pm Sat.

Average 650F. **Set menus** (lunch only)
260F, 380F.
This handsome restaurant, full of silver,
crystal and valuable *bibelots*, is the stage for
chef-owner Michel Rostang and his sophisticated, varied cuisine which blends elements
of the classic, modern and his native region
of Isère. The friendly and attentive service is
overseen by the charming Madame
Rostang. One of the two dining-rooms is
reserved for non-smokers.
*Babies, children welcome. No-smoking room.
Vegetarian dishes on request.*

Le Plaza Athénée
*25 avenue Montaigne, 75008 Paris
(47.23.78.33). Metro Franklin D Roosevelt.*
Open 12.30-2.30pm, 7.30-10.30pm, daily.
Average 600F.
Credit AmEx, DC, MC, F£$TC, V.
The Régence, the more formal and expensive of the two restaurants of the Plaza
Athénée hotel, remains a bastion of the
classic: fine cuisine, excellent service and
flowery décor. The flower-filled courtyard is
a delightful spot for outdoor dining in good
weather. The other restaurant, Le Relais, is
popular with local models, shoppers and
theatre-goers. The cuisine tends to be 'bistro
de luxe' compared with that of the Régence,
and the thirties décor and see-and-be-seen
atmosphere have a different appeal.
Babies, children welcome.

Taillevent
*15 rue Lamennais, 75008 Paris
(45.63.39.94). Metro Georges V.* **Open** 12.30-
2pm, 8-10.30pm, Mon-Fri. **Average** 700F.
Credit AmEx, DC, MC, F£$TC, V.
A perfect fusion of fine cuisine, exemplary service and elegant atmosphere – tables here are
some of the hardest to book in the world. Any

meal at Taillevent is a celebration. The cooking is firmly rooted in classic French cuisine; the wine list is superlative and fairly priced; and the service is discreet. Three Michelin stars.
Babies, children admitted. Vegetarian dishes on request.

La Tour d'Argent
15-17 quai de la Tournelle, 75005 Paris (43.54.23.31). Metro Maubert-Mutualité. **Open** noon-2.30pm, 8-10.30pm, Tue-Sun. **Average** 800F. **Credit** AmEx, DC, MC, F£$TC, V.
A new chef has recently brought new life to the venerable Tour, in existence since 1582. The famous duck Tour d'Argent remains, but alongside newer, lighter dishes. The service, atmosphere, breathtaking view and wine cellar help keep the Tour among Paris's Michelin three-star restaurants.
Children admitted

CLASSIC

Ambassade d'Auvergne
22 rue Grenier-Saint-Lazare, 75003 Paris (42.72.31.22). Metro Etienne Marcel, Rambuteau. **Open** noon-2.30pm, 7.30-11pm, daily. **Average** 250F. **Credit** MC, F£$TC, V.
This family-run fixture of a restaurant is comfortably dusty with age and is a worthy ambassador of its region, the Auvergne. The rich, hearty cuisine includes *cassoulet* and *aligot* (mashed potatoes with Cantal cheese and garlic); there is a good selection of little-known, local wines.
Babies, children welcome. Vegetarian dishes on request.

L'Ami Louis
32 rue de Vertbois, 75003 Paris (48.87.77.48). Metro Temple. **Open** noon-2pm, 8-10.45pm, Wed-Sun. **Average** 500F. **Credit** DC, MC, FTC, V.
See picture and caption.
Babies, children welcome. Pets admitted.

Au Franc Pinot
1 quai Bourbon, 75004 Paris (43.29.46.98). Metro Pont Marie. **Open** noon-2pm, 7.30-11pm, Tue-Sat. **Average** 300F. **Set menu** 150F (lunch only), 180F (lunch and dinner). **Credit** AmEx, MC, F£$TC, V.
This noted address on the Ile Saint Louis is part wine bar (on the ground floor) and part restaurant (in the cool, stone cellar). Wonderful atmosphere of the *vieux Paris*, and one of the few places on the Ile Saint Louis not to be packed with tourists. Quite good cuisine is prepared by a chef who trained with Joël Robuchon of Jamin/Robuchon (*see above* **Haute Cuisine**).
Babies, children welcome. Vegetarian dishes on request.

Bacchus Gourmand
21 rue François 1er, 75001 Paris (47.20.15.83). Metro Champs-Elysées. **Open** noon-2.30pm, 7.30-10.30pm, daily. **Average** 450F. **Set menu** (lunch only) 290F. **Credit** AmEx, MC, TC, V.
A summer terrace and nightly live music venue. The atmosphere here is friendly.

Les Chants du Piano
10 rue Lambert, 75018 Paris (42.62.02.14). Metro Château Rouge. **Open** 8-11pm Mon;

noon-2pm, 8-11pm, Tue-Sat; noon-2pm Sun. **Set menu** 139F, menu dégustation 220F. **Credit** AmEx, DC, MC, V.
On a tiny street near Montmartre, this elegant little restaurant is the brainchild of chef-owner Michel Derbane, a perfectionist who seems to always be creating new dishes. Excellent quality for the price. A newly-opened *salon* can be hired for private dinners (holds 10).
Babies, children admitted.

Chiberta
3 rue Arsène-Houssaye, 75008 Paris (45.63.77.90/45.63.72.44). Metro Charles de Gaulle-Etoile. **Open** noon-2pm, 7-10.30pm, Mon-Fri. **Average** 450F. **Credit** AmEx, DC, MC, F£$TC, V.
A perennially popular restaurant, just off the Champs-Elysées, with a striking, dark-lacquered décor and beautiful flower arrangements. The excellent, modern cuisine is beautifully presented. Owner Louis-Noël Richard and his professional staff will give you a warm welcome.
Babies, children welcome. Vegetarian dishes on request.

Clodenis
57 rue Caulaincourt, 75018 Paris (46.06.20.26). Metro Lamarck-Caulaincourt. **Open** noon-2pm, 8-10pm, Tue-Sat. **Average** 300F. **Set menu** 160F lunch, 190F dinner. **Credit** MC, F£$TC, V.
This pretty, beige-and-salmon restaurant is one of the best in Montmartre. Chef-owner Denis Gentes prepares an original cuisine with its heart in Provence. Quiet and discreet.
Babies, children welcome.

Olympe
8 rue Nicholas Charlet, 75015 Paris (47.34.86.08). Metro Pasteur. **Open** noon-2pm, 8-11pm, Tue-Fri; 8-11pm Sat, Sun. **Average** 350F. **Set menu** (lunch only) 220F. **Credit** AmEx, DC, MC, F£$TC, V.
Olympe Nahmias – perhaps the best-known woman chef in Paris – recently inaugurated a new menu. This emphasizes a more rustic, homey cuisine than in the past, transformed, as always, by her personal ways with quality products. A very Parisian crowd appreciates the thirties décor. Excellent lunch menu.
Babies, children welcome.

Le Petit Montmorency
5 rue Rabelais, 75008 Paris (42.25.11.19). Metro Franklin D Roosevelt. **Open** noon-2.30pm, 7.30-10.30pm, Mon-Fri. **Average** 400F. **Credit cards** MC, F£$TC, V.
Daniel Bouché, chef-owner of this comfortable restaurant in the heart of the art gallery district, made an acclaimed entrance on the Paris restaurant scene in the seventies and continues to impress with his highly personalized cuisine.
Children admitted. Vegetarian dishes on request.

Pile ou Face
52bis rue Nôtre-Dame des Victoires, 75002 Paris (42.33.64.33). Metro Bourse, Rue Montmartre. **Open** noon-2pm, 8-10pm, Mon-Fri. **Average** 300F. **Credit** MC, F£$TC, V.
This small neighbourhood restaurant was recently discovered by an international crowd that enjoys the fine cuisine of chef Claude Udron, based on quality products.

The most beautiful restaurant in Paris, according to many, is **Le Grand Véfour** *(listed under* **Haute Cuisine***). Established in the Palais Royal in the eighteenth century, the Grand Véfour is enjoying a renaissance. The historically listed décor has recently been restored and young chef Jean-Claude Lhonneur has brought back interest in the Véfour's menu.*

It's somewhat crowded, although this is compensated by the amiable service of the young staff.
Babies, children welcome. Vegetarian dishes by arrangement.

La Table d'Anvers
*2 place d'Anvers, 75009 Paris (48.78.35.21).
Metro Anvers.* **Open** noon-2pm, 7.15-11pm, Mon-Fri; noon-2pm Sat. **Average** 500F. **Set menus** 170F, 240F. **Credit** MC, FTC, V.
Though La Table is not the prettiest of restaurants, the father and son team of the Conticinis prepares some of the most flavourful, interesting food in Paris (with a neat line in theme menus). The pastries are simply fabulous. Located in the heart of Montmartre.
Babies, children welcome. Vegetarian dishes on request.

Le Vivarois
192 avenue Victor Hugo, 75016 Paris (45.04.04.31). Metro Pompe. **Open** noon-2.30pm, 8-10pm, Mon-Fri. **Average** 500F. **Set menu** (lunch only) 315F incl ½ bottle of wine. **Credit** AmEx, DC, MC, FESTC, V.
Explosive chef Claude Peyrot is one of France's most skilful with fish and pastry. His Vivarois has inspired countless other chefs, and while there is a certain uneveness to Peyrot's cooking, meals here are often unforgettable. The décor is rather stark, consisting of marble and wood.
Children admitted.

MEDIUM
RANGE

L'Amazonial
3 rue Sainte Opportune, 75001 Paris (42.33.53.13). Metro Châtelet, Sainte Opportune. **Open** noon-2.30pm, 7pm-1am, Mon-Fri. **Average** 60F-150F. **Credit** MC, TC, V.
A restaurant serving French cuisine in an unconventional setting in Les Halles.

L'Ardelène
24 rue des Lombards, 75004 Paris (42.77.71.71). Metro Châtelet. **Open** noon-2pm, 7-11.30pm, Tue-Sun. **Average** 150F. **Set menus** 70F, 130F.
Credit AmEx, DC, MC, FTC, V.
The Ardelène – located in a Halles sidestreet – offers diners modern French cuisine in two elegant dining-rooms.
Babies, children welcome. Vegetarian dishes on request.

Au Pied de Fouet
45 rue de Babylone, 75007 Paris (47.05.12.27). Metro Vaneau, Sèvres-Babylone. **Open** noon-2pm, 7-9pm, Mon-Fri; noon-2pm Sat. **Average** 100F.
No credit cards.
This tiny (seats about 16 people), always-crowded neighbourhood restaurant is popular with students and anyone on a tight budget. Plan on a quick meal of solid dishes, including many stews and other long-simmering recipes. Décor and service are on the minimal side, but then, so is the bill. Lingering over coffee is not encouraged here.

La Belle France
First floor, Eiffel Tower, 75007 Paris (45.55.20.04). Metro Champ de Mars. **Open** noon-3pm, 5-9pm, daily. **Average** 250F. **Set menus** 90F, 170F. **Credit** V.
The cuisine of the Belle France, the Eiffel Tower's tourist restaurant with brasserie overtones, has few pretensions. The restaurant is primarily a fine spot from which to enjoy the city below. *See also above* **Jules Verne**, listed under **Haute Cuisine**.
Babies, children welcome. Vegetarian dishes on request.

Bernard Chirent
28 rue du Mont Thabor, 75001 Paris (42.86.80.05). Metro Concorde. **Open** 12.15-2.30pm, 7.30-10.30pm, Mon-Fri; 7.30-10.30pm Sat. **Average** 150F. **Set menu** 170F incl ½ bottle of wine. **Credit** MC, FESTC, V.
This new little restaurant near the Place de la Concorde and the Tuileries Gardens has as chef-owner a talented young chef who trained with the renowned Troisgros. It's a pleasant 'boutique restaurant', the staff are eager to please, and prices are quite low considering the area.
Babies, children welcome. Vegetarian dishes on request.

La Cave Drouot
8 rue Drouot, 75009 Paris (47.70.83.38). Metro Richelieu Drouot. **Open** noon-2pm Mon-Sat. **Average** 200F. **Credit** MC, V.
Part restaurant, part wine bar, the Cave Drouot faces the enormous Drouot auction house and is a fine place to relax in after making – or watching – a bid there. Good *charcuteries* and an emphasis on Beaujolais and Rhône Valley wines.
Babies, children welcome.

Le Châtelet Gourmand
13 rue des Lavandières, 75001 Paris (40.26.45.00). Metro Châtelet. **Open** 12.15-2.30pm, 7.30-10.30pm, Tue-Sat. **Average** 300F. **Set menus** 130F-250F.
Credit AmEx, DC, MC, FTC, V.
This pleasant establishment just off the place du Châtelet is well-known chef Guy Girard's third restaurant. The house *foie gras* is excellent, there is a large assortment of grilled meats, and prices are reasonable.
Children admitted.

Chez Fernand (Les Fernandises)
17 rue de la Fontaine au Roi, 75011 Paris (43.57.46.25). Metro République. **Open** noon-10.30pm Mon-Fri; 8-10.30pm Sat. **Average** 200F. **Set menu** 110F.
Credit MC, FTC, V.
This rather plain, family-run restaurant near the Place de la République is a price-for-quality marvel. Chef-owner Fernand Asseline's hearty, well-prepared cuisine is inspired by his native Normandy. That region's Camembert cheese is presented ripened in five different ways.
Babies, children welcome.

Le Comptoir
14 rue Vauvilliers, 75001 Paris (40.26.26.66). Metro Châtelet, Les Halles. **Open** noon-2am daily.
Average 90F. **Credit** MC, V.
The *à la mode* restaurant/tapas bar of Dominique Nahmias (alias Olympe, *see above* **Classic**) is open throughout the day, serving drinks and mostly tapas-sized portions of Mediterranean-inspired food. The crowd is very mixed, although there seems to be a predominance of local, funky Halles residents.
Babies, children welcome. Pets admitted.

L'Ami Louis *(listed under* **Classic***) is almost always full, despite its surprisingly run-down furnishings and service that can be curt. Known for its* foie gras, lamb, potatoes *and* game *in season, it remains one of the last bastions of rich, classic French cuisine with no concessions made to diet – or wallet.*

Daniel Météry
*4 rue de l'Arcade, 75008 Paris
(42.65.53.13). Metro Madeleine.* **Open**
noon-2.15pm, 7.45-10.15pm, Mon-Fri; 7.45-
10.15pm Sat. **Average** 300F. **Set menu** 165F.
Credit MC, F£$TC, V.
This unassuming chef has cooked in
restaurants around Paris for years and
has built up a faithful clientele. These regular diners have followed him to his small
new restaurant off the place de la
Madeleine. The menu is limited but varied and prices are reasonable.
Babies, children welcome.

L'Escargot Montorgueuil
*38 rue de Montorgueil, 75001 Paris
(42.36.83.51). Metro Les Halles.* **Open** noon-
3pm, 8-11pm, Tue-Sun. **Average** 300F.
Set menu 150F lunch, 220F dinner.
Credit AmEx, DC, MC, F£$TC, V.
It is said that this was the first restaurant in
Paris to serve snails; and snails are still a speciality. The original 1830s décor is magnificent
and the chef specializes in modern cuisine.
Babies, children welcome.

Marius
*82 boulevard Murat, 75016 Paris
(46.51.67.80). Metro Porte d'Auteuil, Porte
de Saint Cloud.* **Open** lunch by advance
booking only; dinner 7.30-10.30pm Mon-Sat.
Average 230F. **Credit** MC, V.
New owners have recently taken over this
16th *arrondissement* standby. The simple cuisine, with a seafood emphasis, is especially
appreciated in warm weather, when it can be
enjoyed on the terrace. Prices are reasonable considering the area.
Babies, children welcome.

La Niçoise
*4 rue Pierre Demours, 75017 Paris
(45.74.42.41). Metro Charles de Gaulle-Etoile,
Ternes, Argentine.* **Open** noon-2pm, 7.30-
10.45pm, Mon-Fri; 7.30-10.45pm Sat. **Average**
200F. **Credit** AmEx, DC, MC, F£$TC, V.
One of the few Paris restaurants specializing in the cuisine of the region of Nice; an
interesting assortment of the sunny,
herbal dishes of the south of France is
offered here. This small restaurant is decorated in Tiffany glass and posters depicting the south coast.
Children admitted.

L'Oulette
*38 rue des Tournelles, 75004 Paris
(42.71.43.33). Metro Chemin Vert, Bastille.*
Open noon-2.15pm, 8-10.15pm, Mon-Fri.
Average 200F. **Set menu** 120F.
Credit MC, V.
This tiny, plain restaurant-bistro in the
heart of the Marais was recently discovered by the world at large and tables here
are now very difficult to book. Chef Marcel
Baudia prepares delicious food (remarkable quality for the price), strongly influ-
enced by his native Quercy in central
France. The service can be slow.
Babies, children welcome.

Le Petit Doué
*65 rue de Douai, 75009 Paris (45.96.06.81).
Metro Place de Clichy.* **Open** noon-2pm, 7-
11pm, Tue-Fri; 7-11pm Sat, Sun. **Average**
180F. **Set menu** 80F (lunch only), 130F.
Credit MC, FTC, V.
This small local restaurant near the Place
Pigalle is unpretentious, with unremarkable but well-prepared cuisine in a area

where this is quite a rare treat. The reasonable prices, too, are atypical of this
tourist-intensive area.
*Babies, children welcome. Vegetarian dishes
on request.*

Le Rond de Serviette
*16 rue Saint Augustin, 75002 Paris
(49.27.09.90). Metro Quatre Septembre.*
Open noon-2.30pm, 7-11pm, Mon-Fri; 7-
11pm Sat. **Average** 150F.
Credit MC, FTC, V.
Chef André Genin's large, bright establishment serves some of the dishes that you will
also find at his famous nearby bistro, Chez
Pauline (*see below* **Bistros**). Other tasty
bistro fare is served at a reasonable price.
Babies, children welcome.

La Rôtisserie du Beaujolais
*19 quai de la Tournelle, 75005 Pris
(43.54.17.47). Metro Maubert.* **Open** 7.30-
11.30pm Tue; noon-2.30pm, 7.30-11.30pm,
Wed-Sun. **Credit** MC, FTC, V.
Well situated on the Seine *quais* and with
a view of Nôtre Dame, this animated
bistro belongs to the owner of La Tour
d'Argent (*see above* **Haute Cuisine**).
Many products come directly from Lyon
and the Beaujolais region; spit-cooking
meats are a speciality, and there is a full
selection of Beaujolais wines.
Children admitted.

BISTROS

Benoit
*20 rue Saint Martin, 75004 Paris
(42.72.25.76). Metro Saint-Germain-des-
Prés.* **Open** noon-2pm, 8-10pm, Mon-Fri;
Average 350F. **No credit cards** but cash in
any currency is accepted.
Benoit has greatly evolved since starting as
a simple coachman's bistro in 1912. Today it
sparkles with polished brass fixtures, lace
curtains and cut glass. Few bistros in Paris
do the classic repertoire better; the *com-
potier de boeuf*, the *boeuf mode* and other
dishes are wonderful.
Babies, children welcome. Pets admitted.

La Cagouille
*10-12 place Constantin Brancusi, 75014
Paris (43.22.09.01). Metro Gaité.* **Open**
noon-2pm, 9.45-10.30pm, Tue-Sat.
Average 300F. **Credit** MC, V.
The bear-like owner, Gérard Allemandou, a
native of the Charentes region, describes his
large, bright restaurant as a 'bistro
charentais'. Very fresh fish is served here,
cooked and presented as simply as possible.
Babies, children welcome. Pets admitted.

Chardenoux
*1 rue Jules Vallès, 75011 Paris (43.71.49.52).
Metro Charonne.* **Open** noon-2pm, 8-11pm,
Mon-Sat; 8-11pm Sat. **Average** 200F.
Credit AmEx, MC, FTC, V.
Nothing has been altered here since this
local bistro was founded at the turn of the
century. The cuisine is robust, drawing on
many of the French provinces, and the service is familial and unpretentious. You can't
fail to notice the marble-and-zinc bar; 17 different types of marble were used.
*Babies, children welcome. Pets admitted.
Vegetarian dishes on request.*

Claimed to be the oldest brasserie in Paris, **Bofinger** *(listed under*
Brasseries*) is certainly one of the most beautiful. The menu is a predictable
one: shellfish, choucroute and so on. Ask to be placed on the ground floor,
under the dome.*

Chez Pauline
5 rue Villedo, 75001 Paris (42.96.20.70).
Metro Pyramides. **Open** noon-2.15pm, 7.30-
10.30pm, Mon-Fri; 7.30-10.30pm Sat.
Average 300F. **Credit** V.
This second-generation bistro near the
Opéra is a Paris classic. Chef-owner André
Genin successfully combines traditional
cuisine from the Lyon region with his
own, modern dishes. One of the prettiest
bistros in Paris.
Babies, children admitted. Pets admitted.

Le Macadam
23 rue de Turbigo, 75002 Paris
(42.36.52.32). Metro Etienne Marcel. **Open**
8am-2am Mon-Sat. **Average** 200F. **Set**
menus 95F (lunch), 100F, 155F (dinner).
Credit MC, V.
A hip bistro, popular with French media
celebrities and journalists. Traditional
cooking with a twist includes *maatjes fla-*
mand (herring served with blinis); don't
miss the *fondant au chocolat*, a luscious
chocolate pudding.

Le Maquis
69 rue Caulaincourt, 75018 Paris
(42.59.76.07). Metro Larmarck-
Caulaincourt. **Open** noon-2.30pm, 7.30-
10.30pm, Tue-Sat. **Average** 180F. **Set menu**
(lunch only) 109F. **Credit** MC, FESTC, V.
This tiny Montmartre bistro is one of the
best price-for-quality places in the area. The
cuisine is simple and flavourful. There is a
very pleasant, tree-shaded terrace, that's
open in good weather.
Children admitted.

Le Petit Marguery
9 boulevard du Port Royal, 75013 Paris
(43.31.58.59). Metro Gobelins. **Open** noon-
2pm, 7.30-10.30pm, Tue-Sat.
Average 350F. **Set menu** 290F.
Credit AmEx, DC, MC, FESTC, V.
The rather inaccessible location of this bistro
does not deter a knowing group of regulars,
who enjoy its repertoire of classic French
dishes and friendly service. Seasonal game
is a speciality.
Babies, children welcome. Pets admitted.

Le Petit Zinc
25 rue de Buci, 75006 Paris (46.33.51.66).
Metro Mabillon. **Open** noon-3am daily.
Average 200F. **Set menu** 130F. **Credit**
AmEx, DC, MC, FTC, V.
A perennially popular, crowded bistro on the
picturesque rue de Buci, one of the finest food
market streets in Paris. Good quality for the
price, given the area. In fine weather, be sure
to request an outdoor table when booking.
Babies, children welcome.

Savy
23 rue Bayard, 75008 Paris (47.23.46.98).
Metro Franklin D Roosevelt. **Open** noon-
3pm, 7.30-11pm, Mon-Fri. **Average** 580F.
Credit MC, V.
A bit of the Aveyron region of central
France, off the avenue Montaigne and its
haute couture houses. You won't find modern cuisine here, but solid country classics
that have been served by the Savy for the
past 27 years – ham with lentils, stuffed cab-
bage – and are now back in vogue.
Babies, children welcome.

Le Trou Gascon
40 rue Taine, 75012 Paris (43.44.34.26).
Metro Daumesnil. **Open** noon-2pm, 7.30-
10pm, Mon-Fri. **Average** 300F. **Set menu**
190F. **Credit** AmEx, DC, MC, V.
This charming *belle époque* bistro in the distant 12th *arrondissement* is the favourite
restaurant of many Parisians. Owner Alain
Dutournier and his wife have the gift of finding the best food products of south-west
France, and serving them in original ways.

BRASSERIES

Le Balzar
49 rue des Ecoles, 75005 Paris
(43.54.13.67). Metro Cluny, Odéon. **Open**
8am-1am daily. **Average** 150F-200F.
Credit AmEx, MC, FTC, V.
This unpretentious brasserie is now a Latin
Quarter fixture. A noisy mix of students,
Parisians and tourists sit crowded together,
enjoying simply prepared brasserie items,
such as herring and *choucroute*.
Babies, children welcome.

Bofinger
5 rue de la Bastille, 75004 Paris
(42.72.87.82). Metro Bastille. **Open** noon-
3pm, 7.30pm-1am, daily. **Average** 220F. **Set**
menu 155F incl ½ bottle of wine.
Credit AmEx, DC, JCB, MC, FESTC.
See **picture and caption.**
Babies, children admitted.

Brasserie Scossa
8 place Victor Hugo, 75016 Paris
(45.01.73.67). Metro Victor Hugo. **Open**
7am-1am daily. **Average** 160F.
Credit AmEx, DC, V.
This 16th *arrondissement* brasserie serves
standard brasserie food. Worth popping into
if you're in the area.

La Brasserie Wepler
14 place de Clichy, 75018 Paris
(45.22.53.29). Metro Place de Clichy. **Open**
11-1am daily. **Average** 150F. **Set menu** 250F.
Credit AmEx, DC, JCB, MC, FTC, V.
A classic Parisian brasserie on Place de
Clichy. Fine shellfish and good value, if you
can put up with the overdone décor, noise
and hurried (yet attentive) service.
Babies, children welcome.

Charlot 1er
128bis boulevard de Clichy, 75018 Paris
(45.22.47.08). Metro Place de Clichy. **Open**
noon-2.30pm, 7pm-1am, daily. **Average** 200F.
Credit MC, FTC, V.
Seafood specialities are served here. This
place is not to be confused with Charlot Roi
des Coquillages *below.*

Charlot Roi des Coquillages
12 place de Clichy, 75009 Paris
(48.74.49.64). Metro Place de Clichy. **Open**
noon-3pm, 7pm-1am, daily. **Average** 300F.
Credit AmEx, DC, MC, FTC, V.
A brasserie-cum-institution, facing the
animated place de Clichy. Recent renovation has dusted off the original thirties
décor and a new chef has considerably
improved the cuisine. Specialities include
bouillabaisse and, of course, copious
shellfish platters.
Babies, children welcome.

*Recently restored by new owner, brasserie king Jean-Paul Bucher, **La Coupole**
(listed under **Brasseries**) is ready for the nineties. Almost a synonym for the
word 'brasserie', La Coupole has the largest shellfish stand in Paris and a large
menu of typical brasserie fare. Watching the customers, though, is half the fun.*

La Coupole
102 boulevard Montparnasse, 75014 Paris
(43.20.14.20). Metro Vavin. **Open** 7am-2am
daily. **Average** 200F.
Credit AmEx, DC, MC, FTC, V.
See **picture and caption**.
Babies, children welcome. Pets admitted.

Flo
7 cour des Petites Ecuries, 75010 Paris
(47.70.13.59). Metro Château d'Eau. **Open**
noon-3pm, 7pm-1.30am, daily. **Average** 250F.
Set menu (lunch only) 140F.
Credit AmEx, DC, MC, FTC, V.
An authentic turn-of-the-century brasserie
with a warm Alsatian atmosphere. This is
another Jean-Paul Bucher establishment
(*see above*), with a menu similar to those at
all his other addresses. Alsatian wines are
available by the pitcher.
Babies, children welcome.

Julien
16 rue du Faubourg Saint Denis, 75010
*Paris (47.70.12.06). Metro Strasbourg-Saint-
Denis.* **Open** noon-1.30am daily. **Average**
250F. **Credit** AmEx, DC, JCB, MC, FTC, V.
This genuine *belle époque* brasserie
(another Bucher address, *see above*), has
a dazzling décor and the now-familiar
menu to be found at other Bucher establishments (minus the shellfish stand). It's
always crowded, noisy and merry.
*Babies, children welcome. One vegetarian
dish daily.*

La Taverne Kronenbourg
24 boulevard des Italiens, 75009 Paris
(47.70.16.64). Metro Les Halles. **Open**
11.30am-2am daily. **Average** 160F. **Credit**
AmEx, DC, MC, FTC, V; £, $ accepted in cash.
Located near the Opéra on the animated boulevard des Italiens, this big
brasserie is a fine example of the genre,
and even tries harder than most: an
orchestra plays here in the evening.
Fine shellfish and hearty Alsatian
favourites, including *choucroute*, are
house specialities.
Babies, children welcome.

Vaudeville
29 rue de Vivienne, 75002 Paris
(42.33.39.31). Metro Bourse. **Open** 11-2am
daily. **Average** 200F. **No credit cards.**
A Bucher brasserie (*see above* **La
Coupole**) that is located opposite the
Bourse (stock exchange). As is to be
expected, it is always crowded and offers
fine shellfish, house *foie gras, plats du
jour* (dishes of the day) and a large
dessert selection. Handsome *faux* marble
and mirrored furnishings complete the
interior design.
Babies, children welcome.

SEAFOOD

Augusta
98 rue de Tocqueville, 75017 Paris
(47.63.39.97). Metro Malesherbes. **Open**
12.15-1.30pm, 7.30-9.30pm, Mon-Sat.
Average 350F. **Credit** V.
This restaurant specializing in fish dishes is
famous for its *bouillabaisse* with potatoes,
but everything is fresh and good. Owner
Didier Berton takes scrupulous care of

*Many cafés offer quick, reasonably priced dishes throughout the day.
Sitting outside will probably incur extra charges, but the show is worth it.
See also chapter* **Cafés & Salons de thé.**

each client. Prices are extremely fair; it's
also one of the few good fish restaurants to
be open on Monday.

Bar à Huitres
112 boulevard de Montparnasse, 75014 Paris
(43.20.71.01). Metro Vavin. **Open** noon-
2am daily. **Average** 200F.
Credit AmEx, MC, FESTC, V.
This is perhaps the only restaurant in Paris
to specialize in all types of oysters and other
shellfish. A separate menu contains cooked
dishes. Try to get a seat at the bar; this is
where all the action takes place.
Babies, children welcome.

Chez Armand
6 rue de Beaujolais, 75001 Paris
(42.60.05.11). Metro Louvre, Palais Royal.
Open noon-2.30pm, 7.30pm-2am, Mon-Sat.
Average 250F. **Set menus** 145F, 180F.
Credit AmEx, DC, MC, FESTC, V.
A welcoming restaurant facing the back of
the Palais Royal; the candle-light, warm
beams and rich upholstery make it a particularly romantic spot. Chef Ferron prepares a
largely – but not exclusively – fish menu, at
very reasonable prices.
Babies, children welcome.

LeDivellec
107 rue de l'Université, 75007 Paris
(45.51.91.96). Metro Invalides. **Open** 12.30-
2pm, 8-9.30pm, Tue-Sat. **Average** 600F. **Set
menus** (lunch only) 250F, 350F.
Credit AmEx, DC, MC, V.
LeDivellec is perhaps the top fish restaurant
in Paris, with two Michelin stars and a very

elegant clientele. Chef Jacques LeDivellec is
a master at bringing out the true flavour of
simply prepared fish. This is reputedly the
first restaurant in Paris to serve black squid
ink and green seaweed pasta.

VEGETARIAN

Au Grain de Folie
24 rue de Lavieuville, 75018 Paris
(42.58.15.57). Metro Abesses. **Open** 7-
11.30pm Mon; noon-2.30pm, 7-11.30pm,
Tue-Sun. **Average** 75F. **Credit** MC, V.
Known as the non-vegetarian's vegetarian
restaurant, the Grain de Folie is one of
Paris's more liberal veggie eateries: smoking
is allowed, wine (including organic wine) is
available, and fish forms a big part of the
menu. Portions are generous. A good place
to seek out French *baba-cool* (ex-hippies).
Babies, children welcome. Pets admitted.

Country Life
6 rue Daunou, 75002 Paris (42.97.48.51).
Metro Opéra. **Open** *café*: 11.30am-2.30pm
Mon-Fri; *shop*: 10am-4.30pm Mon-Thur;
10am-5pm Fri. **Average** 65F. **Credit** FTC.
A large hot and cold buffet of nutritious
goodies from the Paris branch of this international chain.
Babies, children welcome.

La Macrobiothèque
17 rue de Savoie, 75006 Paris (43.25.04.96).
Metro Saint Michel. **Open** noon-2pm, 7-

10pm, Mon-Sat. **Average** 80F.
Set menu 70F. **No credit cards.**
A friendly café-cum-restaurant with an appropriate pastoral feel to it, selling imaginative vegetarian and macrobiotic dishes. Smoking is not encouraged (but it's tolerated); unfortunately it's unlicensed.
Babies, children welcome.

Naturalia
107 rue Caulaincourt, 75018 Paris (42.62.33.68). Metro Lamarck-Caulaincourt. **Open** *café:* 11.30am-3pm Mon-Fri; *shop:* 10am-7.30pm Mon-Fri; 10am-1.30pm, 3-7.30pm, Sat. **Average** 80F.
No credit cards.
This lunch-time café is attached to a healthfood shop. The café is not exclusively vegetarian (fish and chicken feature on the menu), but there is a first-class range of vegetarian dishes. Organic wines are available.
Babies, children welcome.

Natural's
15 rue Grenier-Saint-Lazare, 75003 Paris (48.87.09.49). Metro Rambuteau. **Open** *winter:* 11am-7pm Mon-Sat; *summer:* 11am-9pm Mon-Sat. **Average** 50F. **Set menu** 45F. **Credit** FTC.
A wonderful macrobiotic café (takeaways are also available), with tasty tofu burgers, vegetable sashimi and sugar-free pastries. Licensed to serve alcohol with full meals only; smoking is 'not allowed'.
Babies, children welcome. Takeaway service.

Piccolo
6 rue des Ecouffes, 75004 Paris (42.72.17.79). Metro Saint Paul. **Open** noon-3pm, 7pm-midnight, daily.
Average 60F. **Credit** AmEx, DC, MC, V.
From salads to carrot caviar, a friendly and relaxed atmosphere in a wood-and-stone setting.

CHEAP

Aux Deux Saules
91 rue Saint Denis, 75001 Paris (42.36.46.57). Metro Châtelet, Les Halles. **Open** noon-midnight daily. **Set menu** 56F incl one drink. **Credit cards** MC, F£$TC, V.
Reliable bistro fare in a *belle époque* setting, in the heart of the Halles.
Babies, children welcome. Pets admitted.

Chartier
7 rue du Faubourg Montmartre, 75009 Paris (47.70.86.29). Metro Rue Montmartre. **Open** 11am-3pm, 6-9.30pm, daily.
Average 70F. **Credit** FTC.
Originally a bouillon where the working class enjoyed simple meals, Chartier is now on every student's and tourist's list for inexpensive, basic French food. Tables in this vast, authentic 1900s hall are shared; expect to queue for seats (no bookings accepted).
Children admitted.

Le Commerce
51 rue du Commerce, 75015 Paris (45.75.03.27). Metro Commerce. **Open** noon-midnight daily. **Average** 70F.
Credit AmEx, DC, MC, V.
Once associated with Chartier *above*, the Commerce has recently attempted to

upgrade its image. It has been given a new coat of paint and prices have been raised, though the quality-price ratio is still excellent.
Babies, children welcome.

Hamilton's Noted Fish & Chips
51 rue de Lappe, 75011 (48.06.77.92). Metro Bastille. **Open** noon-2.30pm, 6-11.30pm, Mon-Sat; 6-11.30pm Sun. **Average** 30F. **Credit** FTC.
Yes, a British fish & chips shop, dealing primarily in take-aways. The best of the genre in Paris, but then there's no real competition.
Takeaway service.

Polidor
41 rue Monsieur-le-Prince, 75006 Paris (43.26.95.34). Metro Odéon. **Open** noon-2.30pm, 7pm-1am, Mon-Sat; noon-2.30pm, 7-11pm, Sun. **Average** 100F. **No credit cards.**
See picture and caption.
Babies, children welcome.

INTERNATIONAL

AMERICAN & MEXICAN

American Style
2 place Gustave Toudouze, 75009 Paris (48.78.30.50). Metro Saint Georges. **Open** noon-2.30pm, 7pm-midnight, daily.
Average 200F. **Credit** AmEx, DC, JCB, MC, FTC, V.
Boston cooking twenties-style that can be downed with one of the many wines from California. Chef JP Machuret has a vast experience in recipes of yesteryear; he collects

antique cookery books, including *The Original Boston Cooking School Book.*
Babies, children welcome.

Chicago Meatpackers
8 rue de la Coquillière, 75001 Paris (40.28.02.33). Metro Châtelet, Les Halles. **Open** 11am-1am Mon-Fri; 11am-1.30am Sat, Sun. **Average** 120F. **Credit** MC, V.
A typical Yankee restaurant, serving all-meat specialities: ribs, hamburgers, and so on. Chicago gold beer is brewed especially for the restaurant. Good for kids.

Del Rio Café
12 rue Princesse, 75006 Paris (43.26.79.95)/15 rue du Cygne, 75001 Paris (42.21.10.57). Metro Les Halles for both. **Open** 10am-2pm, 6.30pm-midnight, Mon-Thur, Sun; 10am-2pm, 6.30pm-2am, Fri, Sat. **Average** 130F.
Credit AmEx, V.
This Tex-Mex hotspot is mostly Mex, down to the imported beers. Check out the 'authentic' Mexican toilet.

Marshal's Bar & Grill
63 avenue Franklin D Roosevelt, 75008 Paris (45.63.21.22). Metro Saint Philippe du Roule. **Open** noon-3pm, 7.30pm-midnight, Mon-Fri; 12.30-4pm, 7.30pm-midnight, Sat; 12.30-4pm, 8.30pm-midnight, Sun. **Average** 200F. **Credit** AmEx, DC, JCB, MC, V.
French-owned and run, Marshal's is nevertheless the only American restaurant in Paris to try to present North American cuisine seriously. Brunch is served on Saturday and Sunday. Have drinks at the attractive stone bar and enjoy the up-beat atmosphere.
Babies, children welcome.

*The **Polidor** (listed under **Cheap**) continues to delight regular diners. A classic, budget, late-night establishment, it somehow manages to retain its charm throughout the years, with its lace curtains and faux bois, columns, and tables set with paper cloths. Simple cooking, very reasonably priced.*

La Perla

*28 rue François Miron, 75004 Paris
(42.77.59.40). Metro Hôtel de Ville, Saint
Paul.* **Open** noon-3pm, 7-10pm, daily.
Average 60F. **Credit** MC, FTC, V.
Primarily a bar, La Perla is a popular Marais
spot for Mexican *botanas* or fingerfood, and
tequilla drinks. There is a limited number of
hot dishes.
Babies, children admitted lunch.

The Studio

*41 rue du Temple, 75004 Paris
(42.74.10.38). Metro Rambuteau.* **Open**
7.30pm-1am Mon-Fri; 12.30-3pm, 7.30pm-
1am, Sat, Sun. **Average** 120F. **Credit** MC, V.
Tex-Mex cuisine and ambience in a pleasant
courtyard in the Marais. The Texas BBQ
and New York cheesecake are typical of the
food served here. The Studio serves brunch
on Saturday and Sunday.

ITALIAN

Chez Vincent

*56 rue Saint Georges, 75009 Paris
(42.85.02.79). Metro Saint Georges.* **Open**
noon-2pm, 6.30-10pm, Mon-Fri; **Average**
80F. **Credit** FTC.
A friendly, family-run restaurant. The
chef may be Italian, but he juggles his
native cuisine and traditional French
dishes with great flair.
Babies, children welcome.

Da Graziano

*83 rue Lepic, 75018 Paris (46.06.84.77).
Metro Abbesses.* **Open** noon-3pm, 8pm-
12.30am, daily. **Average** 250F. **Set menus**
60F lunch, 155F dinner.
Credit MC, F£$TC, V.
A bit of Italy on the picturesque rue Lepic
that winds up to Montmartre. The owner is
'authentic Italian' and tries to squeeze into
the menu as many of his country's dishes as
is possible. There's a pleasant garden for *al
fresco* eating in good weather.
Babies, children welcome.

Sormani

*4 rue du Général Lanrezac, 75017 Paris
(43.80.13.91). Metro Charles de Gaulle-
Etoile.* **Open** 12.15-2pm, 7.45-10pm, Mon-Fri.
Average 350F. **Credit** MC, F£$TC, V.
Possibly the best Italian restaurant in Paris.
Chef Fayet is as French as he is Italian, and
is not afraid of combining the two cuisines in
creative, very successful ways. Recently
redecorated in a fresh Italian-inspired style.
Children admitted.

NORTH AFRICAN

Chez Hamadi

*12 rue Bouterie, 75005 Paris (43.54.03.30).
Metro Saint Michel.* **Open** noon-3pm, 4pm-
midnight, Mon-Sat; noon-midnight Sun.
Average 80F. **Set menu** 70F incl ½ bottle of
wine. **Credit** FTC.

The huge **Nioullaville** *(listed under* **International/Oriental***) in the
Belleville area – the new Chinatown of Paris – specializes in the cuisines of
China, Thailand and Vietnam. The great speciality of dim sum is wheeled in
on a trolley. The menu is about 30 pages long.*

Modest in appearance, this restaurant is nevertheless very popular – and with good reason. The food is inexpensive and is consistently good.
*Babies, children welcome. Pets admitted.
Vegetarian dish (couscous).*

Martin Alma

*44 rue Jean Goujon, 75008 Paris
(43.59.28.25). Metro Alma Marceau.* **Open**
noon-2.30pm, 7-11pm, Mon-Sat; noon-
2.30pm Sun. **Average** 150F. **Credit** MC, V.
The fresh, patio-theme décor of Martin Alma
in the *haute couture* district is one of the reasons for visiting this North African restaurant; the other is the wide range of *couscous*,
and the good paella prepared on certain
days of the week.

Timgad

*21 rue de Brunel, 75017 Paris
(45.74.23.70). Metro Argentine.* **Open** noon-
2.30pm, 7-11pm, daily. **Average** 400F. **Credit**
AmEx, DC, MC, V.
This is many Parisians' favourite
Moroccan restaurant; it even has one
Michelin star, which is quite a feat. The
Moorish décor is sumptuous. Famous
for its *couscous*.

ORIENTAL

Matsuri Sushi

*36 rue Richelieu, 75001 Paris (42.61.05.73).
Metro Palais Royal.* **Open** noon-2.30pm, 7-
10.30pm, Mon-Thur; noon-2.30pm, 7-
11.30pm, Fri; 7-11.30pm Sat. **Average** 160F.
Credit MC, FTC, V.
This bright, clean Japanese restaurant two
blocks from the Louvre specializes in
sushi; it claims to be the only one in Paris
to have the traditional sushi service from a
moving counter.
Babies, children welcome.

Le Nioullaville

*32-34 rue de l'Orillon, 75011 Paris
(43.38.95.23). Metro Belleville.* **Open** noon-
3.30pm, 6.30pm-1am, Mon-Sat; noon-1am
Sun. **Average** 90F.
Credit MC, V.
See **picture and caption**.
Babies, children welcome.

Pagoda

*50 rue de Provence, 75009 Paris
(48.74.81.48). Metro Chaussée d'Antin.*
Open 11.30am-2.30pm, 7-10.30pm, Mon-Fri;
7.30-11pm Sat. **Average** 160F. **Set menus**
80F, 90F (both for one person) 200F-320F for
two people. **Credit** MC, V.
One of the better 'ethnic' restaurants in
Paris, faithful to no particular region of Asia
but combining the cuisines of many countries. The décor is less kitsch than at most
Paris Asian restaurants and the service is
quite attentive.
Babies, children welcome. Vegetarian dishes.

Tong Yen

*1bis rue Jean Mermoz, 75008 Paris
(42.25.04.23). Metro Franklin D Roosevelt.*
Open noon-2.30pm, 7pm-midnight, daily.
Average 300F.
Credit AmEx, DC, MC, F£$TC, V.
A two-storey restaurant with a huge menu of
Chinese, Vietnamese and Thai specialities. A
favourite among the *beau monde*.
Children admitted.

Bars

Socialize and be merry; the bars in the capital are over-flowing with the Devil's brew.

COCKTAIL BARS

Bar Alexandre
53 avenue George V, 75008 Paris
(47.20.17.82). Metro George V. **Open** 10.30-
2am Mon-Sat. **Credit** AmEx, DC, MC, V.
Favoured by smartly dressed Parisians for
pre-dinner cocktails or after-dinner brandies,
this attractive bar off the Champs-Elysées has
a posh yacht-club look – lots of leather and
polished wood – that is comfortable, discreet
and conducive to seductive conversation.

Le Bar des Maîtres Nageurs
6 rue Léopold-Robert, 75014 Paris
(43.21.69.49). Metro Vavin. **Open** 7pm-2am
Mon-Sat. **No credit cards.**
It's new, and cool as a dip in the pool – the
Life Guards' bar is another reason, along
with the Closerie, the Rosebud and La
Coupole, to keep Montparnasse in your
nightlife address book. Dig smooth recorded
jazz and classic cocktails in the company of
pretty faces that may look faintly familiar.

Bar du Céladon
Hôtel Westminster, 13 rue de la Paix, 75002
Paris (42.61.57.46). **Open** 11am-midnight
daily. **No credit cards.**
True to its name, this elegant bar – vestibule
of the vaunted Céladon restaurant – is decorated in tender shades of green; the house
cocktail is of a similar hue. But a choice
selection of premium blended and single-
malt whiskies is on hand, just as well for
those who wouldn't be caught dead drinking
anything pastel.

Bar du Meurice
228 rue de Rivoli, 75001 Paris
(42.60.38.60). Metro Tuileries. **Open** 10-
2am daily. **Credit** AmEx, DC, EC, MC, V.
To the bar proper, we prefer the salon
Pompadour, the decoration of which visitors
find either sumptuous or silly, depending on
their tolerance for velvet and gilt. A piano
player tickles the ivories discreetly in the
background, while you sip a well-made cocktail or *coupe de champagne.*

Bar du Pont-Royal
7 rue de Montalembert, 75007 Paris
(45.44.38.27). Metro Rue du Bac.
Open 11-1am Mon-Sat; closed whole month
of August. **Credit** AmEx, DC, MC, V.
Editors and writers from neighbouring publishing houses (Gallimard, notably) sink regularly into the leather armchairs of this comfortable hotel bar. They have no trouble
hoisting themselves out again, even after a
couple of whiskies, for the drinks are poured
with uncommon stinginess.

Bars du Ritz
(Cocktail Room, l'Espadon, Bar Hemingway)
15 place Vendôme, 75001 Paris
(42.60.38.30). Metro Concorde, Tuileries.
Open *Cocktail Room, l'Espadon:* 11-1am
daily; *Bar Hemingway:* 7pm-3am daily.
Credit AmEx, DC, EC, MC, V.
Finely wrought examples of the barman's
art are priced at just under 100F. Big
spenders will be pleased to learn that they
can shell out several times that sum for a
snifter of old Armagnac (something over
900F) or antique Cognac (1,400F).

Le Bélier
Bar de l'Hôtel, 13 rue des Beaux-Arts, 75006
*Paris (43.25.27.22). Metro Saint-Germain-
des-Prés.* **Open** 24 hours daily.
Credit AmEx, DC, EC, MC, V.
Cross the lobby of this exclusive Left-bank
hotel – where Oscar Wilde once laid his
head – and discover one of the city's most
romantic bars. A discreet pianist sets the
mood for sleek, chic creatures who
exchange murmured conversation over
expertly mixed cocktails.

Birdland
8 rue Guisarde, 75006 Paris (43.26.97.59).
Metro Mabillon. **Open** 10pm-6am daily.
No credit cards.
Just down the street from the super-exclu-
sive Castel, this democratic bar is open to
night-hawks of all ages and persuasions who
appreciate moderately priced libation, low
lights and judiciously chosen recorded jazz.
The staff thoughtfully leave the album sleeve
out for listeners to peruse.

China Club
50 rue de Charenton, 75012 Paris
(43.43.82.02). Metro Ledru-Rollin. **Open** 9-
1.30am Mon-Sat; noon-1am Sun. **Credit** V.
The new Bastille hot spot for the young and
pretty is a good place to test your tolerance for
fairly lethal mixtures of spirits and fruit juice. If
you wish to keep your aplomb, do order some
of the tasty, vaguely Chinese food to keep those
cocktails company. At the convivial bar downstairs, or in the *fumoir* one flight up, drinks are
sold two-for-one on Sundays, 7pm to 9pm.

La Closerie des Lilas
171 boulevard du Montparnasse, 75006
Paris (43.26.70.50). Metro Vavin/RER
Port-Royal. **Open** noon-2am daily.
Credit AmEx, DC, MC, V.
See **picture and caption.**

Le Forum
4 boulevard Malesherbes, 75008 Paris
(42.65.37.86). Metro Madeleine. **Open** 11.30-
2am Mon-Fri; 5.30pm-2am Sat, Sun. **Credit** V.
Since 1930 the Forum's resident chemists
have delighted Parisians with their ingenious
inventions. Pick your chosen potion from a
list of 150 cocktails and a superb collection of
premium whiskies, then enjoy it ensconced in
a comfortable chair. The bar is at its restful
best at cocktail hour, around 7pm.

Harry's New York Bar
5 rue Daunou, 75002 Paris (42.61.71.14).
Metro Opéra. **Open** 10.30-4am daily.
No credit cards.

Good piano music, great cocktails, fine whiskies and a classy clientele sprinkled
with literary and media celebs: it's a successful formula that makes **La Closerie**
des Lilas *(listed under* **Cocktail Bars**) *invulnerable to the vagaries of fashion.*

The mustachioed giant who used to run **Le Café de la Nouvelle Mairie** *(listed under* **Wine Bars***) has gone off to greener arrondissements. The new proprietors pour equally tasty Loire Valley wines with a generous hand. In warm weather, tables are set outside overlooking the paulownia trees on the place de l'Estrapade.*

What's your pleasure? A mint julep as good as any you'd taste on Derby Day in Lexington, Kentucky? A he-man Manhattan? Or a state-of-the-art Bloody Mary (said to have been invented right here at Harry's)? The expert mix-masters at *sank Roo Doe Noo* (play on the street name) have also concocted a potion for sickly lovers; the Blue Lagoon with two straws.

L'Helium
3 rue des Haudriettes, 75003 Paris (42.72.81.10). Metro Rambuteau. **Open** noon-2.15pm, 5pm-1am, daily. **Credit** AmEx, DC, MC, V.
Funky denizens of Les Halles and assorted eccentrics make for an amusing mix at this noisy watering hole, which was once at the cutting edge of Paris nightlife. An all-new hi tech décor has replaced the hi-kitsch of yore.

La Mousson
9 rue de la Bastille, 75004 Paris (42.71.85.20). Metro Bastille. **Open** 7pm-1.30am daily. **Credit** V.
Neo-colonial nights at the Bastille: young hipsters slouch decoratively in wicker armchairs while ceiling fans turn lazily above their heads. As the evening wears on, tropical cocktails, jazz and the crush of bodies combine to ignite something very like jungle fever. The Happy Hour is from 7pm to 9pm.

Le Normandy
7 rue de l'Echelle, 75001 Paris (42.60.30.21). Metro Palais-Royal. **Open** 11am-1pm, 6pm-midnight, daily. **Credit** AmEx, DC, V.
Sink into a cushy Chesterfield armchair and savour an expertly mixed cocktail (around 50F) before setting off to see Lorenzaccio at the Comédie Française. In winter, a log fire adds its crackling warmth to this picture-perfect hotel bar.

La Perla
26 rue François-Miron, 75004 Paris (42.77.59.40). Metro Hôtel-de-Ville. **Open** noon-2am daily. **Credit** V.
Connoisseurs of tequila and of killer margaritas pack this popular Mexican spot. Weaker constitutions can settle for a bottle of good Mexican beer and a gratifyingly authentic array of bar snacks.

Polly Magoo
11 rue Saint-Jacques, 75005 Paris (46.33.33.64). Metro Saint-Michel. **Open** noon-4am daily. **No credit cards.**
Welcome back to the sixties. Crossing the threshold of this Latin Quarter institution is like going back in time. Graduate students and others who plan never to graduate quaff beer and sturdy red wine in a friendly, bohemian ambience.

Le Rosebud
11bis rue Delambre, 75014 Paris (43.35.38.54). Metro Vavin. **Open** 7pm-2am daily; closed whole month of August. **No credit cards.**
Le Rosebud has been around so long now, that the very mention of the place makes some Parisians get nostalgic and misty-eyed. We have never shared the popular enthusiasm for the (soupy) house chilli, but the drinks, the lighting, the music and an 'expectant' atmosphere make this spot special.

Tahonga Club
PLM Saint Jacques Hôtel, 17 boulevard Saint-Jacques, 75014 Paris (40.78.79.80). Metro Saint-Jacques. **Open** 6pm-3am daily. **Credit** V.
Quiet and almost totally cut off from the bustling city, the Tahonga offers little in the way of South Seas atmosphere. However, after downing a couple of the potent house cocktails, you probably won't care there's not more of the desert island about the place. Live jazz (in the form of a pianist or trio) can be heard in the evenings from Thursday through to Saturday.

Le Train Bleu
Gare de Lyon, First floor, 20 boulevard Diderot, 75012 Paris (43.43.09.06). Metro Gare de Lyon. **Open** 11am-10pm daily. **Credit** AmEx, DC. MC, V.
Your train is late? Lucky you...spend that extra time in a cushy armchair of the bar, an altogether decent cocktail in hand, staring in amazement at one of the most beautiful Belle-Epoque décors in Paris.

BEER BARS

Au Caveau Montpensier
15 rue Montpensier, 75001 Paris (47.03.33.78). Metro Palais-Royal/bus 21, 27, 68, 81. **Open** 4pm-1am daily. **Credit** AmEx, DC, MC, V.
An authentic English pub behind the Comédie Française: a round of darts, a pint of stout, and you'll feel right at home. The Queen's English is both spoken and understood in this friendly, casual spot.

Au Général Lafayette
52 rue La Fayette, 75009 Paris (47.70.59.08). Metro Le Peletier, Cadet. **Open** 11-3am Mon-Fri; 3.30pm-3am Sat. **Credit** MC, V.
Admire the Belle-Epoque trimmings while the mustachioed owner draws you a pint of Guinness – or for that matter any of the other ten brews on draught. A friendly, mostly French crowd jokes and jostles around the bar; an equally jolly crew munch snacks at the tables.

Au Métro
138 rue de la Roquette, 75011 Paris (43.79.75.01). Metro Voltaire. **Open** 10-4am Mon-Sat. **Credit** V.
After a tour of the rockin' rue de la Roquette, join the crowd of locals and tourists on the red velvet banquettes of the Métro. The good Belgian beers are on tap (sample the bière blanche), and are all served with a smile.

Bar Belge
75 avenue de Saint-Ouen, 75017 Paris (46.27.41.01). Metro Guy-Môquet/bus 31, 81. **Open** 3.30pm-1am Tue-Sun. **No credit cards.**
The oldest Belgian beer house in Paris is well off the usual nightlife circuits, but true amateurs willingly make the trip. Sample any of the 30 Belgian brews on offer, along with some excellent Flemish *charcuteries*, in a warm, rather jolly atmosphere.

Kitty O'Shea's
10 rue des Capucines, 75002 Paris (40.15.00.30). Metro Opéra. **Open** noon-1.30am daily. **Credit** AmEx, DC, V.
Quaff a pint of draught Guinness or Smithwick's in this convivial, but not over-

look to the less-celebrated areas of Bordeaux – to Côtes de Castillon, Côtes de Bourg, Côtes de Blaye, Fronsac and Lalande-de-Pomerol – and to the oft-overlooked Burgundians – the Hautes-Côtes de Beaune and the Hautes-Côtes de Nuits. These minor wines offer much better value than their more-famous compatriots, and even young vintages can be very drinkable.

Here's a taster of what's on offer in Paris. We've selected a number of good establishments but urge oenophiles to explore on their own as there are hundreds more in town. Look out for awnings that boast *Bistro à vin, dégustation de vins de propriété* (wine tastings). And if said awning adds that the establishment in question has been awarded the *Coupe du Meilleur Pot* (Best Jug of Wine Trophy), then don't hesitate and head right on in.

Down a quaint side-street is **Le Rubis** *(listed under* **Wine Bars***), an old fashioned, bistro-style bar that has a faithful following. It's known throughout the area as being a friendly meeting point where you can try all types of Beaujolais wines. In the summer, drinkers spill over into the street where they chat while eating the house speciality: tartines. Hot dishes are also served, but only at lunch times.*

crowded, Irish bar. Nearly a dozen fine Irish whiskies are on offer as well. If you feel peckish, sample the smoked salmon; the other dishes are unremarkable.

La Micro-Brasserie
106 rue de Richelieu, 75002 Paris (42.96.55.31). Metro Richelieu-Drouot. **Open** 11-1am Mon-Sat. **No credit cards.**
The house beer, which goes by the fetching name of Morgane, is brewed right on the premises in the big brass vats that look so decorative behind the bar. A good, inexpensive set meal is available; for a snack, try one of the robust cheeses from northern and eastern France.

Pub Saint-Germain
17 rue de l'Ancienne-Comédie, 75006 Paris (43.29.38.70). Metro Odéon. **Open** 24 hours daily. **Credit** AmEx, DC, EC, MC, V.
More than a score of excellent beers on draught, hundreds of others in bottles: the Pub should be a haven for anyone who appreciates a good brew. But the unappealing décor, uncomfortable surroundings and mindless music that bleats away night and day make many beer lovers think twice before entering what was once the house of Doctor Guillotin, the inventor of guess what...

Le Sous-Rock
49 rue Saint-Honoré, 75001 Paris (40.26.46.61). Metro Pont-Neuf. **Open** 11-5am daily. **Credit** V.
We've heard some sturdy souls are working their way through all the 500 beers in this bar's stock. Go wish them luck, and decide, perhaps, to take up the challenge yourself. Cocktails are on hand, along with dishes like

chilli, goulash and Irish stew. A giant video screen, golden oldies and country music may or may not add to your heart-burn.

The Twickenham
70 rue des Saints-Pères, 75007 Paris (42.22.96.85). Metro Sèvres-Babylone. **Open** 9-2am Mon-Fri; 9am-6pm Sat; closed whole month of August. **Credit** V.
Publishing clones from Grasset and Fayard and writers and rugby fans belly up regularly to the Twick's mahogany bar. First-timers may find the service polite, verging on the chilly, at this British-style corner pub. A hot *plat du jour* is served at lunch and dinner along with a score of international beers.

WINE BARS

A little knowledge is a dangerous thing, especially when it comes to buying wine. Perhaps the saddest sight is someone laying out 300F for a mediocre bottle from a well-known vineyard, when they could spend a fraction of that on a far more palatable wine from a lesser-known producer. The best way to avoid falling into this trap is to skip the big names altogether; instead of splashing out on Nuits Saint Georges, Gevrey Chambertin, Pomerol and Pauillac, the listwise opt instead for the neglected areas of Alsace and the Loire (with the costly exception of Sancerre) and Rhone Valleys. They

Aux Bons Crus
7 rue des Petits-Champs, 75001 Paris (42.60.06.45). Metro Bourse , Palais-Royal. **Open** 8am-10pm Mon-Fri; closed whole month of August. **No credit cards.**
A plate of lentil salad, some good charcuteries and a glass or two of delicious Muscadet, Vacqueyras or Sancerre are the simple but satisfying pleasures to be found in this noisy, cramped and friendly little bistro near the Bibliothèque Nationale.

Aux Négociants
27 rue Lambert, 75018 Paris (46.06.15.11). Metro Château-Rouge. **Open** noon-8pm Mon, Wed, Fri; noon-10pm Tue, Thur; closed whole month of August. **No credit cards.**
Back behind the Sacré-Coeur, where the tourists almost never go, is an appealing little *bistro à vin* in the true Montmartrois tradition. The local crowd indulges in sturdy French country fare at lunch, washed down by lip-smacking Bourgueil, fruity white Jasnières and frisky Beaujolais.

Le Café de la Nouvelle Mairie
19 rue des Fossés-Saint-Jacques, 75005 Paris (43.26.80.18). Metro Cluny-la-Sorbonne/RER Luxembourg. **Open** 9-1am Mon-Fri; 6pm-1am Sat. **No credit cards.**
See **picture and caption.**

La Cave Drouot
8 rue Drouot, 75009 Paris (47.70.83.38). Metro Richelieu-Drouot. **Open** 7.30am-9.30pm Mon-Sat; closed Saturdays in July, August. **No credit cards.**
Appraisers, auctioneers and the mischievous Basque *patron* provide lots of ambience in this colourful bistro. Best bets from the wine list are the superb Burgundies and Beaujolais; to go with them, order a copious *plat du jour* and finish up with a portion of tangy sheep's milk cheese.

Le Coude Fou
12 rue du Bourg-Tibourg, 75004 Paris (42.77.15.16). Metro Hôtel de Ville, Saint

Paul. **Open** noon-4pm, 6pm-2am, Mon-Sat; 6pm-2am Sun. **Credit** V.

The wine list of this likeable little bistro is studded with treasures. On any given day one can sample a solid red Saint-Joseph from central France, a superlative Domaine de Torraccia from Corsica or a charming Mondeuse from Savoie. What's more, the food is fresh and inventive. Our only gripe: the service can be excruciatingly slow.

Le Duc de Richelieu
110 rue de Richelieu, 75002 Paris (42.96.38.38). Metro Les Halles. **Open** 7-5am Mon-Sat. **No credit cards.**

This typically Parisian, award-winning bistro specializes in wines of the Beaujolais: try the seldom-seen white variety, or a fragrant Fleurie. They also serve hearty Lyonnais *plats du jour* (set meals of the day).

L'Ecluse
15 quai des Grands-Augustins, 75006 Paris (46.33.58.74). Metro Saint-Michel. **Open** noon-2am Mon-Sat. **Credit** AmEx, DC, V.

This bar was the first link in the Ecluse chain, now also present in the 1st, 8th and 9th arrondissements. Bordeaux wines are showcased here, with some 70 châteaux represented. These are always first-rate, as are the pricey little dishes (*foie gras, carpaccio,* San Daniele ham) that accompany them.

Jacques Mélac
42 rue Léon-Frot, 75011 Paris (43.70.59.27). Metro Charonne. **Open** 9am-7pm Mon, Wed, Fri; 9am-10.30pm Tue, Thur; closed mid July to mid August. **No credit cards.**

Everybody's favourite wine bar is still as friendly and unpretentious as ever. Mélac's stock of good but inexpensive bottlings includes a tasty Cahors – a rarity because so many are woody and hard – excellent Chinon and a variety of high-quality country wines. Omelettes, *charcuterie* and other snacks are served at lunch and for dinner twice a week.

Juvenile's
47 rue de Richelieu, 75001 Paris (42.97.46.49). Metro Palais-Royal. **Open** 6-11pm Mon, Sat; 11am-11pm Tue-Fri. **Credit** V.

The Spanish-style snacks known as tapas make for tasty snacks with the marvellous wines chosen by Mark Williamson and Tim Johnston. Sherries headline the list, but bottles from many regions, French and foreign, are on hand also. Juvenile's also serve sophisticated sandwiches and delicious salads.

Ma Bourgogne
133 boulevard Haussman, 75008 Paris (45.63.50.61). Metro Miromesnil. **Open** 7am-8.30pm Mon-Fri. **Credit** V.

At lunch-time the place bursts with solidly built businessmen who relish *patron* Louis Prin's *charcuterie* and bistro dishes. For a quiet glass of Beaujolais (the house speciality), Saint-Véran or Hautes-Côtes-de-Beaune, come after the crowds have departed.

Millésimes
7 rue Lobineau, 75006 Paris (46.34.22.15). Metro Saint-Sulpice. **Open** 10-1am Mon-Sat. **Credit** V.

Hurry over to this little bistro near the Marché Saint-Germain where Chico Sewlce has put together a vast and exemplary collection of French and imported wines. He serves them with robust *charcuteries* and other cold dishes, and asks for very little money in return.

L'Oenothéque
20 rue Saint-Lazare, 75009 Paris (48.78.08.76). Metro Trinité. **Open** 10am-10.30pm Mon-Fri; closed last three weeks of August. **Credit** V.

Here's a wine bar where you can sample a glass of some of the very good and unusual vintages chosen by sommelier David Hallé, before you buy a bottle in the shop. Moderately priced dishes are served in the adjoining restaurant.

Le Père Tranquille
30 avenue du Maine, 75015 Paris (42.22.88.12). Metro Montparnasse. **Open** 10am-8pm Tue-Sat. **No credit cards.**

One hesitates to recommend a place where the owner is unfriendly but if you can overlook Monsieur Nouyrigat's ill humour, you may enjoy the savoury terrines, cheeses and *plats du jour* he proposes to accompany a slew of delicious Loire Valley wines.

Le Rallye
6 rue Daguerre, 75014 Paris (43.22.57.05). Metro Denfert Rochereau. **Open** 9.30am-8pm Tue-Sat; closed whole month of August. **Credit** V.

For a glass of what may well be the best Beaujolais in town, head for the rue Daguerre. This family-run bistro is as friendly a spot as one is likely to find for satisfying *charcuterie* and wines from all ten crus of the Beaujolais region (the Chenas is superlative).

Le Rubis
10 rue du Marché-Saint-Honoré, 75001 Paris (42.61.03.34). Metro Tuileries. **Open** 7am-10pm Mon-Fri; closed whole month of August. **No credit cards.**
See **picture and caption.**

La Tartine
24 rue de Rivoli, 75004 Paris (42.72.76.85). Metro Hôtel de Ville. **Open** 8am-10pm Mon, Thur-Sun; noon-10pm Wed; closed whole month of August. **No credit cards.**

This colourful bar is a classic spot for an inexpensive lunch or snack. Wine lovers from all walks of life drop in to hoist a glass filled with one of some 50 different French growths, all judiciously chosen. A selection of cold dishes and excellent cheeses is on offer as well.

Willi's Wine Bar
13 rue des Petit-Champs, 75001 Paris (42.61.05.09). Metro Bourse. **Open** noon-11pm Mon-Sat. **Credit** V.
See **picture and caption.**

Try **Willi's Wine Bar** (*listed under* **Wine Bars**) *to savour a unique choice of wines. The team of Williamson and Johnston have put together an exemplary list of wines from the Rhône, the Bordeaux area, and as far afield as California and Australia. Each week brings interesting new 'suggestions' for an aperitif. The adjoining restaurant is no longer just a place to be seen in: it's now a great place to eat.*

Cafés & Salons de Thé

Where to sip, dream and while away the afternoons: Paris's cafés and tea-rooms remain ever popular for a drink and unhurried conversation.

CAFES

Acrid, metallic coffee; 'house' Sauvignon smelling distinctly of *pipi de chat*; sandwiches consisting of a lonesome slice of plastic-packed ham on a length of stale *baguette*; *croque monsieurs* that emerge from the toaster oven with dried-out edges and stringy cheese that manages to be cold and burnt at the same time; all these delights served forth in an atmosphere thick with smoke and the tinny din of pinball machines. Such, alas, is the situation in too many of Paris's 12,000 cafés. Our advice to visitors is: if you want a decent cup of coffee, try a tea room. Salons de thé (like wine bars and brasseries) are also a good bet for a light lunch or snack.

Still, the *terrasse* of a Parisian café is an unbeatable observation post for taking the pulse of the city, so visitors in the know should possess a list of at least a dozen strategically placed establishments. Herewith some of our favourites:

Brûlerie San José
30 rue des Petits-Champs, 75002 Paris (42.96.69.09). Metro Pyramide.
Open 8am-7pm Mon-Fri; closed whole month of August. **No credit cards.**
After a shopping binge on the place des Victoires or the avenue de l'Opéra, stop for a reviving cup of espresso or cappuccino at this Italian-style bar. No tables, no pastries, just fine, fragrant coffee, roasted and ground on the premises.

Café Beaubourg
100 rue Saint-Martin, 75004 Paris (48.87.89.98). Metro Châtelet.
Open 8am-2am daily. **Credit** AmEx, DC, V.
An equally huge, similarly chilly, slightly less manic reprise of the **Café Costes** (*see below*). Comparing the merits of the two is a favourite pastime with trendy denizens of Les Halles.

Café Costes
4 rue Berger, 75001 Paris (46.08.54.39). Metro Les Halles. **Open** 8am-2am daily. **No credit cards.**
Post-modern mecca where young Parisians and their cosmopolitan *confrères* can get a first taste of café society. A swell place to idle away an afternoon observing the fauna and writing postcards to the folks back home.

Café de Flore
172 boulevard Saint-Germain, 75006 Paris (45.48.55.26). Metro Saint-Germain-des-Prés/bus 39, 48, 63, 86, 95.
Open 7am-1.30am daily. **No credit cards.**
The other fabled *café littéraire* of Saint-Germain (*see* **Les Deux Magots**). The Flore's terrasse is perhaps a better place to people-watch than the Deux Magots; it's quieter, and patrons are less hassled by aggressive street performers.

Café des Hauteurs
Musée d'Orsay, 1 rue de Bellechasse, 75007 Paris (40.49.48.14). Metro Solférino/RER Musée d'Orsay/bus 24, 73, 84, 88, 89.
Open 10.30am-6pm Tue, Wed, Fri; 10.30am-9pm Thur; 9am-6pm Sat. **No credit cards.**
High atop the Musée d'Orsay, this café is a godsend for exhausted art lovers in need of a restorative cup of tea – or glass of wine. The panoramic view of Paris is not the least of this establishment's attractions.

Café de Madrid
6-8 boulevard Montmartre, 75009 Paris (48.24.97.22). Metro Richelieu-Drouot. **Open** 8am-2am daily. **Credit** AmEx, DC, MC, V.
Founded in 1854, the Madrid originally provided *boulevardiers* with sustenance and refreshment. Its glory days are just a memory now, but actors from the Théâtre des Variétés across the street still drop in for a drink or a dozen oysters at this venerable, slightly sad café.

Café Mouffetard
118 rue Mouffetard, 75005 Paris (43.31.42.50). Metro Monge. **Open** 7am-9pm Tue-Sat; 7am-noon Sun. **No credit cards.**
A café that makes its own croissants? Incredible but true. What's more, they're delicious. Munch a couple while you watch the shoppers at the bustling Mouffetard market.

Café de la Paix
12 boulevard des Capucines, 75009 Paris (42.68.12.13). Metro Opéra.
Open 10am-1.30pm, 2.30pm-midnight, daily. **Credit** AmEx, DC, EC, MC, V.
A Parisian landmark. Inside, look for the Second Empire frescoes and décor by Charles Garnier, best known for his Opéra across the street. Outside, on the covered terrasse, enjoy a wide-angle view of the bustling boulevards. Expensive, packed with tourists, but charming all the same.

Les Deux Magots
6 place Saint-Germain-des-Prés, 75008 Paris (45.48.55.25). Metro Saint-Germain-des-Prés/bus 39, 38, 63, 86, 95.
Open 7am-1.30am daily; closed second week of January. **No credit cards.**
See **picture and caption.**

Le Fouquet's
99 avenue des Champs-Elysées, 75008 Paris (47.23.70.80). Metro George V. **Open** 8.30am-2am daily. **Credit** AmEx, DC, V.
In spring and summer, the terrasse of Le Fouquet's (pronounce the 't') is arguably the prettiest spot on the Champs-Elysées for sipping coffee and observing the Parisian scene. Expensive.

Ma Bourgogne
19 place des Vosges, 75004 Paris (42.78.44.84). Metro Saint-Paul. **Open** 7am-1.30am daily; closed whole month of February.
Under the arcades of the place des Vosges, join the lively eclectic crowd that frequents this Marais landmark for breakfast, lunch, drinks and/or dinner. Don't forget to check out the wine bar upstairs.

Mollard
113 rue Saint-Lazare, 75008 Paris (43.87.50.22). Metro Saint-Lazare.
Open noon-1am daily.
Credit AmEx, DC, EC, MC, V.
Whether your train is pulling into or out of the Gare Saint-Lazare, make a point of stopping at this turn-of-the-century café/brasserie. The sumptuous art nouveau décor alone is worth a detour.

Pause Café
41 rue de Charonne, 75011 Paris (48.06.80.33). Metro Ledru-Rollin.
Open 8am-2am daily. **No credit cards.**
A relaxed atmosphere prevails in this café favoured by Bastille hipsters. Drop in after a look-in at the local art galleries or before going to the **China Club** (*see chapter* **Bars**).

Le Select
99 boulevard du Montparnasse, 75006 Paris (45.48.38.24). Metro Vavin.
Open 8.30am-2am daily. **Credit** V.
It's fashionable to give Le Select short shrift, but eccentrics, non-conformists and sundry colourful characters insist on visiting this spot instead of the trendier Montparnasse watering holes. Good beers.

Zimmer
1 place du Châtelet, 75001 Paris (42.38.74.03). Metro Châtelet.
Open 8.30am-2am daily. **Credit** AmEx, V.
A large, brightly lit café-brasserie; a good place to discuss the evening's performance after a concert or show at one of the nearby theatres. The delicious fresh fruit juices are a must.

SALONS DE THE

A la Cour de Rohan
59-61 rue Saint-André-des-Arts, 75006 Paris (43.25.79.67). Metro Odéon.
Open noon-6pm Tue-Thur; noon-midnight Fri, Sat; 2.30-8pm Sun; closed last two weeks in August. **No credit cards.**
A precious address for this quiet corner that is just off the noisy boulevard Saint-Germain. Cosy and stylish, this two-storey salon de thé offers savoury tarts and light lunch dishes as well as a wide range of teas and appealing pastries.

Angélina
228 rue de Rivoli, 75001 Paris (42.60.82.00). Metro Tuileries.
Open 9.30am-7pm daily; closed whole month of August. **Credit** AmEx, DC, V.

Though it is to be avoided at lunch (mediocre *plat du jour*, astronomically priced), Angélina is to be cherished at teatime. Along with your divine hot chocolate, drink in the Belle Epoque atmosphere and nibble at a lush *Mont Blanc* (whipped cream, meringue and chestnut purée).

Brocco
180 rue du Temple, 75003 Paris (42.72.19.81). Metro République.
Open 7am-7.30pm daily. **Credit** V.
Marble, mirrors and sculptured mouldings adorn this adorable tea room near the place de la République. Prices here are more in keeping with the downscale neighbourhood than with the lush décor, so take a seat at one of the little triangular marble tables and stuff yourself with delicious, inexpensive pastries; try the rich *Malgache au chocolat*. Great coffee, too.

Café de la Mosquée de Paris
39 rue Geoffroy-Saint-Hilaire, 75005 Paris (43.31.18.14). Metro Censier-Daubenton.
Open 11am-8pm daily. **No credit cards**.
Sweet mint tea, authentic loukoums and sticky pastel pastries are served in a most leisurely fashion here at the Paris mosque, a huge moorish edifice near the Botanical Gardens (Jardin des Plantes).

Casa Diva
27 rue Cambacérès, 75008 Paris (42.55.46.52). Metro Miromesnil. **Open** 11.30am-6.30pm Mon-Sat. **No credit cards**.
To enjoy the arias in peace, come after lunch and settle down in the cosy, classy décor with a sublime cup of tea and a generous slice of chocolate mousse cake.

Dailoyau
2 place Edmond-Rostand, 75006 Paris (43.29.31.10). RER Luxembourg
Open 9.30am-7.30pm Mon-Sat; 9am-7pm Sun. **Credit** AmEx, V.
On weekend afternoons it's hard to get a table in the prim little upstairs tea room; but on, say, a Thursday morning, you'll have the place to yourself. And a lovely place it is, with a view of Luxembourg Gardens across the street, a cup of tea or very good coffee, and a dainty pastry or two.

Le Flore en L'Ile
42 quai d'Orléans, 75004 Paris (43.29.88.27). Metro Pont-Marie.
Open 10am-1am daily. **Credit** V.
Real brewed tea, honey cakes, Berthillon ice creams and sorbets, good salads and *plat du jour* are surely reason enough to visit this popular café-cum-tea room. Le Flore en L'Ile also boasts a fabulous view of the Seine and Nôtre Dame.

Ladurée
18 rue Royale, 75008 Paris (42.60.21.79). Metro Madeleine. **Open** 8.30am-7pm Mon-Sat; closed whole month of August. **Credit** V.
Don't let yourself be tempted to lunch in these lovely, distinguished surroundings; the food is ho-hum and too expensive. But, by all means enjoy a late breakfast of wonderful croissants and coffees, or better still, a tea-time treat of Ladurée's far-famed raspberry, chocolate and vanilla *macarons*.

Mariage Frères
30-32 rue du Bourg-Tibourg, 75004 Paris (42.72.28.11). Metro Saint-Paul.
Open 11am-7.30pm Tue-Sat; noon-7.30pm Sun. **Credit** AmEx, DC, V.
Hundreds of rare and exotic teas perfume the air of this extraordinary shop. The salon de thé proposes forgettable light lunch dishes, but the pastries served with, for example, a cup of golden-tipped Grand Yunnan are perfectly delicious. Smokers are segregated in a room upstairs.

Muscade
36 rue de Montpensier, 75001 paris (42.97.51.36). Metro Palais-Royal.
Open *winter*: noon-8.30pm daily; *summer*: noon-11pm daily. **Credit** AmEx, V.
A limited recommendation for this establishment, where meals are usually quite disappointing. However, the setting is delicious, especially for tea in summer, amidst the flowers and fountains of the Jardin du Palais-Royal. Tea, coffee and pastries are served from 3.30pm to 7pm.

La Paradis du Fruit
29 quai des Grands-Augustins, 75006 Paris (43.54.51.42). Metro Saint-Michel.
Open 11.30am-1.30am daily. **Credit** V.
Revive flagging spirits with a vitamin-packed cocktail of fruit or vegetable juice; or watch Parisian life roll by on the *quais* while tucking into fresh salads, fruit pastries and luscious ice-creams. Also featured are premium teas from Mariage Frères.

Patachou
9 place du Tertre, 75018 Paris (42.51.06.06). Metro Abbesses.
Open 8am-midnight daily. **Credit** AmEx, V.
A diversified pastry, chocolate, ice-cream and tea shop, Patachou proposes inventive sweet treats in warm surroundings of polished wood and antique tiles. A haven from the touring hordes of the Butte Montmartre.

A Priori Thé
36 Galerie Vivienne, 75002 Paris (42.97.48.75). Metro Bourse. **Open** noon-6.30pm Mon-Sat; 1-6pm Sun. **Credit** V.
When sunlight filters through the glass roof of the Galerie Vivienne, it's hard to resist the inviting wicker armchairs set out before this charming salon de thé. From 3pm on, an interesting range of English teas is served, along with French and American-style pastries, set out for your inspection. Lunch and weekend brunches are also served.

Tea Follies
6 place Gustave-Toudouze, 75009 Paris (42.80.08.44). Metro Saint Georges/bus 30, 67, 74. **Open** 9am-9pm Mon-Sat, 9am-7pm Sun. **Credit** V.
On a delightfully shady little square just south of Pigalle, indulge in scones and tea, or the considerably more calorific *Ardéchois* (a chocolate and chestnut confection). A good selection of wines is available by the glass. On Sundays, a 100F note will buy you a very good brunch.

*Paris's literary café, **Les Deux Magots** (listed under **Cafés**) still glories in its long list of deceased clients – Mallarmé, Breton, Gide, Hemingway, Sartre and the rest. Unlike today's patrons, they didn't have to shell out 30F for a double espresso. The coffee is quite good, however, and so is the rich hot chocolate, best savoured indoors in a mahogany booth.*

Shops and Services

The boulevards and streets of
Paris are lined with outlandish
and elegant boutiques that rival
those of any other capital city.
The profusion of fashion retailers, specialist shops and food
outlets makes Paris the ultimate
destination for the discerning
consumer. We review all types
of establishment, from those
that sell caviar or specialize in
children's shoes to those that
display designer hats or stock
the latest block-busters. And,
should you require the services
of a Parisian paper engraver, tailor or antiques valuer, we show
you the way. We not only list
emergency services offered by
dentists and dry-cleaners, but
also detail the more luxurious
services that specialist companies offer, such as champagne
breakfast home-delivery and
beauty therapy.

CONTENTS:

Fashion

Parisian boutiques put many of Europe's cities to shame. Below we give a resumé of what's going on in the fashion scene and where you're likely to pick up something to your taste.

Boutiques are the backbone of retailing in Paris. Shopping as a form of pleasure is the goal; customers enjoy individual attention in each shop instead of the self-service mass-retailing which is prevalent in other countries. Certain streets are famous for the types of boutiques which line the pavements. For example, **rue du Cherche-Midi** and **rue de Grenelle** in the 6th arrondissement are *de rigueur* for top quality shoes, bags and leather goods. *Haute Couture* clothes are sold on **rue du Faubourg-Saint-Honoré** and **avenue Montaigne** in the 8th arrondissement. Trendies will think they died and went to heaven as they stroll up **rue Etienne Marcel** to **place des Victoires** bordering the 1st and 2nd arrondissements.

For self-service shopping *à l'américaine*, there are colossal and crowded department stores. The famous rivals, **Galeries Lafayette** and **Printemps**, are flagshipped side by side on boulevard Haussmann in the 9th arrondissement and carry designer, brand name and private label merchandise. Even they have speciality boutiques under their magnificent domes.

WHERE NOT TO SHOP

Sad to say, Paris's former bastion of fashion and class, the **Champs-Elysées**, is now a neon strip of fast food, banks, airline offices, malls and cinemas. The exception to the rule, however, is the **Guerlain Perfumerie** (at No.68) which evokes turn-of-the-century elegance with its curved staircase, gilt bottles and mysterious scents. Also of interest, and a relatively recent arrival, is the mammoth, neo-classical style **Virgin Megastore** (at No.52-60) which stocks a vast selection of records, tapes and CDs. **Les Halles**, though an important shopping area, does have drawbacks. It's best to avoid the giant, subterranean shopping centre, Forum des Halles, a tacky temple of snack bars,

cinemas and more than 180 stores connected by a maze of escalators and mall-walks. It's guaranteed to give anyone a headache.

COUTURE

The world of *Haute Couture*, the ultimate in fashion chic and design, originated in France. *Haute Couture* garments are custom draped, beaded or embroidered for individual clients and cut precisely to their exact measurements. Prices reflect this professional and personalized service. With garments costing 20,000F to 50,000F or more, it's not surprising that this style of dress is beyond the reach of most women's purse-strings.

The French taste for luxury and exclusivity spawned Haute Couture at the beginning of the Industrial

Revolution. By the thirties it reached its pinnacle, led by sleek, New Woman couturiers Madeleine Vionnet, Gabrielle Chanel and Elsa Schiaparelli. It was briefly revived after World War II by Christian Dior's New Look. However, by the swinging sixties, a young, modern and natural style began to emerge — the invention of *prêt-a-porter* (ready-to-wear) garments. Suddenly, scores of fashion designers were parading ready-made collections each season. These new lines are today sold by Couture Houses, such as Yves St Laurent, Chanel and Dior, and, though strictly not *Haute Couture*, they are the closest most women get to wearing the real thing.

After the sixties, out-priced *Haute Couture* became an elitist dinosaur. That is, until 1987, when **Christian Lacroix** opened his fashion house and re-infused *Haute Couture* with wit and opulence. Glamour-starved society ladies, tired of cookie-cutter clothes, are today eating it up. Lacroix's pieces range from 50,000F to-the-sky's-the-limit. The average creation time is 150 hours. Though garments from the Couture Houses

What does an Arab prince do when he's in the Seychelles but needs a new suit? He phones **Pythagore/Purcell** *(listed under* **Designer Boutiques/Around the Arc de Triomphe**)*, who not only have his measurements stored on computer, but will send him (by courier) a swatch book to select the fabric for his tailored 12,000F suit. The more run-of-the-mill stock includes off-the-peg suits (from 6,900F) from Byblos, Zegna, Valentino and Christian Dior as well as P/P's own label.*

may be expensive, if you want to spend a million and look like you have, you'll have to visit Lacroix.

SALES, EXPORT SCHEME & HOLIDAYS

Those visiting Paris at the beginning of January or the beginning of July can take advantage of the discounts during the **sales** (soldes) of 30 to 50 per cent on items such as clothing, shoes, accessories and furnishing fabrics. Seasonal sales generally occupy prime floor space for a month and are then relegated to the back of the store when the new stock arrives. Department stores hold their big sales during two weeks each season: at the end of June to mid-July and from the end of December until mid-January.

Almost all retailers provide **Detaxe** (export scheme) for foreign customers claiming the 18.6 per cent tax refund if purchases reach over 1,200F for non-EEC residents or 2,400F for EEC residents. Present the form to customs when leaving France. Your refund will be credited to you within about six weeks. Retailers providing this service will be noted below with Detaxe.

All stores close on 1 January, 1 May, 14 July and 25 December, but are generally open during other bank holidays. Stores which close during the month of August (the traditional French *vacances*) are noted in the listings.

DESIGNER BOUTIQUES

AROUND THE ARC DE TRIOMPHE

Façonnable
25 rue Royal, 75008 Paris (47.42.72.60). Metro Madeleine/bus 52. **Open** 2-7pm Mon; 10am-7pm Tue-Sat. **Credit** AmEx, CB, DC, EC, MC, FTC, V.
A male anglophile's haven where new suits smell like old money and the wearer is most likely to be as at home in the boardroom as in his country pad. Upstairs you'll find the urbane suits averaging 4,500F, shoes (expect to pay 2,000F for oxblood 'weejun' moccasins) and leather and nylon luggage. The ground floor stocks outdoor-style hunting jackets, jeans, an impressive range of silk ties (325F) and Liberty print boxer shorts (200F).
Alterations. Export scheme (detaxe).
Branch: 174 boulevard Saint Germain, 75006 (40.49.02.47).

Pythagore/Purcell
62 rue du Faubourg Saint-Honoré, 75008 Paris (47.42.88.02). Metro Concorde/bus 52. **Open** 10am-7.30pm Mon-Sat. **Credit** AmEx, CB, EC, DC, MC, F$DM£YenTC, all currencies.
See **picture and caption.**
Alterations. Bespoke tailoring. Custom orders for shoes. Delivery (free delivery by DHL). Export scheme (detaxe). Fax and phone service. Thé salon.
Branches: 74 avenue des Champs-Elysées, 75008 (42.25.63.38); 26 avenue des Champs-Elysées, 75008 (42.89.02.01).

Loft Design By
12 rue du Faubourg Saint-Honoré, 75008 Paris (42.65.59.65). Metro Concorde/bus 52. **Open** 10am-7.30pm Mon-Sat. **Credit** AmEx, CB, DC, EC, MC, F$TC, V.
Brick walls, a wooden staircase, suspended lanterns and a tailor's corner complete with antique sewing machines, give this unisex shop the feeling of an old sewing mill from the Industrial Revolution. The prices even hark back to bygone days: on our visit, a summer-weight khaki suit cost 2,750F, a winter tweedy wool blazer 990F, an oilskin raincoat 800F and shirts (Oxford, classic stripes and pre-laundered cotton) 295F each. Smart casual pullovers and sweatshirts are 395F. There's an impressive array of ties and a selection of shoes.
Alterations. Delivery. Export scheme (detaxe). Mail order.

LES HALLES

Agnes B
2, 3, 6, rue du Jour, 75001 Paris (women 45.08.56.56/men 42.33.04.13). Metro Les Halles, Etienne Marcel/bus 29. **Open** 10.30am-7.30pm Mon-Sat. Credit AmEx, CB, EC, MC, F$TC, V.
There's an Agnes B boutique for everyone on rue du Jour: women's wear at No.6, men's wear at No.3 next to her Lolita shop for teens, and children's wear at No.2. Her style is casual and modern, using basic fabrics. The ubiquitous Agnes B cardigan, a boxy fleece with pearl snaps, in a rainbow of colours, is 390F. Prices average about 700F for trousers, 1,500F for jackets. When trying clothes on, allow for shrinkage. The women's shop and changing rooms are always mobbed and staff seem harrassed.
Export scheme (detaxe).
Branches: 13 rue Michelet, 75006 (46.33.70.20); 17 (women) and 25 (men) avenue Pierre 1er de Serbie, 75008 (women 47.20.22.44/men 47.23.36.69).

Barbara Bui
23 rue Etienne Marcel, 75001 Paris (40.26.43.65). Metro Etienne Marcel/bus 29. **Open** 10.30am-7pm Mon-Sat. **Credit** AmEx, CB, EC, MC, FTC, V.
This Eurasian designer creates decidedly feminine women's wear in linen, silk, crêpe, cotton, chiffon and velour. Diaphanous blouses cost 1,300F and full trousers are 1,500F. In the basement of this airy boutique, men's jackets with subtle draping go for about 2,500F and trousers for 1,200F. The

*Serge Bensimon of **Autour du Monde** (listed under **Designer Boutiques/Le Marais**) began in the surplus clothing business and soon created a traveller's outfittery which stocks timeless, authentic casual wear at good prices and for all ages. The safari image follows through on field watches, luggage, scarves, socks and survival gear. Fragrances from Geo F Trumper of Mayfair and Cutler and Gross sunglasses bring British colonialism to Paris.*

Catherine Baril
Two Boutiques

DELUXE
SECOND-HAND
DESIGNER CLOTHING
14, RUE DE LA TOUR
PARIS 16TH
45.20.95.21

DELUXE
SECOND-HAND
DESIGNER CLOTHING
25, RUE DE LA TOUR
PARIS 16TH
45.27.11.46

OPEN DAILY 10-7
MONDAY 2-7

VISA/CARTE BLEUE ACCEPTED

SAINT LAURENT

GUY LAROCHE

PIERRE CARDIN

TED LAPIDUS

GIVENCHY

UNGARO

CHANEL

colourful embroidered waistcoats are particularly special and are priced 800F.
Alterations. Brochure. Delivery. Export scheme (detaxe).

Creeks
98 rue Saint Denis, 75001 Paris (42.33.81.70). Metro Etienne Marcel, Les Halles/bus 29. **Open** 11am-7.30pm Mon; 10.30am-7.30pm Tue-Sat. **Credit** AmEx, CB, EC, MC, FTC, V.
Architect Philippe Starck's stainless steel shopfront hides three levels of unisex casual wear, shoes and indispensable accoutrements for the 'clean jean' crowd. Fifties' style Chevignon campus jackets and Perfecto biker jackets (1,500F to 3,000F) are a hit with kids whose parents wore the originals. Creeks own jeans and chinos start at 300F.
Export scheme (detaxe).
Branches: 155 rue de Rennes, 75006 (45.48.26.36); 43 boulevard Saint Michel, 75005 (43.54.21.98); 119 rue de la Pompe, 75016 (45.53.59.49); 129 rue de la Pompe, 75016 (47.27.40.22); 2 rue Gustave-Courbet, 75016 (47.27.07.07).

Gaultier Junior
7 rue du Jour, 75001 Paris (40.28.01.91). Metro Les Halles, Etienne Marcel/bus 29. **Open** 10am-7pm Mon-Sat. **Credit** AmEx, CB, DC, EC, JCB, MC, FSDM&TC, V.
Jean-Paul Gaultier's clever ideas are now more affordable in his Junior line – a reference not to age but to wallet size and attitude. He emphasizes youth being an attitude rather than an age by employing octogenarian models. Gaultier's a whiz at revitalizing old classics like the jean jacket, parka and desert boot. His hour-glass shaped coloured denim jackets are already collectors' items (from 850F). Be sure to try clothes on – the sizes are Italian and not always consistent.
Export scheme (detaxe).

Kiliwatch
100 rue Saint Denis, 75001 Paris (42.21.99.37). Metro Etienne Marcel, Les Halles/bus 29. **Open** 10am-8pm Mon-Sat. **Credit** AmEx, CB, DC, EC, MC, FTC, V.
A jumbled assortment of avant-garde young designers from Paris and London: Gaultier Junior, Cyclopo Loco, Yorke and Cole, Red or Dead and English Eccentrics, mingle with mad jewellery by Billy Boy, vintage clothing and jeans. Shame about the bumper-to-bumper racks and makeshift fitting rooms.
Export scheme (detaxe).

Scooter
10 rue de Turbigo, 75001 Paris (45.08.89.31). Metro Etienne Marcel, Les Halles/bus 29. **Open** 2-7.30pm Mon; 10.30am-7.30pm Tue-Sat. **Credit** AmEx, CB, EC, MC, FTC, V.
Specializing in bangle and bauble costume jewellery and their flirty, colourful junior range called Mademoiselle Zaza, Scooter is a haunt for models and trendy art students. All their gear can be carried in a variety of Mlle Zaza nylon bags in 15 colours, ranging from 75F to 290F.
Export scheme (detaxe).

Un Après-Midi de Chien
10 rue du Jour, 75001 Paris (40.26.92.78). Metro Etienne Marcel, Les Halles/bus 29. **Open** 10.30am-7.15pm Mon-Sat. **Credit**

Christian Lacroix *(listed under* **Haute Couture***) is the real thing* – Haute Couture *at its most extravagant and expensive. Cross the decorating styles of Marie Antoinette and Wilma Flintstone and you have his colourful, baroque and animate boutique. The three seasonal collections, Prêt-a-Porter, Luxe and Haute Couture, fit almost every budget – that is, of the rich and famous. A Prêt suit can cost 6,000F to 10,000F depending on detail. A Luxe outfit, of velvet, satin or silk, averages 20,000F while a customized Couture starts at 50,000F.*

AmEx, CB, EC, MC, FTC, V.
A sugar and spice world, right out of a Shirley Temple movie, for pre-teens and teens. Retro-style dresses and pinafores are about 1,000F and a wide selection of embroidered cotton blouses average 450F each. Teddy bears and scottie dogs adorn T-shirts that cost about 250F. Even the Doc Martens are laced up with pussy-cat bows.
Export scheme (detaxe).

LE MARAIS

À La Bonne Renommée
26 rue Vieille du Temple, 75004 Paris (42.72.03.86). Metro Saint Paul/bus 69, 76. **Open** 11am-7pm Mon-Sat; closed two weeks mid-August. **Credit** CB, EC, MC, V.
Sumptuous folkloric patchworks of damasks, velvets, silks and ribbons on clothes, accessories and furnishings make this shop look like a Chekov Christmas scene all year round. The timeless clothes are more like heirlooms than fashion items. Festive wrap jackets are 2,400F, silk blouses cost 1,300F and coats 1,600F to 3,400F. The pouches (between 250F to 560F) make great gifts.
Postal delivery. Export scheme (detaxe).
Branch: 1 rue Jacob, 75006 (46.33.90.67).

Autour du Monde
12 rue des Francs Bourgeois, 75003 Paris (42.77.16.18). Metro Saint Paul/bus 29, 69,

76, 96. **Open** 2-7.30pm Mon, Sun; 11am-7.30pm Tue-Sat. **Credit** CB, EC, MC, V.
See **picture and caption.**
Alterations. Export scheme (detaxe).

Azzedine Alaia
17 rue du Parc-Royal, 75004 Paris (42.72.19.19). Metro Saint Paul/bus 29, 69, 76, 96. **Open** 10am-7pm Mon-Sat. **Credit** AmEx, CB, DC, EC, MC, FSETC, V.
Five years ago, when women's wear was uniformly baggy and masculine, Azzedine Alaia swung the pendulum with his second-skin, blatantly female couture. Curve-hugging dresses run at about 3,000F and his forties' style shoes are 1,500F. Alaia groupies include Grace Jones, Tina Turner and Annie Lennox.
Alterations. Export scheme (detaxe).

Il Pour L'Homme
13 rue du Roi de Sicile, 75004 Paris (42.76.01.81). Metro Saint Paul/bus 69, 76, 96. **Open** 11am-7pm Tue-Sat; closed whole month of August. **Credit** AmEx, CB, EC, MC, V.
Stylish men's accessories and furnishings for the post matt black era: Shaker chairs with basketweave canvas seats, curved thermos hip flasks, chemistry lab copper and chrome coffee makers and dandy wooden bow ties. The unique shirts, by Yoshi Ishikawa, cost 670F.
Export scheme (detaxe).

Step into **L'Apache** (listed under **Vintage Clothes**) and you're beamed back to the thirties: Edith Piaf songs, fan photos of Jean Gabin and Arletty and a huge selection of vintage clothes for men and women. Not as cheap as the flea market (300F for dresses, 250F to 400F for blazers), but the clothes are in much better shape and are also well selected. With staff and customers looking like a Brassaï photo, it's hard to tell who works here.

Branches: 209 rue Saint-Honoré, 75001 (42.60.43.56); 68 rue de Grenelle, 75007 (45.44.98.27).

Inna Kobja
23 rue des Francs Bourgeois, 75004 Paris (42.77.41.20). Metro Saint Paul/bus 29, 69, 76, 96. **Open** 2-7pm Mon, Sun; 11am-7pm Tue-Sat. **Credit** AmEx, CB, EC, CB, MC, F$TC, V.
An eclectic mix of ethnic prints and feminine styling in what looks like a forties' boudoir. Whimsical souvenir scarf minis are 400F and the sudden urge to own the latest season's *de rigueur* embroidered vests from India can be satisfied for 500F. Check the seams – the quality is sometimes dodgy and it can be difficult returning goods.
Export schemes (detaxe).

Othello
24 rue du Roi de Sicile, 75004 Paris (42.77.55.65). Metro Saint Paul/bus 69, 76, 96. **Open** 2-7pm Mon, Sun; also open 2-7pm Sun Sept-March; closed whole month of August. **Credit** AmEx, CB, DC, EC, MC, F$£TC, V.
Othello is a small, friendly boutique carrying the avant-garde creations of British (Ozbek, Galliano), Parisian (Garçonnière) and Swedish (Creatis by Marcel Marongire) designers.
Alterations. Delivery. Export scheme (detaxe).

Plassier
10 rue Ferdinand Duval, 75004 Paris (42.76.00.70). Metro Saint Paul/bus 69, 76, 96. **Open** 2-7pm Mon, Sun; 11am-7pm Tue-Sat. **Credit** CB, EC, MC, V.
Stéphane Plassier's cheeky boutique sports a fantastic mosaic on the floor, flashy Perfecto biker jackets made of chintz (990F) and a cache of never-worn men's and women's shoes from the fifties. Each month, he exhibits the work of new artists, for example hand-painted waistcoats (1,500F) and cartoon-like clocks and radios assembled from salvaged parts (up to 3,000F). For the slightly more serious dresser, he does smart business suitables: 900F for a linen jacket, 450F for a skirt.

Tehen
5bis rue des Rosiers, 75004 Paris (40.27.97.37). Metro Saint Paul/bus 69, 76, 96. **Open** 11.30am-7.30pm Mon-Sat; 2-7.30pm Sun. **Credit** AmEx, CB, EC, MC, V.
Designer Irena Gregori creates a comely collection from knit, jersey and natural fabrics. Distinctive elements are the colour range (each style comes in ten colours), fluid draping and minimalist details. These coordinates work well from day into evening wear and the prices are reasonable: no more than 1,500F for a two-piece outfit. Enthusiasts call it intellectual design.
Export scheme (detaxe).

NORTH OF THE LOUVRE

Adolfo Dominguez
2 rue Catinat, 75001 Paris (47.03.40.28). Metro Bourse/bus 29. **Open** 10am-7pm Mon-Sat. **Credit** AmEx, CB, DC, EC, FTC, MC, V.
Spain's best-known fashion export relies on natural fabrics in earthy colours and unconstructed draping to appeal to professional men and women. Men's suits run from 3,500F to 5,000F; women's separates are about 1,700F; cottons shirts cost 700F.
Alterations. Export scheme (detaxe).

Comme des Garçons
40-42 rue Etienne Marcel, 75002 Paris (42.33.05.21 women/42.36.91.54 men). Metro Bourse, Etienne Marcel/bus 29. **Open** 11am-7pm Mon-Sat; closed first two weeks in August. **Credit** AmEx, CB, DC, EC, MC, F$TC, V.
Rei Kawakubo, once the Yoko Ono of fashion for her severe minimalism and androgyny, has now become downright girlish in her choice of crisp or floaty fabrics and cheery colours. At No.40 is men's wear for suits (7,000F), shirts (700F to 2,600F) accessories and shoes. Women's wear at No.42 features dresses between 2,000F and 4,000F, blouses from 2,000F and shoes at 2,600F. Dramatic draping and quirky details are Comme des Garçons' trademarks.
Alterations. Brochure. Export scheme (detaxe).

Equipment
46 rue Etienne Marcel, 75002 Paris (40.26.17.84). Metro Bourse/bus 29, 67. **Open** 1.30-7pm Mon; 10.30am-7pm Tue-Sat. **Credit** AmEx, CB, EC, DC, MC, F$TC, V.
Equipment's designing mixture of yin and yang make these shirts perfect for both women and men. Choose from their popular big spot style, in a new colour range each season, in rayon at 550F, or a heavy silk uniform style at 850F. They pay special attention to collars on their white cotton shirts which start at 550F.
Export scheme (detaxe).

Henry Cottons
52 rue Etienne Marcel, 75002 Paris (42.36.01.22). Metro Bourse/bus 29. **Open** 10am-7pm Mon-Sat. **Credit** AmEx, CB, DC, EC, MC, F$TC, V.
A brightly designed store that allows you a glimpse of the hidden courtyards behind those massive Parisian doors. Henry Cottons is Italy's answer to Ralph Lauren, outfitting the entire family in BCBG (yuppie) classic sportswear. Suits for men and women in cotton, wool and silk average 2,700F to 4,600F. The hardy parka in canvas and leather is 5,000F. Complete the well-bred look with their shoes, accessories and perfume.
Export scheme (detaxe). Postal delivery.

L'Homme Invisible
43 Galerie Vivienne, 75002 Paris (40.20.03.33). Metro Bourse/bus 29, 67. **Open** noon-7pm Mon-Sat. **Credit** CB, EC, MC, F$£TC, V.
Unabashedly sexy, the unquestionably comfortable unmentionables in cotton and Lycra for men and women run from 90F to 250F. You'll also find swimwear, sleepwear, cyclist shorts and skimpy corset minis (1,500F) to vogue the night away at the latest hot spot.
Delivery. Export scheme (detaxe).

Island
4 rue Vide Gousset, 75002 Paris (42.61.77.77). Metro Bourse/bus 29. **Open** 10.30am-7pm Mon-Sat; closed third week in August. **Credit** AmEx, CB, DC, EC, MC, F$TC, V.

Island sells the kind of casual sportswear, Jack Kennedy-style, for men who would rather be sailing than shopping in Paris. Avirex poplin and rubberized jackets average 900F, oilskin raincoats (in red, yellow or khaki) from England's James Calder are 1,000F to 1,500F. Shoe brands include Sperry Topsider and Vans. Oxford shirts run at about 260F and colourful striped shirts range between 340F and 450F. There's an excellent selection of Hamilton watches (between 900F and 600F), sunglasses by Anglo-American Optical (from 250F to 450F) and leather belts at 300F.
Alterations. Export scheme (detaxe).
Branch: 3 rue Montmartre, 75001 (42.33.15.74).

Jean-Paul Gaultier
6 rue Vivienne, 75002 Paris (42.86.05.05). Metro Bourse/bus 29. **Open** 10am-7pm Mon-Sat. **Credit** AmEx, CB, DC, EC, FSDMTC, V.
Once the *enfant terrible* of French fashion, Gaultier now seems destined for Renaissance manhood. His witty and irreverent clothes have become icons for trendy men and women and are cleverly displayed in this spacious boutique that must resemble the lost city of Atlantis. Check out Gaultier's House music video or latest fashion show in the porthole video screens in the floor.
Delivery service. Export scheme (detaxe).

Moholy-Nagy
2 Galerie Vivienne, 75002 Paris (40.15.05.33). Metro Bourse/bus 29. **Open** 11am-7pm Mon-Sat; closed every Sat during August. **Credit** AmEx, CB, EC, MC, FSTC, V.
A homage to the white shirt. Designer André Frings, grandson of the photographer Lazlo Moholy-Nagy, creates close to 100 styles per season for men and women in natural cotton, silk and Viyella. Prices range from 600F to 700F.
Export scheme (detaxe).

Marithé and François Girbaud
38 rue Etienne Marcel, 75002 Paris (42.33.54.69). Metro Etienne Marcel/bus 29, 67. **Open** 10.30am-7.30pm Mon-Sat. **Credit** AmEx, CB, MC, EC, DC, FSTC, V.
A hi-tech monolith, three storeys high, houses this imaginative range of casual designer clothes and accessories for men and women, as well as the children's line, 'Reproductions'. The labels include Marithé and François Girbaud for shirts and separates, Momento Due for men's city wear, Closed for jeans and casual wear and Maille Party for knitwear. Jeans start at 650F and jackets run betweeen 1,500F and 3,500F. A favourite clothier among media types.
Alterations. Brochure. Delivery. Export scheme (detaxe).

Ventilo
27bis rue du Louvre, 75002 Paris (42.33.18.67). Metro Bourse/bus 29, 67. **Open** noon-7pm Mon; 10.30am-7pm Tue-Sat; closed two weeks in August. **Credit** AmEx, CB, EC, MC, FTC, V.
This earthy, woody store resembles a sprawling ranch house. The basement carries Italian labels Stone Island and Boneville for men. The three floors for women have Ventilo's own label for casual

Since 1837, **Hermès** *(listed under* **Accessories***) has been outfitting the country set with everything from hand-crafted equestrian gear to classic clothing. Their trademark silk scarves, entrenched in the uniform of the rich, come in hundreds of bordered prints for about 970F. For men, they offer John Lobb custom-made shoes (3,000F) and riding boots (18,500F), which take about six months to be made up for the first pair. Upstairs in this luxury emporium is a vast jewellery department.*

wear and feminine, work-worthy separates. There's a plain and fancy selection of cotton shirts that starts at 500F. The delightful *salon de thé* makes up for the sometimes snooty staff.
Alterations. Export scheme (detaxe). Salon de thé (12.30-6pm Mon-Sat; closed August).

SAINT GERMAIN

Et Vous
62-64 rue de Rennes, 75006 Paris (45.48.56.93). Metro Saint-Germain-des-Près/buses 39, 48, 96. **Open** 10.30am-7.30pm Mon-Sat. **Credit** AmEx, CB, DC, EC, MC, FSTC, V.
Kit yourself out with the total look of nostalgic, sugar-coated western gear for Bostonians at a dude ranch. Et Vous's own smart jeans and khakis climb from 350F, chambray and Equipment shirts start at 550F and tooled leather belts are a pricey 700F. Staff are often more interested in each other than in dealing with customers.
Alterations. Export scheme (detaxe). Postal delivery.

Irié
8 rue du Pré-Aux-Clercs, 75007 Paris (42.61.18.28). Metro Rue du Bac/buses 39, 48, 69. **Open** 10am-7pm Mon-Sat; closed first two weeks in August. **Credit** CB, EC, MC, FSETC, V.
Seek out this hidden street for sporty, stretch leggings, T-shirts and minis made

feminine by lace trim and bright floral print (from 300F to 500F). For those of us not blessed with bionic figures, Irié does elongated silk blazers (1,600F) and flowing skirts (980F) in brilliant colours and exotic motifs in the spirit of his mentor, Kenzo.
Export scheme (detaxe).

Kashiyama
147 Boulevard Saint-Germain, 75006 Paris (46.34.11.50). Metro Saint-Germain-des-Près/buses 39, 48, 63, 95. **Open** 11am-7pm Mon-Sat. **Credit** AmEx, CB, DC, EC, JCB, MC, FSTC, V.
Featuring the new guard of fashion's capital: Ozbek, Gigli, Girbaud, Sybilla, lingerie from La Perla and Ferre and shoes by Staphan Kélian. You'll pay top prices (an average of 3,500F per item), but then others will be able to tell you've got money, if nothing else.
Alterations. Export scheme (detaxe). Postal delivery.

Matsuda
25 boulevard Raspail, 75007 Paris (45.49.12.03). Metro Rue du Bac/buses 63, 68, 84, 94. **Open** 11am-7pm Mon; 10.30am-7pm Tue-Sat; closed one week mid-August. **Credit** AmEx, CB, DC, EC, MC, FSTC, V.
As one of the quietest of the wave of Japanese designers to emerge from the late seventies, Matsuda relies on subtle tailoring and impeccable sewing to appeal to

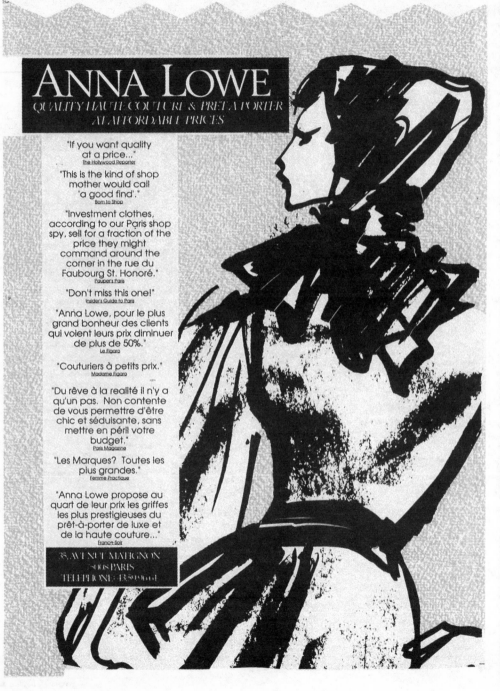

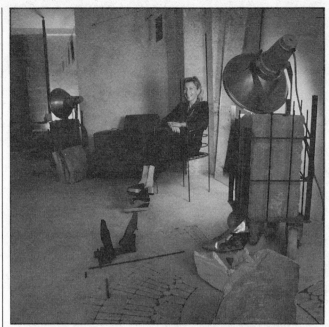

Inoui *(listed under* **Accessories**) *sell shoes by new Japanese designer AKA, Jan Jansen from Holland, Jean-Pierre Figlea and an upcoming collection – still in its prototype stage – by Marie-Christine Frison. Other items are museum pieces: shoes from the thirties to the sixties, sculptures and photographs.*

both women and men. Don't expect to pay less than 5,000F for a suit made of state-of-the-art rayon, silk or wool. Retro style accessories include two-tone shoes, boater hats and marvellous tortoiseshell glasses that are, in some people's book, worth every penny at 1,800F.
Alterations. Brochure. Export scheme (detaxe). Delivery.

TOWARDS THE BOIS DE BOULOGNE

Hemispheres
1 boulevard Emile Augier, 75116 Paris (45.20.13.75). Metro La Muette/bus 32, 52. **Open** 10.30am-7pm Mon-Sat; closed every Mon during August. **Credit** AmEx,CB, DC, EC, JCB, MC, F$Yen£TC, V.
Classic sportswear is the order of the day for Parisian men and women, and that's what Hemispheres specializes in. You'll find a host of striped shirts, ties and sweaters in strange colour combinations, such as purple and green (apparently a favourite with French men), as well as some very special chambray shirts embroidered with barnyard animals (750F to 850F each). Blazers, made in England, Italy or Austria, average 3,000F, although they can cost as much as 6,800F. The women's wear encompasses gold button cardigans in lamb's wool (at 940F) or cashmere (at 3,480F) to frivolous swirling fiesta-style skirts. The shoe department is in the basement.
Alterations. Delivery. Export scheme (detaxe).

Réciproque
95, 101 and 123 rue de la Pompe, 75016 Paris (47.04.82.24/47.04.30.28). Metro Rue de la Pompe/bus 52, 63. **Open** 10am-6.45pm Mon-Sat; closed last week of July, whole month of August. **Credit** CB, EC, MC, V.
Got couturier taste on a thrift shop budget? Réciproque's three side-by-side boutiques are your answer for almost-new designer clothes and accessories for men and women. For example, we found a jet beaded chemise from Jean-Louis Scherrer in tip-top shape priced 500F. One well known Japanese stylist swears by this shop.
Export scheme (detaxe).

COUTURE HOUSES

Couture Houses, such as **Christian Dior, Givenchy, Hermes, Chanel, Pierre Balmain, Yves Saint Laurent** and **Emanuel Ungaro** are all grouped around the Champs-Elysées, in particular avenue Montaigne, avenue George V, rue du Faubourg Saint Honoré and rue François 1er. If your budget doesn't allow for a spending spree in these chic shops, check the dates of their sales – Parisian women swear by them.

HAUTE COUTURE

Christian Lacroix
73 rue du Faubourg Saint-Honoré, 75008 Paris (42.65.79.08). Metro Concorde/bus 52. **Open** 10am-7pm Mon-Sat. **Credit** AmEx, CB, EC, DC, MC, FYen$£TC, V.
See **picture and caption.**
Alterations. Customized orders. Delivery. Export scheme (detaxe).

VINTAGE CLOTHES

L'Apache
45 rue Vieille du Temple, 75004 Paris (42.71.84.27). Metro Saint Paul/bus 69, 76, 96. **Open** 2-7pm Mon; 11am-7pm Tue-Sat. **Credit** CB, EC, MC, F$£TC, V.
See **picture and caption.**

Fuchsia
2 rue l'Avé Maria/1 rue Saint Paul, 75004 Paris (48.04.75.61). Metro Pont Marie, Sully Morland/bus 67. **Open** noon-7pm daily. **Credit** AmEx, CB, EC, MC, FTC, V.
A peek into a feminine boudoir pre-suffragettes: lacy, fine lingerie, dolls, dresser sets and a myriad of perfume flagons. The starchy linen petticoats and camisoles make romantic daywear. Fuchsia buy, as well as sell, heirlooms.
Delivery.

Rag Time
23 rue du Roule, 75001 Paris (42.36.89.36). Metro Châtelet, Les Halles/bus 75. **Open** 2-7.30pm Mon-Sat. **Credit** FTC.
Don't be put off by all the gowns hanging from the rafters and jammed on the racks of the thimble-sized shop. Inside you'll find a veritable museum dedicated to *Haute Couture* dating from the turn of the century to the fifties. Choose and excellent-condition gown with beads, flapper's fringe or thirties' siren simplicity. Prices can soar to 4,000F but you can also rent gowns for 350F to 500F per day. There are also matching hats, bags and a few pairs of collectable Roger Vivier shoes for about 600F.

ACCESSORIES

Adeline Albinet
24 rue du Roi de Sicile, 75004 Paris (42.78.92.78). Metro Saint Paul/bus 69,76, 96. **Open** 2-7pm Mon; 11am-7pm Tue-Sat; also open 2-7pm Sun Sept-March. **Credit** AmEx, CB, EC, MC, F$DM£TC, V.
Albinet combines geometric shapes, rich leathers, clever details and fashion colours for bags (from 750F to 2,000F), belts (from 300F to 700F) and hats (between 250F and 500F). A bargain for the pleasure of wearing them.
Customized orders. Export scheme (detaxe). Postal delivery.

Destination Paris
9 rue 29 Juillet, 75001 Paris

(49.27.98.90). Metro Tuileries. **Open**
10.30am-7.30pm Mon-Sat. **Credit** AmEx,
CB, EC, MC, JCB, FTC, V.
Skip all the tacky souvenir pedlars on the
rue de Rivoli and head for Destination Paris
for the most original Paris memorabilia.
Great housewares and accessories, including original and reworked jewellery from
the forties and fifties, abound in this trendy
shop. Unforgettable gifts at the same price
you'd pay for the boring stuff elsewhere.
Delivery. Export scheme (detaxe).

La Droguerie
*9-11 rue du Jour, 75001 Paris (45.08.93.27).
Metro Les Halles, Etienne Marcel/bus 29.*
Open 2-6.45pm Mon; 10.30am-6.45pm Tue-
Sat. **Credit** $FTC.
La Droguerie is a do-it-yourselfer's best
friend: baubles, beads and buttons come in
every conceivable colour and shape and can
be selected individually or by the scoopful.
There are metres of ribbons, knick-knacks,
feather boas and yarns galore to knit into
'die-for' sweaters. Let your imagination have
a free-for-all.
Delivery.

Hermès
*24 rue du Faubourg-Saint-Honoré, 75008
Paris (42.65.21.60). Metro Concorde/bus 52.*
Open 10am-1pm, 2.15-6.30pm, Mon, Sat;
10am-6.30pm Tue-Fri; July, August only:
10am-1pm, 2.15-6.30pm, Mon-Sat. **Credit**
AmEx, CB, DC, EC, JCB, MC,
FYen$DM£TC, V.
See **picture and caption.**
*Alterations. Brochure. Export scheme
(detaxe). Made-to-measure footwear. Postal
delivery. Watch repair.*

Inoui
*9 rue Keller, 75011 Paris (40.21.81.29).
Metro Ledru-Rollin, Bastille/bus 69.* **Open**
11am-8pm Mon-Sat. **Credit** AmEx, CB, EC,
JCB, MC, FTC, V.
See **picture and caption.**
Delivery. Export scheme (detaxe).

Jack Gomme
*12 rue Rochebrune, 75011 Paris
(40.21.06.43).* **Open** 10am-1pm, 2-7pm, Mon-Sat.
Credit CB, EC, MC, £$FTC, V.
Finding this boutique may seem like being

on a treasure hunt, but once you've tracked
it down, you'll probably want to buy the
clever, fun and practical accessories
designed by two rising stars: Paul Droulers
and Sophie Renier. These designers create
bags, belts, braces and backpacks in leather
and canvas, as well as novel fabrics like fun
fur, giraffe prints and rubber. Some accessories double up as souvenirs; for example,
Eiffel Tower-shaped braces and bags. A new,
more classic line of leather handbags might
just become the new 'Kelly' shape. Though
prices are moderate, you'll cash in on the
compliments.
Delivery. Export scheme (detaxe).

Lunettes Beausoleil
*21 rue du Roi de Sicile, 75004 Paris
(42.77.28.29). Metro Saint Paul/bus
69,76,96.* **Open** 9am-7pm Mon-Sat. **No
credit cards.**
See **picture and caption.**
*Customized orders. Delivery. Export scheme
(detaxe). Guarantee. Delivery.*

Marie Mercie
*56 rue Tiquetonne, 75002 Paris
(40.26.60.68). Metro Etienne Marcel/bus 29.*
Open 11am-7pm Mon-Sat. **Credit** AmEx,
CB, EC, MC, £$FTC, V.
Marie Mercie hand-makes about 160 hats
per year and sells them from her boutique
that looks like an old-fashioned millinary
shop, complete with charming striped hat
boxes. One of her recent summer collections was entitled 'We'll all go to Heaven'; it
was fashioned in black, ivory and gold and
was inspired by Audrey Hepburn. Hats are
priced from 250F to 5,000F, but you'll find
many wonderful styles in the affordable
500F to 600F bracket.
Custom orders. Export scheme (detaxe).

Miller Et Bertaux
*17 rue Ferdinand Duval, 75004 Paris
(42.78.28.39). Metro Saint Paul/bus 69, 76,
96.* **Open** noon-7pm Mon; 10.30am-7pm
Tue-Sat; closed last two weeks in August.
Credit AmEx, CB, DC, EC, MC, F$£TC, V.
Minimalist nature lovers will appreciate
the quiet ethnicity of African and South
American clothing and ikats sold here.
Accessories and objects in leather,
wood and basketweave abound.
Unusual gift items, for example ancient
tin oil pitchers, can be picked up for as
little as 50F.
Export scheme (detaxe).

Les Montres
*58 rue Bonaparte, 75006 Paris
(46.34.71.38). Metro Saint Sulpice/bus 63,
70, 84, 86, 87, 96.* **Open** 10am-8pm Mon-
Sat. **Credit** AE, CB, EC, DC, MC, S£TC, V.
Les Montres has status symbol watches
for any occasion; attending the opera,
scuba-diving or piloting a jet. Here you'll
find the cream of the Swiss and American
crop of watches for men and women,
including Breitling, Corum, Hamilton,
TAG, Porsche Design, Chopard and – the
Rolls Royce of watches – Jaeger-Le-
Coultre. There are also collectors'
watches, such as vintage Rolexes, dating
from the thirties to the fifties.
Delivery. Export scheme (detaxe).
Branches: 16 rue Vieille du Temple, 75004
(42.72.20.87); 6 rue Gustave Courbet, 75016.

Frederic **Beausoleil** *(listed under* **Accessories***) designs spectacles on a
grand scale. His client list reads like an all-star band; Stevie Wonder, Miles
Davis, Serge Gainsbourg, Ray Charles, Jean-Michel Jarre and Tania Maria are
all aficionados. Designers Billy Boy and Hanae Mori also shop in this boutique.
Once you spy his special series of frames crafted from tortoiseshell, cellulose and
antique fixtures (from 450F up to 900F, or over 1,000F for customized orders),
other specs will seem to be of the Thunderbirds-Brains variety.*

Philippe Model
33 Place du Marché Saint-Honoré, 75001 Paris (42.96.89.02). Metro Pyramides. **Open** 10.30am-7.30pm Mon-Sat. **Credit** AmEx, CB, DC, EC, MC, F$TC, V.
Philippe Model's storybook high-fashion hats are fit for a princess – Caroline of Monaco and Gloria von Thurn und Taxis top their looks with his fantasy *chapeaux*. Our favourite was a bird's-eye target straw hat wider than Joan Collins' shoulder pads going for 1,080F. Sculptured-heel shoes average 1,200F and compact, boxy purses are about 2,500F. There's also a wide selection of ladies' gloves to choose from. Model's one-off creations are scene-stealers at the Prix de Diane-Hermès, France's equivalent to Ascot. *Customized orders. Export scheme (detaxe).*

SHOES

Antoine Mercadal
3 place des Victoires, 75001 Paris (45.08.84.44). Metro Bourse. **Open** 10am-7pm Mon-Sat. **Credit** AmEx, CB, DC, MC, V.

Mercadal has an exciting range of shoes for women. Not only does he sell the classic shoe but he also gives attention to a few more imaginative styles. He's particularly good on keeping up with the seasons' changing weather.

Colisée de Sacha
64 rue de Rennes, 75006 Paris (40.49.02.13). Metro Saint-Germain-des-Près/bus 39, 48, 96. **Open** 10.30am-7.30pm Mon-Sat. **Credit** CB, EC, MC, V.
Fun, young and fashion-conscious women's shoes that won't hurt your feet or your wallet. Details like pilgrim buckles and Turkish slipper toes give sparkle to basic shapes. Prices average 600F.
Export scheme (detaxe).
Branches: 50 rue Turbigo, 75002 (45.08.13.15); 43 avenue Wagram, 75017 (46.22.81.82).

Stephane Kélian
13bis rue de Grenelle, 75007 Paris (42.22.93.03). Metro Sèvres-Babylone. **Open** 10.30am-7pm Mon-Sat. **Credit** AmEx, CB, EC, MC, FTC, V.
Women's shoes from the sublime to the sen-

sational, with prices to match. Kélian's own smart suede pumps start at 895F and his siren couture shoes for Claude Montana average 1,700F. Ethnic trinkets adorn his basketweave sandals.
Delivery. Export scheme (detaxe).
Branches: 90 rue du Faubourg Saint Honoré, 75008 (42.65.27.36); 36 rue de Sévigné, 75003 (42.77.82.00); 6 place des Victoires, 75002 (42.61.60.74); 42 avenue Victor Hugo, 75016 (45.00.31.59); 66 avenue des Champs-Elysées, 75008 (42.25.56.96).

Tokio Kumagaï
52 rue Croix Des Petits-Champs, 75001 Paris (42.36.08.01). Metro Bourse, Palais Royal/bus 29, 48. **Open** 10am-7pm Mon-Fri; 11am-7pm Sat. **Credit** AmEx, CB, DC, EC, JCB, MC, F$DM£TC, V.
The witty, *trompe-l'oeil* shoes of racing cars and mice at Tokio Kumagaï required double-takes. Sadly, since his death, the spirit of the line seems a bit safe. Italian-made shoes for women average 950F to 1,000F and men's start at 1,100F. Also available are bags, watches, leather goods and a women's wear collection.
Export scheme (detaxe).

DEPARTMENT STORES

Galeries Lafayette
40 boulevard Haussmann, 75009 Paris (42.82.34.56/fashion show reservations 42.82.30.25). Metro Chausée d'Antin, Opéra/RER Auber/buses 20, 21, 22, 27, 42, 53, 68, 81, 95. **Open** 9.30am-6.30pm Mon-Sat. **Credit** AmEx, CB, DC, EC, JCB, MC, V, F$DMYen£TC, all currencies.
See picture and caption.
Alterations. Beauty salon. Bureau de change. Catalogue. Delivery. Duty free. Export scheme (detaxe). Fashion shows. Guides and interpreters. Parking garage. 1-hour photo service. Restaurants (4). Travel and theatre ticket agency. Watch and shoe repair.
Branch: inside the Montparnasse Building, 22 rue Départ, 75014 (45.38.52.87).

Printemps
64 boulevard Haussmann, 75009 Paris (42.82.50.00). Metro Havre-Caumartin, Saint-Lazare, Opéra/RER Auber. **Open** 9.35am-6.30pm Mon-Sat. **Credit** A/c, AmEx, CB, DC, EC, MC, Takashiyama, V, all TC and all currencies.
A sampling of the world of fashion under one roof: all the big names, as well as new rising stars like Myrène de Prémonville, Romeo Gigli and Martine Sitbon. Goods are well displayed in this vast Aladdin's cave.
Alterations. Beauty institute. Birth and wedding lists. Bureau de change. Delivery and 24-hour shopping pick-up. Duty free. Export scheme (detaxe). Fashion shows twice per week (request invitations only). Food Halls (7). Guides and interpreters. Gift vouchers. Repair to own goods. Restaurants (3). Travel and theatre ticket agency. Watch repair.
Branches: 30 avenue d'Italie, 75013 (45.81.11.50); 10 place de la République, 75011 (43.55.39.09); 25 cours de Vincennes, 75020 (43.71.12.41); 30 avenue des Ternes, 75017 (43.80.20.00).

The **Galeries Lafayette** (listed under **Department Stores**) is the Louvre of department stores, with over 75,000 brand names, including the high fashion in-house boutiques of Christian Lacroix, Claude Montana, Thierry Mugler and Yohji Yamamoto, a vast array of housewares and an entire floor devoted to lingerie. There's a fashion show-cum-breakfast every Wednesday at 10.30am – attendance is free, but phone to make a reservation.

Food & Drink

Let's face it, this is what you came to Paris for. You've toured the restaurants and had your fill; now it's time to ransack the shops for that little extra morsel.

BREAD & PASTRY

Bernard Ganachaud
150-154 rue de Ménilmontant, 75020 Paris (46.36.13.82). Metro Pelleport/bus 60, 61.
Open 2.30-8pm Tue; 7.30am-8pm Wed-Sat; 7.30am-1.30pm Sun; closed whole month of August. **No credit cards.**
Award-winning *boulanger* Bernard Ganachaud bakes 30 different types of bread in his wood-fired ovens up on the heights of Ménilmontant. Treat yourself to a *pain aux noix* chock-full of fresh walnuts, a delicious orange-scented *gâche vendéenne* (brioche) or Ganachaud's country-style apple tart.

Christian Constant
26 rue du Bac, 75007 Paris (42.96.53.53). Metro Rue-du-Bac/bus 68.
Open 8am-8pm daily. **Credit** V.
Sophisticated, imaginative cakes and sweets in the modern mode are Constant's claim to (considerable) fame. His powerfully flavoursome low-sugar chocolates are prized by connoisseurs, though some may find them too bitter.
Branch: 37 rue d'Assas, 75006.

Gérard Mulot
2 rue Lobineau, 75006 Paris (43.26.85.77). Metro Mabillon. **Open** 6.45am-8pm Mon, Tue, Thur-Sun; closed whole month of August. **No credit cards.**
Mulot's shop is worth visiting if only to admire the truly dazzling fresh fruit tarts in the window, as colourful as the Provençal fabrics sold at Souleiado across the street. Why not go inside and treat yourself to a cushiony almond macaroon or a bright-tasting lemon tartelette?

Jean-Luc Poujauran
20 rue Jean-Nicot, 75007 Paris (47.05.80.88). Metro Latour-Maubourg. **Open** 8.30am-8.30pm Mon-Sat; closed whole month of August. **No credit cards.**
With Ganachaud and Poilâne, young Jean-Luc Poujauran is one of the three best *boulangers* in Paris. By all means try his crusty, chewy *baguette* and his authentic *pain de campagne* (country loaf), but don't neglect the rustic specialities of Poujauran's native South-west: *cannelés de Bordeaux* with creamy caramel, or the vegetable pie called *torte landaise aux légumes*.

Lionel Poilâne
8 rue du Cherche-Midi, 75006 Paris (45.48.42.59). Metro Saint-Placide or Sèvres-Babylone/bus 39,70. **Open** 7.15am-8.15pm Mon-Sat. **No credit cards.**
Author and international media celebrity Lionel Poilâne remains a baker first and foremost; his dense, toothsome sourdough bread, made from stoneground flour and baked in a wood-fired oven, is unsurpassed.
Branch: 49 boulevard de Grenelle, 75015.

Pâtisserie Clichy
5 boulevard Beaumarchais, 75004 Paris (48.87.89.88). Metro Bastille/bus 20.
Open 8.30am-8.30pm Tue-Sat; 8am-8pm Sun. **Credit** V.
Master pastry chef Paul Bugat creates a full range of traditional French sweets, from cakes and tarts to chocolates and ice-cream. Sample his wares on the spot, in the little tea room adjoining the shop. We recommend the macaroon-and-chocolate mousse confection called *le Paris*. Bugat's glazed chestnuts are the best in town.

DELICATESSEN

La Cigogne
61 rue de l'Arcade, 75008 Paris (43.87.39.16). Metro Saint-Lazare.
Open 8am-7pm Mon-Fri; 8.30am-7pm Sat; closed whole month of August. **Credit** V.
A vast array of robust Alsatian specialities: a phalanx of regional sausages, and lots of sumptuous sweets, including bilberry, cherry or plum tarts, kugelhupf, sweet pretzels and sachertorte. Helpful sales staff will guide your choice.

Flo Prestige
42 place du Marché-Saint-Honoré, 75001 Paris (42.61.45.46). Metro Pyramides. **Open** 8am-11pm daily. **Credit** AmEx, DC, V.
For a better class of take-out fare, come to Flo. Everything one might need for a de luxe picnic or midnight snack is on hand: wines and champagnes, smoked salmon, *foie gras*, all sorts of cold meats, cheeses and desserts. Most are available in individual portions.

La Galoche d'Aurillac
41 rue de Lappe, 75011 Paris (47.00.77.15). Metro Bastille/bus 69.
Open 10am-midnight Tue-Sat; closed whole month of August. **No credit cards.**
Sample the authentic Auvergne *charcuteries* and cheeses on the spot or take them with you to enjoy later. Especially worth trying are the *pounti* (a rustic meatloaf), the dried *saucisses de Marcolès*, earthy wines and eaux-de-vie from the Auverge region.

Pou
16 avenue des Ternes, 75017 Paris (43.80.19.24). Metro Ternes/bus 43.
Open 9.30am-1.15pm, 3.30-7.15pm, Tue-Sat. **Credit** DC, V.
A shining example of what a typical upmarket Parisian *charcuterie* can be like. The lip-smacking displays of terrines, *pâtés en croûte*, huge York hams (all prepared in the sleek kitchen-laboratory), Lyonnais sausages, *foie gras* and inventive salads are guaranteed to rev up your appetite. Courteous, accommodating service.

CHEESES

Androuët
41 rue d'Amsterdam, 75009 Paris (48.74.26.90). Metro Liège/bus 81, 95.
Open 10am-7pm Tue-Sat.
Credit AmEx, DC, V.
Still a highly reliable cheese shop (though Pierre Androuët sold the place years ago). Pungent Livarots, Epoisses, Munsters and Maroilles mature in a warren of cellars beneath the shop; display cases overflow with farmhouse Brie, triple-cream Lucullus and tangy goat cheeses.

Fromagerie de Monmartre
9 rue du Poteau, 75018 Paris (46.06.26.03). Metro Jules-Joffrin/bus 31, 60.
Open 9am-12.30pm, 4-7.30pm, Tue-Sat. **No credit cards.**
Hundreds of cheeses, many of them matured on the premises, are attractively presented in this bright, spotless shop on the northern side of Montmartre. Madame Delbey is duly proud of her stock, and is a mine of information on how to keep and serve cheese.

La Maison du Bon Fromage
35 rue du Marché-Saint-Honoré, 75001 Paris (42.61.02.77). Metro Pyramides. **Open** 9am-2pm, 4-8pm, Tue-Sat.
If you aren't already an enthusiastic consumer of farmhouse goat and sheep's milk cheeses, the Eletufes (Alain and Michèle) will convert you. Whether you prefer your *chèvre* creamy or *sec*, this couple will select a cheese at just the degree of ripeness you require.

Marie-Anne Cantin
12 rue du Champ-de-Mars, 75007 Paris (45.50.43.94). Metro Ecole-Militaire/bus 28, 49, 80, 82. **Open** 8.30am-1pm, 4-7.30pm, Tue-Sat; 8.30am-1pm Sun. **No credit cards.**
To savour authentic French farmhouse cheeses lovingly ripened and sold at the peak of their form, head for this charming *fromagerie* and sample the Saint-Marcellin, the picture-perfect Camembert, or the buttery Fourme d'Ambert.

CONFECTIONERY

Duc de Praslin
44 avenue Montaigne, 75008 Paris (47.20.99.63). Metro Franklin D Roosevelt.
Open 10am-7pm Mon-Sat.
Credit AmEx, DC, V.
The Duc de Praslin (or his pastry cook, to be precise) invented the delectable almond and caramel confections that bear the duke's name: for pralines, this is the place. All the house chocolates and confectionery are bagged or boxed in covetable gold-and-white wrappings, ideal for gift giving.

Lenôtre
44 rue du Bac, 75007 Paris (42.22.39.39). Metro Rue-du-Bac/bus 69. **Open** 9am-8pm Mon-Sat; 9am-1pm Sun; closed whole month of August. **Credit** AmEx, V.
Lenôtre is perhaps better known as a pastry chef, *glacier* and caterer, but his chocolates are nothing short of sublime. His intensely flavoured truffles and *palettes d'or* are simply not to be missed. Other shops are located in the 9th, 15th, 16th and 17th *arrondissements*.

*If you can't face entering **Fauchon** (listed under **Gourmet Goodies**) and risking the scorn of the supercilious staff – affability seems to be reserved for those who roll up in limos – admiring the fabulous window displays is a treat in itself. The shop is a reliable last resort source of hard-to-find foodstuffs.*

La Maison du Chocolat
225 rue du Faubourg-Saint-Honoré, 75008 Paris (42.27.39.44). Metro Ternes/bus 43, 93. **Open** 9.30am-7pm Tue-Sat; closed whole month of August. **No credit cards.**
The guru of chocolate in Paris is indisputably Monsieur Robert Linxe. We can only urge you to visit his divinely fragrant shop and discover for yourself the thrill of wrapping your tastebuds around a handsome chocolate-coated bonbon filled with an incomparably suave *ganache* flavoured with raspberry, rum, lemon or caramel among others – the list is endless.

A la Mère de Famille
35 rue du Faubourg-Monmartre, 75009 Paris (47.70.83.69). Metro Le Peletier/bus 67, 74. **Open** 7.30am-1.30pm, 3-7pm, Tue-Sat; closed whole month of August. **Credit** V.
Sweets and confections from all the regions of France (calissons d'Aix, pralines de Montargis, macarons de Mortmorillon) as well as a dizzying assortment of boiled sweets, chocolates, caramels, jams and biscuits are collected in this singularly picturesque emporium, founded in 1793.

Richart
258 boulevard Saint-Germain, 75007 Paris (45.55.66.00). Metro Chambre des Députés. **Open** 2-7pm Mon; 10am-7pm Tue-Sat. **Credit** V.
Sensational chocolates from a Lyon-based firm are offered in this attractive boutique. Expert advice on matching wines with your chocolate desserts is dispensed, free of charge.

WINES & SPIRITS
Les Caves Taillevent
199 rue du Faubourg-Saint-Honoré, 75008 Paris (45.61.14.09). Metro Ternes/bus 43. **Open** 2-7pm Mon; 9am-7pm Tue-Fri; 9am-5pm Sat; closed for three weeks mid-summer. **Credit** V.

Now wine buffs can purchase bottles chosen by Jean-Claude Vrinat without booking weeks ahead at his vaunted Parisian restaurant, Taillevent. There are offerings for every budget, from modest but well-made country wines to lordly Burgundies and clarets, along with brandies, ports, sherries and liqueurs.

Jean Danflou
36 rue Mont-Thabor (in the courtyard), 75001 Paris (42.61.51.09). Metro Concorde/bus 72. **Open** 8am-1pm, 2-6pm, Mon-Fri; closed first two weeks in August. **Credit** AmEx, DC, V.
Full-flavoured French eaux-de-vie that taste like the very essence of the fruit from which they are made: cherry, pear, raspberry and plum, each being remarkable. Danflou also proposes a range of fine Cognacs and Armagnacs, and a good house champagne.

Lucien Legrand
1 rue de la Banque, 75001 Paris (42.60.07.12). Metro Bourse/bus 29. **Open** 8.30am-7pm Tue-Fri; 8.30am-1pm, 3-7pm, Sat. **Credit** V.
Opinionated, mischievous Lucien Legrand is famous for his flair in tracking down well-made, inexpensive wines from the Midi and the Loire. Above the bins of bonbons and chocolates in his charming old-fashioned *épicerie* you'll also discover some fine Armagnacs and an unusual marc de Gewurztraminer from Alsace.

Le Repaire de Bacchus
40 rue Damrémont, 75018 Paris (42.52.27.78). Metro Lamarck-Caulaincourt/bus 80. **Open** 3.30-8pm Mon; 10.30am-1.30pm, 3.30-8pm, Tue-Sat; 10.30am-1pm Sun. **Credit** AmEx, DC, V.
Bacchus would feel right at home in this lair among the superb Burgundies, Guigal's powerful wines from the Côtes

du Rhône, a small but choice selection of foreign bottlings and some inexpensive country growths selected by English wine pro Steven Spurrier. There are other branches in the 8th, 15th, 16th and 17th *arrondissements*.

GOURMET GOODIES
Au Bon Marché
38 rue de Sèvres, 75007 Paris (45.49.21.22). Metro Sèvres-Babylone/bus 68, 94. **Open** *supermarket:* 8.30am-8.30pm Mon-Sat. **Credit** AmEx, DC, V.
Foodies love this store, the biggest, most complete gourmet supermarket in Paris. Take home tins of *confit de canard*, sachets of French-grown *tisanes* (herb teas), bars of excellent chocolate, premium coffees, cheeses, mustards, bottled or dried mushrooms or any of the whole range of Fauchon products (*see below*).

Fauchon
26 place de la Madeleine, 75008 Paris (47.42.60.11). Metro Madeleine/bus 42, 52. **Open** 9.40am-7pm Mon-Sat. **Credit** AmEx, DC, MC, V.
See **picture and caption.**

Hédiard
21 place de la Madeleine, 75008 Paris (42.66.44.36). Metro Madeleine/bus 42, 52. **Open** 9.15am-11pm Mon-Sat. **Credit** AmEx, DC, V.
The best of just about everything you might want to buy on the food front. Prices are high, but the selection is vast and the staff is courteous and knowledgeable. A source of greatly appreciated gifts.
See also chapter **Services.**

Soirée Gourmande
16 boulevard Richard-Lenoir, 75011 Paris (43.38.99.11). Metro Bastille/bus 69. **Open** 10am-7pm Mon-Sat. **No credit cards.**
The house motto is: 'Madeleine quality at Bastille prices.' In other words, the same fine foodstuffs – caviar, duck and goose *foie gras*, smoked salmon, champagne, and more – that are sold in the high-price emporiums of the 8th *arrondissement* are available here for less: 20% to 50% less.

Soleil de Provence
6 rue du Cherche-Midi, 75006 Paris (45.48.15.02). Metro Sèvres-Babylon/bus 68, 94. **Open** 9.45am-7pm Tue-Sat; closed whole month of August. **No credit cards.**
Visit this shop on a cold, grey day: the fragrance of sunny Provence will do wonders for your morale. Buy a few jars of delicious olives, some superior olive oil (cold-pressed, extra virgin, of course), unctuous lavender honey, high quality dried herbs and soaps.

Les Vieux Vins de France
56 rue Jean-Jacques-Rousseau, 75001 Paris (42.33.46.85). Metro Louvre/bus 21, 81. **Open** 2-7pm Mon; 9am-12.30pm, 2-7pm, Tue-Sat. **No credit cards.**
Stock up on canned and bottled gourmet treats (mushrooms, oils, vinegars, spices and condiments of all sorts) at this old-fashioned *épicerie*. Wines and *foie gras* are available too, at attractive prices.

Specialist Shops

Whatever your passion, Parisian shops will fulfil your secret acquisitive desires. We give you the best, quirkiest, most value-for-money shops in town.

Whether you're hoping to buy up half of Paris or simply enjoy looking at the window displays, Parisian shops are an integral part of the cityscape that every visitor should indulge in. Opening hours are variable throughout the city; as a rule of thumb, most shops tend to stay open till 7pm, although many close for an hour at lunch. For further information on Bank Holidays, sales and the export scheme (detaxe), *see page 130* **Fashion.**

BEAUTY PRODUCTS

Grain de Beauté
9 rue du Cherche-Midi, 75006 Paris (45.48.07.55). Metro Saint Sulpice/bus 63, 70, 86, 87, 96. **Open** 2.30-7pm Mon; 10.30am-7pm Tue-Sat. **Credit** CB, EC, MC, V.
A quaint boutique reminiscent of a Victorian chemist's, that stocks British fragrances: Penhaligon, Floris and Geo F Trumper. Other sweet scents include potpourri (80F per scoop), clove-studded oranges (130F) and lavender potions (220F).

Guerlain
68 avenue des Champs-Elysées, 75008 Paris (43.59.31.10). Metro Franklin D Roosevelt/bus 32, 73. **Open** 9.30am-6.45pm Mon-Sat. **Credit** CB, EC, MC, £FYenDM$TC, V.
See **picture and caption.**
Beauty salon. Catalogue. Delivery. Export scheme (detaxe).
Branches: 35 rue Tronchet, 75008 (47.42.53.23); 2 place Vendôme, 75001 (42.60.68.61); 93 rue de Passy, 75016 (42.88.41.62); 29 rue de Sèvres, 75016 (42.22.46.60); Centre Maine-Montparnasse, 75015 (43.20.95.40).

Simon's
164 rue Saint Martin, 75003 Paris (48.87.32.31). Metro Rambuteau, Châtelet, Les Halles/bus 29, 75. **Open** 11am-3pm, 4-7.30pm, Mon-Fri; 10am-8pm Sat. **No credit cards.**
Englishman Simon Allchin is banking on Parisians taking up the Green issue – he's opened the first ever ecologically sound boutique that specializes in natural soaps and cleaning products. Stock includes the full range of Belgian Ecover products, recycled stationery and pure soap blocks from Marseille (15F each or five for 70F).
Delivery.

GIFTS

André Bissonnet
6 rue du Pas-de-la-Mule, 75003 Paris (48.87.20.15). Metro Chemin Vert/bus 29, 65. **Open** 2-7pm Mon-Sat. **No credit cards.**
The antique harpsichords, string and brass instruments for sale here hark back to an age when strains of their music filled the rooms in Maison Victor Hugo in nearby place des Vosges. As well as buying and selling seventeenth- to nineteenth-century instruments, André Bissonnet runs a restoration service from his workshop at the back of the store.
Delivery.

Boutique Duo 29
29 rue du Roi de Sicile, 75004 Paris (42.71.90.25). Metro Saint Paul/bus 69, 76, 96. **Open** 11am-7pm Tue-Sat. **Credit** CB, EC, MC, V.
A small, friendly boutique that rivals the Moscow Airport duty-free shop in its selection of behind-the-Iron-Curtain-ware. For example, Ukranian Easter eggs abound; they cost 35F to 95F for the popular style, 200F to 1,500F for those hand-painted by artists. The folkloric embroidered boleros from Yugoslavia and Poland (685F to 2,500F for the antique ones) fit the bill for the latest hippy revival, as do the many pieces of amber jewellery.

Cocody
1bis rue Ferdinand Duval, 75004 Paris (42.77.28.82). Metro Saint Paul/bus 69, 76, 96. **Open** 11.30am-7.30pm daily; closed every Mon Sept-March. **Credit** AmEx, CB, EC, MC, £F$TC, V.
Cocody stocks fabrics, accessories and decorative items from the Ivory Coast, Ghana, Mali and Burkina-Faso. You can pick up colourful basketweave bracelets for as little as 30F, or boxer shorts in bouboudima fabric for 100F. Belts that are made from material go for 450F to 1,200F. There's also a large selection of fun, big bangle earrings and rings in brass, stones and carved wood.
Exports scheme (detaxe).
Branch: 14 rue Descartes, 75005 (43.26.92.27).

Di Maria
45 rue des Francs Bourgeois, 75004 Paris (42.71.02.31). Metro Saint Paul/bus 29, 96. **Open** 10am-6.30pm Mon-Fri; 2-6pm Sat. **Credit** AmEx, CB, DC, EC, MC, FTC, V.
For 15 years, the Di Maria brothers have been buying and selling antique postcards, old books and stacks of ephemera dating from the nineteenth century to the fifties.

Shoppers can pick up a one-off postcard for as little as 6F, and although most go for 30F it's possible to pay as much as 600F for collectors' pieces. The children's books are rare and magical. A leather-bound old photo album in pristine condition will set you back 300F, though you may find one, in a less than perfect state, for 60F.
Delivery.

Galerie Beaubourg
23 rue du Renard, 75004 Paris (42.71.20.50). Metro Les Halles, Rambuteau/bus 75. **Open** 11am-1pm, 2.30-7pm, Tue-Fri; 10am-7pm Sat. **Credit** CB, EC, MC, FTC, V.
A cartoon shop with fixtures created by Hervé and Richard Di Rosa, Paris's pop graffiti artists. Galerie Beaubourg has gadgets that are signed by all the alternative, comic artists of the eighties. Their laughing stock includes T-shirts designed by the Di Rosa brothers, Tinguely and Ben (160F), badges (80F) and caps (200F) by Keith Haring. And, for piss-artists, a 250F-case of four bottles of Bordeaux, each decorated by a different artist.

Kimonoya
11 rue du Pont Louis-Philippe, 75004 Paris (48.87.30.24). Metro Pont Marie, Saint Paul/bus 69, 76, 96. **Open** 1.30-7pm Mon; 11am-7pm Tue-Sat. **Credit** CB, EC, MC, £F$TC, V.
As the name suggests, Kimonoya has an impressive selection of kimonos: short and long, new and ancient, cotton and silk. You can get away with spending 380F for a printed cotton kimono, or up to 2,000F for an ancient ceremonial silk one. The shop also carries a selection of those little lacquer and clay dishes that make Japanese table settings so delicate.
Delivery. Export scheme (detaxe).

Laïmoun
2 rue de Tournon, 75006 Paris (43.54.68.00). Metro Odéon/bus 63, 70, 86, 87. **Open** 2-7pm Mon; 10.30am-7pm Tue-Sat. **Credit** AmEx, CB, DC, EC, MC, £F$YenTC, TCB.
Part souk, part grotto, the Laïmoun displays Middle Eastern objects around a still pool. Men's and women's clothes and accessories are designed and manufactured in Lebanon by Lina Oudi, who works primarily in cotton and silk. The marble soap sets (400F) or the excellent laurel and olive oil soaps (from 15F to 25F) make excellent gifts.
Catalogue. Export scheme (detaxe)

Madeleine Gély
218 boulevard Saint Germain, 75007 Paris (42.22.63.35). Metro Rue du Bac/bus 69. **Open** 9.30am-7pm Tue-Sat. **No credit cards.**
It's probably safe to say that this shop, spilling over with umbrellas and canes, hasn't changed since it opened in 1834. Short or long, plain or fancy, there's an umbrella or cane here to suit people from all walks of life. Animal lovers can indulge in the veritable zoo that is this selection of carved wooden or silver handles – you can even choose your breed of dog – that go to make up over 400 styles of walking sticks. Umbrellas can be custom-made to order.
Export scheme (detaxe). Repair service. Umbrellas made to order.

Marais Plus
20 rue des Francs Bourgeois, 75003 Paris

(48.87.01.40). Metro Saint Paul/bus 29, 96.
Open 9am-midnight Mon-Sat; 9am-7pm
Sun. **Credit** AmEx, CB, DC, EC, MC,
£$FTC, V.
It's possible to spend hours browsing in this
friendly boutique, where there is an entire
wall-full of clever, comical and charming
ceramic teapots and pitchers. Suspended
from the ceiling are inflatable globes of
almost every size imaginable. There is a
small, but interesting choice of books on art
and Paris as well as fun, unusual publications and toys for kids. Don't leave without
sampling the delights in the *salon de thé.*
Café. Delivery.

Pylones
57 rue Saint Louis en L'ile, 75004 Paris
(46.34.05.02). Metro Pont Marie/bus 67.
Open 11am-7pm daily. **Credit** CB, EC, MC,
$FTC, V.
Pylones specializes in colourful, squiggly
rubber jewellery and braces. You'll also find
the full range of IDC sunglasses from the
most simple design (160F) to the more elaborate creation (500F), as well as the famous
backpacks by Jean-Paul Goude for the
Bicentennial celebrations. Other goods
which make on-spec presents include reflective coffee cups and saucers and T-shirts
designed by spray-can artist Speedy
Graphito.

Robin des Bois
15 rue Ferdinand Duval, 75004 Paris
(48.04.09.36). Metro Saint Paul/bus 69, 76,
96. **Open** 10.30am-7pm Mon-Sat; 2-7pm
Sun. **Credit** FTC.
Robin des Bois has a cause: save the planet
Earth. This boutique carries wonderful gift
ideas, all of which are made from recycled
products or ecologically sound. These
include stationery, jewellery and vegetal
ivory – a dead ringer for the real thing that
might put elephant poachers out of business. The shop also stocks a large number
of eco-friendly literature that tells you how to
join the crusade.
Catalogue. Export scheme (detaxe).

Tumbleweed
6 passage Thiéré, 75011 Paris (40.21.81.47).
Metro Bastille/bus 69. **Open** 11am-7pm Tue-
Sat. **Credit** FTC.
Expat American Lynn Rovida combs all the
US craftsfairs for the most unique cottage
industry items. These end up in her thimble-
sized shop that is located in a hard-to-find
passage in the Bastille district. There are
precious hand-stitched Amish quilts
(8,000F) for sale, as well as some patchwork
made-in-Vermont quilts (1,000F to 5,000F).
Unusual decorative objects abound. One
that caught our eye was a one-off buckeye
wooden puzzle box (650F), origins of which
Lynn explained in detail.

HOME ACCESSORIES

Argenterie des Francs Bourgeois
17 rue des Francs Bourgeois, 75004 Paris
(42.72.04.00). Metro Saint Paul/bus 29, 96.
Open 2-7pm Mon; 10.30am-7pm Tue-Sat;
11am-1pm, 2-7pm, Sun. **Credit** CB, EC, MC, V.

Tip the scales with pieces of estate and old
hotel silverware at 400F per kilo, which
usually equals about 15 pieces.
Alternatively, choose from the plentiful supply of antique silver tea and coffee sets,
including some from Cristofle, which cost
on average 5,000F for a five-piece service
with tray.

Au Bain Marie
8 rue Boissy d'Anglas, 75008 Paris
(42.66.59.74). Metro Concorde/bus 52.
Open 10am-7pm Mon-Sat. **Credit** AmEx,
CB, DC, EC, MC, £F$TC, V.
See **picture and caption.**
Catalogue. Delivery. Export scheme (detaxe).
Wedding lists.

La Chaise Longue
8 rue Princesse, 75006 Paris (43.29.62.39).
Metro Saint-Germain-des-Près/bus 96. **Open**
11am-7pm Mon; 11am-8pm, 9pm-1am, Tue-
Sat. **Credit** AmEx, CB, EC, MC, V.
La Chaise Longue specializes in re-editions of
accessories and gadgets from the thirties, forties and fifties. Polished burwood photo frames
start at 250F and radios cost between 1400F
and 1750F. You can pick up IDC sunglasses
(costing 80F to 800F) to go with the colonial
black electric fans that sell at 950F a piece.
Branches: 30 rue des Croix des Petits
Champs, 75001 (42.96.32.14); 20 rue des
Francs-Bourgeois, 75003 (42.71.56.07).

Collections Orient Express
15 rue Boissy d'Anglas, 75008 Paris
(47.42.24.45). Metro Concorde/bus 52.
Open 10am-6.30pm Mon-Fri; 10am-

1pm, 2.15-6.30pm, Sat. **Credit** AmEx,
CB, DC, EC, MC, £F$TC, V.
Now you don't have to board the Orient
Express to re-create the golden age of train
travel. All the original porcelain, silver, blan-
kets, bath accessories and desk pieces,
encrusted with the famous logo, are on sale
at Collections. Depending on your budget,
you'll be able to pick up a special edition
Lalique box for 4,600F, a leather conductor's
bag for 2,600F or natty terry cloth slippers
for 190F. Also high on the nostalgia stakes
are the signed and numbered art deco
lithographs and posters.
Catalogue. Delivery. Export scheme (detaxe).

E Dehillerin
18 and 20 rue Coquillière, 75001 Paris
(42.36.53.13). Metro Les Halles, Louvre/bus
58, 69, 70, 72, 74, 76. **Open** 8am-12.30pm,
2-6pm, Mon-Sat. **Credit** CB, EC, MC, V.
First stop for most cooks touring Paris: E
Dehillerin have supplied many of the great
European chefs since 1820 with all manner
of culinary items. Whether you're cooking
for an army or just yourself, you'll find any
size pot or pan in copper, cast iron and alu-
minium. The crockery section offers buyers
the same range of choice. If you need help,
ask to see one of the English-speaking assistants – they tend to be friendlier to foreigners than their mono-lingual colleagues.
*Delivery. Export scheme (detaxe). Wedding
lists.*

L'Entrepot
50 rue de Passy, 75016 Paris (45.25.64.17).
Metro La Muette, Passy/bus 32. **Open**

One of the last vestiges of the golden age of the Champs-Elysées, the **Guerlain**
perfumery (listed under **Beauty Products**) *is in stark contrast to the neon-clad
stores and cinemas that line this boulevard today. Many of the fragrances for
women and men were created with royal or Proustian inspirations. The
innovative Guerlain cosmetics are renowned the world over; for example, the
translucent face powders, Les Météorites are perfectly spherical cosmetic powders
that go for 150F each. A facial in the upstairs Institut de Beauté costs 400F.*

10.30am-7pm Mon-Fri; 10.30am-7.30pm Sat.
Credit CB, EC, MC, F£TC, V.
Whether you've got 5F or 5,000F to spend, you'll discover that L'Entrepot has gadgets for everyone on your gift list. The vast selection of party supplies alone is enough to inspire anyone to throw a shinding. There are also home accessories ranging from kitsch kitchenware to tools for the serious gourmet. Smart Italian and French casual wear and accessories for men, women and children are also available.
Café (open same hours as shop). Export scheme (detaxe).

Jardins Imaginaires
9bis rue d'Assas, 75006 Paris (42.22.90.03). Metro Rennes. **Open** 2-7pm Mon; 10.30am-7pm Tue-Sat. **Credit** AmEx, CB, EC, MC, FTC, V.
Those with green fingers and a desire to enhance their garden will find Jardins Imaginaires' supplies the perfect addition to their back yard. Pots in terracotta or blue Oriental ceramic come in all shapes and sizes and range from 50F to 2,500F. There's a full range of gardening tools, hand-woven baskets and even Mary Poppins-style park benches.
Delivery. Export scheme (detaxe).

Mariage Frères
30 and 32 rue du Bourg Tibourg, 75004 Paris (42.72.28.11). Metro Hotel de Ville/bus 69, 76, 96. **Open** 11am-7.30pm Tue-Sun. **Credit** AmEx, CB, EC, MC, V.
Parisians from all over town brave the queues at Mariage Frères so as to have a tea

consultation. Staff impart advice on the 350 varieties of tea that are available. What's more, there are almost as many styles of tea service to suit all tastes; Oriental tea ceremony experts and traditional tea makers can select their ideal set from the cleverly-designed pots, cups and saucers. If you survive the long wait, sample your purchase with a luscious patisserie from the delightful *salon de thé.*
Café (noon-7.30pm Tue-Sat). Catalogue. Catering service. Delivery. Export scheme (detaxe).

CONTEMPORARY DESIGN

Duo Sur Canapé
3 rue de Turbigo, 75001 Paris (42.33.37.12). Metro Les Halles, Etienne Marcel/bus 29. **Open** 10.30am-1pm, 2-7pm, Mon-Sat. **Credit** AmEx, CB, EC, MC, £$FTC, V.
Philippe Starck ravers can browse to their hearts' content among his repertoire of creations of tableware, gadgets and furniture. Other designers featured in this gallery include Castiglione and Borek Cipek, who create distinctly modernist, but never outrageous, interiors.
Delivery. Export scheme (detaxe). Wedding lists.

Ego
40 rue de Sévigné, 75003 Paris (42.78.35.30). Metro Saint Paul/bus 29,

96. **Open** 2-7pm Mon-Sat. **Credit** AmEx, CB, EC, MC, FTC, V.
The pure white space of Ego is in sharp contrast to its baroque neighbour, the Musée de Carnavalet (*see chapter* **Museums**). The minimalism carries through to Ego's wares; light-as-a-feather chrome tube chairs and stools by Japanese designers such as Shiro Kuramata, double-face cotton Japanese scarves (400F to 700F) or fabric (500F per metre) and unique desk accessories (90F to 1350F). The non-furniture section resembles a museum gift shop – with prices to match – but a fun bargain is the red rubber banana bag for 100F.
Export scheme (detaxe).

En Attendant les Barbares
50 rue Etienne Marcel, 75002 Paris (42.33.37.87). Metro Bourse/bus 29, 67. **Open** 10.30am-7pm Mon-Fri; 11am-6.30pm Sat. **Credit** AmEx, CB, EC, MC, FTC, V.
Whether you're waiting for the barbarians – as the shop's name suggests – or for Godot, you can do it with wit and flair in this showcase dedicated to the new crop of irreverent, contemporary young designers. Rising stars such as Garouste, Bonetti and Jean-Philippe Glaizes, blend baroque, primitive and salvage styles to create furniture that's poetic, functional and artistic. Pick up Migeon and Migeon bicolour resin candlesticks for 950F or a Marie Antoinette-type *chaise longue* by Eric Schmidt for 7,000F.
Delivery. Export scheme (detaxe).

Espace Cath'art
13 rue Sainte Croix de la Bretonnerie, 75004 Paris (48.04.80.10). Metro Hotel de Ville/bus 29, 69, 76, 96. **Open** 10am-7pm Mon-Sat; 4-8pm Sun. **Credit** AmEx, CB, EC, MC, FTC, V.
Stepping into this furniture gallery is like being invited to Pee-Wee Herman's playhouse; trying to sit on the spiney, anamorphic chairs could pose a problem for most physiques. Most of the furniture-art is painted and shellacked in toy-box colours. The sandwiched wood, anatomically curved chairs by Caspen – who keeps away from Paris and hand-creates his furniture against the grain – are particularly noteworthy.
Delivery. Export scheme (detaxe).

Lieux
5 rue Sainte Croix de la Bretonnerie, 75004 Paris (42.77.63.94). Metro Hotel de Ville, Saint Paul/bus 29, 69, 76, 96. **Open** noon-7pm Tue-Sat. **Credit** CB, EC, MC, FTC, V.
The newest design space in a 'gallery alley' devotes its front window to the cartoon, stone age living-room ensemble by Garouste and Bonetti. No less primitive is the mystic backboard bed with an iron canopy by Philippe Renaud, as well as his fossils-under-glass mirrored tables. Lieux stock includes a range of Hilton McConnico for Daum Cactus glassware and Hilton McConnico's cactus place settings.
Export scheme (detaxe).

Au Bain Marie (*listed under* **Home Accessories***) dedicates itself to the art of fine dining, with elegant displays of new, or perfectly preserved old tableware, linens, crystal, silver, bar accessories and knick-knacks. The impressive selection of books includes publications on cuisine, presentation and decoration.*

FABRICS

Marché Saint Pierre
2 rue Charles Nodier, 75018 Paris (46.06.92.25). Metro Anvers/bus 30, 54. **Open** 9.30am-1.30pm Mon; 9.30am-6.30pm

Shakespeare & Co *(listed under* **Books***) was a regular haunt for the Lost Generation. Founder Sylvia Beach was the editor for and den mother to the likes of James Joyce, Ernest Hemingway and other expat writers. Today, septuagenarian keeper-of-the-flame, George Whitman may invite you upstairs for tea, poetry readings and to rub shoulders with the literary ghosts as you're shuffling through stacks of new, used and antique books arranged to confound any librarian.*

Tue-Sat. Credit $FTC.
Even if you're not in the mood for buying fabric, joining the cacophony of remnant scavengers that combs the five storeys of the Marché for material to make curtains or costumes is a truly Parisian experience. The top two floors have linens and home furnishing fabric; the second floor stocks fine silks, velvets and fantasy fabrics; the first, wool and synthetics; and the ground floor is littered with a little of everything. Bargains abound.
Delivery. Export scheme (detaxe).

Simrane
23-25 rue Bonaparte, 75006 Paris (43.54.90.73). Metro Saint-Germain-des-Prés/bus 39, 48, 63. **Open** 10am-7pm Mon-Sat. **Credit** AmEx, CB, DC, EC, MC, FTC, V.
Simrane sells all types of goods; exotic and colourful fabrics on the roll or made up as bedspreads, table mats and pillow cases. The big cotton scarves, edged in beads or silver bells (250F) make great pareos. Ceramic blue and white doorknobs come in all sizes (60F to 95F).
Export scheme (detaxe).

Souleiado
78 rue de Seine, 75006 Paris (43.54.62.25). Metro Mabillon/bus 39, 63, 70, 84, 87. **Open** 10am-7pm Mon-Sat. **Credit** AmEx, CB, DC, EC, MC, FTC, V.
Souleiado (known as Pierre Deux in North America) specializes in those lovely, bright provençal prints that go to make French country interiors as warm as the sun on the Cote d'Azur. Prints come on cotton, silk and cashmere. There are also bags, pouches and clothing stitched up from Souleiado fabrics. Sales assistants can be downright rude at times; a shame as the winding boutique and fabrics are a treasure.
Export scheme (detaxe).
Branch: 83 avenue Paul Dourmer, 75016 (42.28.99.34).

Wolfe et Descourtis
18 Galerie Vivienne, 75002 Paris (42.61.80.84). Metro Bourse/bus 29. **Open** 11am-7pm Mon-Fri; noon-7pm Sat. **Credit** AmEx, CB, DC, EC, MC, V.
While strolling through the lovely Galerie Vivienne, visit this shop that has supplied couturiers since 1875 with exotic materials and fabrics. Sumptuous silks range from 280F to 400F per metre and beautiful wool flannels, in a dozen colours, are sold off the bolt for 110F per metre. Staff speak English and will ship your chosen material home on request.
Delivery. Export scheme (detaxe).

BOOKS

Artcurial
9 avenue Matignon, 75008 Paris (42.99.16.16). Metro Franklin D Roosevelt/bus 32, 73. **Open** 10.30am-7.15pm Tue-Sat. **Credit** AmEx, CB, DC, EC, MC, $FTC, V.
Situated in the midst of several art and *objets d'art* galleries you'll find the Artcurial bookstore, specializing in twentieth-century *beaux-arts* books. These cover painting, sculpture, photography, interior and architectural design, graphics, civilization and fashion and textiles. A *de rigueur* visit for contemporary art lovers.
Catalogues of gallery exhibitions. Delivery. Export scheme (detaxe).

Astrolabe
46 rue de Provence, 75009 Paris (42.85.42.95). Metro Chaussée d'Antin. **Open** 10am-7pm Mon-Fri; 10am-1pm, 2-7pm, Sat. **Credit** V.
A specialist travel book and map shop.

Galignani
224 rue de Rivoli, 75001 Paris (42.60.76.07). Metro Tuileries/bus 72. **Open** 9.30am-7pm Mon-Sat. **Credit** CB, DM, EC, MC, £$YenTC, V.
The Galignani store is reputed to have been the first English bookstore in continental Europe, established over two centuries ago. It's a traditional bookshop – the warm, woody shelves and literary sales assistants give it an olde worlde feel – yet its stock is up-to-the-minute. It sells the most recently published art and coffee table books in English and French.
Delivery. Export scheme (detaxe).

Shakespeare & Co
37 rue de la Bûcherie, 75005 Paris (no phone). Metro Maubert-Mutalité/bus 63, 86, 87. **Open** noon-midnight daily. **No credit cards.**
See **picture and caption.**

Super Heroes
175 rue Saint Martin, 75003 Paris (42.74.34.74). Metro Les Halles, Etienne Marcel/bus 29. **Open** 11am-8pm Mon-Sat. **Credit** CB, EC, MC, FTC, V.
Comic books are serious business at Super Heros. Alongside characters such as Tintin and Batman, there are the very adult sophisticated and nihilistic strips of Enki Bilal on sale. You'll find rare and old books and comic books, posters and lots of gadgets and gift items posing as your favourite characters.
Catalogues. Delivery. Export scheme (detaxe).

La Table d'Emeraude
21 rue de la Huchette, 75005 Paris (43.54.90.96). Metro Saint Michel/bus 21, 24, 27, 38, 85, 96. **Open** 12.30-7pm Mon; 10.30am-7pm Tue-Sat. **Credit** CB, EC, MC, FTC, V.
La Table d'Emeraude stocks books and manuals on astrology, occultism, sects, clairvoyance, alchemy and mysticism. You also have a large selection of tarot cards to choose from.

WH Smith
248 rue de Rivoli, 75001 Paris (42.60.37.97). Metro Concorde. **Open** 9.30am-7pm Mon-Sat. **Credit** V.
Specialists in British and American press publications and mainstream books. There's a good selection of children's books. *Time Out* is available on Fridays.

RECORDS & HI-FI

Bonus Beat
1 rue Keller, 75011 Paris (40.21.02.88).

Metro Bastille, Ledru-Rollin, Voltaire/bus 61, 69, 76. **Open** 1-8.45pm Tue-Sat. **Credit** CB, EC, MC, V.

Before opening Bonus Beat, Sal Russo was the musical director of the Radical Party in Italy. These days, Sal is capitalizing on direct imports from the USA and the UK, of CDs, LPs and EPs of Techno, House, Acid, Latin, Hip-Hop, Rap and New Beat electronic music. At night, Sal spins his playlist when he DJs at venues around Paris.

Crocodisc
42 rue des Ecoles, 75005 Paris (43.54.47.95). Metro Maubert-Mutualité/bus 63, 86, 87. **Open** 11am-7pm Tue-Sat. **Credit** CB, EC, MC, FTC, V.

Good value, new, used and off-beat records can be bought at Crocodisc and its branch Crocojazz. In addition to the normal pop, rock and funk records, they carry reggae, Oriental, folk, African and country music. Crocojazz specializes in jazz, blues and gospel.
Branch: Crocojazz, 64 rue de la Montagne-Sainte-Geneviève, 75005 (46.34.78.38).

Paralleles
36 rue des Bourdonnais, 75001 Paris (42.33.60.00). Metro Châtelet, Les Halles/bus 58, 69, 70, 72, 74, 85. **Open** 10am-7pm Mon-Sat. **Credit** CB, EC, MC, V.

Paralleles buy and sell records, cassettes, CDs and books. This branch specializes in jazz, classical and golden oldies – used records can be picked up for as little as 10.30F – cinema, cookery and sci-fi books, posters and rock 'n' roll postcards. At the other branch in rue Saint Honoré, they stock pop and rock music, literature, political and comic books, fanzines and badges. Rockabillies, Dead Heads and jazz lovers should make a beeline for Paralleles, so as to seek out that elusive pirate tape.
Branch: 47 rue Saint Honoré, 75001 (42.33.62.70).

Virgin Megastore
52 avenue des Champs-Elysées, 75008 Paris (40.74.06.48). Metro Franklin D Roosevelt/bus 32, 73. **Open** 10am-midnight Mon-Sat; noon-midnight Sun. **Credit** AmEx, CB, DC, EC, JCB, MC, £$YenDMFTC, V.
See **picture and caption.**
Café.. Delivery. Export scheme (detaxe).

STATIONERY

Art du Bureau
47 rue des Francs Bourgeois, 75004 Paris (48.87.57.97). Metro Saint Paul/bus 29, 69, 76, 96. **Open** 10am-7pm Mon-Sat. **Credit** AmEx, CB, EC, MC, FTC, V.

A vast array of must-have-for-the-nineties office accessories that are sure to arouse envy among colleagues and impress the big cheese. Most coveted agendas and accessories are stocked here: Filofax, Mulberry, and Nava, which is designed in Italy. Lamps and desk objects have built-in panache.
Export scheme (detaxe).

Calligrane
4-6 rue du Pont Louis Philippe, 75004 Paris (48.04.31.89/40.27.00.74). Metro Saint Paul, Pont Marie/bus 69, 76, 96. **Open** 11am-7.30pm Tue-Sun. **Credit** CB, £F$TC.
For Pharisee-style present wrapping, try the

giant money bills sold here. Choose from dollars, yen or francs, all priced 30F each. There is also a wide choice of fillers for personal organizers.
Delivery. Export scheme (detaxe).

Marie-Papier
26 rue Vavin, 75006 Paris (43.26.46.44). Metro Vavin/bus 58, 82. **Open** 10am-7pm Mon-Sat. **Credit** CB, EC, MC, V.

Marie-Paule Orluc designs elegant but simple paper products, dossiers and photo albums. Prices are high and definitely out of the art student's league. The best buy is the lizard-print wrapping paper, in dozens of colours, at 26F per sheet.

Melodies Graphiques
10 rue du Pont Louis Philippe, 75004 Paris (42.74.57.68). Metro Saint Paul, Pont Marie/bus 69, 76, 96. **Open** noon-7pm Mon; 11am-7pm Tue-Sat. **Credit** AmEx, CB, EC, MC, FTC, V.

This boutique has the most exquisite Florentine paper in classic publisher's bookbinding patterns that would make even a grocery list poetic. Proust would be proud of the calligraphy pens, inks, writing papers, photo albums, frames and hat boxes.

Papier +
9 rue du Pont Louis Philippe, 75004 Paris (42.77.70.49). Metro Saint Paul, Pont Marie/bus 69, 76, 96. **Open** noon-7pm Mon-Sat. **Credit** CB, EC, MC, FTC, V.

Hand-cut papers, a rainbow of pencil shades, wooden boxes and dossiers in various sizes are a number of goodies that paper lovers can snap up. The two adjoining shops have well-laid out displays.

MH Way
17 rue des Saints Pères, 75006 Paris (42.60.81.65). Metro Rue du Bac, Saint Germain-des-Prés/bus 63. **Open** 3-7.15pm Mon; 10.30am-7.15pm Tue-Sat. **Credit** AmEx, CB, EC, MC, FTC, V.

The MH stands for Japanese designer Makio Hasuike, whose philosophy is to bring imagination, technology, function and aesthetics into those everyday objects we thought we knew so well. Brightly-coloured briefcases, portfolios, back-packs and agendas in hi-tech materials like rubber, nylon and moulded plastic are among his collection.
Export scheme (detaxe).

POSTERS & PRINTS

Librairie Clair Obscur
161 rue Saint Martin, 75003 Paris (48.87.78.58). Metro Rambuteau/bus 29, 75. **Open** 1-7pm daily. **Credit** AmEx, CB, DC, EC, MC, FTC, V.

No film *aficionado* will be able to pass by this store. It's a veritable shrine to celluloid, from

*The sprawling **Virgin Megastore** (listed under **Records & Hi-Fi**), decked out in neo classical, state-of-the-art décor, contains a vast selection of music in all forms (records, cassettes and CDs), videos and electronic games, as well as the latest gadgets to play them on: stereos/hi-fi equipment, video recorders and cameras, personal computers and televisions. The classical music department has an imaginative listening area and on the lower level, there are books on all subjects.*

La Petite Gaminerie (listed under Children/Children's Fashion) is where rock and film stars dress their offspring in their own likeness. The shop carries the trendiest labels for 'show-biz babies kids': Klimagers, Bill Tornade, Liberto jeans, Catimini, Oilily and Pom d'Api shoes. Furniture, decorations for the nursery and traditional gift sets are also available. Even if you don't have children, stick around for the autographs.

the most obscure films (as the name suggests) to box office blockbusters. Every inch of space is packed with film posters and photo stills, an impressive selection of film books in French and English and marvellous dangling marionettes and masks from around the world. Don't miss the charming Passage Molière just next door to Clair Obscur.
Export scheme (detaxe).

Galerie Documents
53 rue de Seine, 75006 Paris (43.54.50.68). Metro Saint Germain des Prés/bus 63, 87, 96. **Open** 10.30am-12.30pm, 2.30-7pm, Tue-Sat. **Credit** CB, EC, MC, FTC, V.
The Galerie specializes in etchings and original posters from the art nouveau to art deco periods – namely 1890 to 1940 – by masters such as Toulouse-Lautrec and AM Cassandre. The mail order service allows collectors to order even after they leave Paris.
Catalogue. Delivery.

MARKETS

Marché aux fleurs
Place Louis-Lepine on Ile de la Cité, 75001 Paris. Metro Cité/bus 21, 38, 85, 96. **Open** 8am-4pm daily.
The sights and smells of this market are a rare treat for the eyes and nose. Blossoms

and plants, be they ordinary or rare, are always brought in every day fresh from the French Riviera, Holland and exotic locales. This market celebrates the simple and elaborate joys of nature. Prices here are cheaper, on average, than at florists'.

Marché aux livres
Parc Georges Brassens, rue Brancion, 75015 Paris. Metro Porte de Vanves. **Open** 9.30am-6pm Sat, Sun.
Antiquarian and second-hand books abound at this weekend specialist market. Prepare yourself for some hard haggling.

Marché aux Puces Saint Ouen
outside Metro Porte de Clignancourt, 75018 Paris. **Open** 5am-7pm Mon, Sat, Sun.
Reputedly the largest flea market in Europe, the puces Saint Ouen is made up of five markets selling antique clothes, accessories, furniture and African art. It's very pricey – unless you get there between 5am and 6am when you can pick up some bargains – and very crowded. Watch out for pickpockets.

Marché aux timbres
cour Marigny, 75008 Paris. Metro Champs-Elysées Clémenceau. **Open** 10am-sunset Thur, Sat, Sun.
A stamp collector's dream: vintage stamps and postcards from all over the world are sold here at the cour Marigny.

Marché de Vanves
avenue Georges Lafenestre (on bridge after Périphérique), 75014 Paris. Metro Porte de Vanves. **Open** 7am-1pm Sat, Sun.
To find this flea market, walk past the food market, turn right and the maché is on the bridge. It's a good place to find any sort of bric-à-brac. The Square des Artistes is taken over at the weekends by artists who display and sell their work in jewellery, painting and sculpture.

CHILDREN

CHILDREN'S FASHION

Chipie
49 rue Bonaparte, 75006 Paris (43.29.21.94). Metro Saint-Germain-des-Prés, Saint Sulpice/bus 39, 48, 96. **Open** 10.15am-7.30pm Mon-Sat. **Credit** AmEx, CB, EC, MC, FTC, V.
This boutique, decorated *à là* Norman Rockwell, sells children's spin-offs of their unisex junior jeanswear. The clothes on sale here are for kids aged six months to pre-teens. Retro jeans cost between 300F and 400F; denim jackets start at 460F. School clothes, mainly for boys, include preppie cotton plaid blazers (640F), traditional crested wool blazers (795F) and classic striped shirts (275F to 340F). The shop also carries canvas shoes, accessories and the Chipie fragrance.
Export scheme (detaxe).
Branches: 31 rue de la Ferronerie, 75001 (45.08.58.74).

Claude Vell
8 rue du Jour, 75001 Paris (42.33.75.94). Metro Les Halles, Etienne Marcel. **Open** 10am-7pm Mon-Sat. **Credit** AmEx, CB, DC, EC, MC, FTC, V.
Tucked away in a little courtyard are the side-by-side boutiques of Claude Vell, specializing in co-ordinated separates for new babies to pre-teen kids. Though the styles and fabrics are simple, each one does come in 16 colours. Clothes are on the pricey side; expect to pay over 300F per item.

Dominique Clairmond
45 rue Bonaparte, 75006 Paris (43.26.58.19). Metro Saint-Germain-des-Prés, Saint Sulpice/bus 39, 48, 96. **Open** 10am-7pm Mon-Sat. **Credit** AmEx, CB, DC, EC, JCB, MC, F$£TC, V.
Traditionalists of the blue-for-boys, pink-for-girls variety should feel at home in this doll's house of a boutique. There are clothes, accessories and gifts for babies to children aged six. Labels include Floriane, Barbar the Elephant and Baby-gro. Prices range from 170F for booties to 935F for a baby's snow parka.
Alterations. Export scheme (detaxe). Postal delivery.

Elisabeth de Senneville
38 Place du Marché Saint Honoré, 75001 Paris (42.60.08.10). Metro Pyramides. **Open** noon-7pm Mon; 10am-7pm Tue-Sat. **Credit** AmEx, CB, EC, MC, F$£TC, V.
The innovator of 'clothing for the computer age' has now branched out into children's wear. De Senneville's thoroughly modern computer print-outs, digital numbers, graphic stripes and photographic faces – on black, red or grey fleece or denim – dress whiz-kids aged three months to 12 years.

Prices for co-ordinated separates take off from 350F. Fleece and denim maternity clothes by de Senneville, children's accessories by Marithé and François Girbaud and shoes by Pom d'Api are also stocked.
Children's hair salon by appointment. Export scheme (detaxe). Videos for children.
Branches: 3 rue Turbigo, 75001 (42.33.90.83); 55 rue Bonaparte, 75006 (46.33.57.90).

Miki House
1 Place des Victoires, 75001 Paris (40.26.23.00). Metro Bourse/bus 29. **Open** 10am-7pm Mon-Sat; closed 5-21 August. **Credit** AmEx, CB, EC, MC, FTC, V.
One of the most popular children's wear labels in Japan, Miki House specializes in appliqués and crayon colours for clothes, hats, shoes and accessories for kids aged three months to seven years. Expect to pay adult prices: appliquéd polo-necks cost about 260F, trousers with braces 490F and denim overalls embroidered with mini Father Christmases 850F. Miki also stocks children's furniture – for example mini Chesterfield sofas at 3,000F – for parents with nothing else to spend their money on.
Alterations. Delivery. Export scheme (detaxe).

Naj-Oleari
1bis rue du Vieux Colombier, 75006 Paris (40.46.00.43). Metro Saint Sulpice/bus 36, 39. **Open** 10am-7pm Mon-Sat. **Credit** AmEx, CB, EC, MC, FTC, V.
Remember Marimeko? Well, Naj-Oleari is the eighties' Italian version available in Paris with its naïve, mini prints in bolts of fabric, clothes for babies to women's wear, multitudes of bags and stationery. Children's wear in cotton or wool, printed with paper doll cut-outs and twee animals are reasonably priced and can co-ordinate with printed school supplies and sturdy, plasticized book satchels (450F). Notebooks, pencils and quilted pouches cost 100F to 235F. For do-it-yourselfers, NO cotton fabric costs 170F per metre and plasticized coating 220F per metre.
Alterations. Delivery in Paris. Export scheme (detaxe).
Branches: 130 avenue Victor Hugo, 75016 (47.55.67.45).

La Petite Gaminerie
32 rue du Four, 75006 Paris (42.22.05.58). Metro Saint-Germain-des-Prés, Saint Sulpice/bus 39,48,96. **Open** 10.15am-7pm Mon-Sat. **Credit** AmEx, CB, DC, EC, MC, F$£TC, V.
See **picture and caption.**
Catalogue for furniture. Delivery. Export scheme (detaxe). Play area.

Pom d'Api
13 rue du Jour, 75001 Paris (42.36.08.87). Metro Les Halles, Etienne Marcel. **Open** 10.30am-7pm Mon-Fri; 10.30am-7.30pm Sat. **Credit** AmEx, CB, DC, EC, MC, F$£TC, V.
See **picture and caption.**
Export scheme (detaxe).
Branch: 28 rue de Four, 75006 (45.48.39.31).

TOYS & BOOKS

Attica 3
23 rue Jean de Beauvais, 75005 (46.34.62.03). Metro Maubert Mutualité/bus 63, 86, 87. **Open** 2-7pm Mon; 10am-7pm Tue-Fri; 10am-1pm, 2-7pm, Sat. **Credit** AmEx, V.
Learning can be child's play – Attica's slogan is literature for pleasure, for English speakers or those wanting to learn English. As well as a large stock of TEFL literature, you'll also find all the British children's classics on sale: *Mr Men*, Beatrix Potter, Roald Dahl and Raymond Briggs. Introduce your children to the English translations of *Asterix*, *Tintin* and other French comics.
Play area.

Au Nain Bleu
406-410 rue Saint-Honoré, 75008 Paris (42.60.39.01). Metro Concorde/bus 24, 42, 52, 842. **Open** 9.45am-6.15pm Mon-Sat. **Credit** AmEx, CB, EC, MC, £$FTC, V.
The most prestigious toy shop in France – and reputedly the oldest, having been established in 1836 – selling original toys from around the world. This could well be the most magical toy store in Paris. There's a dazzling collection of dolls and dolls' houses, musical instruments and the latest in electronic toys. The big, beautiful dolls on the ground floor beckon you in and invite you for a tea party with their elaborately packaged tea sets (720F to 3,000F). There are dozens of jars brimming over with gadgets that cost under 50F. Upstairs you'll find games, lab equipment and models, while downstairs are reliable cars, rocking horses and baby carriages. Too bad about the sales ladies who seem like the nannies before Mary Poppins arrived.
Delivery. Export scheme (detaxe).

Baby Train
9 rue du Petit Pont, 75005 Paris (46.33.90.79). Metro St Michel/bus 24, 27. **Open** 10am-6.45pm Mon, Wed-Sat; 10am-9pm Tue. **No credit cards.**
A model train shop selling everything for enthusiasts of all ages – locomotives, stations, viaducts, buffers and points. There are also model boats, aeroplanes, cars and lead soldiers on sale.

Chantelivre
13 rue de Sèvres, 75006 Paris (45.48.87.90). Metro Sèvres-Babylone, Saint Sulpice/bus 39, 63, 70, 84, 87. **Open** 1-6.50pm Mon; 10am-6.50pm Tue-Sat. **Credit** CB, EC, MC, FTC, V.
See **picture and caption.**
Export scheme (detaxe).

Le Ciel Est à Tout le Monde
10 rue Gay-Lussac, 75005 Paris (46.33.21.50). Metro Luxembourg/bus 21, 27, 38, 84, 89. **Open** noon-7pm Mon; 10am-7pm Tue-Sat. **Credit** MC, V.
This shop sells anything that flies: kites, boomerangs and flying discs either in kit form or ready-made (from 50F to 2,3000F). There is also a selection of puppets, wooden toys and pocket-money toys.

Corvinus
16 rue des Halles, 75001 Paris (42.33.68.97). Metro Châtelet, Les Halles/bus 67, 69, 70, 72, 74. **Open** 2.15-7.15pm Mon; 10.45am-7.15pm Tue-Sat. **Credit** AmEx, CB, EC, MC, £$FTC, V.
Children and lovers of miniatures will be charmed by the tiny, detailed dolls' houses –

From the people who brought you Freelance, the de rigueur *junior shoe line, here is* **Pom d'Api** *(listed under* **Children/Children's Fashion***), a colourful miniaturzed version of our favourite shoes (Doc Martens, desert boots, 'Convers' hi-tops, 'top-siders' and pony skin rockers) for babies and pre-teen children. Manufactured in France in leather, the makers work on the comfort, fit and quality and only then add the aesthetic touch which brings squeals of delight from passers-by. Shoes range from 150F to 400F, with the average being 300F.*

available in kits from 570F to 2,200F – and the furnishings sold here. Even Scrooge would have delighted in the macabre music boxes of skeletons that cost between 390F and 790F. Other old-fashioned toys include kaleidoscopes (starting at 98F), marionettes and Victorian paper dolls.
Export scheme (detaxe). Postal delivery.

L'Epée de Bois
12 rue de l'Epée de Bois, 75005 Paris (43.31.50.18). Metro Censier-Daubenton, Place Monge/bus 47. **Open** 11am-7.30pm Tue-Sat; 11am-1pm Sun. **Credit** MC, V.
A delightful toy shop selling a good range of quality toys for younger children. Most items are in the traditional vein: rocking horses, wooden animals, puppets, musical instruments and an appetising display of sweet jars stuffed with toys and novelties for under 10F each.

Jouets & Cie
11 boulevard de Sébastopol, 75001 Paris (42.33.67.67). Metro Châtelet, Les Halles/bus 38, 47. **Open** 10.30am-7.30pm Mon-Sat. **Credit** AmEx, CB, EC, MC, V.
You know you've found the biggest toy store in Paris when you spy the giant gold baby, one of Philippe Starc's early creations, in the window. Inside this labyrinth on two levels, almost every toy or game currently manufactured – as well as costumes and party

supplies – is on display. Wendy houses, trains, computer games and all the major brand names are available. All goods carry a three-month guarantee. No fancy displays, no messing about – great.
Delivery service on request. Telephone ordering service.

Madame Pierre Fain
34 rue Saint Louis en l'Ile, 75004 Paris (43.26.44.72). Metro Pont Marie/bus 67. **Open** 10am-3pm, 4-8pm, daily.
No credit cards.
At least two generations of school children on the Ile Saint Louis have bought all their pencils, notebooks and other stationery supplies from Madame Pierre Fain. She rewards their crayon artwork by pasting it up all around her tiny store that is crammed with books, toys, cards, dogs and cats. Madame Pierre Fain is much loved and virtually an institution on the Ile Saint Louis.

Multicube
5 rue de Rivoli, 75004 Paris (42.77.10.77). Metro St Paul/bus 69, 76, 96. **Open** 10am-7pm Mon-Sat. **No credit cards.**
A small shop specializing in tasteful and traditional wooden toys, imported mainly from Germany and Scandinavia. Mobiles, music boxes, hand puppets and spinning tops abound.

La Pelu--cherie
Galerie des Champs, 84 avenue des Champs-Elysées, 75008 Paris (43.59.49.05). Metro Franklin D Roosevelt, George V/bus 32, 73. **Open** noon-7.30pm Mon; 10am-7.30pm Tue-Sat. **Credit** AmEx, EC, MC, V.
A spacious shop with thousands of furry toys artistically displayed; there's a veritable jungle of koalas, monkeys, chickens, lions et al, in all sizes and at all prices. A mouse goes for 59F and an elephant could set you back 15,000F. There is also a range of baby clothes and christening presents.

ANTIQUES

Art Depot
3 rue Pont Louis Philippe, 75004 Paris (42.77.99.02). Metro Pont Marie, Saint Paul/bus 96, 69, 76. **Open** 1-8pm Tue-Sun. **Credit** AmEx, FTC.
Classy kitsch from the thirties to the fifties, the stuff on sale here is made up of those appliances that brought oohs and aahs from Tomorrow's World audiences. There's giant picture tube televisions circa 1957 (9,000F) that they will rewire for French systems, Cobra fifties' telephones (650F navy, 900F red) and a multitude of those stylish chrome lamps from the twenties and thirties.
Delivery.

Dolce Vita
25 rue de Charonne, 75011 Paris (43.38.26.31). Metro Bastille/bus 59. **Open** 11am-2.30pm, 3-7pm, Tue-Sat. **Credit** AmEx, CB, EC, MC, £$FTC, V.
Noel Coward would feel at home among these furnishings from the twenties to the forties. Items, such as a Joan Pasco mirrored dresser from the thirties, are typical of the stock. There's a bizarre Tam Tam table from the famous Colonial Expo of the thirties – the table-top is a stretched zebra skin and zebra hoofs hold it up – that looks as if it was pinched from Hemingway's house, cost: 15,000F.
Delivery.

Meubles Peints
32 rue de Sévigné, 75004 Paris (42.77.54.60). Metro Saint Paul/bus 29, 96, 69, 76. **Open** noon-7pm Tue-Sun. **No credit cards.**
Artisan Jean-Pierre Besenval scouts around for antique armoires, dressers and other pieces and then painstakingly restores them to their eighteenth-century glory and paints bucolic and folkloric scenes on them. Depending on the size and complexity of design, Besenval's painted antiques run from 15,000F to 40,000F, although he does admit to liking a bit of haggling.
Delivery.

Monsieur Renard
6 rue de l'Echaude, 75006 Paris (43.25.70.72). Metro Mabillon/bus 39, 63, 70. **Open** 2.30-7pm Mon-Sat. **Credit** AmEx, CB, DC, EC, MC, V.
The tiny boutique of Monsieur Renard is a veritable museum dedicated to nineteenth-century dolls. Monsieur Renard's dolls come in all shapes and sizes; they're all in perfect condition. Modern-day collectors can purchase them for 6,000F to 40,000F. Monsieur Renard will also buy and repair dolls.
Delivery.

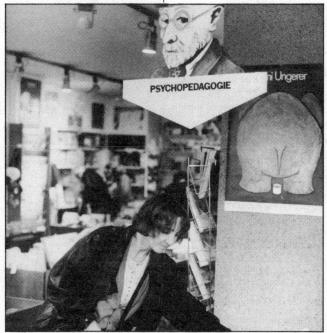

Going to **Chantelivre** *(listed under* **Children/Toys & Books***) can be a family outing. Children enjoy spending time in the play or reading area or joining in special classes for drawing or mime. There are over 10,000 titles, from books for infants to adolescents as well as health and psychology publications for expectant mothers and parents. There's a wide selection of records, cassettes and videos, educational toys and games and fun party supplies. They have an English department for books and records too.*

Services

Want a video nasty at midnight? A tuxedo that fits just right? Wheels, with or without an engine or gourmet catering for 2,000? Paris can deliver it all.

Whatever slings and arrows of outrageous fortune are cast your way, like a toothache or an empty fridge, Paris can usually come up with some soothing balm to calm the nerves. If you find yourself invited to some terrifying party where everyone has to dress up as Beethoven, Paris will throw its urbane arm round your shoulder and whisper 'It's alright, I know this little place that does a great outfit' in your ear. If Mother Nature has daubed your particular oil painting with wild and frizzy hair or baggy skin, Paris will rally round to knead and push, cut and bend whatever details of the fizog or body beautiful require seeing to. If life becomes just too difficult and all you want to do is lie under the double duvet repeating *The Owl and the Pussycat* to yourself over and over again, Paris will send pizzas, chocolates and flowers to your bedside to try and encourage you to once more face *le monde*. Then finally you will be ready to go out and hire a car and drive at high speed the wrong way round the Arc de Triomphe.

Over the following pages we review a myriad of services that are at your fingertips, sometimes available around the clock. Along with the services listed below, there are several help, information and assistance referrals at your disposal. Paris has a system of emergency (SOS) numbers which may be found in the phone directory or in the back of magazines such as the English-language monthly *Paris Passion*. Many SOS numbers are non-profit making or social service agencies. However, there do exist commercial enterprises that preface their name with SOS to connote speedy service. Many of the emergency numbers are listed in the *chapter* **Survival**.

The **French Government Tourist Office** (42.20.88.98) maintains a 24-hour English language information phoneline. Tourist information offices around Paris provide maps, directions to shopping areas, monuments and main government offices as well as information on tourist sites. Hotel bookings can also be made through them. The main tourist office is the **Office de Tourisme de Paris** *(see below* **More Information**). Should you lose something, there's a chance you may get it back if you check with the lost and found office; the **Bureau des Objets Trouvés** *(see below* **More Information**).

CONSUMER COMPLAINTS

When that antique Second Empire clock you mortgaged your home for reveals itself to have about the same lifespan as an African violet in Iceland, contact the **Direction Départmentale de la Concurrence, de la Consommation, et la Répression des Fraudes** *(see below* **More Information**).

MORE INFORMATION

Bureau des Objets Trouvés
36 rue des Morillons, 75015 Paris. Métro Convention. **Open** 9am-6pm Mon-Fri.
If you've lost or mislaid something, fill out a form at the Bureau. They don't deal with phone enquiries.

Direction Départmentale de la Concurrence, de la Consommation, et la Répression des Fraudes
Boîte 5000, 8 rue Froissart, 75153 Paris 15003 (42.71.23.10).
Write to this subdivision of the Ministry of Finance with any consumer complaints. They will investigate, put pressure on the seller to satisfy you or, if he or she refuses, instigate litigation. Be sure to include an explanation of the problem, copies of your receipt and any correspondence with the seller in your letter to the agency.

Office de Tourisme de Paris
127 avenue des Champs Elysées, 75008 Paris (47.23.61.72). Métro George V. **Open** 9am-8pm daily.

FASHION

COSTUME HIRE

Costumes de Paris
21bis rue Victor Massé, 75009 Paris (48.78.41.02). Métro Pigale/bus 67. **Open** 9am-6.30pm Tue-Sat. **Credit** CB, EC, MC, V.

This large costume warehouse resembles a historical tour. Among the 20,000 costumes for men and women must be every change of clothes in history, from the time Adam traded in his fig leaf for more respectable clothes, to futuristic fashions. Manager Madame Roubleu emphasizes that each costume is as authentic as possible, with details created with the original techniques. The average rental price with accessories is 500F for the weekend; a deposit of about 3,000F is required. Modern designer cocktail dresses and evening gowns are also available for hire.

Sommier
3 passage Brady, 75010 Paris (42.08.27.01). Métro Château d'Eau. **Open** 10am-6pm Tue-Sat. **Credit** CB, EC, MC, V.
Fulfil a Fellini fantasy or re-create your wardrobe from a past life at this costumier which specializes in fancy dress for women, men and children. All costumes are pre-1925. Prices range from 150F to 1,000F for a weekend rental.

CUSTOM TAILORING

A Sulka & Co.
2 rue de Castiglione, 75001 Paris (42.60.38.08). Métro Tuileries. **Open** 10am-6.30pm Mon; 9.30am-6.30pm Tue-Sat. **Credit** AmEx, CB, DC, EC, MC, TC, V.
A Sulka & Co menswear has over a century of custom-tailoring under its belt. Their exceptional quality, traditional haberdashery includes a large selection of off-the-peg suits, cashmere sweaters and homewear. The custom-made shirts in cotton are an addictive luxury (starting at 1,750F), as are the made-to-measure suits and tuxedos in English and Italian fabrics, to the tune of 10,000F and more. *Delivery service. Export scheme (detaxe).*

Pythagore/Purcell
62 rue du Faubourg Saint-Honoré, 75008 Paris (47.42.88.02). Métro Concorde. **Open** 10am-7.30pm Mon-Sat. **Credit** AmEx, CB, EC, DC, MC, FSDMÆYenTC, all currencies.
P/P's customized suits, made from the finest British and Italian fabrics, take about four weeks to tailor. It is however possible to have an order made up in three days. Prices for tailor-made suits average 12,000F. Off-the-peg suits (from 6,900F) are available; labels include Byblos, Zegna, Valentino, Christian Dior. Other items include hand-made shoes, trendy tuxedos and bespoke shirts.
Alterations. Bespoke tailoring. Custom orders for shoes. Delivery (free delivery by DHL). Export scheme (detaxe). Fax and phone service. Thé salon. **Branches:** 74 avenue des Champs-Elysées, 75008 (42.25.63.38); 26 avenue des Champs-Elysées, 75008 (42.89.02.01).

DRY-CLEANING & ALTERATIONS

Allô Pressing
Cité Tules-Auffret, rue du Bois-du-Groslay, 93700 Drancy (48.30.56.95). **Open** 7am-7.30pm Tue-Sat. **No credit cards.**
Whatever you need cleaned or repaired, Allô Pressing can probably do it: they will clean clothing, shoes, leather goods, suitcases, fur coats, as well as carry out alterations. They will pick up the item on the day you phone and have it back to you three days later. The service is courteous and efficient. Dry-cleaning prices are about aver-

age; 50F for a coat, 22F for trousers and 70F for a bedspread. There is also a washing and ironing service (50F per kilogramme).
Delivery service.

NEEDLECRAFT

Pelote
40 rue des Francs-Bourgeois, 75003 Paris (42.78.65.65). Metro Saint Paul/bus 29.
Open 10.30am-7pm Mon, Tue, Thur-Sat. **Credit** AmEx, CB, DC, EC, MC, £$FTC, V.
A sweet little shop with a surprisingly full range of knitting and needlework supplies, simple and elaborate patterns and handcraft kits. They carry all the Arry Blatt yarns and if you're stuck on a stitch, proprietor Christine Perlmutter is more than happy to help you out.
Catalogue. Delivery service. Export scheme (detaxe).

Tapisserie au Point
128 Galerie de Valois, 75001 Paris (42.61.44.41). Metro Palais Royal.
Open 1-6pm Mon-Fri. **No credit cards**.
Have you got a worn needlepoint cushion, an ancient cross-stitch heirloom or a damaged rug in need of restoration? Madame Claudine Brunet is a wizard at restoring patterns and needlework on chairs, pillows, rugs and tableaux. She will make up designs to order, be they contemporary or traditional designs, as well as sell her own needlework creations from the shop.

TUXEDO RENTAL

Latreille
62 rue Saint-André-des-Arts, 75006 Paris (43.29.44.10). Metro Odéon, Saint Michel.
Open 2-6.30pm Mon; 9.45am-6.30pm Tue-Sat. **Credit** AmEx, CB, EC, MC, £$FTC, V.
Call them black-tie or tuxedos, the helpful staff will suit you up. They have an admirable selection and size range and they prefer to fit the gentleman eight days before the ceremony or occasion. The average rental fee for a tux is 525F from Friday afternoon to Tuesday morning. They also sell shoes at 500F to 600F.
See also chapter **Study & Business.**

UMBRELLAS

Madeleine Gély
218 boulevard Saint Germain, 75007 Paris (42.22.63.35). Metro Rue du Bac/bus 69.
Open 9.30am-7pm Tue-Sat.
No credit cards.
See picture and caption.
Export scheme (detaxe). Repair service.

GENERAL SERVICES

ALL-PURPOSE RENTAL & REPAIR

Bazar de l'Hôtel de Ville (BHV)
Shop: 52-64 rue de Rivoli/DIY hire annexe 13 rue de la Verrerie, 75004 Paris (shop 42.74.90.00/ DIY hire 42.74.97.23). Metro Hôtel de Ville. **Open** 9am-6.30pm Mon-Sat.
Credit AmEx, CB, EC, MC, SC, V.

Founded in 1834, **Madeleine Gély** *(listed under* **Fashion/Umbrellas***) has a kaleidoscopic selection of umbrellas and canes on sale. The staff will take orders for custom-made umbrellas, no matter the quirky design or size. Choose from carved wooden or silver handles – there are over 400 styles – to suit any walk of life.*

The BHV is the leading department store for furnishings, lighting, decoration, camera cleaning and repair, shoe repair, photocopying and auto parts. The DIY rental annexe has tools, ladders, wallpaper strippers and carpet shampooers, all at competitive daily rental rates.
Delivery service. Export scheme (detaxe).

HAIR & BEAUTY

BATHS & SAUNAS

Hammam de la Mosquée
19-39 rue Geoffroy-Saint-Hilaire, 75005 Paris (43.31.18.14). Metro Censier Daubenton.
Open *women:* 11am-7pm Mon, Wed; 11am-9pm Thur; 10am-7pm Sat; *men:* 11am-7pm Fri, Sun. **Admission** 60F. **No credit cards**.
Transport yourself to Morocco without leaving the 5th *arrondissement*. Beneath the ornate tile domes and around the marble fountain of this hammam (Turkish bath) that forms part of a mosque, are baths, steam rooms and four progressively hotter saunas, the last of which can reach 90ºC (about 190ºF). After your session, try the mint tea and honey pastries in the *salon de thé*.

Hammam Saint Paul
4 rue des Rosiers, 75004 Paris (42.72.71.82). Metro Saint Paul/bus 29, 69, 76, 96. **Open** *women:* 10am-8pm Wed, Fri; *men:* 10am-8pm Thur, Sat. **Admission** 95F. **No credit cards**.

For an entry fee of 95F, soothe your body and soul in the facilities of the baths, water jets, saunas and steam rooms. Additional fees will get you a massage (90F), pedicure (90F), manicure (50F to 70F) and an appointment in the hair salon or with an beautician.
Café.

HAIR SALONS

Carita
11 rue du Faubourg Saint Honoré, 75008 Paris (women 42.65.79.00/men 42.65.10.70). Metro Concorde. **Open** 9am-7pm Mon-Sat. **Credit** AmEx, CB, DC, EC, JCB, MC, V.
These hair and skin specialists for men and women provide facials (300F to 800F), manicures (100F) medical pedicures (240F) and hair colourings. Private tanning booths are available: 92F for the face only, 230F for the entire body.

Desfossé
19 avenue Matignon, 75008 Paris (43.59.95.13). Metro Franklin D Roosevelt.
Open 9.30am-6.30pm Mon-Sat.
Credit CB, EC, MC, TC, V.
For over 100 years, heads of state have entrusted their bonces to Desfossé, the elite gentlemen's grooming parlour, frequented by politicians, celebrities and business barons. Hair treatments (from 210F) include cutting, styling, dyeing and curling. Also available are facials (270F), manicures (100F) and pedicures (165F). Allow three hours for the full works, including a sauna and massage (350F). Make your appointment at least two days in advance.
Bar. Restaurant.

SKIN CARE SALONS

Guerlain Institut de Beauté
68 avenue des Champs-Elysées, 75008 Paris (43.59.31.10). Metro Franklin D Roosevelt.
Open 9am-6.45pm Mon-Sat.
Credit AmEx, CB, DC, EC, MC, V.
See picture and caption.
Catalogue. Delivery service. Export scheme (detaxe).
Branch: 29 rue Desèvres, 75006 (42.22.46.60).

Institute Payot
10 rue de Castiglione, 75001 Paris (42.60.32.87). Metro Tuileries.
Open 9.30am-7.30pm Mon-Sat.
Credit AmEx, CB, DC, EC, MC, V.
Dr Nadine Grégoire, a Russian emigrée and dermatologist, founded the Payot skin care salon in 1919. Separate salons provide facials, make-up application for day and evening, waxing, eyelash and brow tinting and body massage. Payot creams and gels are intensive, revitalizing and generally very effective, and can be purchased at the Institute along with Pavlova perfume, that was created in honour of the ballerina.
Export scheme (detaxe).

HEALTH

For full details of health and counselling services in Paris, *see chapter* **Survival**.

EMERGENCY HEALTH CARE

SOS Médecins
(47.07.77.77/43.37.77.77).
Open 24 hours daily. **No credit cards**.
If you don't know of any doctors or are too ill to leave your bed, this service specializes in dispatching doctors for house calls. Anything will be taken on board, from emergency action to treating and prescribing medication for a cold. A normal home visit in Paris or its suburbs costs 150F before 7pm, 262F after 7pm.

Urgences Dentaires de Paris
9 boulevard Saint Marcel, 75013 Paris (47.07.33.68). Metro Saint Marcel.
Open 24 hours daily.
No credit cards.
If you're struck down by an annoying toothache, put yourself in a comfortable chair and call Urgences Dentaires de Paris. These stomatologists (mouth and dental specialists) will make emergency house calls within the hour. Appointments are taken for treatment at your home or in their office. Normal fees are 300F to 600F, plus 100F to 150F for home visits.

PHARMACY

Swann
6 rue de Castiglione, 75001 Paris (42.60.72.96). Metro Tuileries.
Open 9am-7.30pm Mon-Sat.
Credit AmEx, CB, EC, MC, £$FTC, V.

This pharmacy specializes in British and American products, including homoeopathic, over-the-counter and prescription-only medication. They also stock health and dietary food and Floris fragrances, and they're the only Parisian outlet for Tom's of Maine natural beauty and health products. If they don't have an item you're looking for, they can probably get it from their correspondents in New York and London. Don't worry about any language problems when asking for aspirin, for example; between them, the staff speak nine languages.
Delivery service. Export scheme (detaxe).

LEISURE

AUCTIONS & APPRAISALS

The French government controls auctions and does not permit the big international auction houses (for example Sotheby's and Christies) to hold sales in France.

Hôtel Drouot
9 rue Drouot, 75009 Paris (48.00.20.20). Metro Le Pelletier. **Open** 11am-noon, 2-6pm, Mon-Sat; by appointment Sun. **No credit cards**.
Paris auctions are held here, in one of 16 exhibition halls. Dealers and spectators alike are sure to enjoy the plethora of antique furniture, artwork and jewellery going, going, gone on the auction block. Experts will value items you bring to the appraisal desk free of charge, or alternatively they will visit your home. The house takes a commission (normally 10% to 18%) whether you're buying or selling.

BOOKS

Télélibrairie
Boite Postale 37, 92173 Vanves Cedex (46.45.41.41). **Open** 24 hours daily.
Credit AmEx, CB, EC, MC, V.
This handy book delivery service lets you build up your library without leaving home. Call them up with the title, author's name and, if possible, the publisher and, if the book is available in France, it will be on its way to you by courier. Delivery takes from 48 hours to one week. Along with the price of the book, you'll pay a 17.90F delivery charge no matter how many books you order .
Delivery

FLOWER DELIVERY

Interflora
4bis rue de la Gare, 92303 Levallois Perret (numero vert/free phone 05.20.32.04).
Open 8.30am-5.30pm Mon-Fri; 8.30am-5pm Sat. **Credit** CB, EC, MC, V.
Staff at Interflora's head office will refer callers to the nearest member florist. Bouquets can be delivered anywhere in Paris, France or abroad. There are catalogues of standard flower arrangements to choose from: prices start at 80F for delivery in Paris. Alternatively, bouquets can be made up to individual specifications (from 200F). Credit card orders can be taken over the phone.
Catalogue. Delivery service.

The **Guerlain Institut de Beauté** *(listed under* **Hair & Beauty/Skin Care Salons***), overlooks the once elegant Champs Elysées, a befitting tribute to Guerlain's Proustian past. Beauty treatments, including facials (400F) and cosmetic make-overs, are skillfully applied in private salons using Guerlain's recently developed skin care line,* Evolution, *anti-ageing and rehydrating creams and gels. All the Guerlain lines have UVA filters to protect against sun exposure and the cosmetics are innovative and wonderfully packaged in art deco-style.*

*A delightful grocer's, **Hédiard** (listed under **Leisure/Food & Drink**) has sold luscious candies and gourmet dishes since 1854. Taste the mouth-watering food in the restaurant upstairs, buy from their delicatessen or have their delicacies delivered. The catering service is personalized, whether it's a meal for two or for 2,000. Monsieur Oliver, the knowledgeable manager of their excellent wine cellar, will be happy to recommend the right wine for your meal and one that fits your budget.*

Lachaume
10 rue Royale, 75008 Paris (42.60.57.26). Metro Concorde, Madeleine/bus 52. **Open** 9am-7pm Mon-Sat; 9am-6pm Sun. **Credit** AmEx, CB, EC, MC, V.
This is probably Paris's most regal flower shop, founded in 1845. The aristocratic sniff from the staff is not meant for the flowers alone. Yet, if you want to impress someone with a bouquet, and spend a king's ransom doing it, you'll find Lachaume's exquisite arrangements and the reputation behind the name just the thing. Call before 2pm for same-day delivery in Paris or the nearby suburbs.
Delivery service.

FOOD & DRINK

Allô Fruit
(42.27.05.24). **Open** 9am-7.30pm Mon-Sat. **Credit** V.
Enjoy a healthy (or otherwise) breakfast in bed; Allô Fruit specializes in delivering fruit baskets and breakfast trays. Full breakfasts range from 200F to 800F for two. For 200F you receive a tray with tea, coffee or hot chocolate and patisseries (no cutlery provided); the 800F breakfast includes all the above, plus gift-wrapped champagne and caviar.

Flo Prestige
42 place du Marché-Saint-Honoré, 75001 Paris (42.61.45.46/45.54.76.94). Metro Tuileries. **Open** 8am-11pm daily. **Credit** CB, EC, MC, V.

From the cooks who make Café Flo an institution, here's the fast food equivalent. Their delectable dishes are available from six take-away outlets. They'll also deliver to your door so long as you give them two hours advance notice. Prices are very reasonable; escalope of salmon is 57F per portion and the *plat du jour* starts at 35F. The delivery charge is 100F until 6pm, and 130F afterwards.
Delivery service.
Branches: 102 avenue du President Kennedy, 75016 (42.88.38.00); 61 avenue de la Grande Armée, 75016 (45.00.12.10); 352 rue Lecourbe, 75015 (45.54.76.94); 211 avenue Daumesnil, 75012 (43.44.86.36); 36 avenue de la Motte Picquet, 75007 (45.51.91.36).

Hédiard
21 place de la Madeleine, 75001 Paris (42.66.09.00). Metro Madeleine. **Open** 9.15am-6.30pm Mon-Sat. **Credit** AmEx, CB, DC, EC, MC, £$FTC, V.
See **picture and caption.**
Delivery service.

Jacques Hesse
71 rue Guynemer, Issy-les-Moulineaux, 92130 (40.93.05.05). **Open** 8am-11pm daily. **Credit** AmEx, CB, EC, MC, V.
See **picture and caption.**
Delivery service.

Nicolas
8 avenue de Wagram, 75008 Paris (42.27.22.07). Metro Etoile. **Open** 9am-midnight Tue-Sat. **Credit** AmEx, MC, V.

One of the shops that form part of a national chain of wine shops and off-licences. Any branch will take orders over the phone for home delivery, but this one is the only branch to stay open till midnight. The minimum order is 200F (delivery charge 20F within Paris) and 24 hours' notice is required.

Slice Pizza
62 rue Monsieur Le Prince, 75006 Paris (43.54.18.18). Metro Odeon. **Open** 11am-11pm Mon-Sat. **No credit cards**.
Pizza delivery has finally hit Paris. Slice will bike your order to you within 30 to 45 minutes. The toppings aren't terribly ambitious, but the pizzas are tasty, with a thin, crispy crust. A pizza for four costs between 90F and 130F, and you can add coleslaw, brownies and soft drinks to the order. There is a minimum order of 90F for free delivery.
Delivery service.

SPORT

Allô Sports
(42.76.54.54). **Open** 10.30am-5pm Mon-Thur; 10am-4.30pm Fri.
A free information hotline; operators can answer all questions about where to practice your chosen sport, as well as giving opening hours of municipal facilities, clubs and federations, information about on-going sports activities for adults and children, and more. There is usually an operator on duty who speaks English, but you can always request your hotel concierge to ring them.

STATIONERY

Cassegrain
422 rue Saint Honoré, 75001 Paris (42.60.20.08). Metro Concorde. **Open** 9.30am-6.30pm Mon-Sat. **Credit** AmEx, CB, DC, EC, MC, FTC, V.
Cassegrain's engraved stationery and cards have been crafted in the same careful manner for over 70 years. Prices are slightly higher than at the average printer, but they have an abundant selection of typography to choose from and you can be assured of the quality of the paper, engraving and embossing. Allow three weeks for delivery. You'll also find handsome leather agendas and desk accessories and desirable gold-nibbed pens.
Delivery service. Export scheme (detaxe).

THEATRE BOOKING

If you are staying in a hotel during your visit to Paris, it's worth remembering that the hotel may offer a free booking service or may even have access to seats reserved for their guests. Be sure to ask at the front desk of your hotel if these services are available.

Agence Cheque Théâtre
2nd floor, 33 rue Le Peletier, 75009 Paris (42.46.72.40). Metro Le Peletier/bus 42, 67,74. **Open** 10am-7pm Mon-Sat. **No credit cards.**
This agency sells tickets to all types of entertainment venues by phone, by post and in person.

Alpha-FNAC
3rd level down (– 3), Forum des Halles, 75001 Paris (40.26.81.18). Metro Châtelet, Les Halles/bus 67, 69, 70, 72, 85.
Open 2pm-7.30pm Mon; 10am-7.30pm Tue-Sat. **Credit** V.
An agency that supplies tickets for all types of entertainment. Phone the main number above for details of the branch nearest you.

Jeunesses Musicales de France
56 rue de l'Hôtel de Ville, 75004 Paris (42.78.19.54). Metro Hôtel de Ville/bus 69, 76, 96. **Open** 10am-7pm Mon-Sat; 10am-6pm Sun. **Rates** 150F over-30s; 80F 18-30s; 15F under-18s. **No credit cards.**
A membership organization that offers 50% discounts at all major theatres on certain days. They're very helpful and have a reciprocal arrangement with the British organization, Youth and Music.

Kiosque Théâtre
across from 15 place de la Madeleine, 75008 Paris. Metro Madeleine/bus 42, 52.
Open 12.30-8pm Tue-Sat; 12.30-4pm Sun. **No credit cards.**
Queue up between the monumental Church of the Madeleine and a fish market for discount and half-price tickets for same-day matinée and evening performances of theatre, dance, opera and other events throughout Paris. Tickets are rarely available for the most popular shows.
Branch: Châtelet RER station, 75001.

VIDEO & CASSETTE RENTAL
Reels On Wheels
7 rue Decrès, 75014 Paris (45.42.58.66). Metro Plaisance. **Open** 10am-10pm Mon-Sat; noon-10pm Sun. **Credit** AmEx, CB, EC, MC, F£DM$TC, V.
Film fans and couch potatoes, get your popcorn ready. Ian and Colin, a Scot and a Brit respectively, stock over 2,200 films (in the original lingo), from Hollywood classics to new features. For an annual subscription fee of 500F, you can either rent a film at 25F per night or have it delivered to your home for 50F per night. They will also rent out a PAL-SECAM VCR and 10 cassettes for 600F per month.
Catalogue. Delivery service.

TRANSPORT

BICYCLE RENTAL
Bicyclub
8 place de la Porte Champerret, 75017 Paris (47.66.55.92). Metro Porte Champerret.
Open 9am-1pm, 2pm-6pm, Mon-Fri; 9am-1pm Sat. **Credit** TC.
The healthiest getaway from Paris is on two wheels. Bicyclub rent bikes from such bucolic locations as Saint Germain-en-Laye and Rambouillet forests, Boulogne and

Jacques Hesse *(listed under **Leisure/Food & Drink**) is getting ready for 1992 with a daily-changing menu that offers customers the cuisine of Europe delivered to their door. The range of menus is bewildering; choose goodies for breakfast, brunch, lunch, cocktails or supper. Alternatively, there are prepared dishes that only need to be re-reheated. A complete meal costs about 150F per person and the delivery is free. Lunch can be ordered up to 11am.*

Vincennes woods and Versailles castle, by the hour, day or week (*see chapter* **Sport** for full details). You can pedal further afield on their package tours of the French provinces, Holland, Ireland and Hungary. Daily rental for a three-speed bike is 60F, a ten-speed is 80F and a mountain bike is 100F. A returnable deposit of 1,000F to 2,000F is required.

CAR HIRE
Europcar
145 avenue de Malakoff, 75016 Paris (45.00.08.06/central reservation line 30.43.82.82). Metro Porte Maillot.
Open 8am-8pm daily. **Credit** AmEx, CB, DC, EC, JCB, MC, V.
This is one of the largest car rental network agencies in France. Rent their models of European cars, such as Renault, Peugeot, BMW or Mercedes, in the Budget category (starting at 223F per day plus 3.21F per km), Mid-size category (from 363F per day plus 5.36F per km) or the Superior category (from 562F per day plus 6.39F per km). Pick up your car from several Paris locations or have it delivered to your hotel, office or home. You can return the car at any Europcar office in France, and in many cases in Europe.
Delivery service.

Wills Location
84 avenue de Versailles, 75016 Paris (42.88.40.04). Metro Mirabeau.
Open 8.30am-7pm Mon-Sat.
Credit AmEx, CB, DC, EC, MC, V.
Rent a Ford Fiesta for 169F per day plus 2.30F per km, or a Rolls Royce Silver Spur at 5,000F per day plus 19F per km. They'll deliver the car for no extra charge during office hours; a 200F delivery charge is added after 7pm Monday to Saturday and all day Sunday.
Delivery service.

HITCH-HIKING
Allô Stop
84 passage Brady, 75010 Paris (42.46.00.66). Metro Château d'Eau.
Open 9am-7.30pm Mon-Fri; 9am-1pm, 2-6pm, Sat. **No credit cards.**
Need a lift? This company puts hitch-hikers in touch with drivers. There's an initial fee of 40F, payable to Allô Stop, plus shared toll fees and petrol costs (maximum charge 16 centimes per km). You can also subscribe yearly to this matchmaking organization at a cost of 150F. Most people we have spoken to who have used the service say that it's generally faster and probably safer than thumbing it on the road.

SHIPPING
TAT Express
Zone de Fretnord-Bat 290, 94394 Orly airport (46.87.02.02). **Open** 24 hours Mon-Fri. **No credit cards.**
Call TAT before 1pm and they will pick up your package the same day, to be delivered anywhere in France within 24 hours, or internationally. Costs vary according to weight and destination. The maximum weight per package is 140kg (308lb).

Art Galleries and Museums

In the following pages you'll find the best of the capital's museums and commerical art galleries. Old masters and young unknowns, gargoyles and Gauguins, religious icons, fakes or rare tapestries, Paris's museums have it covered. We tell you which salons to investigate and which to avoid, where to find the liveliest exhibitions and how to beat the crowds. Take a deep breath and prepare to experience the great collections of the world.

CONTENTS:

Art Galleries

Whether you just want to browse or are looking to buy, Parisian galleries offer the connoisseur an eclectic range of works by old masters and young innovators.

Paris long held the reins of the art world, magnetically attracting the leading lights of avant-garde movements from all over the world, particularly eastern and southern Europe. However, the increase in the size of art markets during the last few decades in the US – notably New York – and in countries such as West Germany, has resulted in Paris being left behind on the international market stakes. Today, after a dormant period of 25 years, Paris is beginning to reassert itself as a melting pot for ambitious new work and, consciously or not, seems to be vying for the cultural driver's seat in the Europe of 1992. The number of collectors is multiplying and international artists can yet again look to this capital as a major exhibition venue.

Parisian galleries that specialize in particular movements tend to cluster around specific areas. For example, the Left Bank galleries show fairly classical paintings, whether figurative or abstract, although a number of them do concentrate on works from the fifties and sixties. The galleries around Beaubourg and the low-lying Marais district all profess to be resolutely avant-garde, showing the very latest and most innovative work. Many of the pieces shown consist of 'museum art' – installations and large-scale works – that are hardly appropriate for private collectors, unless your name is Saatchi or Getty. Until the mid-eighties, the Bastille district – originally called Paris's East Village – was very much the domain of artists, craftsmen and furniture manufacturers. Times have changed in some respects. Mitterrand's people's Opera House dominates the Place de la Bastille and brightly lit sushi-bars now occupy the premises where unlicensed bohemia once thrived. But the side-streets are burgeoning with young galleries that have sprung to life over the last four or five years. Though they are still searching for a common identity, this small circuit, which teems with fun bars, cafés and shops, shouldn't be missed.

SALONS

Annual events such as *Salons* – a tradition going back to the nineteenth century – can feature quality work. In particular, the Salon de Montrouge, which usually takes place in May, deserves attention. Mass salons at the Grand Palais, such as the Indépendants, should be avoided because they tend to be both over-subscribed and over-rated. The annual art fair – FIAC, short for the Foire Internationale de l'Art Contemporain – which takes place in October, provides rich pickings drawn from galleries worldwide. Artists from Paris's East Village organize a series of studio open days during the FIAC.

EXHIBITION CENTRES

A number of public bodies own exhibition spaces that are regularly used to display art. Although unrelated to any particular permanent collection, temporary exhibitions are generally of a high standard. For detailed information on the major art museums in Paris, such as the **Musée National du Louvre** *see chapter* **Museums.**

Bibliothèque Forney
Hôtel des Archevêques de Sens, 1 rue du Figuier, 75004 Paris (42.78.14.50). Metro Pont Marie, Saint Paul./bus 67. **Open** 1.30-8pm Tue-Sat. **Admission** 15F adults; 10F under-12s, students, OAPs, UB40s. **No credit cards.**
Set in the lavish surroundings of the oldest of the Marais' mansions, this library is famed for its documentation on the applied arts and has a wing given over to temporary displays. The exhibitions provide an opportunity to catch up on the graphic design innovations or specific designers of the early twentieth century in an almost monastic hush.
Shop. Reference library. Wheelchair access.

Bibliothèque Nationale
Galerie Mansart, 58 rue de Richelieu, 75002 Paris (47.03.81.26)/Galerie Colbert, 6 rue Vivienne, 75002 Paris (47.03.81.26). Metro Bourse/bus 39, 48, 67. **Open** Galerie Mansart: noon-6.30pm Mon-Sat; Galerie Colbert: noon-6pm Mon-Sat. **Admission**
Galerie Mansart: 20F adults; 12F under-12s, students; *Galerie Colbert:* free.
Before building work starts on the 'world's biggest library' – nicknamed the TGB or *Très Grande Bibliothèque* – in the south-east of Paris, make the most of this ageing institution where all French publications covered by copyright are miraculously stored. The Galerie Mansart has regular exhibitions ranging from Indian miniatures to contemporary etchings while the Galerie Colbert, situated in the library annexe, hosts some interesting contemporary photography and print displays.

Centre National de la Photographie
Palais de Tokyo, 13 avenue du Président-Wilson, 75016 Paris (47.23.36.53). Metro Iéna/bus 63. **Open** 9.45am-5.15pm Mon, Wed-Sun. **Admission** 25F adults; 15F 18-25s, OAPs; 12F 10-25s; free under-10s. **No credit cards.**
After a chequered museological career, this immense building facing the Eiffel Tower has finally been given a new *raison d'être* and has become the national centre for photography. Three shows are always held simultaneously, covering work by historical and contemporary photographers. Often crowded at the weekend, the Palais de Tokyo makes a worthwhile weekday destination and can be combined with the neighbouring Musée d'Art Moderne de la Ville de Paris.
Shop.

Ecole Nationale des Beaux Arts
17 Quai Malaquais, 75006 Paris (42.60.34.57). Metro Saint-Germain-des-Prés/bus 24, 27, 39, 48, 95. **Open** 1-7pm Mon, Wed-Sun. **Admission** 18F adults; 10F under-13s, students. **Credit** A, EC, TC, V.
The exhibition halls of France's central art college, the Ecole Nationale des Beaux Arts, are used four times a year for thematic exhibitions which vary considerably in both scale and content. Enormous banners, easily legible from across the Seine, announce the forthcoming events.
Bookstore. Reference library.

Grand Palais (Galeries Nationales)
avenue du Général Eisenhower, 75008 Paris (42.89.54.10; recorded information 42.56.09.24). Metro Champs-Elysées-Clémenceau/bus 42, 73, 83, 93. **Open** 10am-8pm Mon, Thur-Sun; 10am-10pm Wed. **Admission** *Mon-Fri, Sun:* 32F adults; 21F 13-25s, students, OAPs; free under-13s; *Sat:* 21F adults, 13-25s, students, OAPs; free under-13s. **Credit** V.
See picture and caption.
Café and bookstore in section on avenue G. Eisenhower. Wheelchair access.

Institut Français d'Architecture
6 rue de Tournon, 75006 Paris (46.33.90.36). Metro Odéon/bus 58. **Open** 12.30-7pm daily. **Admission** free.
A must for anyone with even a fleeting interest in architecture: the various worldwide exhibitions on current projects are always comprehensive and imaginatively presented.
Catalogues. Wheelchair access.

Pavillon de l'Arsenal
21 boulevard Morland, 75004 Paris (42.76.33.97). Metro Sully-Morland/bus 67,

86, 87. **Open** 10.30am-6.30pm Tue-Sat;
11am-7pm Sun. **Admission** free.
This recently opened centre presents urban
design and architectural projects to the public in the form of drawings, plans and the
occasional maquette. An illuminated 50-
metre (165ft) square model of Paris is per-
manently exhibited, giving the visitor an
ideal platform for putting the city and its various landmarks in perspective.
Small bookshop. Guided tours. Wheelchair access.

Pavillon des Arts
*101 rue Rambuteau, 75001 Paris
(42.33.82.50). Metro Les Halles/bus 29.* **Open**
11.30am-6.30pm Tue-Sun. **Admission** 25F
adults; 15F students, OAPs; free under-5s.
Located next to the Forum des Halles,
this first-floor gallery shows an eclectic
programme of exhibitions with little
apparent continuity of subject from sculpture to photography. You may happen
upon something of major interest or you
may prefer to walk by.
Wheelchair access.

COMMERCIAL GALLERIES

SAINT GERMAIN

Galerie Berggruen & Cie
*70 rue de l'Université, 75007 Paris
(42.22.02.12). Metro Solférino/bus 69.*
Open 10am-1pm, 2-7pm, Tue-Sat. **Credit** V.
Located at the western end of the Saint
Germain gallery circuit, Berggruen is well
known for its rich collection of drawings and
prints. Works in stock include Ernst,
Gautrier, Kandinsky, Klee and Masson as
well as pieces by living artists such as
Arroyo, Béringer and Horst Janssen.

Claude Bernard
*7-9 rue des Beaux Arts, 75006 Paris
(43.26.97.07). Metro Saint-Germain-des-
Prés/bus 39, 48, 63, 95.* **Open** 9.30am-
12.30pm, 2.30-6.30pm, Tue-Sat.
No credit cards.
If you are looking for figurative work, this
gallery should be able to satisfy you somehow . Extensive stock of work has been built
up since the sixties; the collection includes
paintings by Bacon, Botero, Hockney, Saul
Steinberg and Kitaj.

Isy Brachôt
*35 rue Guenégaud, 75006 Paris
(43.54.22.40). Metro Odéon/bus 58, 70, 87,
96.* **Open** 11am-12.30pm, 2-7pm, Tue-Sat.
No credit cards.
With its main branch in Brussels, this
gallery has changed course over the last few
years, moving away from a predominantly
figurative emphasis to featuring more conceptual work. Nonetheless, Magritte seems
to have withstood the change of focus and is
particularly well represented. Other
favoured artists include Broodthaers, Beuys,
Gina Pane and Bijl.

Jeanne Bucher
*53 rue de Seine, 75006 Paris (43.26.22.32).
Metro Odéon/bus 39, 63, 70, 84, 87.* **Open**
9am-1pm, 2-7pm, Tue-Fri; 10am-12pm, 2.30-
6.30pm, Sat. **No credit cards.**

Under its domed glass and iron roof, the **Grand Palais** *(listed under*
Exhibition Centres) is a striking leftover from the 1900 Universal Exhibition.
Its various galleries are now used for important historical exhibitions – Turner,
Gauguin and Monet are just a few of the masters to have been featured to date.
The building is also divided into artists' salons and is used for the annual Foire
Internationale de l'Art Contemporain that takes place in October.

This large sky-lit gallery set back from the
street is one of the oldest in the area – established in 1925 – and is mainly geared to
showing abstract paintings from the fifties,
including work by Bissière, Dubuffet, Asger
Jorn and Vieira da Silva.

Galerie Di Meo
*5 rue des Beaux Arts, 75006 Paris
(43.64.10.98). Metro Saint-Germain-des-
Prés/bus 39, 48, 63, 95.* **Open** 10am-1pm,
2.30-7pm, Tue-Sat. **No credit cards.**
A visit to this fairly traditional gallery that
specializes in abstract art from the fifties and
sixties should be rewarded with a selection
of work by Fontana, Matta or Cy Twombly.

Jean-Jacques Dutko
*5 rue Bonaparte, 75006 Paris (43.26.96.13).
Metro Saint-Germain-des-Prés/bus 39, 48, 63,
95.* **Open** 10.30am-12.30pm, 2.30-7pm, Tue-
Sat. **No credit cards.**
While in the Saint Germain area, take
advantage of the concentration of dealers
trading in very high quality art deco furniture and *objets d'art*. The thirties movement is much in evidence at this gallery
that hangs work by Masson, Fougeron,
Gleizes, Marcoussis, Zadkine, Faultrier
and Georges Noel.

Yves Gastou
*12 rue Bonaparte, 75006 Paris
(46.34.72.17). Metro Saint-Germain-des-
Prés/bus 39, 48, 63, 95.* **Open** 11am-1pm, 2-
7pm, Tue-Sat. **No credit cards.**
For some of the latest furniture designs,
which look forward to the nineties, this is
one of Paris's most informed showcases.
Accompanied by historical pieces from the

fifties and sixties, the designs by Sottsass,
Kuramata, Ron Arad and Tom Dixon take
centre stage.

Samy Kinge
*54 rue de Verneuil, 75007 Paris
(42.61.19.07). Metro rue du Bac/bus 69.*
Open 10.30am-1pm, 2.30-7pm, Tue-Sat. **No**
credit cards.
Down by the Musée d'Orsay (*see chapter*
Museums) this small venue is active in promoting contemporary European art. Despite
the limited space, the gallery has a wide
panorama of art on display that includes
work by Martin Bradley, Samios and Thek.

Galerie Krief
*50 rue Mazarine, 75006 Paris
(43.29.32.37). Metro Odéon/bus 39, 63, 70,
84, 87.* **Open** 10.30am-7pm Tue-Sat.
Credit AmEx, V.
The gallery enthusiastically promotes a variety of young artists, including a generous
helping of native protégés. Rémy Blanchard,
Jean-Luc Poivret, Chambas and Babou have
all emerged during the eighties to carry the
French standard and get comprehensive
exposure in this gallery.

Adrien Maeght
*42 & 46 rue du Bac, 75007 Paris
(45.48.45.15). Metro rue du Bac/bus 69.*
Open 10.30am-1pm, 2-6.30pm, Mon-Sat.
Credit AmEx, DC.
Here we have the French equivalent of
Dynasty being acted out before the
appreciative gaze of the Parisian *beau*
monde. Originally set up by Aimé
Maeght's son, Adrien, the gallery is now
run by Aimé's grand-daughter, Yoyo. The

Alice.

Il manquait une librairie
à la place de la Madeleine.

Au 1er étage.
De très bonnes bouteilles
avec tout pour les
ouvrir, apprécier leur
température ou
les servir en carafe.

Un endroit agréable
pour découvrir vins
connus et méconnus.

Au rez-de-chaussée.
Une étonnante sélection
de petits vins de pays.

Nous vous rappelons
que nous pouvons
vous conseiller et livrer
vos choix à domicile.

Au 1er étage.
La librairie avec les
meilleurs livres et revues
sur le vin. A acheter
ou à compulser.

Au rez-de-chaussée.
Une impressionnante
collection de vins
de France et d'ailleurs.

A la cave.
Des millésimes depuis
1900.

31, place de la Madeleine.

Up on the first floor, overlooking the Cour du Bel Air, the dynamic, young **Michel Vidal** *gallery (listed under* **Commercial Galleries/Bastille***) has an interesting* mélange *of work by young French artists and more established names from the sixties and seventies such as Alain Jacquet, Spoerri, Kosuth, Rancillac and Villegle.*

relationship between the two has proved less than idyllic; a monumental legal wrangle is currently being fought between dad's heirs. In the meantime, they use the generous double-gallery space to exhibit young artists – from the brightly coloured canvases of Kuroda to the neo-primitive style of Hélène Delprat. The stock of twentieth-century artists is enviable and ranges from Miro to Calder.

Galerie Montenay
31 rue Mazarine, 75006 Paris (43.54.85.30). Metro Odéon/bus 39, 63, 70, 84, 87. **Open** 11am-1pm, 2.30-7pm, Tue-Sat. **No credit cards.**
This expansive sky-lit gallery, which started life as a garage, is now cheerfully used for exhibiting contemporary artists with conceptual leanings – completely out of place in this 'quartier' which is becoming increasingly traditional in character. Tom Drahos, Ange Leccia – who once exhibited a Mercedes at the Venice Biennale – Donald Baechler, Not Vital, Brice Marden and Keith Sonnier are all regular exhibitors.

Galerie de Paris
6 rue du Pont de Lodi, 7506 Paris (43.25.42.63). Metro Pont-Neuf, Odéon/bus 58, 70. **Open** 2.30-7.30pm Tue-Sat. **No credit cards.**
If you want a surprise, this gallery should be able to accommodate your taste for the unexpected: go straight downstairs where installations by young artists are given prominence. French artists such as Richard Baquié – who incorporates neon into photoworks – or Présence Panchounette, alter-

nate with international artists such as Art & Language and Braco Dmitrijevic.

Galerie Stadler
51 rue de Seine, 75006 Paris (43.26.91.10). Metro Odéon/bus 39, 63, 70, 84, 87. **Open** 10.30am-12.30pm, 2.30-7pm, Tue-Sat. **Credit** MC, V.
Opened in the fifties in the heart of what was then the hub of avant-garde Paris, Stadler remains faithful to the field of abstract expressionism. Works can be found by Tapiès or Arnulf Rainer, as well as by younger protagonists such as Maya Andersson, David Budd, Damian and Sauran.

Galerie Patrice Trigano
4bis rue des Beaux-Arts, 75006 Paris (46.34.15.01). Metro Saint-Germain-des-Prés/bus 39, 48, 63, 95. **Open** 10am-1pm, 2.30-6.30pm, Tue-Sat. **No credit cards.**
In a street which harbours a number of established galleries, Patrice Trigrano, is another ardent defender of the Ecole de Paris of the fifties and sixties that launched the abract work of Lanskoy, Messon and Schneider. The gallery also represents anomalies such as the British Pop artist Allen Jones and the committed graphics of Velickovic.

Aline Vidal
70 rue Bonaparte, 75006 Paris (43.26.08.68). Metro Saint-Sulplice/bus 63, 70, 86, 87, 96. **Open** 2-7pm Tue-Sat. **No credit cards.**
A short way from the main exhibiting nucleus of the Left Bank, Aline Vidal's gallery is worth visiting if you want to see conceptual work by

some interesting young artists. British 'ephemeral' sculptor Andy Goldsworthy has exhibited here, as has photographer Keiichi Tahara and young French artists such as Eric Fonteneau and Hélène Mugot.

BEAUBOURG & LE MARAIS

Galerie Beaubourg
23 rue du Renard and 3 rue Pierre-au-Lard, 75004 Paris (42.71.20.50/48.04.34.40). Metro Hôtel-de-Ville/bus 38, 47, 75. **Open** 10.30am-1pm, 2.30-7pm, Tue-Sat. **No credit cards.**
This is one of Paris' most important contemporary art galleries, securing a steady flow of international crowd-pullers. Past dignitaries have included the sculptors Arman and Cesar with paintings by Rauschenberg, Dokoupil, Combas and Larry Rivers. A second gallery, which recently opened across the road, is an impressively spacious affair, particularly suited to larger work.

Galerie Alain Blondel
4 rue Aubry-le-Boucher, 75004 Paris (42.78.66.67). Metro Châtelet, Rambuteau/bus 38, 47. **Open** 11am-1pm, 2-7pm, Tue-Fri; 2-7pm Sat. **No credit cards.**
Situated just across the square from the Beaubourg (Pompidou Centre), this gallery appeals to those who prefer a realist style of painting, typical of the early twentieth century. Apart from being the recognized dealer for paintings by the thirties society artist, Tamara de Lempicka, Blondel represents mainly French figurative artists such as Van Hove, Claude Yvel, J-M Lango and J-M, Poumeyrol.

Gilbert Brownstone
9 & 15 rue Saint-Gilles, 75003 Paris (42.78.43.21). Metro Chemin Vert/bus 38, 47. **Open** 11am-7pm Tue-Sat. **No credit cards.**
At the far end of the Marais and within throwing distance of the Bastille, the American Gilbert Brownstone remains committed to showing work based on geometric abstractions and minimalist styles. Keen to fuse the older masters with some new blood, he has featured major international names alongside lesser known artists. The gallery does have some heavyweights on its books, though, so don't be surprised to encounter works by Albers, Soto, Honegger, Mosset, Ed Ruscha or Christian J Jaccard hanging in this very sleek setting.

Farideh Cadot
77 rue des Archives, 75003 Paris (42.78.08.36). Metro Arts-et-Métiers/bus 38, 47, 75. **Open** 11-7pm Tue-Sat. **No credit cards.**
Farideh Cadot's celebrated studio is situated on the first floor of this building. A pioneer in his field – he was the first to move into this part of the Marais and to search out avant-garde movements in the early eighties – Cadot's gallery is a centrepiece for both provocative and imaginative work. A sister gallery in New York helps maintain close links with American artists. Georges Rousse's photoworks are now widely appreciated while Joël Fisher, David Tremlett, Juan Uslé, Marcus Raetz and Connie Beckley have gained international acclaim in a variety of media.

DAY IS GREY

THE NIGHT IS BLACK & WHITE

Black&White
Scotch Whisky

TRADUISEZ : LE JOUR EST GRIS. LA NUIT EST BLACK & WHITE. SACHEZ APPRÉCIER ET CONSOMMER AVEC MODÉRATION.

Galerie Charles Cartwright
6 rue de Braque, 75003 Paris (48.04.86.86).
Metro Rambueau/bus 29. **Open** 11am-1pm,
2-7pm, Tue-Sat. **No credit cards.**
This third-floor gallery is one of Paris' liveliest showcases and remains in step with the
latest movements. Mixed-media works by
young French artists such as Laurent
Joubert, Philippe Hurteau and Jean-Sylvain
Bieth are displayed.

Galerie Crousel-Robelin/Bama
40 rue Quincampoix, 75004 Paris
(42.77.38.87). Metro Châtelet,
Rambuteau/bus 29. **Open** 11am-1pm, 2-7pm,
Tue-Sat. **No credit cards.**
One of the longest-standing galleries in this
street, the Galerie Bama once pioneered conceptual work at a time when few others were
interested in showing such artists. Two
years ago Chantal Crousel joined forces with
the gallery; today it continues to present a
cohesive programme of artists of prime international relevance, including Sigmar Polke,
Tony Cragg, Jochen Gerz, John Armleder,
Wolfgang Laib and Jon Kessler.

Durand-Dessert
3 rue des Haudriettes & 43 rue de
Montmorency, 75003 Paris (42.77.63.60).
Metro Rambuteau/bus 29. **Open** 2-7pm Tue-
Fri; 11am-7pm Sat. **Credit** V.
A well-established venue with international
pull, this gallery is geared towards conceptual work with two exhibitions generally
being held simultaneously. The gallery at 3
rue des Haudriettes has the more substan-
tial space. You are just as likely to walk in on

an exhibition in the *arte povera* vein as one
with a minimalist or conceptual theme.
Major French artists exhibited here in the
past have included François Morellet,
Gérard Garouste and Bertrand Lavier.
Mario Merz, Kounellis, Tosani and Barry
Flanagan are also regulars.

Jean Fournier
44 rue Quincampoix, 75004 Paris
(42.77.32.31). Metro Châtelet,
Rambuteau/bus 29. **Open** 10am-12.30pm,
2.30-7pm, Tue-Sat. **Credit** MC, V.
This spacious gallery hidden away in a
courtyard is particularly representative of
the French seventies movement *Support-
Surface* and shows artists such as Claude
Viallat, Buraglio, Shirley Jaffé, Sam Francis
and Piffaretti. Part of the gallery is devoted
to a well-stocked arts bookshop.

Galerie de France
50-52 rue de la Verrerie, 75004 Paris
(42.72.38.00). Metro Hôtel-de-Ville/bus 69,
76, 96. **Open** 10am-6pm Mon; 10am -7pm
Tue-Sat. **No credit cards.**
See picture and caption.

Galerie Karsten Greve
5 rue Debelleyme, 75003 Paris
*(42.77.19.37). Metro Saint Sébastien-
Froissart/bus 20, 65.* **Open** 10am-1pm, 2-
7pm, Tue-Sat. **No credit cards.**
This important gallery, originally set up in
Cologne, has now been relocated in Paris –
a sign, perhaps, of the imminent approach
of 1992. Major twentieth-century artists are
exhibited, such as Albers, Fontana,
Picasso, Manzoni, De Kooning and
Fautrier. You may discover the occassional

wild card such as Grauber, Nicola de Maria
or Blinky Palermo.

Galerie Ghislaine Hussenot
5bis rue des Haudriettes, 75003 Paris
(48.87.60.81). Metro Rambuteau/bus 29.
Open 10.30am-7pm Tue-Sat.
No credit cards.
Uncompromisingly committed to conceptual
work, this gallery invariably features an
impressive range of established names. The
most notable recent inclusions have been
Boltanski, Wall, Koons and Schütte.

Galerie Laage-Salomon
57 rue du Temple, 75004 Paris
(42.78.11.71). Metro Rambuteau/bus 29.
Open 10.30am-12.30pm, 2.30-7pm, Tue-Fri;
11am-7pm Sat. **No credit cards.**
In the heart of the Beaubourg gallery circuit
and tucked away at the back of a secluded
courtyard, Laage-Salomon is a gallery with an
international reputation. Ambitious exhibitions
in the past have included Christo's land-pro-
jects and the forceful neo-Expressionist work
of the German artists Balelitz and Lüpertz.

Galerie Lacourière Frelaut
23 rue Sainte Croix de la Brétonnerie,
75004 Paris (42.72.02.30). Metro
Rambuteau/bus 29. **Open** 10am-12.30pm,
1.30-7pm, Tue-Sat. **No credit cards.**
In a traditional vein, this gallery deals in
figurative work. The selection of etchings
and other prints originating from the
famous Montmartre print-workshop –
which gave birth to the gallery itself – are
of particular interest. Dado's weird reptil-
ian world or Suzzoni's exaggerated human
forms offer a fantastical aside from the con-
formity of the main displays.

Yvon Lambert
108 rue Vieille-du-Temple and 5 rue du
Grenier Saint-Lazare, 75003 Paris
(42.71.09.33/42.71.04.25). Metro Filles du
Calvaire/bus 20, 69. **Open** 10am-1pm, 2.30-
7pm, Tue-Sat. **No credit cards.**
As one of Paris' pioneering forces in the seventies, Lambert is rarely intimidated by convention in his choice of artists. He is responsible for launching a number of French artists,
among them the comic-strip hero Combas,
the more subtle J-C Blais and Philippe 'small
is beautiful' Favier. Lambert also exhibits
some more familiar names from across the
Atlantic – Schnabel, Bruce Nauman, Haim
Steinbach, Cy Twombly, Sol LeWitt – and
major Europeans, such as Clemente and
Barcelo. The gallery at No.108 is a gigantic
warehouse-type space while the venue at
No.5 is the more modest original gallery.

Badoin Lebon
34 rue des Archives, 75004 Paris
(42.72.09.10). Metro Hôtel-de-Ville,
Rambuteau/bus 29. **Open** 9am-7pm Mon-
Sat. **No credit cards.**
This pleasant, spacious gallery has an eclectic mixture of exhibitions ranging from the
eccentric Popo and Fluxus artist Ben to the
disturbing photographic world of Joel-Peter
Witkin. Works by American artists, such as
the late Robert Mapplethorpe and Warhol
also surface from time to time.

Galerie Sylvana Lorenz
13 rue Chapon, 75003 Paris (48.04.53.02).
Metro Rambuteau/bus 29. **Open** 2-7pm
Tue-Sat. **No credit cards.**

The **Galerie de France** *(listed under* **Commercial Galleries/Beaubourg**
& Le Marais*) contains a wide and challenging range of contemporary artists'*
work exhibited in a superb, three-tiered space situated almost directly behind the
BHV department store. Alain Jacquet, Pistoletto, Soulages, Niki de Saint-
Phalle, Rebecca Horn and exponents of the Soviet avant-garde are all well rep-
resented. Will more artists from behind the crumbling Iron Curtain exhibit here
in the future? Time will tell.

This baby of the art world was quickly absorbed into the Marais gallery nucleus, probably because its owner has such an inimitable personality. The gallery has a particularly eccentric leaning. You are quite likely to be given a personal tour of the exhibition works by conceptual artists – that are usually three-dimensional pieces – such as Michael Corris, Martin Kippenberger, Chuck Nanney, G Rockenschaub and Wolfgang Stähle.

Galerie Nikki Diana Marquardt
9 Place des Vosges, 75004 Paris (42.78.21.00). Metro Bastille, Saint Paul/bus 69, 76. **Open** *10am-7pm Tue-Sat.* **No credit cards.**
The American owner of this spectacular gallery has used the space to exhibit the work of young artists who are developing in a variety of directions. British sculptor David Mach has created pieces *in situ*, Antoine Poupel shows his slickly reworked photos, Harald Vlugt his architecturally-inspired sculptures and collages and Dan Flavin his minimalist neon sculptures.

Gabrielle Maubrie
24 rue Sainte Croix de la Bretonnerie, 75004 Paris (42.78.03.97). Metro Hôtel-de-Ville/bus 69, 76, 96. **Open** *2-7pm Tue-Sat.* **No credit cards.**
Located on the second floor of this building, this gallery is under American stewardship, showing some important conceptual artists who work in a variety of media. Some of the more eminent exhibitors have included Dennis Adams, Alfredo Jaar and Muntades.

Galerie Néotu
25 rue du Renard, 75004 Paris (42.78.96.97). Metro Hôtel de Ville/bus 38, 47, 75. **Open** *9am-7pm Mon-Sat.* **No credit cards.** *See picture and caption.*

Alain Oudin
47 rue Quincampoix, 75004 Paris (42.71.83.65). Metro Rambuteau/bus 29. **Open** *11am-1pm, 2-7pm, Tue-Sat.* **No credit cards.**
Mainly concerned with showing installations, Alain Oudin represents a number of young French artists who work in the multimedia field. Many of the projects patronized by Oudin are developed outside the gallery.

Claudine Papillon
59 rue de Turenne, 75003 Paris (40.29.98.80). Metro Chemin-Vert/bus 20, 29, 65. **Open** *11am-7pm Tue-Sat.* **No credit cards.**
A relative newcomer to this area, located at the back of a courtyard, this gallery is committed to contemporary European artists such as Tony Carter, Erik Dietman, Raymond Hains, Sigmar Polke and Dieter Roth. Hangings and installations are always innovative and flamboyant.

Regards
11 rue des Blancs-Manteaux, 75004 Paris (42.77.19.61). Metro Rambuteau/bus 29. **Open** *2.30-7pm Tue-Sat.* **No credit cards.**
This long-established gallery specializes in exhibitions of abstract contemporary artists. Works are generally of a high standard and painters such as Christian Sorg are always worth searching out.

Samia Saouma
2 Impasse des Bourdonnais, 75001 Paris (42.36.44.56). Metro Châtelet/bus 58, 67, 69, 70, 72, 74, 76, 85. **Open** *1-7pm Tue-Sat.* **No credit cards.**
Originally committed to displaying photographs, this gallery is now less specialized and includes a broader range of work. It houses an eclectic mixture of art that ranges from the subtle textural paintings of Gérard Traquandito to the irreverent ink sketches of Glen Baxter that mimic the public school icons of the *Boy's Own* comic strip.

Daniel Templon
30 rue Beaubourg, 75003 Paris (42.72.14.10). Metro Rambuteau/bus 29. **Open** *10am-7pm Tue-Sat.* **No credit cards.**
As a major vehicle for the promotion of contemporary art in Paris, this gallery is well worth a visit. Representing American conceptual and minimalist artists, such as Carl André, Do Judd, Bruce Nauman and Richard Serra, Daniel Templon's gallery also houses a large assortment of European artists from Alberola to Paladino. You name it – Daniel has it all.

BASTILLE

Claire Currus
30-32 rue de Lappe, 75011 Paris (43.55.36.90). Metro Bastille/bus 69, 76. **Open** *10.30am-7pm Tue-Sat.* **No credit cards.**
Past the night-clubs and the late-night bars is this small-fronted gallery, one of the first to set up in the area. Concentrating on more extreme conceptual works, you may see some pieces by Ian Hamilton Finlay or, perhaps, one of Felice Varini's optical games on display.

Antoine Candau
17 rue Keller, 75011 Paris (43.38.75.51) Metro Bastille/bus 61, 69. **Open** *9am-noon, 2-7pm, Tue-Sat.* **No credit cards.**
Mid way along the rue Keller, which is fast becoming the main gallery strip of the Bastille, Antoine Candau's progressive gallery is committed to showing some difficult mixed-media work by young French and foreign artists. Olivier Tome's wall sculptures and Nechvatel's drawings are of particular interest.

Galerie du Génie
23 rue Keller, 75011 Paris (48.06.02.93). Metro Bastille/bus 61, 69. **Open** *10am-12.30pm, 2-7pm, Tue-Fri; 2-7pm Sat.* **No credit cards.**
Although limited in space, this gallery manages to pack in a broad and colourful range of work, from Nam June Paik's stacks of old TV sets and Villegle's torn layers of street-posters – *à la Rotella* – to some younger, unknown artists whose work updates the venue's appeal.

Gutharc-Ballin
47 rue de Lappe, 75011 Paris (47.00.32.10). Metro Bastille/bus 69, 76. **Open** *11am-7pm Tue-Sat.* **Credit** *AmEx.*
Some unconventional young artists exhibit here; the Japanese artist Endo has carved some fascinating pieces in wood, while David Newman's photographs open an eerie window into another world.

Lavignes-Bastille
27 rue de Charonne, 75011 Paris (47.00.88.18). Metro Bastille/bus 69, 76.

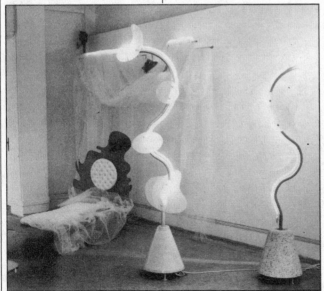

Step inside the **Galerie Néotu** *(listed under* **Commercial Galleries/Beaubourg & Le Marais***) if you want to see the latest in avant-garde furniture design. Temporary exhibitions and a permanent stock downstairs give visitors an opportunity to experience the exciting work of Martin Szekely, Garouste and Bonetti, Pucci di Rossi, Borek Sipek, Gérard Dalmon, François Bauchet, Dan Friedman and Marco Zanuso Jnr. Eat your heart out, Conran.*

Open 11am-7pm Tue-Sat. **Credit** AmEx, V.
This large three-tiered gallery has assembled a selection of mainly realist work, often with a neo-Pop bias. American hyper-realist Hohn Kacere, German neo-Expressionist Lukaschewski and the Scottish painter Calum Fraser are all regulars. Andy Warhol's last Parisian show took place here.

Michel Vidal
56 rue du Faubourg Saint-Antoine, 75012 Paris (43.42.22.71). Metro Bastille./bus 69, 76. **Open** 11am-1pm, 2-7pm Tue-Sat. **No credit cards.**
See **picture and caption.**

LES CHAMPS-ELYSEES

Louis Carré
10 avenue de Messine, 75008 Paris (45.62.57.07). Metro Miromesnil/bus 28, 49. **Open** 10am-12.30pm, 2-6.30pm, Tue-Sat. **No credit cards.**
Located in what was once the recognized core of the gallery circuit, this historic venue is now run by the grandson of its founder. Previously concentrating on exhibiting works by the likes of Calder, de Staël, Delaunay, Kupka and Jacques Villon, the gallery has recently focused on contemporary French artists such as Peter Klasen and Jean-Pierre Raynoud.

Galerie Lelong
13 & 14 rue de Téhéran, 75008 Paris (45.63.13.19). Metro Mironesnil/bus 28, 49. **Open** 9.30am-1pm, 2.30-6pm Mon-Fri; 2-7pm Sat. **Credit** EC, MC, V.
The gallery name of Aimé Maeght evaporated in the early eighties after the painter's death; eventually it was changed to that of one of his co-directors, Lelong. Notwithstanding the new name, the gallery lost none of its considerable standing within the art world. These two adjacent venues continue to show work by major twentieth-century artists such as Bacon, Miro, Kounellis, Takis and Saul Steinberg. Limited edition prints, catalogues and books are sold in the downstairs gallery.

Galerie Montaigne
36 avenue Montaigne, 75008 Paris (47.23.32.35), Metro Franklin D Roosevelt/bus 42, 80. **Open** 11am-7pm Tue-Sat. **No credit cards.**
Conveniently situated between Nina Ricci and the Musée d'Art Moderne de la Ville de Paris (*see* chapter **Museums**), this recently opened gallery should be an interesting addition to an area better known for its *Haute Couture.* It intends to follow a fairly adventurous path, alternating shows of contemporary artists – for example, Marie-Jo Lafontaine – with retrospectives of artists such as Man Ray, Picabia and Duchamp.

PHOTO GALLERIES

If photography is your preferred medium, then Paris offers an unrivalled opportunity to view some of the most exciting work being produced today. Every even year, Paris hosts a proliferation of photo exhibi-

Agathe Gaillard *(listed under* **Photo Galleries***) was one of the first people to open a photography gallery in Paris. She remains faithful to her Seine-side location, opposite the Île-Saint-Louis. Master photographers, such as Kertesz, Ralph Gibson, Cartier-Bresson, Boubat and Alvarez Bravo, are all exhibited here. Prices start at 2,000F and rise to 20,000F. There is an exhaustive selection of publications and cards available, for those who don't want to break the bank.*

tions that take over almost one hundred different spaces under the banner of *Le Mois de la Photo.*

Comptoir de la Photographie
Cour du Bel Air, 56 rue du Faubourg Saint-Antoine, 75012 (43.44.11.36). Metro Bastille/bus 86. **Open** 11am-7pm Tue-Sat; 3-6pm Sun. **Credit** A, V.
Located within a courtyard, lush with creepers and exotic blooms, the gallery is stocked with an excellent selection of works by contemporary photographers, including Erwitt, Strettner and Jean-Loup Sieff. Prices range between 3,000F and 110,000F.

Michèle Chomette
24 rue Beaubourg, 75003 Paris (42.78.05.62). Metro Rambuteau/bus 29. **Open** 2-7pm Tue-Sat; outside these hours by appointment. **No credit cards.**
Just up the road from the Centre Pompidou, this second-floor gallery exhibits and promotes both historical and contemporary photographic work ranging from Eugène Mailland to Alain Fleischer. Books and literature on the subject are produced in-house.

Viviane Esders
40 rue Pascal, 75005 Paris (43.31.10.10). Metro Gobelins/bus 86. **Open** 2.30-7pm Tue-Sat. **No credit cards.**
Located some way from the main focus of atten-

tion in Paris, this gallery is nevertheless active, with a lively exhibition programme of contemporary photographers including Elizabeth Lennard, Grete Stern, Morel Donfler. Prices are in the 9,000F to 10,000F range.

Agathe Gaillard
3 rue du Pont Louis-Philippe, 75004 Paris (42.77.38.24). Metro Pont-Marie/bus 67. **Open** 1-7pm Tue-Sat. **Credit** V.
See **picture and caption.**

Studio 666
6 rue Maître-Albert, 75005 Paris (43.54.59.29). Metro Maubert-Mutualité/bus 63, 86, 87. **Open** 2-7pm Tue-Sat. **No credit cards.**
Hidden down a narrow Left Bank side-street, Studio 666 regularly puts on exhibitions of young and innovative photographic talent. *Gallery publications.*

Zabriskie
37 rue Quincampoix, 75004 Paris (42.72.35.47) Metro Châtelet/bus 38, 47, 75. **Open** 11am-7pm Tue-Sat. **No credit cards.**
A cornerstone in the world of photography galleries and sister of the New York venue of the same name, Zabriskie hangs some of the world's most celebrated enlargements. You can find photographs by Brassai, William Klein, Lee Friedlander and Stieglitz. You can also spend one million francs on a photograph, should you so wish.

Museums

Paris clocks in high on the Great-Museums-of-the-World list. We give you the low-down of where to go and what to see.

The government's *grands projets* – which have come to fruition in the late eighties – have successfully focused international attention on the city. Visitors should aim to take in a few of these post-modern masterpieces. Top of the list of priorities might be a handful of museums constructed during Mitterrand's time, such as the **Musée d'Orsay**, the 'new, improved' **Musée du Louvre** (*see below* **Art & Design** for both), the **Institut du Monde Arabe** (*see below* **Oriental Arts**), the **Cité des Arts et de l'Industrie** (*see below* **Science & Technology**) or the **Musée des Arts de la Mode** (*see below* **Applied Art & Crafts**).

Most major museums are in central Paris, so transport is not a problem. You can quite easily walk from the Pompidou Centre (known as **Beaubourg**) to the **Louvre** and across the Seine to the **Musée d'Orsay**. The lesser-known museums tend to be further out and getting to them can involve a trek across town; check their opening hours before setting off as they occasionally close for renovation. The same applies to the châteaux dotted around the perimeter of Paris, that seem to use any public holiday as a good excuse to pull up the drawbridge. Dates to watch out for are January 1, May 1, August 15, November 1, and December 25.

Parisians regard museum-going as a normal cultural pastime, to be indulged in at weekends. You should therefore aim to visit any major exhibition on a weekday, preferably at lunch-time, if you want to view exhibits without having to fight off the crowds. It's also worth taking advantage of late opening hours. For example Beaubourg (*see below* **Centre National d'Art et Culture Georges Pompidou**, *listed under* **Art & Design**) stays open until 10pm daily. A note of caution; many museums close on either Mondays or Tuesdays.

Though reduced admission charges for certain categories of people do exist, make sure you have an up-to-date identity card or a passport proving your status if you want to stand any chance of not paying the full price. Ticket vendors are rarely flexible or open to persuasion. In some cases even valid cards, such as non-French old age pensioner passes, may not be accepted.

COUNTRY PURSUITS

A trip to the country can make a welcome change after fighting the hordes in the city. So we've listed a number of châteaux within easy reach of the city centre (*see below* **Outside Paris**) that are either renowned for their collections of paintings and furniture or because they're of particular architectural interest. A concerted attack on the châteaux circuit should be planned with great care; it's a tiring business. Work out beforehand where your interests really lie, then target your visits accordingly.

APPLIED ART & CRAFTS

Manufacture Nationale des Gobelins

42 avenue des Gobelins, 75013 Paris (48.87.24.14). Metro Gobelins/bus 22, 47, 83. **Open** by guided tour only, 2pm and 3pm Tue-Thur. **Admission** 22F adults; 12F under-18s. **No credit cards.**
Named after Jean Gobelin – a fifteenth-century dyer – this working museum is housed in a group of buildings where state tapestries, carpets and furniture have been made since the seventeenth century. Under Louis XIV this manufacturing trade flourished and became a booming business. However, this century has seen sales figures drop and business slacken off. In the early eighties, Jack Lang, Minister of Culture, took it upon himself to resurrect this antediluvian trade by pouring hard cash into the Gobelins-based business. This financial boost has enabled the museum to put on interesting exhibitions. Apart from witnessing the laborious process of tapestry weaving, visitors can tour the traditional Savonnerie carpet workshops.

Musée des Arts Décoratifs

107-109 rue de Rivoli, 75001 Paris (42.60.32.14). Metro Palais Royal/bus 39, 48, 67, 68, 69, 72. **Open** 12.30-6pm Wed-Sat; 11am-6pm Sun. **Admission** 20F adults; 14F under-25s, OAPs. **Credit** (shop only) DC, MC, V.
See **picture and caption.**
Shop (10am-7pm daily). Reference library (2-5.30pm Mon; 10am-5.30pm Tue-Sat). Wheelchair access.

Musée des Arts de la Mode

109 rue de Rivoli, 75001 Paris (42.60.32.14). Metro Palais Royal/bus 39, 48, 67, 68, 69, 72. **Open** *during exhibitions only* 12.30-6pm Wed-Sat; 11am-6pm Sun; closed between exhibitions. **Admission** usually 20F adults; 15F under-25s, OAPs. **Credit** (shop only) TC, V.
Opened in 1986, assisted and encouraged by the erstwhile Minister of Culture, Jack Lang, the museum of fashion produces some imaginative temporary exhibitions of both historical and contemporary couture, from shoe designs to film costumes. At present, the comprehensive collection is not on display, so the museum is closed between exhibitions.
Reference library 2-7pm by appointment only. Shop. Wheelchair access.

Musée Baccarat

30bis rue de Paradis, 75010 Paris (47.70.64.30). Metro Château d'Eau/bus 32. **Open** 9am-5.30pm Mon-Fri; 10am-noon, 2-5pm, Sat. **Admission** free. **Credit** (shop only) MC, TC, V.
In 1832 the celebrated glass-maker Baccarat moved his company, established in 1764, to the building which today houses the Musée Baccarat. The techniques employed in making elegant glassware are as inventive and varied as the exhibits themselves. If you're short of glassware, however, the rue de Paradis is still the street to come to, with its numerous manufacturing outlets.
Shop.

Musée Christofle

12 rue Royale, 75009 Paris (42.60.34.07). Metro Concorde/bus 24, 42, 52, 84, 94. **Open** 10am-6pm Mon-Sat. **Admission** free.
In this chic street, which runs from the Concorde to the Madeleine, you can browse round the showroom and first-floor museum where the accomplishments of Christofle – the man who gave the people silver-plated cutlery – is celebrated. By developing the use of silver-plate rather than solid silver, Christofle not only enabled the growing, nineteenth-century middle-classes to acquire ornately designed items, but also made himself a small fortune. The display spans 150 years of silver work; look out for the marrow-shaped samovar of 1880, the water-lily tray and the carrot vase. The art deco examples are, of course, somewhat more conventional.

Musée de l'Holographie

Forum des Halles, Niveau -1, 75001 Paris (40.39.96.83). Metro Châtelet, Les Halles/bus 67, 69, 70, 72, 76, 85. **Open** 10am-7.30pm Mon-Sat; 1-7pm Sun. **Admission** 28F adults; 22F students, OAPs; free under-18s. **Credit** (shop only) V.
Located in the depths of the Forum des Halles shopping centre, this small museum colours the air with illusory 3-D images and

makes a fun stop for the kids. However, lasers and holograms, having appeared on beer-taps, credit cards and night clubs, have lost much of their initial appeal. The examples shown here are not over-stimulating, with the exception of the holographic classical statues, but new developments may make for more inventive display in the future.
Shop. Workshops.

Musée de la Mode et Costume
Palais Galliera, 10 avenue Pierre 1er de Serbie, 75116 Paris (47.20.85.23). Metro Iéna/bus 32, 63. **Open** 10am-5.40pm Tue-Sun. **Admission** 25F adults; 15F students; free under-7s. **No credit cards.**
Not far from the Musée d'Art Moderne (*see below* **Art & Design**) and the Palais de Tokyo, this elegant nineteenth-century mansion houses the costume museum belonging to the Ville de Paris. Its temporary and changing exhibitions show a succession of accessories and clothes dating from 1735 to the present. A mainstay of the 'seizième grannies' – elderly, Gucci handbag-wearing women who live in the smart sixteenth arrondissment – it provides great intellectual fodder for sociologists.
Library (by appointment only, 10am-1pm Tue-Fri).

Musée National de Céramique de Sèvres
place de la Manufacture, 92310 Sèvres (45.34.99.05). Metro Pont de Sèvres/bus 160, 169, 171, 179, 420. **Open** 10am-noon, 1.30-5pm, Mon, Wed-Sun. **Admission** 15F (special exhibitions 22F) adults; 8F (13F) 18-25s, OAPs; free under-18s. **Credit** (porcelain showroom only) DC, MC, TC, V.
Originally founded here in 1738 as a private concern, the Sèvres porcelain factory was rapidly nationalized by the State. On display are finely painted, delicately modelled pieces, together with ceramics and porcelain from other European centres including Saxe, Delft and Nevers. Italian majolica and Spanish ceramics dating from the Middle Ages and some superb early Islamic pieces also feature.
Shop and showroom. Wheelchair access.

Musée de la Publicité
18 rue de Paradis, 75010 Paris (42.46.13.09). Metro Château d'Eau/bus 32. **Open** noon-6pm Mon, Wed-Sun **Admission** 18F adults; 10F under-25s, OAPs; free under-7s. **Credit** (bookshop only) FTC, V.
This former china and porcelain warehouse was converted into a museum in 1978, leaving intact a spectacular ceramic-tiled courtyard at the entrance. Only the second of its kind in the world, this advertising museum holds regular thematic exhibitions. These can be anything from posters – there are 40,000 examples dating from 1750 to the present day – or other advertising milestones such as the latest hits in cinema and television commercials (the oldest date from 1912). Upstairs is a documentation and research centre that is open to the public.
Bookshop. Slide and video library (ioam-5pm Mon-Fri).

Musée de l'Armée
Hôtel des Invalides, Esplanade des Invalides, 75007 Paris (45.55.37.67). Metro Varenne, Latour-Maubourg/bus 28, 49, 69, 93. **Open** 10am-5pm daily. **Admission** (valid for 2 consecutive days) 23F adults; 11.50F under-18s, students, OAPs; free under-7s, soldiers in uniform. **No credit cards.**
Apart from housing the monolithic tomb of Napoleon, which rests under an impressive ribbed dome, the Musée de l'Armée should be a real feast for young and not-so-young boys prone to war fantasies. Military history is explained through prints, paintings, diagrams, maps, plans, uniforms, weapons and armour (both with and without bullet holes), up to World War II. This collection can be visited over two consecutive days, but interest tends to wane after a couple of hours. There are exhaustive displays of military hardware, such as oriental armour with weapons and model soldiers. Within this Army Museum is the **Musée des Plans-Relief**, an unusual collection of about 80 large models of French forts built between the seventeenth and nineteenth centuries. The entire Invalides edifice was built during the reign of Louis XIV, later becoming a home for army pensioners – hence the name.
Cinema (films on World War I at 2.15pm; World War II at 4.15pm). Shop. Wheelchair access to half the museum.

Atelier-Musée Henri Bouchard
25 rue de l'Yvette, 76016 Paris (46.47.63.46). Metro Jasmin/bus 22. **Open** 2-7pm Wed, Sat; other times by appointment only.
Admission 35F adults; 20F students; free under-7s, OAPs. **Credit** (bookshop only) DC, MC, FTC, V.
This small studio museum displays the work of sculptor Henri Bouchard (1875-1960) who undertook government commissions. The museum, although not a prime destination for most visitors, has an amusingly genteel character and you will be well looked after by the sculptor's son and daughter-in-law, who run the establishment. *Wheelchair access.*

Centre National d'Art et de Culture Georges Pompidou
Plateau Beaubourg, 75004 Paris (42.77.12.33/recorded information 42.77.11.12). Metro Châtelet, Hotel de Ville, Rambuteau/bus 29, 38, 47. **Open** noon-10pm Mon, Wed-Fri; 10am-10pm Sat, Sun. **Admission** to MNAM: 23F adults; 17F 18-25s, OAPs; free under-18s; *Galeries Contemporaines:* 16F adults; free under-13s; *CCI:* 15F adults; free under-13s; *temporary exhibitions:* admission varies; *Day-pass to all exhibitions:* 50F adults; 45F 13-25s, OAPs; free under-13s. **Credit** (bookshop only) DC, MC, V.
The Centre Pompidou is a crucially impor-

The north-west wing of the Palais du Louvre is occupied by the fascinating **Musée des Arts Décoratifs** *(listed under* **Applied Art & Crafts**). *The five upper floors contain* objets d'art, *furniture and furnishings from the Middle Ages to the present day. Art nouveau and art deco styles are comprehensively displayed, along side pieces by contemporary designers. Certain sections, such as those textiles and wallpaper, can only be seen by appointment with the curator.*

tant part of Paris's architecture and a prime example of a seventies' hi-tech edifice. Designed by Piano and Rogers and opened in 1977, Beaubourg (as it is more commonly known) has become its own worst enemy as an arts centre. The superb panoramic view from the roof attracts an average 25,000 visitors daily – few of whom seem to be interested in the exhibitions – which creates serious overcrowding problems, particularly in the spring and summer. To avoid the crush, take advantage of the evening opening hours. Using the lifts, rather than the ponderously crawling escalators, to reach the upper floors allows for a romantic view of Paris. The fifth floor houses the **Grandes Galeries** where major temporary exhibitions are held; the *cinémathèque* has an excellent daily film programme. Avoid the café-restaurant; the food is less inspired than the building. On the fourth floor is the superb collection of the **Musée National d'Art Moderne** with works from 1905 to 1965; art from 1965 to the present day can be found on the third floor. The ground floor has the **Galeries Contemporaines**, which houses temporary exhibitions of contemporary art, in addition to an industrial design gallery and library. A photographic gallery is housed on the ground floor, and dance performances and concerts take place in the basement. The Centre is a must for the first-time visitor to Paris. Recently, there has been mounting criticism of both the lack of ambitious exhibitions and the general running of the Centre. *See also* **picture and caption.**
Bookshop; design shop. Café, restaurant. Guided tours (3.30pm daily). Music research unit (IRCAM). Reference library; slide, video and record library. Wheelchair access.

The **Centre National d'Art et de Culture Georges Pompidou** *(listed under* **Art & Design***) is more commonly known as Beaubourg. It's extraordinary façade continues to amaze the thousands of visitors who come to see the extensive, numerous and flamboyant modern art collections.*

Fondation Le Corbusier
8-10 place du Docteur Blanche, 75016 Paris (42.28.41.53). Metro Jasmin/bus 22. **Open** 10am-12.30pm, 1.30-6pm, Mon-Fri; closed whole month of August. **Admission** 5F. **No credit cards.**
Housed in Villa La Roche and designed by the artist himself in 1923, this collection shows the breadth of Le Corbusier's talents. His paintings, sculpture and furniture are exhibited here; the adjoining Villa Jeanneret houses an extensive library with microfilm on his designs and drawings.

Musée d'Art Moderne de la Ville de Paris
11 avenue du Président Wilson, 75116 Paris (47.23.61.27). Metro Iéna/bus 63. **Open** 10am-5.30pm Tue, Thur-Sun; 10am-8.30pm Wed. **Admission** 35F adults; 20F students; free under-7s, OAPs. **Credit** (bookshop only) A, DC, MC, FTC, V.
See **picture and caption.**
Bookshop. Café, restaurant (tables outside: terrace). Jazz concerts. Wheelchair access.

Musée de Boulogne-Billancourt
26 avenue André Morizet, 92100 Boulogne-Billancourt (46.84.77.38). Metro Marcel Sembat/bus 175. **Open** 10am-noon, 2-5.30pm Mon, Wed-Sun. **Admission** free.
This western suburb of Paris was home to a number of artists back in the twenties and this modest museum houses a collection of their work. There are paintings by Gris, Maurice Denis, Emile Bernard, Carrière, Huet, Masson, Lipska and sculptures by Bouchard, Poupelet and Muller, among oth-

ers. An architectural section contains plans, drawings, photos and maquettes of buildings in the area. The museum is also rich in designs from the same period, exhibiting work by Mallet-Stevens, Auguste Perret, Le Corbusier and Lurçat.
Wheelchair access.

Musée Bourdelle
16 rue Antoine-Bourdelle, 75015 Paris (45.48.67.27). Metro Montparnasse, Falguière/bus 48, 89. **Open** 10am-6.40pm Tue-Sun. **Admission** 12F adults; 6.50F students, OAPs; free under-7s. **No credit cards.**
Once the studio of the sculptor Antoine Bourdelle (1861-1929), this delightful museum contrasts markedly with the particularly unappealing sight of the near-by Tour and Gare Montparnasse. The pieces on show contrast Bourdelle's flamboyant beginnings with the more conformist style that emerged after he began to work under the master sculptor, Rodin. Over 100 sculptures as well as maquettes and sketches are displayed throughout this pleasantly dusty studio and garden.
Reference library (researchers only). Wheelchair access.

Musée et Hôtel de Cluny
6 place Paul-Painlevé, 75005 Paris (43.25.62.00). Metro St Michel, Cluny/bus 21, 27, 38, 85, 87, 96. **Open** 9.45am-12.30pm, 2-5.15pm, Mon, Wed-Sun. **Admission** 18F adults; 8F 18-25s, OAPs; free under-18s. **No credit cards.**
See **picture and caption.**
Bookshop.

Musée Cognacq-Jay
Hôtel Denon, 8 rue Elzévir, 75003 Paris (no telephone). Metro Saint Paul/bus 29. **Open** 10am-5.40pm Tue-Sun. **Admission** free.
Put together by the founders of the La Samaritaine department store, Ernest Cognacq and his wife Louise Jay, the collection concentrates on the eighteenth century. The founders amassed furniture, *objets d'art* and paintings – Boucher, Chardin, Canaletto, Fragonard, and even Reynolds, are represented.

Musée Delacroix
6 rue Furstenberg, 75006 Paris (43.54.04.87). Metro Saint-Germain-des-Prés/bus 39, 48, 63, 70, 96. **Open** 9.45am-12.30pm, 2-5.15pm, Mon, Wed-Sun. **Admission** 10F adults; 5F 18-25s, OAPs; free under-18s. **No credit cards.**
This leafy enclave, just behind Saint Germain, offers a welcome break from the frenzied shoppers of the neighbouring boulevard. The Musée Delacroix is an added incentive. Delacroix (1798-1863) had this studio built just a few years before his death. Today, together with its small garden, the studio continues to retain an authentic period atmosphere. Apart from the somewhat alarming self-portrait – depicting the artist as Hamlet – most of his paintings are at the Musée d'Orsay (*see below*); it's mainly drawings, prints and personal documents that are on display here.

Musée Gustave Moreau
14 rue de la Rochefoucauld, 75009 Paris (48.74.38.50). Metro Trinité/bus 26, 32, 43, 49, 79. **Open** 10am-12.45pm, 2-5.15pm, Mon,

Wed-Sun. **Admission** 15F adults; 8F 15-18s, OAPs; free under-15s. **No credit cards.**
The Symbolist painter Gustave Moreau (1825-1898) lived, worked and taught his art in this neo-Renaissance building. Pupils included Matisse, Rouault, Fauves Marquet and Puy. The museum makes a fascinating visit and will transport any visitor back into the mysticism and dreamy abstraction of an artistic movement that peaked in the late nineteenth century. An impressive display includes Moreau's drawings and luminous, highly detailed paintings with, of course, the notorious *Salomé* prominently displayed. His personal apartment, closed since 1903, is due to be opened to the public.
Bookshop. Library (by appointment only).

Musée Jacquemart-André
158 boulevard Haussmann, 75008 Paris (45.62.39.94). Metro Miromesnil, Saint Philippe du Roule/bus 22, 43. **Open** 11am-6pm daily; permanent collection closed Mon, Tue. **Admission** 35F adults; 25F under-25s, students.
No credit cards.
Yet another impressive example of a marital team amassing an aesthetic hoard of no mean proportions (*see above* **Musée Cognacq-Jay**). The collection was assembled in the late nineteenth century and concentrates mainly on eighteenth-century French paintings and furnishings, together with works culled from the Italian Renaissance. The elegant mansion, which is beautifully maintained, has paintings by Rubens, Rembrandt, Van Dyck and Frans Hals. These complement the Watteaus, Bouchers and Lancrets. Uccello's *Saint George* and a number of della Robbia terracottas have also survived the centuries. Temporary exhibitions held here are often ambitious in scope.

Musée Marmottan
2 rue Louis-Boilly, 75016 Paris (42.24.07.02). Metro Muette/bus 32. **Open** 10am-5.40pm Tue-Sun. **Admission** 25F adults; 10F 18-25s, OAPs; free under-18s. **No credit cards.**
An excursion into the sixteenth arrondissement, through the Ranelagh Gardens filled with nannies, au-pairs and their wards, will bring you to this major collection of Impressionist paintings. Originally a private collection of furniture, objects and paintings from the Napoleonic period, the museum achieved its fame with Michel Monet's legacy, which includes 165 works by his father, as well as paintings by Sisley, Renoir, Pissarro, Berthe Morisot and Caillebotte, among others. By an embarrassing burglary in 1985, the museum was deprived of Monet's *Impression Soleil Levant* – the painting that gave the movement its name – as well as other major works. In 1987 compensation was provided in the form of the Duhem donation that included works by Gauguin, Renoir, Corot, Sisley. Apart from these major pieces, displayed on the recently redecorated first floor, you can see the magnificent Wildenstein collection of 230 medieval illuminated manuscripts. Because of its relative distance from the city centre, the museum is rarely overcrowded and possesses an atmosphere of calm.
Shop.

Musée des Monuments Français
Palais de Chaillot, place du Trocadéro, 75016 Paris (47.27.35.74). Metro Trocadéro/bus 22, 30, 32, 63. **Open** 9am-6pm Mon, Wed-Sun. **Admission** 15F adults; 8F under-25s, OAPs; free under-18s. **No credit cards.**
Another inhabitant of the imposing Palais de Chaillot (*see below* **Musée du Cinéma Henri Langlois** *under* **Cinema & Music**; **Musée de l'Homme** *under* **Ethnography**; and **Musée de la Marine** *under* **Maritime Interests**), this museum was founded by Viollet-le-Duc as an exercise in collecting celebrated counterfeits of French sculpture and architecture. Everything here is a copy or a mould – whether of murals, gargoyles or stained glass – and gives a quick and concentrated overview of what you could otherwise spend a few weeks travelling to see throughout France. Don't miss Guibal's baroque fountain. The original is in Nancy but once turned on, the cascade is almost indiscernible from the real thing.
Shop.

Musée National Hébert
85 rue du Cherche-Midi, 75006 Paris (42.22.23.82). Metro Vaneau/bus 39, 70, 89. **Open** 2-6pm Mon, Wed-Sun.

Admission 10F adults; 5F students, OAPs; free under-18s. **No credit cards.**
A favourite spot for the bright young things of Paris, the rue du Cherche-Midi should be Michelin-starred for its variety of typically Left Bank shops, restaurants and cafés. After succumbing to the many enticements that will come your way, don't miss out on this museum devoted to the works of Ernest Hébert (1817-1908). He was a fairly orthodox, society painter who dabbled with the Symbolist movement.

Musée National Jean-Jacques Henner
43 avenue de Villiers, 750017 Paris (47.63.42.73). Metro Monceau/bus 94. **Open** 10am-noon, 2-5pm, Tue-Sun. **Admission** 12F adults; 7F under-15s, students, OAPs. **No credit cards.**
North of the Parc Monceau is a surprising one-man museum. It houses more than 700 paintings, sketches and drawings by the prolific Henner (1829-1905), a rather modest, solitary character, never satisfied with the official honours that were poured over him. 'I'm not ambitious, I'm not looking for drama or outstanding subject-matter ... sometimes I think I've succeeded with one detail and the next day I don't like it' he complained. This extensive col-

Take a break from instruments of war at the **Musée de l'Armée** *(listed under* **Armed Services**) *to collect yourself at Napoleon's tomb! A cinema at the museum screens simulations and rare footage of French battles.*

lection is interesting, not so much for the quality of the works (which varies considerably), but as an illustration of how Henner obsessively reworked and transformed the same subjects.

Musée National du Louvre
rue de Rivoli, 75001 Paris (40.20.51.51). *Metro Palais Royal, Louvre/bus 21, 24, 69, 72, 74, 76, 85.* **Open** *permanent collection:* 9am-9.45pm Mon, Wed; 9am-6pm Thur-Sun; *temporary exhibitions:* noon-10pm Mon, Wed-Sun. **Admission** 25F adults; 13F 18-25s, OAPs; free under-18s. **Credit** (bookshop only) A, V.
See **picture and caption.**
Art shop and bookshop. Bureau de change. Café, restaurant. Nursery. Post office. Wheelchair access.

Musée National Picasso
Hôtel Salé, 5 rue de Thorigny, 76003 Paris (42.71.25.21). *Metro Chemin Vert, Saint Paul/bus 29.* **Open** 9.15am-5.15pm Mon, Thur-Sun; 9.15am-10pm Wed. **Admission** 21F adults; 11F 18-25s, students, OAPs; free under-18s. **No credit cards.**
See **picture and caption.**
Bookshop. Restaurant. Wheelchair access.

Musée Nissim de Camondo
63 rue de Monceau, 75008 Paris (45.63.26.32). *Metro Monceau, Villiers/bus 94.* **Open** 10am-noon, 2-5pm, Wed-Sun. **Admission** 15F adults; 8F 18-25s, OAPs; free under-18s. **No credit cards.**
A homogeneous private collection, set in an elegant 1911 town house – that was inspired by the Petit Trianon at Versailles –

backing onto the Parc Monceau. The Camondos were a rich banking family who settled in Paris in 1867 and became fervent collectors of eighteenth-century furniture, paintings and *objets d'art*. Much of this collection originated from royal residences and there are some superb examples of marquetry, lacquering, Savonnerie and Aubusson carpets. The porcelain room bulges with sets of Sèvres, Chantilly and Meissen porcelain, numerous enough to serve a small army. You will also see oddly specialized furniture such as two *voyeuses* – low chairs for watching gambling – designed by Sené in 1789.

Musée de l'Orangerie
place de la Concorde, 75001 Paris (42.97.48.16). *Metro Concorde/bus 24, 73, 84, 94.* **Open** 9.45am-5.15pm Mon, Wed-Sun. **Admission** 15F adults; 8F 18-25s, OAPs; everyone on Sunday; free under-18s. **No credit cards.**
Across the Tuileries Gardens from the now defunct Jeu de Paume (awaiting conversion into a contemporary art gallery) is the Orangerie – a very airy museum which houses Monet's *Water Lilies* as well as the collection of Jean Walter and Paul Guillaume that dates from the Impressionists to the twenties. The eight gigantic panels of *Water Lilies* were conceived for these oval rooms and left as a 'spiritual testimony' by Monet. Presented to the public in 1927, a year after his death, they still impart an extraordinary freshness and depth – meditation is an option some find hard to resist. Upstairs the Walter-Guillaume collection is a little patchy, despite possessing some big names such as

Soutine, Cézanne, Renoir, Sisley, Picasso, Derain, Matisse, Rousseau and Modigliani.
Shop. Wheelchair access.

Musée d'Orsay
1 rue de Bellechasse, 75007 Paris (40.49.48.14/recorded information 45.49.11.11). *Metro Solférino/bus 24, 68, 69.* **Open** 10am-6pm Tue, Wed, Fri-Sun; 10am-9.15pm Thur. **Admission** 23F adults; 12F 18-25s, OAPs; free under-18s. **Credit** (bookshop only) AmEx, MC, V.
See **picture and caption.**
Bookshop. Café, restaurant. Guided tours. Library. Wheelchair access.

Musée du Petit Palais
avenue Winston Churchill, 75008 Paris (42.65.12.73). *Metro Champs-Elysées-Clémenceau/bus 42, 63, 73, 93.* **Open** 10am-5.40pm Tue-Sun. **Admission** 15F adults; 8.50F 7-18s, students; free under-7s; additional charge for temporary exhibitions. **Credit** (bookshop only) V.
Standing sedately across the road from the **Grand Palais** (*see chapter* **Art Galleries**), the Petit Palais contains rather a hotchpotch of private collections donated to the city. There are, however, some major works here and eighteenth- and nineteenth-century enthusiasts should not ignore this museum. Greek pottery, Chinese porcelain, Beauvais tapestries and paintings from the Dutch school will lead you to works by Millet, Delacroix, Géricault, Daumier, Courbet, Odilon Redon and a good selection of Impressionists. Vuillard and Bonnard are particularly well represented. Occasional temporary exhibitions are held at this venue.
Bookshop. Library. Wheelchair access.

Musée Rodin
Hôtel Biron, 77 rue de Varenne, 75009 Paris (47.05.01.34). *Metro Varenne/bus 69.* **Open** 10am-5pm Tue-Sun. **Admission** 18F adults; 8F 18-25s, OAPs; free under-18s, art students. **Credit** (bookshop only) V.
See **picture and caption.**
Bookshop. Wheelchair access.

Musée Zadkine
100bis rue d'Assas, 75006 Paris (43.26.91.90). *Metro Port Royal/bus 83.* **Open** 10am-5.40pm Tue-Sun. **Admission** 10F adults; 7F students; free on Sundays. **No credit cards.**
In the heart of Montparnasse, close to La Closerie des Lilas – a favourite haunt of intellectuals and untethered egos – lived the Cubist sculptor Ossip Zadkine (1890-1967). His house, studio and garden contain drawings, gouaches and, of course, numerous sculptures giving a complete vision of this artist's development.
Wheelchair access.

The monumental **Musée d'Art Modern de la Ville de Paris** *(listed under* **Art & Design***), was built in 1937 to house the municipal collection of modern art. The museum is particularly strong on the Cubists, the Fauves, the Delaunays, Rouault, Gromaire, Soutine, Modigliani and the Ecole de Paris. An innovation for the French bicentenary was the re-hanging of the museum's collection, mixing pieces by contemporary artists such as Boltenski, Lavier, Ange Leccia, Sarkis and Buren, with works by old masters. The upper floor is occupied by the contemporary department, ARC, which co-ordinates some of the most ambitious and adventurous art exhibitions in Paris.*

CINEMA & MUSIC

Musée du Cinéma Henri Langlois
Palais de Chaillot, place du Trocadéro, 75116 Paris (45.53.74.39). *Metro Trocadéro/bus 22, 30, 32, 63.* **Open** guided tours only, 10am, 11am, 2pm, 3pm, 4pm, Mon, Wed-Sun. **Admission** 20F. **No credit cards.**

Much trumpet-blowing accompanied the opening of the new, improved, **Musée National du Louvre** *(listed under* Art & Design*) in the French Revolution Bicentenary year. Architect Pei's notorious glass pyramid, which was erected in the Cour Napoléon, now makes a spectacular and crowded main entrance to the museum's various departments. In its opening year, the pyramid saw an average 18,000 visitors per day. The museum's rich collections range from Oriental, Greek, Egyptian, Etruscan and Roman antiquities to European painting and sculpture from the fourteenth to the nineteenth centuries*

Paris really is sacred ground for cinema enthusiasts and this museum is testimony to Henri Langlois, who set up the Cinémathèque (*see chapter* Film). It presents the evolution of the art, from its very early days – magic lanterns and Louis Lumière's 1895 first movie camera– to the present day. Memorabilia ranges from scripts, photos, posters and costumes to film-sets and a reconstruction of Mélies' studio. The guided tour includes some film screenings but don't forget the adjoining Cinémathèque and its rich daily programme of all those gems you missed the first time around.

Musée Edith Piaf
5 rue Crespin-du-Gast, 75011 Paris (43.55.52.72). Metro Ménilmontant. **Open** by appointment only, 1-6pm Mon-Thur. **Admission** voluntary donation.**No credit cards.**
The small private Musée Edith Piaf up in the faubourgs is dedicated to Paris's famous 'sparrow' – as she was known – with her clothes, tiny shoes, letters and posters as well as photos and paintings of her, all displayed and maintained with Gallic devotion. All the recordings she ever made and a collection of 8,000 photos can be scanned by the public.

Musée des Instruments de Musique Mécanique
impasse Berthaud, 75003 Paris (42.71.99.54). Metro Rambuteau/bus 38, 47, 75. **Open** 2-7pm Sat, Sun, Public Holidays; other times by appointment. **Admission** 25F adults; 15F under-12s. **No credit cards.**
Over 100 examples of automated musical instruments are displayed here – it's a source of great amusement for kids to watch invisible

hands playing the keys of a Steinway, or a barrel organ churning out its merriment. Pianolas that play out music composed by Debussy or Stravinsky, automated violins, cylinder-operated nickelodeons, sitars and trumpets, mechanical harmoniums ... all work perfectly and are enthusiastically demonstrated by the owner-collector and his daughter.

Musée de l'Opéra
1 place Garnier, entrance on rue Auber side of Opéra, 75009 Paris (40.17.33.33.). Metro Opéra/bus 21, 22, 27, 29, 52, 53, 66, 68, 95. **Open** 10am-5pm Mon-Sat. *(The museum will be closed for renovation until 1991).* **No credit cards.**
Between gazing at Charles Garnier's extravagant opera house (built in the 1870s) and shopping at Galeries Lafayette, you might want to drop in on this little museum. It's squeezed in next to the huge Opéra library, which contains the scores of all operas and ballets performed at l'Opéra, as well as drawings and photos of costumes and sets. At the museum you can see some nineteenth-century to scale models of opera sets and other opera-related memorabilia such as Debussy's desk, Nijinsky's sandals, Pavlova's tiara and portraits of other less eminent patrons.

Musée de Radio-France
116 avenue du Président Kennedy, 75016 Paris (42.30.21.80). Metro Ranelagh, Passy/bus 70, 72. **Open** guided tours only, 10.30am, 11.30am, 2.30pm, 3.30pm, 4.30pm, Mon-Sat. **Admission** 10F adults; 5F students. **No credit cards.**

On the second floor of this building, which houses the offices and recording studios of France's national radio stations, is this museum. Starting a fair way back with Roman fire beacons (clumsy but cost-effective), the collection takes you through Chappe's telegraph, a number of Marconi originals, crystal receivers from the twenties, those imposing thirties art deco radios, early television sets and the latest colour models.

ETHNOGRAPHY

Musée des Arts Africains et Océaniens
293 avenue Daumesnil, 75012 Paris (43.43.14.54). Metro Porte Dorée/bus 46. **Open** 9.45am-noon, 1.30-5.15pm, Mon, Wed-Fri; 12.30-6pm Sat, Sun. **Admission** 22F adults; 15F 18-25s, OAPs; free under-18s. **No credit cards.**
Set on the far eastern side of Paris at the entrance to the Parc de Vincennes, this museum is often overlooked by tourists. Its façade has an astonishing bas-relief, an exotic homage to colonialism – the museum was in fact designed for the 1931 Exposition Coloniale – and there is some remarkable art deco furnishing inside. Not strictly ethnographic, its important collection concentrates more on the arts and crafts of Africa (including the Maghreb with its particular emphasis on fabrics and embroidery) and from the Pacific, the emphasis on this area stemming from France's historic role in those regions, now somewhat discredited by the exposés of Greenpeace. A major attraction with children is the enormous tropical aquarium, while the near-by park is a useful outlet for pent-up energies. *See chapter* Children.
Bookshop. Wheelchair access.

Musée des Arts et Traditions Populaires
6 avenue du Mahatma Gandhi, 75116 Paris (40.67.90.00). Metro Sablons/bus 73. **Open** 9.45am-5.15pm Mon, Wed-Sun. **Admission** 15F adults; 8F 18-25s, OAPs; free under-18s. **No credit cards.**
This important centre of French ethnography is located close to the Bois de Boulogne. As a break from the cycle of palaces and aristocratic collections, it gives a wide perception of 'peasant' France in those halcyon, pre-industrial days. All the activities of rural life – work and leisure – are explained and illustrated with tools, objects, furniture, reconstructed interiors and models. Don't miss the waffle irons, skittles and early toys. Demonstrations are given of certain craft techniques and audio-visual material supplements the exhibits.
Auditorium. Bookshop. Library and archive material. Record collection.

Musée Dapper
50 avenue Victor Hugo, 75116 Paris (45.00.01.50). Metro Etoile/bus 52. **Open** during exhibitions only, 11am-7pm daily. **Admission** 15F adults; 7.50F students, schoolchildren, OAPs; free under-12s. **Credit** TC, V.
This attractive museum exhibits some

superb pieces of African art, in rotation and according to a chosen theme or region. Set up by a Dutch foundation in 1986, it is housed in a limited but beautifully designed space with a verdant garden that sets the tone perfectly. Three or four exhibitions are arranged every year; the museum is closed between exhibitions. The specialist library can be visited by appointment.
Library.

Musée de l'Homme

Palais de Chaillot, place du Trocadéro, 75116 Paris (45.53.70.60). Metro Trocadéro/bus 22, 30, 32, 63. **Open** 9.45am-5.15pm Mon, Wed-Sun. **Admission** 16F adults; 8F students, schoolchildren, OAPs; free under-4s. **Credit** (bookshop only) A, EC, V.
Through costumes, weapons, jewellery, sculpture and other ornamental artefacts, the museum traces the development of the human race. The African and European displays are on the first floor; Asia, the Americas and the Pacific are on the second. The Salon de la Musique displays a weird and wonderful collection of musical instruments, while a series of recordings – some as rare as the exhibits themselves – act as background music for visitors. Some fantastic objects are shown here ranging from Maori earrings to African masks. Gory highlights of our tribal past include the life-sized King Béhanzin, 'shark-man', in the African section, the Easter Island head and a selection of 'decorative' human skulls, with reconstructed faces, from the Pacific. A number of activities are arranged with children in mind; consequently this colourful, exotic collection is often a great hit with them.
Café, restaurant. Cinema (2.30pm Wed-Sun). Concerts. Guided tours. Lecture room. Library. Wheelchair access.

FAKES

Musée de la Contrefaçon

16 rue de la Faisanderie, 75016 Paris (45.01.51.11). Metro Porte Dauphine/bus PC. **Open** 2-4.30pm Mon, Wed; 9.30am-noon Fri. **Admission** free. **No credit cards.**
Any designer will tell you that the counterfeit industry is big business these days. Although we're hardly in the same league as Taiwan or Hong Kong, an impressive selection of forgeries awaits you. The museum shows how this lucrative business dates back to 200BC – for example, there are displays of fake wine from Narbonne – and continues in Portugal with Audak (Kodak) cameras and in Italy with countless handbags (Louis Vuitton being particularly popular). Big-name labels now have enormous 'defence' budgets to try to prevent these ingenious counterfeits and the museum takes care to underline the penalties awaiting you in case you're tempted.

Musée Grévin

10 boulevard Montmartre, 75009 Paris (47.70.85.05). Metro Rue Montmartre/bus 20, 39, 48, 67. **Open** term-time: 1-6pm daily; *school holidays:* 10am-6pm daily. **Admission** 40F adults; 28F 6-14s; free under-6s. **No credit cards.**
See picture and caption.

HUNTING & FISHING

Musée de la Chasse et la Nature

Hôtel Guénégaud, 60 rue des Archives, 75003 Paris (42.72.86.43). Metro Hôtel de Ville/bus 75. **Open** 10am-12.30pm, 1.30-5.30pm, Mon, Wed-Sun. **Admission** 20F adults; 10F under-10s. **No credit cards.**
The museum is housed in a delightfully proportioned mansion, built in 1654 and set against a garden that unfortunately, can only be admired from inside the museum itself. This rather exceptional collection, exhibited over three floors, contains weapons – from ivory crossbows to ebony halberds and etched silver daggers – hunting trophies and some stuffed and mounted beasties from Asia, America and Africa that tragically oversee the proceedings. To finish off, there is a superb collection of paintings by Cranach, Brueghl, Rubens, Oudry, Chardin and hunting scenes by the eighteenth-century court painter François Desportes.

LITERARY

Maison de Balzac

47 rue Raynouard, 75016 Paris (42.24.56.38). Metro Passy/bus 32. **Open** 10am-5.40pm Tue-Sun. **Admission** 12F adults; 6.50F students, OAPs; free under-7s. **No credit cards.**
Although Balzac kept moving from house to house, this pretty little edifice and gar-

When the **Musée National Picasso** *(listed under* Art & Design*) opened in 1985 it was a major Parisian event, as it symbolized the culmination of years of well-reported legal wrangles following Picasso's death. His heirs managed to negotiate paying death duties by handing over artworks to the state – a first in French legal history. The museum houses 203 paintings, 158 sculptures, 3,000 drawings and etchings, not to mention ceramics, collages and other pieces by Picasso. His own collection of works by his contemporaries – 60 pieces by Cézanne, Derain, Braque, Miro and Matisse, among others – is also displayed.*

*Converted from a station designed in 1900 by Laloux, the **Musée d'Orsay** (listed under **Art & Design**) now bears the controversial stamp of designer Gae Aulenti – whether you like it or not, the bunker style of natural stone blocks is unforgettable. The extensive and multifarious collection covers the period 1848 to 1914: fine arts, decorative arts, architecture and photography are all represented. The museum houses the main Impressionist collection in Paris, as well as art nouveau pieces and modern sculpture.*

den managed to keep Balzac at home from 1840 to 1847. This is where he churned out most of the chapters of *La Comédie Humaine*. It makes a charming one-man museum, providing background colour in the form of portraits of Balzac and his favourite mistress, Eva Hanska. There's a collection of walking-sticks, engravings, letters, critical reviews of his work, the desk over which he brooded and publications by many of his contemporaries. *Library.*

Maison de Victor Hugo
Hôtel de Rohan-Guéménée, 6 place des Vosges, 75004 Paris (42.72.16.65). Metro Bastille/bus 29. **Open** 10am-5.40pm Tue-Sun. **Admission** 16F. **No credit cards.**
The legendary Victor Hugo lived at the Maison de Victor Hugo between 1832 and 1848. The luxurious apartment witnessed the composition of part of Les Misérables and a number of poems and plays. When not writing, the author kept himself busy drawing, decorating, carving – much of the furniture is his work – and engraving.

HISTORY

Musée Carnavalet
23 rue de Sévigné, 75003 Paris (42.72.21.13). Metro Saint Paul/bus 29. **Open** 10am-5.40pm Tue-Sun. **Admission** 15F adults; 8.50F students, teachers; free

under-7s. **Credit** (bookshop only) A, V.
If the history of Paris at the Musée Grévin (*see above* **Fakes**) was a little light-weight for you, this is where you should head for. The mansion dates from the sixteenth and seventeenth centuries. The writer Madame de Sévigné lived here from 1677 to 1696. In 1880 it was transformed into a museum that covers the history of Paris and its arts and crafts, from the sixteenth century onwards. It now houses a rich collection of paintings, furnishings and architectural elements, such as gilded panelling and – at the other end of the scale – tavern signs, engravings, maps and topographical models, with special sections devoted to the Revolution. Well placed right in the middle of the Marais and with a suitably sedate little garden, it is worth visiting. Temporary exhibitions often cover major twentieth-century photographers. *Bookshop. Guided tours (12.30pm Wed, 2.30pm Fri). Reference section. Wheelchair access.*

Musée de l'Histoire de France
Hôtel de Soubise, 60 rue des Francs-Bourgeois, 75004 Paris (40.27.62.18). Metro Rambuteau/bus 29. **Open** 1.30-5.45pm Mon, Wed-Sun. **Admission** 12F adults; 8F students, teachers, OAPs; free under-18s. **No credit cards.**
See picture and caption.

Musée de Montmartre
12 rue Cortot, 75018 Paris (46.06.61.11). Metro Lamarck-Caulaincourt. **Open** 2.30-6pm Tue-Sat; 11am-6pm Sun. **Admission** 20F adults; 10F students, OAPs; free under-

8s. **No credit cards.**
If you're up in the heights of Montmartre and want a rest from the tourist junk and hustlers, visit this charming seventeenth-century house and its small garden that overlooks the last working vineyard in Paris. The history of Montmartre, its buildings, the eccentric and, at times, illustrious inhabitants, a collection of local Clignancourt porcelain, some original Toulouse-Lautrec posters and a homage to the famous local bistro, Le Lapin Agile, make up the museum's contents. *See also chapter* **Paris By Area.**

MARITIME INTERESTS

Institut Océanographique
195 rue Saint Jacques, 75005 Paris (46.33.08.61). Metro Luxembourg. **Open** 10am-12.30pm, 1.15-5.30pm, Tue-Fri; 10am-5.30pm Sat, Sun; closed whole month of August. **Admission** 15F adults; 9F 4-18s, students under 25; free under-4s.**No credit cards.**
Jacques Cousteau, the deep-diving doyen of French oceanography, set up this enchanting museum. It's a great place for diverting the kids, as it possesses no fewer than 12 aquariums (*see chapter* **Children**). Other exhibits give detailed explanations on Cousteau's ambitious underwater operations that pioneered the development of the aqua lung in the sixties and seventies. An accompanying film is shown on Wednesdays, Saturdays and Sundays at 3pm and 4pm. *Wheelchair access.*

Musée de la Marine
Palais de Chaillot, place du Trocadéro, 75016 Paris (45.53.31.70). Metro Trocadéro/bus 22, 30, 32, 63. **Open** 10am-6pm Mon, Wed-Sun. **Admission** 20F adults; 10F 5-12s, soldiers, sailors; free under-5s. **Credit** (bookshop only) V.
This is a favourite among mariners craving the smell of the sea or the pull of the tides; the museum houses the largest maritime collection in the world. Apart from Vernet's imposing series of 13 paintings of the ports of France (1754-1765), the collection boasts the Emperor's barge that was built when Napoleon's illusions of grandeur were reaching their zenith in 1811. There are also carved prows, numerous models of ships, old maps, antique and modern navigational instruments, underwater equipment and a model of a nuclear submarine as well as more romantic maritime scenes, mainly from the eighteenth century. There are regular temporary exhibitions on related themes. *Shops. Guided tours. Lectures. Wheelchair access.*

MEDALS & COINS

La Monnaie de Paris
11 Quai de Conti, 75006 Paris (40.46.56.66). Metro Pont-Neuf/bus 24, 27, 58. **Open** *museum:* 11am-5pm Tue, Thur-Sat; 1-9pm Wed; *workshop:* 2.15-3pm Tue, Fri. **Admission** 10F. **No credit cards.**
The National Mint and its museum are

housed in this spectacular Louis XVI edifice overlooking the Seine. Coins and medals from all epochs are displayed, as are drawings, projects, models and relevant tools and objects. The workshops themselves can be visited on Tuesday and Friday only.
Shop (9am-5.30pm Mon-Fri; 10am-1pm, 2-5.30pm, Sat). Wheelchair access.

Musée du Cabinet des Médailles
Bibliothèque Nationale, 58 rue Richelieu, 75002 Paris (47.03.83.30). Metro Bourse/bus 39, 48, 67. Open 9am-5pm Mon-Sat. Admission 20F adults; 12F students, OAPs; free under-12s. No credit cards.
This major collection of coins and medals is housed on the first floor of the Bibliothèque Nationale. It's intended for the initiated as it contains some 400,000 specimens, including the world's largest collection of cameos and intaglios. If your eyes begin to blur after focusing on such small exhibits, there are also works of art on show. Of particular interest is King Dagobert's throne, in addition to various items of silverwork and a selection of paintings, including Boucher and Van Loo.

NATURAL HISTORY

Musée National d'Histoire Naturelle
57 rue Cuvier, 75005 Paris (40.79.30.00). Metro Monge, Jussieu/bus 67, 89. Open *Gallery of Anatomy & Paleontology:* 10am-5pm Mon, Wed-Sun; *Tropical greenhouses:* 1-5pm Mon, Wed-Sun; *Zoo, menagerie:* 9am-5.30pm daily; *temporary exhibitions:* 10am-5pm Mon, Wed-Sun. Admission *Gallery of Anatomy & Paleontology:* 18F adults; 12F students, 4-16s, OAPs; free under-4s; *Tropical greenhouses:* 12F adults; 8F students, 4-16s, OAPs; free under-4s; *Zoo, menagerie:* 22F adults; 10F students, under-16s, OAPs; *temporary exhibitions:* prices vary. No credit cards.
About 2.5 million visitors come to this museum every year, many of them amoeba-like groups of schoolkids catching up on the dinosaurs and other such exhibits. On a par with the British Museum in London and the Smithsonian Institute in Washington, the Musée National possesses vast collections that are spread around its numerous departments: from botany and mineralogy to paleontology, geology and zoology. The gardens are favourite weekend promenading areas. The zoo is cramped and a sad sight despite the beauty of some of the surrounding centennial trees and plants. Much admired, the museum and its setting has long inspired artists, including Victor Hugo who wrote a poem about it, the painter Rousseau who specialized in painting the contents of the tropical greenhouses, and the designers of the latest Hermès porcelain tableware.
Library. Shops.

ORIENTAL ARTS

Institut du Monde Arabe
23 quai Saint Bernard, 75005 Paris (40.51.38.38). Metro Jussieu, Cardinal-Lemoine/bus 24, 63, 89. Open *museum:* 1-8pm Tue-Sun; *library:* 1-8pm Tue-Sun; *temporary exhibitions:* 10am-10pm Tue-Sun. Admission *museum:* 20F adults; 10F students, 18-25s, OAPs; free under-18s; *temporary exhibitions:* usually the same as museum; mixed tickets available.
No credit cards.
See picture and caption.
Bookshop. Café, restaurant (noon-midnight Tue-Sat; noon-6pm Sun). Cinema. Guided tours (2.30pm, 4.30pm, Tue-Sun). Lectures. Library. Wheelchair access.

Musée Cernuschi
7 avenue Velasquez, entrance at 111 boulevard Malesherbes, 75008 Paris (45.63.50.75). Metro Villiers, Monceau/bus 94. Open 10am-5.40pm Tue-Sun. Admission 12F adults; 6.50F students, OAPs; free under-7s; extra charge for temporary exhibitions. No credit cards.
You may find you're the only one wandering around this rather sad museum with its cat-napping guards. The mixed collection of Chinese art ranges from neolithic terracottas (several millenia BC) to Han and Wei dynasty funeral statues, a T'ang spitting vessel and a superb stoneware leaf-form pillow of the Sung dynasty. A gigantic Buddha sits high up in his throne room. Though the museum now belongs to the city of Paris, its collection was originally built up in the late nineteenth century by Cernuschi who frantically scoured the East to assemble works. The museum is next to the entrance to the Parc Monceau and around the corner from Nissim de Camondo's museum (*see above* Art & Design).
Wheelchair access.

Musée Kwok-On
41 rue des Francs-Bourgeois, 75004 Paris (42.72.99.42). Metro Saint Paul/bus 29. Open 10am-5.30pm Mon-Fri. Admission 10F adults; 5F under-12s, students under 25, OAPs. No credit cards.
This fantastically colourful private collection of objects relating to the Asian performing arts was originally built up in Hong Kong before being brought to Paris and installed in the Marais. Since then it has been enlarged by a number of private organizations and is now presented according to the origins of the pieces. The Japanese show-case contains some perfectly sculpted heads used for their doll theatre, unique outside Japan, while the Chinese opera costumes are unrivalled in their rich fabrics and complex embroidery.
Documentation centre. Library (books, photos, video and sound recordings). Wheelchair access.
See also picture and caption.

Musée National Guimet
6 place d'Iéna, 75116 Paris (47.23.61.65). Metro Iéna/bus 32, 63, 82. Open 9.45am-5.15pm Mon, Wed-Sun. Admission 17F adults; 9F students, OAPS, everyone on Sundays; free under-18s. No credit cards.
Much time can be spent exploring this museum, which houses the national collection of Oriental art. Afghanistan, India, Nepal, Thailand, Cambodia, Vietnam, China, Korea and Japan are all represented by pieces which are stunning both in scale and quality.

The **Musée Rodin** (listed under **Art & Design**) *is a favourite with visitors to Paris. Combining a superb collection of Rodin's sculpture – which he left to the state on his death in 1917 – with the refined setting of this 1723 mansion, the museum has a charm which is hard to beat. Recent additions to the collection include a number of works by Rodin's pupil and mistress Camille Claudel. The museum houses Rodin's most celebrated works including* The Kiss, Adam and Eve, The Hand of God, *in the garden, the* Gate of Hell, *the still undecided* Thinker, Balzac *and the terminally desperate* Burghers of Calais.

The ground floor is a maze of Cambodian Khmer sculpture, each Buddha's countenance more enigmatic than the next – this is the so-called 'Angkorian smile' from the civilization of Angkor Wat. More exuberant are the pieces from Indonesia, while Tibetan art is even more ornate, with statues studded with coloured stones and a series of mandala wall hangings showing the life of Buddha. Upstairs you will move from India (more Buddhas, marble bas-reliefs, stone sculpture from South India, bronzes of the Hindu goddess Shiva and a number of fine gouaches from the Mogul and Rajput periods) through treasures from Pakistan and Afghanistan, before arriving at some fine Chinese and Japanese pieces. All in all it makes an enjoyably concentrated trip East.
Bookshop. Library. Photographic reference section. Wheelchair access.

POSTAL HISTORY

Musée de la Poste
34 rue de Vaugirard, 75015 Paris (43.20.15.30). Metro Montparnasse/bus 48. **Open** 10am-5pm Mon-Sat. **Admission** 10F adults; 5F 18-25s, OAPs; free under-18s. **No credit cards.**
Although postage stamps must be among the smallest possible exhibits – one of the reasons for the popularity of philately as an investment is the fact that the treasure is transportable and easily hidden – a walk around this museum is quite an undertaking as the 15 rooms cover five floors. On display are drawings by artists such as Miro, Dali and Buffet, examples of different methods of communication and transport, postmen's uniforms, letter-boxes, stamps and their printing methods, and a miscellaneous collection of related instruments and tools. Recent developments in telecommunications and future projects are also covered. *Shop.*

RELIGION

Musée d'Art Juif
42 rue des Saules, 75018 Paris (42.57.84.15). Metro Lamarck-Caulaincourt. **Open** 3-6pm Mon-Thur, Sun; closed whole month of August, Jewish holidays. **Admission** 10F adults; 5F under-16s. **No credit cards.**
This museum, close to the Musée de Montmartre, is in the centre of this most Bohemian of districts. Founded in 1948, this sanctuary of Jewish art and artefacts possesses some rare pieces: a beautiful wooden eighteenth-century tabernacle from Italy, ornamental plaques, incense burners and candlesticks, to list but a few. A collection of model Central European synagogues is another rarity. The art collection contains photos, prints, sculpture and paintings, with works by Chagall, Benn, Mane-Katz and Lipschitz. *Library.*

Musée de la Franc-Maçonnerie
16 rue Cadet, 75009 Paris (45.23.20.92). Metro Cadet/bus 26, 32, 42, 85. **Open** 2-6pm Mon-Sat. **Admission** free. **No credit cards.** Situated at the back of the Masonic Temple, the displays at this museum are of insignia, paintings glorifying the brotherhood, objects used in ceremonies and documents relevant to the Society's past. While trying to fathom what all this esotericism is about, beware the six-fingered handshake.

SCIENCE & TECHNOLOGY

Cité des Sciences et de l'Industrie
Parc de la Villette, 30 avenue Corentin-Cariou, 75019 Paris (40.05.72.72/recorded information 46.42.13.13). Metro Porte de la Villette/bus 75, PC. **Open** 10am-6pm Tue-Sun. **Admission** *cité:* 30F adults; 15F students, schoolchildren; free under-7s; *planetarium:* 15F. **Credit** V.
Three times the size of the Centre Georges Pompidou (*see above* **Art & Design**), the Cité des Sciences has been riding high since its opening in 1986; it's a great pole of attraction for hordes of schoolchildren. Surrounded by a moat and set within the growing complex of the Parc de la Villette, it is another of Paris's architectural showcases. Its ambitious design and the permanent Explora show which whisks the visitor through 30,000 square metres (323,000 sq ft) of 'space, life, matter and communication', with scale models of satellites, planes and robots, make the journey an exciting one. The Planetarium (sessions at 10.30am, 12.30pm, 2pm, 3pm and 5pm) is on the second floor and is reached by transparent lifts. The lower floors house temporary exhibitions, documentation centres and the like. Outside stands the spectacular Géode, a 36 metre (108ft) diameter sphere covered with plates of stainless steel, another technical feat of complete irrelevance. Inside, a hemispherical cinema shows a programme of specially-adapted wide-angle films. While visiting, discover the park, described by its architect Bernard Tschumi as 'an urban park for the twenty-first century'. The gradually emerging sculptural follies sprouting from the grass certainly have nothing rural about them. The Grande Halle, dating from 1867, is now used for temporary exhibitions. *Bookshop. Café. Cinema. Conference centre. Library (multimedia). Wheelchair access and hire.*

Musée National des Techniques
270 rue Saint Martin, 75003 Paris (40.27.22.20). Metro Arts et Métiers/bus 20, 38, 47, 75. **Open** 10am-5.30pm Tue-Sun.

The **Musée Grévin** *waxworks (listed under* **Fakes***) is over a hundred years old and was originally inspired by Madame Tussaud's in London. It gives a quick, animated overview of French history. On the ground floor you can keep up with the latest hot news on the personality front; for example, who is the Prime Minister, among other things. Needless to say, children love it. An annexe in the Forum des Halles (40.26.28.50, open 10am-6.45pm daily) presents scenes of Paris in the 1900s – complete with* son et lumière *light relief.*

Admission 15F adults; 8F students, OAPs, everyone on Sunday; free under-12s. **No credit cards.**

This rather surprising and often overlooked technical museum occupies the site of a former priory. The church now contains vintage cars and planes and the library is housed in the thirteenth-century refectory. It was also the first school for 'the masses', founded immediately after the Revolution in 1794, and its first director was a certain Mr Montgolfier, the inventor of the hot air balloon. The collection is fascinating for both adults and children. Look out for the 1893 Peugeot car or the plane Louis Blériot used to cross the Channel in 1909. The section on printing, photography, film and broadcasting has some wonderful exhibits, including cameras used by Daguerre, Niepce and Lumière, as well as an early 'mole' design – a 5mm (0.20in) thick camera hidden in a cravat, dating from 1884 and intended for a little bit of Gallic espionage. Astronomy, electricity, acoustics, optics, mechanical toys (including one that belonged to Marie Antoinette), are all well represented here. Clocks are included in this section; there are some stunningly ornate pieces by illustrious eighteenth-century horologists such as Lepaute and Bréguet. There's also glasswork from Daum, Lalique, Gallé, Baccarat and Murano.

Library (1-8pm Tue-Sun). Wheelchair access.

Palais de la Découverte

avenue Franklin D Roosevelt, 75008 Paris (40.74.80.00)/recorded information 43.59.18.21). Metro Franklin D Roosevelt/bus 28, 49, 72, 83, 93. **Open** 10am-6pm Tue-Sun. **Admission** *Palais:* 20F adults; 10F under-18s, OAPs; *planetarium:* 13F adults; 9F under-18s, OAPs. **No credit cards.**

This is Paris's original science museum, housing works and designs from Leonardo da Vinci's extraordinary inventions onwards. Replicas, models, audio-visual material and real apparatus are used to bring the displays to life. Housed at the back of the Grand Palais, it is far more conveniently located than the Cité des Sciences (*see above*) and teems with crowds of young children. The Planetarium has shows at 2pm, 3.15pm and 4.30pm (extra sessions during school holidays and at weekends), and films are screened in the cinema at 2.30pm and 4pm. The newly-opened permanent displays cover man and his biology, light and the thrills of thermo-dynamism. For the budding genetic engineers in the audience, scientific experiments are conducted at 11am and 3pm.

Bookshop. Cinema. Guided tours.

TOBACCO

Musée de la SEITA

12 rue Surcrouf, 75007 Paris (45.56.60.17). Metro Invalides, Latour-Maubourg/bus 69. **Open** 11am-6pm Mon-Sat. **Admission** free. **No credit cards.**

Though you may choose to call this propaganda, you'll at least be able to trace the development of the lowly weed that came from relative obscurity to becoming a household name in most hospitals throughout the world. All thanks to Jean Nicot (Nicot/nicotine) who, in 1561 introduced it to France in his diplomatic bag. International smoking

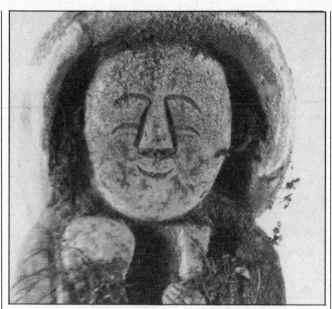

A wonderful miscellany of theatrical objects greets you at the **Musée Kwok-On** *(listed under* **Oriental Arts***): richly embroidered costumes, both crude and sophisticated masks – gods and devils, delicate string and shadow puppets – and superbly crafted instruments among other pieces.*

devices are displayed. Others have have literary connotations, such as Georges Sand's favourite pipe, or astrological links, such as the model pipe engraved with the Zodiac signs. Now who, you may be asking yourself, would wish to set up such a strange museum? The answer is SEITA, the state-run tobacco company and French equivalent of BAT, which since the thirties has sponsored artists and designers – including Max Ponty, the creator of that famous blue silhouette adorning the Gitanes packet – in an attempt to keep its image clean. It's a small museum that makes interesting and amusing viewing. Surprisingly, smoking is forbidden within the confines of the museum.

OUTSIDE PARIS

For further information on châteaux and other sights outside Paris *see chapter* **Trips out of Town.**

Château d'Anet

28260 Anet (16-37.41.90.07). **Getting there** *by car:* approx 20km north of Dreux; take the Autoroute de Normandie from Paris towards Rouen, exit at Nantes-Sud; *by train:* no direct lines. **Open** *Easter-Oct:* 2.30-6pm Mon, Wed-Sat; 10am-11.30pm, 2.30-6pm, Sun; *Nov-Easter:* Sat, Sun 2-5pm. **Admission** 24F adults; 16F 8-13s; free under-8s. **No credit cards.**

Henri II's beautiful and ambitious mistress, Diane de Poitiers, resided here in relative splendour. To keep herself active, she expanded and rebuilt the castle, using the much-respected architect Philibert Delorme. When Henri inherited the throne he offered her the more spectacular château of Chenonceau, but on his death she was unceremoniously ousted from there by his widow, Catherine of Medici. Diane returned here where she eventually died. The eye-catching remains include the superb Chapelle Royale, together with the main entrance and one wing .

Restaurant. Shop.

Château de Champs

77420 Champs-sur-Marne (60.05.24.43). **Getting there** *by train:* RER line A4 to Bry-sur-Marne then bus 220 or 213B to the Mairie (buses do not run on Sundays). **Open** *May-Sept:* 10am-noon, 1.30-5.30pm Mon, Wed-Sun; *Oct-April:* 10am-noon, 1.30-4pm Mon, Wed-Sun. **Admission** 22F adults; 5F 7-17s; free under-7s. **No credit cards.**

This early eighteenth-century château is one of the most charming of its genre in France. Most of the furniture is French Regency and there is some beautiful rococo decoration. The Chinese rooms decorated by Christophe Huet are quite superb. Once rented by the notorious Madame de Pompadour, there is still a lingering sense of crumbling morality and court intrigue. Unfortunately you can only visit the château itself with regular guided tours, but the simple grounds compensate to a certain extent.

Château de Chantilly

Musée Condé, 60500 Chantilly (16-44.57.08.00/telephone information 16-44.57.03.62). **Getting there** *by car:* take the Autoroute du Nord, A1 exit at Survilliers; *by train:* from Gare du Nord to Chantilly. **Open** *April–Oct:* 10am-6pm Mon, Wed-Sun; *Nov–March:* 10.30am-5pm Mon, Wed-Sun **Admission** 30F adults; 7F under-12s; *park only:* 12F adults; 7F under-12s. **Credit** (bookshop only) V.

The château is something of an architectural hotchpotch, having been added to at various stages between the fifteenth and the nineteenth centuries. It stands in a beautiful park designed by Le Nôtre, and the grounds feature carp-infested lakes, canals, various aristocratic outbuildings and a surrounding forest. The Musée Condé, housed in the castle, is rich with lavish furnishings and works from the Italian and French Renaissance – Poussin, Van Dyck, Watteau, Lancret, Ingres, Delacroix, Fromentin and Gérome – and tapestries and eighteenth-century porcelain are all on display. The miniatures and illuminated manuscripts include Etienne Chevalier's *Book of Hours* (1453-1460) and the famous *Très Riches Heures du Duc de Berri* (1416). The library contains other medieval and Renaissance documents and some stunning bindings. In the gallery leading to the Chapel are drawings by, among others, Dürer and Raphael.

Bookshop. Library. Restaurant. Wheelchair access.

Château de Compiègne

place du Général de Gaulle, 60200 Compiègne (16-44.40.02.02). **Getting there** *by car:* take the Autoroute du Nord A1, exit at Compiègne; *by train;* from Gare du Nord to Compiègne. **Open** 9.30-11.15am, 1.30-4.30pm, Mon, Wed-Sun. **Admission** 21F adults; under-18s free. **No credit cards.**

Surrounded by one of the largest remaining forests in France that was once a favoured royal hunting ground, this vast château dates from the fourteenth century. In 1430 it was the scene of Joan of Arc's imprisonment. Both Louis XV and XVI indulged in expensive rebuilding and it was further restored by Napoleon, who, spurred on by thoughts of imperial grandeur, was also responsible for the redesigning of the park, in his case to celebrate his marriage to Marie-Louise. The interiors are lavish, particularly the Empress's richly-adorned apartments. There are guided tours at the weekend only.

The Musée de la Voiture possesses a unique collection of 150 vintage cars.
Bookshop.

Château d'Ecouen

Musée National de la Renaissance, 95440 Ecouen (39.90.04.04). **Getting there** *by car:* take the N16 from the Porte de la Chapelle, through St Denis to Ecouen; *by metro:* to Saint Denis-Porte de Paris, then bus 268C to Ezanville. **Open** 9.45am-12.30pm, 2-5.15pm, Mon, Wed-Sun. **Admission** 15F adults; free under-18s. **No credit cards.**

This large château, built in the mid-fifteenth century for the Constable Anne de Montmorency, now houses a museum dedicated to the French Renaissance. Many exhibits were unearthed from the cellars of the Cluny museum (*see above* **Art and Design**). On display are some masterful woodcarvings, decorative architectural elements such as fireplaces, friezes, hand-painted encasements and, above all, an astonishing series of sixteenth-century tapestries entitled The Story of David and Bathsheba which further promotes a sense of elitist grandeur. Not on the main tourist circuit, this museum is often pleasantly deserted even in midsummer. However, the surrounding park is rather featureless and lacks the formal elegance of other major châteaux gardens around Paris.
Shop. Wheelchair access.

Château de Fontainebleau

77300 Fontainebleau (64.22.27.40). **Getting there** *by car:* take the Autoroute du Soleil A6, exit at Fontainebleau. **Open** 9.30am-12.30pm, 2-5pm, Mon, Wed-Sun (ticket office closes 45 minutes before the château itself) **Admission** 23F adults; 12F 18-25s, OAPs; free under-18s. **No credit cards.**

Arguably the most captivating château in France, Fontainebleau with its Disney-like façades, was built by François I in 1528. He intelligently ordered much of the interior mural decoration to be carried out by Italian craftsmen and artists; this undoubtedly would have helped a later resident Pope to feel more at home. Numerous illustrious royals have passed through and most have left their mark, none more indelibly than the great pretender himself, Napoleon. The Cour des Adieux, the main entrance courtyard, is where the Emperor bade farewell to crowds of fans before being banished to a life on exile on Elba. His apartments and those of Josephine contain important Napoleonic souvenirs as well as rich Louis XV/XVI decoration and Empire furniture. Marie Antoinette's apartments deserve special attention, particularly her bedroom and throne room with its original Louis XIII painted ceiling. The 64 metre (208ft) long Galerie François I contains the highly prized excesses of Rosso il Fiorentino whose ornate work embellishes the gallery. The park is extensive and its sweeping views remain very much as they must have looked to the pint-sized despot Napoleon as he patrolled his domain.
Shop. Wheelchair access.

Château de Maisons Laffitte

avenue Carnot, 78600 Maisons-Laffitte (39.62.01.49). **Getting there** *by train:* RER line A1 to Maisons-Laffitte. **Open** 9am-noon, 2-6pm, Mon-Fri; 9am-noon, 2-4pm, Sat; 2-6pm Sun; closed for refurbishment Jan-June 1990. **Admission** 22F adults; 12F students, OAPs;

Expand on the knowledge gained at the Musée Carnavalet by visiting the **Musée de l'Histoire de France** *(listed under* **History***) that forms part of the National Archives. It displays historical documents from the Middle Ages to the Hundred Years War, while two rooms are devoted to the French Revolution. Although the proliferation of paper may become slightly tiresome, keep in mind that this is the Marais mansion which outshines all others and as such receives continued attention. Dating from 1712, it was decorated by such artists as Boucher, Natoire, Restout and Van Loo and is superbly maintained.*

5F 7-17s; free under-7s. **No credit cards.**
Better known for its race course, this small
town just north of Saint-Germain-en-Laye
possesses a remarkable château with quite a
chequered history. It was built in the mid-
seventeenth century by the architect
François Mansart, but during the Revolution
most of its contents were scattered. When
Jacques Laffitte bought it in the thirties, he
proceeded to demolish the stables and sell
off the land. The next owner, a Russian
artist, was no less a speculator and continued along this mercenary path. Early this
century the remains of the château were
saved *in extremis*, purchased by the French
state and extensively restored. Despite the
Louvre quickly moving in to gobble up some
of the more valuable works of art, it still contains some early eighteenth-century
Gobelins tapestries, the print collection of
the Salle des Gravures with its *trompe-l'oeil*
ceilings, and the domed *Cabinet aux Miroirs*
with its marquetry floor.

Château de Malmaison
avenue du Château, 92500 Rueil-Malmaison
(47.49.20.07). **Getting there** *by train:* RER
line A1 to La Défense then bus 158A. **Open**
Sept-April: 10am-noon, 1.30-4.30pm, Mon,
Wed-Sun; *May-Sept:* 10am-noon, 2-5pm Mon,
Wed-Sun. **Admission** 22F adults; 11F students, OAPs; free under-18s.
Empress Josephine moved into this seventeenth-century château in 1798 and it
became her favourite retreat following her
divorce from Napoleon in 1809 until her
death in 1814. The château is littered with
artefacts dating from their reign: Napoleon's
throne from Fontainebleau, his desk and
armchair, a reconstruction of his bedroom
with original furniture and hangings, his
death-mask, clothing, the camp-bed on
which he breathed his last in 1821 and the
brocade that covered his coffin. Is that the
end of him you may ask. Well, no, as out in
the park, which is much reduced in size
since Josephine's day, are his gala coach and
the summer-house where he used to while
away the salad days of his First Consulship.
And if you are still hungry for further
Napoleonic relics, go to the Musée du
Château de Bois-Préau a few minutes' walk
away, where the entire Bonaparte family
seems to be honoured. At long last you will
see that familiar, long grey coat and triangular hat. Admission to the Bois-Práu museum
is included in the Malmaison château ticket.
*Bookshop. Guided tours only. Limited
wheelchair access.*

Château de Sceaux
Musée de l'Ile de France, 92330 Sceaux
(46.61.06.71). **Getting there** *by train:* RER
to Parc de Sceaux or Bourg-la-Reine. **Open**
2-5.30pm Mon, Fri; 10am-noon, 2-5.30pm
Wed, Thur, Sat, Sun. **Admission** 9F adults;
4.50F students, OAPs; free under-16s.
Le Nôtre's work still remains visible in the
lay-out of this superb park even though the
original seventeenth-century château was
completely rebuilt in 1860. The 'new' building now contains a museum covering the
history and topography of the Paris area. On
display are Sceaux ceramics, Sèvres and
Saint Cloud porcelain, and numerous paintings of the area. Don't miss the lovely seventeenth-century *orangerie* in the park, scene
of chamber music concerts throughout the
summer, nor the Pavillon de l'Aurore of the
same period, built by Claude Perrault. The

park occasionally flirts with the twentieth
century and hosts rock concerts at various
times throughout the year.
Library.

Château de Versailles
78000 Versailles (30.84.74.00). **Getting
there** *by train:* RER line C or train from Gare
Montparnasse. **Open** *château:* 9.45am-5pm
Tue-Sun; *Grand Trianon:* 9.45am-noon, 2-
5pm, Tue-Sun; *Petit Trianon:* 2-5pm Tue-
Sun. **Admission** *château:* 23F adults; 12F 18-
25s, OAPs, everyone on Sun; free under-18s;
Grand Trianon: 15F adults; 8F concessions
as above; free under-18s; *Petit Trianon:* 10F
adults; 5F concessions as above; free under-
18s; *park:* free.
The château of Versailles is commonly
referred to as the biggest palace in the
world. It is mainly the effort of Louis XIV
who in 1661 decided to leave this rather
understated little reminder of his worth to
the nation. Versailles remains a fantastic
symbol of the undisciplined excesses of the
royals that fired the Revolution. 'Let them eat
cake' were reputedly Marie Antoinette's mis-
placed last words as the mob closed in to
haul her away for the ultimate show-case in
the Republic's staged executions. Versailles
was the jewel in the aristocratic crown and
the pillaging that followed was so frenzied
that it took over hundred years to restore
the palace and its contents. Since then it has
continued to play a symbolic political role,
witnessing the signing of peace treaties –
after World War I for example – and the
meetings of heads of state. The vast château
is a challenge for visitors. You can't see
everything in one visit, but make sure you
go down the Galerie des Glaces (an opulent
display of original Louis XIV furnishings by
Mansart) and the various royal apartments.
These are a reasonably harmonious mixture
of original features and works of art with
more recent reconstructions or copies. Le
Nôtre had a field day designing the formal
gardens and, with their fountains that don't
always function, ponds, tree-lined alleys, terraces and sculptures, they provide a tranquil
backwater away from the main attraction.
*Guided tours. Cafés, tea-rooms. Shop.
Wheelchair access.*

Opened in 1987, the **Institut du Monde Arabe** *(listed under* **Oriental Arts***)
is yet another of Mitterrand's grands projets. The 242 south-facing windows are
equipped with electro-photographic diaphragms, which react to the sun's strength,
creating an evenly filtered light reminiscent of traditional Arab musharabia
screens. The permanent collection has been furnished from various Parisian museums, including the Louvre. Meanwhile the museum awaits further donations from
the 20 Arab countries that initially subscribed to the project.*

Arts and Entertainment

Before the bars and boutiques claim your last centime, seek out one of the many entertainment venues in Paris. Whether you're alone in town or the family's in tow, you'll find something that's to your liking. We review a kaleidoscopic range of places: the capital's top music and nightlife hot-spots, film and cabaret venues, student life and sport locations. And when you want to crash out we tell you what's on the telly, where to look for food in the wee hours and who'll mind the kids while you laze at a spa.

CONTENTS:

Cabaret

Piaf chansons, leggy showgirls and dancing hermaphrodites – whatever your passion, the capital's cabaret venues are sure to tickle your fancy.

There has always been a tradition of singing, dancing and acting in the auberges, cafés and bistros of Paris. They've been popular watering holes, usually equipped with an open stage where new or established artists could perform their latest piece. Aristide Bruant, Jeanne Avril, Georges Brassens, Juliette Greco – not forgetting Edith Piaf and Charles Trenet – all started out in these bars.

But times have changed. The price of property in Paris has rocketed in the last decade and driven lowly cabaret venues out of business. The result? All that is truly popular entertainment has been forced out of town. Music halls, cabarets and revues – once the people's palaces – have almost all been superceded by contemporary mass entertainment; cinemas, jazz clubs and wine bars. What remains are the dazzling cabaret shows, in the grand old tradition immortalised by Toulouse-Lautrec: the Moulin Rouge, the Folies Bergères and their successors, the Lido, the Crazy Horse and the Paradis Latin. These draw audiences made up mostly of foreign businessmen and non-Parisians who want to see – what they erroneously believe to be – the show of a lifetime. Parisians seem to stay clear of these tits-and-feather spectacles.

But Paris does still have a number of smaller cabaret revues that nightly strive to recreate the *ambiance* of a bygone era. Here the choice comes down to how much you are willing to pay for an evening's entertainment. You can fork out a basic 90F or a stinging 450F for the same singalong of *Sous les Ponts de Paris*. You can dine or simply have a drink (at a price) while singers, comics (northern style), magicians and ventriloquists ritually follow one another onto a tiny stage. Depending on the venue, the audience and your frame of mind, it's possible to have a good night out. However, don't expect to be challenged intellectually in any way.

ALTERNATIVE CABARET

So where do young, switched-on Parisians go for entertainment these days? The closest equivalent to our 'alternative' cabaret circuit is the *Café-Théâtre* fringe theatre. *Café-théâtre* venues are renowned for their intimate size and the off-beat shows they put on. Popular in the early seventies, these cabarets are often a spring-board for comics, actors and singers – among them Depardieu, Miou-Miou and Coluche – who then went on to work in the established theatre, the cinema and television. For example, Coluche who died in 1987, was a radical comic who criticized French politics and social attitudes, to the extent of putting himself forward as a joke candidate for the 1981 Presidential elections. He was the recognised spokesman for the '68 generation and had such a backing that polls at the time showed him to have won over 12 per cent of potential voters, 6 per cent fewer than for Mitterrand.

Café-théâtre today, frequented almost exclusively by Parisians, continues to promote young and obscure talent. One-man/woman shows, stand-ups (called Sketchman) and singer-songwriters are most common. Most venues change their programme every few months but some have shows that have been running for years – Blancs-Manteaux is into its 10th year – an indication perhaps of their contemporary appeal. Parisians with an ear to the ground will tell you what's worth seeing if your French is up to largely non-visual, verbal theatrical pieces. Have a few drinks before you go; *café-théâtres* do not usually have bars.

TITS & FEATHERS

Moulin Rouge
82 boulevard de Clichy, 75011 Paris (46.06.00.19). Metro Blanche/bus 30, 54. **Open** 8pm-2am daily. **Show** 8pm, 10pm & midnight daily. **Admission** *dinner & dance:* at 8pm, from 530F per person (includes

tourist menu and half bottle champagne); *show only:* at 10pm & midnight, from 365F per person (includes half bottle champagne). **Credit** AmEx, DC, MC, V. *See* picture and caption. *Advance booking advisable. Beware of pickpockets as you leave. English-speaking waiters. Dress: smart.*

Folies Bergères
32 rue de Richer, 75009 Paris (42.46.77.11). Metro Cadet, rue Montmartre/bus 48, 67, 74, 85. **Open** 9-11.30pm Tue-Sun; closed whole month of January. **Show** 9-11.30pm Tue-Sun. **Admission** *show only, standing behind stalls:* 82F; *show only, stalls:* maximum 360F. **Credit** EC, MC. *See* picture and caption. *Dress: smart.*

Crazy Horse Saloon
12 avenue George V, 75008 Paris (47.23.32.32). Metro Alma-Marceau/bus 42, 80. **Open** doors open 30 minutes before show starts. **Show** 9pm & 11.30pm Mon-Thur, Sun; 8.15pm, 10.35pm & 12.45am Fri, Sat. **Admission** *standing at bar:* 195F (includes one drink, second drink 50F); *seated:* 495F (includes half bottle champagne). **Credit** AmEx. DC, MC, V.
The entrance in avenue George V, discreet in itself, is marked by bouncers dressed in full Canadian Mountie uniform, a taster of the military feel that will dominate the rest of the evening. The audience, predominantly male from Japan or the USA, is herded by officious waiters into a small auditorium that's as bland and featureless as any international airport business lounge and where loud taped music precludes any pre-show conversation. Impresario Alain Bernadin worships the nude female form and sees his girls as moving sculptures; accordingly he picks for his team ice-cold beauties of identical height and vital statistics. Baptised when they join Bernadin's army with names like Betty Buttocks, Friday Trampoline or Blondy Corridor, they are required to be capable of simultaneously thrusting their breasts and buttocks as far as is humanly (or rather inhumanly) possible. Throughout the dozen or so numbers they thrust and splay themselves with military precision into stylised tableaux of erotic fantasies, while mouthing the words of playful songs. Top marks for ingenuity go to the costume designer for finding constantly new and exciting things to do with a G string and a pair of epaulettes. But the real genius of the show is the lighting designer who tastefully dresses these statuesque blow-up dollies in spots, stripes and tiger skins of laser light. Two novelty acts break the antiseptic monotony of breasts and laminated wigs. Separated from their public by a dense, though invisible, wall of sound and light, there is no risk of anyone catching any germs here; not a pubic hair out of place, and that goes for the audience too. At the slightest whiff of over-excitement or dissent, bouncers remove the offender with the efficiency of storm-troopers. If you like your sex on a cold slab, the Crazy Horse is for you. As convenient as an automatic, self-flushing super-loo with about as much atmosphere.

Alcazar
62 rue Mazarine, 75006 Paris (43.29.02.20). Metro Odéon/bus 58, 70. **Open** 9.45pm-midnight Mon-Sat; closed

17th July-end August. **Show** 10pm Mon-Sat. **Admission** *dinner:* at 8pm, 510F-900F (includes half bottle champagne); *show only:* at 10pm, 350F (includes half bottle champagne). **Credit** AmEx, DC, EC, MC, V.

A sparkly, tits-and-feathers revue which has gone somewhat downhill since the demise of Jean-Marie Rivière who opened it 20 years ago. Michel Lavigne, your compère, puts in rather too much energy to save the sinking ship. However, the young and fulsome team of dancers seem to be moving with the times: apart from the obligatory French CanCan, there's also Michael Jackson, David Bowie and Yma Sumac numbers. Though a little iffy, it's probably the cabaret most frequented by Parisians. *Dress: smart or evening.*

Paradis Latin

28 rue Cardinal Lemoine, 75005 Paris (43.25.28.08). Metro Cardinal Lemoine/bus 47. **Open** 8.30pm-midnight Mon, Wed-Sun. **Show** 8.30pm Mon, Wed-Sun. **Admission** *dinner:* 510F (includes quarter bottle of champagne or half bottle of Bordeaux); *show only:* 350F (includes half bottle champagne). **Credit** AmEx, DC, EC, MC, V.

Although the show celebrates ten years in this theatre – which was constructed by Gustave Eiffel – the 500 costumes, the 30 *artistes* and the 17 scenery changes are still not enough to make it a memorable show. The choreography is a bit loose and the girls look as if they've just left school. Nonetheless, Mister Sergio, your effervescent compère, makes a huge effort to wake the slumbering audience and his team of waiters is lively and charming. All in all, this cabaret has seen better days. Expect to sit among lots of Japanese coach parties.
Dress: smart or evening

Le Lido

116 avenue des Champs Elysées, 75008 Paris (45.63.11.61). Metro George V/bus 73. **Open** 8pm-2am daily. **Show** 8pm, 10.15pm & 12.30am daily. **Admission** *dinner:* at 8pm, 510F; *show only:* at 10.15pm & 12.30am, 350F. **Credit** AmEx, DC, EC, MC, V.

The 60 Bluebell Girls put on dance routines that are of a high standard though short on innovation. This ranks alongside the Crazy Horse as being one of the most sterile revues in town, frequented mainly by Japanese businessmen and American tourists. The show is grandiose but regimented, with superb special effects that are good enough to take your breath away. The feathers, fishnets and furs are livened up by two of the best novelty acts in town.

TRADITIONAL CABARETS

Caveau de la Bolée

25 rue de l'Hirondelle (6 place Saint Michel), 75006 Paris (43.54.62.20). Metro Saint Michel/bus 21, 27, 38, 85, 96. **Open** 8pm-3am Mon-Sat. **Show** 8.30pm, 10.30pm & 1.30am Mon-Sat. **Admission** *dinner:* at 8pm, 200F (includes one drink); *show only:* 10.30pm & 1.30am, 100F (includes one drink). **Credit** V.

Tucked away down a picturesque alley in the Latin Quarter, is this cosy bar where you can eat or meet for a friendly game of chess. In the basement, is the cellar bar where you can watch classic cabaret of superior quality. Renowned stand-ups, such as Smaïn and Matthieu, began their careers here. The formula of singalong-Piaf means that punters get to hear the resident *chanteuse* – a laidback crooner – singing touching ballads or bawdy community songs. What's more, a magician with a good line in audience participation makes a regular appearance, as does a stand-up comic who's generally better than the kind you're likely to find in a *café-théâtre*. Though the acts change every three or four months, the formula remains the same. Performers are relaxed and professional and the acoustics good. The atmosphere is convivial and the audience is young, noisy and receptive. Don't hesitate to have a chat with your neighbour; the chances are that you won't be able to move anyway. Go with a group for a good night out. Well worth a visit.

Caveau du Cloître

19 rue Saint Jacques, 75005 Paris (43.25.19.92). Metro Saint Michel/bus 21, 27, 38, 85, 96. **Open** 8.30pm-midnight Tue-Sat. **Show** 8.30pm & 10.30pm Tue-Sat. **Admission** *one show:* 75F (includes one drink); *two shows:* 130F. **No credit cards.**

A small cabaret in an intimate cellar bar in the Latin Quarter. The management produce an ever-changing programme of stand-

At the **Folies Bergères** (listed under **Tits & Feathers***) the dancers have all the hallmarks of belonging in a big spectacular; long gloves and diamante jewellery, naked breasts peeking out of a sea of feathers. Acts include the American in Paris-style Apache dance, crinolined ladies at the Viennese court and Yolanda Graves (a black jazz singer) who fills the obligatory Josephine Baker slot. The dome of the Great Hall with its merry-go-round of rampant horses is where the Tiller Girls used to descend astride their plaster mounts over the heads of the audience, until the day one of them fell.*

One hundred years old this year the **Moulin Rouge** *(listed under* **Tits & Feathers***), high temple of kitsch and haunted by the spectre of Toulouse-Lautrec, still captures the atmosphere of the gay Paris of Montmartre. Expect a thousand gasps as the stage is flooded with exotic plumed creatures, the famous Doriss Girls. For two hours, they flaunt their oh-so-perfect wares with great energy and flair; the costumes and the décor are sumptuous, the choreography imaginative and the standard of dancing and singing is high. The Moulin is – for many – a once in a lifetime experience.*

ups and double acts. Ring for details of current programmes.

Caveau des Oubliettes
11 rue Saint Julien-le-Pauvre, 75005 Paris (43.54.94.97). Metro Saint Michel/bus 21, 24, 27, 38, 47, 85, 96. **Open** 9pm-2am Mon-Sat. **Show** 9pm Mon-Sat. **Admission** 100F (includes one drink). **No credit cards.**
A medieval-style, tiny vaulted cellar, piano bar where Anne-Marie Belin interprets Piaf and Gérard Delord plays the hurdy-gurdy. Meanwhile, expect to be entertained by minstrels, troubadours and serving wenches who sing ballads, drinking songs and sea shanties from the eleventh to the nineteenth century. After the show, the audience can take part in a guided tour of the dungeons to see a guillotine, a chastity belt and a collection of weapons from the days when the cellar was part of the prison of Petit Châtelet.

L'Ane Rouge
3 rue Laugier, 75017 Paris (45.62.52.42). Metro Ternes/bus 30, 31, 43, 93. **Open** 9pm-2am daily. **Show** 10.30pm daily. **Admission** *dinner:* 150F, 250F & 350F (wine not

included) Mon-Fri, Sun;,200F Sat, Public Holidays. **No credit cards.**
The l'Ane has all the ingredients of a typical Parisian cabaret: a choice of menu, an intimate restaurant crowded with French provincials and well-dressed foreign business people, and a tiny stage. The emphasis is on laughs. The entertainment formula is singer, magician, comedian, followed by a ventriloquist, all of whom, at the end of their 25 minute act, slip off to do another show at a similar venue. Regulars include Gilles Olivier – a genial, singer-cum-guitarist with a beautiful voice – who has a talent for getting everyone to join in, and a comedian in a frilly shirt and medallions who serves up northern-style, liberal one-liners. Audience participation is the order of the day, which makes l'Ane a perfect venue for a work outing or a birthday party. Wine costs 100F per person and you can drink as much as you like. Alternatively pay 150F for a half bottle. Surprise birthday cakes for two to four people cost 100F.

Au Lapin Agile
22 rue des Saules, 75018 Paris (46.06.85.87). Metro Lamarck/bus 80.

Open 9pm-2am Tue-Sun. **Show** 9pm Tue-Sun. **Admission** 90F (includes one drink, second drink 22F-25F). **No credit cards.**
If at nightfall, after having wandered the little cobbled streets and alleys of the Butte Montmartre, you want to pay one last homage to this historic and poetic quarter, visit one of its best known houses. The Lapin Agile (Agile Rabbit), which considers itself to be the 'Doyen of Cabarets', first became a revue bar in 1860. In those halcyon days, it was a favourite meeting place for Montmartre's more bohemian residents: at the end of the nineteenth century Verlaine and Renoir, and more recently Apollinaire, Max Jacob and Picasso, the latter having one evening paid for a meal here with one of his paintings (the *Harlequin*). Worth keeping an eye out for are the signed poems and paintings on the charcoal-blackened walls that bore witness to this artistic period. The artists have now been replaced by a team of well-intentioned performers who warmly invite you into their parlour, sit you on a wooden stool and fix you a drink as if you were an old friend popping in to say hello. And then – with stultifying reverence and sickly sentimentality – they attempt to bring the past to life with three songs from the eras of Marie-Antoinette and Music Hall. It's a bit like being in an aunt's front room while having to endure endless party pieces. The night we visited the Lapin, 30 or so young Japanese and German tourists seemed to be gazing vacantly through their empty glasses at the comedians, not understanding the puns and unable to join in, but clapping politely. Another 20 and the room would have been full. Beware – once you're inside, it's very difficult to escape without getting the feeling that you're personally ruining the performers' evening if you do. When we left after an hour and a half of forced jollity, a third of the audience followed our lead. This place is ideal for historians and waxworks enthusiasts. We vote they rename the Lapin Agile the Lame Tortoise. Dress: mourning.

Madame Arthur
75bis rue des Martyrs, 75019 Paris (42.64.48.27). Metro Pigalle/bus 30, 54.
Open 10pm-midnight daily. **Show** 10.15pm daily. **Admission** *dinner:* at 8.30pm, 250F (includes wine); *show only:* at 10.15pm, 165F (includes one drink, second drink 95F).
Credit EC, MC, V.
Madame's puts on a burlesque transvestite and drag show that won the 1988 Laurier d'Or award. Inside this small cabaret venue in Pigalle, where you're obliged to knock on the door before being admitted, Madame Arthur presents a non-stop show of bizarre transvestites, drag artists and transsexuals, who mime extreme caricatures of female singers (for example, Mireille Mathieu and Chantal Goya) or historic scenes, such as Caligula or the French Revolution. Laughs turn to grimaces as you watch this parade of actors; the make-up is as heavy and grotesque as the double-entendres. The pre-recorded music is so loud and the speakers are of such low quality, that not only are you deafened but also prevented from commiserating with your neighbour as you are forced to applaud the costumes, the tacky sets and the four sparklers which represent fireworks. However, Madame Arthur himself does have camp value and does his best to insult everyone equally; those of a sensitive disposition, bald men and people who wear specs should

refrain from sitting at the front. As a finale, a number of pretty boys try and get unlucky members of the audience to do the conga in celebration of this strange and tiring evening. *Reserve in advance.*

Chez Michou
80 rue des Martyrs, 75018 Paris (46.06.16.04). Metro Pigalle/bus 30, 54. **Open** 9pm- midnight daily. **Show** 9pm daily. **Admission** *dinner:* 480F (includes cocktail & wine). **No credit cards.**
Visit Michou if you want to experience a burlesque drag and parody show. It is very funny, very high camp and has impressive cossies.

CAFE THEATRES

This form of cabaret is anti-conformist, marginal, experimental and, at times, absurd. Venues are small and intimate; admission prices affordable. Between 1970 and 1980 the *café-théâtres* located around the developing Halles area, resembled the cabarets of the early fifties. The *café-théâtres'* post-'68 revolution humour – as popularised by the now defunct weekly satirical journal Charlie Hebdo – reflected the views and aspirations of a generation. Today, those outspoken stars of the seventies, are the stars of TV and cinema. The revolutionary genre is in a state of petrification. One woman/man shows, which usually comprise of an hour of mediocre monologue, are currently in vogue because they are cheap and easy to put on. Many of the 'plays' aren't even up to the standard of end-of-term school productions; they wouldn't last a night in clubs and fringe theatres in London, Edinburgh or New York. Nevertheless, fans of twentieth-century theatre will be spoilt for choice, so long as what they want to see are small productions of Ionesco, Giraudoux, Boris Vian or Beckett.

TRADITIONAL

Café de la Gare
41 rue du Temple, 75004 Paris (42.78.52.51). Metro Hôtel de Ville/bus 69, 76, 96. **Open** 8pm-midnight Tue-Sat. **Show** 8pm & 10.15pm Tue-Sat. **Admission** 80F-100F. **No credit cards.**
See picture and caption.
Reservations by phone 2-6pm.

Café d'Edgar
58 boulevard Edgar Quinet, 75014 Paris (43.20.85.11). Metro Edgar Quinet or Montparnasse/bus 28, 58, 82. **Open** 8pm-midnight Mon-Sat. **Show** 8.15pm, 9.30pm & 10.30pm Mon-Sat. **Admission** 50F-65F one show; 100F two shows. **No credit cards.**

An intimate theatre opened in 1973 by Alain Mallet, which, like so many other such venues, has no bar. Actors usually put on plays, although one man/woman shows are not uncommon. The standard of acts is usually high and delivery professional.
Reservations by phone 2.30-7.30pm.

Au Bec Fin
6 rue Thérèse, 75001 Paris (42.96.29.35). Metro Palais-Royal/bus 21, 76, 81. **Open** 7pm-midnight daily. **Show** 7pm, 8.30pm & 10pm daily; extra show at 11pm on Sat. **Admission** 65F one show, or 200F one show plus meal; 115F two shows, or 250F two shows plus meal. **Credit** V.
This ground-floor restaurant has an intimate 60-seater theatre in the basement. You can eat either before or after the show, and are allowed to take drinks into the theatre. Two hundred francs buys you a three course meal, *à choix*, or for 250F you can order seven *plats de dégustation*. This venue changes its programme quite regularly; expect to see short plays, comic sketches and *chansons paillards* (bawdy songs). There are hilarious public auditions on Sunday evenings when new, usually comic talents stagger onto the stage and try their hand at entertaining. Its friendly, convivial atmosphere makes Au Bec Fin a cabaret worth visiting.

Points Virgule
7 rue Sainte-Croix-de-la-Bretonnerie, 75004 Paris (42.78.67.03). Metro Hôtel de Ville/bus 69, 76, 96. **Open** 8pm-midnight Tue-Sun. **Show** 8pm, 9.30pm & 10.45pm. Tue-Sun. **Admission** 75F. **No credit cards.**
A somewhat cramped and dark 100-seater fringe theatre that has a reputation for putting on recently-discovered talents. The small stage lends itself to one man/woman shows; both Gustave Parking and Pierre Palmade have recently played here to full houses. Like other such cabarets, it's a venue without a bar. Consult the publicity boards outside for reviews of current shows. *Wheelchair access.*

Blancs-Manteaux
15 rue des Blancs-Manteaux, 75004 Paris (48.87.15.84) Metro Hôtel de Ville, Rambuteau/bus 69, 76, 96. **Open** 8pm-midnight Mon-Sat. **Show** 8.15pm, 9.30pm & 10.30pm Mon-Sat. **Admission** 45F one show Mon; 65F one show Tue-Fri; 100F two shows Mon-Sat. **No credit cards.**
The Blancs is made up of two seperate, 100-seater theatres; the bar is located between the two. Members of the audience are prohibited from taking drinks into the auditorium. Frequented by a young, buzzing crowd, this is where the long-running

The **Café de la Gare** *(listed under* **Café-Théâtres/Traditional***) has been the home to the same cabaret company for twenty years. Originally led by Romain Bouteille and now by Sotha, the artists produce their own pieces and regularly invite performer friends they admire to rent the space. The Café spawned comic and theatrical talents such as Coluche, Patrick Dewaere, Miou-Miou, Romain Bouteille and Gérard Depardieu. Housed in the former mews of a coaching inn, the Café is surrounded on all four sides by the Dance Centre of the Marais.*

Areu=MC2 – a play about three babies who take over the world – is still performed after ten years in its original form. The 10.30pm show is often a one man/woman production, highly popular with the Parisian crowds.

SHOWCASES FOR NEW TALENT

Le Tourtour
20 rue Quincampoix, 75004 Paris (48.87.82.48). Metro Châtelet-Les-Halles/bus 38, 47. **Open** 8.30pm-midnight Thur only. **Admission** 40F. **No credit cards.**
A restaurant and café-théatre where Daniel and Chantal Olive – themselves struggling artists – rent the vaulted cellar bar to provide a space for young actors and comedians. It's used as a showcase in order to attract press reviews and to publicize shows they are putting on elsewhere. Auditions are held in front of 30 or so actors and public impresarios who are on the look-out for good acts. The audience is young, earnest and polite, and so are the acts. Usually, there will be three acts, including stand-ups and singer-songwriters. The cellar bar holds about 60 people; you sit in the round on stools. It has bar and drinks are allowed inside the cellar. However, smoking is not allowed. Try it out.

Tintamarre
10 rue des Lombards, 75004 Paris (48.87.33.82). Metro Châtelet-Les-Halles/bus 29. **Open** 8-11pm Tue-Sat. **Admission** 60F-80F show; 30F audition 2.30pm Sat. **No credit cards.**
Tintamarre is famous for its public auditions of young one man/woman shows, stand-ups, orators and singers. Those that pass the audition get a regular spot in the theatre, usually at 9.30pm. Save yourself some money and savour potential talent on Saturday afternoons.

IMPROVISATION

Bataclan
50 boulevard Voltaire, 75011 Paris (47.00.30.12). Metro Voltaire/bus 56. **Open** 9pm-after midnight Mon only. **Admission** to be announced.
A *match d'improvisation*, along the lines of theatre-sports, but more formalised. Two teams of actors improvise on a theme while the audience acts as a jury, voting with bits of coloured card. Slippers are readily available if you want to show your displeasure; they are thrown at the players when the improvising gets really bad.

FOOD & LAUGHS

A number of restaurants and bars offer diners and drinkers entertainment of questionable quality; sometimes one man/woman shows, more often singers. Go for the food and don't expect great things of the show - you may be pleasantly surprised.

Au Movies
15 rue Michel Lecomte, 75003 Paris (42.74.14.22). Metro Rambuteau/bus 29. **Open** *restaurant:* noon-2.30pm, 7.30pm-midnight, Mon-Fri; 7.30pm-midnight Sat. **Show** at 7.30pm Thur-Sat. **Admission** 40F diners; 60F non-diners. **Credit** AmEx, DC, EC ,V.
Au Movies is a restaurant run by Richard Kalfa – an ex-Paradis Latin dancer – who enjoys taking the cinema-theatre theme through from the decor to the food. Housed in a charming old building, the food here is good and reasonably priced. Try *Les Misérables* (a mixed salad), *Moby Dick* (a crab salad) or *Gandhi* (curried chicken). On most Thursdays, Fridays and Saturdays, the bar area is turned into a stage, so get your drinks in early. The curtains are drawn, the sound man sets his gear up by the front door and under the beams of the main room a show unfolds. Consult the publicity in the window before you commit yourself, as getting past the sound man, if you don't like the show, can be tricky. Smoking is prohibited during acts.

Le Grenier
3 rue Rennequin, 75017 Paris (43.80.68.01). Metro Ternes/bus 30, 31, 43, 93. **Open** 7.30pm-after midnight Tue-Sun. **Show** at 10pm Wed-Sat. **Admission** 40F diners; 50F non-diners. **Credit** CB.
A small crêperie restaurant that puts on late shows, usually one man/woman acts, four nights a week.

Le Limonaire
88 rue de Charenton, 75012 Paris (43.43.49.14). Metro Ledru Rollin/bus 46, 76, 86. **Open** 8pm-1am Mon-Sat; closed whole month of August. **Show** 10-11pm Wed-Sat. **Admission** no admission fee, but hat is passed round after show. **No credit cards.**
A local bistro in the 12th arrondissement, just around the corner from the noisy bustling Aligre market. Baptised in 1985 by Philippe Duval, who is the mime artist, street singer, and artist of the *Limonaire*, the barrel organ. Since being taken over by Daniel Tartier, it offers excellent and reasonably priced wine to accompany an *à la carte* meal that costs around 80F per head. The entertainment is usually musical, but you'll sometimes find comics and poets doing their stuff. A classic in its genre.

Nostalgie
27 avenue des Ternes, 75017 Paris (42.27.65.25). Metro Ternes, Porte Maillot/bus 43. **Open** 9pm-3am Tue-Sat; closed whole month of August. **Show** at 10pm Tue-Sat. **Admission** *diner:* 350F (includes wine); *drink & show:* from 100F. **Credit** AmEx, CB, DC, EC, MC, V.
See **picture and caption.**

Petit Casino
17 rue Chapon, 75003 Paris (42.78.36.50). Metro Arts et Métiers, Rambuteau/bus 29. **Open** 8pm-midnight Tue-Sun. **Show** at 9pm & 10.30pm Tue-Sun. **Admission** *dinner & 2 shows:* 230F (includes drink); *one show only:* 60F. **No credit cards.**

Nostalgie *(listed under* **Food & Laughs***), a large restaurant with a fifties-rock, is linked to the Nostalgie FM radio station. It can seat 200 to 250 people, serves up good food, puts on a fun cabaret, and has a large stage, video screen and good sound system. Acts are varied; there's the ubiquitous string of ventriloquists and magicians, some good raunchy jazz singers, and try-outs for amateurs in the audience. Dress is mixed; DJs or designer T-shirts are just the job. Expect members of the audience to be Parisian yups .*

A restaurant and small fringe theatre, that is a trendy haunt for those seeking out reasonable food, one man/woman shows, double acts and short plays.

La Vieille Grille
1 rue du Puits de l'Ermite, 75005 Paris (47.07.22.11). Metro Censier Daubenton/bus 47. **Open** 8pm-midnight Tue-Sat. **Show** at 8.30pm Tue-Sat. **Admission** 80F. **No credit cards.**
Once the bastion and pioneer of radical comedy, experimental theatre, folk, jazz and just about everything, the Vieille Grille, a cosy bar-cum-theatre that has gone through many phases. It continues to present a varied menu of entertainment, such as singer-songwriters, Greek tragedy plays, stand-up comics, and classical music, though not all on one evening. The telephone pre-recorded message gives details of the current shows.

An African in Paris
9 rue Marcadet, 75018 Paris (42.23.87.98). Metro Marcadet. **Open** 7.30pm-midnight Mon-Sat. **Credit** AmEx, EC, MC, V.
An African-Antillais restaurant in the African quarter to the North of Paris that's run by a mixed partnership of a French ex-Maxim's patisseur and a Senegalese chef. The average price of a main course is 60F, and the set menu is 100F, all included. There is excellent and authentic African and West Indian food on the menu. The atmosphere is friendly and African musicians, playing instruments such as the kora, belafon, drums and so on, perform at weekends. Phone for details of shows. Dress city casual.

LAID BACK
SHOWS

Chez Georges
11 rue des Cannettes, 75006 Paris (43.26.79.15). Metro Mabillon/bus 70, 87, 96. **Open** noon-2am Tue-Sat; closed whole months of July and August. **Show** at 10.30pm Tue-Sat in the cellar. **Admission** 50F. **No credit cards.**
See **picture and caption.**

René Cousinier – La Branlette
4 impasse Marie Blanche (2nd left off rue Lepic), 75004 Paris (46.06.49.46). Metro Blanche/bus 30, 54. **Admission** free, although obligatory drink starts at 80F. **No credit cards.**
On the slopes of Pigalle, far from the noise and the peep shows, is a grubby little cellar bar. Here René Cousinier, a living legend, will, if your French is up to it, keep you chuckling for a good hour and a half. If his nickname means anything to you, you'll already have a good idea of the tone of his humour. Nobody knows how long he has propped up the same shady corner, regaling the mainly young and relaxed audience with his salacious stories that are related machine-gun style in his inimitable Provençal accent. Vulgar, obscene, truculent and extremely funny, he's full of pertinent observation and philosophical – and sometimes poetic – charm. Not a show for the prudish.

Au Vieux Paris
72 rue de la Verrerie, 75004 Paris (no telephone). Metro Châtelet/bus 69, 76, 96. **Open** 3pm-4am Tue-Sat. **Admission** free, although obligatory drink starts at 15F. **No credit cards.**
There's no admission fee; just ring the bell. If Madame Françoise likes the look of you, she'll let you in. Better still, pop in for a drink in the early evening and introduce yourself. You are drawn inside this very ordinary little Parisian café by the sounds of Mexican accordionist extraordinaire Sergio Valagez and then invited to sing your heart out. Somebody hands out the words and everyone harmonises through Piaf, Trenet, Brel and Latin American favourites till the early hours. It's a real taste of old Paris; it's therefore all the more astonishing to find it here in the 4th arrondissment, only a stone's throw from trendy, touristy Les Halles. But beware, Madame Françoise, patronne behind the zinc counter for 34 years, runs an orderly house and doesn't let just nay old punter in. Football supporters and drunken revellers should keep walking ... even clapping is discouraged here.

Trottoirs de Buenos Aires
37 rue des Lombards, 75001 Paris (42.33.58.37). Metro Les Halles/bus 29. **Open** 8.30pm-midnight daily. **Show** at 8.30pm & 10.30pm daily. **Admission** 90F. **Credit** AmEx.
A pleasant, dingy bar in the middle of the Les Halles area that specializes in genuine Argentinian Tango. The room seats about 100 people, seated around small tables. The 8.30pm show is usually a French singer-songwriter, although you might sometimes come across more exciting contemporary music from the likes of the excellent Michel Musseau and his Bal Contemporain. And for the 10.30pm show, impresario and patron Alain Houzel plays host to the best Argentinian Tango in town.
Reserve in advance at weekends

Le Piano Zinc
49 rue des Blancs-Manteaux, 75004 Paris (42.74.32.42). Metro Rambuteau, Hôtel de Ville/bus 29, 69, 75, 76. **Open** 7pm-2am Tue-Sun; closed Public Holidays. **Admission** free. **Credit** MC.
The seven-year-old Zinc – slang for a bar – is like no other in Paris. Though its clientèle is predominantly gay, everyone is made welcome. The three bars are stacked one on top of the other. Sandwiched in the middle is the famous piano. When you enter into *Paradise*, grab a draught lager (18F) or a whisky cola and wander down through the *melée* into *Purgatory*, the piano bar. Here, surrounded by faded posters of Dietrich, Hayworth and Monroe, anyone can get up to the mike, and – with the help of the resident pianist who'll accompany you – you can sing your way through the great Broadway hits, or chansons of Piaf and Trenet. The songs are sometimes good, sometimes bad, moving, funny, bawdy or sentimental, but always spontaneous and unpretentious. From midnight on, it's impossible to find a place to stand, so penetrate down into *Hell*, where the excellent singers upstairs are relayed by closed circuit TV to the revellers below. Not primarily a pick-up joint, but a meeting place for conviviality, tenderness and a good singalong.

Chez Georges (*listed under* **Laid Back Shows**) *is a place to eat, drink and be merry without the whole experience costing you an arm and a leg. This classic, old, French bar – now a rarity in increasingly chic Saint Germain – has been run by Georges, patron très sympa, as a family concern since 1952. His grandson now runs the cabaret and his daughter works behind the bar in the afternoons. Georges's clientèle is ageless, cosmopolitan and animated, and the beer is cheap (12F for a half lager) and good. This place has a real pub atmosphere.*

Children

Paris offers parents far more than just an endless chain of hamburger joints and cinemas. Below we list the alternatives intended to keep your *enfants terribles* out of mischief.

Paris is not a place we generally associate with children and you may sometimes wonder if, like the children of Hamelin, Parisian kids haven't been enticed away by a dancing flautist. The sad fact is that as property prices in Paris rise, families are increasingly forced out of the city to the distant suburbs. But open any park gate, or go to any museum on a Wednesday, Saturday or Sunday (children's days off from school) and you'll discover jostling herds of youngsters who've come into central Paris for the day. What's more, the Mairie de Paris (the central municipal body) ensures that there are ten square metres (105 square feet) of green space per inhabitant and that every patch of green is utilized to its maximum. This means that city kids can let off steam in relative safety.

Up to the age of about five, a child that finds a sand-pit is as happy as the proverbial sandboy. Paris is well serviced by public squares and gardens for toddlers. For information on these and where to find your local square *see below* **Green Areas** *and chapter* **Survival**. Teenagers will generally find their own entertainment and are happy snapping the sights to show off to their schoolmates back home. Put them on a bus or a boat (*see below* **Supervised Activities**; *see also chapter* **Travelling Around Paris**) and give yourselves a couple of hours off. In theory, at least.

Most television channels show children's programmes and cartoons in the morning between 7am and 8am and again at around 5pm and 6pm on weekdays. Television on Wednesday and Saturday is dedicated almost entirely to children's programmes. Watch out for familiar characters such as Batman or Denver, the last dinosaur (*Denver, le dernier dinosaur*) in French.

Local town halls (*mairies*) provide information on crèches and children's activities in the borough, including *ludothèques*. The latter are game-playing spaces with facilities for toy-borrowing, which usually are available only on seasonal subscription to long-term visitors. All *arrondissements* have public libraries and most of these have a children's corner and some literature in English. All *mairies* are listed in order of *arrondissement* under 'Mairies' in the phone book (white pages).

Full details of events and activities for children can be found in the weekly *7 à Paris* and *Pariscope* and the monthly, English-language *Paris Passion*. For enquiries concerning children's health, rights, sport and leisure activities, contact **Inter-Service Parents**, *see below* **Child-minding**. *See also chapter* **Survival** for information on children's hospitals.

CHILD-MINDING

Most baby-sitting agencies expect parents to leave food for the sitter if she or he is minding during normal eating hours. At the end of the evening you must make sure that the sitter gets home safely. Always leave a phone number where you can be reached in case of emergency.

Fees vary depending on what time of day your child needs minding; below we give average hourly rates. Extra charges may be made if sitters have to work until very late or during public holidays.

Inter-Service Parents
(43.48.28.28). **Open** 9.30am-12.30pm, 1.30-5pm, Mon-Tue, Fri; 9.30am-12.30pm Wed; 1.30-5pm Thur. **No credit cards.**
See **picture and caption.**

Ababa
8 rue du Maire, 75015 Paris (45.49.46.46).
Open 24 hours daily. **Rates** 22F-24F depending on time of day; 42F booking fee (discounts for frequent use). **No credit cards.**
Renowned for its competent, efficient team, Ababa offers a 24-hour, all-year service. The company has about 350 English-speaking babysitters on its books, both male and female. You must give the agency two hours' notice if you want to use the service. Ababa also caters for weekend sitting, takes children out for the day and arranges children's tea parties.

American Church
65 Quai d'Orsay, 75006 Paris (47.05.07.99/crèche 47.05.66.55). *Metro Invalides/bus 63, 83*. **Open** 9am-10.30pm Mon-Sat; 9am-8pm Sun. **Rates** average 30F per hour; no booking fee. **No credit cards.**
English-speaking minders offer baby-sitting services via a bulletin board at the church. Go to the church and consult the board yourself – and do your own selecting over the phone. There is also a crèche which is part of a bilingual French/English school. Various children's activities are organized by the centre, including t'ai chi, kung fu, yoga and toddlers' dancing classes. Phone for details.

Kid's Service
17 rue Molière, 75001 Paris (42.96.04.16/42.96.04.17). **Open** 9am-1pm, 2-8pm, Mon-Fri; 10am-1pm, 2-8pm, Sat; reduced hours Aug; closed public holidays. **Rates** 23F-25F per hour depending on time of day; 230F for 10 consecutive hours day or night; 50F booking fee. **No credit cards.**
One of the oldest baby-sitting agencies in Paris, with over 20 years' experience. The selection process is rigorous and the young, friendly team is highly dependable. Qualified nannies, governesses or play-school supervisors are available at 30F an hour.

Service Social de la Cité Universitaire
19 boulevard Jourdain, 75014 Paris (45.89.67.57, extension/poste 276). **Open** 2-5.30pm Mon-Fri. **Rates** 28F per hour first child, plus 2F for each additional child; 250F for 8 hours; no booking fee. **No credit cards.**
A student-run agency, providing occasional or regular sitters. The sitter's return journey must be arranged. Students also do housework for 35F per hour.

Zabou
Boite Postale 397-75962, Paris Cedex 20 (46.36.03.76). **Open** 24 hours daily. **Rates** 22F per hour; 190F per day; 160F per night; 30F booking fee. **No credit cards.**
A 24-hour agency service that guarantees the arrival of a sitter within one hour of your making a telephone booking. Sitters will come out at any time. Zabou employs young people, the idea being that children treat them like a big brother or sister, as someone they can really play with. The company's insurance covers both the sitter and the children. This agency is one of the few that's open full hours during August. Children's parties can also be organized, at a cost of 30F per hour plus a 60F booking fee.

SUPERVISED ACTIVITIES

Give yourself and the kids a break. Both the **Atelier des Enfants** and the **Jardin des Enfants aux Halles** offer supervised activities and the guided bus and river trips listed below are happy to take unaccompanied children. Be sure to check picking-up times.

Atelier des Enfants (Children's Workshops)

Centre Georges Pompidou, entrance to the right of Centre main door, Plateau Beaubourg, 75004 Paris (afternoons only 42.77.12.33). Metro Châtelet, Les Halles, Hotel de Ville, Rambuteau/bus 38, 47, 75. **Sessions** 2.30-4.30pm Wed, Sat; reserve a place in person 30 minutes before session starts. **Admission** free.

This workshop space for kids is run on a first come, first served basis. If you get there early enough you can leave your child (age 6 to 12) in the capable hands of assistants who supervise activities, such as constructing a twenty-first-century town out of polystyrene bricks. A visit to the museum of modern art upstairs (*see chapter* **Museums**), will show the children where their work might end up one day. Although workshop activities are mainly manual and creative, children will need a smattering of French to get by. Afterwards take them for tea in the nearby rue Saint-Merry that overlooks a fantastic water-garden with humorous kinetic sculptures by Tinguely and Nikki de Saint Phalle. *See also below* **Salle d'Actualité de Jeunesse**.

Cityrama

4 place des Pyramides, 75001 Paris (42.60.30.14). Metro Palais Royal, Pyramides/bus 39, 48, 67, 72. **Tours** 9.30am, 10.30am, 1.30pm, 2.30pm, daily. **Tickets** 110F adults; 55F 6-10s; under-6s free if accompanied; group discounts available. **Credit** AmEx, MC, V.

Cityrama runs tours of Paris in double-decker buses; the English-language voice-over is on personal cassette. The two-hour tour takes in all the major tourist sites: Nôtre Dame, the Eiffel Tower and, inevitably, the abysmal Parisian traffic system. Your children cannot get off the bus during the tour, so make sure all is in order before they set off. The hostess will keep an eye on them if approached diplomatically and voilà, you've got two hours to yourself.

Jardin des Enfants aux Halles (Children's Garden in the Halles)

105 rue Rambuteau, 75001 Paris (45.08.07.18). Metro Les Halles/bus 58, 67, 69, 70, 72, 74, 76, 85. **Open** *May-Oct:* 9am-noon, 2-6pm, Tue, Thur, Fri; 10am-6pm Wed, Sat; 1-6pm Sun, Public Holidays; *Nov-April:* 9am-noon, 2-4pm, Tue, Thur, Fri; 10am-4pm Wed, Sat; 1-4pm Sun, Public Holidays; reserve a place in person, one hour before garden opens. **Admission** 2.20F per hour. **No credit cards.**

An open-air children's activity garden for kids aged 7 to 11 that's plumb in the middle of the busy Les Halles area. It's constructed as a concrete labyrinth made up of slides, underground tunnels, rope swings, secret dens and 'swimming pools' of coloured ping-pong balls where kids can indulge their every whim. The garden is well supervised by a team of *animateurs* and children can join in group activities or scramble about on their own. Adults are not allowed in except on Saturdays between 10am and 2pm, when they can also bring younger children. Places are limited, so do arrive one hour ahead to book.

Salle d'Actualité de Jeunesse (Children's library)

Centre Georges Pompidou, entrance at 18 rue Beaubourg, 75004 Paris (42.77.12.33).

Metro Les Halles, Rambuteau/bus 38, 47, 75. **Open** noon-7pm Wed; 1-7pm Sat, Sun. **Admission** free.

Children over the age of six can be left unaccompanied to browse through a large selection of books, comics and video films, mainly in French but some in English. Depending on your luck, you may or may not find an attendant who speaks English. Adults are admitted at all times.

Vedettes du Pont Neuf

place du Vert-Galant, entrance behind the equestrian statue in the middle of the Pont Neuf, 75001 Paris (46.33.98.38). Metro Louvre, Pont Neuf/bus 24, 27, 58, 67, 70, 72, 74, 75. **Cruises** 10.30am, 11.15pm, noon, then half-hourly 2-5pm, daily. **Tickets** 30F adults; 15F under-10s; group discounts available. **No credit cards.**

A small, friendly company that operates river trips from Nôtre Dame to the Eiffel Tower and back, taking in views of the Louvre, the Musée d'Orsay, the Grand Palais and the Invalides (*see chapters* **Museums** and **Sightseeing**). The tours take one hour and have a commentary in English, French and German. Children can be left unaccompanied at their parents' discretion. If you feel they're old enough, leave them to enjoy their cruise and head across the road for some good company, excellent and reasonably-priced wine and a plate of *charcuterie* at the Henri IV wine bar. Robert Cointepas will willingly relate how he was possibly the last man to see the writer Simenon alive.

GREEN AREAS

Lac de Vincennes (Lac Daumesnil)

by main entrance on route de Ceinture du Lac Daumesnil, Bois de Vincennes, 75012 Paris. Metro Porte Dorée. **Open** *park:* 24 hours daily; *boat house:* 10am-dusk daily. **Tickets** 38F-42F per boat per half hour, depending on number of people; deposit 50F. **No credit cards.**

A boat trip on the lake is the perfect end to a family day out at the zoo (*see below* **Animals**). It's a bit pricey, and a tip for the boat boys is expected, but it's a grand way of seeing this large man-made lake.

Jardin d'Acclimatation

Bois de Boulogne, 75016 Paris (40.67.90.80). Short stroll down rue des Sablons from Metro Porte Maillot/bus 73. **Open** *Bois de Boulogne* 24 hours daily; *Jardin d'Acclimatation* 10am-6pm daily. **Admission** *pleasure train:* 7F adults; 3.50F under-16s; *Jardin d'Acclimatation:* 7F adults; 3.50F under-16s; *combined ticket:* single journey plus admission 10.50F adults, 7F under-16s; return journey plus admission 14F adults, 10.50F under-16s; group discounts available, phone for details. **No credit cards.**

For over 125 years, the Jardin d'Acclimatation has been a promised land

---

Inter-Service Parents (*listed under* **Child-Minding**) *is a free telephone advisory service giving details of baby-sitting agencies, child-minding associations and children's activities around Paris. Although this is not specifically a service for visitors, staff will do their best to help in any language.*

for Parisian parents and every year about 1.5 million people religiously stream through its turnstiles. The journey starts with *'le petit train'*, a miniature pleasure train which unhurriedly chugs its way past the picnickers and *clochards* (tramps) in the woods of the Bois de Boulogne to the Gates of Fun City. The train leaves from behind **L'Orée du Bois** restaurant, outside the Porte Maillot metro, and runs every ten minutes throughout the day on Wednesday, Saturday, Sunday and public holidays (from 1.30pm during school holidays). If you want to relax and enjoy the taste of unleaded oxygen, issue the kids with a limited amount of cash and let them loose. Some of attractions cost extra: donkey rides, dodgems, remote-control model speed boats or a trip down the 'enchanted river' cost on average 5F to 7F. But there's a lot that's free once you've paid the main admission price: the hall of mirrors, the children's zoo, the *Guignol* theatre (*see below* **Theatre & Guignol**) and the all-wooden under-12s playground. The Musée en Herbe, an educational centre with activities and occasional shows aimed at children, is located within the grounds. It also houses re-creations of both a village set in the time of *Asterix* and one set around the time of the Revolution (*phone* 40.67.97.66 for a programme of events), giving a wide range of activities to occupy the kids.

Jardin des Plantes
place Valhubert/quai d'Austerlitz, or rue Cuvier/rue Buffon, 75005 Paris. Metro Gare d'Austerlitz, Jussieu/bus 24, 58, 63. **Open** *dawn-dusk daily.* **Admission** *to park:* free; *to galleries of Entymology, Mineralogy, Paleontology, hot-house, Alpine garden:* prices vary.
The Jardin des Plantes is a large area of aromatic and verdant splendour in a relatively calm district of Paris. A children's playground features a giant wooden dinosaur, its massive tail forming a slide, and the rest a climbing frame. Sand-pits, see-saws and swings, a labyrinth, donkey rides, a menagerie and a vivarium are all part of the attraction. There are several kiosks and small cafés for drinks and snacks. One visit will not be enough to explore all the riches of this delightful haven.

Le Parc Floral de Paris
route de la Pyramide, Bois de Vincennes, 75012 Paris (43.43.92.95). Metro Château de Vincennes then 112 bus to Parc Floral or 15-minute walk. **Open** *summer:* 9.30am-8pm daily; *winter:* 9.30am-5pm or 6pm.
Admission 4F adults Mon-Fri, 8F Sat, Sun, public holidays; 2F 6-10s Mon-Fri; 4F Sat, Sun, public holidays; under-6s free.
No credit cards.
Situated in the Bois de Vincennes, a major leisure and recreation park on the eastern edge of Paris, the Parc Floral has a slower pace than its western counterpart, the Jardin d'Acclimatation in the Bois de Boulogne (*see above*). On schooldays it's full of pensioners admiring the prize dahlias and young mums pushing buggies around the aromatic flower beds. All very pleasant, but perhaps a little soporific. However, at the far end of the garden is a good, large playground with the usual slides, climbing frames and swings, plus ping-pong tables, pedal karts (for 4 to 10 year-olds) and a miniature train that costs 4F per ride. It's mainly a place for gardening enthusiasts

and ecologists (worksheets, in French only, are available in various nature chalets), but there is also the Astral Theatre which presents children's shows on Wednesdays, Saturdays, Sundays and public holidays; phone the main office for details.

THEATRE & GUIGNOL

THEATRE
There is a tradition of theatre and *guignol* (puppet shows akin to Punch and Judy) for children in Paris. Many of the fringe theatres (*cafés-théatres*) have children's shows on Wednesday, Saturday and Sunday afternoons and during school holidays. The quality of these fringe shows is extremely variable but they can usually be relied upon to put on something that'll amuse the kids. Below we give full details of the English-language company in Paris; people with a smattering of French should phone the other venues listed for ticket prices and show times as these vary depending on the season and play.

Galerie '55' Underground
55 rue de Seine, 75006 Paris (43.26.63.51). Metro Odéon, Saint Germain, Mabillon/bus 39, 63, 70, 84, 87. **Office open** *phone bookings:* 11am-5pm daily. **Shows** *mid Oct-end Dec, school holidays only:* 3pm Wed, Sat (extra shows during school holidays).
Tickets 65F adults; 60F under-15s.
No credit cards.
A English-language theatre for children during school holidays and the run-up to Christmas. Past shows have included *The Wizard of Oz, Alice in Wonderland, Dracula* and *The Jungle Book*. There's also evening plays for adults, for example Sam Shepard's *True West*.

Centre d'Animation des Batignolles
75bis rue Truffaut, 75117 Paris (47.37.30.75). Metro Brochant/bus 54, 74.

Café d'Edgar
58 boulevard Edgar Quinet, 75014 Paris (43.22.11.02). Metro Edgar Quinet/bus 28, 58, 68.

Au Bec Fin
6bis rue Thérèse, 75001 Paris (42.96.29.35). Metro Palais Royal/bus 21, 69, 76, 48, 68.

Le Lucernaire
53 rue Nôtre Dame des Champs, 75006 Paris (45.48.39.70). Metro Nôtre Dame des Champs, Vavin/bus 58, 68, 82.

Point Virgule
7 rue Sainte-Croix-de-la-Bretonnerie, 75004 Paris (42.78.67.03). Metro Hôtel de Ville/bus 69, 76, 96.

Paris has a large number of squares and play areas specifically designed for small children. Each arrondissment will have one of two of these green oases, equipped with sand-pits, slides and swings.

Cité Universitaire/bus 21. **Shows** 3pm, 4pm, Wed, Sat, Sun; daily during school holidays. **Tickets** 12F.

Théâtre Guignol
square de Choisy, 75013 Paris (43.66.72.39). Metro Place d'Italie, Tolbiac/bus 47, 83. **Shows** weather permitting, 3.30pm Wed, Sat, Sun; closed whole months of July and August. **Tickets** 7F.
This is the most traditional *Guignol* in Paris.

Théâtre Guignol-Anatole
Parc des Buttes Chaumont, entrance opposite town hall, 75019 Paris (43.98.10.95). Metro Laumière/bus 5. **Shows** 3pm Wed, Sat, Sun; daily during school holidays. **Tickets** 7F.

CINEMA

A list of films for children appears in the weekly *L'Officiel des Spectacles*. For further information on cinemas *see chapter* **Film**.

Action Ecoles
23 rue des Ecoles, 75005 Paris (43.25.72.07). Metro Cardinal Lemoine, Maubert Mutualité/bus 10. **Tickets** 35F adults; 25F under-16s. **No credit cards.** Tex Avery and Walt Disney cartoons are shown here. Phone for details.

Le Saint Lambert
6 rue Péclet, 75015 (45.32.91.68/48.28.78.87). Metro Vaugirard/bus 49, 70, 80. **Tickets** 30F adults; 20F under-16s; group discounts available. **No credit cards.**
This is one of the few Parisian cinemas specializing in children's films. Programmes include classics such as *Gulliver's Travels* or French comic-strip heroes *Tintin*, *Lucky Luke* and *Asterix*, all in VO (*version originale*, original language). Children can be left unaccompanied at their parents' discretion.

ACTIVITY MUSEUMS

Most museums in Paris have special programmes for children on Wednesday afternoons. These do not generally cater for non-French speakers, but the activities listed below are visually orientated and have become great favourites with children of all ages and nationalities. For more information on which museums are popular with children, *see chapter* **Museums**.

L'Inventorium
30 avenue Corentin Cariou, Cité des Sciences et Industrie, 75019 Paris (46.42.13.13). Metro Corentin Cariou, Porte de la Villette/bus PC. **Open** *Inventorium* sessions: 11am, 12.30pm, 2pm, 3.30pm, Tue, Thur, Fri; extra session 5pm Wed, Sat, Sun. **Admission** day pass to Cité des Sciences: 30F adults; 12F under-16s

The **Cité des Sciences et de l'Industrie** (*see* L'Inventorium *listed under* **Activity Museums***) is the largest centre of its kind in the world. Take the kids for the day and they'll learn through 'hands-on' experiments about science and how the world goes round.*

Sentier des Halles
50 rue Aboukir, 75002 Paris (42.36.37.27). Metro Sentier/bus 20, 39.

Théâtre Astral
Parc Floral de Paris, 75012 Paris (43.55.78.33). Metro Château de Vincennes/bus 46, 56.

Théâtre les Cinq Diamants
10 rue des Cinq Diamants, 75013 Paris (45.80.51.31). Metro Place d'Italie/bus 27, 47, 57, 67, 83.

Théâtre des Enfants
4 boulevard des Filles du Calvaire, 75011 Paris (47.00.23.77). Metro Filles du Calvaire/bus 20, 65.

Tintamarre
10 rue des Lombards, 75004 Paris (48.87.33.82). Metro Châtelet/bus 38, 47.

Tourtour
20 rue Quincampoix, 75004 Paris (48.87.82.48). Metro Châtelet/bus 38, 47, 75.

GUIGNOL

Guignol started as the mouthpiece of the striking weavers of Lyon at the beginning of the nineteenth century and has evolved to become the French equivalent of Punch and Judy shows. There's no wife-battering here but the policeman comes in for some flak, and there's always lots of audience participation. These shows are great for language-learning because you can take children back to see exactly the same routine several times and they never seem to tire of it. *Guignol* theatres are often located in parks, enabling children to get some fresh air as well as entertainment. The following theatres are recommended:

Guignol du Jardin d'Acclimatation
boulevard des Sablons, 75016 Paris (40.67.90.82). Metro Porte Maillot/bus 73. **Shows** several from 3pm Wed, Sat, Sun; every day during school holidays. **Tickets** *to shows*: free; *to Jardin d'Acclimatation*: 7F adults, 3.50F under-12s.

Marionettes du Guignol de Paris
Parc des Buttes Chaumont, 75019 Paris (46.36.32.01). Metro Buttes Chaumont/bus 76. **Shows** 3pm Wed, Sat, Sun; daily during school holidays. **Tickets** 7F.

Marionettes de Montsouris
Parc Montsouris, entrance avenue Reille/rue Gazan, 75014 Paris (46.65.45.95). Metro

(extra charge for Discovery Space and Planetarium); *ticket for Inventorium only:* 15F per session. **Credit** A, MC, V.

The Inventorium runs four or five 'discovery' sessions a day, encouraging children (alone or accompanied) in hands-on experiments to discover science and develop their curiosity through play. Young children can learn how water flows by dabbling in the waterfalls and pumps or playing 'Pooh sticks' through streams. They can learn how to make music by stamping and rolling over giant piano keys and musical stepping-stones. But the best bit, according to one five-year-old, was the mini-construction site with its bricks, wheelbarrows and cranes, complete with regulation hard hats and jackets. Older children may enjoy seeing what a skeleton looks like when riding a bike, how sound travels through tubes and telephones or what ants do underground. There are also computer games – used to compare genetic types – that test skin type, eye and hair colour. Screen monitors are on hand but are rarely needed as in our experience children are excitedly occupied for the duration of the sessions. There are few language problems as most activities are visually self-explanatory and the space is both self-contained and well managed, so there is no risk of children wandering off unsupervised. The place is spotlessly clean and great regard is paid to safety. Parents can either join in or browse around the rest of the centre. Animated lectures and demonstrations occur throughout the day and cafés are located throughout the complex offering your enlightened off-spring some well-earned refreshments.

See also **picture and caption**.

Musée d'Orsay

1 rue Bellechasse, 75007 Paris (40.49.48.14/recorded information 45.49.11.11). Metro Solférino/RER Musée d'Orsay/bus 26, 68, 69, 73. **Open** 10am-6pm Tue, Wed, Fri, Sat; 10am-9.45pm Thur; 9am-6pm Sun, Public Holidays. **Admission** 23F adults; 12F 18-25s, OAPs; free under-18s. **No credit cards**.

This turn-of-the-century railway station has been converted to the magnificent Musée d'Orsay housing objets d'art that date from 1848 to 1914. The museum prints English-language worksheets to help focus children's attention and interest on specific paintings, architectural features, geometrical shapes and even the view over Paris from the windows. Smaller children may need some help, but that will only add to your enjoyment of this astonishing museum. There is a café and a restaurant, but they tend to be very crowded at meal-times.

See also chapter **Museums**.

Parc Océanique Cousteau

Forum des Halles, 75001 Paris (40.28.98.98/99). Metro Châtelet, Les Halles/bus 38, 47. **Open** noon-7pm Tue-Sun (last ticket 5.30pm). **Admission** 75F adults; 52.5F 5-14s; free under-5s; group discounts available. **No credit cards**.

The Cousteau Oceanic Park opened in July 1989 and has already proved to be a big hit with Parisians and tourists alike. Plunge into a Cousteau-like world in the depths of the Forum des Halles in a shell-like module – without getting your feet wet – and descend into a world of coral reefs, ship-wrecks, giant octopuses and sharks. If you're expecting fish tanks full of exotic sea creatures you'll be disappointed. Cousteau loves and respects the sea and its inhabitants so much that he wouldn't harm a scale on their backs by having them in a museum. Once gently

deposited on the seabed you are ushered through a series of well-designed audio-visual underwater experiences. In the cinema you are assaulted by giant 3-D monsters, to the chorus of 'What's that, mum?' around you. But for many budding explorers, the highlight of the trip is being swallowed by a blue whale, the largest mammal on earth (as big as a DC10) and which has been so rarely filmed in the wild. The tour lasts about one and a half hours. As you leave by the escalator that softly ejects you into the gift shop, the voice of Jacques Cousteau beseeches you to 'protect the things you love'.

ANIMALS

Galerie d'Anatomie Comparée et de Paléontologie

57 rue Cuvier, in the Jardin des Plantes, 75005 Paris (40.79.30.30). Metro/RER Austerlitz/bus 24, 61, 63, 65, 67, 89. **Open** 10am-5pm Mon, Wed-Fri, Sun; 11am-6pm Sat. **Admission** 18F adults, 12F under-16s. **No credit cards**.

This is just one of the galleries that make up the Museum of Natural History, which was built in 1898, and is a classic example of steel and glass architecture. The building houses a collection of skeletal remains ranging from prehistoric times to some more

contemporary animals, including turtles, whales and insects. One can do no better than bring kids here to see the bony frames of these ancient beasts, reconstructed in this enormous pavilion where the dust of years only adds to their charm. Possibly because of lack of funds, the gallery is a little short of factual information, but children are enraptured by sights such as the stegosaurus that stomped the earth 140,000 years ago. Also in the Jardin des Plantes is the Ménagerie, *see below*.

Une Journée au Cirque (A Day at the Circus)

Le Cirque de Paris, avenue de la Commune de Paris/avenue Hoche, 9200 Nanterre (47.24.11.70). RER Nanterre Ville, line A. **Sessions** 10am-5pm Wed, Sun, Public Holidays, school holidays; closed during July-Oct. **Tickets** *show only:* 55F-140F adults, 35F-90F under-12s; *day at circus and one meal:* 195F-270F adults, 155F-195F under-12s. **No credit cards**.

In 1945, at the age of 14, François Schoeller began setting up the Royal Circus with a schoolmate. Two years later he bought a tent from a flea market and began building up a stock of animals: cats, dogs, lizards and white mice. During his military service he continued with his dream, recruiting among his *confrères* jugglers, magicians and acrobats, while he adopted the role of clown. In 1973 he established the Cirque de Paris and now invites children of all ages to participate in his dream

The tour of the **Musée Grévin** *(listed under* **Thrills and Chills***) waxworks starts with a hall of mirrors leading to a magnificent rococo 'palace' brimming over with celebrities from history and today's world of pop, films, politics and popular myth. The fun lies in recognizing the wax figures; kids will have no trouble spotting, among others, Michael Jackson, Charlie Chaplin, JR and Alfred Hitchcock, who shares a railway compartment with the Invisible Man.*

by spending a day at the circus. The day starts at 10.15am, training with the artists and discovering the various disciplines of the circus: clowning, make-up, trapeze and tightrope. Lunch is taken with the artists in the ring, followed by the 3pm show: two hours of chimps, clowns, magicians and all the razzamatazz of the fair. After the show, lion-tamer Thierry le Pontier, who speaks English, Italian and German, takes the children on a tour of the big cats. The only problem will be dragging your child away.

The Ménagerie
Jardin des Plantes, 57 rue Cuvier, 75005 Paris (43.36.19.09). Metro/RER Austerlitz/bus 24, 61, 63, 65, 67, 89. **Open** 9am-6pm daily. **Admission** 22F adults; 10F under-18s. **No credit cards.**
See **picture and caption.**

Tropical Aquarium
Musée National des Arts Africains et Océaniens, 293 avenue Daumesnil, 75012 Paris (43.43.14.54). Metro Porte Dorée/bus 46. **Open** 9.45am-noon, 1.30-7.30pm Mon, Wed-Fri; 10am-6pm Sat, Sun. **Admission** 15F adults; free under-18s. **No credit cards.**
Created in 1931, this museum set out to exhibit the spoils of colonial occupation. The main museum has an astonishing collection of African art. Downstairs in the tropical aquarium, a dark hall full of exotic creatures holds small children in a trance-like state. Crocodiles and piranha lie in wait, seemingly dormant but primed to gorge on whatever the keeper drops into their tanks. The museum is ideal for babies and toddlers – they'll love the colours and movement.

Zoo de Vincennes
53 avenue de Saint Maurice, 75012 Paris (43.43.84.95). Metro Porte Dorée/bus 46. **Open** 9am-6pm daily in summer; till 5pm in winter. **Admission** 30F adults; 15F 4-9s; free under-3s; family discounts. **No credit cards.**
Thanks to some ingenious landscaping, reinforced steel, caves and plateaux, the zoo provides enclosures sympathetic to the animals' respective habitats in the wild. Lions, tigers, elephants and rhinos wander in relative freedom, separated from the ogling public by a system of high walls and moats. The spacious paths make it easy to push buggies and prams. Perennial favourites are the monkeys, seals and sea-lions (feeding time is 4.30pm), hippos and giraffes. If at all possible, avoid the busy Wednesday afternoons and weekends; in summer there's likely to be a queue at the turnstiles whatever time you go. There are numerous kiosks and a restaurant. A miniature train goes round the zoo (no stops) and the park.

THRILLS & CHILLS

The Catacombs
1 place Denfert Rochereau (access in the middle of the square), 75014 Paris (43.22.47.63). Metro Denfert Rochereau/bus 38, 68. **Open** 2-4pm Tue-Fri; 9-11am, 2-4pm, Sat, Sun. **Admission** 15F adults; 8.50F under-18s. **No credit cards.**
The catacombs are a massive underground labyrinth of interconnecting galleries that

*The **Jardin des Plantes** was established in 1640 as a royal garden, and soon became an important centre for natural science research. Within the grounds are several museums, a hot-house and the **Menagerie** (listed under **Animals**). The small zoo features a collection of wild beasts (monkeys, big cats, camels and bisons), several open enclosures with farmyard animals, avivarium of nasty creepy-crawlies and a huge reptile house. You can feed the residents with their own specially prepared food and all the cages are well documented.*

run for miles beneath central Paris. Originally carved out by the Romans to provide stone for the construction of the city, they were later used as both a shelter by the persecuted Christians in the eighth century, and much later as the central communications headquarters of the Resistance, under the very feet of the German occupation. The visit starts with an interminable descent down a spiral staircase. Then, 600ft (180m) down, you leave the staircase to start weaving through dank corridors charged with history. Suddenly above the portals of an entrance, a sign declares 'Stop, you are entering the Empire of Death'. The catacombs are in fact an enormous ossuary as the bones of about five or six million ex-Parisians are stacked here. Notices (in French only) explain the mysteries behind these ghoulish remnants. Bring a warm jacket, some stout shoes and a torch and don't wander off the indicated route. Wine bottles scattered among the bones, paint a scene of cadaverous remains reassembling into skeletons that enjoy an unseen soirée once the visitors have moved on.

Les Egouts de Paris (the sewers)
place de la Résistance (entrance at junction of pont de l'Alma), 75007 Paris (47.05.10.29). Metro Alma-Marceau/bus 42, 63, 80, 92. **Open** 3-7.30pm Wed-Sun. **Admission** 12F; free under-6s. **No credit cards.**
The sewers are both the entrails and the central nervous system of Paris and who else but the French, obsessed by their digestion, would offer up the capital's pungent

waste system as a major tourist attraction. Notice boards in various languages relate the history of the Parisian sewers. Did you know that at the time of François I the stench in the streets of Paris was so bad that the Royals had to move out? Or that the cholera epidemic of 1832 was the inevitable result of human and industrial waste deposited directly into the Seine? Each year 15,000 cubic metres of solid waste are drawn from the network – the equivalent of a six-storey building. Apparently a fully-grown crocodile was discovered some time ago behind a partition; no-one knows how it got there, but it's now alive and kicking in the Brest zoo. Anything subterranean and hidden is a mystery and children love nothing better than the mysteries of *caca*. To our great dismay, and despite avid scrutiny of the flowing effluent, we saw nothing really revolting, but the smell is guaranteed to live up to all expectations.
Shop.

Musée Grévin (waxworks)
10 boulevard Montmartre, 75009 Paris (47.70.85.05). Metro Rue Montmartre/bus 20, 39, 48. **Open** 10am-7pm daily. **Admission** 40F adults; 28F 6-14s; free under-6s. **No credit cards.**
The Musée Grévin waxworks is well presented, with few annoying sound-effects, except in the cellar which makes the perfect setting for scenes of Revolutionary plotting and skullduggery. Kids love it. This branch is not to be confused with the one at the **Forum des Halles** – a series of tableaux of Paris in the Belle Epoque, accompanied by *Son et*

Lumière (40.26.28.50, open 10am-6.45pm daily). The Son is too loud and only in French and the Lumière defines how long you have to stand at each tableau. Whereas the main branch gives you delicious cold shivers, the Forum branch simply left us cold.
Shop.

FOR
TEENAGERS

The Eiffel Tower
Champs de Mars, 75007 Paris (45.50.34.56/recorded information 45.55.91.11). Metro Bir Hakeim, Ecole Militaire, Trocadéro/bus 82. **Open** *summer:* 9.30am-midnight daily; *winter:* 10am-11pm daily. **Admission** *by lift:* 14F-35F adults, depending on floor; 6F-20F under-12s; free under-4s; *by stairs to 2nd floor:* 7F adults; free under-4s; group discounts available.
No credit cards.
The Paris landmark was first opened in March 1889 for the Great Exhibition. Designed by Stephen Sauvestre, it took Gustave Eiffel two months and five days to build. For those who are interested, the tower is 320.75m high (1,052ft) and weighs 10,100 tons; 2,500,000 rivets hold the 18,000 pieces of iron together; and if you placed Nôtre Dame under the Tower, it would nestle comfortably beneath the four pillars. *See also chapter* **Sightseeing**.
Café, restaurant. Shops.

La Main Jaune
square de l'Amérique Latine, Porte de Champerret, 75017 Paris (47.63.26.47). Metro Porte de Champerret. **Open** 2.30-7pm Wed, Sat, Sun. **Admission** 40F; 25f under-14s (Wed only); skate hire 10F.
No credit cards.
The only roller-skating rink in Paris, La Main Jaune doubles as a disco in the evening. In the afternoon alcohol is taken off the drinks list and 'life-guards' are on hand to patch up grazed limbs. Bring your own roller-skates if you've got them or hire them for 10F. Roller-skating is not obligatory: lots of kids come just to boogie, bop and pose in front of the huge mirrors. Mirror balls, neon lighting, loud music and pinball machines make this a great place to leave your children for a few hours while you browse around the boutiques at the nearby Palais des Congrès. There is no age limit, but most children are between 8 and 16.

La Samaritaine
19 rue de la Monnaie, 75001 Paris (40.41.20.20). Metro Châtelet, Louvre, Pont Neuf/bus 24, 27, 69, 72. **Open** 9.30am-7pm Mon, Wed, Thur, Sat; 9.30am-8.30pm Tue, Fri. **Admission** free.
This turn-of-the-century department store, overlooking the Ile de la Cité and the Louvre, boasts one of the best panoramic views in Paris from its roof-top terrace. The terrace has a telescope and a picture map to pick out the main landmarks, though it hasn't been updated to include the Pompidou Centre or the Montparnasse Tower. Inside the store itself, admire the craftsmanship of the staircases, the frescos and the glass roof.
Café. Travel agency.

TRIPS OUT
OF PARIS

A number of Disneyland-type theme parks around Paris are currently in dire straits, mainly because they charge exorbitantly high entrance fees. Some have already folded and even those within easy driving reach of Paris face the threat of closure. They are likely to be totally eclipsed by the new Euro Disneyland park already under construction. However, if you have a flexible budget, an enjoyable day out can be had at one of them, especially if you avoid weekends and school holidays, when unending queues for the many stomach-churning attractions may prove more daunting than the rides themselves.

Asterix Parc
Plailly (16-44.62.32.10). Take the Autoroute A1 towards Calais, exit Parc Asterix. **Open** 10am-6pm Mon-Fri, Sun; 10am-10pm Sat, Public Holidays. **Admission** 120F adults; 90F 4-12s; free under-3s. **No credit cards.**
Just 35kms (22 miles) from Paris, this amusement theme park dedicated to the French comic-strip hero Asterix, offers an enjoyable escape back to the days of gladiators, slave auctions and feasts of wild boar. There are rides, games, parades, music, puppeteers, roving actors and food for all tastes and budgets. English, Spanish, German and Italian are spoken. There are half-hour queues for the more popular rides at weekends.

π
Park de Saint Vrain
(64.56.10.80). Take the Autoroute A6, exit at Vizy-Fleury. **Open** *spring, summer:* 10am-6pm Mon-Sat; 10am-5pm Sun, Public Holidays. **Admission** 54F adults; 44F 2-10s; free under-2s. **No credit cards.**
An open-air safari park only 45km (28 miles) from Paris, with an impressive array of free-roaming beasts and birds with outdoor scenes featuring dinosaurs and prehistoric men. Take it in by either riverboat or monorail. There are cafeteria and picnic facilities.

Parisian parks are brimming over with see-saws, sand-pits and sports facilities for children. Take the kids for the afternoon to the **Jardin d'Acclimatation** *or the* **Parc Floral de Paris** *(both listed under* **Green Areas***) and watch them run around while you relax in one of the many cafés that line the boulevards.*

Dance

Though most French dance companies step into Paris tutu rarely, we show you where to find the best arabesques in town.

While Paris is ordinarily the centralized hub of all French culture, this is less true in the realm of dance. Many top companies are located out in the wilds. Fashionable modernist Régine Chopinot is based in the Atlantic seaside city of La Rochelle; Jean-Claude Gallotta runs one of the most innovative national companies in Grenoble; Roland Petit is in Marseilles; ex-Parisian *danseur étoile* Patrick Dupont directs the stylish Ballet de Nancy and Dominique Bagouet is in Montpellier. This is almost entirely due to the fact that the French Cultural Ministry has followed a programme of subsidizing companies which don't operate from the capital, in order to bring 'culture' to the rest of the country. The French dance scene has been so expertly decentral-ized that, for example, when the Paris-based Ile-de-France Opera Ballet began to organize its regional Iles de Danse festival, it discovered that virtually all the local talent had to be imported from out of town.

The up-side of funding those who stay away from Paris is that young, French dance companies are getting fancy commissions and generous government travel grants. Consequently, dancers who receive generous State commissions, are making their mark on the international dance scene, as travel costs and training expenses can now be met with relative ease. These new, subsidized companies frequently travel to Paris but have no fixed venue where they regularly perform.

As a result, in Paris it is important to keep your eyes glued to marquees and metro billboards. Big-draw French and foreign companies put on shows all over town. Maurice Béjart, Alvin Ailey, Antonio Gades, Bob Wilson, the American Indian Theatre, or the Bolshoi Ice Dancers may be headlining at the Palais des Sports, the Grand Palais, the Casino de Paris, the Palais des Congrès convention centre or north of town in Saint-Denis or Bobigny. The new French companies to look out for include L'Esquisse, La P'tite Cie, and Ris et Danceries Company. Check also the weekly listings in *L'Officiel des Spectacles* or the listings in the monthly English-language magazine *Paris Passion*. As a general rule, count on seeing the most *avant-garde* works by up-and-coming choreographers in the small dance spaces near the Bastille. That is, at least until construction of the Maison de la Danse – a large-scale project that is still at the pre-planning stages at the Ministry of Culture – which will host major dance events and festivals.

*The **Maison de la Culture de Créteil** (listed under **Dance Venues**) is at the forefront of innovative dance in Paris. Maguy Marin, choreographer, is based in Créteil, an otherwise dreary eastern suburb of Paris. Her troupe is subsidized by the Ministry of Culture, the Créteil Municipality and the Val-de-Marne General Council. Marin sky-rocketed to international fame with her Cendrillon for the Lyon Opera Ballet in 1985. Consistently praised for her daring and dark humour, Marin's performances are well worth the long metro ride from Paris.*

DANCE VENUES

Café de la Danse
5 passage Louis-Philippe, 75011 Paris (48.05.57.22). Metro Bastille/bus 69. **Box office open** *by telephone:* in advance; *in person:* 30 minutes before show. **Tickets** 80F-100F. **No credit cards.**
Located at the end of a dusty little cul-de-sac off the prime party-bar street in the Bastille district, the Café de la Danse is an unprepossessing hole-in-the-wall with a fifties' beatnik décor. The audience perches awkwardly on tiered, wooden benches; the dancers perform audaciously against a red-brick backdrop.

Centre Mandapa
6 rue Wurtz, 75013 Paris (45.89.01.60). Metro Glacière/bus 21, 62. **Box office open** 2-8.15pm daily. **Tickets** 30F-80F. **No credit cards.**
The 120-seat Mandapa Centre is dedicated to traditional dance forms. Speciality companies from India, China, the Middle East, the Maghreb and Eastern Europe regularly visit this *avant-garde* hall. There is also a school dedicated to Indian Dance on the premises.

Maison de la Culture de Créteil
place Salvador Allende, 94000 Créteil (49.80.18.88, noon-7pm Tue-Sat). Metro Créteil-Préfecture. **Box office open** *by telephone:* in advance noon-6pm Mon-Fri; *in person:* noon-7pm Tue-Sat. **Tickets** 85F-110F. **No credit cards.**
See **picture and caption.**

The **Théatre Contemporain de la Danse** (listed under **Dance Venues**), which is intrumental in producing prominent new dance groups in venues throughout Paris, has a subscription service offering tickets at lower prices. Professional dancers who become members of CTD have access to a Dance Documentation Centre, which compiles information on modern dance, and free or discounted studio time.

Opéra de Paris
place de l'Opéra, 75009 Paris (47.42.57.50). Metro Opéra/bus 21, 22, 27, 29, 42, 52, 68, 81, 95. **Box office open** by telephone: noon-6pm Mon-Sat; in person: 11am-7pm Mon-Sat. **Tickets** 20F-300F. **Credit** FTC, V.
The glamourous Paris Opera building, designed by Charles Garnier in 1875, is one of the largest theatre venues in the world (11,000 sq m/118,404 sq ft). There is a complete slice-away maquette (model) of the amazingly ornate Second Empire edifice in the Musée d'Orsay (see chapter **Museums**), but anyone with an architectural gilt complex should make a personal pilgrimage to the glimmering Great Staircase. The immense stage has room for 450 players and the auditorium – under a ceiling painted by Marc Chagall – has 2,200 seats. Until the opening of the Bastille Opera (see chapter **Music: Classical**), Gisèle and Sleeping Beauty had to share their stage-space with Mimi and Aida. The Opéra dance company is as electryfing and dramatic as its director, Rudolf Nureyev, and prone to strike at the oddest times (for example, in 1989, the dancers marched off minutes before a benefit gala given for themselves). Furthermore, at the time of going to press, Nureyev has been temporarily suspended from his duties, for having missed the opening of the 1989-1990 season. The final outcome has yet to be decided. The Ballet has a summer season in the Louvre courtyard.

Théatre Contemporain de la Danse (CTD)
9 rue Geoffroy l'Asnier, 75004 Paris (42.74.44.22). Metro Pont Marie/bus 67, 69, 76, 96. **Box office open** by subscription: in advance; in person: from 24 rue Geoffroy l'Asnier, 75004 Paris **Tickets** prices vary. **No credit cards.**
See **picture and caption.**

Théatre de la Bastille
76 rue de la Roquette, 75011 Paris (43.57.42.14). Metro Bastille/bus 69. **Box office open** by telephone: in advance; in person: 30 minutes before performance. **Tickets** 90F; group discounts available. **No credit cards.**
A young, adventurous dance programme in the heart of the Paris club district. The theatre seats 250 people.

Théatre des Champs Elysées
15 avenue Montaigne, 75008 Paris (47.23.47.77). Metro Alma Marceau/bus 42, 80. **Box office open** by telephone: only three weeks in advance call 47.20.36.37.,2-6pm Mon-Fri; in person: 11am-7pm Mon-Sat. **Tickets** 40F-300F. **Credit** CB, V.
This elegant 1,900-seat theatre – located only a few doors from Dior, Valentino and Chanel – attracts a well-heeled, well-dressed crowd for the Bolshoi, the New York City Ballet and the Leningrad Ballet Theatre.

Théatre de la Ville
2 place du Châtelet, 75001 Paris (42.74.22.77). Metro Châtelet/bus 21, 58, 67, 69, 70, 72, 74, 75, 76, 81, 85. **Box office open** by telephone: 11am-6pm Mon, 9am-8pm Tue-Sat; in person: 11am-8pm Mon-Sat. **Tickets** 60F-175F. **No credit cards.**
This 1,000-seat theatre (restored and re-opened in 1980) presents the most consis-

tently pleasing programme of modern dance in town: Trisha Brown, Nederlands Dans Theater, Karine Saporta, Alwin Nikolais generally play here. However, this theatre also introduces new groups (like the daring ISO Dance, the latest off-shoot of MOMIX) at the less expensive, 6.30pm preview shows. The spring 1990 schedule includes the dancers Pina Bausch, danse-nouvelle partisan Dominique Bagouet, Jean-Claude Gallotta, Carolyn Carlson, and Belgium's Anna Teresa de Keersmaker. The theatre runs a subscription service, which, though handy for those living in Paris, is not such an invaluable service because individual tickets go on sale two weeks before performances anyway.

CLASSES & INFORMATION

Casta Diva
56-58 rue Vieille-du-Temple, 75003 Paris (42.72.63.49). Metro Saint Paul/bus 29. **Open** 11am-8pm daily. **Credit** AmEx, CB, DC, V.
This tiny shop specializes in hard-to-find classical dance and opera records, books and tapes.

Centre de Danse de Paris
252 rue Faubourg Saint Honoré, 75008 Paris (45.63.40.21). Metro Châtelet/bus 30, 73, 92. **Open** 8.45am-8pm mon-Sat. **No credit cards.**
The Centre holds classes in ballet and contemporary dance in the atmospheric studios above the Salle Pleyel concert hall, for beginnners and advanced students. Many of the professors are associated with the Paris Opera. Individual classes cost 65F; a subscription for ten ballet classes is 600F; modern or contemporary subscriptions are 500F.

Fédération Française de la Danse
12 rue Saint Germain l'Auxerrois, 75001 Paris (42.36.12.61). Metro Châtelet/bus 69, 72, 81. **Open** 9am-5.30pm Mon-Wed.
A tiny, non-profit making clearing house with information on classes, studio rentals, auditions, festivals and workshops throughout France. Telex Danse magazine is also an excellent source of information on master classes, auditions and dance festivals. It costs 90F per year subscription fee; write to the Federation for an application form to receive their publication.

Rock'n'roll Dance Centre
6 Impasse Levis, 75017 Paris (43.80.90.23). Metro Villiers/bus 30. **Open** 11am-11pm Mon-Thur; 11am-7pm Fri; 11am-6pm Sat. **No credit cards**
Everything you need to swing in Paris – classes in boogie, samba, tango, acrobatic rock, and even trapeze. They also teach juggling and high-wire circus stunts. A ten -class subscription costs 550F.

Stanlowa
250 rue du Faubourg Saint-Honoré, 75008 Paris (45.63.20.96). Metro Etoile. **Open** 10am-7pm Mon-Sat. **Credit** CB, V.
Shoes, practice wear and costumes for all dance disciplines can be purchased at this speciality shop.

Film

Film-buffs will think they died and went to heaven when visiting Paris; there's over 350 screens, showing blockbusters, arty movies and special retrospectives.

Despite the continuing vitality of cinema's 'official' predecessors – architecture, music, painting, sculpture, poetry and dance – a look at the plentiful listings in the capital's weekly entertainment guides might sway one into thinking 'the seventh art' really deserves top billing. For although doomsayers have been declaring for decades that there's a crisis in the cinema world and movie houses continue to close at an alarming rate, there still remain about 350 screens within the Paris city limits. Commercial cinemas alone offer some 275 different films each week. And that's without taking into account the remarkably varied programmes at the Cinémathèque and the Pompidou Centre, film projections at (despite its name) the Vidéothèque and special retrospectives at the many foreign cultural centres around town. In Paris you can see a different film every day of the year, and that's a boast few, if any, other cities can make.

FLIC THROUGH THE MAGS

Film programmes change on Wednesdays, which is when the weekly entertainment guides – available at any news-stand – come out. Among the most noteworthy publications is **L'Officiel des Spectacles**, which is neatly organized and costs only 2F. For those whose tastes run to specific genres ('I simply must see a Western tonight') **Pariscope** at 3F offers readers cinema listings by category as well as by arrondissements. If you can read French, you might want to try **7 à Paris** (cost 6F), a more comprehensive city magazine that includes articles of varying quality; the title is a pun on the aforementioned seven arts and, when pronounced in French, means 'What's on'.

WHAT TO X-PECT

Unless deliberately setting out to see a French feature, you'll probably want to pay special attention to

whether a given film is being presented in **VO** or **VF**. The previous, VO, stands for *version originale*, which means that the film is in the language in which it was made – be it English, Russian or Serbo-Croat – with French subtitles. VF, which stands for *version française*, tells viewers that the film has been dubbed into French. If, as is increasingly the case, a French-speaking director has made an English-language film, you may come across the designation VA (*version anglaise*).

Most cinemas list two show times for each presentation. The first, known as the *séance* (nothing to do with contacting the spirit world), consists of anything from 10 to 40 minutes of coming attractions and commercials. Theoretically, the house lights are to be only partially dimmed, leaving patrons the option of reading, knitting or otherwise ignoring the ads. However, if you've never seen topless women touting the Yellow Pages or simulated sex acts masquerading as publicity campaigns for beer, you may want to direct your attention to the screen. For recent hit films you'd best arrive for the *séance* to be assured of a good seat.

The ubiquitous usherette or *ouvreuse* – a position once filled chiefly by war widows and other unskilled women who survived on the tips they received – has, in recent years, given way to salaried personnel. The smartly uniformed employees of the major chains, for example Pathé, Gaumont, UGC, no longer expect a tip, but the ushers at art houses and a few first-run cinemas still rely entirely on your generosity. A minimum *pourboire* of 2F per person is polite.

Ticket prices range from 33F to 45F, with student and senior citizen discounts running roughly 10F cheaper. Student discounts (*réduction étudiant/tarif réduit*) are available at most venues during the week and at some over the weekend. Thanks to a policy

begun in 1980 everyone, city-wide, is entitled to a 30 per cent discount each Monday.

If you're planning to do a lot of mainstream filmgoing, you may want to invest in the magnetic debit cards offered by Pathé and UGC for exclusive use in their respective theatres. The rechargeable Pathé card, encoded with 10 admissions and valid for 18 months from initial use, works out at 28F per entry for you and as many friends as you care to take along. The UGC debit card, valid for 30 days and available in the form of four admissions for one person or six admissions for one or two people, offers similar savings and priority entry. Bargain matinées (20F to 24F) are offered at the Forum Horizon, Forum Orient Express and Gaumont Les Halles (all in the 1st arrondissement), Saint-Germain-des-Prés, Racine and 14 Juillet Odeon (all in the 6th arrondissement) and the George V and Triomphe (in the 8th).

If you're debating where to see the latest English-language blockbuster, opt for one of the following three cinemas: Max Linder Panorama (9th arrondissement), Kinopanorama (15th), or the THX *salle* at the Forum Horizon (1st). Barring that, you should get your money's worth on the Champs-Elysées where nearly all of the cinemas are respectably equipped and nicely maintained. Recommended are screens listed as *grande salle, salle prestige*, or *Gaumont Rama,* which guarantee a large screen, comfortable seating and high standards of projection and sound.

LAST RESPECTS

Die-hard film buffs can pay their last respects at the commemorative plaque that marks the spot where, on 28 December 1895, France's Lumière brothers held the world's first public film screening. The plaque is at at 14 boulevard des Capucines, 75001 Paris.

COMMERCIAL CINEMAS

Since you really can't go wrong on the Champs-Elysées, we've chosen to highlight individual cinemas in other parts of town. These are listed below by arrondissement.

1ST ARRONDISSEMENT

Forum Horizon
7 place de la Rotonde, Nouveau Forum des Halles, 75001 Paris (45.08.57.57). Metro Châtelet, Les-Halles/bus 58, 67, 69, 70, 72, 74, 76. **Tickets** 35F-45F/reduced 23F-39F; student reductions daily.
See **picture and caption.**
Air-conditioned. Wheelchair access.

2ND ARRONDISSEMENT

Le Grand Rex
boulevard Poissonière, 75002 Paris (42.36.83.93). Metro Bonne-Nouvelle/ bus 20, 39. **Tickets** 36F/reduced 28F; student reductions 1-5pm Tue-Fri.
Although there's an annoying propensity toward dubbed films at this venue, it's a magnificent setting and with 2,800 seats the Grand Rex is the city's largest cinema. An enormous screen, cushy seats and dreamy, movie palace décor – complete with projected clouds wafting across the star- sprinkled ceiling – make it unique. If the feature film is being presented in *Grand Large*, you'll have to forgo the comfortable stalls for the upper reaches of the balcony because the management has installed a colossal retractable screen that supersedes the proscenium screen and leaves something to be desired in the sharp-focus department. Late shows are on Friday and Saturday nights.
Air-conditioned. UGC debit card accepted. Wheelchair access.

5TH ARRONDISSEMENT

Accatone
20 rue Cujas, 75005 Paris (46.33.86.86). Metro Luxembourg, Cluny-La-Sorbonne/bus 21, 27, 38, 85. **Tickets** 34F/reduced 25F 6pm Mon-Fri.
Excellent repertory programming, with a distinct flair for otherwise unavailable Eastern Bloc films, distinguishes this mini-cultural centre with a small screen, 115 seats and Dolby stereo sound system. Polish director Krzysztof Zanussi, Hungary's Miklos Jancso and the UK's Derek Jarman have all put in appearances. A fine selection of specialized books, a modest exhibition space and a pleasant wine bar two doors down, round out the premises.

Action (Mini-chain)
This independent mini-chain, founded in 1967, prides itself on obtaining the negatives of terrific old movies and striking fresh prints. Their showpiece installation is the **Action Rive Gauche** with its panoramic screen, 240 comfortable seats and Dolby sound system. The Action's other screens (three in the 5th, four in the 6th and the Mac-Mahon in the 17th arrondissment) are on the small side. Action excels at theme retrospectives – Lubitsch, Hitchcock, Bogart, Garbo, the Marx Brothers, Billy Wilder, Woody Allen, Clint Eastwood, Jack Nicholson and so on – and frequently sells out, so arrive early. A free *carte de fidelité*, stamped each time you buy a ticket, entitles you to a sixth film free of charge for every five paid admissions. Founders Jean-Marie Rodon and Jean-Max Causse have almost flawless taste, compounded by the good sense to honour student ID cards seven days a week.

Action Ecoles
23 rue des Ecoles, 75005 Paris (43.25.72.07). Metro Maubert-Mutualité , Cardinal-Lemoine/bus 63, 86, 87. **Tickets** 35F/reduced 25F.

Action Rive Gauche
5 rue des Ecoles, 75005 Paris (43.29.44.40). Metro Cardinale-Lemoine/bus 63, 86, 87. **Tickets** 35F/reduced 25F.

Action Christine
4 rue Christine & 10 rue des Grands-Augustins, 75006 Paris (43.29.11.30). Metro Odéon, Saint-Michel/bus 24, 27. **Tickets** 35F/reduced 25F.

Le Champo
51 rue des Ecoles, 75005 Paris (43.54.51.60). Metro Odéon, Saint-Michel/bus 63, 86, 87. **Tickets** 35F/reduced 25F.
Truffaut, among others, has written of the happy hours he spent at this cinema that celebrated its 50th anniversary in 1989. It's been recently redecorated, and pays tribute to the French comic Jacques Tati. Two small but charming screen-rooms fill up fast for theme retrospectives: James Bond, Pier Paolo Pasolini, Jean Renoir, Sacha Guitry, Jacques Tati and so on.
Air-conditioned. Wheelchair access to street-level theatre.

Pantheon
13 rue Victor-Cousin, 75005 Paris (43.54.15.04). Metro Luxembourg/bus 21, 27, 38, 65. **Tickets** 34F/reduced 24F Mon-Fri.
A wonderful one-screen cinema with 229 seats, character-laden décor and a Dolby stereo system. The façade features the stylized outline of a film projector and the no-frills box office has its own unique charm. Although the Pantheon showed *Diva* for ages, it can now be relied upon to offer different current art films every few weeks.
Wheelchair access.

Studio Galande
42 rue Galande, 75005 Paris (43.54.72.71). Metro Saint-Michel/bus 24, 47. **Tickets** 35F/reduced 23F Mon-Wed.
For travellers who can't get along without their weekly dose of *The Rocky Horror Picture Show*, this valiant hole-in-the-wall institution, with 92 seats, keeps the tradition alive. You can catch the film from Thursday through to Sunday night, with an extra post-midnight show on Friday and Saturday evenings.

Studio des Ursulines
10 rue des Ursulines,75005 Paris (43.26.19.09). Metro Luxembourg, Port-Royal/bus 38, 82, 83, 91. **Tickets** 34F/reduced 25F Mon-Fri.
This, the city's oldest art house that opened on 21 January 1926, is still in operation as a cinema having taken time out over the years to be a legitimate stage. Small – it has only 150 seats – and dignified, it has an intimate lobby, comfortable armrests and a quaint balcony with excellent sightlines. It's known for its impeccable repertory programmes (*Last Tango in Paris, The Last Temptation of Christ, Blue Velvet*) and its faithful clientele.
Air-conditioned.

Comfort and quality projection are assured in the six-screen subterranean complex of **Forum Horizon** *(listed under* **Commercial Cinemas/1st Arrondissement***), making it the multiplex (apart from the Champs-Elysées) at which to see new releases. The* Grande Salle THX, *with 600 seats and the steepest admission price, is the showpiece of the bunch. An outstanding feature here is the discount for the first show of the day from 11.30am to 1pm, seven days a week. This means you can see the likes of* Lawrence of Arabia, Batman *or the latest James Bond film under ideal conditions for only 23F. Midnight shows are on Saturday night.*

6TH ARRONDISSEMENT

Action Christine
See above **Action** *under*
5th Arrondissement.

Le Bretagne
*73 boulevard Montparnasse, 75006 Paris
(42.22.57.97). Metro Montparnasse/bus 28,
48, 82, 83, 91, 92.* **Tickets** *40F/reduced
30F Mon-Fri.*
The *Grande Salle* – with 860 seats, a large
screen, Dolby stereo system and glow-in-
the-dark clocks – is a pleasant setting for
major releases, provided they're in VO.
The smaller theatre seems to have been
an afterthought.
Air-conditioned.

Cosmos
*76 rue de Renne, 75006 Paris (45.44.28.80).
Metro Saint-Sulpice/bus 48, 89, 95, 96.*
Tickets *33F/reduced 23F.*
A large, agreeably shabby and comfortable
one-screen cinema specializing in Soviet films.

Lucernaire Forum
*53 rue Nôtre-Dame-des-Champs, 75006
Paris (45.44.57.34). Metro Nôtre-Dame-
des-Champs/bus 48.* **Tickets** *34F/reduced
24F Mon-Fri.*
These three very small but acceptably
equipped screening rooms consistently
show excellent art films that have pretty
much exhausted their runs elsewhere. The
cinemas form just one part of the pleasant
arts complex; there are two theatres, a bar, a
restaurant and a gallery space.

Saint-André-des-Arts
*30 rue Saint-André-des-Arts, 75006 Paris
(43.26.48.18) & 12 rue Git-le-Coeur, 75006 Paris
(43.26.80.25). Metro Saint-Michel/bus 24, 27,
58, 65, 70.* **Tickets** *35F/reduced 25F Mon-Fri.*
The Saint-André complex is renowned for its
sensational programming – Wim Wenders,
Mike Leigh, Krzysztof Kieslowski – in
medium-sized theatres.
Wheelchair access to salle 2.

Saint-Germain-des-Prés
*place Saint-Germain-des-Prés, 75006 Paris
(42.22.87.23). Metro Saint-Germain-des-
Prés/bus 39, 48, 63, 95.* **Tickets**
34F/reduced 24F; bargain show at noon,
student reductions daily.
A dandy one-screen theatre with black walls,
conscientious programming (arty new
releases and arty re-releases) and a
respectable-size screen.

Les 3 Luxembourg
*67 rue Monsieur-le-Prince, 75006 Paris
(46.33.97.77). Metro Luxembourg,
Odéon/bus 21, 27, 38, 58, 85.* **Tickets**
33F/reduced 23F; student reductions daily.
It's often the case that the best programming is featured in some of the least
impressive *salles*. The three screens and
seating at Luxembourg border on the
totally clapped out, but the film selection is
so good, that you feel you've got to forgive
the management their failings on the cinema's comfort side. Claude Lanzmann's
Shoah played here, as did Marcel Ophuls'
Hotel Terminus. Cheerier fare has
included Frank Capra and François
Truffaut retrospectives. The cleverly
anchored multi-media collage on the
façade is worth spying out.

The **Pagode** *(listed under* **Commercial Cinemas/7th Arrondissement***) only
remaining cinema in the posh 7th arrondissement was built in 1896 as a private
ballroom for one of the directors of the nearby Bon Marché department store. The
basic framework and wooden ornamentation were imported from Japan and most
of the lavish glass and ceramic detailing was created by skilled decorators here in
Paris. The Pagode, a cinema since 1931, was declared a historical monument in
1982. The exotic main auditorium (listed as salle chinoise in the guides) is exquisite
inside and out, although the screen itself is not particularly large. The utilitarian
smaller screening room is distinguished only by the types of film shown.*

7TH ARRONDISSEMENT

La Pagode
*57 rue de Babylone, 75007 Paris
(47.05.12.15). Metro Saint-François
Xavier/bus 28, 49, 87.* **Tickets** *37F/
reduced 27F Mon-Fri.*
See **picture and caption.**
*Salon de thé (open 4pm-10pm Mon-Sat, 2pm-
8pm Sun). Wheelchair access to salle only.*

8TH ARRONDISSEMENT

Cinemas to watch out for are the
Gaumont Ambassade (*Gaumont
Rama*), the **George V**, the **Pathé
Marignan Concorde** and the
Publicis Elysées. The large theatre
at the **Balzac** – the only art house in
the vicinity– is also good.

UGC Ermitage
*72 Champs-Elysées, 75008 Paris
(45.63.16.16). Metro Franklin D Roosevelt/bus
32, 73, 92.* **Tickets** *38F/30F Mon.*
One of the three screening rooms (*salle prestige*) was completely redone in mid-1969 to
exacting SHOWSCAN specifications. This
means that in theory, at least, SHOWSCAN
films can be shown here at their full, glorious
best. To the uninitiated, the story behind
these type of movies goes thus. American
special effects wizard Douglas Trumbull – he
worked on *2001: A Space Odyssey, Close
Encounters of the Third Kind* – found that
film, when shot and projected back at 60
frames per second (two and a half times the
conventional sound speed of 24 fps), completely satisfied the brain's appetite for information, because the screen 'disappeared' and
the viewer was drawn into motion pictures of
astonishing realism. The hitch is that, thus
far, no feature has been made in the new format and there are only a handful of SHOWS-
CAN shorts. Other UGC screen that we
highly recommend are the *grandes salles* of
the **UGC Normandie** and **UGC Biarritz**.

9TH ARRONDISSEMENT

Max Linder Panorama
*24 boulevard Poissonnière, 75009 Paris
(48.24.88.88). Metro Rue Montmartre,
Bonne Nouvelle/bus 20, 39, 48.* **Tickets**
40F/reduced 30F Mon-Fri.
See **picture and caption.**
Air conditioned. Wheelchair access.

11TH ARRONDISSEMENT

Republic Cinemas
*18 faubourg du Temple, 75011 Paris
(48.05.51.33). Metro République/bus 75.*
Tickets 34F/reduced 25F daily.
A slightly down-at-heel, 200-capacity theatre
with very comfortable seats and fine repertory programming that runs the gamut from
Nosferatu to Tex Avery.

13TH ARRONDISSEMENT

Escurial Panorama
*11 boulevard du Port-Royal, 75013 Paris
(47.07.28.04). Metro Gobelins/bus 83, 91.*
Tickets 37F/reduced 26F Mon-Fri.
The ultimate in kitsch; red velveteen seats, a
spiffy lobby with brass and neon trim and swell
portraits of the stars adorning the walls. The

very large screen – don't sit too close – would be perfect if only the image were a bit sharper edge-to-edge. No complaints about the sound or the selective first-run programming.
Wheelchair access to the main theatre.

14TH ARRONDISSEMENT

Apart from the two cinemas listed below, we recommend a trip to the *Gaumont Rama salles* of the **Gaumont Alesia** (73 avenue du Général-Leclerc, 75014), which sometimes show films in VO, and the **Gaumont Parnasse** (82 boulevard du Montparnasse, 75014), which always show films in VO.

Denfert
24 place Denfert-Rochereau, 75014 Paris (43.21.41.01). Metro Denfert-Rochereau/bus 38, 68. **Tickets** 34F/reduced 25F daily.
The Denfert is a valiant little place – 120 seats – with outstanding repertory programming that seems to include all the films you've always meant to see but haven't got around to yet. Past films include vintage Chaplin, Buñuel and Lang to Welles, Kubrick and Greenaway.
Wheelchair access.

L'Entrepot
7-9 rue Francis de Pressensé, 75014 Paris (45.43.41.63). Metro Pernety/bus 58.
Tickets 32F/reduced 24F daily; block of 10 tickets 240F.
This cinema has three bare screening rooms, each with 100 seats and excellent optics. The management puts on terrific and often exclusive art house fare, including thorough retrospectives along the lines of Alan Rudolph, Marguerite Duras and Krzysztof Kieslowski. The Entrepot (French for warehouse) is a multi-media treasure trove with cable and satellite television reception, video conference facilities, a wonderful specialized bookshop and an attractive restaurant and bar complete with video monitors that are tuned in to a wide variety of international broadcasts. A successful blend of hi-tech decor and intimate atmosphere.
Air-conditioned. Restaurant (open noon-midnight daily). Shop (open 2-8pm Mon-Sat). Wheelchair access to salle 1.

15TH ARRONDISSEMENT

Le Grand Pavois
364 rue Lecourbe, 75015 Paris (45.54.46.85). Metro Balard/bus 42.
Tickets 35F/reduced 25F Mon-Fri.
Le Grand Pavois (listed under Commercial Cinemas/15th Arrondissement) has two cosy salles – the Tribord, with 130 seats, and the Babord, with 160 – each outfitted with a very wide, if somewhat shallow, curved screen and a crisp sound system. This venue specializes in a blend of art and mainstream films that have been around for a while, such as Bladerunner, The Name of the Rose, The Last Emperor, E.T., Dune. Shows are generally in VO unless the session is aimed at children.

Kinopanorama
60 avenue de La Motte-Picquet, 75015 Paris (43.06.50.50). Metro La Motte-Picquet-Grenelle/bus 80. **Tickets** 40F/reduced 30F

Mon-Fri, last two shows Sun.
A splendid and extremely popular establishment with a huge curved screen, 70mm projection and Dolby stereo six-track sound. There are 620 seats; tickets for 250 of them can be purchased up to three days in advance for each show. The orchestra seats that are straight ahead as you enter the auditorium, are more comfortable than the normal stalls, but the balcony, which is to your left, is a superior vantage point. Posters over the doors commemorate the theatre's 'greatest successes', including *West Side Story*, *Gone With the Wind, 2001: A Space Odyssey*, and *Lawrence of Arabia*.
Air-conditioned. Wheelchair access.

Saint-Lambert
6 rue Péclet, 75015 Paris (45.32.91.68/ 48.28.78.87). Metro Vaugirard/bus 39, 49, 70, 80. **Tickets** 30F/reduced 20F Mon-Fri (including under-18s).
A family-run local cinema that could easily bring a tear to the eye of any traveller who comes from a place where such charming venues no longer exist. It's strictly second-run and repertory, consisting of children's films interspersed with adult sessions such as *Amarcord, Kiss of the Spider Woman, and Patti Rocks*. This is the only place in town that thinks children should pay less than adults.
Wheelchair access to the main floor theatre.

16TH ARRONDISSEMENT

Ranelagh
5 rue de Vignes, 75016 Paris (42.88.64.44). Metro Muette/bus 22, 52. **Tickets** 35F/reduced 25F Mon-Fri.
This building, that houses the only remaining cinema in the well-to-do 16th arrondissement, dates from 1890. It's daintily elegant and, in keeping with the seizième image, shows the likes of Marcel Carné's *Children of Paradise* or a classic of similar vintage. The cinema also hosts plays and the occasional concert.
Wheelchair access.

17TH ARRONDISSEMENT

Mac-Mahon
5 avenue Mac-Mahon, 75017 Paris (43.29.79.89). Metro Etoile/bus 92. **Tickets** 35F/reduced 25F.
The Mac-Mahon, a very quaint local cinema with 200 seats, celebrated its fiftieth anniversary in 1989. Staff here seem to be part of the furniture: the curious Madame Odile has been seating patrons for 50 years, while Monsieur Jean has been working as the cinema projectionist since 1959. This venue forms part of the **Action** mini-chain (*see above* **5th Arrondissement**). Although the wonderful auditorium, with concealed video facilities, is used for private screenings

Founded in 1919 by Chaplin's idol, the great French comic Max Linder, the **Max Linder Panorama** (*listed under* **Commercial Cinemas/9th Arrondissement**) *was gutted and re-opened in late 1987 as a magnificent state-of-the-art screening facility. This is the only cinema in this part of town that has a VO policy. It also has a trendy lobby complete with refreshment bar, a colossal screen, textured black walls, plush seating, exacting projection standards and THX sound. Hint: the first row on the mezzanine level is the ideal vantage point, and either balcony is preferable to the main floor. You can reserve your seat up to one week in advance. You'd have to be crazy to see a film somewhere else if it was playing at the Max Linder.*

during the week, it does show choice revivals at the weekend. Student cards are always honoured when used to get a reduction in the admission price.

18TH ARRONDISSEMENT
Studio 28
10 rue Tholozé, 75018 Paris (46.06.36.07). Metro Abesses, Blanche/bus 30, 54. **Tickets** 26F/reduced 21F Wed-Fri; block of five tickets 100F (valid 2 months).

Founded in its namesake year of 1928, the Studio was later described by the infamous Jean Cocteau as 'a masterpiece of theatres, the theatre of masterpiece'. This unique venue was torn apart by a scandalized public when Salvador Dali and Luis Buñuel's *L'Age d'Or* premièred here in 1930. The film was then banned in the name of public order, and was not officially released again in Paris until 1981. This family-run enterprise features a different, recent film every two days that is always shown in VO. In honour of Studio 28's sixtieth anniversary, the lobby was redecorated by veteran art director Alexandre Trauner. If you have to wait when you go to see a film, hang around at the quaint bar or in the small courtyard garden before being allowed into the auditorium. Check out the kitsch wall sconces in the theatre itself. This is the only VO cinema in the 18th arrondissement and the least expensive place in town. It's closed on Mondays and Tuesdays, and during most of August.

19TH ARRONDISSEMENT
La Géode
26 avenue Corentin-Cariou, 75019 Paris (42.46.13.13). Metro Porte de la Villette/bus 150, 152, PC. **Tickets** 40F/reduced 30F Tue-Fri.

This, the city's only OMNIMAX cinema, is housed in a glorious geodesic dome that's covered with hundreds of triangular reflective panels. You can see the impressive projectors that handle the 70mm film, which is shot and projected horizontally, as you pass the projection booth on your way out. Hourly shows from run from 10am to 9pm Tuesday through to Sunday. It's advisable to book; reservations are accepted. Furthermore, it's possible to buy a combination ticket for the film and the adjacent Science and Industry Museum. In autumn of each odd-numbered year, the Géode plans to host an international festival of films produced in this eye-popping format. Another OMNIMAX screen is planned for La Défense. *Wheelchair access.*

REPERTORY
La Cinémathèque Française
Palais de Chaillot, place de Trocadéro (avenue Albert de Mun & avenue du Président Wilson), 75016 Paris (47.04.24.24). Metro Trocadéro/bus 32, 63. **Tickets** 20F/members 12F.

Founded in 1936 by film fanatics Georges Franju and Henri Langlois, the Cinémathèque is where the members of the French New Wave got their education. Langlois (1914-1977) believed that every film had the potential to be a masterpiece and therefore col-

lected *everything,* lest some as yet unappreciated gem got away. He also believed that films should be shown, not carefully preserved for the musty musings of scholars. The 400-seat theatre that Langlois designed in the basement of the left-hand wing of the Palais de Chaillot, has a large screen and was recently equipped with a Dolby stereo sound system. Three or four different films are shown from Tuesday through to Sunday; information on these can be obtained from the box office. The clientele ranges from rabid *cinéphiles* debating the true identity of the second assistant director of some obscure Hungarian silent film to ordinary folk who've wandered in off the street. Due to administrative squabbling and money woes, plans to open additional theatres a few blocks away at the Palais de Tokyo have been postponed until 1993 when the Cinémathèque's outstanding film reference library and still photo collection will be housed under one roof.

Musée du Cinéma-Henri Langlois
Palais de Chaillot, 75016 Paris (45.53.74.39). Metro Trocadéro/bus 22, 30, 32, 63. **Admission** 20F.

Salle Garance
Centre Pompidou, 75004 Paris (42.78.37.29). Metro Rambuteau, Hotel de Ville/bus 38, 47, 75. **Tickets** 20F.

The box office is to the rear of the Pompidou Centre and the theatre itself, which hosts excellent comprehensive retrospectives at a reasonable price, is two flights up. This is also the site of the annual ethnographic film festival *Cinéma du Réel*.

Vidéothèque de Paris
2 Grand Galerie: Porte Saint-Eustache, Forum des Halles, 75001 Paris (40.26.34.30). Metro Châtelet-Les-Halles/bus 58, 67, 69, 70, 72, 74, 85. **Tickets** 18F per day; membership available.

For 18F you can stay as long as you like at the Vidéothèque de Paris. Opened in 1988 as a public archive of film and video documents on Paris, there are video consoles for research. The screening rooms are impeccable, if a little sterile, with each room being named after the number of seats it contains. Salle 300 is the most popular. When a film features some aspect of Paris – such as in the Eiffel Tower scene in Superman II or the letter of introduction scene in Babette's Feast – the chances are that the Vidéothèque already has it or is planning to get it, no matter how brief the relevant clip. There's a hi-tech café on the premises.

*Anyone even remotely interested in film history will be delighted by Langlois' brilliantly eclectic vision of the evolution of moving images at the **Musée du Cinéma** (listed under **Repertory**). This is illustrated by means of a peerless collection of cinemabilia, including costumes, posters, set designs and props from all over the world; the designers of London's Museum of the Moving Image took their inspiration from Langlois' museum. Guided tours (in French) are at 10am, 11am, 2pm, 3pm and 4pm, and last approximately 90 minutes.*

Gay & Lesbian

The best places to meet up, where to shop and who to contact when you're in town - the comprehensive guide to gay life in Paris.

There is no longer a proper gay 'community' in Paris. In the last decade, gays and lesbians have integrated so succesfully into public life that there are no longer easily identifiable gay areas in the city. However, not so long ago in the seventies, there was a recognised gay district in Saint Germain on the Left Bank; in the early eighties the gay community moved to the Marais on the Right Bank. Today, wander through public spaces everywhere and you'll see that gays are mixing in with the rest of Paris's residents. The pressure is off. There's no longer the need to be self-sufficient. It's believed that out of the 100,000 gays living in central Paris, only 5,000 of them visit Paris's gay areas on a regular basis.

This chapter should help you find those places that are frequented by members of the gay community. In the reviews take the term 'mixed crowds' to mean places that are used by both straight and gay people.

INFORMATION

Gay Switchboard
3bis rue Clairaut, 75017 Paris (46.27.49.36). Metro La Fourche.
Open 10am-midnight daily.
Run by a gay Christian organization, the Centre du Christ Libérateur (CCL for short) provides counselling. Basic, non-specialized information for gay men and women is also available.

RHIF
(46.30.93.91). **Open** 8-10pm daily.
Phone the RHIF for free legal advice and information.

Aids Helpline
(47.70.98.99). **Open** 7-11pm daily.
This organization specialises in counselling and gives direct support to PWAs (People With Aids). It also helps with research and distributes basic information to the public.

MIEL (Mouvement d'Information et d'Expression des Lesbiennes)
(43.79.61.91). **Open** recorded information line.
A general information line, giving details of current activities for women in Paris.

PRESS & CONTACTS

The magazines listed below are widely distributed and are available at most newsstands throughout the country. They're also on sale at the gay bookshop **Les Mots à la Bouche** (*see below* Shopping).

Lesbia
Monthly; price 19F.
Put together by a band of volunteers, this monthly magazine writes about lesbian life in France. Reminiscent of Spare Rib, it has something of a militant spirit about it.

Gai Pied Hebdo
Weekly (from Friday); price 20F.
Established ten years ago, this 84-page weekly gay news publication is the main magazine for gays in France. There's a national and international news section, features, reports, stories, consumer advice, an arts section, plus ten pages of personal ads. Gai Pied also produce an annual guide to gay life in France, Switzerland and Belgium price 40F. It comes out in June and is available every summer from newsagents and major bookshops, and throughout the year at Les Mots à la Bouche (*see below* Shopping); by post from *Gai Pied, 45 rue Sedaine, 75011 Paris (43.57.52.05).*

Gay Info
Monthly; price 10F.
A monthly gay news magazine: reports, fiction, consumer guide, arts section.

Minitel
Minitel is an interactive information service pioneered by French Telecom, the state-owned phone company. All telephone customers are issued with a special computer, through which they have access to hundreds of services (hotel reservations, train timetable information, electronic telephone directory and so on), including dozens of 'dating' services. This tremendously popular dating system costs 60F per hour. Unfortunately, because of the cost and limited interest, very few public Minitel systems (in hotels, libraries, town halls and so on) carry these contact services. Should you have access to a private Minitel and want more information on these dating lines, contact Gai Pied Hebdo (*see above*).

Telephone contact lines
A few gay groups and party lines are available on any phone: callers join an open line and are free to strike up conversation, exchange information or just listen. It costs from 1F to 3F per unit (a unit lasting about three minutes). The most popular numbers are: *36.65.38.38, 36.65.75.55* and *49.09.90.90.* These lines are only available from Paris and the suburbs.

SHOPPING

BOOKS

Les Mots à la Bouche
6 rue Sainte Croix de la Bretonnerie, 75004 Paris (42.78.88.30). Metro Hôtel de Ville.
Open 11am-8pm Mon-Sat. **Credit** MC, V.
Paris's main gay bookshop has an extensive choice of gay literature from around the world, including most of the international gay magazines, and a wide range of art books and postcards. There's also an exhibition gallery.

La Librairie des Femmes
74 rue de Seine, 75006 Paris (43.29.50.75). Metro Odéon. **Open** 10am-7pm Mon-Sat. **Credit** AmEx, MC, V.
A large bookshop that specialises in general books for women, including subjects that are of particular interest to lesbians. *Lesbia* is the leading magazine.

SEX SHOPS

A rapidly expanding industry, Paris's sex shops usually have videos – cost approximately 800F, although some from 100F – magazines, cards, calendars and accessories for sale.

French Art
64 rue de Rome, 75008 Paris (45.22.57.35). Metro Europe. **Open** 10am-7pm Mon-Sat.
No credit cards.
A large video shop, stocking all of producer Jean-Daniel Cadinot's films and hundreds of others, priced 190F to 550F.

IEM
208 rue Saint Maur, 75010 Paris (42.41.21.41). Metro Goncourt. **Open** noon-7.30pm Mon-Sat; 2-7.30pm Sun. **No credit cards.**
See **picture and caption.**
Branches: 4 rue Bailleul, 75001 (42.96.05.74); 33 rue de Liège, 75008 (45.26.69.01).

BARS AND CAFES

The majority of Parisian bars are fairly welcoming. You won't get hassled if you're by yourself; on the

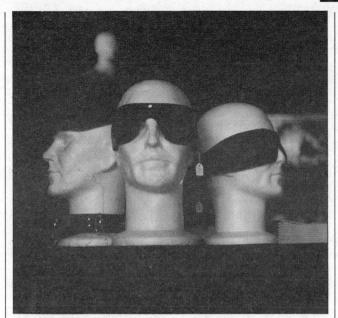

*Rather like a supermarket, at 3,000 square metres (32,280 square feet), this particular branch of **IEM** (listed under **Shopping/Sex Shops**) claims to be the biggest sex-shop in France. Videos, magazines, rubber and leather gear can all be bought here. All clothes and equipment can be altered and individual commissions are accepted.*

contrary, Parisians are quite keen on making contact with foreigners and trying out their English. The bars listed below are not expensive. Drinks such as coffee and draught beer usually have a fixed price, though expect to pay more if you sit at a table as opposed to merely standing at the bar. During the summer it costs extra to sit outside. After 10pm some bars and cafés charge more for all drinks sold. All establishements must display a price list. Don't be embarrassed about asking how much something costs before ordering; it's usual practice.

Bar Le Central
33 rue Vieille-du-Temple, 75004 Paris (42.78.11.42). Metro Hôtel de Ville. **Open** 4pm-2am daily. **Credit** MC, V.
This is one of the oldest bars of the gay Marais. At one time this place was mainly used by macho men, but a change in the music two years ago has made this bar more accessible to a younger, more relaxed crowd.

Broad-side
13 rue de la Ferronnerie, 75001 Paris (42.33.35.31). Metro Les Halles. **Open** 11.30am-3am Mon-Sat; 2.30pm-3am Sun. **Credit** MC, V.

This central, trendy bar lends itself to late afternoon meetings. It's a little on the expensive side (coffee 10F).

Café Moustache
138 rue du Faubourg Saint Martin, 75010 Paris (no phone). Metro Gare de l'Est. **Open** 4pm-11pm Mon-Thur; 4pm-1am Fri-Sun. **Credit** MC, V.
Moustaches are favoured in this friendly local bar.

Coffee-Shop Central
3 rue Sainte Croix de la Bretonnerie, 75004 Paris (42.74.71.52). Metro Hôtel de Ville. **Open** noon-midnight daily. **Credit** MC, V.
A nice little place for tea or coffee and a bite to eat (alcohol is served with meals only). Choose from mixed salads or a set two-course menu, then relax at the bistro-like, marble-topped tables.

Le Duplex
25 rue Michel le Comte, 75003 Paris (42.72.80.86). Metro Rambuteau. **Open** 8pm-2am daily. **No credit cards.**
The Duplex is a warm little bar that thankfully never gets too crowded and is populated with chatty, faithful regulars. Avant-garde exhibitions are held regularly.

H2O
50 rue Godefroy Cavaignac, 75011 Paris (40.09.90.92). Metro Voltaire. **Open** 8pm-2am daily. **Credit** MC, V.
A trendy bar on the edge of the Bastille area. The main speciality is cocktails, although

there's a good range of beers (from 20F). The interior is decked out in fake fifties' décor; plastic and metal.

Hollywood Bar
12 rue du Plâtre, 75004 Paris (48.87.58.18). Metro Rambuteau. **Open** 4pm-2am daily. **No credit cards.**
Jeans and moustache clones predominate here. Small and crowded.

Le Keller
14 rue Keller, 75011 Paris (47.00.05.39). Metro Bastille. **Open** 10pm-2am daily. **Credit** MC, V.
The Keller is most notable for its pool table, not commonly found in Parisian bars. Welcoming regulars wear leather.

Objectif Lune
19 rue de la Roquette, 75011 Paris (48.06.46.05). Metro Bastille. **Open** 6pm-2am daily. **Credit** MC, V.
There's lots of chrome and house music in this trendy fashionable place close to the new Bastille Opera House.

Le Piano Zinc
49 rue des Blancs-Manteaux, 75004 Paris (42.74.32.42). Metro Hôtel de Ville. **Open** 6pm-2am Tue-Sun. **Admission** 40F Fri, Sat. **Credit** MC, V.
Two bars and a stage on three floors make this bar somewhat unique. The nightly entertainment, which includes cabaret, is very popular and there's a terrific atmosphere, helped by the fact that staff and customers are welcome to take the microphone and do a turn on stage. Mixed crowd.

Le Quetzal
10 rue de la Verrerie, 75004 Paris (48.87.99.07). Metro Hôtel de Ville. **Open** noon-2am Mon-Fri; 2pm-2am Sat, Sun. **No credit cards.**
The famous and lively Le Quetzal is a large, crowded bar, with videos and loud, chart music. Hugely popular.

Le Swing
42 rue Vieille-du-Temple, 75004 Paris (42.72.16.94). Metro Hôtel de Ville. **Open** noon-2am daily. **No credit cards.**
See **picture and caption.**

Le Transfert
3 rue de La Soudière, 75001 Paris (42.60.48.42). Metro Tuileries, Pyramides. **Open** 11pm-5am daily. **Credit** V.
Leather-clad dress code is the norm here.

The Trap
10 rue Jacob, 75006 Paris (43.54.53.53). Metro Saint-Germain-des-Prés. **Open** 11pm-4am daily. **Admission** 50F. **No credit cards.**
The bar is on the ground floor. An elaborate iron staircase leads to the busy, dark and cruisey first floor. A door policy operates; bouncers can be quite choosy but friendly, if you're not too pushy.

RESTAURANTS

We don't have to re-emphasize how much the French like to socialize around a table. While the

English will cement a recent friendship in a pub, it's common for the French to eat out together almost immediately after meeting. The following restaurants are run mostly by gay people, although the clientele is made up of a mixed crowd. However, **Au Mauvais Garçons, Fond de Cour** and **Le Petit Prince** cater specifically for gay diners.

Average prices listed below are based on the price of a starter, a main course and dessert, but do not include drink.

L'Amazonial
3 rue Sainte Opportune, 75001 Paris (42.33.53.13). Metro Châtelet, Les Halles. Open noon-3pm, 7pm-1am, Mon-Fri; 7pm-1am Sat, Sun. **Average** 150F; set menus 80F-160F. **Credit** AmEx, DC, MC, V.
A very lively 120-seat restaurant with a mock-tropical décor. The cuisine is inventive classical French, with a smattering of Brazilian dishes. All the patisserie is made on the premises. People often come here after a show.

L'Ange Heurtebise
2 rue de la Verrerie, 75004 Paris (42.72.41.88). Metro Hôtel de Ville. Open 8pm-1am Tue-Sun. **Average** 250F. **Credit** AmEx, MC, V.
Decorated rather like a chocolate box in hues of blue and pink, L'Ange Heurtebise opened in May 1989. Classical French recipes with a twist form the basis of the menu here; salmon and trout feature heavily, and there's a smattering of meat dishes. Seats 60; bookings recommended.

Aux Mauvais Garçons
4 rue des Mauvais Garçons, 75004 Paris (48.87.96.98). Metro Hôtel de Ville. Open noon-11.30pm Tue-Sat; 7-11.30pm Sun. **Set menu** 90F. **Credit** AmEx, MC, V.
A cosy, relaxed atmosphere prevails at this restaurant – despite the rather overpowering salmon pink colour scheme – partly because it only seats 60 people. The food is traditional French *cuisine bourgeoise*.

Au Rendez-Vous des Camionneurs
72 quai des Orfèvres, 75001 Paris (43.54.88.74). Metro Pont-Neuf. Open noon-2pm, 8pm-11pm, Mon-Fri. **Average** 120F. **Credit** MC, V.
Traditional French cuisine served in a small, family-run restaurant. Booking is recommended.

L'Aviatic
23 rue Sainte Croix de la Bretonnerie, 75004 Paris (42.78.26.20). Metro Hôtel de Ville. Open noon-2am daily. **Average** 180F. **Credit** AmEx, MC, V.
L'Aviatic mixes hi-tech metallic décor with an American-influenced menu; burgers, mixed salads and ice-cream. Fashionable, but slightly expensive.

Le Beautreillis
18 rue Beautreillis, 75004 Paris (42.72.36.04). Metro Bastille, Saint Paul.

Open noon-2.30pm, 7.30-11pm, Mon-Sat. **Average** 130F; set menus 50F, 90F. **Credit** AmEx, MC, V.
Oak-panelled walls and wooden tables and chairs convey a rustic atmosphere to this unpretentious and simple restaurant. The 50F set menu might feature salad with warm goats' cheese, poached fish and home-made cakes.

La Bergerie
20 rue Beautreillis, 75004 Paris (42.72.05.84). Metro Bastille, Saint Paul. Open noon-2.30pm, 7pm-3am, daily. **Average** 150F; set menu 80F. **No credit cards.**
Regulars of this popular, rustic restaurant appreciate classic French cuisine; boeuf bourguignon and veal with tarragon sauce often feature on the menu.

Caviar and Co
5 rue de Reuilly, 75012 Paris (43.56.13.98). Metro Faidherbe-Chaligny. Open noon-2pm, 7.30pm-midnight, Mon-Fri; 7.30pm-midnight Sat, Sun. **Average** 180F; set menu 80F. **Credit** AmEx, MC, V.
Caviar, *foie gras* and smoked salmon are, not surprisingly, served here by friendly staff. English is spoken.

L'Equinox
47 rue Rochechouart, 75009 Paris (40.16.98.60). Metro Cadet, Anvers. Open noon-2.30pm, 7pm-11pm, Mon-Wed; 7pm-midnight Thur-Sat. **Average** lunch set menu only, 60F; average dinner 150F. **Credit** MC, V.
Innovative and ambitious cuisine based on traditional recipes, served in new-tech surroundings.

Fond de Cour
3 rue Sainte Croix de la Bretonnerie, 75004 Paris (42.74.71.52). Metro Hôtel de Ville. Open noon-2pm, 8-11.30pm, Mon-Fri; 8-11.30pm Sat. **Average** 250F; set menu *lunch:* 90F, 130F; *dinner:* 160F, 300F (5 courses). **Credit** MC, V.
Part of this charming, but expensive restaurant is set in a courtyard. The menu changes every month. Sophisticated cuisine (*croquant de saumon fumé, cuisse de lapereau au thym*) and elegant décor make this a good choice for special occasions.

Le Pierrot de la Butte
41 rue de Caulaincourt, 75018 Paris (46.06.06.97). Metro Place de Clichy, Lamarck-Caulaincourt. Open noon-2pm, 7.30-11.30pm, Mon-Sat. **Average** 180F; set menu *lunch:* 60F; *dinner:* 90F. **Credit** MC, V.
Popular with local theatre-goers as an after-show venue, this restaurant with a pink-and-black décor serves TFC (traditional French cuisine).

Le Remedium
11 rue Rodier, 75009 Paris (48.78.27.80). Metro Nôtre Dame de Lorette, Anvers. Open 7pm-midnight Mon-Sat. **Average** 190F; set menu 130F. **Credit** MC, V.
Polish and Russian specialities are served at this pleasant little restaurant. Examples of slavic cuisine include smoked fish and goulash; and vodka is available. Guitar-playing by the owner is not unheard of here. The cosmopolitan staff speak most European languages, except Italian.

Le Swing (*listed under* **Bars & Cafés**) *is a small bar, decorated with a touch of fifties' style. There's a young, mixed, hard-drinking crowd (no food is served) and lots of atmosphere.*

Vision Quai
*1 rue de Poissy, 75005 Paris (43.26.37.28).
Metro Maubert-Mutualité, Cardinal
Lemoine.* **Open** 7.30pm-midnight Mon-Sat;
noon-4pm, 7.30pm-midnight, Sun. **Average**
180F; set menu 110F, 160F. **Credit** MC, V.
Specialities from south-western France, such
as succulent *foie-gras*, are a main feature
here, although smoked salmon is also
served. The large, white-walled room (which
seats 40) lends itself perfectly to the exhibitions that are held on the premises on a regular basis. *See also* **picture and caption.**

Xica da Silva
*47 rue des Batignolles, 75017 Paris
(42.93.22.98). Metro Rome, Place de Clichy.*
Open 5pm-2am Mon-Sat. **Average** 200F.
Credit AmEx, MC, V.
If you should tire of French cuisine, Xica
da Silva specializes in Brazilian cuisine in a
décor to match: plastic palm trees and
fruit, and strings of different coloured
lightbulbs. The attached bar draws customers as much as the food does. There is
occasional late-night cabaret.

CLUBS &
DISCOS

Most of the clubs and discos listed
below are rather small and situated in converted basement cellars – a restriction imposed by the
size of Parisian buildings. Music
doesn't get given high priority in
most clubs; sound systems are
often not as refined or impressive
as in Britain. The admission
charge always includes one drink.

Le BH
*7 rue du Roule, 75001 Paris (no phone).
Metro Louvre, Châtelet, Les Halles.* **Open**
11pm-7am daily. **Admission** free Mon-Thur,
Sun; 30F Fri, Sat. **Credit** MC, V.
It's impossible to categorize the sort of
person who comes here; the clientele are
a very mixed bunch. The crowd-puller is
the frenetic dance music, which makes
up for the rather insignificant décor. Very
busy and cruisey at weekends, this place
shouldn't be missed if you enjoy a variety
of cultures.

Le Boy
*6 rue de Caumartin, 75009 Paris
(47.42.68.05). Metro Madeleine, Havre-
Caumartin, Opéra.* **Open** from 11pm-6.30am
daily. **Admission** free Mon-Thur, Sun; 60F
Fri, Sat. **Credit**, MC, V.
A young and lively mixed crowd dance
at this newly opened disco. At the forefront of the Parisian gay night scene and
hot on House (although there's a seventies' night on Monday), this club is
probably the most talked about venue at
the moment.

Broad Connection
*3 rue de la Ferronnerie, 75001 Paris
(42.33.93.08). Metro Châtelet, Les Halles.* **Open**
11pm-7am Wed-Sun. **Admission** free Wed,
Thur, Sun; 50F Fri, Sat. **Credit** AmEx, MC, V.
Two bars, a small dance floor and domed
ceilings make up this disco for the young
and trendy.

Le Club
*14 rue Saint Denis, 75001 Paris
(45.08.96.25). Metro Châtelet.* **Open** from
11.30pm-6am daily. **Admission** free Mon-
Thur, Sun; 50F Fri, Sat. **Credit** MC, V.
Especially popular among teenagers, the
majority of Le Club's clientele are adolescent
boys, although girls are admitted. Predictably,
chart hits are played in dark, mirrored rooms
with rather basic flashing lights.

Gay Tea Dance at Le Palace
*8 rue du Faubourg Montmartre, 75009 Paris
(42.46.10.87). Metro Rue Montmartre.*
Open 5-11pm Sun. **Admission** 60F.
Credit AmEx, MC, V.
Paris's oldest gay disco is located in an old
converted theatre, which dates from the
twenties.: it's now a listed building. The
Sunday afternoon gay tea dance has been
going for ten years now and is still *the* event
of the week. Sweat, muscles and pretty
faces. Not to be missed.

La Luna
*28 rue Keller, 75011 Paris (40.21.09.91).
Metro Bastille.* **Open** 11pm-late Wed-Sun.
Admission free Wed-Thur, Sun; 50F Fri, Sat.
Credit MC, V.
Growing success for this new club, popular
as a starting point for the evening.

Scorpion 4
*25 boulevard Poissonnière, 75002 Paris (no
phone). Metro Richelieu-Drouot, Montmartre.*
Open 11pm-5am daily. **Admission** free
Mon-Thur, Sun; 50F Fri, Sat. **Credit** MC, V.
A men's club linked to the lesbian club of the
same name (*see below* **Women**). The clientele here is extremely varied – leather fans,
transsexuals, young and old, and women. A
cabaret show is performed every night.

SAUNAS

All establishments listed below are
for men aged over 18. For more
information on women's health centres and saunas, *see chapter* **Sport.**

Continental Opéra
*32 rue Louis-le-Grand, 75002 Paris
(42.66.37.24). Metro Opéra.* **Open** noon-2am
daily. **Admission** 100F before 10pm; 60F after
10pm; 60F under-26s at all times. **Credit** MC, V.
This lavish centre is decorated with pseudo-
greek mosaics and includes a hammam
(Turkish bath), a sauna, a swimming pool, a
gym, a solarium, a bar, a restaurant, shops
and video screens.

Euro Men's Club
*8-10 rue Saint Marc, 75002 Paris
(42.33.92.63). Metro Rue Montmartre,
Bourse.* **Open** noon-11pm Mon-Sat; 1-
11pm Sun. **Admission** 90F; 55F under-
26s. **No credit cards.**

On the banks of the River Seine, **Vision Quai** *(listed under* **Restaurants***) is a
rather special place with excellent food and a relaxed atmosphere. Jean-Philippe, the
English-speaking owner, often welcomes cutomers personally and quite obviously
cares about detail.*

Wander along the Jardin des Tuileries to the **Terrasse du Bord de L'Eau** *(listed under* **Summer Specials***) and take in the sights: a fantastic park and a medley of people promenading along the famous terrasse. In the summer, this is probably the most popular place to meet up.*

Popular with men of all ages; regulars are aged 18 to 70 years old. There are three floors; a ground floor and 2 storeys below it, housing a sauna and a Turkish bath, a Jacuzzi, a swimming pool, a video room, sun beds, a resting room and of course a bar.

IDM
4 rue du Faubourg Monmartre, 75009 Paris (45.23.10.03). Metro Rue Montmartre. **Open** noon-1am daily. **Admission** 90F; 60F under-26s. **No credit cards.**
A bath house and fitness centre, this is the self-proclaimed biggest American-style sauna in Paris.

King Night
70 avenue de Saint Ouen, 75018 Paris (42.29.08.44). Metro Guy Mocquet. **Open** 10pm-9am daily. **Admission** 75F before midnight; 60F under-27s before midnight; 45F for all midnight-5am. **Credit** MC, V.
This sauna opens when King Sauna *below* closes. Strictly for night owls.

King Sauna
21 rue Bridaine, 75018 Paris (42.94.19.10). Metro Rome. **Open** 1pm-midnight daily. **Admission** 65F; 45F under-25s. **Credit** MC, V.
A small, popular sauna.

SUMMER SPECIALS

There's more to Paris gay life than bars and clubs. During the summer especially, socializing takes place out of doors. Below we list a few suggestions for lazy summer days.

Bastille Day Ball
Quai Saint Bernard, 75006 Paris. Metro Pont-Marie, Maubert-Mutualité. **Date** 13 July, 10pm-dawn, every year. **Admission** free.
Organized by gay people, but open to everyone, this ball takes place on the eve of Bastille Day. Situated on the embankment, up to four thousand people turn up for one of the biggest social events of the Parisian calendar. The music is impressively loud and there are two bars; sandwiches are normally served. The dancing continues until dawn, when those with any stamina left stagger into the nearby cafés for breakfast. Although this event has up until now been a yearly occasion, a special licence has to be obtained from the municipal offices every year and there is no guarantee it will be issued in future. For further information, phone *Gai Pied* (43.57.52.05).

Cimetière du Père Lachaise
boulevard de Ménilmontant, 75020 Paris. Metro Gambetta, Père Lachaise, Philippe Auguste. **Open** *mid March-early Nov:* 8am-6pm Mon-Fri; 8.30am-6pm Sat; 9am-6pm Sun, public holidays; *early Nov-mid March:* 8am-5.30pm Mon-Fri; 8.30am-5.30pm Sat; 9am-5.30pm Sun, public holidays.
The tombs of the famous can be found in this cemetery, now a lovely park. For example Oscar Wilde, Edith Piaf and Jim Morrison are buried here. A beautiful spot to take a picnic or go walking as there are lots of trees and grassy slopes. *See chapter* **Sightseeing**.

Parc des Buttes-Chaumont
rue Botzaris, 75019 Paris. Metro Buttes-Chaumont, Botzaris. **Open** dawn-dusk daily.
A beautiful English park with hills, dales and a waterfall. In the summer there's plenty of young people lazing on the smooth grass.

Parc de Sceaux
RER Parc de Sceaux, Sceaux, La Croix de Berny (15 minutes from Châtelet-Les Halles). **Open** dawn-dusk daily.
There's an outside swimming pool on the outskirts of these grand French gardens, where people go jogging or take picnics. Ponds and avenues of trees make this a pleasant place to while away the afternoon.

Piscine Deligny
25 quai Anatole France, 75007 Paris (45.51.72.15). Metro Concorde, Chambre des Députés. **Open** *May to October.* 8.30am-10pm daily. **Admission** 40F. **Credit** MC, V.
This floating swimming pool on the river Seine is frequented by a mixed crowd of sunbathers. There's also a bar, a restaurant, a solarium and a gym.

Tata Beach
port des Tuileries, 75001 Paris. Metro Concorde/RER Orsay.
In the summer the river bank is packed with sun worshippers. A strong smell of sun cream pervades the air.

Terrasse du Bord de l'Eau
in Jardin des Tuileries, 75001 Paris. Main entrance: place de la Concorde. Metro Concorde. **Open** dawn-dusk daily.
This is probably the oldest gay spot in Paris. Gays have made this terrace their favourite afternoon promenade for over two centuries. *See also* **picture and caption**.

WOMEN

La Champmeslé
4 rue Chabanais, 75002 Paris (42.96.85.20). Metro Les Halles. **Open** 6pm-2am Mon-Sat. **Credit** AmEx, DC, V.
A well-known women's bar, with the accent on feminism rather than lesbianism. Men are admitted as guests. The décor is rustic; bare stone walls and wooden tables. There's cabaret on Thursday nights, when drinks are slightly more expensive than usual (admission is free).

Le Katmandu
21 rue de Vieux Colombier, 75006 Paris (45.48.12.96). Metro Saint Sulpice. **Open** 11pm-6am daily. **Admission** 90F.
Opened 15 years ago by a feminist writer Ellula Perrin, this is reputed to be the oldest lesbian club in Paris. The door policy ensures that only the *crème de la crème* is admitted (no men allowed). The best nights to go are Wednesday and Thursday. Expect to pay 100F per drink (the first drink is included in the admission charge).

Scorpion
50 rue de la Chaussée d'Antin, 75009 Paris (42.80.69.40). Metro Chaussée d'Antin. **Open** 11pm-5am Wed, Fri, Sat. **Admission** 50F.
A new (opened autumn 1989), large club, already quite popular with young lesbians.

Music: Classical & Opera

From opera classics to new, experimental, and sometimes free concerts, Paris offers the music lover a wide range of sounds.

Paris offers up strong, if not remarkable, orchestras. These include the **Ensemble Orchestral de Paris, Orchestre National de France, Orchestre de Paris** and **Orchestre Philharmonique de Radio France.** Other high quality guest orchestras and foreign and French chamber music groups – such as **The Beaux Arts Trio, The Borodine Quartet** and **The Amadeus Quartet** – add to the already wide spectrum.

If you are willing to break away from the most expensive venues and the 'stars' in town, you'll find a large number of individuals and organizations that want to bring good music to the public. Paris has several churches – for example, **Saint Julien-le-Pauvre** and **Saint Eustache** – that have well established and respected concert series. Both the **Louvre** (with its beautiful new auditorium) and the **Musée d'Orsay** also have wonderful classical music series and there's an almost infinite number of festivals that celebrate music.

BOOKING AHEAD

For a comprehensive list of ticket booking agencies *see chapter* **Services**. These agencies accept credit card bookings; a useful service as not one music venue accepts them. To tap into what's on during your stay, be on the look-out for promotional posters or pick up a copy of *Pariscope, 7 à Paris,* or *L'Officiel des Spectacles.* For further-ranging activities, try *Le Monde de la Musique,* the music fanatic's monthly. Alternatively, page through *Paris Passion's* 'Calendar' section for a small, selective listing of the month's performances.

CONCERT HALLS

L'Auditorium des Halles
les Halles, Porte Saint Eustache, 75001 Paris (42.33.00.00). Metro Les Halles/bus 29, 38, 47, 67, 74, 85. **Open** *box office:* 11am-7pm daily; *telephone booking:* 11am-7pm Mon-Sat. **Tickets** 35F-200F. **No credit cards.**
A welcome addition to the Paris classical music scene, this hall brings in some of the best, if not always well-known, musicians around. Acoustically, it's just about fair.

Bobigny
1 boulevard Lenine, 93000 Bobigny (48.31.11.45/45.26.72.52). Metro Bobigny-Pablo Picasso. **Open** *box office:* 3-7pm Mon-Sat; *telephone booking:* 10am-7pm Mon-Sat. **Tickets** phone for details. **No credit cards.**
Not in Paris proper, this opera house in the north-western suburbs nonetheless merits a visit. Productions here are frequent and good. Whether or not you can get tickets to the Bastille, the opera here is something to sing about.

Centre Georges Pompidou/IRCAM
main entrance on rue Saint Martin, 75004 Paris (42.77.12.33). Metro Hôtel de Ville, Rambuteau/bus 38, 47, 75. **Tickets** contact the Ensemble InterContemporain, *42.78.79.95,* for all box office and ticket information. **No credit cards.**
IRCAM is an organization devoted to the development of and experimentation in contemporary music. The Ensemble InterContemporain is the sister company that performs the avant-garde music. That can mean that programmes presented here are sometimes no more than random thumps and squeaks. But, occasionally, they can make for a refreshing change. The auditorium is serviceable and modern.

Opéra Bastille
place de la Bastille, 75012 Paris (43.12.55.02). Metro Bastille/bus 20, 29, 65, 69, 76, 86, 87, 91. **Open** *box office:* phone for details. **Tickets** phone for details. **No credit cards.**
See **picture and caption.**

Palais/Opéra Garnier
8 rue Scribe, 75009 Paris (47.42.57.50). Metro Opéra/bus 20, 21, 22, 27, 29, 42, 53, 66, 68, 81. **Open** *box office:* 11am-7pm Mon-Sat. **Tickets** phone for details. **No credit cards.**
Just around the corner from the glorious old Opéra de Paris, it is this venue that presents opera and opera excerpts fairly frequently. It isn't bad stuff, but the best is found elsewhere (such as at the **Théâtre Musical de Paris,** *see* below).

Radio France
116 avenue du President Kennedy, 75016 Paris (42.30.22.22). Metro Javel, Passy, Ranelagh/bus 22, 52, 70, 72. **Open** *box office:* phone for details. **Tickets** phone for details. **No credit cards.**
The Radio France building houses an interesting auditorium complex that is important to the livelihood of classical music in France. Radio France has its own renowned Philharmonic which puts on a good performance. Visitors might also chance upon soloists and chamber groups, the music of which is usually broadcast on Radio France airwaves (*see* chapter **Media**).

Salle Favart
5 rue Favart, 75009 Paris (42.96.12.20). Metro Richelieu Drouot/bus 20, 39, 48, 67, 74, 85. **Open** *box office:* 11am-6.30pm Mon-Sat. **Tickets** 50F-160F. **Credit** (group bookings only) CB, V.
An old hall, often given over to opera productions and lightweight musical programmes. The classical music is sometimes good here, but it generally doesn't compare with the likes of **Pleyel** or **Gaveau** *(see below)*.

Salle Gaveau
45 rue de la Boétie, 75008 Paris (49.53.05.07). Metro Miromesnil/bus 28, 32, 49, 80. **Open** *box office:* 11am-6pm Mon-Fri, Sun; 11am-4pm Sat. **Tickets** phone for details. **No credit cards.**
An old-fashioned, red-velvet covered interior predominates at the Gaveau, but the music is good, so who cares? The intimacy of the seating and warmth of the sound makes for a very enjoyable evening.

Salle Pleyel
252 rue du Faubourg-Saint-Honoré, 75008 Paris (45.61.06.30). Metro Ternes/bus 30, 31, 43, 93. **Open** *box office:* 11am-6pm Mon-Sat. **Tickets** phone for details. **No credit cards.**
Chopin played his last recital in this hall, and it hasn't aged badly in the more than 100 years since then. The exterior doesn't look too impressive, but the interior is lovely and has respectable sound, too.

Théâtre de la Ville
2 place du Châtelet, 75004 Paris (42.74.22.77). Metro Châtelet/bus 21, 38, 47, 58, 67, 69, 70, 72, 74, 75, 76, 81, 96. **Open** *box office:* 11am-6pm Mon, Sun; 11am-9pm Tue-Sat; *telephone booking:* 11am-6pm Mon, Sun; 9am-8pm Tue-Sat. **Tickets** 60F-145F. **No credit cards.**
Although this theatre is more likely to host performances that are part of a festival or special series, it does put on classical recitals on a regular basis. Check around for current programming during your visit. *Wheelchair access.*

Théâtre des Champs-Elysées
15 avenue Montaigne, 75008 Paris (47.23.37.21; telephone booking 47.20.08.24). Metro Alma Marceau/bus 42, 80. **Open** *box office:* 11am-7pm daily; *telephone booking:* 2-6pm Mon-Fri. **Tickets** 90F-250F. **No credit cards.**
The Théâtre des Champs-Elysées is the most celebrated classical music venue in Paris. Even though a few rotten apples do appear on the programme these days, fine musicians and groups play here regularly. The orchestra seats are some of the best in Paris in terms of sound quality. The Théâtre sometimes breaks away from standard concert programming in order to stage an

opera. The operas are almost always big-name productions and only last a few nights. Concerts by great solo opera singers are also hosted.

Théâtre Musical de Paris (Châtelet)
2 rue Edouard Colonne, 75001 Paris (40.28.28.40). Metro Châtelet/bus 21, 38, 47, 58, 67, 69, 70, 72, 74, 75, 76, 81, 96. **Open** *box office:* 11am-7pm daily. **Tickets** phone for details. **No credit cards.**
When **Opéra Bastille** (*see above*) opens and presents its first full season, it may be the thing that finally knocks the Châtelet site off the map as Paris's most complete opera venue. For several years, Châtelet had been gaining ground as the only place in Paris to present anything close to a full opera season. Still, even with the new opera house in town, the folks at Châtelet are planning to keep bringing progressive, well-made productions to the people. They even hope not to reduce the number of productions they stage. Check listings carefully before you decide on an opera to see. On the whole, this is a popular venue that presents everything from opera and voice recitals to soloists and full-blown orchestral concerts.

Théâtre National de Chaillot
place du Trocadéro, 75016 Paris (42.27.81.15). Metro Trocadéro/bus 22, 30, 32, 63. **Open** *box office:* 11am-7pm Mon-Sat; 11am-5pm Sun; *telephone booking:* 11am-7pm Mon-Sat.* **Tickets** phone for details. **No credit cards.**
Mega-monster concerts are often held here; the ones with a lot of financial backing and big name musicians. The programming can

be a bit cock-eyed at times – it's not always a sure bet – but generally, this theatre doesn't waste time on the mediocre.

SERIES

There are several organizations that arrange series of concerts in various venues throughout Paris. For further information on the performers, venues and ticket prices, phone the numbers listed below.

Concerts Boeringer
In various churches in Paris (42.62.40.65). **Tickets** phone for details.
A good chamber group and ensemble concert series. Noted for presenting the *Trompettes de Versailles* on Saturday evenings at Saint Julien-le-Pauvre.

Concerts Lamoureux
In various concert halls in Paris (45.63.60.62). **Tickets** phone for details.
A wide-ranging series of programmes, often taking place in the **Salle Pleyel** (*see above* **Concert Halls**). You can hear choirs, chamber groups and soloists alike. Concerts usually start around 5.45pm.

Concerts Pasdeloup
In various churches in Paris (43.87.41.50). **Tickets** phone for details.
This is a primarily 'top ten' music series, often held in the **Salle Pleyel** (*see above*

Concert Halls). Not to say that it's poor in quality, but only the tried and true as well as popular pieces and arias are performed. However, the concerts are done quite well and they do serve the purpose of bringing new listeners to classical music.

Musée du Louvre
34 quai du Louvre, 75001 Paris (40.20.51.51). Metro Palais-Royal/bus 21, 24, 27, 37, 48, 67, 68, 69, 72, 76. **Open** *box office:* phone for details. **Tickets** phone for details.
Les Midis du Louvre is a series of lunch-time concerts of solo and chamber music as well as evening concerts that are part of an upgraded programme to make more use of the Louvre's fine, newly constructed auditorium. By virtue of their name, the concerts draw talented musicians, and the auditorium has a good, though somewhat bright, sound.

Musée d'Orsay
1 rue de Bellechasse, 75007 Paris (45.49.48.14). Metro Solferin/bus 24, 68, 69, 73. **Open** *box office:* opens half hour before each concert. **Tickets** phone for details.
The Musée d'Orsay puts on a popular and well-done concert series, that presents lunch-time (generally 12.30pm), early evening (generally 6.30pm) and evening (generally 8.30pm) recitals. Both soloists (including singers) and chamber groups perform.

Théâtre du Rond-Point (Théâtre Renaud Barrault)
2bis avenue Franklin D Roosevelt, 75008 Paris (42.56.60.70). Metro Champs Elysées-Clémenceau, Franklin D Roosevelt. **Open** phone for details. **Tickets** 80F.
A very popular Sunday morning concert series, scene of many a young soloist's debut in Paris. The hall looks a little odd and hollow, but the sound is good. There's a small restaurant in the basement level of the theatre, but after the concert everyone heads off to the Champs-Elysées cafés.

CHURCHES

The churches cited below are, at the time of going to press, sponsoring regular concerts as part of their own series or of a larger series. It is essential to call ahead to verify programmes since the churches often change their plans and programmes. Should you have difficulty reaching a specific church by phone, phone the **Paris Tourist Bureau** (*see below* **Festivals**) for more information. Ticket prices are generally no more than 100F.

Chapelle Saint Louis de la Salpêtrière
47 boulevard de l'Hôpital, 75013 Paris (45.70.27.27). Metro Saint Marcel/bus 24, 42, 52, 84, 94. **Tickets** phone for details.
Very beautiful organ music and vocal recitals can be heard here. The small church (tucked into a very large one), has a lovely sound.

Eglise de la Madeleine
place de la Madeleine, 75009 Paris (39.61.12.03). Metro Madeleine.

The **Opéra Bastille** (*listed under* **Concert Halls**) *multi-functional performance space has been the topic of conversation in Paris's opera world for over three years. With its official opening scheduled for April 1990, opera lovers will judge once and for all just how successful a European opera centre it is. It will also host various concert and dance programmes. The glorious old Opéra – in the place de l'Opéra – is now only used for ballets.*

Tickets phone for details.
Big and beautiful with a lovely sound, this church often sponsors voice concerts (being near the old opera, and all).

Eglise Saint Eustache
2 rue du Jour, 75002 Paris (42.36.31.05).
RER Châtelet-Les -Halles/bus 39, 48, 63, 65, 70, 86, 87, 95, 96. **Tickets** phone for details.
See **picture and caption.**

Eglise Saint Germain des Prés
3 place Saint Germain des Prés, 75006 Paris (43.25.41.71). Metro Saint-Germain-des-Prés/bus 39, 48, 63, 65, 70, 86, 87, 95, 96.
Tickets phone for details.
It had to be – Paris's second most famous church couldn't *not* present a musical programme. A very pretty interior and a great neighbourhood to wander through after the evening's performance.

Eglise Saint Julien-le-Pauvre
1 rue Saint Julien-le-Pauvre, 75005 Paris (43.54.20.41). Metro Saint Michel.
Tickets phone for details.
This pretty little church near Shakespeare and Co presents some very fine solo programmes as well as the much-lauded *Trompettes de Versailles* as part of the **Concert Boeringer** series (*see above* **Series**).

Eglise Saint Louis-en-l'Ile
19 rue Saint-Louis-en-l'Ile, 75004 Paris (45.23.18.25). Metro Pont-Marie/bus 24, 67.
Tickets phone for details.
A plain little church on the fashionable Ile Saint Louis that draws a good crowd to its presentations. You can't get a more centrally located concert in Paris than this. The sound, alas, is so-so.

Eglise Saint Séverin
1 rue des Prêtres Saint Séverin, 75005 Paris (48.04.98.01). Metro Saint Michel/bus 24, 47, 63, 86, 87. **Tickets** phone for details.
A good venue for organ concerts. They also do voice and some soloist programmes.

FESTIVALS

The musical festivals reviewed here are the most popular and important in Paris. The sites and venues for festival performances are numerous. Below, we list only the festival name, its approximate dates, its general theme and/or purpose and the telephone number of either the organizers or people that will give out further information. Unfortunately, these numbers can change over the course of the year, as the festival draws nearer. Should you have any trouble obtaining further details on a festival you wish to attend, phone the **Paris Tourist Bureau** at one of three locations: *Gare du Nord (45.26.94.82); Gare de Lyon (43.43.33.24);* and *Gare*

The **Eglise Saint Eustache** (*listed under* **Series/Churches**) *is gaining much deserved popularity for great sound in a beautiful church. Good soloists perform here regularly as well as fantastic choir groups.*

d'Austerlitz (45.84.91.70) for the latest information on how to reach the headquarters of that festival.

Festival de Paris
Mid May-June *(40.27.82.25).*
A young festival, begun in 1988, the Festival de Paris is sponsored by the city and brings together as many as 25 different nations through its presentation of music, theatre and dance.

Fête de la Musique
June 21 *(Paris Tourist Bureau; 45.26.94.82).*
This one day each year is set aside by the whole of France, including the city of Paris for revelling in the joy of music. There are lots of free, open-air concerts to be heard and enjoyed.

Festival Saint Denis
June-early July *(42.43.77.72).*
Completely dedicated to the celebration of classical music, this festival draws large crowds and great musicians.

Festival International d'Opéra
July *(42.68.23.32).*
Opera, opera, and nothing but opera for two weeks out at Versailles. If you love to hear the fat lady sing, don't miss it.

Festival Estival de Paris
July-September *(48.41.98.01).*
A classical music, opera and dance festival that has been held annually for over a quarter of a century. It is sponsored by the French Ministry of Culture and the city of Paris.

Festival de Jazz de Paris
Summer or early autumn *(47.83.84.06).*
All the big names in jazz visit Paris during the peak season to make two weeks' worth of jazz. A very popular, chic event.

Festival d'Automne
September-end December *(42.96.12.27).*
This is the second biggest event – the first is the city's **Festival Estival** (*see above*) – of the year. Music, theatre, dance, art and opera are all on deck. You can't go anywhere in Paris during the autumn without realizing it's all around you.

Fêtes d'Automne
September-December *(43.29.21.75).*
Not to be confused with the Festival d'Automne *below*, this one is just as much fun, if only a little scaled down. Music, theatre, art and discussions are held at cultural sites in the 5th *arrondissement.*

Festival d'Art Sacré
October-November *(42.77.92.26).*
Primarily held in churches, this festival celebrates not only the artworks found in religious celebration and practice, but the music. Some truly fabulous concerts of song and voice take place at this time.

Festival des Instruments Anciens
March *(Paris Tourist Bureau; 45.26.94.82).*
A festival that takes place in various churches and halls throughout Paris, in tribute to music from the past.

Music: Rock, Folk & Jazz

Feel the beat of the rhythmic sounds at Paris's top or sleazy jazz and rock venues.

Although Paris is a home for expatriates of all nationalities, the major forces of musical interest are powered by African and American artists. Through the corridors of the metro echo the drums of African musicians who tomorrow may grace the stage of the **Chappelle des Lombards** (*see* **Clubs**) and next month might be playing at the **Zenith** (*see* **Large-Scale**). Artists as varied as Johnny Clegg and Manu Dibango first achieved success in France.

In the clubs, it's the American singers that still occupy the elite position. Many – such as Lavelle, Bruce Johnson and Jane X – come for a short stay and end up adopting Paris as a home, because respect for their work is more forthcoming here than in America. This has long been the case with black, American jazz musicians, like Dee Dee Bridgewater, who found success in Paris when it had eluded them Stateside.

In a city of fashion victims, live music has had difficulty finding a toehold but enthusiasm for it is on the increase. At least now for every club that closes, new venues seem to pop up or re-open almost as quickly. In addition, independent musicians are also taking the initiative organizing concerts at clubs and other venues around town that wouldn't normally have a music policy.

The lack of an important live rock scene is compensated for by a large selection of jazz clubs presenting respected American musicians as well as the French jazz powerhouses Michel Petrucciani, Paul Motion, Claude Boling and Michel Portal; and hot newcomers such as Carl Schlosser and Sylvain Kassap.

MONEY MATTERS

In Paris opening your ears also means opening your wallet — wide. Bargains are few and far between and generally confined to govern-ment-subsidized venues and events. A club date will set you back at least 100F and concert tickets often run to 150F or more. If you think the prices are exorbitantly high, consider that club owners here pay enormous taxes. Hopefully, in 1992, the economic unification of Europe might ease the strain. Until then, don't be surprised to have to fork out 80F for a beer.

With the exception of jazz there are usually only a couple of bands per night representing the various musical styles of the day. Paris is hopping when ten groups doing original material appear simultaneously on the city's stages. Surprises, nevertheless, can occur. A good night at the **New Moon** (*see* **Clubs**) could find you face to face with Vic Moan and his Franco-American blend of swamp psychedelia with a folk-funk beat. The Kingsnakes could be churning out some fine rhythm 'n' blues at the **Gibus** or the **Rex**; Les Doryphores (from Viet Nam and Paris) could be setting up somewhere in the 14th *arrondissement* (*see* **Clubs**). Even the occasional impromptu bar gig does exist, that is until the police swoop.

And if you're still feeling blue, barely a night goes by when somewhere in Paris a reedman of the highest calibre isn't wailing his guts out to ease his heart and yours. Almost makes you forget the drink prices.

LARGE-SCALE

The major venues that do not have their own box office often sell tickets through a chain of ticket booths called **FNAC**. For more information, *see* chapter **Services/Booking Agencies**.

La Bataclan
50 boulevard Voltaire, 75011 Paris (47.00.30.12). Metro Oberkampf. **Open** *box office:* 10.30am-7pm Mon-Sat; concerts usually in the evening, once a week. **Admission** 90F-100F; *tea dance:* 60F. **No credit cards.**

A theatre with the seats removed, this hall recently accommodated Jane Birkin's first ever live performances. A raised section with tables and chairs along the perimeter of the hall offers an excellent view of the large stage. The hall's round design somehow gives one a cosier feeling than in similar venues of this size (1,200 capacity). Unfortunately this venue doesn't see as much use as it should. Local bands, generally of the French punk variety, occasionally rent it *en masse* for special events, and the occasional touring band does come through – for example, the Woodentops and the Alarm. The Sunday afternoon tea dance (from 4 to 9pm) is an amusingly kitsch institution for the whole family, featuring pancakes for brunch and ridiculous entertainment on stage. Hopefully this will continue.

Casino de Paris
16 rue de Clichy, 75009 Paris (42.85.26.27; box office 49.95.98.98.). Metro Trinité. **Open** *box office:* 11am-7pm Mon-Sat; evening concerts most nights. **Admission** 90F-130F. **No credit cards.**

Despite the name, the only gamble here is on the music. There are 1,500 plush but deteriorating and cramped seats; the hall boasts an orchestra pit and was probably more suited to vaudeville and operetta than rock 'n' roll. A lot of *variété française* comes through here for extended runs. Recent features have included Gérard Blanchard – the king of the accordion who had a big neo-aka hit 10 years ago and has been living off it ever since – and Canada's female version of Klaus Nomi; Diane Dufresne. Bands do occasionally play here and the acoustics are generally better, and the prices lower, than in similarly sized venues around town.

La Cigale
120 boulevard Rochechouart, 75018 Paris (42.23.38.00). Metro Pigalle. **Open** concerts two or three times a week, phone for details. **Admission** 110F-150F. **No credit cards.**

Probably the best concert space in Paris. Another old vaudeville house with the seats removed, the place has been tastefully and functionally renovated. The high stage affords an excellent view from the floor or the balcony, and somehow acoustics always seem a notch above the competition. Maybe it's the bands that play here; Willy DeVille, BAD, REM, Chris Isaak, Rita Mitsouko. The only negative point is the deranged, power-hungry bouncers (former Hell's Angels), who make you understand that possessing a ticket is only the beginning of the battle for entry.

Elysée Montmartre
72 boulevard Rochechouart, 75018 Paris (42.52.25.15). Metro Anvers. **Open** *box office:* noon-7pm Mon-Fri; evening concerts most nights. **Admission** 80F-120F; free gigs once a month. **No credit cards.**
See picture and caption.

Grand Rex
1 boulevard Poissonière, 75002 Paris (45.08.93.89). Metro Bonne Nouvelle. **Open** phone for details; concerts from 8pm each evening. **Admission** prices vary; approximately 150F. **No credit cards.**

This is the largest movie theatre in Europe and it has some kind of pretension to competing with New York's Radio City Music Hall. The place is tackier than its American cousin and much smaller, although 3,000 capacity can hardly be considered tiny. There are wonderful leather seats to sink your behind into, though as in most French venues, nowhere to stick your legs. Concerts tend to be sedate, 'important' events. Many of the big names in jazz play here when a club is considered too small – Phillip Morris Jazz Band, Art Blakey, Sonny Rollins – and recent shows have included REM and Tracy Chapman.

Olympia
28 boulevard des Capucines, 75009 Paris (47.42.82.45). Metro Opéra. **Open** *box office:* 10am-7pm daily; concerts from 8pm each evening. **Admission** 150-170F. **Credit** CB, MC.
More plush décor here than at the Casino *above*, there's more leg room, and the graffiti gets cleaned up quickly. This is the Olympia after all, the past home-away-from-home for Piaf, Trenet, Aznavour, Montand and other old-timers. The history of French music hall is contained in this venue, the sleek lines of the balcony and the discreet lighting being the best in art deco. Long off limits to rock shows, the Olympia has recently been the scene of spectacular concerts by Lou Reed, Tom Waits and Elvis Costello. *Variété française* is still the main source of music.

Palais Omnisport Bercy
8 boulevard de Bercy, 75012 Paris (43.41.72.04). Metro Bercy. **Open** *box office:* 11am-6pm daily; concerts from 8pm most nights. **Admission** from 155F. **No credit cards.**
It might be fun to play in front of 16,000 people at this vast stadium, but sitting among the punters is not our idea of a good time. The Cure and Dépêche Mode regularly pack the place several nights running, something only Johnny Halliday, among the locals, has been able to accomplish. Miles Davis tried. Everything, from the 15F flat cokes to the insane ticket prices, is a rip-off, and the sound is usually bad even for a stadium gig.

Zenith
211 avenue Jean Jaures, 75019 Paris (42.45.91.48). Metro Porte de Pantin. **Open** phone for details; concerts once a week. **Admission** prices vary, from 150F. **No credit cards.**
Nadir would be a more appropriate monicker for this hangar of a structure. Its logo is in fact an airplane — at a perilous angle of descent. Somehow the Zenith manages to actually look and feel bigger than it really is. The acoustics are terrible, but it's easier to move than at **Bercy** (*see above*) and despite the cavernous feeling, it's still less than half the size. Prices are also generally lower than at the sports palace. All the big groups that don't book into Bercy come here, including, of late, The Pogues, Iggy Pop and Aerosmith.

CLUBS

Chappelle des Lombards
19 rue de Lappe, 75011 Paris (43.57.24.24). Metro Bastille. **Open** 10.30pm-dawn Mon, Thur-Sun. **Admission** 60F; drinks from 30F. **No credit cards.**
The premiere venue for hearing African music at its finest. Toure Kounda were regulars here before making it big and the space

The **Elysée de Montmartre** (*listed under* **Large-Scale***) has become the rock 'n' roll mecca of Paris. A turn of the century theatre with a historic façade, the walls of this hall bear witness to decades of magic, striptease, animal shows, boxing, vaudeville, jazz and – since its renovation two years ago – almost exclusively rock 'n' roll music. Every touring combo in the world has or will come through here. Once a month there is a free concert, featuring a fairly well-known French act and two up-and-coming bands. Past shows have included Marc Minelli, Noir Désir, Les Innocents and Daniel Darc – some of the cream of French rock.*

has also welcomed Youssou N'dour and Salif Keita. Samba and salsa music make an occasional appearance as well. Xalam, a band from Senegal now based in Paris, is probably the finest of the new breed. It gets so sweaty on the dance floor that you could lose more weight shaking it for a night here than being pursued by Mike Tyson round a small boxing ring. Bands play on Thursdays, Fridays and Saturdays, and the discotheque takes over on Sundays and Mondays. The friendlier-than-average door staff can sometimes be induced to give impromptu group rates.

Fahrenheit
31 boulevard Gambetta, Issy les Molineaux, 92130 (45.54.67.28). RER line 'C' to Issy les Molineaux. **Open** phone for details; concerts almost every Friday night. **Admission** 50F; beer 10F. **Credit** MC, V.
There's a long video bar and a well equipped stage in this venue that somehow reminded us of London's Dingwalls. Mostly local bands, though just about all of the big name rock 'n' roll outfits of France, have played here over the last five years. A rowdy, beer drinking, rock crowd, but it's still definitely worth the 20 to 30 minute train ride. The club uses the hall of the local culture and youth centre.

Le Gibus
18 rue de Faubourg du Temple, 75011 Paris (47.00.78.88). Metro République. **Open** 11pm-5am Tue-Sun. **Admission** 50F; beer 30F. **No credit cards.**
The Gibus celebrated 20 years of existence last year and is the oldest club in Paris to have continuously presented live music. The place

reeks of rock 'n' roll. Unfortunately, the sound system also celebrated its twentieth birthday and if the groups don't bring their own crew, the assault on the ears can be disastrous. In general, the staff – the door people, the bartenders and the sound techs – couldn't care less who's playing and they show it. Nevertheless, the stage is good for a small club and Le Gibus is, believe it or not, one of only two venues in a city of about 2.5 million (this does not include Greater Paris)where original bands perform every night. Due to this extraordinary situation, Le Gibus played host to the likes of Deep Purple in the early seventies, and more recently to the Police, the Stray Cats and Rita Mitsouko in their infancy. Wreckless Eric, who lives in town, and Johnny Thunders, who used to, make regular appearances to rake in the bucks for the management. The Gibus can be painfully empty at times. This club is the Marquee of Paris.

Le Golf Druot (Au Bus Palladium)
6 rue Fontaine, 75009 Paris (48.74.54.99). Metro Blanche. **Open** 8pm-midnight Wed. **Admission** 50F, includes one drink; subsequent beers 30F. **Credit** MC, V.
The Golf Druot is an old name on the Paris club scene, but its new incarnation, sponsored by Kanterbrau beer, is a once-a-week affair that invades a club called the Bus Palladium, another dinosaur – The Beatles and the Stones hung out here in the sixties. Every Wednesday the Golf puts on a national battle of the bands with hopefuls from all over France playing 20-minute sets in front of an 'industry' jury. At 11pm there is

a concert by an already established French band, before this Cinderella of a club turns into a pumpkin. At midnight sharp, the live music must stop and the Golf becomes the Bus. The programming isn't bad; recent concerts have included performances by Kingsnakes, Pijon and Christine Lidon. The contest bands can also surprise — one of last year's finalists could be one of France's great pop bands someday: The Alice Lovers.

La Locomotive
90 boulevard de Clichy, 75018 Paris.
(42.57.37.37). Metro Blanche. **Open** 10pm-dawn daily. **Admission** 50F, includes one beer; subsequent beers 30F. **Credit** MC, V.
This mammoth club boasts three levels, the bottom tier built around the old power plant to next-door neighbour Le Moulin Rouge. The venue is sponsored by Lee Cooper jeans, so all the seating is covered in denim and giant mock-ups of Lee Cooper back pockets adorn the stage curtain. Too big and clean and industry-minded to qualify as a rock venue, and not hip enough to appeal to fashion snobs and other Parisian trendsetters, the Locomotive is a fairly yuppy establishment. There is something for everyone here: a billiard and game room; an upstairs lounge with softer music; the aforementioned boiler room which tends to watered down House and hip-hop; and, oh yes, the main level with a beautiful, large stage and a great PA. The local bands that occasionally play here usually get ripped off on the sound, as the house technicians can't be bothered to use the whole mixing board. On the up-side, visiting groups usually have a great sound here. Among some of the outstanding bands that have played the Loco recently are Los Lobos, Tom Verlaine and The Fleshtones.

New Moon
66 rue Pigalle, 75009 Paris (45.95.92.33).
Metro Pigalle. **Open** *club:* 11pm-dawn Mon-Sat; bands each night. **Admission** 50F, includes one beer; subsequent beers 30F.
No credit cards.
The other regular rock venue after **Le Gibus** (*see above*), New Moon is a tiny club, with a capacity of 200 and real atmosphere. It was previously a lesbian porn palace and before that a slightly seedy cabaret venue. The walls, which date from the twenties, are said to have been painted by an assistant to Picasso. Because it's recently been given a face-lift – new paint on the big seashell above the door, enlarged stage and a new PA – the countless local bands that play here now sound quite good. The DJs tend to play greatest hits of post-punk music, but you could do worse than Buzzcocks, XTC, Talking Heads and the Clash. Stiv Bators appeared here backed by Paris rhythm 'n' blues greats, the Dee Dees, while his girlfriend recently presented New York trash band the Raunch Hands.

Le Palace
8 rue du Faubourg Montmartre, 75009 Paris (42.46.10.87). Metro Rue Montmartre.
Open 11pm-6am daily. **Admission** 120F; drinks 80F. **Credit** AmEx, MC, V.
Le Palace has been in the news of late: closed for six months by the authorities in December 1989, this club will supposedly reopen in the summer of 1990. The reason for the closure? One of the punters over-dosed in the toilets and the manager purportedly threw him out onto the pavement, where he later died. The venue has recently been bought by a British company, that will be under taking extensive renovations. There

are performances and playbacks and the occasional mini-concert by the likes of Kraze and local heroine Yianna Katsoulos. The venue has a gorgeous balcony with a fine view of the goings-on down below. It's a pity the dance floor is so small for a place this size; it's more fun (and expensive) to lounge around on the couches drinking 1,000F-bottles of champagne. You might even catch a glimpse of your favourite model or the likes of Serge Gainsbourg or Rupert Everett. Occasionally the Palace is rented for evening concerts (tickets in advance; *see above* **Large-Scale** for where to buy tickets).

Le Plan
Avenue d'Aunette, Ris Orangis (69.43.11.14). Take the train from Gare de Lyon to Orangis station; a 25 minute ride. **Open** 9.30pm-2am daily; concerts usually on Fridays and Saturdays. **Admission** 70F; beer 15F. **No credit cards.**
A purpose-built venue for rock shows like no other in the Paris area, it's definitely worth the trip. Just the right size (500 capacity) and state of the art sound. The owners are real music lovers, which is rare in this business. Groups on tour are from all over the world and have included Dr Feelgood, the Fleshtones, Elliot Murphy and the Del Lords, preceded by a local support act.

Rex Club
5 boulevard Poissonière, 75002 Paris (42.36.83.98). Metro Bonne Nouvelle. **Open** 11pm-dawn Mon-Sat; 7pm-1am Sun. **Admission** 60F; 30F Sun; beer 30F.
No credit cards.
There used to be concerts here every night at 8pm, but the movie theatre upstairs couldn't live with the noise so bands now have to play after midnight. At the moment live music is on Tuesday and Friday nights. The best Paris bands play here – standards are higher than at Gibus and New Moon and the place is comfortable for musicians and audience alike. Look out for Charley Bad Goose (terrible name, but good R 'n' R), The Imperials (a bunch of maniacs doing forties' and fifties' pre-rock swing), and Big Eyes (like Iggy Pop sung by Nina Simone). Musicians come to the Rex to see and hear their friends. Sunday evenings this venue is home to *Les Aprem's a Toto*, an art school night with various performances, video shows and exhibitions; intellectual fun for the whole family.

Studio A
49 rue de Ponthieu, 75008 Paris (42.25.12.13). Metro George V. **Open** 11pm-4am daily. **Admission** 80F includes drink; subsequent beers 40F. **Credit** MC, V.
A very rich and very young crowd from the Champs Elysées area of Paris frequent this club. Boring music and weak drinks abound in a nondescript, but not ugly space and there's plenty of room to dance. This is life on the edge of the gold-plated razor blade set. The occasional live bands may surprise, though. So-Oh from England and Paris popstars Fish on Friday have played here.

Trois Mailletz
58 rue Galande, 75005 Paris (43.54.00.79). Metro Maubert-Mutualité. **Open** 6pm-6am Tue-Sun. **Admission** 60F charge for music downstairs; beer 30F. **Credit** MC, V.
This is one of the zaniest venues around, presenting anything from the tackiest rock 'n' roll cover band to good blues, jazz, show-

In the wake of **Négresses Vertes** *(see above photo) and Gypsy Kings international success, many groups have abandoned second-rate Anglo-rock posturing in favour of the accordion, tin-whistle and French cabaret lyrics, creating a kind of French world-music that appeals to a foreigner's idea of what 'real' French music should sound like. With a rock 'n' roll mentality and street musician image, the Négresses, Mano Negra and OTH have spurred a nationwide boom in home-grown music.*

tunes, Latin and the occasional original band. The staff seems mostly Chinese and they are the only sober people on the premises. Just behind the Sorbonne, this club attracts a serious student crowd, but is also replete with a healthy dose of freaks, refreshingly un-Parisian in dress and eager for a dance and a laugh. The last time we visited, we had the pleasure of listening to some Mexican yodelling Elvis Presley songs – we kid you not. Light dinners are served upstairs.

JAZZ

Au Duc des Lombards
42 rue des Lombards, 75001 Paris (42.36.51.13). Metro Châtelet. **Open** phone for details; music every night from 11pm. **Admission** free; drinks from 60F. **Credit** AmEx, DC, V.
A bit too much of a lounge atmosphere and something of a tourist trap, the Duc boasts a white grand piano usually competently played, and various crooners doing blues, showtunes and standards. Trios and quartets, occasionally with drums, also play here. It's very dark in this venue; could be romantic.

Les Bouchons
19 rue des Halles, 75001 Paris (42.33.28.73). Metro Châtelet les Halles. **Open** 10.30pm-2pm daily. **Admission** free; drinks from 40F. **Credit** AmEx, DC, V.
A beautiful, wooden staircase leads down from the restaurant to this elegant and pleasant room. One of the few nightspots where they don't assault you with the drink list every five minutes. The music runs from good piano bar to small ensembles artfully interpreting the standards. New Year's Eve offers an all-night celebration with the best jazz voices in Paris jamming 'till the liquor runs out. One of the most comfortable jazz venues in town.

Café de la Plage
59 rue de Charonne, 75011 Paris (47.00.91.60). Metro Bastille. **Open** 10pm-2am Tue-Sun. **Admission** free; drinks from 50F. **Credit** MC, V.
The upstairs has been a hip, arty bar for a couple of years. With the support of radio France Inter and tasteful posters, the 'cave' is making a bid for major jazz club status. Unfortunately, it's just a little too small to house the big names and so far the quality of the music has been disappointing, run of the mill be-bop. Always full, though, and with a pretentiousness quotient lower than most jazz venues.

Caveau de la Huchette
5 rue de la Huchette, 75005 Paris (43.26.65.05). Metro Saint Michel. **Open** 9.30pm-2.30am Mon-Fri; 9.30pm-4am Sat, Sun. **Admission** 40F-55F; beer 15F. **No credit cards.**
Sister venue of the Slow Club *below*, the Caveau is a friendly cruising joint, full of lots of little dresses on little girls out for a twist and a flirt. The door personnel ensure against patrons of the down and dirty variety. Downstairs, the cavernous space is usually packed, while couples smooch in the wooden booths. Competent swing, Dixieland and oldies bands power the night from the high stage.

Eustache
37 rue Berger, 75001 Paris (40.26.23.20). Metro Les Halles. **Open** 11am-2am Mon-Sat; music from 10pm-2am. **Admission** free; drinks from 50F before 2am; 25F after 2am. **Credit** MC, V.
This is one hopping joint; look in from the street through the big window, and you'll see the piano in the middle of the floor and hear the horns wailing. There's lots of wood and a no-frills party atmosphere. The sound gets a bit lost around the edges, but the band is right there with you, playing their guts out. The whole venue is a stage. Food is served until 10pm.

Le Flamingo
134 rue Saint Jacques, 75005 Paris (43.54.30.48). RER Luxembourg. **Open** 9pm-2am Tue-Sat. **Admission** free; drinks from 40F. **Credit** MC, V.
A post-hippy – called *baba-cool* in France – establishment, where blues and jazz can be heard floating through the alcoholic haze. The young, pretentious, political student crowd balances the simple, homely atmosphere.

Hilboquet
13 rue Saint Benoit, 75006 Paris (45.48.81.84). Metro Saint-Germain-des-Prés. **Open** 8pm-1am Mon-Sat; music 10pm-3am. **Admission** 100F; drinks 100F . **Credit** AmEx, DC, MC, V.
Standard jazz ensembles play loudly to a middle-aged tourist crowd at this Saint Germain venue. The run-down *belle époque* décor complete with Monet reproductions sets the tone. There's a good menu, though, and it's not as snobby as the money grabbing doorman suggests.

Latitudes
7-11 rue Saint Benoit, 75006 Paris (42.61.53.53). Metro Saint-Germain-des-Prés. **Open** *piano bar;* 6pm-2am Mon, Tue; *concerts;* 10pm-2am Wed-Sat. **Admission** free, but first drink 85F; subsequent beers 25F. **Credit** AmEx, DC, MC.
By far the most up-market venue of the three jazz clubs on the rue Saint Benoit. The tastefully modern downstairs of a hotel lobby, this jazz lounge attracts an elegant clientele. Comfortably spaced tables provide a civilized environment to listen to the high calibre music played here.

Mécene
6 rue des Lombards, 75004 (42.77.40.25). Metro Châtelet. **Open** free; beer 40F-70F. **Credit** AmEx, MC, V.
A friendly, little jazz hole with a good stage. It's decorated in glass and chrome with a touch of the zebra stripe. Vaguely seventies in look and sound as well – often played by musicians who were toddlers at the time. Wednesday is often Brazilian or salsa night.

Le Méridien
81 rue Gouvion-Saint-Cyr, 75017 Paris (40.68.34.34). Metro Porte Maillot. **Open** 10pm-2am Mon-Sat. **Admission** free, drinks from 55F. **Credit** AmEx, CB, MC, V.
The Lionel Hampton Bar situated in one of Paris's premier hotels has become a prestige jazz venue in the same league as the New Morning *below*. A polished, marble floor leads to a large room with a distinctly 'blue' atmosphere. Plush leather seats allow 300 auditors a comfortable

Jane X *is a long-standing member of Paris's vocal elite. Originally from Philadelphia, her distinguished and versatile voice lends itself particularly well to jazz, rock, and her soulful brand of blues. Gordon Russell (ex-Dr Feelgood) accompanies her on guitar.*

view of the small stage, and the large bar affords good access. Most people come to listen – even the tourists – and they do it in suits; even to the hair-raising zaniness of the brilliant Screamin' Jay Hawkins, a regular at the Méridien.

Le Montana
28 rue Saint Benoît, 75006 Paris (45.48.93.08). Metro Saint-Germain-des-Prés. **Open** 6pm-3am daily; music from 10.30pm-2.30am daily. **Admission** free; drinks 85F. **Credit** AmEx, DC, MC, V.
Programming runs from jazz to 'chanson' to showtunes. With limited sound and space, this venue is essentially a rip-off. Soon to begin jazz brunches from Wednesdays to Sundays in the more spacious restaurant.

New Morning
7 rue des Petites Ecuries, 75010 Paris (45.23.51.41). Metro Château d'Eau. **Open** phone for details; concerts almost every night at 9.30pm. **Admission** 80F-100F; beer 30F. **No credit cards.**
World famous, New Morning is the centre of jazz life in Paris. Every big name from Miles Davis to Oscar Peterson, Chet Baker to Carla Bley has played here. Spacious seating and a clean, tight sound make it a pleasure to attend a concert at this venue. More of a hall, really, than a club, it has a capacity of 600. The management has recently begun renting the space to pop bands; the Pixies were among the first of these bands to play here. Don't be fooled by the ugly, concrete, shopping mall exterior; this venue is worth the price of admission. Tickets are on sale at

the usual locations (*see above* **Large-Scale**) and at the door one hour before the show.

Petit Journal
71 boulevard Saint Michel, 75005 Paris (43.26.28.59). RER Luxembourg. **Open** 10pm-2am daily. **Admission** 80F, includes first drink; subsequent beers 50F.**Credit** MC, V.
Leather and wooden booths give this venue a pub-plush look. Long and narrow with a low ceiling, the place seems cramped and the awkward position of the seating alcoves give a very limited view of the stage inadequately compensated by the closed-circuit TV system.

Petit Journal Montparnasse
13 rue du Commandant-Mouchotte, 75014 Paris (43.21.56.70). Metro Montparnasse. **Open** 9pm-2am Mon-Sat. **Admission** free, but first drink 80F.
Credit AmEx, DC, MC, V.
Sister club to the Petit Journal at Saint Michel (*see above*), this establishment is larger and more modern. Though graced with a design more in line with a fancy American diner – Howard Johnson's and the like – the character of the place comes from the music which includes the bigger names on the international cicuit, with a concentration of the French stars. A big plus is the fact that you can see and hear well from just about anywhere in this joint.

La Pinte
13 carrefour de l'Odéon, 75005 Paris (43.26.26.15). Metro Odéon. **Open** 6pm-2am Mon-Sat; music 10pm-2am. **Admission** free; drinks from 45F. **No credit cards.**

A tiny bar with a video monitor showing the action down below – of which there is very little. The place holds about 30 people, but is rarely full. This venue would make a good folk club, but they insist on programming basic, bad jazz.

Slow Club
130 rue de Rivoli, 75001 Paris (42. 33.84.30). Metro Châtelet. **Open** 9.30pm-2.30am Tue-Thur; 9.30pm-3am Fri; 9.30pm-4am Sat. **Admission** 50F; drinks from 30F. **Credit** AmEx, MC, V. .
The neon couple dancing atop the door is an indication of the old-fashioned atmosphere at this ballroom-cum-club. Swing and Dixieland form the bulk of the programming, with the occasional big-band and rhythm 'n' blues thrown in. Refreshing in its unpretentiousness. Watch out for Mighty Flea featuring Paris's outstanding sax virtuoso Carl Schlosser.

Le Sunset
60 rue des Lombards, 75001 Paris (40.26.46.60). Metro Châtelet. **Open** 10pm-4am daily; concerts every night from 10pm. **Admission** 40F-80F depending on band. **Credit** MC, V.
Basic jazz bands set up in the corner of this small, L-shaped 'cave'. Occasionally trombonist Frank Lacey comes in and raises the level ten notches. At least the bands usually play their originals, so there's a chance you might run into something interesting. A venue for the studious jazz set. Lots of tweed jackets.

BAR-LIKE VENUES

The following venues don't really have a club atmosphere, neither do they come close to the populist British idea of a pub. They offer musical entertainment in a variety of styles – at Paris prices – and the policy is more oriented towards cover bands that blend into the décor. Because Paris offers such a paucity of real music clubs, the following bunch deserve a mention; the occasional interesting combo does grace their stages.

Baiser Salé
58 rue des Lombards, 75001 Paris (42.33.37.71). Metro Châtelet.. **Open** 8pm-dawn daily; rock bands from 9-11pm; jazz-rock, funk and world music after midnight. **Admission** free; beer 60F; cocktails 80F. **Credit** MC, V.
Cramped and uncomfortable with an impolite staff, the Baiser Salé inspires instant dislike. If you manage to stay for the music, however, the occasional hot Afro beat will make you forget for a moment the price of your warm beer. Many pick-up bands that really swing, perform here. Forget the jazz and jazz-rock, though, unless third-rate Journey, Santana and Pat Metheney is your cup of tea.

Caf' Conc
6 rue Saint Denis, 75001 Paris (42.33.42.41). Metro Châtelet. **Open** 9.45pm-4am daily. **Admission** free; drinks from 50F. **Credit** AmEx, MC, V.

The larger venues in Paris, such as the **Grand Rex** *(listed under* **Large-scale**) *often welcome US and British bands such as Dr Feelgood, The Fleshtones and Carmel, that never cracked it big at home but are stars in France.*

Elli – *Elli Mediros and Ramuntcho Matta – really hit the the French music scene with their album* Bom Bom, *that came out in the early summer of 1987. The rest of that year saw them touring Europe in a frenzied programme of concerts, the only break in the music routine coming about only because Elli gave birth to a baby boy, César. Their latest album offering carries the group's name only:* Elli.

The owner is a sometime drummer who puts together house bands with atrociously vulgar singers doing all the top hits you never wanted to hear again from 1980 to the present with an occasional Beatles tune thrown in. There's a hi-tech stage with electronic drums that you can see from the street, and many video screens. Popular with rich Third-World tourists and French country folk on vacation in Paris. Always full.

Canal Quatro
38 rue de Montreuil, 75011 Paris (43.67.41.41). Metro Faidherbe Chaligny. **Open** *restaurant:* 8pm-2am daily; *music:* 9pm-midnight daily. **Admission** free; beer 25F. **No credit cards.**
Opened in the latter part of 1989, this vaguely hippy venue is a colourful addition to an already hopping part of town. The young, enthusiastic owners wish they could bring you more, but for now decent ensembles get all excited on the stage that's no higher than the table you eat your hearty meal on. Apparently they even have drums here, though where they put them is anyone's guess. Decent art on the walls, too.

City Rock
13 rue de Berri, 75008 Paris (43.59.52.09). Metro Georges V. **Open** 6pm-2am daily; bands every night from 10pm. **Admission** free; drinks 50F. **Credit** V.
Modelled vaguely on the spirit of the Hard Rock Café, the upstairs features a decent hamburger, shake and ribs joint. Downstairs the bands grind out the rock 'n' roll, country and rockabilly to a mainly

tourist audience liberally sprinkled with Americans. Generic get-down music for young lawyers on vacation.

Le Corail
140 rue Montmartre, 75002 Paris (42.36.39.66). Metro Bourse. **Open** 24 hours Tue-Sun; music 10pm-3am. Wed-Sat **Admission** 50F; beer 25F. **Credit** MC, V.
An ordinary looking Paris bar from the outside, this venue is one of the few to stay open 24 hours, giving it a bit of the killer look by 4am. If you can get past the drunks upstairs, the 'cave' below is a clean, pleasant space to listen to samba, salsa and the occasional rhythm 'n' blues or rock band till the wee hours of the morning. Just enough room to dance. The Jane X band is by far the standout here.

Distrito
49 rue Berger, 75001 Paris (40.26.91.00). Metro Les Halles. **Open** *restaurant;* 7pm-midnight; *music* 10pm-2am Mon-Sat. **Admission** free; beer 40F. **Credit** AmEx, DC, MC, V.
A hangout for bridge and tunnel people, preppies and worn-out music industry regulars. It's all grey, metal and glass; nouvelle cuisine and nouveau yuppie. The music is in the cellar and the low volume makes up for bad sound. Uncomfortable seating and outrageous prices, but yes folks, Joe Strummer did walk in here and jam with the R&B outfit on stage. The music runs the gamut from soul and funk to country and R&B. Must to avoid: Paul Breslin. Not a bad night out: Bruce Johnson. There's a happy hour from 8pm till 10pm; drinks half price.

5th Avenue
2bis avenue Foch, 75016 Paris (45.00.00.13). Metro Porte Dauphine. **Open** 11pm-dawn daily; bands at 1am Wed, Sun. **Admission** 110F; drinks from 50F. **Credit** AmEx, DC, MC, V.
This latest addition to the Paris scene is one huge, swanky dive. An underground discotheque featuring nude dancers and other distractions, this is the place to come when you want to see a Parisian idea of American chic. Pick-up bands play covers on music nights. The large dance floor allows patrons to get down again as soon as the band stops.

Hollywood Savoy
44 rue Nôtre Dame des Victoires, 75002 Paris (42.36.16.73). Metro Rue Montmartre. **Open** 7pm-2am Mon-Sat. **Admission** free; drinks from 50F. **Credit** AmEx, DC, MC, V.
Basically this is a supper club. The Transcontinental Cowboys, nominally from Texas, have been away from Austin so long they'd be hard pressed to tell a tequila from a Singapore Sling. Monday, Thursday and Saturday are 'rock' nights with the Cowboys; they have a R&B act, a country set and a rock set and they play it all asleep on their feet. Other nights are reserved for jazz. Cynthia McPhersen and Sarah Lazarus have enough humour to cut through the bullshit. The Savoy is also the home of the singing waitress – the staff does the second set with the band. This venue is the centre of American-tackiness-in-exile and as such can be considered a tourist attraction. It's near the stock market, so it also attracts French yuppies who wish they were American.

Le Metro
18 boulevard Pasteur, 75015 (47.34.21.24). Metro Pasteur. **Open** 6pm-2am Mon-Sat; music 11pm-2am Fri, Sat. **Admission** free; beer 35F. **No credit cards.**
Just a corner Paris bistro; a bit cleaner and hi-tech looking than average. The podium in the corner allows the surly owner to put bands on it and double his drink prices. As is usual in Paris, America is the model: 70 hats from all over the Big Country are pinned to the wall over the bar. Good blues here, on occasion.

OTHER VENUES

Auditorium de Châtelet
Forum des Halles, Porte Saint Eustache, 75001 Paris (40.28.28.14). Metro Les Halles. **Open** 11am-7pm daily; concerts on various nights. **Admission** 175F-395F. **Credit** MC, V.
This brand new venue is a smaller version of the Théâtre de la Ville *below.* The superlatives reserved for the latter establishment also hold true for this hall. Often home to classical chamber music concerts, the city presents a fair amount of jazz at this venue. The auditorium is located on the edge of an underground shopping complex, but don't let this put you off. Look for the yellow-trimmed, white posters announcing events here.

Café de la Danse
5 passage Louis Philippe, 75011 Paris (48.05.57.22). Metro Bastille. **Open** box

office: 11am-6pm Mon-Fri; performances 8pm, 10pm, most nights. **Admission** 100F. **Credit** MC, V.

A gorgeous structure of brick and wood that despite its name produces all sorts of theatre and music with the latter tending to bizarre jazz and 'New Age'. There is a high percentage of female performers; the venue is run by a trio of lesbians. Go to the occasional post-performance piano bar on the balcony – to do this you'll unfortunately have to pay a small, extra cover charge.

Le Dunois
28 rue Dunois, 75013 Paris (45.84.72.00). *Metro Nationale.* **Open** phone for details; concerts on various nights, fairly regularly on weekends, showtime usually 9pm. **Admission** 50-80F. **Credit** MC, V.

A 200-seat theatre in an out of the way corner of Paris, Le Dunois has developed a reputation for presenting avant-garde and free jazz. The terraced seating offers an excellent view and the sound is adequate for even a big band performance. Once or twice a month, usually on Sundays or Wednesdays, the venue is invaded by hard core and punk bands presented by the promoters SG Warhead and *Sortie de Garage* (out of the garage). The sound system tends to be allergic to the decibels put out on these occasions. Tickets are available from **FNACs** (*see* **Large-Scale**).

Palais des Congrès
place Porte Maillot, 75008 Paris (46.40.28.20). *Metro Porte Maillot.* **Open** 12.30-6.45pm daily. **Admission** 140F. **No credit cards.**

Currently starring for an indefinite run is Charles Trenet. Many of the biggest names in French variety music put on their 'spectacle' here, so if you're into show-biz. The Bolshoi ballet has also performed here in the past.

Sentier des Halles
50 rue d'Aboukir, 75002 Paris (42.36.37.27). *Metro Sentier.* **Open** shows at 6.15pm, 7.15pm, 8.30pm, 10.30pm. **Admission** usually around 50F. **No credit cards.**

This venue is rented by any number of groups and organizations. A lot of *chanson*; some experimental theatre or mime; and the occasional rock or jazz show. Ideal for small, acoustic ensembles. A pleasant place.

Théâtre de la Ville
place du Châtelet, 75001 Paris (48.87.54.42). *Metro Châtelet.* **Open** *box office:* 11am-7pm Mon, Sun; 11am-8pm Tue-Sat. **Admission** 120F-135F. **No credit cards.**

A superb modern hall inside a historic theatre building in the heart of Paris. Beautiful sight lines and a spacious stage. Lots of wood make for great acoustics. Programming by the city of Paris includes the best in international dance, jazz and modern classical. The 6pm concerts are a bargain at 50F.

Théâtre du Tourtour
20 rue Quincampoix, 75004 Paris (48.87.82.48). *Metro Rambuteau.* **Open** *box office:* tickets on sale 20 minutes before each show; shows at 7pm, 8.30pm, 10pm. **Admission** 60F. **No credit cards.**

A tiny theatre where the management actually takes an interest in what goes on rather than just renting the venue. Tends towards *chanson française*, but the modern and intelligent variety. *Restaurant.*

Théâtre Ruteboeuf
16 allée Léon Gambetta, Clichy 92210 (47.56.14.85). *Metro Mairie de Clichy.* **Open** *box office:* 2.30-6.30pm Tue-Sat; one or two concerts per month. **Admission** 60F-120F. **No credit cards.**

The rhythm 'n' blues capital of Paris, even if it is a couple of metro stops beyond the city's border. It feels like a US high school gym. A basic, unpretentious good-time place to hear Dr Feelgood, Rufus Thomas, Isaac Hayes, Eddy Floyd, Bobby Womack. Not excessively advertized, so there's usually plenty of space to dance.

TLP Dejazet
41 boulevard du Temple, place de la République, 75003 Paris (42.74.20.50). *Metro République.* **Open** *box office:* 10am-6pm daily; shows at 8.30pm. **Admission** 80F-120F. **No credit cards.**

A slightly run-down mid-size theatre that is often home to up-and-coming or down-and-out French *variété* artists. Though the venue is traditionally French, it nevertheless welcomed 1988's First Annual Festival of American Music.

Trottoirs de Buenos-Aires
37 rue des Lombards, 75001 Paris (42.33.58.37). *Metro Châtelet.* **Open** 8pm-1am Tue-Sun; shows at 8.30pm, 10.30pm. **Admission** 90F; half price after midnight. **Credit** AmEx.

This is the unofficial Argentine cultural attaché to France. Traditional music to tango to, though more in a dinner-theatre setting. Looks and sounds like the real thing; Saturday evenings at 6pm are reserved by solo guitar recitals; Sunday is tango day hosted by Carmen and Victor with classes and dancing till 1.30am.

Utopia
1 rue Niepce, 75014 Paris (43.22.79.66). *Metro Pernety.* **Open** phone for details; music from 10pm Tue-Sat. **Admission** free; drinks from 30F. **Credit** MC, V.

The only venue in Paris where hippy folk music survives. There's a lot of blues and occasional *chanson française* on the small podium. Decoration is more on the line of a canteen than a club, but you can nurse a pint of Guinness while listening to American blues harp ace John Ratikan.

Virgin Megastore
52 avenue des Champs Elysées, 75008 Paris (40.74.06.48). *Metro Franklin D Roosevelt.* **Open** 10am-midnight Mon-Sat; noon-midnight Sun.
Credit *shop:* AmEx, DC, MC, V.
See **picture and caption.**

Mini acoustic concerts in the store's lobby often take place at the **Virgin Megastore** *(listed under* **Other Venues***), usually on the day of a group's Paris concert. They're really glorified record signings, but there have been some real moments: Elvis Costello played for almost half an hour once. There are now at least one or two concerts per week, so if you're in the area, it's worth popping in. Check the music listings every Monday in* Libération.

Nightlife

The glitzy groove for the nineties is the hip-hugging, spangle-belted Eastern rhythm. We tell you where to find it and get on down.

Following Ravi Shankar's appearance at the **Rex Club** (*listed under* **Les Grands Boulevards**), trendy night-clubbers are now into indie-alternative music. There's also been a return to the disco decade, and open-shirted Travolta lookalikes groove again with dolls in ballooning skirts.

For atmosphere, 'World Beat' venues are packing in sensation-hungry crowds fed up with single-style one-nighters, and ethnic music like rai and Puerto Rican salsa inspire the feet of today's modish twosomes. Elsewhere Molsky, Squalaly and other black rappers are packing venues like the **Java** (*listed under* **Bastille**) with its 'sardine soirées' on Thursdays. House music is on the way out, except in the gay clubs.

Increasingly, Parisian clubbers are getting to bed early during the week (before 3am) to report fit for work by ten in the morning. Night buses do run in the capital, but the best way to get home is still by taxi.

BASTILLE

Le Balajo
9 rue de Lappe, 75011 Paris (47.00.07.87). Metro Bastille. **Open** 11pm-5am Mon, Thur-Sat. **Admission** 100F. **No credit cards.**
A survivor of the *belle époque*, Le Balajo is still going strong. The bar was once propped up by the likes of Edith Piaf, Marcel Cerdan, and Jean Gabin, and the superb period décor and ritzy mouldings remain. Today's bright young things dance the tango and retro 'musette' on Mondays, under the guidance of Nouvelle Eve DJ Albert.

Chalet du Lac
Orée du Bois de Vincennes, close to the Mairie, 75012 Paris (43.28.09.89). Metro Saint Mandé-Tourelles. **Open** phone for

details. **Admission** 60F Mon-Sat; free for girls on Friday until midnight; 15F Sun, free for girls until 4pm. **No credit cards.**
A huge smoke-filled, red-plush venue with potted plants and lights on all the tables. Chalet du Lac is on the edge of town, and attracts a young crowd who come for its mood and laser sounds.

Chappelle des Lombards
19 rue de Lappe, 75011 Paris (43.57.24.24). Metro Bastille. **Open** 11.30pm-5am daily. **Admission** 70F-80F. **No credit cards.**
Once a women's prison, this has become the hottest tropical dance spot in Paris. Touré Kounda started out here, and the club now features salsa stars and Caribbean blues crooners. The over-thirties come as much to listen as for the groin-grinding beats.

Le Gibue
18 rue du Faubourg du Temple, 75011 Paris (47.00.78.80). Metro République. **Open** 11pm-5am Tue-Sat. **Admission** 70F. **No credit cards.**
In its time Le Gibue was home to such names as The Clash and The Police. Now, Tuesday is a heavy metal night for body-beautiful gym jocks. Brylcreem boys and suburban pop-pickers mingle here, on the lookout for the latest Anglo-Saxon band.

La Java
105 rue du Faubourg du Temple, 75011 Paris (42.02.20.52). Metro Belleville. **Open** Mon-Thur, Sun, phone for opening times; live band 9.30pm -5am Fri-Sat. **Admission** 30F-75F. **No credit cards.**
The musette-style dance hall where Piaf made her name, La Java has become a retro fetish night-spot. The seats are beginning to show their age, as are the jivers, who now come here with their children. It's a lively, attractive venue for performance tango, and on weekdays lively disco nights attract a soul and sixties dance crowd.

CHAMPS ELYSEES

Keur Samba
79 rue de la Boétie, 75008 Paris (43.59.03.10). Metro Franklin D Roosevelt. **Open** 11pm-10am daily. **Admission** 100F. **Credit** V.
This stylish club, with day-glo painted décor and subtle lighting, is popular with the black establishment and wealthy Lebanese crowd. The haunt of insomniacs, it comes into its own at 6am when the Jaguars and Mercedes drop off their loads of all-night party-goers. To get in you need to be smartly dressed and relaxed about everything, including money.

Lord Byron (Là-Bas)
6 rue Balzac, 75008 Paris (45.63.12.39). Metro Franklin D Roosevelt. **Open** 11pm-dawn Mon-Sat. **Admission** 100F. **No credit cards.**
Philippe Starck's unforgettable décor of plush-covered walls and funeral black marble is witty, if slightly grotesque. Less memorable are the punters: come here if you want to see France's answer to Hooray Henries raving to Hendrix or vintage Stones.

Olivia Valère
40 rue du Colisée, 75008 Paris (42.25.11.68). Metro Franklin D Roosevelt. **Open** 11pm-5am Mon-Sun. **Admission** members & guests

Warm Afro-Latin, reggae, salsa and tango beats have been attracting a lushly sensuous dance crowd to **Le Tango** (*listed under* **Les Halles**) *for years. On Fridays and Saturdays veteran Serge Kruger plays his mix of up-front and retro style music. Dress casual rather than smart.*

L'AMAZONIAL

Restaurant

RESTAURANT

3, RUE SAINTE-OPPORTUNE 75001 · PARIS · TELEPHONE: 42.33.53.13

The epitome of the cellar discotheque, **La Locomotive** *(listed under* **Pigalle***) three-tiered basement is home to the newest and best in speciality recordings, especially little-known labels crossing the Channel into the continent. Three one-nighters in one attract a young and trend-seeking weekday crowd; there's more suburbanites at weekends.*

only; membership 3,500F per year.
Credit AmEx, DC, M, TC, V.
Queen of the Paris nightclub scene, Olivia Valère is second home to hordes of fashion models and ageing celebrities. Soraya and Guy des Cars can be seen here, but it's a no-go area for non-Sloanes.

LES HALLES

Les Bains
7 rue du Bourg-l'Abbé, 75003 Paris (48.87.01.80). Metro Etienne Marcel. **Open** midnight-5am daily; restaurant and sushi bar 9pm-3am. **Admission** 120F (club). **Credit** V.
Housed in what were once Turkish baths, Les Bains is the capital's trendiest and would-be most exclusive club. Stiflingly intimate on busy nights, this is the 2am venue most favoured by showbiz and fashion personalities. Watch out for Marilyn's unpredictable door policy, as there's

no telling if your face will fit. A late supper is served to the right sort of person, but otherwise stay off the food, or stick to low-risk sushi.

Le Baiser Salé
58 rue des Lombards, 75001 Paris (42.33.37.71). Metro Châtelet. **Open** 8pm-5am daily. **Admission** 80F Mon-Thur, Sun; 90F Fri, Sat (includes concert and drink). **Credit** V.
A small, plain but comfortable venue. Sit at the 'U'-shaped bar on the ground floor under the giant video screen and sip freshly-pressed fruit juice or natural sorbet. Upstairs, the tiny smoke-choked room is home to a different jazz band every night.

Le Broad
3 rue de la Ferronnerie, 75001 Paris (42.36.59.73). Metro Châtelet. **Open** 11pm-4am daily. **Admission** free Mon-Thur; 45F Fri-Sun. **Credit** AmEx, DC, MC.

For older men of thirtysomething, this is a classic club on the gay circuit. Halles-dwellers, dandies and snappy dressers make up a large part of the crowd, attracted by the relaxed and friendly ambience. The different levels resound to House music, rap and recent videos.

La Plantation
45 rue Montpensier, 75001 Paris (49.27.06.21). Metro Palais-Royal. **Open** 11pm-5am Tue-Sun. **Admission** 80F. **No credit cards.**
An Afro-Caribbean club with tropical décor that's been hosted by Yaffa for the last 25 years, La Plantation attracts a relaxed and cosmopolitan crowd. Wednesday is theme night, while Sunday's the great bingo day.

La Scala
188 rue de Rivoli, 75001 Paris (42.60.45.64). Metro Palais-Royal. **Open** 11pm-5am daily. **Admission** 80F; free for girls except Fri, Sat.
Credit AmEx, DC, MC, V.
The club of the moment, La Scala attracts the capital's largest young crowd – over 40,000 a month. Disco, top 50, funk or tropical sounds are spun for an easy-going, conventional crowd with a smattering of tourists. Huge light shows, lasers and a video screen complete the show.

Le Slow Club
130 rue de Rivoli, 75001 Paris (42.33.84.30). Metro Châtelet, Pont Neuf. **Open** 10pm-3am Tue-Sat. **Admission** 50F Tue-Thur; 70F Fri-Sat. **Credit** V.
The oldest jazz club in Paris, Le Slow has been recently renovated though still conserving its retro décor. Meanwhile, students and flower-powered bimbos hip-hop three basements down.

Le Sunset
60 rue des Lombards, 75001 Paris (40.26.46.60). Metro Châtelet. **Open** 10pm-5am Mon-Sat. **Admission** 40F-80F depending on band. **Credit** V.
An unlikely jazz club where actress Miou-Miou meets her café-theatre friends and other *habitués* of Les Halles quarter. The draw is the food, the metro-style wall tiles, and up-beat sounds along with the best in the French jazz tradition.

Le Tango
13 rue Au-Maire, 75004 Paris (48.87.54.78). Metro Arts et Métiers. **Open** 11pm-4am Tue-Sat. **Admission** 50F-80F. **No credit cards.**
See **picture and caption.**

Les Trottoirs de Buenos Aires
37 rue des Lombards, 75001 Paris (42.33.58.37). Metro Châtelet. **Open** 8pm-1am Tue-Sat; 6pm-1.30am Sun. **Admission** 90F Mon-Sat; 70F Sun; *show times:* 10.30pm Mon; 8.30pm & 10.30pm Tue-Sat.
No credit cards.
The later sessions at Les Trottoirs are for Gardel's tango, following the traditional French 'chanson' at 8.30pm. Sundays used to be the preserve of old-timers who came to enjoy tea and tangos. Writer Julio Cortázar's favourite café-concert now attracts a more mixed crowd, but the concertina still sends shivers down your spine.
See also chapter **Cabaret & Chanson.**

PIGALLE

La Locomotive
90 boulevard de Clichy, 75018 Paris
(42.57.37.37). Metro Blanche.
Open 11pm-6am daily.
Admission 50F-90F. **Credit** AmEx, V.
See **picture and caption.**

SAINT GERMAIN

Bobino
20 rue de la Gaîté, 75014 Paris
(43.27.24.24). Metro Gaîté. **Open** 11pm-
4am Tue-Sun. **Admission** 100F. **Credit** V.
This is France's largest mega-disco. Once
a music hall, the two storeys have been
transformed with décor *à la* New York as
well as the addition of *objets*, like a
bomber and the odd telephone kiosk. On
Fridays there's a one-nighter with
Zoopsie and the grooviest of Paris's
trendsetters, Marthe Lagache.

LATIN QUARTER

Le Saint
7 rue Saint-Séverin, 75005 Paris
(43.25.50.04). Metro Saint Michel. **Open**
11pm-5am Tue-Sat. **Admission** free Mon,
Tue, Sun; 50F-70F Wed-Sat.
Credit AmEx, V.
Le Saint has three inter-communicating cav-
erns which reverberate to varying levels of
decibels. A mix of World Beats, more
relaxed rhythms and old acid head numbers
– such as quirky, French-style Jacques
Dutronc – play to an audience of students
and inquisitive tourists.

Zed Club
2 rue des Anglais, 75005 Paris
(43.54.93.78). Metro Maubert-Mutualité.
Open 10.30pm-3.30am Wed-Sat.
Admission 90F. **No credit cards.**
A Spartan whitewashed cavern, the Zed
attracts rock 'n' roll groovers of all ages who
vie for attention on the dance floor. The bar
specializes in dispensing giant glasses of *cit-
ron pressé* and Coke. Smart dress essential.

LES GRANDS
BOULEVARDS

Le Boy
6 rue Caumartin, 75009 Paris
(47.42.68.05). Metro Havre Caumartin.
Open 11pm-9am daily. **Admission** free
Mon-Thur, Sun; 50F Fri-Sat.
Credit AmEx, M, V.
Le Boy is back in the limelight as *the* gay
club and favoured haunt of all-night
groovers. The décor is high kitsch and
schmaltzy, with a half-moon dance floor,
tiered balcony surrounds and torch-bearing
nymphs. Currently it's packed all night till
nine in the morning with pretty boys and
smart girls fazed out by House music.

Bus Palladium
4 rue Fontaine, 75009 Paris (48.74.54.99).
Metro Pigalle. **Open** 11pm-5am Tue-Sun.
Admission 110F. **No credit cards.**
Aspiring salespersons flock here to Paris's
best pop session to blow their first pay-
packet. Usually packed with a young and
eager crowd, at the weekends the uniform
is 501s and Chevignon jackets. Wednesday
is revival night for the legendary Golf-

Drouot, guaranteed to catapult small rock
groups into celebrity. The Palladium is difficult to get into, so make sure you look
good or be prepared to slip a backhander
to get past the door.

La Main Jaune
Place de la Porte Champerret (47.63.26.47).
Metro Porte de Champerret. **Open** 2.30-6am
Thur; 10pm-5am Fri-Sat. **Admission** 110F.
No credit cards.
Get your skates on! This huge venue
with glitzy, witty Philippe Starck décor
has two dance floors, two bars and lots
of little stuccoed nooks for canoodling
in. A trendy young crowd resorts here
from the monied west side and the suburbs. The more daring roller-skate to
rap, soul and funk, while the timid just
go in their Reeboks.

Le Palace
8 rue du Faubourg Montmartre, 75009 Paris
(42.46.10.87). Metro Rue Montmartre.

Open 11pm-6am daily.
Admission 120F. **No credit cards.**
See **picture and caption.**

Le Rex Club
5 boulevard Poissonnière, 75002 Paris
(42.36.83.98). Metro Bonne Nouvelle.
Open 11.30pm-5am Tue-Sun.
Admission 90F. **No credit cards.**
The minor rock groups have disappeared,
to be replaced by Le Rex's *Aprem's à Toto*
Sunday afternoons (3-10pm), now the prime
venue for young live artists in Paris. At night
rap, funk and soul attract a relaxed, jeaned
and Perfectos'-loving crowd.

Le Scorpio
50 rue de la Chaussée-d'Antin, 75009 Paris
(42.80.69.40). Metro Havre Caumartin.
Open 11pm-5am Tue-Sun. **Admission** 60F.
Credit AmEx, V.
Once a haunt of gay men, Scorpio is now
popular with lesbians. Cropped hair and
leather jackets mix easily with high heels
and fish-net stockings.

Home to the top trendsetters, **Le Palace** *(listed under* **Les Grands**
Boulevards*) is Paris's best-known club, complete with rococo swirls, stucco*
mouldings and theatrical red plush. Closed down for six months at the end of
1989, it's due to re-open in the summer of 1990. The reason for the closure?
Some punter over-dosed in the toilets and the manager purportedly threw him
out onto the pavement, where he later died. So if you're feeling off-colour, give it
a miss. Otherwise, Wednesday remains the most popular night with French Kiss
and fashionable photographer Jean-Claude Lagrèze in attendance. House
music has fallen victim to retro discos and the swinging sixties. Sunday's tea
dance is still a favourite haunt of the capital's brightest beaux. Dress up – you'll
have to be fiendishly stylish (and different) if you want to be noticed.

The Early Hours

The party's over and you need a late-night snack, a packet of condoms or a taxi home. Look no further; we review those places that are open all hours.

Scratch the surface of Paris and you'll find hundreds of places open in the early hours. There's no shortage of restaurants or shops where you can stop off for a quick bite or buy up the store. We also give a lowdown on where to go in an emergency. For more information on what's open when, *see chapters* **Services** and **Survival**. Those who want to carry on bopping should *see chapter* **Nightlife**.

EATING & DRINKING

Paris, gastronomical capital of the world, is full of cafés and restaurants open well past midnight. Areas where one can always find something open include the Latin Quarter and Les Halles, and around the main train stations such as Gare du Nord. For a comprehensive selection of restaurants, bars and cafés, many of which are open very late (or early), *see chapter* **Eating & Drinking**. Below we list a selection.

FOOD TO TAKE AWAY

L'An 2000
82 boulevard des Batignolles, 75017 Paris (43.87.24.67). Metro Rome/bus 30. **Open** 5pm-1am Mon-Sat; 11-1am Sun, Public Holidays. **Credit** V.
Paella, the house speciality, is always on the menu, which also includes a daily-changing selection of cooked dishes to take away, usually in two-person portions.

Le Cochon Rose
44 boulevard de Clichy, 75018 Paris (46.06.86.25). Metro Place de Clichy/bus 30, 68, 74. **Open** 6pm-6am Mon-Wed, Fri-Sun. **Credit** FE$TC.
Sandwiched between two grocers, this caterer is open throughout the night. It's strong on delicatessen and traditional, ready-cooked meals, patisseries and drinks – excellent for night-time binges.

Layrac
29 rue de Buci, 75006 Paris (43.25.17.72; telephone orders 46.34.21.40). Metro Odéon/bus 63, 87, 96. **Open** 9-3am daily. **Credit** AmEx, DC, EC, MC, V.
Here you will find everything you need for a full-scale meal: first course, main course, dessert, wine and other drinks. Home deliveries are available until midnight, provided the order comes in before 11.45pm. Good, but expensive.

RESTAURANTS

Au Pied du Cochon
6 rue Coquillère, 75001 Paris (42.36.11.75). Metro Les Halles/bus 58, 69, 76, 85. **Open** 24 hours daily. **Average** 250F. **Credit** AmEx, DC, EC, TC, V.
Two minutes from the vibrant Les Halles complex, the Pied du Cochon's doors are open day and night. A sophisticated cuisine is on offer, with excellent meat, fish and seafood dishes.

Au Chien Qui Fume
33 rue du Pont Neuf, 75001 Paris (42.36.07.42). Metro Pont Neuf/bus 58, 70. **Open** noon-2am daily. **Average** 180F. **Credit** AmEx, DC, EC, MC, V.
A late-night restaurant with a family atmosphere and animal posters covering the walls. A word of advice: leave room for dessert, in particular for the famed chocolate mousse.

Bar à Huitres
33 boulevard Beaumarchais, 75003 Paris (48.87.98.92). Metro Bastille/bus 20, 29, 65. **Open** 11.45-2am daily. **Average** 200F. **Credit** AmEx, V.
If you want to savour shellfish after Cinderella time, this is a good place to go. Freshness and quality can be relied on, and you'll be served up to 2am.

La Champagne
10bis place de Clichy, 75009 Paris (48.74.44.48). Metro Place de Clichy/bus 30, 54, 74, 81. **Open** noon-2.25am daily. **Average** 300F. **Credit** AmEx, V.
Loup flambé (flambéed sea perch), fish and seafood will be served up to 2.25am precisely. Not always the friendliest of places, and don't bank on spending less than 300F per head.

Le Dieu Gambrinus
62 rue des Lombards, 75001 Paris (42.21.10.30). Metro les Halles/bus 38, 47. **Open** 11-6am daily. **Average** 120F; set menu 70F. **Credit** V.

This old-style brasserie in the heart of Les Halles provides plentiful food at reasonable prices. Choose from French favourites: mussels, *coq au vin* or Alsatian sauerkraut.

Gari's
63 avenue des Champs-Elysées, 75008 Paris (42.25.96.16). Metro Franklin D Roosevelt/bus 73. **Open** 9-2am daily. **Average** set menu 120F. **Credit** AmEx, DC, EC, MC, V.
The excellent regional cuisine served here will give you an insight into some of the culinary richness France can offer. In addition to the basic 120F menu, there's a different speciality for every day of the week: leg of lamb on Tuesday, Toulouse cassoulet on Wednesday, pot-au-feu on Thursday, and bouillabaisse (fish soup) on Friday.

Le Kikana
3 avenue du Maine, 75015 Paris (45.44.71.88). Metro Montparnasse/bus 28, 58. **Open** noon-7am daily. **Average** 180F. **Credit** V.
The atmosphere in this African restaurant is warm, enlivened by drum-beat background music. The house speciality is Tarot: a puréed root vegetable with spices, served with goat meat. The Kikana is one of the few African restaurants to offer this traditional dish.

Old Navy
150 boulevard Saint Germain, 75006 Paris (43.26.88.09). Metro Odéon/63, 70, 86, 87, 96 bus. **Open** 9.30-5am (approx) Mon-Sat; 10.30-5am (approx) Sun. **Average** 50F. **No credit cards.**
Five minutes from tourist and student-packed Saint Michel, the Old Navy brasserie stays open until 4am or 5am depending on the customer and the management's mood. All hot dishes cost 39F, but sandwich and salad eaters are also catered for. There's a relaxed, fun-loving atmosphere.

Le Pigalle
22 boulevard de Clichy, 75017 Paris (46.06.72.90). Metro place Clichy/bus 30, 54, 61, 95. **Open** 7.30-5am daily. **Average** 200F; set menu 160F. **Credit** AmEx, DC, V.
Fun and fizz all night long in this unassuming, friendly local café. Cure culinary cravings with the day's speciality.

Restaurant d'Alsace
39 avenue des Champs-Elysées, 75008 Paris (43.59.44.24). Metro Franklin D Roosevelt/bus 73. **Open** 24 hours daily. **Average** 300F. **Credit** DC, MC, V.
Alsatian regional specialities are available at all hours of the day and night at this celebrated Champs-Elysées eating house. Try out the sauerkraut or spindler veal escalope.

La Tour Monthlhery
5 rue des Prouvaires, 75001 Paris (42.36.21.82). Metro les Halles/21, 67, 69, 74, 76, 85 bus. **Open** 24 hours Mon-Fri. **Average** 180F. **Credit** V.
The regulars never go 'chez Tour Monthlhery', but 'chez Denise'. This well-established restaurant offers excellent and plentiful traditional cuisine at all hours of the day and night. There's just one thing you must never do: forget to reserve.

Le Verre Bouteille
85 avenue des Ternes, 75017 Paris (45.74.01.02). Metro Ternes/bus 43, 93. **Open** noon-3pm, 7.30pm-5am Mon-Fri. **Average** 100F. **Credit** AmEx, DC, V.

If you want a quirky décor come here, and admire walls festooned with draught boards and *jeu de l'oie* (a snakes and ladder-type traditional French game, based on geese). Bistro cuisine at its best is served here: simple meat dishes, sandwiches and salads. The genuinely friendly welcome will have you longing to return as soon as you leave.

SHOPPING

For a comprehensive list of shops *see section* **Shopping & Services**. Below we review the stores that are open after midnight.

BAKERIES

Two bakeries stay open after midnight:

Boulangerie de l'Ancienne Comédie
10 rue de l'Ancienne Comédie, 75006 Paris (43.26.89.72). Metro Odéon/bus 87, 96. **Open** 24 hours Mon-Sat; 7am-8pm Sun. **No credit cards.**
Bread, patisseries and *viennoiseries* to deal with that empty feeling just before dawn.

Boulangerie Trojette
2 rue Biot, 75017 Paris (43.87.68.84). Metro Place de Clichy/bus 30, 54, 74, 81. **Open** 11-2am Mon, Wed, Thur-Sun. **No credit cards.**

In addition to bread and *viennoiseries*, the shop also sells 'emergency' foods, dairy products, drinks and delicatessen.

BUTCHERS

Boucherie Bruneau
1 rue Monmartre, 75001 Paris (42.36.40.97). Metro Rue Monmartre/bus 20, 39, 48. **Open** 4.30am-7pm Tue-Fri; 4.30am-6pm Sat; 4.30-11am Sun. **No credit cards.**
This butcher's opening times are geared to its restaurant and mass catering clients, but there's nothing to stop individuals from taking advantage of the services.

DRUGSTORES

'Drugstores' in Paris are nothing like the basic American or British version: here they stock a great variety of generally top-quality goods: foodstuffs, gifts, cigarettes, alcohol and even books. There are several late-night ones dotted around Paris:

Drugstore Etoile
133 avenue des Champs-Elysées, 75008 Paris (47.23.54.34). Metro Georges V/bus 73. **Open** 10-2am daily. **Credit** AmEx, DC, V.

Drugstore Matignon
1 avenue de Matignon, 75008 Paris (43.59.38.70). Metro Franklin D Roosevelt/bus 32, 73. **Open** 10-2am daily. **Credit** AmEx, DC, EC, MC, V.

Drugstore Saint-Germain
149 boulevard Saint-Germain, 75006 Paris (42.22.92.50). Metro Saint-Germain-des-Prés/bus 39, 48, 63, 95. **Open** 10-2am daily. **Credit** AmEx, DC, EC, MC, V.

Multistore Hachette-Opéra
6 boulevard des Capucines, 75009 Paris (42.65.83.52). Metro Opéra/bus 42, 52. **Open** 11am-midnight daily. **Credit** AmEx, DC, EC, MC, V.
Stock up on your bed-time reading.

LOCAL FOODSTORES

Local shops that stay open till late (about 10pm) are generally run by North African immigrants and are found in most areas of Paris. The two listed below, open all night, are both in the 18th *arrondissement* and sell all basic products.

Libre Service
33 boulevard de Clichy, 75018 Paris (42.85.16.38). Metro Place de Clichy/bus 30, 54. **Open** 4pm-6am Mon, Tue, Thur-Sun. **No credit cards.**

Chez Salem
20 boulevard de Clichy, 75018 Paris (46.06.60.03). Metro Place de Clichy/bus 30, 54. **Open** 9pm-5am Mon; 24 hours Tue-Sun. **No credit cards.**

MUSIC SHOPS

Night-time music lovers in need of a new number after the FNAC has closed will find all kinds of music, records, cassettes or CDs in one place only – the Champs Elysées.

Champs Musique
84 avenue des Champs Elysées, 75008 Paris (45.62.65.46). Metro Franklin D Roosevelt/bus 73. **Open** 9.30-2am daily. **Credit** AmEx, DC, V.

Lido-Musique
68 avenue des Champs Elysées, 75008 Paris (45.62.65.46). Metro Franklin D Roosevelt/bus 73. **Open** 10-1am Mon-Sat; noon-1am Sun. **Credit** AmEx, DC, EC, MC, V.

POST OFFICE

PTT
52 rue du Louvre, 75002 Paris (40.28.20.00). Metro Louvre/bus 67, 74, 85. **Open** 8am-midnight Mon-Thur, Sun; 24 hours Fri, Sat. **No credit cards.** The last pick-up for international post is about 7pm, and anything later will have to wait till the next day.
Photocopying machine available.

SUPERMARKETS

There are only two very late-opening supermarkets in Paris:

As Eco
11 rue de Brantôme, 75003 Paris (42.74.30.19). Metro Rambuteau/bus 29. **Open** 9am-12.30am Mon-Fri; 9am-10pm Sat. **Credit** V.

Paris is still buzzing after-hours when most cities are fast asleep. Traffic jams are not uncommon, particularly in the Latin Quarter and around the Arc de Triomphe, when night-clubs close and happy boppers make for their homes or hotels.

*Pharmacies have a monopoly on issuing medication, and even on certain brands of deodorant, shampoo and skin-care lotion. Staff at pharmacies can provide basic medical attention (for a small fee) and will indicate the nearest doctor on duty. The **Pharmacie des Champs** (listed under **Health/Pharmacies**) is open 24 hours daily.*

Dentists: SOS Dentistes
(42.61.12.00). **Open** 24 hours daily.
Contact for emergency dental treatment.

PHARMACIES

There is only one, yes one, pharmacy open round the clock in Paris, the **Pharmacie des Champs** (*see below*), and it is, of course, in the Champs Elysées. A number of others remain open until 2am.

Delaître
149 boulevard Saint Germain, 75006 Paris (42.22.80.00). Metro Saint Germain-des-Prés/bus 39, 63, 70, 87. **Open** 9-2am Mon-Sat; 10-2am Sun. **Credit** AmEx, DC, EC, MC, V.

Finkel
133 avenue des Champs Elysées, 75008 Paris (47.20.39.25). Metro Franklin D Roosevelt/bus 73. **Open** 8.30-2am Mon-Sat. **Credit** AmEx, DC, EC, MC, V.

Matignon
2 rue de Matignon, 75008 Paris (43.59.86.55). Metro Franklin D Roosevelt/bus 32, 73. **Open** 8.30-2am Mon-Sat; 10-2am Sun. **Credit** AmEx, DC, EC, MC, V.

Pharmacie des Champs
84 avenue des Champs Elysées, 75008 Paris (45.62.02.41). Metro Franklin D Roosevelt/bus 73. **Open** 24 hours daily. **Credit** V.

TRANSPORT

At around 12.45am the metro closes its doors. On the bus front, all services stop at midnight, if not much earlier. So there are only two ways to get round Paris at night: for those who are patient, there are the **Noctambus** (*see below*), and for the rest, taxis.

NOCTAMBUS

Nine night buses start running at about 1am and stop at 5am, all starting or ending at the place du Châtelet. *Carte Orange* (season ticket) holders travel free; otherwise tickets have to be bought on the bus. For further information, pick up a night-bus map at any metro station, or contact **RATP** *(43.46.14.14)*. *See also chapter* **Travelling Around Paris.**

TAXIS

The following taxi firms take telephone bookings 24 hours daily.

Alpha Taxis *(45.85.85.85).*
Artaxi *(42.21.50.50).*
Taxis Bleu *(49.36.10.10).*
Taxi Etoile *(42.70.41.41).*
Taxi G7 *(47.39.33.33).*

As Eco used to be open even longer hours. It was a major disappointment when this supermarket, two minutes from the Pompidou Centre, re-scheduled its opening times – for security reasons, it would appear.

Prisunic
109 rue de la Boétie, 75008 Paris (42.25.27.46). Metro Franklin D Roosevelt/bus 32, 73. **Open** 9.45am-midnight Mon-Sat. **Credit** V.
If you suddenly have an urge to buy clothes at night, the Champs Elysées Prisunic is the only place to do it. You can buy anything from a pair of socks to Petit Lu biscuits here, taking in toiletries on the way.

HEALTH

Stomach-ache, a nasty fall, toothache...acute pain requires rapid relief. We list below a few useful telephone numbers; for full details of medical and counselling services, *see chapter* **Survival.**

EMERGENCY AND S.O.S

Ambulance service: Samu
(45.67.50.50). **Open** 24 hours daily.
Phone for emergency ambulance service.

Fire department: Sapeurs Pompiers
(18). **Open** 24 hours daily.
Phone for fire and other emergency services.

Doctors: SOS Médecins
(47.07.77.77). **Open** 24 hours daily.
Contact for emergency doctor service. House calls only, charges start at 150F.

Heart failure: SOS Cardiologues
(47.07.50.50). **Open** 24 hours daily.
Call for emergency heart treatment; the doctors are trained cardiologists.

Sport & Fitness

Burn off those ballooning calories by simply trying to reach one of the outlying sports parks in Paris.

Nearly every imaginable sport is available somewhere in the Paris area, whether you want to spectate or participate. The problem is getting to it. Because the good Baron Haussmann – Napoléon III's favourite builder – decided to build *up* rather than *out*, the city is very compact. This means that apart from the parks, there are virtually no open spaces in central Paris that have sports facilities.

Tennis courts are to be found near the *portes* (gates) of Paris. Swimming pools are mostly underground or outside the city proper. Even getting to a gym or a park for a bit of exercise can mean an hour's ride on the metro. There are of course the two big parks, the **Bois de Boulogne** and the **Bois de Vincennes** (*see below* **Big Venues**), but the thought of having to trek across Paris to reach them puts many people off. And to play on a real golf course – a recent French craze – you have to catch a train out into the suburbs.

To make matters worse, once you get where you're going the facilities may be closed because of strange opening hours. You may encounter problems trying to get in as many places insist on you being a member of the club or association. It's not unusual to pay a nominal membership fee, even if you're only going to use the facilities once in your life. Some of the private fitness centres offer day passes or week passes, others allow visitors in as long as they're guests of members. Sports parks (*see below* **Big Venues**) are located in Paris's suburbs; they have a selection of sporting facilities that people can use on a daily basis.

Spectator sports pose a different problem; it's not so much the distance you have to travel, but the crowds you have to endure. Every year people fight for seats to spectate at Roland-Garros – the French Open Tennis Tournament – while tickets to major soccer matches

remain as elusive as a parking space near the Parc des Princes stadium. If you're determined to get in to major sporting events, you'll have to be highly motivated, well-informed and know exactly where you're going. Being able to speak a bit of French will stand you in good stead.

KEEPING INFORMED

A good magazine to keep you up with what's happening sports-wise is *Le Figaro*'s Wednesday supplement, called *Figaroscope*. Here you'll find a weekly list of most of the major – and some minor – sporting events taking place throughout the French capital. If you're not in town on a Wednesday try the all-sports daily called *L'Equipe*. This newspaper gives details on every possible sport with practical information and in-depth articles. It's perfect, so long as you can read French.

Allô-Sports

(42.76.54.54). **Open** 10.30am-5pm Mon-Thur; 10.30am-4.30pm Fri.
Municipal phoneline, giving information on sports and sporting events in the Paris area.

BIG VENUES

THE PARKS

Just outside the huge exterior boulevard are two large parks called **Bois de Boulogne** and **Bois de Vincennes**. Both offer any prospective athlete countless sporting possibilities. To find your way around, consult the maps posted at most of the entry points. We give a breakdown of what you'll find in these green havens.

Bois de Boulogne

Metro Porte d'Auteuil, Porte Dauphine, Porte Maillot, Sablons/bus 73, 244. **Open** dawn till dusk.
Surrounded by the 16th *arrondissement* to

the east, Neuilly to the north and a big loop in the Seine to the west, this 863-hectare (2,132 acres) park takes its name from a church that Philippe IV (1268-1314) had built here upon his return from a pilgrimage to Boulogne. Today it's a favourite place for Sunday *promeneurs* and sports-minded Parisians. In the south-west and south-east corners are the Longchamp and Auteuil Race Tracks. It's in the former that the two biggest French racing events take place every year: the Prix de l'Arc de Triomphe and the Prix du Président de la République. Situated between the two is the famous Roland-Garros Stadium where the French Tennis Open is played (*see below* **Spectator Sports**). *See also* **picture and caption**.

Bois de Vincennes

Metro Château de Vincennes, Porte de Charenton, Porte Dorée /RER Fontenay-sous-Bois, Joinville/bus 46, 56, PC. **Open** dawn till dusk.
On the east side of the city is the 995-hectare (2,458 acres) Bois de Vincennes. Less chic than its sister-park on the other side of Paris, it is nonetheless as crowded at the weekends and just as charming. And it does have the advantage of not being so full of cars. Like the Bois de Boulogne, you can rent rowing-boats on the two lakes or go jogging around them. There are several soccer and rugby fields as well as handball courts in the eastern half of the park. Although these are used by many private associations, they are open to the public. There are 21 public tennis courts in the Plaine de Saint-Hubert which can be rented for a nominal fee (*see below* **Tennis**). At the Porte Dorée entrance and next to the Lac des Minimes you'll find stands for renting bicycles. There are also private riding clubs and a large zoo with an impressive fake mountain.

MULTI-SPORTS COMPLEX

Aquaboulevard

4 rue Louis-Armand, 75015 Paris (40.60.10.00). *Metro Balard/RER Boulevard Victor/bus 42, 169*. **Open** 8am-1am daily. **Admission** *Aquatic Park*: 60F adults; 45F 3-12s; under-3s free; *water sports plus gym*: 140F. **No credit cards.**
This new, ultra-modern sports complex, recently opened near the boulevard Périphérique, is today's response to the age-old question: how to bring the country to the city? Here you'll find putting greens, palm trees, a wave pool, giant water slides, 12 tennis courts, six squash courts, and a bowling alley. Other diversions include video games, clothing boutiques, restaurants and sun-bathing areas. The whole complex is run by Forest Hill, a local (despite the English name) company that also runs rather expensive private tennis clubs and gyms. Many activities go on till 1am and you can either take an annual membership or go à la carte as many times as you like.

SPORTS PARKS

Below we list three of the better equipped parks.

Parc d'Antony

148bis, avenue du Général de Gaulle, 92160 Antony (43.50.39.35). *RER Croix de Berny (RER line B)*. **Open** dawn to dusk.

Located next to a regional forest, just ten minutes from central Paris by RER, this park has ten tennis courts (only open to the public during the week), five soccer fields, and an outdoor olympic-sized pool with a high diving area. Obviously the pool is closed during the cold season (Oct-May). Take the RER line B to the station Croix de Berny, then walk towards the Parc de Sceaux. There will be signs indicating the entrance.

Parc de Puteaux
Ile de Puteaux, 92800 Puteaux (45.06.68.12; pool 45.06.15.98). Metro Pont de Neuilly, then bus 144. **Open** dawn to dusk.
Just a skip up the river from the skyscrapers of la Défense, this island is a good place to get sporty in a natural setting not far from central Paris. An olympic-size, outdoor swimming pool (closed Oct-May) with lots of room for sunbathing, 24 tennis courts and five soccer fields await you.

Parc du Tremblay
11 boulevard des Alliés, 94500 Champigny sur Marne (48.81.11.22). RER Joinville (line A), then bus 108N. **Open** dawn to dusk.
This 73-hectare (180 acre) park is a bit further out than the other parks, but it's well worth the trip. The very dynamic local government has made an effort to offer sports facilities catering for all ages: from soccer fields (10) and tennis courts (17) to *boules* rinks and roller-skating tracks. The soccer fields and tennis courts are only open to residents of Paris or Val de Marne. They also have handball courts, archery ranges and bicycle paths. Set in a hilly forest near the Marne River, it's an excellent place for a hearty jog in the woods.

KEEPING FIT

In the last ten years, Paris has seen an explosion in the gym and fitness market. Working out used to take place in small, dusty local gyms, each with a handful of clients, or in huge swimming pools. All that has changed. Today it's a big business with lots of top-market chic locations, buy-outs by big corporations and constant improvements to beat the competition.

GARDEN GYM
This chain of gyms offers a book of ten tickets (for ten visits) at 450F to non-members, making it one of the best deals if you're only in Paris for a short time. But if you're staying for more than two weeks, invest in a monthly pass for the same price. **Garden Gym** have seven gyms throughout Paris and will soon be opening another under the monumental Arche de la Défense, renamed Arche de la Fraternité. Smaller and more intimate than the **Gymnase Club** chain (*see below*), the atmosphere is less that of a fitness factory and more of a club, and the gyms are more family-orientated. Unfortunately the gyms are too small for the lunch hour or rush hour crowds, so plan

accordingly. The **Garden Gym Molitor**, though far from the centre of town, is set in a pleasant, art-deco swimming pool and next to the Bois de Boulogne where they take jogging groups. There are also two very centrally located gyms which are hard to come by in such an old city: the **Palais-Royal**, which offers 1,000 square metres (10,780 square feet) of fitness space as well as jogging in the Tuileries Gardens ; and the **Drouot**, situated in the heart of the banking and auction house area of Paris.

Garden Gym Beaugrenelle
208 rue de Vaugirard, 75015 Paris (47.83.99.45). Metro Volontaires/bus 39, 49, 70. **Open** 7.30am-9.30pm Mon-Fri; 9am-5pm Sat; 9am-2pm Sun. **Admission** *see above.* **Credit** AmEx, V.

Garden Gym Drouot
2 rue Drouot, 75009 Paris (42.46.60.14). Metro Richelieu-Drouot/bus 20, 39, 48. **Open** 8.30am-9pm Mon-Fri; 10am-5pm Sat. **Admission** *see above.* **Credit** V.

Garden Gym Elysées
65 avenue des Champs-Elysées, 75008 Paris (42.25.87.20). Metro Franklin D Roosevelt/bus 32, 73. **Open** 9am-10pm Mon-Fri; 10am-5pm Sat. **Admission** *see above.* **Credit** AmEx, DC, V.

Garden Gym Javel
62 rue de Javel, 75015 Paris (45.77.18.32). Metro Javel/bus 42, 62. **Open** 7.30am-9.30pm Mon-Fri; 9am-5pm Sat; 9am-2pm Sun. **Admission** *see above.* **Credit** V.

Garden Gym Molitor
12 avenue de la Porte-Molitor, 75016 Paris (46.51.10.61). Metro Michel-Ange-Molitor/bus 52, 123, PC. **Open** 10am-9pm Mon-Fri; 10am-4.30pm Sat. **Admission** *see above.* **Credit** AmEx, V.

Garden Gym Neuilly
123 avenue Charles de Gaulle, 92100 Neuilly (47.47.62.62). Metro Sablon/bus 73. **Open** 8.30am-10pm Mon-Fri; 9am-5pm Sat; 9am-3pm Sun. **Admission** *see above.* **Credit** AmEx, DC, V.

Garden Gym Palais-Royal
147bis rue Saint Honoré, 75001 Paris (40.20.03.03). Metro Palais-Royal/bus 21, 27, 29, 39, 48, 81. **Open** 8am-10pm Mon-Fri; 9am-5pm Sat. **Admission** *see above.* **Credit** AmEx, V.

GYMNASE CLUB
This multi-million franc chain is the biggest on the market. Their gyms are often spacious and offer a great variety of fitness programmes and facilities. The clientele is generally young and flashy. You can buy a book of 10 tickets for 500F, plus a 220F registration fee. If you want to take out a year's membership, expect to pay between 2,600F and 3,100F. Gymnase Club also offer services like free towels and a golf card, giving you reductions at certain golf courses. For certain services or activities you may be charged more, so ask first. Most of the gyms have a particularly strong feature, such as the driving range for golfers in the **Porte Maillot** gym; the wall for cliff-scalers in **La Défense**; the martial arts classes and turn-of-the-century pool in the **Monceau** gym, and the Saturday session for toddlers in the **Montsouris** gym (*see below*).

The **Bois de Boulogne** (*listed under* **Big Venues/The Parks**) *has a vast selection of sports facilities. On the Allée de Longchamps, near the Porte Maillot, is a free roller-skating rink which is open to the public. Around the Lac Inférieur is an excellent and quite popular jogging track measuring 2,350 metres (7,780 feet) in circumference. During the day, you can rent row-boats on this same lake by the hour. At the northern-most point of the lake is the bicycle rental stand; here you can hire a bike for the day and take advantage of the 95 kilometre (59 miles) of roads and paths in the park. You'll also see tennis courts, equestrian centres and swimming pools; these often belong to private, rather exclusive clubs.*

Gymnase Club Denfert-Rochereau
28 avenue du Général-Leclerc, 75014 Paris (45.42.50.57). Metro Mouton-Duvernet/bus 38, 68. **Open** 8am-10pm Mon-Fri; 8am-8pm Sat; 9am-3pm Sun. **Admission** *see above.* **Credit** V.

Gymnase Club Grenelle
8 rue Frémicourt, 75015 Paris (45.75.34.00). Metro Commerce/bus 70. **Open** 8am-10pm Mon-Fri; 9am-8pm Sat; 9am-5pm Sun. **Admission** *see above.* **Credit** V.

Gymnase Club Italie
Centre Galaxie, 16 rue Vandrezanne, 75013 Paris (45.80.34.16). Metro Place d'Italie/bus 47, 57, 62. **Open** 7.45am-10pm Mon-Fri; 7.45am-7pm Sat; 9am-5pm Sun. **Admission** *see above.* **Credit** V. With 18 metre pool.

Gymnase Club La Défense
Les Quatre Temps, Parvis 1 La Défense, Paris (47.78.70.92). RER La Défense/bus 73. **Open** 7.30am-9pm Mon-Fri; 9am-7pm Sat. **Admission** *see above.* **Credit** V.

Gymnase Club La Fayette
10 rue de la Victoire, 75009 Paris (48.74.58.49). Metro Le Peletier/bus 42, 67, 74. **Open** 7.30am-9pm Mon-Fri; 8am-5pm Sat. **Admission** *see above.* **Credit** V.

Gymnase Club Les Champs-Elysées
55bis rue de Penthieu, 75008 Paris (45.62.99.76). Metro Franklin D Roosevelt/bus 32, 73. **Open** 7am-10pm Mon-Fri; 9am- 8pm Sat; 9am-4pm Sun. **Admission** *see above.* **Credit** V.

Gymnase Club Monceau
24 rue de Chazelles, 75017 Paris (43.80.66.14). Metro Courcelles/bus 38, 84. **Open** 8am-9pm Mon-Fri; 8am-6pm Sat. **Admission** *see above.* **Credit** V.

Gymnase Club Montsouris
73 rue Brillat-Savarin, 75013 Paris (45.80.34.16). RER Cité Universitaire (line B)/bus 67, PC. **Open** 9am-9pm Mon-Fri; 9am-6pm Sat; 9am-2pm Sun. **Admission** *see above.* **Credit** V.

Gymnase Club République
11 rue de Malte, 75011 Paris (47.00.80.95). Metro Filles de Calvaire, Oberkampf/bus 20, 56, 65. **Open** 8am-9.30pm Mon, Wed, Fri; 8am-10pm Tue, Thur; 8am-6pm Sat; 10am-2pm Sun. **Admission** *see above.* **Credit** V.

VITATOP

This small chain with three locations in Paris aims for the top of the market. Vitatop's clubs are quite sophisticated; each with a pool, a Jacuzzi and all the modern equipment for a real sweaty workout. For visitors they offer a day pass for 150F which they will reimburse, should you choose to become a card-carrying member (3,800F per year). Here you'll find very personalized service and no charge for extras. In their **Porte Maillot** location *(see below)* they have a wall for cliff-scaling and offer jogging in the nearby Bois de Boulogne. Their **Sofitel** gym is on the 22nd floor of a hotel, bedecked with glass-enclosed elevators (no need to be a client of the hotel). On the roof you'll find a small pool and an area for bronzing your body with a view over Paris. Their **Vaugirard** branch is ideally located near Saint-Germain-des-Prés, an otherwise gymless area.

Vitatop Porte Maillot
58 Boulevard Gouvion-Saint-Cyr, 75017 Paris (40.68.00.21). Metro Porte Maillot./bus PC, 73, 82. **Open** 9am-9pm Mon, Tue, Thur; 9am-10pm Wed, Fri; 9am-7pm Sat; 9am-3pm Sun. **Admission** *see above.* **Credit** V.

Vitatop Sofitel
8 rue Louis-Armand, 75015 Paris (45.54.79.00). Metro Balard/bus 42. **Open** 9am-10pm Mon; 9am-9pm Tue-Fri; 9am-7pm Sat; 9am-3pm Sun. **Admission** *see above.* **Credit** V.

Vitatop Vaugirard
118 rue de Vaugirard, 75006 Paris (45.44.38.01). Metro Raspail/bus 68. **Open** 9am-9pm Mon, Wed, Fri; 9am-10pm Tue, Thur; 9am-7pm Sat; 9am-3pm Sun. **Admission** *see above.* **Credit** V.

SWIMMING POOLS

The city of Paris has 36 swimming pools that are open to the general public: 26 municipal, seven run by private organizations and three privately-owned. Opening times vary tremendously. Phone first to make sure that the pool is open. If you're in need of a quiet swim, avoid the pools on Wednesday and Saturday afternoons because this is when Parisian kids take the place over. Below is a selection of some of the better pools. This is not exhaustive; you'll find a complete list at the local Town Hall *(Mairie)* or simply by calling **Allô Sports** *see above* **Keeping Informed.**

1ST ARRONDISSEMENT

Piscine Suzanne-Berlioux
20 place de la Rotonde, 75001 Paris (42.36.98.44). Metro Les Halles/bus 21, 58, 67, 69, 70, 72, 74, 76. **Open** 11.30am-8pm Mon; 11.30am-10pm Tue, Thur, Fri; 10am-10pm Wed; 9am-5pm Sat, Sun. **Admisson** 18F adults; 14F children; 160F for 10 tickets (adults); 130F for 10 tickets (children). *See* **picture and caption.** *Indoor. No solarium.*

4TH ARRONDISSEMENT

Piscine Saint-Merri
18 rue de Renard, 75004 Paris (42.72.29.45). Metro Rambuteau, Hôtel-de-Ville/bus 38, 47, 75. **Open** 7am-7pm Mon-Sat; 8am-5.30pm Sun. **Admission** 9F adults; 4.50F under-16s.

*The **Piscine Suzanne-Berlioux** (listed under **Swimming Pools**) is a newly opened, underground 50-metre pool with pyramidal skylights. It's one of the two municipal pools to stay open in the evening. The pool is modern and clean, with a touch of greenery thanks to a tropical greenhouse boasting 700 species of plants. Like the local area, the clientele is young and trendy.*

The **Piscine du Marché Saint Germain** *(listed under* **Swimming Pools***) is a rather small, underground pool that has two big advantages: its specially designed, extra-deep diving section and its location – it's in the heart of this quartier.*

Centrally located right behind the Pompidou Centre in an ugly attempt at seventies' architecture. This pool is more intimate than its fashionable neighbour in Les Halles; some even say it's the artists' and intellectuals' pool.
Indoor with solarium. Pool: 25 x 10 metres.

5TH ARRONDISSEMENT

Piscine de Pontoise
19 rue de Pontoise, 75005 Paris (43.54.82.45). Metro Maubert-Mutualité/bus 63, 86, 87. **Open** noon-1.45pm, 5-7.30pm, Mon; noon-1.45pm, 5-9pm, Tue; 11.15am-5.30pm Wed; noon-1.45pm, 5-7.30pm, Thur; noon-1.45pm, 5.30-9.30pm Fri; 10am-7.30pm, Sat; 8am-6pm Sun. **Admission** 19F adults pool only; 16F under-16s.
This old pool, bedecked with a thirties' style skylight and retro tiles, has a very dynamic health and fitness programme with Jacuzzi, sauna and squash courts as well as classes for kids and pregnant women. There's nude swimming every Monday and Thursday from 8pm to 10 pm.
Indoor with solarium. Pool: 33 x 15 metres.

Piscine Jean Taris
16 rue Thouin, 75005 Paris (43.25.54.03). Metro Cardinal-Lemoin/bus 47, 89. **Open** 7am-8am, 11.30am-1.30pm Tue, Thur; 7am-8am, 11.30am-5.30pm Wed; 7am-8am, 11.30am-1pm, 5-8pm Fri; 7am-5.30pm Sat; 8am-5.30pm Sun.
Admission 9F adults; 4.50F children.
Looking out onto the Panthéon and the Lycée Henri IV gardens, this pool is often full of students. Built in 1978, it offers the

delightful advantage of having no chlorine as the water is purified electronically. Open certain nights, phone for details.
Indoor. No solarium. Two pools: 25 x15 metres and 6 x 15 metres.

6TH ARRONDISSEMENT

Piscine du Marché Saint-Germain
7 rue Clément, 75006 Paris (43.29.08.15). Metro Mabillon/bus 39, 63, 70, 87. **Open** 7am-8am, 11.30am-1pm, 5-8pm Tue; 7am-8am, 11.30am-5pm Wed; 7am-8am, 11.30am-1pm Thur, Fri; 7am-6pm Sat; 8am-6pm Sun. **Admission** 9F adults; 4.50F children.
See **picture and caption.**
Indoor. No solarium. Pool: 25 x 12.5 metres.

7TH ARRONDISSEMENT

Piscine Déligny
5 quai Anatole-France, 75007 Paris (45.51.72.15). Metro Solférino/bus 24, 69, 73. **Open** summer only. **Admission** 40F adults; 20F under-16s.
This old Parisian institution (built in 1840) looks more like a barge than a pool as it sits comfortably on the Seine at the foot of the Musée d'Orsay. But it's been the chic place to swim for years, and even more so today, as it now belongs to the owners of the ever-fashionable night club Les Bains (ex-les Bains-Douches). There are 1,500 square metres (16,140 square feet) of sun-soaking space, a bar, a fitness room, and a restaurant. The place stays full all summer despite the

40F entrance fee (remaining chic is priceless) and you can actually swim here since everyone else is busy tanning. On certain nights the pool stays open for soirées and midnight dips.
Outdoor with tanning deck. Pool: 50 x 15 metres.

11TH ARONDISSEMENT

Piscine Oberkampf
160 rue Oberkampf, 75011 Paris (43 57 56 19). Metro Ménilmontant/bus 96. **Open** 11.30am-1pm, 4.30-6.30pm Mon, Thur, Sun; 11.30am-1pm, 4.30-5.30pm Fri; 8.30am-1pm Sat. **Admission** 14F adults; 9F children; 10 entries 120F.
Set in a tiny cul-de-sac in a traditionally middle-class area, here you'll find two old-fashioned pools which are neither very big nor very crowded. One of them is L-shaped and topped-off with a glass dome.
Indoor. No solarium. Two pools: 15 x 6 metres and 9 x 6 meters.

12TH ARRONDISSEMENT

Piscine Roger-LeGall
34 boulevard Carnot, 75012 Paris (46.28.77.03). Metro Porte de Vincennes/bus 46, 56. **Open** noon-2pm, 5-8pm Mon, Tue, Thur; 9am-9pm Wed; noon-2pm, 5-9pm, Fri; noon-7pm Sat; 9am-6pm Sun. **Admission** 17.50F adults; 12.50 F children; 10 entries 150F.
Almost in the suburbs, on the edge of the Bois de Vincennes, this rather calm pool is covered with a tent every winter that comes off during the hot months. As it is run by the municipal swimming team races are occasionally held.
Both indoor & outdoor with solarium. Two pools: 50 x 15 metres and 25 x 12.5 metres.

13TH ARRONDISSEMENT

Piscine Buttes-aux-Cailles
5 place Paul-Verlaine, 75013 Paris (45.89.60.05). Metro Place d'Italie/bus 27, 47, 57, 67, 83. **Open** 7am-8am, 11.30am-1pm, 4.30-6.30pm Tue; 7am-8am, 11.30am-6.30pm Thur, Fri, Sat; 8am-5.30pm Sun. **Admission** 15F adults; 13F children.
Built in 1910 and renovated in 1924, this beautiful pool offers delightful coloured Italian tiles and an art deco, vaulted ceiling. The smaller pool is out of doors and is open during the summer months; they claim it's fed by an artesian well. There is also a special area for older swimmers. Beyond the regular hours, they remain open Thursday and Friday afteroons.
Indoor & outdoor pools. Two pools: 33 x 12 metres and 25 x12.5 metres.

15TH ARRONDISSEMENT

Piscine Armand-Massard
66 boulevard du Montparnasse, 75015 Paris (45.38.65.19). Metro Montparnasse-Bienvenue/bus 28, 48, 82, 92, 95, 96. **Open** 8am-5.30pm Tue, Thur-Sun; 8am-8.30pm Wed. **Admission** 9F adults; 4.50F children.
This vast underground swimming complex, under the famous Montparnasse skyscraper, is quite popular with young Parisians. Here you'll find three pools in all, the smallest of which is for beginners. You can also practise yoga, karate or even basketball in the gymnasium.
Indoor. No solarium. Three pools: 33 x 15metres, 25 x 12.5 metres and 12.5 x 6 metres.

Piscine Emile-Anthoine

9 rue Jean-Rey, 75015 Paris (45.67.10.20).
Metro Bir-Hakeim/bus 82. **Open** 7am-
8am,11.30am-1pm Tue, Thur, Fri; 7am-8am,
11.30am-5.30pm Wed; 7am-5.30pm
Sat; 8am-5.30pm Sun.
Admission 9F adults; 4.50F children.
This ultra-modern pool with gym and outdoor racing track offers a view of the
nearby Eiffel Tower. Here you won't feel closed in;
maybe that's why it's so popular and often
crowded. The pool is ideal for the disabled.
*Indoor with bronzing in terraced garden. Two
pools: 25 x 12.5 metres and 12.5 x 6 metres.*

16TH ARRONDISSEMENT

Piscine d'Auteuil

Bois de Boulogne, Route des Lacs, 75016
Paris (42.24.07.59). Metro Ranelagh/bus
PC. **Open** 7-8am, 11.30am-1pm Tue, Thur,
Fri; 7-8am, 11.30am-5.30pm Wed; 7am-
5.30pm Sat; 8am-5.30pm Sun.
Admission 9F adults; 4.50F children.
Set in the heart of the Auteuil Race Track
in the Bois de Boulogne, it's not surprising
to discover that this pool is closed at noon on
race days. Built underground, but very
bright and with an outdoor sunbathing area,
this uncrowded pool is well worth the hike.
*Indoor with outdoor tanning area. Two pools:
25 x 15 metres and 15 x 6.5 metres.*

Piscine Henry-de-Montherlant

32 boulevard Lannes, 75016 Paris
(45.03.03.28). Metro Porte-Dauphine /bus PC
Open 7-8am, 11.30am-1pm, 5.15-8.30pm Tue,
Wed, Thur, Fri; 7am-5.15pm Sat; 8am-5.15pm
Sun. **Admission** 9F adults; 4.50F children.
Not far from the Bois de Boulogne, this
huge, modern pool has a very chic clientele.
Although it's quite popular, one never really
feels closed in. There are also tennis courts
and a gymnasium for sports fans as well as a
water slide for the wee ones.
*Indoor with large outdoor tanning area. Two
pools: 25 x 15 metres and 15 x 6 metres.*

17TH ARRONDISSEMENT

Piscine Champerret

36 boulevard de Reims, 75017 Paris
(47.66.49.98) Metro Porte de
Champerret/bus 84, 92, 163, 164, 165.
Open 11.30am-2pm, 4.30-8pm Tue, Thur,
Fri; 11.30am-8pm Wed; 9am-7pm Sat, Sun.
Admission 18F adults; 15F children.
This is one of the more recent additions to
the Paris pool collection and like its cousin
in Les Halles, it's open all day long. It's
bright and pleasant, with a big tanning section. The only problem is it's stuck
between the exterior boulevards and the
périphérique, so it's some way away. There
are also tennis courts and a gym, a diving
board and a slide for kiddies.

18TH ARRONDISSEMENT

Piscine des Amiraux

6 rue Hermann-Lachapelle, 75018 Paris
(46.06.46.47). Metro Simplon/bus 56. **Open**
5-7.30pm Mon; 7-8am, 11.30am-1pm Tue,
Thur, Fri; 7-8am, 11.30am-5.50pm Wed; 7am-
5.30pm Sat; 8am-5.30pm Sun. **Admission** 9F
adults; 4.50F children.
Built in 1930 by Henri Sauvage, creator of the
Samaritaine department store, this pool is an
architectural phenomenon. Renovated in 1982,

Located in a former cinema, the **Ecole de Golf de Paris** (listed under
Golf) now offers 14 driving tees and a putting green in a very pleasant setting.
The Ecole claims to be the only place in Paris to have a Swing Analyzer, the
latest US gadget to analyse your golfing methods. There's also a sauna and a
boutique, and the loan of golfing equipment comes free of charge.

it's perfectly equipped for modern needs.
Besides the traditional hours, the pool is open
from 5pm till 7.30pm on Monday nights.
Indoor. No solarium. Pool: 33 x 10 metres.

19TH ARRONDISSEMENT

Piscine Georges-Hermant

4 rue David d'Angers, 75019 Paris
(42.02.45.10). Metro Danube, Ourcq/bus 75
Open 11.30am-1.15pm, 4.30-7.45pm Mon,
Thur; 11.30am-1.15pm, 4.30-6.45pm Tue, Fri;
8.30am-6.45pm Wed, Sat; 8.30am-1.45pm
Sun. **Admission** 15F adults; 11F under-16s;
10 entries 114F (adults), 87F (children).
This is the biggest pool in the French capital.
Set not far from the Buttes-Chaumont park,
this rather old-fashioned pool has a sliding
roof that is opened in the summer for tanning fans. There's also a diving area.
Indoor with sliding roof. Pool: 50 x 20 metres.

20TH ARRONDISSEMENT

Piscine Georges-Vallerey

148, avenue Gambetta, 75021 Paris
(40.31.15.20). Metro Saint-Fargeau/bus 61,
96 **Open** 10am-5pm Mon-Wed, Fri; 11.30am-
10pm Tue, Thur; 9am-5pm Sat, Sun.
Admission 18F adults; 14F children.
This pool was the first to hold swimming
competitions as an Olympic sport back in
1924. It's also where Johnny Weissmuller,
future Tarzan, swam away. Today it's spank-
ing new as it has undergone renovations; it
offers very sophisticated equipment. The
roof comes off from May to September,
affording swimmers a sunny dip.
Indoor with sliding roof. Pool: 50 x 18 metres.

TENNIS

PUBLIC COURTS

The city of Paris has over 160 tennis courts
which are open to public use. Some of them,
like the **Plaine de la Faluère** in the Bois de
Vincennes with its 24 courts, are part of
huge complexes. Others are a single local
court. The price is 51F per hour for an
indoor court, 33F per hour for an outdoor
one with artificial light and 22F per hour for
an outdoor court without lights. The hours,
much like for the municipal pools, are generally organized around the school periods,
but there are a few exceptions. Here are
three good possibilities:

Centre Sportif La Faluère

Bois de Vincennes, 75012, Paris
(43.74.40.93). Metro Château de Vincennes.
Open 8am-8.30pm daily.
Five courts for individual players.

Centre Sportif Henry-de-Montherlant

18 boulevard Lannes, 75016 Paris
(45.03.03.64). Metro Porte-Dauphine.**Open**
7am-10.30pm Mon, Tue, Thur-Sun; 7am-1pm
Wed. **Reserve** 24 hours in advance.
Four courts.

Tennis d'Asnières

32-34 boulevard de Reims, 75017 Paris. Metro
Porte-de-Champerret. **Open** One court reserved
for individuals daily from 7am-10.30 pm Sun-
Tue, Thur-Sat. **Reserve** 24 hours in advance.

MUNICIPAL CLUBS

Joining a club and playing on municipal courts may or may not be costly, it all depends on how long you're intending to stay in Paris. There are clubs that only cost 500F in membership fees, plus the 22F court rental fee. Compared to a private club where you can pay upwards of 200F per hour court rental fee, it's a bargain if you use it as little as three times. For the list of a club near you, contact **Allô Sports** *(see above* **Keeping Informed***)* or go to your *arrondissement's* town hall.

PRIVATE CLUBS

Private clubs are extremely expensive – they often have memberships running into the thousands of francs mark – and also have long waiting lists. Phone **Allô Sports** *(see above* **Keeping Informed***)* for information on where to go if you want private facilities.

GOLF

Fédération Française de Golf
69 avenue Victor-Hugo, 75016 Paris (45.02.13.55). Metro Victor-Hugo/bus 52. **Open** 9.30am-6pm Mon-Fri.
There are four hostesses here who will answer your questions and provide a list of all the golf courses in France.

Club de l'Etoile
10 avenue de la Grande-Armée, 75017 Paris (43.80.30.79). Metro Etoile/bus 73 **Open** 8am-10:30pm Mon-Fri; 9am-5 pm Sat. **Registration** 65F for 30 mins; 450F per month membership; 2,300F per year membership.
Set in a greenhouse on a rooftop, a stone's throw from the Arc de Triomphe, the Club de l'Etoile is one of the oldest and most beautiful practice ranges in Paris. The driving range has seven tees, six of which are equipped with computers designed to analyse your swing. The club is hoping to open a restaurant and sun terrace in the near future.

Ecole de Golf de Paris
5 avenue des Ternes, 75017 Paris (47.63.06.54). Metro Ternes/bus 30, 31, 43, 93. **Open** 8am-10pm Mon-Fri; 9am-6pm Sat. **Registration** 250F registration then 60F for 30 mins; 350F per month membership.
See **picture and caption.**

City Golf
115 rue du Bac, 75007 Paris (45.49.93.93). Metro Sèvres- Babylone. **Registration** 3,500F per year; 300F registration plus 770F for a book of tickets.
This big space, set in an old part of the city, offers a real bunker, with a pond and a real green. Plus there are 10 tees for those who want to practice driving.

SPECTATOR SPORTS

Palais Omnisport Paris-Bercy (POPB)
8 boulevard Bercy, 75012 Paris (43.46.12.21).

Metro Gare de Lyon/bus 24, 87.
The Palais Omnisport Paris-Bercy, more commonly known as Bercy, was opened in January 1983. This vast blue and white metallic structure with hills of grass growing up all four sides was built along the Seine in a rather delapidated district, and can hold up to 17,000 people and accommodate 22 different sports. The Bercy is home to the annual Paris Horse Show and International Jumping Contest, the French International Motocross Championships and major hockey and bicycling events.

Parc des Princes
24 rue du Commandant-Guilbaud, 75016 Paris (42.88.02.76). Metro Porte de Saint-Cloud/bus PC, 22, 62.
This vast municipal stadium set above the exterior boulevards can hold 50,000 spectators within its cement walls. Built in 1972, this is home to the two Parisian soccer teams: Paris-Saint Germain and Racing Paris 1, cross-town rivals to say the least. But it's not just for soccer games: this is where tens of thousands of rugby fans come streaming in to scream over the France-Wales match, for example.

Roland Garros
2 avenue Gordon-Bennett, 75016 Paris (47.43.00.47). Metro Porte d'Auteuil/bus 32, 52, 123, 244N.
This stadium, named after a French aviator – the first to cross the Mediterranean by plane – is home to the world-famous French Tennis Open. Despite the fact that the number of spectators has gone from 70,000 in 1969 to 320,000 nearly 20 years later, it is still possible to obtain seats for

this great event. The tournament takes place the last week of May and the first week of June every year. To reserve, ask for a reservation form before the end of February for the following summer: **FFT,** *Service Réservation, BP 333-16, 75767 Paris Cedex 16.* Tickets are first sold to registered French tennis players before being sold to the public. It is possible to buy seats at the stadium for minor matches at Porte 12. Good luck.

RACE TRACKS

Hippodrome d'Auteuil
Bois de Boulogne, 75016 Paris (42.24.47.04). Metro Porte d'Auteuil. **Admission** 20F.
See **picture and caption.**
Closed during July and August.

Hippodrome de Longchamp
Bois de Boulogne, 75016 Paris (42.24.13.29). Metro Porte d'Auteuil, then shuttle bus on race days. **Admission** 20F.
See **picture and caption.**
Closed during July and August.

Hippodrome de Vincennes
Bois de Vincennes, 75012 Paris (43.68.35.39; reservations for the restaurant 43.68.64.94). RER Joinville, then 10 minute walk/bus PC, 46, 56. **Admission** 15F-20F.
See **picture and caption.**

There are three horse-racing tracks in Paris. Auteuil, home to hurdle races, also organizes the Prix du Président de la République, an annual hurdle race for mostly French horses. Longchamp hosts what is considered to be the top flat race in the world, the Prix de l'Arc de Triomphe, a true contest in international elegance and million dollar steeds. At Vincennes the big annual racing event is the Prix d'Amérique. All three venues are listed under **Race Tracks.**

Media

Tune in on up-beat music, watch the best of French soaps or catch up on the latest news – whatever your chosen medium, we give a critical appraisal of what's on offer.

THE PRESS

What you notice first about French newspapers is their overall quality. Trash tabloids don't really get a look in, although they do exist, for in France newspapers reflect the true, abiding French obsession: politics. Parisians buy their weekend reading on Thursdays, choosing from *Le Nouvel Observateur* (the left-wing weekly magazine), *Le Point* and its historic rival *L'Exprès* (both centre right weeklies) and *L'Evenement du jeudi*, a weekly news magazine. *Le Journal du Dimanche* is the only paper that's available on Sundays.

We list below some of the main French newspapers and magazines, available at any news-stand.

NEWSPAPERS

Le Figaro
The story of *Le Figaro* echoes that of *The Times*: it is an old (1866), respected newspaper, taken over by a right-wing despot. Traditionally conservative – it still bears Beaumarchais' *Marriage of Figaro* quotation 'without the freedom to blame there is no worthwhile praise' – it lost its authority during Mitterrand's first presidency when it consistently attacked the Socialists, becoming a virtual right-wing newsletter under Chirac's two-year rule. However, on Mitterrand's re-election, proprietor Robert Hersant took the extreme action of hiring the editor of leading left-wing weekly *Le Nouvel Observateur*, confusing everybody. It seems to have paid off; *Le Figaro* is slowly regaining some dignity. A morning broadsheet, its layout is busy; buy it for fashion coverage and property ads.

France Soir
If *Le Figaro* (see above) is for educated conservatives, then Hersant's other paper, *France Soir* is for the rest. It consciously seeks a non-political image, carrying very little hard news and lots of consumer affairs. Like *Le Figaro*, its broadsheet format has a messy lay-out with lots of fuzzy colour pictures, spot colour and coloured sports and TV pages. It's much-read by horse racing fans. Supposedly an evening paper, its first edition is in the morning – very confusing.

L'Humanité
Wonderfully sub-titled 'The Organ of the Communist Party', *L'Humanité's* decline in popularity echoes the political reality in France. Founded before World War I by leading socialist Jean Jaurès, it once enjoyed a huge readership. Now, because it follows the traditional hardliners instead of usefully reflecting the current debates within the party, it is only read by the older, faithful few.

Libération
The cult paper of the eighties, Libé has mirrored the evolution of the '68 radicals into today's affluent middle class. Jean-Paul Sartre founded it in the early seventies as an extreme-left paper, at a time when, in France, that meant mainstream. Libé still leans to the left, but with more restraint. Very hip, its arts section is the best around, particularly for music coverage. Articles are full of Parisian slang and Americanisms; layout is clean and innovative with lots of big pictures. Be branché (switched on, cool), read Libé. Out in the morning.

Le Monde
The hallowed *Le Monde* is Paris's most-read newspaper, and the most influential, because of its almost trade mag status with politicians and top businessmen. Created in 1944 by Résistance leaders and owned by its journalists, it has retained its humanist ideology. Its painstaking thoroughness does not always make for easy reading though; articles can run over several days, it has few photographs and its arts section is weak. It is good for top job ads however, and its many supplements range from student life and music to stamp-collecting, depending on the day. It comes out late afternoon.

Le Parisien
The tabloid *Le Parisien* has tried hard to improve its image of late, and a recent redesign and switch to *Le Monde's* printers can only help. Out in the morning.

Le Quotidien
Strictly for those who enjoy full-page interviews with extreme right-winger Jean-Marie Le Pen, and appalling photographic reproduction.

MAGAZINES

Actuel
A glossy, monthly cultural and current events magazine, giving details of forthcoming events in Paris and throughout France. If your French is up to it, the quirky feature stories make fascinating reading, but facts sometimes need to be taken with a pinch of salt.

Le Canard Enchainé
A law unto itself, this weekly eight-page rag has a pre-war look about it. But its influential investigative scoops into political, judicial and economic scandals still carry a punch.

Comics
The French national bed-time reading is considered an art form like any other, and some cartoonists are considered national artists. Comics are big business here, with as many published in book form as in magazine format.

Magazines to look out for especially are **A Suivre** and (for a truly adult read) **Hara Kiri**, but any kiosk will carry many more.

Pariscope, 7 à Paris, L'Officiel du Spectacle
All are weekly guides to film, theatre, cultural events and restaurants. All come out on Wednesday.

Paris Match
Current affairs and who's divorcing who, in pictures.

Paris Passion
Paris's English-language monthly magazine, covering cultural and current events.

TELEVISION

At the time of going to press, all programme details are correct. Programmes change however, and the ones listed below may no longer be showing at the times mentioned. All newspapers carry daily programme information, and most publish weekly schedules and reviews once a week. *Le Monde* (*see above* **Press**), puts out a weekly television supplement in its Sunday/Monday edition.

TF1
Once upon a time back in 1987 Robert Maxwell got into bed with a French builder, thus marking the end of **TF1** as France's flagship public channel. It is now indisputedly the country's leading private service. Selected as the surprise candidate for privatization during the deregulation of French broadcasting in 1987, TF1 was sold off to a variety of shareholders, the two principals being Maxwell's Pergamon Press and Bouygues, France's major construction company.

Early days were tough; its top stars defected to arch-rival **La Cinq** for telephone number salaries. They went on a cloud of hype, they did the same wildly-expensive shows – and nobody watched. Humbled, they crawled back to TF1, did the same shows – and more people watched than ever before.

Since then it has mixed the unashamedly commercial – sitcoms (*Marc et Sophie*), Gallic versions of US game shows (*Jeopardy* and *Roue de La Fortune*), American soaps (*Santa Barbara*) and very popular variety shows (*Sacrée Soirée*) – with expensive French drama (*L'Ami Maupassant*), sensationalist documentaries on prostitution and drugs, quality foreign series (*Jewel in the Crown*) and the excellent puppet satire *Le Bebete Show*. Consistently high-rating and worth a look is *Avis De Recherche* (8.40pm Friday) which unites a star with schoolfriends to discuss the interim years. The result? The French simply cannot get enough. *See also* **picture and caption**.

Antenne 2
Since the privatization of TF1, **A2** has been France's leading public service channel, watched by around 24% of the public. *La Passion, c'est Antenne 2* says its slogan, for

reasons perhaps only known to them. It's funded, like **FR3**, by a mix of advertizing and *la redevance*, the French licence fee.

Some programmes on A2 are institutions: *Les Chiffres et Les Lettres* (6.55pm daily) is a quiz game based on scrabble and mental arithmetic; *Apostrophe* (10pm Friday) is an enormously influential book review show which smacks of a time when French intelligentsia gathered in cafés and debated existentialism; and *Dossier de L'Ecran* (screen-file) makes the most of controversial films, airing them in the context of a debate. Its top-rating show is *Champs Elysées*, an expensive variety show at 8.30pm Saturdays.

A2 caused itself unnecessary grief last year by wooing back top newscaster Christine Ockrent to its airwaves from TF1 at an inflated salary, at a time when staff morale was already low. A strike forced Miss Ockrent to take a cut, as it turns out, rightly, as she has not fulfilled her promise at all. Ratings for the 8pm news have plummeted.She has now resigned as anchor-person (but still works there).

Overall, A2 is a classy service, showing major films, prestigious documentary series such as *L'Architecture au Carrefour* (Architecture at the Crossroads), the patchy but popular music show *Les Enfants du Rock* (11.35pm Friday) and selected American imports such as *Falcon Crest*. And with the current political thinking to stop the costly and pointless competition between the two public channels, unite them under one president and have two distinctively different channels, A2's future looks healthy.

FR3

France's second public channel lumbers along like a dinosaur, weighed down with personnel, regional facilities and a confused policy. And although the plan under the new united front with Antenne 2 is to make FR3 a serious minority channel and to encourage the 12 regional stations to be more productive, especially on the news front, FR3 fears it may become merely a dumping ground for programmes its sister channel doesn't want.

But while the *grands fromages* sort out the new strategies, the show must go on. One positive early change is the decision to challenge TF1 by counter-programming in harness with Antenne 2. **FR3** has recently 'got culture', giving over airtime to its now sister channel **La Sept** to air its ballets and classical concerts. One Bank Holiday it put on an uninterrupted nine hours of Claudel's epic play *Soulier de Satin*. This is a major step forward for the channel, because since deregulation, it has been fighting fire with fire, aping the mainstream entertainment output of the other channels. Its ratings dropped to an average 9.7%.

Now instead of putting an inferior film against the other five movies going out at 8.30pm Sundays, FR3 puts on a strong international documentary in its *Optique* slot. Then stay tuned for *Océaniques*, a weekly look at cultural events in Paris. More general high-brow issues are discussed in the Monday, Wednesday and Thursday editions of *Océaniques* at 10.30pm. Thirteen years old and still making waves is *Thalassa*, an hour-long magazine on the sea (9.30pm Friday). Its main quiz programme *Question pour un Champion* is relatively intelligent, based on the BBC's *Going for Gold*. The about-face is that FR3 is also the home of *Miss France*, an unintentionally hilarious Christmas beauty jamboree hosted by Sacha Distel. And its top-rating show is, wait for it, *Benny Hill*.

English-language newspapers and magazines such as The International Herald Tribune, *The* Guardian, The Times, *The* Independent *and even The* Sun, *and magazines such as* Newsweek *and* Paris Passion *are sold at most kiosks in central Paris. For less mainstream titles, see chapter* **Shopping**, *under* **Books**.

Canal Plus (4)

Created in 1983, **Canal Plus** was born with several silver spoons in its mouth. Even though cinema-going was as automatic to the French as going to Mass, and possibly more sacred, the government didn't want a cot-death on its hands and protected its new movie-channel from market forces.

Even so it had a tough infancy, but a major turning point came with the initiative to air hard-porn late at night at weekends. Subscriptions have now soared to three million households, and viewers have become addicted to the channel's unique blend of rotating new films, good quality children's shows, documentaries and top sporting events. Its customer service is remarkable – for a whole year it sent out leather wallets to subscribers on their saint's day.

Despite the signal being encrypted during most of the day, there are periods when the signal is clear to non-subscribers. This means you can watch *CBS Evening News* at 8am Monday to Friday, the *French Top 50* at 6.50pm Monday to Saturday, *'Allo, 'Allo* at 8pm Friday. Fans of *Rapido*'s Antoine de Caunes can get a double fix with the French *Rapido* (12.30pm Sunday) and in the excellent talk show he co-hosts, *Nulle Part Ailleurs* (7.20pm daily) which consistently pulls in The Best Guests. But the French version of Spitting Image failed.

Now, apart from being the major funder of French cinema, Canal Plus is expanding into Belgium, Germany and Spain and has been awarded two channels on the French high-power satellite TDF1, which can be reached all over Europe. Watch that space.

La Cinq

Since Day One back in 1986, when it was created as France's second private channel, **La Cinq** got it wrong. It's the product of an uncomfortable alliance between two of Europe's biggest media egos, Italian TV magnate Silvio Berlusconi and right-wing French press baron Robert Hersant, and it's been battered and bewildred by TF1's invincible grip on the viewers.

La Cinq is known for its news programmes and the number of badly dubbed American shows it airs, such as *LA Law* (10.20pm Wednesday) and *Deux Flics à Miami* (no prizes for guessing). Broadcasting 24 hours a day, it's losing money at a breathtaking rate, and its audience, never large, is dwindling daily. It suffered further indignity in July 1989 when it was fined a mammoth £7 million for disobeying the strict French content laws.

Berlusconi has publicly called the channel a disaster and is understood to be bailing out. The word is that the government will try and merge La Cinq and **M6** — as far as La Cinq goes, there would be few tears shed.

M6

Created in 1987 as a result of deregulation, **M6**'s viewing figures have trebled in the last year. Another 24-hour channel, it can only be received in half of France, but rest assured, this includes the capital.

Thirty per cent of its programmes must have a music content by law, which means quite a lot of music videos at 5am, but also some not bad jazz at more sociable times. It runs an excellent six-minute, very interesting news bulletin (7.45pm daily) which has no presenter, just subtitles.

Recently M6 has started working with British channels, doing documentaries with the BBC, the remake of *The Saint* with LWT and a Patricia Highsmith series with ITV. Bill Cosby fans passing through Paris can catch a daily dose of *The Cosby Show* (dubbed) at 8pm. And if your hotel can't pick up Canal Plus' blue movies, M6's *Sexy Clip* (Friday) or *Charmes* (Thursday) at 11.20pm might give you a cheap thrill.

La Sept

La Sept is born of that peculiar French mix of pride and stubbornness which renders them oblivious to commercial reality. The latest French government toy, La Sept aims to bring culture to the people – but at a price. From its inception in 1986, it was destined to fly on the French DBS satellite TDF1. But to get viewers used to what they were about to receive, public channel FR3 was told to give over three hours of airtime a day to La Sept's schedule of ballet, theatre, classical music and off-beat documentaries.

Since May 1989, when TDF1 was launched successfully, La Sept has given FR3 back its hours and now broadcasts all over Europe with a top-quality picture and stereo sound – to about half a dozen people. The reason? Well, when the French government laid its plans, it was determined that the dishes and decoders necessary to receive the TDF1 signal should be manufactured in France. The cheapest equipment produced costs about £600, and while some

people seem happy to consume culture when it comes free, they seem less prepared to put *leurs mains dans leurs poches* and fork out for it. The fight is now on to get the signal carried on the struggling French cable networks, where La Sept fans could receive it for a more reasonable £15 per month. Plus it's back on good old FR3.

Quite undeterred by these hiccups, the French government has now struck a deal with the German authorities to provide a dual-language version of La Sept, and is now looking to branch into more culturally-minded Eastern Europe.

RADIO

In France, private FM radio is no longer pirate and certainly not out of phase with the public's desires. Much more, even, than in America, the big FM stations dictate musical taste. **France Inter**, **RTL**, **Europe 1** – virtually the only high-powered stations just a few years ago – are now finding themselves eclipsed by several upstarts with national networks. One station above all stands out in both blandness and popularity: **NRJ**. With a thirty per cent market share and an extremely tight playlist, this radio virtually controls the 'Top 50', and not receiving airplay in Paris all but insures the cut-out bin. Many publishers regularly give points on royalties to NRJ, a form of payola still legally tolerated in France.

The government, initially opposed to any kind of independent competition, relented in 1983 – so long as private broadcasters didn't sell advertizing for profit. NRJ, with heavy start-up funding, was able to get a jump on the other indies by heavily advertizing themselves without bothering to raise revenue. When they were firmly ahead they joined the small fry in demanding the right to function in a normal commercial manner. Since 1984, when all restrictions were lifted, a plethora of small, local stations catering to very specific tastes have been forced to close by NRJ and the other 'super-radios' that have copied NRJ's policy of hits-only radio, including **Skyrock**, **Fun FM**, **Kiss** and a couple of smaller stations. What in 1984 promised to be one of the more exciting airspaces in the world has withered to about 20 stations playing pretty much what you would hear anywhere else in Europe.

LOCAL RADIO

There are quite a few local stations catering for minorities of taste and race; the diversity of the capital's audience is rich enough to support their relatively small enterprises. Several such local stations were forced to group together on the same frequency – broadcasting at different times – for reasons of bandspace as well as economic viability. **Radio Aligre** and **Ici et Maintenant** have long been active in their community – the Bastille area of Paris – and can be heard throughout most of the city on 93.1MHz. The 94MHz slot is occupied by **France Maghreb** and **Soleil Menilmontant**, broadcasting mostly African music and North Paris news. Strange band-fellows have been created in the shuffle, including **Radio Latina** and **Radio Solidarnosc** on 99MHz. The large Jewish community has its station: **Fréquence Juive** on 94.8MHz, and Christians are not to be outdone, with **Radios Chrétiennes** broadcasting on 100.7MHz. Classical music is well represented throughout the bandwidth, more so, probably, than in England. And finally, as

If you can't get to a television screen, you could always check out what's new in moving pictures at the **Musée d'Art Moderne** *(see chapter* Museums*).*

Canal 9 (90.9 MHz)
Rock, blues.

Chérie FM (99.9 MHz)
Just about to go national, Chérie rates fifth in the Paris region. It's difficult to say why, but the familiar recipe of two-thirds French, one third international with a generous pinch of Golden Oldies can be interesting, as can the dating services.

Europe 1 (104.7 MHz)
Currently sporting a 'For Sale' sign, Europe 1 is France's first publicly-listed station (there is currently only one other, NRJ *below*). With a Top 50-based playlist, it snaps at RTL's heels (*see below*), but can occasionally show sparks of originality thanks to its woman musical director Yvonne Lebrun. She claims to have discovered for Gallic listeners Terence Trent D'Arby, Suzanne Vega and Tracy Chapman, and one of her claims to fame was creating the European Lambada craze. More recently, she has laid her money on Bulgarian church music – Les Voix des Bulgares – and has a show of her own on Sunday at 8pm, 'Toutes les Musiques que j'Aime'.

FIP (90.4 MHz)
Useful in the car, as it tells you why you're stuck in a 4km traffic jam, interspread with news of what's on where in Paris if only you could get there, and a mixed bag of jazz, classical and *tubes* (French for hit).

France Infos (105.5 MHz)
This station is the favourite choice for many a radio-alarm, with its revolving, 24-hour programme of international news, economic updates and sports reports.

France Inter (87.8 MHz)
State-run, it broadcasts mostly middle-of-the-road music and too much talk.

France Maghreb and Soleil Menilmontant (94.0 MHz)
A shared bandwave (*see above* **Local Radio**)

France Musique (91.3 MHz and 91.7 MHz)
The national cultural music channel – large concerts, live orchestras, top jazz performances – has recently acquired a new director, who promises new ways of presenting France Musique's repertoire to its 700,000 loyal listeners.

Fréquence Juive (94.8 MHz)
See above **Local Radio**.

Fun (101.9 MHz)
Skyrock (*see below*) by a better name.

Futur Génération and Transitalia (94.4 MHz)
A shared bandwave: business/Italian.

Kiss FM (89 MHz)
Kiss has cooled off recently as far as the natives go, but for foreign ears it still has quite a lot going for it. The music's based, for a change, on album artists, with past and current hits getting equal airtime.

Maxximum FM (105.9 MHz)
Untested by time, Maxximum aims to be the radio of the nineties. Metamorphosing out of the unremarkable Adventure FM, the station

*Like America's CBS with 60 Minutes, **TFI** has discovered that current affairs does very well in the early Sunday evening time-slot. **Anne Sinclair** (pictured above) has been the sole host of Sept sur Sept since 1987, which features a single guest interviewed on the evenings of the week. Sinclair won awards for journalistic excellence in 1985 and 1986, and again in 1988 for best moderator.*

befits the French, there exists a large, middle-brow cultural state network called **France Culture**, generally referred to as 'France Cul' or French bum.

Among the stations primarily devoted to music, two are clearly at the forefront: Radio Nova and Oui. **Radio Nova** (101.5MHz) offers a steady diet of funk, rap, House, African, Latin and the bizarre, with an occasional touch of smart and swampy rock 'n' roll. The talk is brief enough and you can hear what's hip on 'Bons Plans' (7pm Monday to Friday). **Oui** (102.3MHz) is *the* rock radio in Paris (though it occasionally succumbs to the French tendency to forced intellectual eclecticism (such as reggae after a Jesus and the Mary Chain song), and it also has a hand in organizing many of the better Parisian concerts. It must be said that Nova and Oui were already close enough to interfere with each other's signal before NRJ imitator **Fun** squeezed in at 101.9MHz and

practically drowned out both of them. In the rock radio category **Canal 9**, broadcasting since last year 1988 on 90.9MHz could give Oui a run for their money.

TUNING IN
Twiddling the dial in Paris is a mind-blowing experience. With more FM stations than any other city in the world, Parisian airwaves are so crowded that the only bearable way to listen is on digital equipment. Use the list below to aid in Parisian dial-twiddling. Happy hunting.

Aligre and Ici et Maintenant (93.1MHz)
A shared bandwave (*see above* **Local Radio**)

BBC World Service (Radio 648) (648 KHz, Medium Wave)
Continuous, 24-hour English-language broadcasting on Medium Wave, covering international news, current events, pop, drama, and poetry. The station is also available on 198KHz from midnight to 5.30am daily.

has a mission to 'make you move'. Aimed at 15 to 25 year-olds and not based on the Top 50, it used a lot of American market research to come up with its mix of dance tunes. Just bought by RTL (*see below*).

Montmartre (102.7 MHz)
Local community issues, some music.

Oui FM (102.3 MHz)
Claiming to be the only radio station to play rock all day, Oui FM also has close ties with the respected film magazine *Cahiers du Cinéma*. Listen for informed reviews in 'Entrée Libre' (10am and 7pm daily).

NRJ (100.3 MHz)
See above.

Pacific FM (97.4 MHz)
Going for the sunshine sound, Pacific dares to have a playlist, 40% of which is new records, but not neccessarily Top 50. More than half the output is non-French, and it's not half bad really.

Radio Beur (98.2 MHz)
Rai music (North African) and political issues.

Radio Classique (101.1 MHz)
Non-stop classical music with very little conversation.

Radio Courtoisie and Radio Asie (95.6 MHz)
A shared bandwave: general talk shows/Asian interests.

Radio Nostalgie (105.1 MHz)
Music for bathrooms and car stereos, but people obviously appreciate its mainly French oldies. Started in 1984 as an independent network, the station was recently bought by RMC. Very big in Belgium, apparently.

Radio Nova (101.5 MHz)
In a world full of Madonna and Eddie Mitchell, Nova comes as music to the ears – new music and different music at that. If it's happening in Tokyo or New York then Nova will play it. And what's more they'll tell you what's currently trendy to see, do and eat in Paris, thanks to its links with parent publication *Actuel* (*see above* **Press**).

Radio Tour Eiffel (95.2 MHz)
The Mayor's office unofficial station: light music and news.

Réussir FM (99.6 MHz)
The name says it all: Succeed FM. Airs yuppie job ads in between yuppie tunes.

RFM (103.9 MHz)
RFM's moment of glory was having the much-mourned French comedian Coluche as presenter in the early eighties. The British group Crown bought the station in 1989 and switched the target audience to 25 to 40 year-olds. Pretender to the Coluche mantle is now Antoine de Caunes with 'Ba Be Bi Bo Bu' (6pm daily), a whacky, self-indulgent vehicle for the motor-mouth *Rapido* presenter (*see above* **Television: Canal Plus**) and two cohorts. It's pretty impenetrable even to native French speakers, but worth dipping into to marvel how much

Canal Plus's *Rapido is as incomprehensible to the French as the English-language version is to the Brits, but the channel's* Nulle Part Ailleurs *talk-show, also hosted by* **Antoine de Caune** *(pictured above) is more accessible. The motor-mouth star also finds time to host a daily radio programme on* **RFM***.*

some men laugh at their own jokes. Otherwise, 80% international hits follow the excruciating slogan 'Tous les tops, toute la Pop sans les flops'.

RMC Radio Monte Carlo (103.1 MHz)
A middle-of-the-road housewives' station originating in Monte Carlo, but there is one gem; Corinne Madoc's show 'Mers Chaudes' (5pm Saturday and Sunday), devoted to music from the Antilles , Africa, South America and the Mediterranean basin.

RTL (104.3 MHz)
Still France's most listened-to station, the music-and-chat service is meeting the private upstarts' challenge with a new schedule. There's 'Mea Culpa' (7.20pm Monday), where politicians have to justify their actions; 'Place Rouge – Maison Blanche' (Red Square – White House, 8.45pm Saturday), a three-way discussion on East-West relations; and 'Grand Jury' (6.30pm Sunday), which attracts top-drawer political guests to join a debate between the station's own journalists and colleagues from *Le Monde* (*see above* **Press**). The quiz 'Chiffres en Question' (10.30am Monday to Friday) has for nov-

elty its prize money in ECUs (European Currency Unit). The music's rather standard – French popular hits and international standards, although evening listening is better. 'Satell'hit' (8.30pm Monday to Friday) sees the DJ linking up with record-spinners in other parts of the globe, and 'Wango-Tango' (11pm Monday to Friday) can unearth some goodies.

Skyrock (96 MHz)
Any station that boasts about reducing its play-list from 100 titles a week to 40 (60% of them non-French) is strictly for chart fans. Each number is assured between two and seven plays per day.

Tropic FM (92.6 MHz)
Tropic is great. It plays African and West Indian music, presented by DJs with a neat line in pidgin French, intercut with ads for mango juice and the like.

Voltage (97.8 MHz)
Since taking up a dance stance in September 1988, Voltage is blasting onwards and upwards, and is now the fourth-ranking Parisian FM station. With 40% new dance records and the rest funk standards, it leans black and it's hot, man.

Theatre

There are more than 100 theatres in and around Paris but only one with an all-English repertoire.

For those who don't want to take the plunge into the native or adopted language of Racine, Anouilh or Beckett, **Galerie 55** (*see* **Independent Theatres**) is the only English-language theatre in Paris that presents some of the finest – albeit tried and tested – pieces of English and American theatre. It celebrated its tenth anniversary with the1989-90 season.

Depending on your knowledge of French language and English theatre, you'll slowly begin to realize that *Duo pour un soliste* (*Duet for One*) or *L'avantage d'être constant* (*The Importance of Being Earnest*) – to name but a few – are imports from the West End or Broadway. These are adapted with apparent ease; *habitués* learn to look past the metre-high names of stars no-one's ever heard of, in search of the vaguely familiar name of a play. Only then will those in the know spot the author's name, in letters one centimetre high. Original French pieces – though still being put on – are no longer the biggest crowd-pullers in town.

STAGE-FRIGHT

If you come to Paris looking for the Boulevard du Crime, the pantomime buffoonery and the magical mime you first fell in love with in Carné's Barrault-based *Enfants du Paradis* film re-creation, you'll find little more than the harlotry and hucksterring of the Saint-Denis quarter. Time was when Cocteau staged work to music by Satie and the costumes were designed by Picasso. But ask most Parisians today what they think about theatre, and you'll get a long spiel on classical alexandrines that they were force-fed at school or some vague comment on the antiquated but beautiful **Comédie Française.**

So what's the closest thing to theatreland in Paris? Not very much. Theatre in this capital is a far cry from the innovative concentration of work that occurs every year in venues such as Edinburgh. But in the area bounded by the Gare Saint-Lazare, Gare du Nord and place de la République, you'll find a number of venues, one of the most sumptuous theatres in Paris being the **Mogador**. Alternatively, if you're into fringe theatre try the Marais area first: Essaion, Espace Bastille, Théâtre de l'Ile Saint-Louis, Théâtre du Marais, Théâtre de l'Epicerie (consult the weekly listings magazine *Pariscope* for details). These are more accessible than the cluster of progressives that have sprung up around the established 'national' **Théâtre de la Colline.**

BOOKING AGENCIES

Agence Cheque Théâtre
2nd floor, 33 rue Le Peletier, 75009 Paris (42.46.72.40). Metro Le Peletier/bus 42, 67,74. **Open** 10am-7pm Mon-Sat. **No credit cards.**
They offer reservations for all forms of entertainment by phone, by post and in person. They also offer subscription schemes that let you simply call and go.

Alpha-FNAC
3rd level down (– 3), Forum des Halles, 75001 Paris (40.26.81.18). Metro Châtelet-Les Halles/bus 67, 69, 70, 72, 85. **Open** 2pm-7.30pm Mon; 10am-7.30pm Tue-Sat. **Credit** V.
This agency is probably your fastest, simplest option. They book almost all venues for all types of entertainment. Call the main number to find the branch nearest you.

Jeunesses Musicales de France
56 rue de l'Hôtel de Ville, 75004 Paris (42.78.19.54). Metro Hôtel de Ville/bus 69, 76, 96. **Open** 10am-7pm Mon-Sat; 10am-6pm Sun. **Rates** 150F over-30s; 80F 18s-30s; 15F under-18s. **No credit cards.**
A membership organization that offers 50% discounts at all major theatres on certain days. They're very helpful people and have a reciprocal arrangement with members of the British organization 'Youth and Music' at 78 Neal Street, London, WC2H 9PA (081 379 6722).

Kiosque Théâtre
across from 15 place de la Madeleine, 75008 Paris. Metro Madeleine/bus 42, 52. **Open** 12.30-8pm Tue-Sat; 12.30-4pm Sun. **No credit cards.**
The half-price, same-day ticket seller. If you don't mind waiting on line, it's a very good deal.
Branch: Châtelet RER station, 75001 Paris.

Minitel Reservations
(3615 BILLETEL). **Credit** V.
The minitel is a computer linked to the French phone system. You use a terminal to type in your ticket reservation and pay by typing in your Visa card account number. Abandon all hope ye who enter here. It can be done, but Minitel is often more of a headache than it's worth for the visitor to Paris.

NATIONAL THEATRES

Chaillot
Place du Trocadéro, 75016 Paris (47.27.81.15). Metro Trocadéro/bus 32, 63. **Open** *box office:* 11am-7pm Mon-Sat; 11am-5pm Sun; *telephone bookings:* 11am-7pm Mon-Sat. **Tickets** 130F; 60F students; 70F school group guides; 90F under-25s, OAPs. **No credit cards.**
See **picture and caption.**
Advance booking (up to 14 days in advance).
Wheelchair access.

Comédie Française
2 rue de Richelieu, 75001 Paris (40.15.00.15). Metro Palais-Royal/bus 39, 48, 67. **Open** *box office:* 11am-6pm daily. **Tickets** 40F-137F. **Credit** V.
Arguably, the most established theatre in France. Programmes are generally of the Molière ilk, all done well. The edifice exudes history; you'll find the beauty of the building half the pleasure.
Advance booking (up to 14 days in advance).

Odéon Théâtre National
Place Paul-Claudel, 75006 Paris (43.25.70.32). Metro Odéon/bus 63, 70, 86, 87, 96. **Open** *box office:* 11.30am-6.30pm daily. **Tickets** 35F-180F. **Credit** CB, V.
A fraternal twin of the **Comédie Française** *(see above)*, the Odéon counts as a double theatre space *(see below* **Petit Odéon)**, offering a good range of contemporary work in the main house and an interesting mix of plays performed in other languages (with the emphasis on European languages) in the smaller house. No Monday performances.
Advance booking (up to 14 days in advance).

Opéra Comique (Salle Favart)
5 rue Favart, 75002 Paris (42.96.12.20). Metro Richelieu Drouot bus 20, 39, 48. **Open** *box office:* 11am-6.30pm Mon-Sat. **Tickets** 50F-160F. **No credit cards.**
A well-established theatre that puts on musicals. Most of the season's offerings are of high standard and fun to watch, but choose carefully. Some of the pieces are too fluffy for anyone's palate. Dance productions also make an appearance. No Monday performances. *See also chapter* **Music: Classical & Opera.**

Petit Odéon
(Odéon Théâtre National) place Paul-Claudel, 75006 Paris (43.25.70.32). Metro Odéon/63, 70, 86, 87, 90. **Open** 11am-6.30pm daily. **Tickets** 62F; 42F OAPs, under-25s. **Credit** CB, V.
The small branch of **Odéon Théâtre** *(see above)*, features performances in languages other than French. There are no Monday performances.
Advance booking (up to 14 days in advance).

Théâtre de la Colline
*15 rue Malte-Brun, 75020 Paris
(43.66.43.60). Metro Gambetta/bus 60, 61,
69.* **Open** *box office:* 11am-7pm daily. **Tickets**
130F; 100F OAPs, students; 80F groups of
10 or more. **No credit cards.**
A good theatre that's taking the initiative
to present contemporary work. This policy sometimes backfires and the audience
suffers the consequences by having to sit
through incomprehensible plays. Ask
about the night's performance, before
you fork out.
Advance booking (up to 14 days in advance).

Théâtre de la Ville
*(Mairie de Paris) 2 place du Châtelet, 75004
Paris (42.74.22.77). Metro Châtelet.* **Open**
box office: 11am-6pm Mon, Sun; 11am-8pm
Tue-Sat; *telephone booking:* 11am-6pm Mon,
Sun; 9am-8pm Tue-Sat. **Tickets** 60F-145F.
No credit cards.
Though this venue is considered to be the
major contemporary dance space in Paris,
you'll occasionally see original, but inoffen-
sive drama. Many of the presentations are
excellently done. They do musical programmes and special presentations for children also. Call for specific programme
details and prices, as they do vary. There are
no performances on Mondays.
Advance booking. Wheelchair access.

INDEPENDENT THEATRES

Antoine-Simone Berriau
*14 boulevard de Strasbourg, 75010 Paris
(42.08.77.71). Metro Strasbourg-Saint-
Denis/bus 20, 39.* **Open** *box office:* 11am-7pm
Mon-Fri; 11am-3.30pm, 4-7pm, Sat; 11am-
1pm, 4.30-7pm, Sun.* **Tickets** 80F-250F.
No credit cards.
You'll usually find more purely French
works than adaptations at this friendly the-
atre. There are no Sunday evening or
Monday performances.
Car park. Wheelchair access.

Atelier
*place Charles-Dullin, 75018 Paris
(46.06.49.24). Metro Anvers/bus 30, 54.*
Open *box office:* 11am-7pm Mon-Sat; 11am-
1pm, 4.30-7.20pm, Sun. **Tickets** 20F-220F;
150F groups. **No credit cards.**
As the name implies, this is a theatre that
acts as a workshop and aims to be more
experimental and risky than other similar
venues. It usually succeeds, although the
direction is sometimes surprisingly pedestrian. Take note; the traffic congestion in this
area, at the foot of the Sacre Coeur, can be
hellish. There are no Sunday evening or
Monday performances.
Car park (rue Dancourt). Wheelchair access.

Bastille
*76 rue de la Roquette, 75011 Paris
(43.57.42.14). Metro Bastille, Voltaire/bus
69.* **Open** box office: 10am-7pm daily.
Tickets 90F. **No credit cards.**
The Bastille theatre will probably get more
business by virtue of its proximity to the
new Opéra Bastille. Generally speaking, it
deserves credit as a real mover and shaker
for new theatre and dance. Lots of directors
and companies start here and eventually go

The **Chaillot** *(listed under* **National Theatres***) gets some of its elegance from
being close to the Eiffel Tower and some from the well-staged and expensively
produced plays that are put on. Although all mainstream material, there's a
good mix of styles. There are no Monday performances.*

on to financial stability and fame. The low
admission prices means that this venue
makes it onto most visitors' agendas. There
are no Monday performances.

Bateau Théâtre
*Opposite 190 quai de Jemmapes, 75010 Paris
(42.08.68.89). Metro Château Landon/bus
46.* **Open** *box office:* open 15 minutes before
day's 8.30pm performance. **Tickets** 90F, 70F.
No credit cards.
See **picture and caption.**

Bouffes du Nord
*37bis boulevard de la Chapelle, 75010 Paris
(42.39.34.50). Metro La Chapelle/bus 65,
350.* **Open** *box office:* 11am-6pm Mon-Sat.
Tickets 100F; 70F Sat matinée.
No credit cards.
This is Peter Brook's upstart. Good,
although the audience isn't always let in on
what the point of the story is. A little experimentation can be a confounding thing. Still,
they do very good, professional adaptations
of foreign plays.

Bouffes Parisiens
*4 rue Monsigny, 75002 Paris (42.96.60.24).
Metro Quatre-Septembre/bus 20, 29.* **Open**
box office: 11am-7pm daily. **Tickets** 35F-230F.
No credit cards.

A programme of simple comedies and dra-
mas offered up at reasonable prices. Though
a popular mid-town theatre, you won't find
great theatrical productions here. Go if you
feel like seeing something straightforward
and intellectually undemanding.

Bouffon Théâtre
*26-28 rue de Meaux, 75019 Paris,
(42.38.35.53). Metro Colonel Fabien/bus 46,
75.* **Open** *box office:* please phone for details.
Tickets 60F, 40F.
Cheap and quirky, but a popular place. They
present lots of comedy and silliness.

Cartoucherie
*route de Champ-de Manœuvres, 75012 Paris.
Metro Château de Vincennes, then shuttle bus
112/theatre shuttle.* **Tickets** see below.
This multi-theatre complex is considered
to be the most avant-garde theatre space in
Paris. Innovative and wild, productions are
value for your franc because they make
you think and react. The material is sometimes a bit difficult to understand, but the
quality of the staging is good. There is a
buffet and bar for all theatres after 7.30pm.
See the following listings for information
on the three individual theatres. Booking
by phone is strongly recommended.

Théâtre de l'Aquarium
(43.74.99.61). Open *box office:* 10am-7pm daily. Tickets 90F, 70F, 50F. No credit cards.

Théâtre de la Tempête
(43.28.36.36). Open *box office:* 2-7pm Tue-Sun. Tickets 90F, 60F; 40F students. No credit cards.

Théâtre du Chaudron
(43.28.97.04). Open *box office:* 2-5pm daily. Tickets 80F, 60F. No credit cards.

Cinq Diamants
8 rue des Cinq Diamants, 75013 Paris (45.80.51.31). Metro *Place d'Italie.* Open *box office:* 10am-2pm daily. Tickets 80F, 50F. No credit cards.
An ordinary spot for inexpensive light drama and farce. Not bad, but no great shakes, either.

Cité Internationale Universitaire
21 boulevard Jourdan, 75014 Paris (45.89.38.69). Metro *Cité-Universitaire.* Open *box office:* 1-8pm daily. Tickets 100F; 60F groups; 35F OAPs, students. No credit cards.
One of the better local college-level playhouses. Interesting blend of diverse, multinational pieces and performers; even though the performers are a bit inexperienced, they do pretty well.

Comédie des Champs Elysées
15 avenue Montaigne, 75008 Paris (47.23.37.21; telephone bookings 47.20.08.24). Metro *Alma Marceau/bus 42, 80.* Open *box office:* 11am-7pm daily; *tele-*

phone bookings: 2-6pm Mon-Fri. Tickets 90F-250F. No credit cards.
This place is far better known for its classical music wing *(see chapter* Music: Classical & Opera *).* The chances are that you'll have an enjoyable night at the playhouse, even though it won't astound you. All those in the know go to the Bar du Théâtre across the road for a post-theatre dinner, drink and mingle. There are no performances on Sunday evenings or Mondays. *See also below* Studio des Champs-Elysées.

Comédie Italienne
17 rue de la Gaîté, 75014 Paris (43.21.22.22). Metro *Edgar-Quinet/bus 28, 58.* Open *box office:* 2-7pm daily. Tickets 100F; 80F under-26s, OAPs (except Sat and days following Public Holidays). No credit cards.
A good value theatre in the Montparnasse area. It isn't the best in town, but it's quite good and tries successfully to programme a season of both classics and a few modern works.

Edouard VII Sacha Guitry
10 place Edouard VII, 75009 Paris (47.42.59.92). Metro *Opéra, Madeleine/bus 42, 52.* Open *box office:* 11am-6pm daily. Tickets 80F-210F. No credit cards.
An interesting drama venue in a nice neighbourhood where nice people go out for a nice evening. Get the picture? The plays can be a bit stodgy.

Mogador
25 rue de Mogador, 75009 Paris (42.85.45.30/48.78.75.15). Metro *Trinité/bus 26, 32, 43, 49.* Open *box office:* 11am-7pm daily. Tickets 80F-240F. Credit CB, V.
They're trying hard here to grab more of the

Opéra-area audience; they already draw a large number. It is a well set up theatre that shows the likes of *Tango Argentino.* You can get good views of the stage, even in the lower price range seats.

Montparnasse
31 rue de la Gaîté, 75014 Paris (43.22.77.74). Metro *Edgar-Quinet, Gaîté/bus 28, 58.* Open *box office:* 11am-6pm Mon; 11am-7pm Tue-Sun. Tickets *large theatre:* 90F-230F; *small theatre:* 130F. No credit cards.
This is the biggest theatre attraction in the Montparnasse area and one of the biggest in the city. Inside the two playhouses the company puts on lively productions; the season is founded on a variety of solid imported pieces and not-so-mouldy French works. More chances in play production are taken in the small theatre. As an added treat, lunch and wine are served an hour and a half before each show in the larger theatre from Wednesdays to Saturdays. There are no performances on Sunday evenings or Mondays.

Nouveau Théâtre Mouffetard
73 rue Mouffetard, 75005 Paris (43.31.11.99). Metro *Place Monge/bus 47.* Open *telephone bookings only:* 2-6.30pm Tue-Sat. Tickets 100F; 60F students except Sat. No credit cards.
A Latin Quarter spot that is fairly popular; it's inexpensive and the direction and interpretation are pretty good. The production team try hard. There are no performances on Sunday evenings or Mondays.

Olympia
28 boulevard des Capucines, 75009 Paris (47.42.25.49). Metro *Opéra, Madeleine/bus 42, 52.* Open *box office:* 10am-7pm Mon-Sat; 11am-6pm Sun, Public Holidays. Tickets 205F, 160F. No credit cards.
Fun, light farce and operettas are the mainstays here. If the play is right, it's a fine performance space, although to enjoy it, it's best to be in the mood for lightweight entertainment.

Palais-Royal
38 rue Montpensier, 75001 Paris (42.97.59.81). Metro *Bourse, Palais-Royal.* Open *box office:* 11am-7pm daily. Tickets 20F-260F. No credit cards.
This is the genuine article: a beautiful building with productions (primarily light bedroom farce) that are all on the mark. The high-quality staging and performance are at a price range that makes this an option for everyone. A note of caution: don't buy the cheapest seats. The difference in view and enjoyment if you're willing to go up to around 100F is worth it. There are no performances on Sunday evenings or Mondays.

Porte Saint Martin
16 boulevard Saint-Martin, 75010 Paris (42.08.00.32). Metro *Strasbourg-Saint-Denis/bus 20, 39.* Open *box office:* 11am-6pm Mon, Sun; 11am-7pm Tue-Sat. Tickets 80F-200F; 90F students, OAPs. Credit CB, V.
Well, the theatre isn't bad, but the area is. Dodging drug dealers is no way to spend an evening. The plays themselves are quite respectable and not bad in quality. They also do a lot of one-man show material, mostly comedy. There are no performances on Sunday evenings or Mondays.

Cheap, strange and maybe you'll like it; the Bateau Théâtre *(listed under* Independant Theatres*) is possibly the world's only floating theatre. If you don't get sea-sick (although the boat is docked) you'll have a pleasant enough time watching fairly ordinary interpretations of light drama and farce. There are rumours that it may possibly be closing. No performances on Sunday evenings or Mondays.*

Ranelagh

5 rue des Vignes, 75016 Paris (42.88.64.44).
Metro Muette/bus 22, 52. **Open** box office:
11am-7pm daily. **Tickets** 120F, 100F, 80F students. **No credit cards.**
Located in one of the city's more sedate
quarters, this theatre manages to avoid dull
productions. It's comfortable and does some
of the better contemporary pieces in town.
Production standards are high. There are no
performances on Mondays.

Renaud-Barrault

2bis avenue Franklin D Roosevelt, 75008
Paris (42.56.60.70). Metro Champs-Elysées-
Clémenceau, Franklin D Roosevelt. **Open**
box office: 11am-6pm daily. **Tickets** 180F.
No credit cards.
A good two-stage theatre just off the Rond-
Point des Champs-Elysées. The programme is adventurous and well-exe-
cuted. It isn't a particularly attractive
place, but it does sponsor a 'meet the
artist' discussion series. Check their lobby
for promotional flyers or call to find out
who's on deck.
Advance booking (up to 14 days in advance).

Studio des Champs-Elysées

15 avenue Montaigne 75008 (47.23.35.10;
telephone bookings 47.20.08.24). Metro Alma
Marceau/bus 42, 80. **Open** box office: 11am-
7pm daily; *telephone bookings:* 2-6pm Mon-
Fri. **Tickets** 150F; 75F students.
No credit cards.
The baby of the **Comédie des Champs-
Elysées** *(see above)*, productions don't vary
much from Mum except in ticket price. The
plays may be newer and have a more neophyte
cast, but the topics dealt with are of a similar
nature. Still, it's a good choice if you're looking
to visit a small theatre. There are no performances on Sunday evenings or Mondays.

Théâtre à Ciel Ouvert

place du Marché Sainte-Catherine, 75004
Paris (48.77.01.59). Metro Saint-Paul/bus
69, 76. **Open** April-November (dependent
on weather). **Tickets** free.
The cheapest show in Paris and one of the
most enjoyable. The players are enthusiastic
– if sometimes a little amateurish – and the
open-air setting can take your imagination
back to theatre as it once was.

Théâtre de Paris

15 rue Blanche, 75009 Paris (42.80.09.30;
telephone bookings 42.80.59.73). Metro
Trinité/bus 68. **Open** box office: 11am-7pm
Mon-Sat. **Tickets** 170F-280F.
No credit cards.
Not to be confused with the city-funded
Théâtre de la Ville *(see above* **National
Theatres)**, this is one of the older independents
that does a decent, predictable job with what-
ever's hot. *Cats* was playing here for a while.
Advance booking (up to 14 days in advance).

Théâtre Fontaine

10 rue Fontaine, 75009 Paris (48.74.74.40).
Metro Blanche/bus 68, 74. **Open** box office:
11am-6pm Mon-Sat. **Tickets** 150F-250F;
100F students, OAPs. **Credit** CB.
Sort of glitzy with a programme to match,
this place is fun, but not always straight
theatre. It's a good bet if you want to have a
cheerful, touristy night out. Stroll down
closer to the Opéra afterwards for supper.
There are no performances on Sunday
evenings or Mondays.

Théâtre Gaîté-Montparnasse

26 rue de la Gaîté, 75014 Paris
(43.22.16.18). Metro Gaîté/bus 28, 58.
Open box office: 11am-7pm daily. **Tickets**
210F, 170F, 110F. **Credit** CB.
Another good Montparnasse area theatre. This one is quite fun and does lots of
comedy and some good one-man-show
performances. There are no performances on Mondays.
Wheelchair access.

Théâtre Galerie 55 (The English Theatre of Paris)

55 rue de la Seine, 75006 Paris
(43.26.63.51). Metro Odéon. **Open** tele-
phone box office: 11am-7pm Tue-Sat. **Tickets**
100F, 80F, 60F; student reductions.
No credit cards.
Paris's ten-year-old English-language theatre Théâtre Galerie 55 features the likes
of Sam Shepard, Tom Stoppard and
Edward Bond. The troupe also performs a
children's play series each Sunday as a
matinée. The theatre happens to be
located in one of the city's most lively
streets. There are no performances on
Sundays or Mondays.

Théâtre Huchette

23 rue de la Huchette, 75005 Paris
(43.26.38.99). Metro Saint-Michel. **Open**
box office: 5-10pm Mon-Sat. **Tickets** 80F; 60F
students, except Sat; reduced rate if you see
several plays in one evening.
No credit cards.
See **picture and caption.**
Wheelchair access.

Théâtre Jardin Shakespeare

Pré Catelan, Bois de Boulogne, 75016 Paris
(45.27.13.88). Metro Porte Maillot/bus 73.
Open box office: half hour before show, or phone
to reserve seats; phone for details. **Tickets** 60F;
30F OAPs, students.**No credit cards.**
Shakespeare in French goes down a bit
strangely, but the people behind this group
are sincere and talented. It is interesting to
see (although this is not the only place to find
Shakespeare in Paris; some other theatres do
adaptations, too) and hear, but only if you
have time to see other kinds of plays as well
and only if you're a real Shakespeare buff.

Théâtre Madeleine Compagnie Valère-Dersailly

19 rue de Surène, 75008 Paris
(42.65.07.09). Metro Madeleine/bus 42, 52.
Open box office: 11am-7pm Mon-Sat; 11am-
5pm Sun. **Tickets** 65F-240F. **Credit** CB, V.
A critic's favourite that deserves more attention.
They present good theatre, including a sprinkling of experimental works, in a well-planned
space. Almost all seats have a good view.
Wheelchair access.

Théâtre Tristan Bernard

64 rue du Rocher, 75008 Paris
(45.22.08.40). Metro Villiers/bus 30, 53.
Open box office: 11am-7pm daily. **Tickets**
85F-160F. **No credit cards.**
A currently hip theatre to attend. Although
the plays are interesting, too much of the
players' or directors' egos tend to come
through. For the most part, you'll see good
performances at a very fair price.

The Latin Quarter **Théâtre Huchette** *(listed under* **Independent Theatres)**
has been performing Ionesco's The Bald Soprano *for years. They see themselves as*
specialists in Ionesco and stage a number of his plays as double and triple features.
There are no performances on Sundays.

Study & Business

Searching for a secretary to translate a multi-million franc contract? Or are you a student looking for a cheap meal? We show you the way.

BUSINESS INFORMATION

Business is more formal in France than in Britain: communications are by letter, Fax or Telex rather than by phone and all written instructions, advertisements and descriptions must be in French. For a list of foreign banks in Paris, *see chapter* **Essential Information**; for a full list of embassies in Paris and useful reference libraries, *see chapter* **Survival**. Contact the following organizations for advice and information; all are open Monday to Friday.

British Consulate
*16 rue d'Anjou, 75008 Paris (42.66.91.42).
Metro Concorde/bus 42, 52, 72, 84.* **Open** 9.30am-12.30pm, 2.30-5.30pm, Mon-Fri.

British Embassy, Commercial Section
35 rue du Faubourg Saint Honoré, 75008 Paris (42.66.91.42). Metro Concorde/bus 42, 52, 72, 84. **Open** 9.30am-1pm, 2.30-6pm, Mon-Fri. *See* **picture and caption**.

Chambre de Commerce et d'Industrie Franco-Britannique
8 rue Cimarosa, 75016 Paris (45.05.13.08). Metro Boissière/bus 16, 22.
Open 8am-7pm Mon-Fri.
The Franco-British Chamber of Commerce provides help, information, documentation, rag trade check list, reference library (60F members, 40F students), trade research and trade contacts. Staff can also help with import/export procedure. They provide space for conferences and functions and will recommend translators if required. Membership (4,000F per year for corporate membership; 1,200F individual membership) is not required, but gives you some advantages. The associated **Centre d'Affaires** (Business Centre at the same address) offers short and long-term office lets with all facilities.

Chambre de Commerce et d'Industrie de Paris, Direction de Relations Internationales and World Trade Centre
2 rue de Viarmes, 75001 Paris (45.08.36.00/30). Metro Louvre/bus 21, 72, 81. **Open** 1-5.30pm Mon-Fri.
The Chamber provides assistance, orienta-

tion, trade contacts, consultation on all documentation and help with import/export procedure and legal matters.

COFACE (Compagnie Française d'Assurance pour le Commerce Extérieur)
3 rue Caumartin, 75009 (47.42.22.21). Metro Madeleine, Opéra/bus 24, 52, 84. **Open** 9am-5pm Mon-Fri.
The French equivalent of the Export Credits Guarantee Department.

Service des Renseignements Douaniers (Customs Information Service)
192 rue Saint Honoré, 75001 (42.60.35.90). Metro Palais Royal/bus 24, 94. **Open** 9am-5pm Mon-Fri.

Service des Autorisations Financiéres et Commerciales (Export & Import Licence Bureau)
42 rue de Clichy, 75009 Paris (42.81.91.44). Metro Limôge. **Open** *imports:* 9.15am-12.30pm, 1.30-5pm, Mon-Fri; *exports:* 9.15-11.30am, 1.30-5.45pm, Mon-Fri.

CFCE (Centre Français du Commerce Extérieur) (French Overseas Trade Board)
10 avenue d'Iéna, 75016 Paris (40.73.30.00). Metro Iéna/bus 82. **Open** 10am-5.30pm Mon-Thur; 10am-4.30pm Fri.

Greffe et Régistre du Commerce (Companies Registration Office)
1 quai de Corse, 75004 Paris (43.29.12.60). Metro Cité/bus 21, 96. **Open** 9-11.30am, 1-5pm, Mon-Fri. Setting up a company in France is usually a lot more difficult than it is in the UK, and this is the organization to approach for guidance. They can also supply trade information on French companies, such as financial status enquiries.

Préfecture de Police (Central Police Authority)
7 boulevard du Palais, 75004 (42.60.33.22). Metro Cité/bus 21, 96. **Open** 9am-5pm Mon-Fri.
This is where you apply for residence and work permits (which are required if you stay for more than three months). We advise checking with the British Consulate first.

Bureau d'Information de la Communauté Européenne (Press and Information Service of the EEC)
61 rue des Belles Feuilles, 75016 Paris (45.01.58.85). Metro Dauphine/bus 63. **Open** noon-5pm Mon-Thur; noon-4.30pm Fri.

Banque de France
39 rue de la Croix des Petits Champs, 75001 Paris (42.92.42.92). Metro Palais Royal or Bourse/bus 27, 68, 69. **Open** 11am-5pm Mon-Fri.

Bourse (Stock Exchange)
4 place de la Bourse, 75002 Paris (42.33.99.83). Metro Bourse/bus 27, 68, 69. **Open** 11am-1.30pm Mon-Fri.

IMPORT PROCEDURE

For almost any goods imported into France, a customs declaration must be presented. Payment is by documentary letter of credit, and forward contracts for imports arranged in France are not allowed. VAT is payable on all goods entering France (5.5 per cent for foodstuffs, 18.6 per cent standard, 25 per cent for luxury goods).

For import licences on restricted items (such as firearms) applications must be made by a French resident to: **Direction Générale des Douanes et Droits Indirects, Ministère de l'Economie des Finances et de la Privatisation,** *rue de Rivoli, 75001 Paris (42.60.33.00)*.

The value of goods declared at customs should include commissions. All samples must be declared (but duty can be waived by filling in a *carnet*, available from the **London Chamber of Commerce,** *69 Cannon Street, London EC2 (071 248 4444)*. All goods vehicles entering France require permits and British exporters are advised to use an agent (details from **Commercial Section, British Embassy in Paris,** *see above* **Business Information**). If you are operating through a French company, you may be liable to pay French income tax for any earnings made in France.

For more information contact:

Department of Trade and Industry
Sanctuary Buildings, 16-20 Great Smith Street, London SW1 (French desk 071 215 4765). Victoria underground/BR/bus 38, 73. The French desk should be able to advise on both general and specific requests relating to France's export and import markets.

EXPORT PROCEDURE

Centre Français du Commerce Extérieur
10 avenue d'Iéna, 75016 Paris (40.73.30.00). Metro Etoile/bus 22, 52, 73. **Open** 9am-noon, 2-6.45pm, Mon-Fri.

The French Embassy
Commercial Section, 21-24 Grosvenor Place, London SW1 (071 235 7080). Knightsbridge underground/bus 19, 73. **Open** 9.30am-1pm Mon-Fri.
Contact for information and advice.

*The various departments within the **British Embassy's Commercial Section** (Technology, Agriculture, Fashion and so on), listed under **Business Information**, keep lists of companies who wish to establish or extend their business links with the UK.*

French Tourist Office
178 Piccadilly, London W1 (071 491 7622). Piccadilly Circus underground/bus 38, 73. **Open** 9am-5pm Mon-Fri.
The Office's Business Travel Department gives information on conference centres, hotels, banks, and business procedure.

TRADE FAIR SITES

There are around 100 competing exhibition organizers with different calendars, hosting trade fairs in one of these main exhibition halls. It's advisable to contact each venue for a programme listing events. You may also obtain a complete national trade exhibition calendar from:

Imprimerie Nationale
20 rue de la Boétie, 75008 Paris (42.65.11.97). Metro Miromesnil/bus 24, 52, 84.
Stock the *Calendrier des Foires et des Salons* (Fairs calendar), published by the French Ministry of Commerce and priced 35F.

French Trade Exhibitions
197 Knightsbridge, London SW7 (071 225 5566). Knightsbridge underground/bus 19, 73.
This association represents and promotes many French exhibitions, issuing calendars which cover the various events.

Parc des Expositions Paris
Porte de Versailles, 75015 Paris (48.42.87.00). Metro Porte de Versailles/bus 48, 89.

Parc des Expositions Paris Nord
Villepinte, Boite Postale 60004, Paris Nord 2, 95970 Roissy-Charles de Gaulle Cedex (48.63.30.30). RER (line A2) to Parc des Expositions.

Grande Halle de la Villette
211 avenue Jean Jaurès, 75019 Paris (42.49.77.22). Metro Porte de Pantin/bus 75.

Palais des Congrès
2 place de la Porte Maillot, 75017 Paris (46.40.22.22). Metro Porte Maillot/bus 75.

Espace Champerret
rue Jacques Ibert , 75017 Paris (40.55.19.55). Metro Porte de Champerret/bus 30, 31, 43, 93.

BUSINESS SERVICES

PERSONAL COMPUTER HIRE

ISTC
(département Locamicro), 3 rue Sainte Félicité, 75015 Paris (45.32.80.01). Metro Vaugirard/bus 48, 89.
Open 8.30am-5pm Mon-Fri.
Credit V.
Apple and IBM computer rental by the week or month.

Locatel
Head Office 16 rue Barbès 92300 Levallois Perret (47.58.12.00). **Open** 10am-1pm, 2-7pm, Mon-Sat. **Credit** by application only.
This company supplies answerphones, car phones, TVs, satellite TVs, video recorders and hi-fi equipment. There is a minimum rental period of six months, which is the norm in France.

DUPLICATING & PRINTING

Alpha Copy
10 rue du Roule, 75001 Paris (40.26.86.33). Metro Louvre/bus 58, 67, 69, 70, 72. **Open** 9am-1.30pm, 2.30-6.30pm, Mon-Fri.
Black and white and colour photocopying, from one to 1,000 copies. Reductions and enlargements, plus binding, folding and stapling of your documents are available. You can also have letter-heads, posters and envelopes printed in a variety of colours and paper qualities.

Copy Top
4 avenue de l'Opéra, 75001 Paris (42.96.83.88). Metro Pyramides/bus 27, 29, 68, 81, 95. **Open** 8.30am-12.30pm, 1.30-6pm, Mon-Fri.
Photocopying (black and white, colour); photo engraving, off-set printing, binding, word processing, laser printing, mailings and circulars can all be taken care of here.

Copy 2000
30 rue Washington, 75008 Paris (45.63.73.62). Metro George V/bus 73. **Open** 9am-12.30pm, 1.30-6.30pm, Mon-Fri. **No credit cards.**
Black and white and colour copying, four-colour reproduction, off-set printing, production of stationery, press kits, company newsletters and so on are all provided by this company.

SECRETARIES & TRANSLATIONS

Agglomération
25 rue Jean Leclaire, 75017 Paris (42.63.85.45/Fax 42.63.86.68). Metro Guy Moquet/bus 31, 81. **Open** 10am-6pm Mon-Fri. **No credit cards.**
Bilingual services in advertising, communications and marketing are available. There's also hi-tech voice training in French and English.

Société Internationale de Traduction
19 rue de la Paix, 75001 Paris (47.42.79.59). Metro Opéra/bus 22, 52, 53, 66. **Open** 9am-6pm Mon-Fri. **No credit cards.**
This organization specializes in legal translations.

GR Interim
12 rue de la Paix, 75001 Paris (42.61.82.11). Metro Opéra/bus 22, 52, 53, 66. **Open** 9am-6pm Mon-Fri. **Rates** 160F-178F per hour. **No credit cards.**
Qualified bilingual secretaries.

Vrai
32 boulevard Henri IV, 75004 Paris (48.04.39.27/Fax 48.04.73.65). Metro Bastille, Sully Morland/bus 86, 87. **Open** 10am-6pm Mon-Fri. **No credit cards.**
For personalized specialist French-English-French translation, interpreting, copywriting

or re-writing services. English and French native speakers are available as required. The staff are experienced in all fields, including publicity, legal, personal and technical.

See also above **Chambre de Commerce et d'Industrie**, listed under **Business Information**.

DRESS HIRE
Beral
2 rue Caulaincourt, 75018 Paris (43.87.72.37). Metro Clichy/bus 54. **Open** 2-6.30pm Mon; 9am-12.30pm, 1.30-6.30pm, Tue-Sat. **Rates** 300F-900F per evening. **Credit** V.
This company tends to specialize in traditional men's evening wear, favouring tuxedos, cuff-links and stiff collars.

La Femme Ecarlate
42 avenue Bosquet, 75007 Paris (45.51.08.44). Metro Ecole Militaire/bus 28, 49. **Open** 11am-1pm, 2-7pm, Tue-Sat. **Rates** about 400F-1,400F per evening.
No credit cards.
Another shop which favours traditional couture: female evening attire here tends to be wrapped in taffeta and crushed silk.

LANGUAGE COURSES

Alliance Française
101 boulevard Raspail, 75006 Paris (45.44.38.28). Metro Rennes. **Open** phone for details. **Fees** 880F-2,000F per month.
The Alliance Française has a very good reputation, and offers several services to its students, including a *mediathèque*, a French cinema club and lectures on a wide range of topics. Perhaps one of the biggest advantages is that you pay monthly, so you can spread payments. Courses cover all fields, including French language (at all levels), literature and economics. Classes can be attended at seven different times a day.

Berlitz France
29 rue de la Michaudière, 75002 Paris (47.24.13.39). Metro Opéra. **Open** phone for details. **Fees** *four week intensive:* 10,400F. **Credit** FTC.
Expensive, but very well known and effective. There are all types of courses here, at all hours of the day and evening, with several schools around Paris.

British Institute
9 rue Constantine, 75007 Paris (45.55.71.99). Metro Invalides. **Open** phone for details. **Fees** *full time:* 2,490F per term, *part time:* 950F-2,375F per term.
The Institute is linked to the University of London, and courses are open to everyone over 18. You should apply for your registration form two to five months before the start of term. Language classes are held for all levels, with some interesting lectures on French cinema, theatre and other media on the French Civilization course; outings and visits are also arranged. On average, there are 12 hours of class per week for each course. Fees are per term. For details in Britain, contact *Senate House, Malet Street, London WC1 (071 636 8000, ext 3920).*

Fondation Post-Universitaire Internationale
30 rue Cabanis, 75014 Paris (45.89.84.20). Metro Glacière. **Open** phone for details. **Fees** 440F-805F per month. **Credit** FTC.
Situated within the Foyer International, which is essentially for young people, this school accepts all ages and is reasonably priced.

La Sorbonne – Centre de Civilisation
47 rue des Ecoles, 75005 Paris (40.46.22.11, ext 2464). Metro Cluny La Sorbonne, Luxembourg, Saint Michel. **Open** phone for details. **Fees** 2,650F-3,800F per half-year. **Credit** FTC.
See **picture and caption**.

Télélangue Système
31 rue de la Brèche-aux-Loups, 75012 Paris (43.44.48.43). Metro Daumesnil. **Open** 8am-8pm Mon-Fri.
Credit AmEx, CB, EC, MC, FTC, V.
An innovative language-learning system, used by numerous business and busy people to learn any of 14 languages in over 600 specialities (such as medicine or restaurant terminology). It works like this: you take a written test to determine your ability in your chosen language. After meeting your instructor face to face, you make a series of appointments with him or her for twenty minutes of telephone conversation. Your instructor will phone at the appointed time. A 12-week course, of four 20-minute sessions per week, costs 1,200F.
Branch: 65bis rue du Rocher, 75008 (42.94.90.02).

STUDENT INFORMATION

It is possible to live on a low budget in Paris, despite its reputation as one of Europe's more expensive capitals. Many students of all nationalities come here to learn or improve their French, and a wide range of discounts and services are available. To benefit from most of these you should equip yourself either with the *International Student Card* (ISIC, £4, available in France and in Britain) or with the *Carte Jeunes (see below* for details.) Above all, come prepared, so as not to fall into the all too easy trap of overspending. For useful

The **Sorbonne** *(listed under* Language Courses*) is France's most eminent educational institution and the pulse of the Latin Quarter. Courses here are very much along the same lines as those at the British Institute, with variations within the French Civilization course (lectures on politics, history and so on). Language-only courses are also available. Courses are open to everyone over 18, and those with British 'A' levels or equivalent are at a distinct advantage.*

the shortest sea route...

To get to England, go through Calais.
The closest port to England, separated by only 33km of sea, Calais is naturally the Number One Channel Port of Europe and for more than 9 million travellers).

The most up-to-date travel facilities,
grouped together in a first-rate setting: ticket offices, bureau de change, shops, bar, restaurant, self-service cafeteria and more. 30 hectares of parking space, special traffic lanes and two-level footbridges make sure you get on board quickly and easily.

More crossings - more often.
Calais provides up to 104 crossings a day, so you can get to England quicker. With the new generation of car ferries, a pleasant mini-cruise of 75 minutes is all it takes to cross the Channel. And if you go by hovercraft, you can be in Dover in 30 minutes.

For details of sailing times and prices, contact your travel agent or P&O European Ferries and Sealink for car-ferries and Hoverspeed for hovercrafts.
Bon voyage from Calais!

VIA Calais

EUROPE'S No1 PORT FOR CROSSINGS TO ENGLAND

libraries, *see chapter* **Survival**. Contact the following agencies for information and advice.

AJF (Acceuil des Jeunes en France)
119 rue Saint Martin, 75004 Paris (42.77.87.80). Metro Les Halles, Rambuteau. **Open** 9.30am-7pm Mon-Sat.
Situated right opposite the Pompidou Centre, the AJF provides help and information on temporary accommodation, discount train tickets, events, and so on. As they are always busy, it's best just to turn up rather than phone. They operate some youth hostels with bookings on a day-by-day basis (*see below* **Student Accomodation**).
Branch: 139 boulevard Saint Michel (43.54.95.86).

CIDJ (Centre d'Information et de Documentation Jeunesse)
101 Quai Branly, 75015 Paris (45.67.35.85). Metro Bir Hakeim, Champs de Mars. **Open** 9am-7pm Mon-Fri; 10am-6pm Sat. **No credit cards.**
An indispensable address for young people. Staff give information on work and study, as well as social life, hobbies and sports. They have information on job offers, but *not* on accommodation, though they can, however, give you a list of cheap hotels and hostels for short-term stays. Information is not given by phone, so write or go in person. You can buy your *Carte Jeune* here too. It's a good place for finding part-time work to bring in extra cash – the main youth bureau of the **ANPE (Agence Nationale Pour l'Emploi)** is situated within the Centre, *see* **picture and caption.**

CROUS (Centre Régional des Oeuvres Universitaires et Scolaires)
39 avenue Georges Bernano, 75005 Paris (40.51.36.00). Metro Port Royal. **Open** 9am-5pm Mon-Fri. **No credit cards.**
See **picture and caption.**

UCRIF (Union des Centres de Rencontres Internationales de France)
4 rue Jean-Jacques Rousseau, 75001 Paris (42.60.42.40). Metro Louvre. **Open** 10am-6pm Mon-Fri. **Credit** V.
UCRIF operates several cheap hostels throughout France, with 16 in Paris (*see below* **Student Accommodation**). They also organize social events and language courses. There is no age limit for those wishing to benefit from their services.

STUDENT ACCOMMODATION

LONG-TERM

Chambre contre travail
One of the more common forms of accommodation for students (admittedly more for girls rather than boys) is a *chambre contre travail* (free board in exchange for work). You will normally have your own separate room. Just how much babysitting or housework you have to vary does, as does the pos-

At the **Agence Nationale Pour l'Emploi** *(see* **CIDJ**, *listed under* **Student Information***), it is possible to sign on for up to three months' British Unemployment Benefit, by taking Form E303 from the DHSS to the ANPE. They will direct you from there. As with all red tape, this is not as easy as it sounds, and is of course not available to you while you are studying, but it could help to tide you over if you're trying to get a job during the summer holidays.*

sibility of having your own shower and loo. Advertisements of this kind can usually be found through your Course Accommodation Office, or through some of the centres listed in **Student Information** *above.*

Flat-hunting
The name of the game is money, readily available (and preferably in large amounts). As students often cannot provide the required proof of income, a porte-garant (guarantor) is required. This role is usually filled by a parent who writes a letter (in French) declaring that he/she will guarantee payment of your rent. Bring this with you, as you will waste precious time waiting for it to be sent. Be prepared to hand over twice the monthly rent as a deposit (returnable when you leave), plus the first month's payment, plus an agency fee (if applicable) of anything up to the equivalent of one month's rent, in one fell swoop... C'est la vie...

Cité Universitaire
19 boulevard Jourdan, 75014 Paris (45.89.13.37). RER Cité Universitaire. **Open** phone for details.
If you are enrolled on a university-style course (Sorbonne, British Institute and so on) and are under 30, you can apply for a place at the Cité Universitaire – a huge campus of Halls of Residence on the outskirts of the 14th *arrondissement*. Rooms have to be booked for the entire academic year (October to June). Prices range from 1,050F to 1,400F per month for a single room and from 750F to 900F per person for a double. The price range depends on which *maison* you live in, the Maison Américaine and Maison Internationale

being the two most popular. During the summer, rooms are available for rent to anybody holding an International Student Card, on a *tarif passager* of 80F to 100F per night.

SHORT-TERM

For more information on cheap hotels and *pensions*, *see chapter* **Accommodation.**

AJF (Acceuil des Jeunes en France)
119 rue Saint Martin, 75004 Paris (42.77.87.80). Metro Les Halles, Rambuteau. **Open** 9.30am-7pm Mon-Sat.
The AJF operates several highly recommended hostels/residences. It is best to go to one of the main offices to book a place, as they can tell you which hostel has vacancies, and will give you a complete list. Bookings are on a daily first-come, first-served basis, and queues have already formed at 9am. Prices range from 75F to 125F or so per night, depending on whether you share. We list below those hostels that are open throughout the year. There are also a few seasonally-open hostels, giving an extra 3,000 beds. Contact the AJF for details.

Le Fauconnier
11 rue du Fauconnier, 75004 Paris (42.74.23.45). Metro Saint Paul. **Open** 7am-1am daily.
No credit cards
Very pretty converted mansion in the Marais. Very popular and therefore crowded, but one of the nicest.

Fourcy
6 rue de Fourcy, 75006 Paris (42.74.23.45).
Metro Saint Paul. **Open** 7am-1am daily.
No credit cards.
A charge of 80F per night includes breakfast here, which is served from 8am to 10am. There are 224 rooms, each sleeping from two to eight people, with a shower in each room.

Kellermann
17 boulevard Kellermann, 75013 Paris (45.80.70.76). Metro Maison Blanche. **Open** 6.30am-1.30am daily. **Credit** CB, V.
Slightly more out of the way than some of the others, but they have parties, meeting rooms, and other activities.

Maurice Ravel
6 avenue Maurice Ravel, 75012 Paris (43.43.19.01). Metro Porte de Vincennes.
Open 6.30am-1.30am daily.
Credit AmEx, MC, V.
There are 225 beds available at 115F per day, with breakfast included.

Maubuisson
12 rue des Barres, 75004 Paris (42.72.72.09). Metro Hôtel de Ville. **Open** 6am-1am daily. **No credit cards.**
Another Marais mansion. Also very popular, it's a restored seventeenth-century hotel in a fashionable district.

Residence Bastille
151 avenue Ledru Rollin, 75011 Paris (43.79.53.86). Metro Bastille. **Open** 2pm-noon daily. **No credit cards.**
There are 156 beds (77F per person per night, with breakfast included). Most rooms have individual showers, or a shower on the same floor. Three rooms are singles, the rest are shared.

UCRIF (Union des Centres de Rencontres Internationales de France)
4 rue Jean-Jacques Rousseau, 75001 Paris (42.60.42.40). Metro Louvre. **Open** 10am-6pm Mon-Fri. **Credit** V.
UCRIF run many hostels in Paris and throughout the rest of France. *See* **picture and caption** for details. The main, most central Parisian residences are:

Centre International de Paris/Louvre
20 rue J J Rousseau, 75001 Paris (42.36.88.18/40.26.66.43/42.33.82.10). Metro Louvre or Palais Royal. **Open** 6am-2am daily. **No credit cards**
Single and shared rooms (200 beds), from 80F per night with breakfast.

BVJ Les Halles
5 rue du Pélican, 75001 Paris (40.26.92.45). Metro Louvre. **Open** 6am-2am daily. **No credit cards.**
Single and shared rooms (55 beds), from 80F per night with breakfast.

BVJ quartier Latin
44 rue des Bernardins, 75005 Paris (43.29.34.80). Metro Maubert Mutualité. **Open** 7am-1am daily. **No credit cards.**

BVJ Opéra
11 rue Thérèse, 75001 Paris (42.60.77.23). Metro Pyramides or Palais Royal. **Open** 7am-1am daily. **No credit cards.**

CROUS *(listed under* **Student Information***) is best known for its university restaurants – Restos-U (see* Cheap Grub*). It also organizes cheap excursions, sport and cultural events, as well as providing information on student accommodation and jobs.*

Single and shared rooms (68 beds), from 80F per night including breakfast.

CHEAP GRUB

Being on a low budget doesn't mean you have to miss out on eating out; you simply have to be a bit more selective. Once you've settled yourself in you're bound to find your favourite restaurant *du coin* with a 50F menu, but until you do, here are a few useful addresses. *See also* chapter **Restaurants**.

La Casa Miguel
48 rue Saint Georges, 75009 Paris (42.81.09.61). Metro Saint Georges. **Open** noon-1pm, 7-8pm, daily. **No credit cards.**
You have to queue for an hour to get in but it's worth it. It's in the Guinness Book of Records as being the cheapest restaurant in the world. You can have a main course, dessert and wine for the princely sum of 5F (no, it's not a typing error). Simple but good food is served, but opinions are divided as to the freshness of the products used.

Chartier
7 rue du Faubourg Montmartre, 75009 Paris (47.70.86.29). Metro Rue Montmartre. **Open** 11am-3pm, 6-9.30pm, daily.
Average 70F. **Credit** FTC.

This traditional restaurant has been around for over 150 years, and has managed to keep its décor more or less intact. It's filled with locals, impoverished artists and students, and you can eat for 30F to 60F on average. It's a highly popular place, so try and come as early as possible (all tables are shared as required). An institution.

Restaurant des Beaux Arts
11 rue Bonaparte, 75006 Paris (43.26.92.64). Metro Saint Germain des Près. **Open** noon-11pm daily.
No credit cards.
The Beaux Arts (set menu 50F) has got a great atmosphere and it's nice to be able to eat fondue, *boeuf bourguignon* and the rest in this chic area of Paris without paying through the nose.

Resto-U: Albert Châtelet
10 rue Jean Calvin, 75005 Paris (43.31.51.66). Metro Censier Daubenton. **Open** 11.30-1.45pm, 6.30-8pm, Mon-Fri; variable times Sat, Sun, phone for details. **No credit cards.**
CROUS (*see above* **Student Information**) run a chain of *Restos-U* (university restaurants) and this is one of them. Food is not hugely appetising, but the prices are unbeatable. Buy a *carnet* of tickets at 9.30F per ticket for students (18.60F non-students). Get a full list of restaurants from the CROUS head office or the restaurant listed here.

Trips Out of Town

So you're beat and want to get out of town? Feel the novelty of Paris begin to wear thin? Make for the open road and try one of the many destinations we suggest for a breath of fresh air. From Normandy and the Brittany coast to the Alps and the Pyrenees, the range and diversity of rural France is sure to tempt you away from the boulevards of Paris. The section is divided into themes for easy reference, so oenophiles can delve into the chapter entitled Wine & Champagne to get the low-down on the vineyards of France, while architectural buffs or those interested in seeing the Landing Beaches of World War II need only turn to the Special Interest chapter. A day trip or weekend away from the capital is sure to broaden your understanding of the Gallic psyche; visit one of the many locations that we have reviewed and judge for yourself.

CONTENTS:

Leaving Paris

Half the time you're stuck on the metro, the other half fighting the crowds. Want to leave town? Here's the low-down on travelling to some of France's more interesting regions.

You've decided to get out of Paris and see what the rest of the country looks like; to see if what they say about Paris not being typically French is true. The most striking aspect of *la République Française*, with its 99 *départements* divided into 22 *régions*, is its incredible diversity. The Île-de-France, with its vast castles, abbeys and turn-of-the-century suburbs, is altogether different from Aquitaine and its pine forests, vineyards and wide, sandy beaches. From Paris you can spend five hours in the TGV (Train Grande Vitesse, France's high-speed train network) and suddenly find yourself in Alpine grandeur, or on the rocky granite coasts of Brittany. Or if you prefer flying, every nook and cranny of France is within an hour's plane ride from Paris's Orly Airport. But before you go, certain details are worth knowing.

WHEN NOT TO TRAVEL

Since 1936, when France had its first Socialist government, the French have had *congés payés* (paid holidays), traditionally taken in July and August. And since 20 per cent of the French live in the Paris region, when they leave for this holiday it looks a lot like Moses escorting the Israelites across the Red Sea. Weekends to avoid travelling on at all costs are around the beginning, middle and end of July, and again at the end of August. These two months are in fact an ideal time to be in Paris, where high season is in June and September. The other bad time to travel in France is the month from mid-February to mid-March, when all of these holiday-makers don snowsuits and attach wooden boards to their feet for sliding down mountain sides. If you thought the traffic jams to the Riviera were bad, try these, where there are just as many cars and a blizzard to make things more sporting.

Fortunately, the French are starting to take their holidays throughout the year. It's true that the Riviera and the Basque Coast are delightful in mid-September, but·what about sunny May mornings in the Dordogne, brisk November walks along the Normandy shore or warm October afternoons in Provence? Because of this recent change in behaviour, small *auberges* (inns) and restaurants are able to stay open longer. But be informed before you go. It would be a shame to organize a spur-of-the-moment trip during Armistice weekend (11 November) only to discover that everything closed up for the season on All Saints weekend (1 November).

INFORMATION

For information before going to France, contact your local French Tourist Office.

French Tourist Office
178 Piccadilly, London W1V 0AL (recorded information 071 499 6911/direct line 071 491 7622). Piccadilly Circus underground. **Open** 9am-5pm Mon-Fri; closed 14 July.

The Paris Tourist Office on the Champs-Elysées and the annexes in the main train stations (*see below*) are probably the best places to start. Although their primary duty is to promote Paris, they are very efficient at giving information on the rest of France. There are also a number of regional tourist offices in Paris, offering a hotel reservation service and package trips conceived around different themes as well as general information. The full list of **Maisons de Tourisme** in Paris and throughout the rest of France is available from the main Paris Tourist Office; we list a few of the major ones below.

Paris Tourist Office, main office
127 avenue des Champs-Elysées, 75008 Paris (47.23.61.72) Metro George V. **Open** 9am-8pm daily.

Gare du Nord Tourist Office
(45.26.94.82). **Open** *Nov-Easter*: 8am-8pm Mon-Sat; *Easter-Nov*: 8am-10pm Mon-Sat; 1-8pm Sun.

Gare de l'Est Tourist Office
(46.07.17.73). **Open** *Nov-Easter*: 8am-1pm, 5-8pm, Mon-Sat; *Easter-Oct*: 8am-10pm Mon-Sat.

Gare de Lyon Tourist Office
(43.43.33.24). **Open** *Nov-Easter*: 8am-1pm, 5-8pm, Mon-Sat; *Easter-Oct*: 8am-10pm Mon-Sat.

Gare d'Austerlitz Tourist Office
(45.84.91.70). **Open** *Nov-March*: 8am-3pm Mon-Sat; *April-Oct*: 8am-10pm Mon-Sat.

Eiffel Tower Tourist Office
(45.51.22.15). **Open** *May-Sept only*: 11am-6pm daily.

Maison Alpes-Dauphiné (Northern Alps)
2 place André-Malraux, 75001 Paris (42.96.08.43). Metro Palais Royal. **Open** 11am-1.30pm, 2-6pm, Mon-Sat.

Maison d'Alsace
39 avenue des Champs-Elysées, 75008 Paris (42.56.15.94). Metro Franklin D Roosevelt. **Open** 9am-7pm Mon-Fri; 11am-5pm Sat; closed Sat whole month of August.

Maison du Nord-Pas de Calais
18 boulevard Haussman, 75009 Paris (47.70.59.62). Metro Chaussée d'Antin. **Open** 9am-5pm Mon-Fri.

Maison du Périgord (Dordogne)
30 rue Louis-le-Grand, 75002 Paris (47.42.09.15). Metro Opéra. **Open** 10am-1pm, 2-6.30pm, Mon-Thur; 10am-1pm, 2-5.30pm, Fri.

Maison des Pyrénées
15 rue Saint-Augustin, 75002 Paris (42.61. 58.18). Metro Quatre Septembre. **Open** 9am-6pm Mon-Fri.

Maison de la Savoie (Southern Alps)
31 avenue de l'Opéra, 75001 Paris (42.61.74.73). Metro Opéra, Pyramides. **Open** 9.30am-6.30pm Mon-Sat.

TRAVELLING BY TRAIN

The French railroad company, the **Société Nationale des Chemins de Fer (SNCF)** is one of the most efficient in the world. But like all huge, government-run organizations, it has certain drawbacks such as regular strikes, total disinterest in profit making (therefore in the client), strange hours and slow internal exchange of information. Services are very efficient however, and trains almost always leave on time.

Various tariff bands are offered to travellers: **Red, White** and **Blue**. Red is basically 'rush hour'; Blue is 'slow period'; and White is in between. To encourage Red passengers to travel during Blue periods, discounts are offered. These vary with the social profile of the traveller: Senior Citizens, Students, Married Couples, Parents with Children, Salaried Employees, and so on. A concrete example is the **Carré Jeune**. This card, for people between the ages of 12 and 26, allows four one-way trips at 50 per cent discount during the Blue period and a 20 per cent reduction during the White period; the card is valid for one year on both first and second class and costs about 140F. Journeys must start in the relevant period, but can end in another.

No matter what colour period, the **TGV** (Trains Grande Vitesse, or high-speed trains) usually command a supplement. And always, *always* have your ticket stamped at the little orange *composteurs* located by the platforms. Inspectors on trains are authorized to charge for the full price of a ticket, plus fine, if this is not done.

Night trains are no cheaper than regular trains and they're much slower, but they save precious daytime when travelling long distances. Shared sleeper cabins are available for an additional charge; provided you manage to fall asleep with five people snoring around you, they can be quite pleasant and the linen is clean.

The most complicated thing about leaving Paris by train is knowing which station to go to, as each one corresponds to a different region. Leave from **Gare Montparnasse** for *Brittany* and *southern Normandy*; from **Gare Saint-Lazare** for *northern Normandy* and some destinations in *Great Britain*; from **Gare du Nord** for *northern France, Belgium, northern Europe* and other destinations in *Great Britain*; from **Gare de l'Est** for *Strasbourg, Champagne* and *southern Germany*; from **Gare de Lyon** for *Burgundy, the Alps, Provence* and the *Riviera*; and from **Gare d'Austerlitz** for *south-western France (Bordeaux, Poitiers)* and *Spain*. It will be clear from the ticket which station to leave from.

Tickets can be bought on the day of travel or in advance from any train station. Alternatively, they can be booked by phone and collected from any station; make sure you check when they should be picked up..

SNCF Central Information Service
(Information 45.82.50.50/Reservations 45.65.60.60). **Open** 8am-8pm daily. **Credit** V. The central numbers deal with information and reservations for all services and stations.

TRAVELLING BY PLANE

Up until recently, the French national company **Air Inter** had a near-monopoly on domestic flights. **Air France**, also a national company, now offers some flights to major French cities but they've basically adopted the Air Inter prices, which are sometimes cheaper than the train. As with the railroad, flights have been divided into Red, White and Blue periods (clearly a popular leitmotiv for French mass transport). Various types of passenger are entitled to discounts. For example, under-25s or students under the age of 27 get a 50 per cent reduction at certain times; a return flight Paris-Bordeaux could cost about 600F.

Air France
119 avenue des Champs-Elysées, 75008 Paris (45.35.61.61). Metro George V. **Open** 9am-6pm Mon-Sat. **Credit** AmEx, DC, EC, MC, V.

Air Inter
49 avenue des Champs-Elysées, 75008 Paris (45.39.25.25). Metro Franklin D Roosevelt. **Open** 9am-midnight Mon-Sat; noon-midnight Sun. **Credit** V.

TRAVELLING BY CAR

As you can see from any map of France, all roads do not lead to Rome, but to Paris. This has made the French capital notorious for traffic jams. Even the ultra-modern highways have been built along the antique pattern of spokes around a metropolitan hub, leading to a concentration of traffic on main arteries.

Various *portes* (gates) of the *périphérique* (the circular highway around Paris) give access to the main roads out of Paris. To go

south (Lyon, the Riviera) or **south-west** (Tours, Bordeaux) take the *Porte d'Orléans* or *Porte d'Italie*; to go **west** (Versailles, Normandy), take the *Porte de Saint Cloud*; to go **east** (Nancy, Strasbourg), follow the Seine east towards *Bercy*; and to go **north** (Lille, Chantilly), take the *Porte de la Chapelle*. All the other *portes* lead to smaller, slower highways.

French roadways are divided into *Autoroutes* (motorways, featuring an 'A' in front of the number), *Routes Nationales* (national roads, featuring an 'N' in front of the number) and *Routes Départementales* (departmental, or local, roads, featuring a 'D' in front of the number). The motorways were built by private

companies and are toll roads. This may be a deterring factor for some people (the toll from Paris to Lyon is about 100F) but motorways are impeccably well-maintained and have a speed limit of 130 kilometres (80 miles) per hour. This gives them a definite advantage over the *Routes Nationales* and their miserable 90 kilometres (56 miles) per hour limit.

Before you go to France, familiarize yourself with French rules of the road and driving etiquette, which can differ greatly from British ones. Obviously British drivers need to remember to drive on the right. A useful booklet to read is the **Royal Automobile Club**'s *Continental Motoring Guide*, which covers such subjects as regulations for most European countries, international road signs and toll charges. It costs £1.95 from any RAC office, or £2.40 by post. The RAC head office is at *49 Pall Mall, London SW1 5JG (071 839 7050)*.

For details of car repair services, *see chapter* **Survival**.

Around Paris

Spend the day or weekend visiting one of the many attractions in the *environs* of Paris. We review some of the local sights and châteaux and guide you through the countryside.

For more information on the châteaux outside Paris *see chapter* **Museums.**

VAUX-LE-VICOMTE

Not as well-known as Versailles, or nearby Fontainebleau (*see below* for both) and therefore less crowded, this château, some 60 kilometres (37 miles) outside Paris, is an absolute gem. Once you know the rather peculiar history of this fairy-tale castle, your visit will prove to be even more moving.

The land itself was bought by Nicholas Fouquet (1615-1680) in 1641 and at the time the only standing edifice was a medieval ruin. This keen businessman and mem-

ber of the Parisian Parliament was considered one of the wealthiest men in all of France. Benefactor to the nation's biggest names in art (Molière, La Fontaine, Madame de Sévigné), he was also the protégé of the ultra-powerful Cardinal Mazarin, regent of France until Louis XIV came of age. Thus in 1653 Fouquet was named *Surintendant des Finances* (French equivalent of the Chancellor of the Exchequer). This prestigious position apparently brought him more wealth and brought the nation closer to bankruptcy.

Three years later, in 1656, Fouquet decided to have Vaux built. For the occasion he assembled three of France's most talented men: painter Charles Le Brun, architect Louis Le Vaux and land-

scape gardener André Le Nôtre. If these names sound familiar to you it's because they also worked together to build Versailles a few years later. During the five years of construction, Jean-Baptiste Colbert, who later became Finance Minister, tried to convince the King that his friend Fouquet was a dishonest, power-hungry man.

Finally on a warm summer night on 17 August 1661, Fouquet held a huge soirée for the inauguration of his beautiful new house and invited the King. Historians claim that it was the most luxurious party in the history of France. Live, jewel-encrusted elephants decorated the alleys lined with orange-trees. Spectacular imported Chinese fireworks were shot off from the reflecting ponds. Crowned heads from around the world attended or sent gifts. Livid with jealousy, and egged on by Colbert, the King, who was 23 and ruling *de facto* for the first time, decided this ostentatious show of wealth (more than his own) was the last straw. The recent death of Cardinal Mazarin meant that the Finance Minister was unprotected and seen as a threat by the King. He therefore had Fouquet arrested on a trumped-up charge. A court trial was held and Fouquet was declared guilty of *malversation* (embezzlement). His personal effects were taken by the crown and the court sentenced him to exile. But Louis XIV found this sentence too slack and had it changed to solitary confinement, ensuring that Fouquet would never return to power. Some say that Fouquet was the famous Man with the Iron Mask described by Alexandre Dumas. The reason for this theory is that Fouquet was such a popular politician that if people had recognized him in prison it would have caused a public uproar. It was therefore necessary for the King to have Fouquet's face covered.

In the meantime, Fouquet's widow sold Vaux-le-Vicomte before it was even finished. The most moving symbol of this fallen magnate is the unfinished, domed ceiling in the vast, elliptical Grand Salon where Le Brun only had time to paint the cloudy sky and one solitary eagle holding the chandelier in its beak. It's no surprise that 1661 was also the year that Louis, the Sun King, began renovating a rather humble hunting lodge he owned in a subur-

The vast, French-style gardens and the stately yet unimposing, neo-classic façade set in the heart of the countryside make **Vaux-Le-Vicomte** *a most harmonious architectural spectacle. Inside, the period furnishings are impressive and the paintings well worth seeing.*

ban town called Versailles. History recounts that the road between Vaux and Versailles was quite busy with moving waggons that year.

When entering the grounds via the outbuildings, bypass the Carriage Museum unless you've time to spare. A stroll round the interior is fascinating, and particularly moving when it's candle-lit (8.30pm to 11pm Saturday, from May to September). The furnishings, which include a bizarre wicker bathroom suite, reflect the periods of each ownership. Most of the furniture and decoration is the result of the Sommier family who, between 1875 and 1968, saved and restored the château and gardens. And it's the gardens that stun. As you round the moat, the sober frontage doesn't prepare you for the baroque rear aspect. The vista gets ever more breathtaking the further back you venture through the statues, sculpted hedges and pools. Watch out for the fountains that spout from 3pm to 6pm on the second and last Saturday of every month. It's best to take a picnic if heading for the Hercules statue; you'll soon realize why the residents made it a day trip.

Château Vaux-le-Vicomte
77950 Maincy (60.66.97.11/60.66.97.09). **Open** 11am-5pm daily. **Admission** 42F adults; 34F under-16s. *Gift shop. Restaurant.*

MORE INFORMATION
Getting there
From Paris to Château Vaux-le-Vicomte by car: take the motorway **A6** to the Fontainebleau exit; follow signs to Melun, from there follow the signs to the castle. Alternatively, take the **A4** to Melun exit, then N36 and D215; 46km (28 miles) from Paris, 6km (4 miles) from Melun. *By train:* from Gare de Lyon to Melun, 40 minutes. *By tour coach:* try Paris-Vision (42.60.31.25) who organize half-day and day trips from central Paris.

FONTAINEBLEAU

Fontainebleau, recommended by France's horse-riders, cyclists, artists, walkers, climbers and overworked city dwellers as a place to take a break from Paris, is a quiet town, fairly typical of the *environs* of the capital. That is, until you see the sumptuous palace which dominates the town.

Unlike Versailles (*see below*), the palace at Fontainebleau has a

*Once a twelfth-century hunting lodge, the palace at **Fontainebleau** now pulls the crowds who come to ogle at the outrageously rich and fantastic furnishings and the Le Nôtre-designed gardens. It's often difficult for the visitor to imagine such a grandiose place as a private residence. Such is the égalité of democracy.*

charming disunity of design. In 1528, François I transformed Fontainebleau from a neglected royal mansion, using Italian Renaissance craftsmen, but successive monarchs felt so at home here that they added bits of their own – classical wings by Louis XIV and Marie Antoinette's Queen's Room. The final result of all this building is the five skew courtyards, although it was Napoleon Bonaparte who completed the job. The château has suffered a bit since then; over-decorated by Louis-Philippe, made Allied Command HQ after World War II and now besieged by tourists.

Today's town residents, with expensive tastes not unlike those of the *ancien régime*, are wealthy commuters. There's also a floating population of high-flying students and staff from INSEAD, Europe's answer to Harvard Business School. Unfairly portrayed as archetypal yuppies, all are multi-lingual (English is compulsory), so there's no shortage of intelligent conversation in the bars. They've also

inspired a great variety of restaurants and hotels with very high standards at reasonable prices. The ubiquity of Range Rovers and the improbable presence of an Austin-Rover car dealer hint at the dominance of English county fashions. Pricey men's boutiques include British House, Seeving Road and one shamelessly called BCBG (*bon chic, bon genre*; French for yuppy). It's a response to the hordes of Parisians who descend at the weekends on **Fontainebleau Forest**; a ten-minute stroll from town and you're in the woods.

Buy a map of the forest from the Tourist Information kiosk. The map costs 35F and marks all the paths. The endless terrain of ancient woodland and surrealistic glacial rock formations is superb for walking or riding a mountain bike or horse (*see below* for details). Worth driving, or cycling down, is the road from Barbizon to Gorges d'Apremont, the Gorge de Fronchard and the Seine valley.

A fish restaurant where you can catch your own meal, *l'Ile aux*

Truites, 6 chemin de la Basse Varenne (64.23.32.65), will reward a trip to pretty **Vulaines-sur-Seine**, six kilometres (four miles) away. The pastries and the gorge panorama at *Mont Chauvet* restaurant *(64.22.92.87)* are extra reasons for travelling the spectacularly serpentine Route des Hauteurs de la Solle. It's not just wild boar and deer lurking in the undergrowth that make this a trip with a difference. Watch out for the dayglo Lycra of the rockclimbers; the boulders Plutus and Gargantua are uniquely good for practising this sport while showing off to motoring passers-by.

Impressionist artists liked it here too. Home of the school of Corot and Millet, **Barbizon**, 7 kilometres (4 miles) along the N7 and full of expensive restaurants, rather over-relies on tourists visiting the studio of Théodore Rousseau and the many galleries. These display mostly twee derivatives, although there's modern art at *Triade, 6 & 10 rue du 23 Août*. **Moret-sur-Loing** was home to Sisley for 20 years. This medieval town, 10 kilometres (6 miles) away, is also famed for its *son-et-lumière* pageants (light-and-sound shows held outside), which take place on Saturdays from late June to early September (phone the tourist office, 60.70.41.66 for details*)*.

Château de Fontainebleau
(64.22.27.40). **Open** 9.30am-12.30pm, 2-5pm, Mon, Wed-Sun. **Admission** 23F adults; 12F 18-25s, OAPs; free under-18s ; Sun 12F for all.

MORE INFORMATION
Getting there
From Paris to Fontainebleau by car: **A6** to Fontainebleau exit, then **N7**; 65km (40 miles). *By train:* from Gare de Lyon to Fontainebleau-Avon (50 minutes) then bus A or B.

Tourist Information
31 Place Napoléon Bonaparte, 77302 Fontainebleau (64.22.25.68/64.22.66.77/ 64.22.67.08). **Open** *April-Oct:* 9am-noon, 1.45-6pm, Mon-Sat; 10am-12.30pm, 3-6pm, Sun; *Nov-March*: 10am-12.30pm Sun.

Eating and Drinking
Take your pick of the restaurants in **Fontainbeleau**. A typically reliable bet is *Chez Arrighi, 53 rue de France (64.22.29.43, closed Mon)* with set menus at 85F, 130F and 180F. The presentation is as imaginative as their Corsican specialities. Alsatian dishes can be sampled at *La Petite Alsace, 26 rue de Ferrare (64.23.45.45)* and North African cooking at *Le Carthage, 26 rue de France (64.22.68.68)*. The *Franklin Roosevelt, 20 rue Grande (64.22.33.14)* is good value with 47F and 67F menus. Take out a mortgage for the Michelin-recommended *L'Aigle Noire, place Napoléon Bonaparte (64.22.32.65)*, or indulge in its luxury at the piano bar *Le Montijo*; cocktails 48F. Allegedly France's first video-bar, *Les Glaces, 15 rue Grande (64.22.21.82)*, is the best general bar, where the young gather to consume 16F beers and excellent *croque monsieurs* (toasted cheese and ham, 17F). A rowdier crowd sups the 11F English ales at a genuine Whitbread pub, *Le Cygne* (Swan), *30 rue Grande (64.23.45.25)*.

Shopping
This is Brie country and the two superb *fromageries* on *rue de Sablon* can supply the Meaux and more potent Melun varieties. It's hard to be disappointed by the produce in most shops here, but on the main street, rue Grande, these patisseries excel; *B Mesples* at *71* and *la Panetière*, which has a *salon de thé* round the back where you can sample the *tarte aux fraises* (8F). If the Carrefour hypermarket in Villiers-en-Biere (13km/8 miles north on the N7) is out of reach try *Major, rue du Château* or *Champion, avenue F Roosevelt*, 500m from the station. More fun is the market, on *place de la République* (Tue, Fri, Sun mornings); the stalls have quality, but expensive meat, produce, dairy goods and clothes. There are shops for riding, climbing and other sports, and there's evidently a demand for non-essential executive trinkets and luxury chocolates.

Where to stay
There's a good supply of accommodation, from the no-star *Cygne* pub to the four-star *L'Aigle Noire* (*see above* **Eating and Drinking** for details). The tourist office will supply lists of local hotels.

Bicycle hire
Tourist Information office *(see above for details)*. **Rates** 60F per hour; 120F per half day; 160F per day.

Mountain-bike Folie's *246 rue Grande (64.23.43.07)*. **Open** 10am-7pm Tue-Sun. **Rates** 40F per hour; 120F per half day; 150F per day.
Mountain bikes only. Folie's can also provide guides for groups: 50F extra per person, minimum 10 people.

Horse-riding
Société Hippique Nationale *avenue de Maintenon (60.70.22.40)*. **Open** 10am-

*It was Napoleon Bonaparte who put the finishing touches to **Fontainebleau**, only to abdicate later by addressing his troops here in the Farewell Courtyard with its sweeping, double-horseshoe staircase.*

12.30pm, 2-5.30pm, Mon-Fri.
The Society can provide lists of accredited riding centres. Phone for details.

VERSAILLES

Versailles was no more than a simple backwater when Louis XIII decided to build a modest hunting lodge on the property in 1631. At the time, Versailles showed little early promise of becoming France's most celebrated example of monumental architecture. In 1661, however, Louis XIV, not renowned for his restraint and seething with royal jealously, commissioned a structure that would eclipse the Vaux-Le-Vicomte, the magnificent chateau which proved to be the downfall of Louis' own Finance Minister *(see above)*. The greatest names in French architecture and decoration – Louis Le Vaux, Jules Hardouin Mansart, Charles Le Brun and eventually Jacques-Ange Gabriel – were summoned to the task, and André Le Nôtre (the landscape artist of Vaux-le-Vincomte) was chosen to design Versailles' 250-acre gardens.

Largely due to its enormous size, Versailles is not the most beautiful of French châteaux. It certainly lacks the charm of Chenonceaux or Meillant. In fact, the French kings themselves were the first to realize this. Even before work had finished on the Château itself, the kings were building romantic 'escape' châteaux in the back yard (the **Large** and **Small Trianons**) and Marie Antoinette even created a miniature country village on the grounds (the **Hameau**) where she could play out her peasant fantasies.

Today, the swarms of tour buses parked in front of the château can sour the initial impact of the vast neo-classical façade. Nonetheless, everyone should explore Versailles at least once – to marvel at the **Hall of Mirrors**, the **Queen's Bedroom** (where their Royal Highnesses gave birth before witnesses), the **Opera** designed by Gabriel and the **King's Apartments**. Versailles is so large that you can't see everything in one guided tour. If you want to see it properly, Versailles will take the better part of your day, so get an early start from Paris. And, in good weather, you will probably want to spend most of the afternoon exploring the gardens, which are filled with one delight (folies, statues, reflecting pools and so on) after another.

The **town** of Versailles exists mainly for tourism and the French Army, which maintains a strong presence here. There is, however, a seventeenth-century **Hardouin-Mansart church** which deserves a visit, as well as the small eighteenth-century **cathedral of Saint Louis**.

Château de Versailles
(30.84.74.00). **Open** *Château*: 9.45am-5pm Tue-Sun; closed Bank Holidays; *Gardens*: times vary, usually dawn-dusk daily. **Admission** *château*: 23F; *gardens only*: free.

MORE INFORMATION

Getting there
From Paris to Versailles by car: the most scenic route is via the **N185** from Porte de Saint Cloud. *By train*: RER line C from Gare d'Austerlitz, Quai d'Orsay, or Pont de l'Alma to Versailles-Rive Gauche (Warning: the stop at Versailles-Chantiers leaves you far from the centre of town).

Tourist Information Centre
7 rue des Réservoirs (39.50.36.22). **Open** *Nov-April*: 9am-4.15pm Mon-Fri; 9am-5.30pm Sat; *May-Oct*: 9am-7pm Mon-Sat; 9am-5.30pm Sun.

Eating and Drinking
The best restaurant in Versailles is the elegant two-star *Trois Marches, 3 rue Colbert (39.50.13.21, closed Mon, Sun)*. It's expensive, but Chef Gérard Vié's innovations with traditional French cuisine are remarkable. The *Trianon Palace, 1 boulevard Reine (39.50.34.12)* has a garden restaurant with a significant history: the conditions of the Treaty of Versailles were formally presented here in 1919.

Where to stay
This is such an easy day trip from Paris that relatively few visitors stay the night. However, the *Trianon Palace (see above Eating and Drinking, rooms 750F-1,110F)*, a gracious *belle époque* structure whose gardens adjoin the château, is a very tempting place to spend the night. There is access to a swimming pool and health club, and the management will lend bicycles to guests.

At one point, more than 20,000 labourers were employed to drain the marshy fields of **Versailles**, *divert a river, construct 1,400 fountains and build a château large enough to house 3,000 courtiers.*

Special Interest

From the cathedral towns of Chartres and Orléans, to the battlefields of the Great War and the Winter Olympics – we pick a few of the more interesting locations to head for.

THE WORLD WARS

WORLD WAR I BATTLEFIELDS

A sombre alternative to the good life in Paris, would be a visit to the scene of the 'war to end all wars'. You'll need to have private transport or go on a tour, but the main battlefields are easy to reach, just off the motorway between Paris and Calais. You'll need a map and preferably a guidebook (*see below*) to make the most of it.

Vimy Ridge, about 100 kilometres (62 miles) south of Calais, was the scene of bitter fighting in 1917 as the allies, in particular the Canadians, stormed the German-held ridge. A few kilometres north of Vimy is **Nôtre Dame de Lorette**, the French National Memorial and cemetery. The cemetery, which is marked by a large lighthouse tower, contains the graves of 20,000 Frenchmen killed in the locality. A visit here is a never-to-be-forgotten experience, and one which hammers home the horrendous losses and futility of war.

A further 50 kilometres (31 miles) to the south lie the infamous **battlefields of the Somme**. The allied assault here began on 1 July 1916, at a cost of nearly 60,000 British casualties on the first day. There are numerous places of interest on the Somme, the following being three of the most visited. At the **Newfoundland Memorial Park** one can walk across a preserved section of the front line that has grass-covered trenches. Nearby at **Thiepval** stands the British memorial to the missing. This evocative monument lists the names of over 73,000 British soldiers who died on the Somme and who have no

known grave. Finally, at **Baiselle** there is a huge crater left by a British mine exploded on 1 July 1916 in an attempt to dislodge the German defences; the explosion was felt for hundreds of miles.

All the sites are free and open all the year round (except the tunnels at Vimy).

Further reading: *Before Endeavours Fade* (Battle of Britain Prints International) by Rose Coombs is a good, general, large-format guide, with clear maps, directions and illustrations. *The Somme* (Tressell Publications) is cheap and excellent.

MORE INFORMATION
Getting there
From Paris to Vimy Ridge by car: exit from A26 at junction 7, take N17 towards Lens. After 1km (just over half a mile) the trenches and memorial are on the left; for Nôtre Dame de Lorette take D937 (parallel to A26), turn left on D58 just north of the village of Souchez and straight on.
From Paris to the Somme by car: exit from A1 at Bapaume, take D929 towards Albert and Amiens; after 12km (7 miles) turn right at Pozières on D73 to Thiepval. Newfoundland Memorial Park is slightly further. For the crater turn left off the D929 just through the village of La Boiselle.

Tourist Information Centre
The nearest Tourist Office is at Verdun (29.84.18.85). Open 9-10am, 2-5.30pm, Mon-Sat.

WORLD WAR II LANDING BEACHES

Normandy was the hardest-hit of all French regions during World War II. Bombardments scarred its countryside, reduced most of its major cities (Rouen, Caen, Le Havre) to rubble and turned its tranquil beaches into battlefields. The fortunate town of **Bayeux** (*see below*), however, was not only spared the bombing raids, but on 7 June 1944 was the first French city to be liberated from the Germans. Visit the **Museum of the Battle of**

Normandy, which is located just outside Bayeux *en route* to Cherbourg, for an over-view of events during the landings.

Not far from the town of Bayeux, in the little village of **Arromanches**, is the most celebrated beach of World War II. On 6 June 1944, in this tiny tourist resort with no docks or landing facilities, the allies linked together huge sections of pre-fabricated cement structures in order to make an impromtu floating harbour. Code named the Mulberry Harbours, these huge cement boxes were made in Britain and were then floated across the Channel. Today, you can see the remains of this extraordinary construction. The **Musée du Débarquement** tells the story (in 15 different languages) with a diorama and audio-visual display, lasting about an hour and a quarter. After a walk on the beach and along the cliffs, go to nearby **Pont de Bénouville** to see the **Musée des Troupes Aéroportées**, a homage to the Allies who were flown into France from England.

Musée du Débarquement
place du 6 Juin, 14117 Arromanches (31.22.34.31). Open *Sept-mid May:* 9-11.30am, 2-5.30pm, daily (closed 1-22 Jan); *mid May-Aug:* 9am-6.30pm daily **Admission** 15F adults; 10F children; joint ticket with Musée des Troupes Aéroportées 20F adults, 15F children.

Museum of the Battle of Normandy
boulevard Fabien Ware, 14400 Bayeux (31.92.93.41). Open *mid Oct-mid March:* 9am-12.30pm, 2-6pm, daily; *mid March-mid May, mid Sept-mid Oct:* 9am-12.30pm, 2-6.30pm, daily; *mid May-mid Sept:* 9am-7pm daily. **Admission** 16F adults; 9F under-18s.

Musée des Troupes Aéroportées
Pont de Bénouville, 14117 Arromanches (31.44.62.54). Open April-mid Oct only; *April, Sept-mid Oct:* 9.30am-12.30pm, 2-6pm, daily; *July, Aug:* 9am-7pm daily. **Admission** 10F.

MORE INFORMATION
See below **The Bayeux Tapestries** for information on how to get to Normandy, where to eat, shop and stay.

THE BAYEUX TAPESTRIES

Although Normandy was the scene of bitter fighting in World War II (*see above*), most people still think of Bayeux in terms of the Battle of Hastings. This confronta-

*At **Vimy Ridge** (listed under **The World Wars**) visitors can walk through the preserved World War I trenches and will be surprised to see how close the two opposing sides were. Below the ridge is a network of tunnels that contain a hospital, ammunition dumps and the general's headquarters. The tunnels are open in summer, with Canadian students as guides.*

tion in 1066 between William the Conqueror and Harold, King of England, that so conclusively shaped British history, is immortalized in the crewelwork and embroidery of the **Bayeux Tapestries**. These tapestries, on view daily at the **Centre Guillaume le Conquérant**, are ample reward for the two-hour train journey from Paris.

In 58 scenes, the Bayeux Tapestries present a mural-style chronicle of the background and the actual fighting at Hastings. A bilingual French and English text details each segment with its stories of intrigue, betrayal, bloody gore and heavenly intervention thought to have been provided by Haley's Comet. Make sure you grab hold of a cordless phone on the way in; you carry one of these around the exhibit and listen to the explanation in whatever language you wish. They work by homing in on different communication points at each stage of the story, which is told entirely from the eleventh-century French perspective. Embroideries along the borders show sex-starved Anglo-Saxon maid-

ens ripping off their clothes in delight as the well-endowed Norman soldiers advance towards them. You may, however, think that the maidens are more likely than not being raped. Plan to spend a minimum of two hours to see the tapestries and the small museum of Norman history adjoining the centre.

Bayeux itself (population 15,000) is well worth a visit both for its thirteenth-century **Cathedral** and the fourteenth to sixteenth-century half-timbered houses that line its narrow streets.

Centre Guillaume le Conquérant

rue des Nesmond, 14400 Bayeux (31.92.05.48). **Open** *mid Sept-mid March:* 9.30am-noon, 2pm-6pm, daily; *mid March-mid May:* 9.30am-noon, 2-6.30pm, daily; *mid May-mid Sept:* 9am-7pm daily. **Admission** 20F adults; 10F under-18s.

MORE INFORMATION
Getting there
From Paris to Bayeux by car: take the **A13** from Porte d'Auteuil via Lisieux and Caen (268km/166 miles). *By train:* from Gare Saint Lazare (2 hours 25 minutes).

Tourist Information Centre
1 rue Cuisinière, 14400 Bayeux

(31.92.16.26). **Open** *mid Oct-May:* 9am-12.30pm, 2-6.30pm, Mon-Sat; *June-mid Oct:* 9am-12.30pm, 2-6.30pm, daily.

Eating and Drinking
Dieting is nearly impossible here. Norman cuisine is loaded with butter and cream and the Norman cheeses, Livarot and Camembert, are rich and heavy. The local brew is cider (mildly alcoholic) and the local *digestif* is Calvados (wildly alcoholic). One of the best restaurants in **Bayeux** is the one-star *Lion d'Or, 71 rue Saint Jean (31.92.06.90)*, which serves shellfish stews soaked in Calvados and hefty plates of Norman-style veal and potatoes.

Where to stay
In **Bayeux**, the *Lion d'Or (see above* **Eating and Drinking***, rooms 180F-350F)*, was a *relais de poste* (coaching inn) in the seventeenth century and its simply-decorated rooms look out onto a quiet stone courtyard. There are two *Youth Hostels: 39 rue Général-de-Dais (31.92.15.22)* and *21 rue des Marettes (31.92.08.19)* and a camping ground on the *boulevard d'Eidhoven (31.92.08.43)*, open from March to the end of October. The *Château d'Audrieu*, 13km (8 miles) out of town in **Tilly-sur-Seulles** *(31.80.21.52, rooms 605F-1,550F)* is a delightful eighteenth-century château on land that was once deeded to William the Conqueror's personal chef. The small, romantic restaurant here has one Michelin star (leave room for the utterly blissful desserts).

THE LOVE OF MONET

In 1883, Claude Monet moved his largish personal entourage (one mistress, eight children) to **Giverny**, a rustic rural retreat fifty miles north-west of Paris. Until his death in 1926, the leader of the Impressionist School immortalized his flower garden and particularly the water-lilies beneath his Japanese bridge. In 1966, Michel Monet donated his father's property to the Académie des Beaux Arts which, with the financial support of noted art-lovers like Richard Nixon and Henry Kissinger, transformed the modest estate into the major tourist site it is today. Don't be put off by the hordes of tour buses in the car park or by the outrageously enormous gift shop – which appears to have twice the square footage of Monet's house and studio – that must be crossed before arriving at the museum proper. The natural charm of the pink brick house with its cornflower-blue and yellow kitchen, bedrooms lined with Japanese prints and the rare glory of the gardens, survives intact. This is such an easy day trip that it can be concluded in Paris with a visit to the quiet **Musée Marmottan** (*see chapter* **Museums**) which houses the capital's best collection of nympheas (water-lily) paintings.

Claude Monet Museum
Giverny, 27620 Gasny (32.51.28.21).
Open April-October only; *museum:* 10am-12pm, 2-6pm, Tue-Sun; *garden:s* 10am-6pm Tue-Sun. **Admission** 25F.

MORE INFORMATION
Getting there
From Paris to Giverny by car: take the **A13** from the Porte d'Auteuil to Bonnières, where you cross the Seine and follow **D201** to Giverny. *By rail:* trains to nearby Vernon leave from Gare Saint Lazare; then a 5km (3 miles) taxi ride, or stroll along the D5, to Giverny.

Where to stay
La Musardière (32.21.03.18) is a moderately-priced little inn (with a crêperie restaurant) situated at the entrance to the Monet Museum. It is only open from April to October.

CATHEDRAL TOWNS

ORLEANS

Orléans (population 105,000) is only an hour from Paris and is one of the most popular taking-off points for trips to the Loire châteaux. However, this town's greatest glory lies in its strategic importance during the Hundred Years War.

The memory of **Joan of Arc**, who liberated this city from English troops in 1429, lingers almost everywhere in Orléans, although her nineteenth-century equestrian statue in the place de Martrois looks more as though she's saving the city from the armies of tourists. Unfortunately, due to World War II bombing, most of the Joan of Arc memorabilia is modern. The Maison Jeanne d'Arc, housing a small museum featuring a diagram of the siege of Orléans, is a complete restoration. It is the mansion where the Saint was received as a guest in 1429; the building remained virtually intact for 500 years until a direct hit in 1940.

This pleasant little city is also a lesson in how fast retail prices plummet once you get out of the Paris vicinity. Even if your time is limited, consider making a sightseeing day trip just to see the cathedral and to stop for lunch. Orléans has several Michelin-star restaurants with *prix-fixe* menus

Although historians are agreed on the date of the **Bayeux Tapestries** *(listed under* **The Bayeux Tapestries***) being 1077, there is considerable confusion over who commissioned them and who sewed them. The popular theory is that they were devised by Queen Mathilde, William the Conqueror's wife and that they were presented to his brother Eudes, the Bishop of Bayeux.*

which, while not cheap, are a fraction of what one pays in Paris. Count on finding good fish, game and fragrant goat cheeses on the restaurant tables. While in town, experiment with the deliciously flinty local Loire Valley wines, which are quite inexpensive when compared to Bordeaux and Burgundy vintages.

You can shop to your heart's content in Orléans, particularly if you like children's antiques. *Sylviane Dugas (38.53.48.60)* and *Dolet (38.62.13.66),* which sit side by side on the tiny *rue E Dolet,* are especially good for old-fashioned dolls and doll's house accessories. And anyone interested in buying museum-quality antique furniture (without a mega-budget) should visit *Mailfert, 26 rue Nôtre-Dame-de-Recouvrance (38.62.70.61),* which produces France's ritziest 're-edition' (fake) furniture.

MORE INFORMATION
Getting there
From Paris to Orléans by car: take the **N20** from the Porte d'Orléans (130km/81 miles). *By train:* over a dozen daily departures to Orléans/Les Aubrais from Gare d'Austerlitz (one hour).

Tourist Information Centre
place Albert 1er, 4500 Orléans (38.53.05.95).
Open *July, August:* 9am-7pm daily; *Sept-June:* 9am-6.30pm Mon-Sat.

Eating and Drinking
Orléans is a good place to plan some Michelin-star meals at much lower prices than in Paris. Chef Paul Huyart's two-star *La Crémaillère, 34 rue Nôtre-Dame-de-Recouvrance (38.53.49.17)* serves outstanding seafood. At *Les Antiquaires, 2 rue au Lin (38.53.52.35),* local fish and game are served in an antique-shop ambience. *La Poutrière, 8 rue de la Brèche (38.66.02.30)* serves a formal continental cuisine in a quiet beamed-ceiling dining room or an intimate backyard flower garden. (In fact, you have to walk through the kitchen to get to the garden.) Many of the most attractive cafés are located off the *place de Martrois.*

Where to stay

The Sofitel, 44 quai Barentin (38.62.17.39, rooms 495F) is not particularly charming, but it is the most luxurious option in town with passable views overlooking the Loire and quite fine views of the Old City. The Sofitel also has a bar and restaurant. The *Hotel D'Orléans, 6 rue Crespin (38.53.33.34, rooms 220-320F)* is attractive, moderately priced and benefits from a central location.

Events

Joan of Arc Festival, early May (costume parade and pageants).

CHARTRES

The sculptor Auguste Rodin called **Chartres Cathedral** the 'French Acropolis'. Certainly, this twelfth-century Gothic structure with its exquisitely mismatched towers is one of the most striking sights in France. It is also a major religious cult shrine, as it was built to house the *Sacra Camisia* (the lie-in garment of the Virgin Mary) donated to the city in the ninth century by King Charles the Bald of France. This

relic miraculously escaped destruction during several disastrous fires that severely damaged both the cathedral and previous religious structures on the site. The *Sacra Camisia*, only slightly frayed after nearly two millennia, is displayed in state in the Cathedral Treasury.

Our advice is to drive to Chartres. The view of the cathedral from the motorway, unobscured by high-rise blocks and hoardings as it slowly rises over the Beauce plains, is simply extraordinary. From the train, the first impression of the cathedral silhouette is far less dramatic. Or better yet, walk to Chartres with the troops of faithful student pilgrims who file through the Rambouillet Forest to the city every spring. The medieval rite of atonement was revived in modern times by the poet Charles Péguy (1873-1914). Foreign church groups that would like to participate in a pilgrimage should contact the *Paroisse Cathédrale, 11 rue des Lisses, BP 131, 28003 Chartres Cedex*.

Having arrived in Chartres, you'll find that the most famous cathedral tours in town are led in English by the remarkably learned and highly entertaining Malcolm Miller. He specializes in deciphering the medieval picture codes in order to 'read' the messages in the cathedral's fabulous stained-glass windows. Mr Miller's tours, where payment is voluntary, are generally held at 11am and 2.45pm daily. He says that he'll be lecturing at Chartres 'until Doomsday'. However, Mr Miller does have the occasional travel commitment, so it's wise to ring in advance to find out if he's in town *(37.28.15.58)*.

Other sights in Chartres include the Romanesque **Eglise Saint André** (twelfth century), the **Eglise Saint Pierre** (thirteenth century) and **Saint Aignan** (sixteenth century). The Tourist Office has excellent tape tours of the Old City which cost 35F for two (with a refundable 100F deposit on the cassette player). Indoor sights in Chartres include the **International Stained Glass Centre** (beside the cathedral; closed Tuesdays). If you have a car, ask the tourist office for directions to the **Maison Picassiette** just outside town *(22 rue de Repos; closed Tuesday)*, a colourful naïve mosaic house constructed with bits of broken pottery by a former Chartres civil servant.

The glimmering white Gothic towers of the magnificent **Cathédrale de Sainte-Croix** *(listed under* **Cathedral Towns/Orleans***), begun in the thirteenth century and managing to survive a thorough battering by Protestant Huguenots in the sixteenth century, utterly dominate this city. There is an extremely poignant memorial chapel in the cathedral dedicated to Anglo-Saxon soldiers who died in France during the World Wars.*

MORE INFORMATION
Getting there

From Paris to Chartres by car: Take the **A10** (88km/55 miles). *By train:* from the Gare Montparnasse (less than an hour).

Tourist Information Centre

place de la Cathédrale, 28005 Chartres (37.21.50.00). **Open** *May-Sept*: 9.30am-6.45pm daily; *Oct-April*: 9.30am-12.30pm, 2pm-6pm, Mon-Sat.

Eating and Drinking

Due to the tourist presence, Chartres is a fast-food haven. Its graceful ancient streets are crammed with pizza parlours, Turkish kebab stands, cafés, crêperies and oriental take-aways. A good choice for a stylish sit-down dinner is the *Restaurant Henri, 31 rue Soleil d'Or (37.36.01.55)* which has a fine wine cellar and a traditional French menu. It's worth ringing to reserve a table next to the huge second-storey picture windows overlooking the cathedral (which is illuminated at night). *La Serpente Café* near the cathedral, at *2 Cloître Nôtre Dame (37.21.68.81)* has inexpensive meals.

Where to stay

This world-famous pilgrimage city is not over-endowed with comfortable hotels.

Some, but not all, of the rooms in the *Mercure, 8 avenue Johan de Beauce* (37.21.78.00, *rooms 340F-415F*) have views overlooking the cathedral. The *Grand Monarque, 22 Place Epars* (37.21.00.72, *rooms 304F-475F*) has a lovely restaurant and nice public rooms, but many of the bedrooms look out on a very noisy roundabout.

WINTER
OLYMPICS 1992

On the face of it, **Albertville,** in the department of Savoie, is possibly the least attractive town in the French Alps. Its emergence at the core of the 1992 Winter Olympics

was largely due to its proximity to the more scenic resort sites. Thus, the town of Albertville (population 20,000) will host only the opening and closing ceremonies, as well as the figure-skating and speed-skating events in a 30,000-seat arena now under construction. The other events will be scattered throughout Savoie's more prestigious winter sports venues. Ski-jumping, ice hockey and cross-country events will take place in **Courcheval** and **Méribel**; alpine events in **Val d'Isère/Tignes, Les Menuires, Val Thorens** and **Méribel**; biathlon and more cross-country in **Les Saises**; luge and bobsleigh in **La Plagne** and curling in **Palognan**. The **Olympic village** will be based in **Brides-les-Bains,** where the therapeutic hot springs will no doubt be greatly appreciated by the competitors.

The budget for the two-week games (**8 to 23 February 1992**) is estimated at 3.2 billion francs. Currently, the area's airports are being enlarged and highways are being widened and upgraded. Half a million spectators are expected, in addition to 4,000 journalists, 4,500 athletes and support personnel, 20,000 Olympic workers, 1,000

members of the 'Olympic Family' and the 400 members of the Organizing Committee.

So, as you read this, it's probably easier to make it into the Swiss ski team than to book a room in Albertville during the festivities. For those determined to be there, the Albertville Tourist Office advises seeking chalet-shares as far away as Grenoble (86 kilometres/53 miles). Expect your Olympian powers of endurance to be tested to the full.

MORE INFORMATION
Getting there
From Paris to Albertville by car: **A6** to Lyon, then **A43** to Chambery then **N90** to Albertville (*600km/375 miles*). *By train:* TGV (high-speed train) from Gare de Lyon (four and a half hours). *By plane:* the nearest airports are Chambery, Lyon and Grenoble.

Tourist Information Centre
place de la Gare, 73200 Albertville (*79.32.04.22*). **Open** 9am-noon, 2-7pm, Mon-Sat.

Eating and Drinking
Savoie is fondue country, but there are more delicate regional specialities, notably the flaky white Fera fish which shows up on restaurant menus baked, poached and sautéd. *Million, 8 place de la Liberté* (*79.32.25.15*) is a comfortable two-star restaurant in the heart of **Albertville** which offers an enticing selection of local fish and cheeses. *Chez Uginet, pont des Adoubes* (*79.32.00.50*) has a moderately priced *prix-fixe* lunch menu where regional specialities are highlighted in red ink. *Le Ligismond* (*79.32.53.50*) is a one-star restaurant located in the medieval town of **Conflans,** which is just across the Arly River from Albertville.

Where to stay
You'll probably find it impossible getting accommodation in Albertville for the Winter Olympics. The Tourist Office (*see above*) will help in finding rooms and chalets in the area. Normally, however, *Million (see above* **Eating and Drinking,** *rooms 260F-550F*) has a limited number of quiet, understated rooms above its top-flight restaurant. *Fast Hotel, chemin des Trois Poiriers* (*76.37.42.10, rooms 120F*), a standardized chain hotel, opened its doors in April 1989. *La Berjann, 33 route de Tours* (*79.32.47.88, rooms 190F-250F*) is located just outside Albertville centre, on the other side of the Arly River.

Wear comfortable shoes; **Chartres** (*listed under* **Cathedral Towns/Chartres***) is a vertical city with the* ville haute *around the Cathedral, and the* ville basse *on the banks of the* Eure *river, connected by winding roads and steep stone stairways. During the summer months, the Tourist Office runs a more sedentary alternative; a small train with hourly departures from the* Parvis de la Cathédrale *that has a French-speaking guide and English-language cassettes.*

Wine & Champagne

**'That I might drink, and leave the world unseen,
And with thee fade into the forest dim' – Keats.**

For those who have not drunk their fill of life's elixir in Paris, we explore the over-flowing vineyards and hidden watering holes of France.

BORDEAUX & AREA

The Bordeaux vineyards produce about half the total French output of *appellation contrôlée* wines every year. That's on average 400 million bottles per year. Within the *appellations contrôlées* in the Bordeaux area there will usually be various châteaux – normally farms – that produce wine of varying quality and type. You'll find both light and full-bodied reds, as well as dry and sweet whites. The term 'claret', always associated with Bordeaux reds, comes from the word *clairet* which was used by the English nobility during the occupation of the Aquitaine region. Harvest time, during September and October, is the best time to visit the area. However, châteaux have *dégustations* all year round; keep your eyes peeled as you drive along, as these tastings are normally sign-posted.

GETTING STARTED

The best way to see this region is by kicking off with a visit to the **Maison du Vin** (the House of Wine) in **Bordeaux** itself. It's set in a sombre, triangular building, said to have 365 windows – one for every day of the year – that stands on a wide avenue lined with trees. On arrival, all visitors are told of the different wine tours that are possible. In one corner of the vast building is a large bar where you can taste some of the local libations.

Across the street is the **Office de Tourisme** (*see below* **More Information**), where the dynamic staff are well-informed about what the region has to offer. It's also possible to obtain information on neighbouring provinces, for example the Dordogne, the Basque Country, Landes, Gers and so on. The Tourist Office has published a useful series of small brochures that can be used as a sort of self-guided tour of the area. It is possible to see Bordeaux on foot. However, tours outlined in the Tourist Office brochures, that take in the surrounding countryside, will require the use of a car. The publications are compiled with a theme in mind, such as Mauriac's Bordeaux (the turn-of-the-century French novelist), Pigeonniers in the Local Countryside (stately dovecotes built near manor houses in south-western France) or even Antique Door-knockers. There are also boat tours on the river. For information on what to see, where to eat, shop and stay, *see below* **The City of Bordeaux**.

La Maison du Vin

1 cour 30 Juillet, 33000 Bordeaux (56.52.82.82). **Open** *Oct-May:* 8.30am-5.30pm Mon-Fri; 8.30am-6pm Sat; *June-Sept:* 8.30am-5pm Mon-Fri; 8.30am-6pm Sat; 9.30am-noon, 1.30-5pm, Sun; *wine tastings* (bookings required for groups over 10 people) 10.30-11.30am, 2.30-4.30pm, Mon-Sat.

A VISIT TO THE VINEYARDS

Once you've visited the Maison du Vin and the Tourist Office (*see above* **Getting Started**), you will understand how the massive Bordeaux vineyard is divided up into *appellations,* which are in fact geographical regions. Each region has its own specific characteristics, both gustatory and visual, so the choice is quite large. But they all overflow with châteaux, the local name for any vintner's house, be it a shack or a mansion. Obviously many, but not all, are mansions; many can be visited, some are

A trip into the countryside around Bordeaux can be a rewarding experience: vineyards abound and the chateaux will often have dégustations *(wine tastings) where you can sample the region's produce.*

closed to the public. It's all a question of supply and demand: the most famous ones are less likely to be open. But there's more to see than just the wine-presses in each region. We give a breakdown:

MEDOC

Probably the most famous of any of the Bordeaux wine regions, this peninsula, north of the city of Bordeaux, is home to *Margaux, Ducru-Beaucaillou, Beychevelle, Latour* and many others. On a sun-drenched strip of land, affording wonderful views over the Gironde Estuary, the world-famous châteaux are lined up side by side. Here and there you may see *Vente Directe* signs, meaning they sell to the public. The inland town of **Margaux** and the waterside town of **Pauillac** are both ideal for short walks, while some of the smaller villages have delightful churches. If you're driving, which is by far the best way to go, don't hesitate to take the tiny side roads that allow you to see some amazing countryside. The small local train also affords some marvellous views of countryside; you'll have to go back the same way as you came, as the Médoc is a cul-de-sac. Check the timetables: there aren't that many trains.

Maison du Médoc
place du Palais de Justice, 33340 Lesparre (56.41.86.00). **Open** *Sept-June:* 9am-12.30pm, 2-5.30pm, Mon-Fri; *July, Aug:* 9am-12.30pm, 2-6pm, daily..
The best place to get information on local wines and vintners. Tastings can be arranged (reservations required).

GRAVES

Starting in the southern suburbs of Bordeaux and descending south along the Garonne River, this region produces dry white and red wines. Châteaux, for example the seventeenth-century **Carbonnieux** or the eighteenth-century **La Louvière** in the town of **Léognan** are spectacular. Along with the town of **Pessac** – a residential suburb of Bordeaux – these are the communities producing the top Graves wines. *Haut-Brion* and *Fieuzal* are just two examples of the wines you'll find here. As you either drive down the **N113** or take the train into **Portets**, **Podensac** and **Preignac**, the properties become less majestic and have fewer hectares. In the Graves town of **La Brède**, don't miss the

Early in the morning when the rising sun reflects off the Garonne and the fountain, la place de la Bourse *alone makes a trip to* **Bordeaux** *worth while. It is currently home to the Chamber of Commerce, although during the eighteenth century this urban project was the ultimate in chic living for wealthy Bordeaux families.*

moat-surrounded home of Charles de Secondat, Baron de Montesquieu et de La Brède. This is where the famous political writer put his ideas on democracy on paper, thereby inspiring the North American, and later the French, revolutionaries. Within the Graves region is a smaller region called **Sauternes**. This is home to the delicious, sweet white wine made from grapes left to rot on the vines. Towns like **Barsac** and **Preignac** that fall within the region, produce wines from famous names such as **Château Yquem** or **Château de Malle.**

Maison des Vins des Graves
rue François Mauriac, 33640 Podensac (56.27.09.25). **Open** *Sept-June:* 8.30am-12.30pm, 1.30-5.30pm, Mon-Fri; *July, Aug:* 8.30am-12.30pm, 1.30-7pm, daily.
The Maison des Vins des Graves was set up to give out information on local wines. Over 100 vintners are represented, and details of all local vineyards can be obtained here. Tastings are arranged for groups of more than ten people only (booking required).

ENTRE-DEUX-MERS & COTE DE BORDEAUX

These lesser-known *appellations* are located across the Garonne from the Graves region. Take the bridge in **Cerons** (there is no train) to the beautiful city of **Cadillac** where the Duc d'Epernon built an ominous-looking castle. Head down the river towards Bordeaux and visit the delightful waterside towns of **Rions**, a thirteenth-century walled village, and charming **Langoiran**. Located further inland, is the **Entre-deux-mers** region. Local produce is a dry white wine – that seems to have been created solely for accompanying oysters from the nearby **Bassin d'Arcachon** – that is produced in small, very rural, properties. Even the landscape is very different from the other bank, as there are forests, cattle and even hills.

LIBOURNE, SAINT EMILION

The ancient city of Libourne, sitting comfortably on the bank of the Dordogne River, takes its name from its founder, a certain Englishman called Leyburn. Indeed, it goes all the way back to the fourteenth century and the times of the English occupation. Libourne is set in the Saint Emilion *appellation* and boasts

The names of the vineyard villages of **Burgundy** *– Nuits Saint Georges, Montrachet, Chablis and Romanée-Conti – are as magical as the bright, elegantly fruity wines that they produce. A trip through this huge wine-producing area can include excursions to the enchanting towns of Dijon and Beaune.*

famous names such as *Pétrus* and *Cheval-Blanc*. The town of Saint Emilion itself still harbours medieval ruins and tiny streets with delightful houses and shops. There is a marvellous panorama from the top of the hill on which this town is built. All the little white specks you see scattered across the different patches of green are the famous Bordeaux wine châteaux. You can get to Libourne and Saint Emilion by train but you'll have to do a bit of walking. Once again, a car is the best solution.

THE CITY OF BORDEAUX

Bordeaux is the most homogeneous and stunning example of neo-classical architecture in France. Cross the arcaded *Pont de Pierre*, with its triple-branch and candelabra streetlights, and you will see that all the façades overlooking the muddy Garonne River are exactly alike. Thanks to a most fruitful economic boom, this city was almost entirely rebuilt during the eighteenth century. Even up until the early twentieth century, the Bordelais continued to build in this same style. As you walk down the grand avenues or through the tiny,

curving streets of the old quarter, keep an eye out for the laughing *mascarons* (faces carved above windows), elegant wrought-iron balconies and grandiose staircases. Bordeaux is a true treasure chest for architecture buffs.

As you approach the Maison du Vin (*see above* **Getting Started**), you can't help but see the symbol of Bordeaux's neo-classical architecture, the fabulous **Grand Théâtre** (1773-1780) built by Parisian architect Victor Louis. This master of colonnades also built the galleries of the Palais-Royal Gardens in Paris and the Comédie Française theatre. The breathtaking pillars and the majestic staircase – which inspired that of the Paris Opera – are fine examples of this very pure, very stoic architectural period. Inside the theatre you can visit the different salons. The restaurant has a *prix fixe* menu at 35F and gilded woodwork galore. Although the musical season at the Théâtre does not have the same reputation as Monsieur Louis, changes are on the way, thanks to a new musical director. The most important cultural event, the **Mai**

Musical, is held in May in various venues throughout Bordeaux, one of which is the Grand Théâtre.

On descending the stairs of the theatre, look to the right and you'll see a rather kitsch column rising above a wide open space. This is the **Monument aux Girondins,** erected in honour of the members of the Assembly who tried to bring about certain changes within the post-Revolutionary government and consequently were executed for treason (*see chapters* **Revolution** *and* **Empires & Rebellions**). The monument stands in what is said to be the largest public square in Europe, **la place des Quinconces.** This huge open area, that is symmetrically lined with trees, looks out onto the Garonne River. It is home to many public events, that range from the annual antique show to the circus and 14 July Bastille Day celebrations.

Notwithstanding the size of la place des Quinconces, it's not the most beautiful square in Bordeaux. In the heart of the old quarter called Saint-Pierre, is the breathtaking **place de la Bourse,** which was masterminded by the Gabriel family. This father and son team – who worked as Louis XV's royal architects – also built splendours such as the place de la Concorde in Paris, the Opéra of Versailles and the Grand Trianon. At that time, a high iron gate closed it off on both sides, making the garden private. Today that very same garden is a major thoroughfare and a riverside warehouse. From here, head into the old quarter with its narrow streets and elegant buildings. A look inside one of these houses will reveal the impressive majestic staircases in yellowish-white stone typical of the area. These date back to the eighteenth century and are particularly popular in south-west France. Within the Saint-Pierre quarter is the **place du Parlement,** an excellent spot for an evening dinner out of doors.

Bordeaux has several marvellous churches. Enthusiasts of Gothic architecture should make for **Saint André.** Because it is set in a recess, it is difficult to appreciate this church from the outside, particularly when seen from a distance. The best view to be had is probably from the front of the town hall, the latter being a rather imposing, former ducal palace behind which is a **Fine Arts Museum.** Along with its sister church **Saint Michel,** Saint André is unusual because of its bell-tower, which does not form part of the main edifice. The views of the city from the top of Saint André are breathtaking. At Saint Michel, visitors can view the tower only from the outside. On Sunday mornings the square at Saint Michel is a delightful place to look for antiques and other hand-me-downs; the local flea market is held here every week.

Another fine church, which is unfortunately some way from the city centre, is the Romanesque **Sainte-Croix.** Built in the twelfth century, this gem boasts an impressive, intricate façade complete with Tuscan-style colonnades and an equestrian statue. Today it's in the middle of a semi-industrial district. Another good, but less spectacular, example of Romanesque architecture is **Saint-Seurin.** Although smaller in size, this charming church and churchyard is an ideal place not far from the city centre where you can stop off and relax.

If you prefer Baroque styles, try the slightly Italianate **Nôtre-Dame** on the rue place du Châtelet. It once formed part of an abbey and therefore has an incredibly decorative façade. This has recently been cleaned and is a true, shining jewel.

Bordeaux is renowned for the huge archways that occasionally line the streets. These structures at one time were used as gates to the walled city. Some even date back to the time of the English occupation; porte Cailhaud is such an example.

If you feel a need for a breath of contemporary air, try the modern art museum called the **CAPC**, also known by locals as the **Entrepôts Lainé**. This eighteenth-century warehouse, where merchants found out what cargo had arrived for sale, is one of Europe's foremost modern art spaces. An efficient funding programme and a keen eye for daring artists make for surprisingly successful, international exhibitions in this quiet provincial setting.

MORE INFORMATION
Tourist Information Centre
12 cours 30 Juillet, 33000 Bordeaux (56.44.28.41). **Open** *Oct-May:* 9am-6.30pm Mon-Sat; 9.30am-12.30pm Sun; *June-Sept:* 9am-7pm Mon-Sat; 9am-3.30pm Sun.

Getting there
From Paris to Bordeaux by car: take the **A10** all the way (450km/280 miles). *By train:* from Gare d'Austerlitz, journey time currently four and a quarter hours; a new TGV

(high-speed train) is to start operating in the near future, which should cut the time down to three and a half hours.

Shopping
There are two major shopping areas in town. The first is a huge triangle, easy to walk to and find as the Grand Théâtre occupies one of the angles. From the theatre you can either go up the **cours de l'Intendance** or the **allée de Tourny**, the latter being the more up-market of the two. They are joined at both ends by a third side called the **cours Clémenceau**. These three major roads are lined with private banks, fashionable clothing shops and small businesses. In the middle of the triangle are several chic boutiques and foodstores and the soon-to-be-renovated market called the **Marché des Grands-Hommes** (the Big Men Market). The second shopping area, immediately next to the first, consists of two streets that cross one another at right-angles: the **rue de la Porte-Dijeaux** and the **rue Sainte-Catherine**. The latter was the first street in France to be turned into a pedestrian precinct and on a frantic, crowd-filled Saturday morning it looks strangely like Oxford Street during rush hour. The former, which is parallel to the cours de l'Intendance, is adorned at one end by a charming garden called **place Gambetta**, and at the other end by the exquisite **place de la Bourse**. Together they form a slightly more affordable shopping area in addition to several department stores. Visit the wood-panelled *Librairie Mollat* (corner of the *rue de la Porte-Dijeaux* and the *rue Vital-Carles*), the biggest and most complete family-run bookstore in France.

Where to stay
Unfortunately there is no exceptional, love-at-first-sight hotel in the heart of Bordeaux. However, a good, reasonably-priced hotel in central Bordeaux is the *Grand Hôtel Français, 12 rue du Temple (56.48.53.88).* For more upmarket accommodation, try the recently opened four-star *Hôtel Burdigala, 115 rue Georges-Bonnac (56.90.16.16).*

Getting about
As mentioned above, the best way to get to most places is by car. However, it is perfectly possible to visit Bordeaux and some nearby towns by using public transport. The **city buses** leave from the following main areas: the Saint-Jean train station, place Gambetta and place Jean-Jaurès. There are also local slow trains going into regional towns. Keep in mind that they usually cross the industrial areas before getting to the real countryside, so be patient as you leave Bordeaux. There is also a major local **coach** service to take you on short or long trips: *Citram, 14 rue Fondaudège (56.81.18.18).*

BURGUNDY

This wine-producing area is so large and varied – extending from the Côte d'Or all the way south to the

Thanks to the TGV (France's high-speed train network), **Dijon** *is linked to Paris by a journey of less than two hours. Once you step off the train however, you feel that you are two days away from the silvery-grey houses and muted slate roof-tops of Paris. Burgundian civic architecture tends to be flamboyant and the Dijon roof-tops are brightly patterned in geometric designs of yellow, green, black and rust.*

start of the Beaujolais district – that it is virtually impossible to take it all in the context of a brief excursion from Paris. We offer two suggestions for getting an introduction to this amazingly rich (in food, wine, art and history) section of France. One is to tour the individual vineyards by car. The second is to visit the major wine cities by rail and to explore their fine restaurants and museums with only a few trips just outside the city limits.

VINEYARD TOURING

For the true œnophile, this is the only real option. The districts of Burgundy that are closest to Paris are located near **Dijon**. They are the **Côte d'Or**, the **Côte de Beaune**, the **Hautes Côtes de Beaune** (including Chassagne-Montrachet, Meursault, Pommard, Puligny-Montrachet, Savigny-les-Beaune) and the **Côte de Nuits** and **Hautes Côtes de Nuit** (Gevrey-Chambertin, Nuits Saint Georges, Vosné-Romanée, Vougeot). The *Comité Interprofessionel de la Côte d'Or et de*

L'Yonne edits a free pamphlet with names, addresses and phone numbers of wine producers who welcome visitors. This booklet is available from the Dijon Tourist Office (*see below* **Dijon & Beaune**) and can greatly simplify your holiday plans. Among producers who accept both private and group visits are the *Château de Meursault (80.21.22.98)*, just eight kilometres (five miles) from Beaune. This château is open daily from March through to December; wine tastings cost approximately 40F (with a souvenir tasting cup included). Another vintner is *Morin Père et Fils* in Nuit Saint Georges *(80.61.19.51)* open all the year round, who offer tours of the eighteenth-century caves and wine-tastings for between 10F and 30F. Both have wine for sale. Phone in advance and plan your trip carefully. Some producers may be too busy to welcome visitors during the harvest.

DIJON & BEAUNE

The wealth of Burgundy is not only in its vineyards. In the fifteenth century, the Dukes of Burgundy were

so rich that they rivalled the Kings of France in terms of power and wealth. Consequently, the grandiose art and architecture in what was their capital, **Dijon**, is astounding. Furthermore, the smaller town of **Beaune** which is just forty-five kilometres (28 miles) to the south of Dijon carries the hallmarks of their power. Wandering through the streets with a camera, marvelling at the half-timbered fifteenth-century houses, is one of the great pleasures here. Save time for the **Musée des Beaux Arts** (located in the Hardouin-Mansart Hotel de Ville) which boasts one of the best provincial collections in France.

If your major interests are food and wine, both Dijon and Beaune have a lot worth exploring *(see below* **Eating and Drinking**). For historical data, both the **Musée du Vin de Bourgogne** in Beaune and the **Musée de la Vie Bourguignonne** in Dijon are helpful. Also in Beaune, the **Marché aux Vins**, located in the former twelfth to thirteenth-century Eglise des Cordeliers *(rue Nicolas Rolin, 80.22.27.69)*, is worth visiting. It's closed during the latter part of December and the month of January, but is open for visits and wine-tastings (40F) on a daily basis during the rest of the year. Even if you don't have a car, some wine producers, such as the Château de Meursault, are so close to town as to be accessible by taxi at a pinch.

The annual festivals are a great time to visit the area. The **Fête de la Vigne** (Festival of the Vine) in Dijon is celebrated the first week of September. Don't be misled by the name. In fact, the Fête is an international folk festival, the emphasis being more on women and song than on wine. During the first two weeks in November, Dijon hosts the **Foire Gastronomique** (International Food and Wine Fair) in the convention centre on the edge of town. Although geared towards professionals, amateurs can nonetheless enjoy window-shopping as well as all the specialities. Finally, there is the **Trois Glorieuses** (*see* **picture and caption**), the annual wine auction. If you are thinking of visiting Dijon or Beaune during the latter two events, advance hotel reservations are essential.

Festivals in the wine-producing areas of France abound, such as the **Fête de la Fleur** *in Bordeaux (see above photo). The* Trois Glorieuses *(listed under* **Dijon & Beaune***) is held in the third week of November in Dijon. The highlight of this annual fête is the wine auction at the Hospices de Beaune.*

MORE INFORMATION
Getting there
From Paris to Beaune and Dijon by car: take the **A6** autoroute from the Porte de

Centilly (315km/195 miles). *By train*: TGV (high-speed train) from Gare de Lyon to Dijon (1 hour 45 minutes).

Tourist Information Centres

Dijon: *place Darcy, 21100 Dijon (80.43.42.12)*. **Open** *Nov-March*: 9am-noon, 2-6pm, Mon-Sat; 10am-noon, 2-7pm, Sun; *April-June, Oct*: 9am-noon, 2-9pm, daily; *Aug, Sept*: 9am-9pm, daily.

Beaune: *rue de l'Hotel Dieu, 21200 Beaune (80.22.24.51/80.22.26.05)*. **Open** *Nov-March*: 9am-7.15pm Mon-Sat; 9am-noon, 2-6pm, Sun; *April-Oct*: 9am-8pm daily.

Eating and Drinking

This is what made the region famous. Specialities include *boeuf bourguignon*, *escargots* (with plenty of garlic), *jambon au persil* and *coq au vin*. *Cassis* (blackcurrant) is also produced in the area, so kir, a wine-based cocktail, can be considered the regional trademark. Gingerbread is a local speciality, as is (how can one forget) Dijon mustard, supposedly developed at the Burgundian court to mask the flavour of turned meat. Turned meat is no longer a problem in **Dijon**, which has some of the best restaurants in France. Chef Jean-Pierre Billoux's exclusive restaurant in the vaulted cellars of the *Hotel la Cloche, 14 place Darcy (80.30.11.00)* is listed under his own name and he makes a special point of promoting regional recipes. *Thibert, 10 place Wilson (80.67.74.64)* has an exciting young chef, a trim, understated décor and reasonable prices given the high quality of the food. Also worth a try for regional dining is the restaurant in the *Châpeau Rouge Hotel, 5 rue Michelet (80.30.28.10)*. The *Etape Bourgonde, 3 rue Montigny (80.30.20.17)* is located in an eighteenth-century wine cellar and serves inexpensive regional dishes. *La Toison d'Or, 18 rue Sainte Anne (80.30.73.52)* is a hearty, informal restaurant with a large local fan club. In **Beaune**, *escargots* are the speciality at the city's several Michelin-star restaurants, which include the *Rotisserie la Faix, 47 Fauberg Madeleine (80.22.33.33)*; and the *Ecusson, place Malmédy (80.22.83.08)*.

Where to stay

The 76-room *Hotel la Cloche, 14 place Darcy (80.30.12.32, rooms 460F-600F)* is the fanciest hotel in **Dijon**, with a muted interior design that reflects the patterned rooftops of the town. The *Châpeau Rouge, 5 rue Michelet (80.30.28.10, rooms 385F-515F)* has a good central location, while the no-frills *Gresil'h, 16 avenue Poincars (80.71.10.56, rooms 210F-262F)* is notable chiefly for its close proximity to the Dijon convention centre. The hotel landmark in **Beaune** is the *Poste, 1 boulevard Clémanceau (80.22.08.11, rooms 630F-1,200F)*.

COGNAC

Set in the heart of the Charente region, Cognac is a rather dormant, agricultural city similar to hundreds of others throughout France. But the major difference between this one and all the others is the golden-brown libation that bears its name and is known throughout the world: cognac.

This delightful elixir was in fact invented by accident. In the sixteenth century, the region around Cognac and nearby Saintes was producing so much white wine that they couldn't sell it all. Consequently, standards in quality dropped, which resulted in the wine becoming rather acidic with a low alcohol content. This type of wine was terribly difficult to export to northern European countries, because it was undrinkable by the time it arrived at its destination. That's why both the Dutch and English came up with the idea of distilling wine from Cognac upon its arrival, thereby making *eau-de-vie*. It was in the seventeenth century that merchants realized it was cheaper to have the acidic wines distilled while in their native region and then transported, because the quantities were smaller (due to evaporation) and the quality unchangeable once it was distilled. Export of the distilled wine gave way to prosperous trade with the New World and other far-off countries, making cognac a big hit in the eighteenth century (493,000 barrels were exported between 1718 and 1736), not to mention a great source of wealth for the locals. Many of these 'locals' were in fact descendants of the different merchants both French and foreign. These families are still there today, with good French names like Hine and Hennessy. In 1988, Cognac represented 77 per cent of all French spirits exported.

GETTING STARTED

Below we give three different ways of getting orientated.

The first is a visit to the **Musée de Cognac**. Built in 1838 for the Dupuy d'Angeac family, this elegant mansion is set in a 10-hectare (25-acre) park that was the result of the marriage of two private parks belonging

*From barrel-making to glass-blowing, vineyards to shipping, it's all explained in detail at the **Musée de Cognac** (listed under **Cognac/Getting Started**). After a visit, make for the collection of trees and plants in the gardens around the museum.*

to two manor houses. The neighbouring mansion is now the town hall. At the time of fusion, the *boulevard Denfert-Rochereau* was transformed from city ramparts into the wide street you see today. Certain architectural remnants, notably la *Porte Saint-Jacques*, indicate that this was once a walled city. The museum is not just pleasant from the outside; inside is an art collection that once belonged to Emile Pellisson, a Cognac merchant. It contains many paintings and sculptures from the sixteenth to nineteenth centuries. To these have been added paintings by local artists, a collection of regional ware, finds from the various Roman digs, an impressive ceramics and glass collection and a very complete presentation of – what else? – the cognac industry.

Musée de Cognac
48 boulevard Denfert-Rochereau, 16100 Cognac (45.32.07.25). **Open** *June-Sept*: 10am-noon, 2-6pm, Mon, Wed-Sun; *Oct-May*: 2-5.30pm Mon, Wed-Sun. **Admission** free.
See **picture and caption**.

Another good way of understanding what Cognac is all about is to visit one of the **distilleries**. **Hennessy** is an ideal place: big, well-organized for visitors and completely modern while remaining traditional. You will be shown an audio-visual presentation (in several languages), the bottling rooms and a delightful cooperage museum. It's centrally located, so it's walking distance from the rest of the city. And, provided the rain hasn't caused any flooding, you might even be able to take the tiny boat across the Charente to visit the ageing warehouses. Another good distillery worth visiting is the **Otard-Dupuy** house, set in the medieval Château de Cognac – otherwise known as the Château des Valois – where the great pro-Italian king François I was born in 1494. A statue in his honour stands in the rather ugly *place François Ier* in the city. Thanks to an audio-visual show, it's possible to follow the whole history of this building and the city of Cognac. Afterwards, as in most of the distilleries, visitors get a tasting and a chance to buy a bottle or two. A walk along the Charente River is a delightful way of rounding off the visit. On the other side of the bridge is a pleasant park made up of several small islands.

Millions of gallons of cognac have drifted off the barrels over the centuries in what is called la Part des Anges *(the Angel's Share). This mist has draped itself over* **Cognac's** *stone walls, where it has turned into a black fungus. Much like the famous British black-and-white moths during the Industrial Revolution, which turned black as a result of the fumes from the factories, here a local species of spider, that eats miniscule mushrooms growing on the stone walls, has evolved. Appetizing,* n'est-ce pas?

Cognac Hennessy
1 rue de la Richonne, 16100 Cognac (45.82.52.22). **Open** *mid Sept-mid June*: 8.30-11am, 1.45-4.30pm, Mon-Fri; *mid June-mid Sept*: 9am-5.30pm Mon-Sat. **Admission** free.

Cognac Otard-Dupuy
Chateau de Cognac, 16100 Cognac (45.82.40.00). **Open** *Oct-March*: 10-11am, 2-5pm, Mon-Fri; *April-Sept*: 10-11am, 2-5pm, daily. **Admission** free.

A final suggestion for getting to know the region and the city is to jump on a two-hour **boat cruise** (48F adults, 28F children). Leaving central Cognac on a regular basis, pleasure boats take day-trippers upstream to the town of **Saint Brice** and back. Not only will you hear a descriptive narrative of the town's history but you'll also see the surrounding countryside with its vineyards, centuries-old farms and beautiful forests. Because the vintners grew rich as a result of the successful export of their fine drink, they built mansions in place of their humble farms. These

can be seen all around the town; some are stately, some are tatty châteaux. This cruise gives visitors a feeling of what this region is all about, above and beyond the multi-national alcohol firms. There's also the possibility of taking a lunch or dinner cruise (243F or 273F) up to the town of **Bourg-Charente** and back. For more information or to make reservations, contact the Office de Tourisme (*see below* **More Information**).

VISITING THE TOWN
One of the most extraordinary phenomena found in the city of Cognac is what is called *la Part des Anges*, or Angels' Share. This is the poetic way the vintners have of describing the percentage of alcohol that drifts off into space as it evaporates from the porous barrels (*see* **picture and caption**).

Walk through the curving, cobbled streets of the old quarter to discover stunning Renaissance and neo-classical stone houses. Here and there are statuettes, carved doors, ornate windows and façades. Unfortunately none of this is renovated and it all looks a bit abandoned. Even the local pride and joy, **la Maison de la Lieutenance** *(7 rue Grande)*, with its half-timbers and carved beams is rather rundown. The Romanesque church of **Saint-Léger** (twelth, thirteenth and sixteenth centuries) is probably quite beautiful. The main façade alone is rather stunning with its Romanesque arcades and Gothic rose window. On the fourth rung of the arcades surrounding the main gate the different signs of the zodiac are carved in the stone, each with a different task representing the period of the year. But in the lovely city of Cognac trade comes first. The rest of the church is surrounded by shops and boutiques, so you can never really appreciate the whole thing in one go.

AROUND COGNAC

If you have a car, take a drive through the surrounding vineyard area just to get a feel for the land. The dynamic staff at the Tourist Office *(see below* **More Information)** organize several different visits during mid-June to mid-September that take in the vineyards and nearby Romanesque churches.

Another fine way to relax and see some of the nearby countryside is on the newly-opened Cognac golf course. Located in **La Maurie** just 5 kilometres (3 miles) from Cognac on the road to Jarnac in the Charente River valley, this 18-hole course offers rental equipment, a driving range, lessons in French and English and even a restaurant in a charming setting.

Just a 15-minute drive from Cognac on the D736 (follow signs for Rouillac) is the **Château de Ligneres** in the Bisquit Cognac domain. With over 200 hectares (500 acres) of vines, this is the largest cognac vineyard. In pleasant outdoor surroundings you'll see how everything is done from distilling to bottling.

Domaine de Ligneres
16170 Rouillac (45.21.88.88). **Open** 8am-12.30pm, 1.15-5pm, Mon-Fri. **Admission** free.

MORE INFORMATION
Getting there
From Paris to Cognac by car: take the A10 to Saintes (470km/290 miles) then 30km (19 miles) to Cognac. There's a high road and a low road, the latter being close to the river and the more picturesque, but also the slower. *By train:* From the Gare d'Austerlitz, it's a three-hour train trip to Angouleme and then about a half hour by a smaller train.

Tourist Information Centre
16 rue du 14 Juillet, 16100 Cognac (45.82.10.71). **Open** mid Sept-May. 9am-12.30pm, 2-6.15pm, Mon-Sat; *June-mid Sept*: 8.30am-7pm Mon-Sat.

Eating and Drinking
There are no really great restaurants in Cognac, but around the place François I are several reasonable places to eat. Try the *Coq d'Or (45.82.02.56)*, an old brasserie with a good reputation.

Where to stay
The hotels in this small city aren't exactly great. Major cognac clients are usually lodged in the huge manor houses, so for the lowly tourist there's not much available. Try the proper but unsurprising *Hôtel François I, 3 place François I (45.32.07.18)*. The *Hôtel d'Orléans, 25 rue d'Angouleme (45.82.01.26)* is quaint, but the wallpaper may keep you awake at night. If you are only planning to visit for one day, try the town of **Saintes**, half an hour away. Here there is a choice of several different kinds of hotel. The *Logis de Beaulieu (45.82.30.50)*, just 4km (2 miles) outside Cognac on the Saintes road, is a rather up-market three-star, but word has it it's not as good as it used to be.

Few beverages command the abundance of charming trivia associated with that most charismatic of drinks, **champagne**. *Did you know that there are, on average, fifty million bubbles inside each bottle of champagne? That the shape of the original coupe de champagne (champagne glass) was copied from Diane de Poitier's breast? That the good monk Dom Perignon exclaimed 'I'm drinking stars' when he sampled the stuff?*

CHAMPAGNE

As the champagne region (and its celebrity cities, **Reims** and **Epernay**) is barely 140 kilometres (87 miles) from Paris, this fascinating region makes an ideal day or overnight trip from the capital.

Champagne, the most strictly regulated of all alcohol, is produced in a double distillation process from the juice of *pinot noir, chardonnay* and *pinot meunier* grapes grown on the chalky soil of France's 62,000 acres of champagne fields. Each French champagne house maintains its own characteristic taste by blending several vintages into non-vintage champagne. Vintage champagne, made from a single exceptional year, is far more expensive. The distillation process, perfected in the seventeenth century, is fully documented in **Epernay's Musée de Champagne**. However, more fun is to tour the champagne cellars themselves, and almost all the houses offer tours. Among the most popular, **Moët &**

Chandon (the world's largest producer of champagne) attracts some 160,000 visitors each year to its 28 kilometres (17 miles) of subterranean vaults in Epernay. Alternatively, try the attractive cellars of Pommery & Greno (*see* **picture and caption**). Both houses offer tours all the year round, but be sure to ring in advance for exact times and availability of English-speaking guides. Wear your woollies: champagne vaults are cold and clammy. Information numbers for several other major champagne manufacturers are listed below.

Musée de Champagne
13 avenue de Champagne, 51205 Epernay (26.51.90.31). **Open** 10am-noon, 2-6pm, Mon-Sat; 10am-noon, 2-5pm, Sun. **Admission** 6.40F adults; 3.20F under-18s.

Moët & Chandon
20 avenue de Champagne, 51205 Epernay (26.54.71.11). **Open** 9.30am-12.30pm, 2-5.30pm, Mon-Fri. **Admission** free.

Pommery & Greno
5 place Général Gouraud, 51100 Reims (26.05.71.61). **Open** in 1989, 9-11am, 2-5pm, Mon-Fri; 10-11.30am, 2-4.30pm, Sat, Sun; due to change for 1990, phone for details. **Admission** free.

Reims (population 182,000) is worth a visit even from a teetotaller's point of view. The magnificent thirteenth-century cathedral of **Nôtre Dame** – with its winsome 'smiling angel' sculpture – is one of the most beautiful in France, despite heavy shelling in World War I that necessitated extensive renovation. In fact, the Champagne region has often been the scene of bloodshed: Attila's horde of Huns was decimated near Reims in AD451; the Hundred Years War was largely fought in this area and the World War I bombings levelled 80 per cent of the town. Other structures of architectural interest in Reims include the **Basilique Saint-Rémi** and the twentieth-century **Foujita**

Chapel, which is conveniently located across the street from the **Mumm** Champagne headquaters.

Champagne Houses
The following are all based in **Reims**. Ring in advance for visiting times.

Mumm *(26.40.46.13)*
Veuve Clicquot *(26.40.25.42)*
Piper-Heidsieck *(26.85.01.94)*
Louis Roederer *(26.40.42.11)*
Krug *(26.88.24.24)*

MORE INFORMATION
Getting there
From Paris to Reims by car: take the **A4** autoroute leaving from the Porte de Bercy (150km/95 miles). *Epernay* is 26km (16 miles) south of Reims via **D51**. *By train to Reims*: from the Gare de l'Est; the trip is approximately one and a half hours.

Tourist Information Centres
Epernay: *7 avenue de Champagne (26.55.33.00)*. **Open** *mid Oct-mid April*: 9.30am-12.30pm, 1.30-5.30pm, Mon-Sat; *mid April-mid Oct*: 9.30am-6.30pm Mon-Sat; noon-5pm Sun.
Reims: *2 rue Guillaume-de-Machault, 51100 Reims (26.47.25.69)*. **Open** *Oct-mid June*: 9.30am-6.30pm daily; *mid June-Sept*: 9am-7.30pm daily.

Eating and Drinking
Of course you know what you're going to drink and this area is blessed with more than its share of fancy restaurants to wash it down in. If money is no problem, by all means make a pilgrimage to **Reims**'s *haute cuisine* Mecca, Gérard Boyer's restaurant at *Château des Crayeres, 64 boulevard Henri Vanier (26.82.80.80)* which is located in an imposing Second Empire château on the south-east fringe of town. Also in Reims, the *Assiette Champenoise, 40 avenue Paul Vaillant-Couturier (26.04.15.56)* just east of the city limits; the *Florence, 43 boulevard Foch (26.47.12.70)*, and *Le Chardonnay, 184 avenue d'Epernay (26.06.08.60)* have one Michelin star each. Advance reservations are necessary at all the above. The décor (a champagne mini-museum) and the 120 entries on the champagne list make *Le Vigneron, place Paul Jamot (26.47.00.71)* especially popular. Dining possibilities in **Epernay** are far more modest, but the *Royal Champagne, Bellevue*, in Champillon *(26.52.87.11)*, 6km (4 miles) north of town, has a Michelin star, a small hotel, and an attractive garden.

Where to stay
Of the above, *Les Crayeres (rooms 980F-1530F)* with its three-star kitchen and private tennis courts, is the most elegant solution, but the *Assiette Champenoise (rooms 450F)* and the *Royal Champagne (rooms 600F-900F)* are also delightful places to sleep off last night's *brut*. Otherwise, we'd recommend heading back to Paris after a great lunch, a tour of the cathedral and a champagne tour. If you don't wish to take the last train back to Paris and want to spend a few days cheaply, the Reims Tourist Office (*see above*) can arrange less expensive accommodation given five days' notice.

The exceptionally attractive **Pommery & Greno** *cellars in Reims (listed under* **Champagne***), which were fitted into Gallo-Roman chalk mines, are decorated with art nouveau bas-reliefs and Emile Gallé sculptures. If you're thinking of visiting these vaults, wear warm clothing; it can get cold and clammy.*

Further Afield

Stay away from the typical tourist locations and head for the green hills of the Basque country or the wind-swept beaches of Northern Brittany.

NORTHERN BRITTANY

Wide, sandy beaches, azure water, and fabulous fresh seafood characterize Northern Brittany, which is an afternoon's train ride away from Paris. Don't expect to find Druid stone circles or indecipherable Breton signposts. Despite the fact that Saint Malo takes its name from the sixth-century Welsh missionary Saint MacCloud, this scenic section of the Breton coast is curiously devoid of Celtic memorials. It's the seventeenth-century corsairs, whose daring pirate raids wreaked havoc on British merchant shipping, that are famous here.

Saint Malo (population 47,000) is the largest of the towns and sheer paradise for Errol Flynn fanatics. Surrounded by the Atlantic on four sides, the old city (*intra muros*) is the archetypal pirate fortress with massive stone walls and crenellated look-out towers. Although most of it has been restored – it was heavily damaged by Allied bombs in World War II – the swashbuckling charm has survived. Appease the kids right away with the dayglo plastic buckle-on swords that are sold at the town's ubiquitous souvenir stands. There are two small forts (local hero, Chateaubriand, is buried in one of them) that can be waded out to at low tide. There are also guided tours of the Saint Malo château and fortress, a waxwork museum, and a city museum.

Dinan (population 14,000) is a picturesque medieval town 29 kilometres (18 miles) south of Saint Malo. It makes up for its lack of beaches by its near-endless photo opportunities. In summer, the thirteenth to fourteenth-century ramparts that ring this hilly town are perfumed with lushly-cultivated roses and wisteria. Both the fourteenth-century château (now an archaeological and ethnographic museum) and the Saint Sauveur basilica (a happy mélange of Romanesque, flamboyant Gothic and Renaissance architecture) merit visits. As an artistic haven for small craftsmen, Dinan also offers significant attractions for shoppers. The seventeenth-century *rue de Jerzeul* (often painted by Corot) is particularly noteworthy for leather, jewellery and woodworking ateliers and provincial antique shops.

Dinard (population 10,000), a ten-minute ferry-ride from Saint Malo, is a somewhat faded *belle époque* resort dominated by a casino and the ultra-glamorous Villa Hotel Reine Hortense. Hortense – who was Napoleon III's mother – crammed her three-storey beach cottage with every sort of Victorian knick-knack possible, and most of them have been preserved by the present hotel owners. One suite even has Hortense's columned silver bath-tub.

The seaside town of **Cancale**, 34 kilometres (21 miles) from Dinan and 5 kilometres (3 miles) from Saint Malo, is famous chiefly for its magnificent oyster beds and the romantic two-Michelin-star restaurant run by Olivier Roellinger called *De Bricourt (99.89.64.76)*. This is the most expensive gourmet venue in the area and advance reservations are absolutely necessary.

MORE INFORMATION

Getting there
From Paris to Saint Malo by car: **A11** to Rennes then **N137** (400km/250 miles). *By train:* from Gare Montparnasse, change at Rennes; the journey takes approximately four and a half hours.

Tourist Information Centres
Saint Malo: *esplanade Saint Vincent, 35400 Saint Malo (99.56.64.48)*. **Open** Sept-June: 9am-noon, 2-6.30pm, Mon-Sat; *July, Aug:* 8.30am-8pm Mon-Sat; 10am-6.30pm Sun.
Dinan: *6 rue Horloge, 22100 Dinan (96.39.75.40)*. **Open** Oct-March: 9am-12.30pm, 2-6.30pm, Mon-Fri; 9am-12.30pm, 2-7.30pm, Sat; 10am-7.30pm Sun; *April-Sept:* 9am-1pm, 2-7pm, daily.
Dinard: *2 boulevard Féart, 35800 Dinard (99.46.94.12)*. **Open** Oct-June: 10am-noon, 2-6pm, Mon-Sat; *June, Sept:* 9.30am-12.30pm, 2-7pm, daily; *July, Aug:* 9.30am-7.30pm daily.

Cancale: *44 rue du Port, 35260 Cancale (99.89.63.72)*. **Open** Sept-June: 8.30am-12.30pm, 2-6pm, Tue-Sat; *July, Aug:* 8.30am-8.30pm daily.

Eating and Drinking
Dining in Brittany won't cost you an arm and a leg. Inexpensive local specialities include crêpes and fizzy, slightly alcoholic cider, available in countless informal eating places. Alternatively, look for the many 50F-100F *prix fixe* restaurants where you can dine royally on huge platters of mussels in cream sauce washed down with inexpensive Muscadet. Sweet treats include custardy Breton 'far' pastry and tiny marzipan 'pommes de terre'. In **Saint Malo**, the *Duchesse Anne (99.40.85.33)* is the most famous restaurant. Built right into the ramparts, it boasts an outdoor patio, one Michelin star, and (relative to Paris) quite moderate prices. Although the best Breton custard desserts in **Dinan** are served at the one-Michelin-star *La Caravelle, 14 place du Clos (96.39.00.11)*, try one of the many small harbour-side bistros, which have more atmosphere, for a taste of the same pudding.

Where to stay
In **Saint Malo**, the seventeen-room *Hotel Elizabeth, 2 rue des Cordiers (99.56.24.98, rooms 275F-402F)* and the *Central, 6 Grande Rue (99.40.87.70, rooms 270F-480F)* are the finest hotels located within the old city walls. The recently-redecorated *Univers, place Chateaubriand (99.40.89.52, rooms 180F-280F)* is good for budget-conscious holiday-makers. The *Mercure, 2 rue Joseph Loth (99.56.84.84, rooms 340F-460F)*, a large chain-hotel just outside the walls, has a ramp entry and rooms with wheelchair access. The *Brocéliande, 43 chaussée du Sillon (99.56.86.60, rooms 200F-330F)* is a moderately-priced guesthouse on the beach east of the town. Handsome private gardens make **Dinan's** *D'Avaugour, 1 place du Champs Clos (96.39.07.49, rooms 260F-360F)* a good bet, but avoid rooms overlooking the noisy place du Champs Clos. In **Dinard**, the *Emeraude Plage, 1 boulevard Albert Ier (99.46.15.79, rooms 160F-420F)* is a budget-priced hotel with its own share of charm.

MONT SAINT MICHEL

The Mont Saint Michel is a long train ride from Paris (*see below* **More Information**), but only 52 kilometres (32 miles) from Saint Malo (*see above*). During the summer, this remarkable Benedictine abbey, perched on a granite rock and surrounded by a sea of quicksand, is filled with tourists. In the winter, it is almost deserted, a ghost town with only one or two cafés and restaurants open on a rotating basis. But if you can bear the piercing winds, the Mont Saint Michel is at its most romantic without crowds or noise.

Saint Michel first appeared on the Mount in AD708 and asked

Saint Malo (*listed under* **Northern Brittany***) makes a good base from which to tour the area. Its harbour is the take-off point for the ferry service to Mont Saint Michel, Cap Frehel and Jersey. Shorter boat trips are also possible down the Rance waterway to the popular resorts of Dinan and Dinard.*

Aubert, Bishop of Avranches, to build him a chapel. No trace of this first building remains. The earliest parts of the current structure date from AD996, and successive layers of architecture culminate in the austere Gothic chapel, simply called the *Merveille* (marvel). In the eighteenth century, the Mont Saint Michel became a prison. It was not until 1874 that the abbey was officially made a National Monument. In order to keep track of the overlapping historical and architectural layers, arm yourself with a good map. Inside the abbey itself, all visits are accompanied by a guide.

MORE INFORMATION

Getting there
From Paris to Mont Saint Michel by car. **A11** to Rennes then **N175** to Pontorson then **D976** (400km/250 miles). *By train:* TGV (high-speed train) from Gare Montparnasse to Rennes (2 hours) and change for Pontorson/Mont Saint Michel (1hour); then bus or taxi (9km/6 miles).

Tourist Information Centre
March-October: *Cours de Garde des Bourgeois, 50100 Mont Saint Michel* (33.60.14.30).

Open 9am-12.30pm, 2-6pm, daily. November-February, written enquiries only: *BP4, 50116 Mont Saint Michel.*

Mont Saint Michel Abbey
(33.60.14.14). **Open** *mid May-mid Sept:* 9.30am-6pm daily; *mid Sept-mid Nov, mid Feb-mid May:* 9.30-11.45am, 1.45-5pm, daily; *mid Nov-mid Feb:* 9.30-11.45am, 1.45-4.15pm, daily. **Admission** 25F adults; 5F under-18s.

Eating and Drinking
Mont Saint Michel's claim to gastronomic fame are the huge, soufflé-like omelettes served at *Mère Poulard* (33.60.14.01), which also owns the less expensive *Restaurant Terrasses Poulard* (33.60.14.09). Both are on the Mont's main street.

Where to stay
Both of the above restaurants have small hotels: The *Mère Poulard* (rooms 450F-750F) has 27 rooms, while the *Hotel Terrasses Poulard* (rooms 200F-750F) has 29.

THE BASQUE COUNTRY

In a Europe of open borders and internationalization, Basques continue to make a fuss about being an independent nation. When you hear a Basque talk about this small

region – you can cross the French Basque land in about two hours by car – it's with a tremolo in his voice. It's part of the Basque phenomenon, which is indeed a unique one.

Some historians say that the Basques are descended from northern invaders. Others maintain that they are the lost tribe of the ancient city of Atlantis. But most historians agree that the Basques are simply one of those races that have always been there, resisting any kind of invasion or influence, like the Berbers in North Africa. What is bizarre is the fact that Basques have an unusual blood-group. Doctors Eyquem and Saint-Paul of the Pasteur Institute in Paris discovered that 60 per cent of Basques had O blood-grouping and 27 to 35 per cent were Rhesus negative. This led them to conclude that the Basques 'represent the pure descendants of the people who occupied Europe in Palaeolithic times and, throughout the continent, were crossed with Asian invaders'. Whatever the correct theory, the six Basque Regions — Alava, Guipuzcoa and Vizcaya in Spain and La Soule, Le Labourd and Basse-Navarre in France — form one region with a common history, language and culture that are completely different from those surrounding them.

Unlike the Basques in Spain who nurture their language to the point of obsession, the French Basques are more relaxed regarding the whole question of language and identity. This is largely due to the fact that France has been successfully centralized since the Revolution, so people on the whole identify with Paris, far more than their Spanish compatriots do with Madrid. Consequently, French is spoken throughout the region, and in some parts, Basque also. But if you're hoping to pick up a word or two while in the area, beware. Legend has it that when the Devil set out to corrupt the Basques, he realized that he would have to learn their language. After seven years, he was no nearer to pronouncing *akelare* (the witches' sabbath) than he had been at the outset of his mission. Irate and disheartened, he jumped into the river at the base of the Pyrenees, never to be seen again.

GETTING STARTED
The best way to get to know this civilization is to start in the northern-

most Basque city of **Bayonne**. Built on the spot where the Nive and Adour Rivers empty into the ocean, this city is seen as a symbolic marriage of the two cultures, French and Basque. The Nive trickles down from the sheep-covered Pyrenees and the Adour flows in from the lower lands of French Gascony to meet in this town. But even that's not clear as Gascony was once inhabited by the Basques – the name derives from the original Basque word for Gascons, *vasco* – before becoming part of the Duchy of Aquitaine. What's more, at the court of Aquitaine in Poitiers, one of the local delicacies was *chèvre* (goat) cheese, now a local speciality said to have been brought there by the Saracen armies in the eighth century. These advancing armies, which were stopped in Poitiers in the year 732, consisted mostly of Basque mercenaries who settled in that region.

THE SEASIDE TOWNS

Even though **Bayonne** is a big city, it's nevertheless a pleasant place to explore. Walk up the *rue du Port-Castets* lined with arcades that were once slips for boats when this street was a canal. From there you can head toward the **Gothic cathedral**. Around the church, in one of the narrow streets is the first shop in Europe to have sold chocolate. A Jewish Bayonnais is responsible for having brought the continent one of its favourite *gourmandises*. In Bayonne the stoic, eighteenth-century, neo-classical architecture, that's so typically French, stands next to the squat, white Basque houses that have the original owner's name carved above the door. Below many of these houses are elegant vaulted cellars used for stocking goods — Bayonne has always been a trading centre. In some restaurants and boutiques you can see these rooms; one has even been turned into a night-club. If you have the time, spend a few hours at the Musée Basque, which is near the bridge over the Nive. It is currently closed for refurbishment, but is due to reopen in 1991. This extraordinary museum has a collection of all-things-Basque, including flags, regional costumes, furniture, displays on the national sport pelota and sections devoted to the local composer Ravel and native writer Pierre Loti.

To get to the nearby, legendary city of **Biarritz**, you'll have to go through the **Forêt de Chiberta**, which is by the town of **Anglet**. These two towns, with the addition of Bayonne, make up the beautiful municipal centre sometimes called *BAB* (Bayonne-Anglet-Biarritz). The rolling pine forest is speckled with holiday homes and golf courses – it's home to the Ladies' Biarritz Open and the Biarritz Cup – and is bordered by a golden, sandy beach. This is the best place for swimming in the BAB region.

Just up the coast is **Biarritz**. Go there in summer and you'll end up walking through overcrowded streets lined with souvenir shops full of screaming kids with melting ice-cream.. Is this the jewel in the Basque crown? Is this the summer hide-away town of Edward VII, and Napoleon and Eugénie? Democracy has left its marks. If you don't own one of the stunning turn-of-the-century villas or a luxury apartment in one of the old palaces, Biarritz is more a nightmare than a dream. It's true that the countryside is breathtaking: here and there are tiny beaches and gardens full of flowers; the city itself is completely integrated into a grey cliff along a wide, semi-circular bay. But for the most part, Biarritz is to be avoided during peak season.

When in town, take in the stunning casino, the ex-Imperial palace and the Russian church, all of which are interspersed with some interesting modern architecture. If you're into the Parisians-in-bathing-costumes-and-Vuarnet-sunglasses atmosphere, then this is the ideal place for luxury shopping, art gallery browsing, night-clubbing and so on, all served up with a kind of *faux* snobby air.

As you leave Biarritz, heading for the 'other side' — Basques never refer to France or Spain — you will notice a high, black mountain dominating the coast. Straddling the Franco-Spanish border, this symbol of the Basque country is called **La Rhune**. Many a Basque fisherman will sing odes to La Rhune in his strange, native tongue as he slowly returns to shore. A cog-wheel electric train travels to the summit of this mountain, leaving from the picturesque town of **Ascaïn** (phone 59.54.20.26 for details).

Along the coast are the towns of **Guéthary** and **Bidart**, both small,

*The tiny island of **Mont Saint Michel** was first built on by the Church in the eighth century. Then, every stone had to be brought by boat and lifted by pulley. The island is now linked to the mainland by a causeway; beaches on either side of it are submerged at high tide, when the incoming sea can reach speeds of 15 miles per hour.*

orderly and quite quaint. Here the beaches are mostly of pebble and therefore not exactly comfortable. But further on is the truly beautiful town of **Saint-Jean-de-Luz** (about 15 kilometres/9 miles from Biarritz) with a sandy beach among other things.

This city, which is starting to resemble Disneyland thanks to the massive crowds, fortunately is not entirely dependent on tourism. Here fishermen haul in their catch and repair their nets on the docks of the old port. The pedestrian streets are lined with shops that sell ordinary goods, and not the depressing array of souvenirs and post cards. One of the most delightful 'old buildings' is the town church. Saint-Jean-Baptiste is built completely in the Basque style and therefore has wooden balconies around the nave, that are for the exclusive use of men. Mass is said in Basque. In the centre of the nave is an intricate model boat, suspended from the ceiling above the parishioners' heads. It was in this very church, a year after the Franco-Spanish peace treaty of 1659, that Louis XIV, the 22-year-old future Sun King, married the *Infanta* Maria-Teresa of Spain.

TOWARDS THE PYRENEES

Leave the coast and take one of the many winding roads up into the green foothills to see what Basque culture is all about. Once the touristy façade has been scraped away and you get down to the bare bones of a small village, you understand the importance of the house, the family, the church and the pelota court. Add to these elements a great sense of self-preservation and a tinge of machismo and you've got the Basque mentality in a nutshell.

Towns like **Sare**, **Aïnhoa**, and **Ascaïn** are small, impeccably clean, quite rural and overflowing with atmosphere. If you want to see them at their most patriotic, make sure you visit them during the annual festivals, which are held in June, August and September. To find out the exact dates of these festivities, give the local *mairie* a call, and they'll be able to tell you when the jollities kick off. Outside these towns are head-spinning walks in the green hills where today you can still

Some people declare an unconditional love for **Biarritz** *(listed under* **The Basque Country***) and it's true that, on a warm September evening after the crowds have left, it's quite heavenly to take a late afternoon dip, to climb out of the ocean and have a* pastis *and eat some* tapas, *to go back to your hotel to change and then have a seafood dinner in an intimate restaurant.*

see eagles and wild boar. An interesting detour is a visit to the village of **Zugarramurdi** over the border, which is famous for its witches. During the Spanish Inquisition, most of these temptresses were burned to death. Today you can tour the caves where the witches are reputed to have carried out pagan rituals; the festival commemorating the religious fight between the Basques and the Catholic Castillians takes place in June every year.

In the town of **Cambo-les-Bains**, an extremely well-equipped modern spa has been built in a lovely garden setting. Parts of the interior date back to the sumptuous art deco period, when this town became popular for 'taking the waters'. During your stay, you may want to visit the **Musée Arnaga**, the house French playwright Edmond Rostand had built at the end of the nineteenth century. The picturesque house and manicured, formal gardens with a view over the Nive River valley are well worth the trip. Further inland, the gateway to the Pyrenees is the ever-popular town of **Saint-Jean-Pied-de-Port**, famous for the pil-

grims that travel the road across Europe to Santiago de Compostela in western Spain.

MORE INFORMATION

Getting there
From Paris to Biarritz by car: **A10** all the way (750km/465 miles). *By train:* from Gare d'Austerlitz; trip takes about six hours by day, about nine hours by night train. *By plane:* Air Inter have three flights daily.

Tourist Information Centres
Agence Touristique du Pays Basque *BP 247, 64108 Bayonne Cedex (59.59.28.77)*. Letter or telephone enquiries only.
Biarritz: *Office de Tourisme, 'Javalquinto', square d'Ixelles, 64200 Biarritz (59.24.20.24)*. **Open** *mid Sept-mid June*: 9am-12.30pm, 2.15-6.15pm, Mon-Fri; 9am-12.30pm, 5-6pm, Sat; *mid June-mid Sept*: 9am-7.30pm Mon-Sat; 10am-12.30pm Sun.
Bayonne: *Office de Tourisme, place de la Liberté, 64100 Bayonne (59.59.31.31)*. **Open** *mid Sept-June*: 9am-7pm Mon-Fri; *July-mid Sept*: 9am-7pm Mon-Sat; 10am-5pm Sun.

Where to stay
In the centre of **Biarritz** hotels abound, but they are generally expensive and lacking in character. The Tourist Office can supply a full list of hotels and flats in the area. **Inland** try the two-star *Hôtel des Touristes (59.28.61.01, rooms 180F-280F)* a real country inn in the town of **Licq-Athérey**, lost in the Pyrenees.

Survival

The art of survival is an acquired skill in any language and finding a plumber, dentist or all-night garage abroad can prove a crisis in itself. Whether you want to send a Fax or need a vet, we point you in the right direction.

COMMUNICATIONS

TELEPHONES
The minimum fee for a call within Paris is 1F, which allows you to talk for six minutes. A blinking signal indicates it's time to insert another coin. Most cafés have coin phones, but these are generally reserved for customers. Post offices usually have both coin and card phones.

PHONECARDS
As there are fewer and fewer coin phones in Paris, be sure to buy a phonecard (*télé-carte*). These are available at *tabacs* (tobacconists) and post offices. Calls are priced at 80 centimes per unit, and cards are available for 40F and 96F. The phone's digital display gives instructions when the card is inserted and says how much credit is left. Don't forget to remove the card after the call; it's quite common to find cards people have left behind.

DIALLING
From inside Paris
All Paris phone numbers have eight digits; central Paris numbers begin with a 4; suburban numbers might begin with a 3 or a 6.

Out of town
If you're dialling **from Paris to another part of France**, dial 16, wait for the low-pitched, steady tone, then dial the eight-digit number which begins with the area code.
   If you're dialling **from the provinces to Paris**, dial 16, wait for the tone, then dial 1, then the eight-digit Paris number.
   If you're dialling **from province to province**, simply dial your correspondent's eight-digit number.

International calls
Dial 19, wait for the low-pitched, steady tone; then dial the country code, followed by the area code (omitting the 0 for UK codes), and finally your correspondent's number.

International dialling codes
Australia: 61
Canada: 1
Ireland: 353
New Zealand: 64
United Kingdom: 44
United States: 1

If you haven't got your correspondent's country code or area code, or if you have any problems getting your call through, contact the operator (*see below* **Telephone services**).

CHARGES
Charges depend on the distance and duration of the call. Calls within Paris cost 1F for approximately six minutes, standard rate. Within Metropolitan France, calls outside a 100km (60 miles) radius are charged at the same long-distance rate regardless of distance; so a phone call to a French location 120km (75 miles) away will cost the same as one to a spot 350km (217 miles) away. Calls to the UK cost 4.50F standard rate, calls to the US 10F per minute.

Reduced rates
Reduced rates to the UK and Ireland apply from 9.30pm to 8am Monday to Friday; from 2pm Saturday and all day Sunday and public holidays. Cost: 3F per minute.

Reduced rates to the US and Canada: the cheapest rates apply from 2am to noon Monday to Friday; cost 5.70F per minute. Another cheap rate (7.20F per minute) applies from noon to 2pm, and again from 8pm to 2am, Monday to Saturday; from noon to 2am Sunday and public holidays.

TELEPHONE SERVICES
Operator assistance, French directory enquiries (24 hours daily) dial 12.

International directory enquiries (24 hours daily) dial 19.33.12, followed by the country code (if you haven't got the country code, ask operator on 12).

Engineers (24 hours daily) if your phone is out of order, dial 13.

Telegram (24 hours daily) in English dial 42.33.21.11; telegrams in any other language, dial 42.33.44.11.

Time (24 hours daily) dial 36.99.

Alarm calls (24 hours daily) dial 36.88. A recording will ask you to dial your telephone number, then the time you wish. The system uses a 24-hour clock, so you dial four digits. For example, to be woken at 8.30am dial 0830; to be woken at 2.45pm dial 1445.

Weather for specific enquiries on weather around the world, dial 45.56.71.71 (3-6pm Mon-Fri); for a recorded weather announcement for Paris and region, dial 36.65.02.02 (24 hours daily); for recorded information on weather throughout France, dial 64.09.01.01 (24 hours daily).

News international news (French recorded message, 24 hours daily) dial 36.65.44.55.

Traffic news (24 hours daily) dial 48.99.33.33.

PHONE BOOKS
Phone books are found in all post offices and in most cafés (ask the bartender if you don't see them by the phone). The White Pages (three volumes) list names of people and businesses alphabetically. The Yellow Pages (two volumes) list businesses under category headings.

POST OFFICES
Post offices (*bureaux de poste*) are open from 8am to 7pm Monday to Friday; 9am to noon Saturday. All are listed in the phone book: under 'Administration des PTT' in the Yellow Pages; under 'Poste' in the White Pages.

Main post office
52 rue du Louvre, 75001 Paris (40.28.20.00). Metro Louvre, Les Halles. **Open** 24 hours daily for Poste Restante, telephones and telegrams. The best place to get your mail sent to if you haven't got a fixed address in Paris. Mail should be addressed to you in block capitals, followed by Poste Restante, then the post office's address.

Extended hours
71 avenue des Champs Elysées, 75008 Paris (43.59.55.18). Metro George V. **Open** 8am-10pm Mon-Sat; 2-8pm Sun.

POSTCODES
Letters will arrive sooner if they feature the correct five-digit postcode.

Within Paris: postcodes always begin with '750'; if your address is in the 1st *arrondissement*, the postcode is 75001; in the 15th the code is 75015.

Throughout France: postcode information 42.80.67.89. If you've got an address, they've got the postcode for it.

STAMPS & STATIONERY
Get stamps from any post office or in any *tabac* café or shop. Most *tabacs* also sell post cards, though the choice is limited. You'll find more unusual cards around the Pompidou Centre and in the Latin Quarter (especially rue Saint André des Arts). Writing paper and envelopes are sold in *papeteries* (stationers) but can also be found in most supermarkets, and usually at a much lower price.

MINITEL
The Minitel is a small computer screen and keyboard, connected to the telephone line, which allows access to many different services: electronic directory enquiries, airline and train schedule information and ticket reservations, theatre information, and so on. You'll find Minitel terminals in most post offices. Charge is usually about 1F per minute, but they do vary.

Minitel directory in English punch 36.14 on the keyboard, wait for the beep, press 'Connection', then type 'ED'.

FAX & TELEX
Faxing facilities are available at the main post office (*see above* **Post Office**), at most modern hotels and in Telex agencies (listed in the Yellow Pages under 'Telex'.

HEALTH

All EEC nationals staying in France are entitled to take advantage of the French Social Security system, which generally refunds 70 per cent of medical expenses. Other nationals should make sure they take out insurance before leaving home.

The French Social Security system is complex and involves tedious bureaucratic procedures. British nationals should obtain form E111 before leaving the UK (or form E112 for those already in treatment), as this is a prerequisite for any refund you will apply for in France.

If you do get ill while in France, the doctor will give you a prescription and a *feuille de soins* (statement of treatment). At the pharmacy, the medication will feature *vignettes* (little stickers) which you must stick onto your *feuille de soins*. Send this, along with your prescription and form E111, to your local Caisse Primaire d'Assurance Maladie (listed in the phone book under 'Sécurité Sociale' in both the White and Yellow Pages). Refunds can take a month or two to come through. Be sure to make a photocopy of all your receipts, just in case.

EMERGENCIES

The following services are open 24 hours daily.

Ambulance (SAMU) *(45.67.50.50)*.

Fire department *(18)*.
Fire or no fire, they'll be on the spot in record time.

Doctors (SOS Médecins)
(47.07.77.77/43.37.77.77).
House calls only. Charges start at 150F.

Dentists (Urgences Dentaires)
(47.07.44.44).
House calls for the elderly or the handicapped. In other cases, phone (any time, day or night) for an appointment and go see them at *9 boulevard Saint Marcel, 750013 Paris. Metro Saint Marcel*.

Nurses (SOS Infirmiers) *(48.87.77.77)*.
House calls only. For a live-in nurse, charges start at 1,600F per day.

Psychiatrists (Urgences Psychiatres)
(43.29.20.20).
Charges for house calls start at 400F.

HOSPITALS

For a complete list of hospitals in and around Paris, consult the phone book (white pages) under 'Hôpital Assistance Publique', or ring their headquarters, 40.27.30.00. All hospitals have an emergency ward open 24 hours daily. The following is a list of hospitals specializing in particular injuries or fields.

Burns: Hopital Saint Antoine
184 rue du Faubourg Saint Antoine, 75012 Paris (43.44.33.33). Metro Faidherbe-Chaligny.

Most public phone boxes now only accept phonecards (see **Communications***). Those that still accept coins take 20 centimes, 50 centimes, 1F, 5F and sometimes 10F coins. Beware: the machine only returns coins which haven't been used, which means you will not get change of a 5F coin if the call has only cost 1F.*

Children: Hôpital Necker
149 rue de Sèvres, 75015 Paris (42.73.80.00). Metro Duroc.

Dog bites: Institut Pasteur
211 rue de Vaugirard, 75015 Paris (45.67.35.09). Metro Pasteur.

Drugs: Hôpital Marmottan
19 rue d'Armaillé, 75017 Paris (45.74.00.04). Metro Argentine.

The American Hospital in Paris
63 boulevard Victor Hugo, 92202 Neuilly (47.47.53.00). Metro Porte Maillot.
Open 24 hours daily.
This is a private hospital. The French Social Security refunds only a small percentage of treatment costs.

PHARMACIES

There are hundreds of pharmacies throughout Paris and you can spot them from afar by a green neon cross outside the shop door. Pharmacies have a monopoly on issuing medication, and even on certain brands of deodorant, shampoo and skin-care lotion. Ordinary items such as tooth-brushes, disposable razors and the like are usually much cheaper in supermarkets. Most pharmacies are open from 9am or 10am to 7pm or 8pm, sometimes with a break for lunch. Staff can provide basic medical attention (for a small fee) and will indicate the nearest doctor on duty. Below we list late-opening pharmacies, in order of *arrondissement*.

4th arrondissement: Cariglioli
10 boulevard Sébastopol, 75004 Paris (42.72.03.23). Metro Châtelet.
Open 9am-midnight Mon-Sat.

8th arrondissement: Dhéry
84 avenue des Champs-Elysées, 75008 Paris (45.62.02.41). Metro Georges-V.
Open 24 hours daily.

Matignon
2 rue Jean Mermoz, 75008 Paris (43.59.86.55). Metro Franklin D Roosevelt. **Open** 8.30am-2am Mon-Sat; 10am-2am Sun.

9th arrondissement: Caillaud
6 boulevard des Capucines, 75009 Paris (42.65.88.29). Metro Opéra. **Open** 8am-1am Mon-Sat; 8pm-1am Sun.

11th arrondissement: La Nation
13 place Nation, 75011 Paris (43.73.24.03). Metro Nation. **Open** 8am-midnight Mon-Sat; 8pm-midnight Sun.

Relax, you're never very far from a toilet! The streets are crowded with automatic toilets, which cost 1F and play classical music for your money's worth. Many metro stations also have paying toilets. Or you can always walk into any café and head for the (usually free) toilets, which are generally at the back, or downstairs in the bigger cafés.

13th arrondissement: Pharmacie d'Italie
61 avenue d'Italie, 75013 Paris (43.31.19.72). Metro Tolbiac. **Open** 8am-midnight Mon-Sat; 8pm-midnight Sun.

DOCTORS & DENTISTS
You'll find the complete list of practitioners in the Yellow Pages, under 'Médecins Qualifiés'. In order to get a Social Security refund, make sure you choose a doctor or dentist registered with the National Health; look for 'Médecin Conventionné' after the name.

Centre Médical Europe
44 rue d'Amsterdam, 75009 Paris (42.81.93.33/dentists 48.74.45.55). Metro Liège. **Open** 8am-7pm Mon-Fri; 8am-6pm Sat. Here you'll find practitioners in all fields under one roof, charging minimal consultation fees (85F-125F). Appointment advisable but not required.

ALTERNATIVE MEDICINE
ACUPUNCTURE
Association Française d'Acuponcture
1bis Cité des Fleurs, 75017 Paris (42.29.63.63). Metro Brochart. **Open** 9am-6pm Mon-Fri. Phone for information or an appointment with a qualified acupuncturist.

Syndicat National des Médecins Acuponcteurs de France
60 boulevard Latour-Maubourg, 75007 Paris. Send a stamped, self-addressed envelope for a list of recognized acupuncturists.

HOMOEOPATHY
Most pharmacies (*see above*) provide homoeopathic medicine. Practitioners are listed in the Yellow Pages under 'Médecine Spécialisée, orientation homéophathie'.

Académie d'Homéopathie et de Médecines Douces
2 rue d'Isly, 75008 Paris (43.87.60.33). Metro St Lazare. **Open** 9am-6pm Mon-Fri. Phone for an appointment.

Centre d'Homéopathie de Paris
81 rue de Lille, 75007 Paris (45.55.12.15). Metro Champs Elysées-Clémenceau. **Open** 8.30am-6.30pm Mon-Fri; 8.30am-noon Sat. Phone for an appointment.

SEX, CONTRACEPTION, ABORTION
The one family planning centre is open to Paris residents only. Non-residents will need to make an appointment with a gynaecologist (listed in the Yellow Pages under 'Médecine Spécialisée: Gynécologie'), who will advise on methods of contraception suited to your needs. If you are pregnant, the gynaecologist will make an appointment at a hospital for you, where you will see a counsellor to discuss abortion or maternity.

SEXUALLY TRANSMITTED DISEASES
Institut Vernes
36 rue d'Assas, 75006 Paris (45.44.38.94). Metro Rennes. **Open** 8.30am-noon, 1.30-4.30pm, Mon-Fri; 8.30am-noon Sat. Free consultations for all venereal diseases except HIV/AIDS. As appointments are not taken, there's usually a long queue.

HIV/AIDS (SIDA)
There are four centres, all offering free and anonymous testing.

Centre Médico-Social
218 rue de Belleville, 75020 Paris (47.97.40.49). Metro Télégraphe. **Open** 5-8pm Mon-Fri; 9am-12.30pm Sat.

Centre SIDAG
3 rue de Ridder, 75014 Paris (45.43.83.78). Metro Plaisance. **Open** noon-7.30pm Mon-Fri; 9am-12.30pm Sat.

Service de Médecine Interne du Docteur Collin
Hopital Lariboisière, 2 rue Ambroise Paré, 75010 Paris (49.95.65.65). Metro Gare du Nord. **Open** 8.30am-noon Mon-Sat.

Service de Médecine Interne du Docteur Emerit
Hopital Pitié Salpêtrière, 47 boulevard de l'Hopital, 75013Paris (45.70.21.72). Metro Saint Marcel. **Open** 8am-5pm Mon-Fri; 9am-noon Sat.

AIDS Hotline (SIDA AP)
(45.82.93.39). **Open** 9am-5pm Mon-Fri; 9am-noon Sat. Free information and advice.

HELP & ADVICE

ADMINISTRATIVE
CIRA (Centre Interministeriel de Renseignements Administratifs)
(43.46.13.46). **Open** 9am-12.30pm, 2-5.30pm, Mon-Fri. This service answers all enquiries concerning French administrative procedures, or directs you to the competent authorities.

FISCAL
Town Halls: If you need help understanding tax legislation, *mairies* run a weekly fiscal information and advice service. Sessions are from 2pm to 4pm Tuesday for the 1st to the 10th arrondissements; from 2pm to 4pm Friday for the 11th to the 20th arrondissements. A full list of *mairies* can be found in the telephone book under 'Mairies'.

LEGAL
Avocat Assistance et Recours du Consommateur
15 place du Pont Neuf, 75001 Paris (43.54.32.04). Metro Pont Neuf. **Open** 2-6pm Mon-Fri. Here you'll find lawyers charging minimal fees: 150F for a consultation, 800F for a procedure.

Palais de Justice

Galerie de Harlay, Escalier S, 4 boulevard du Palais, 75004 Paris (46.34.12.34). Metro Cité. **Open** 9.30am-noon Mon-Fri.
Free legal consultations. Come early to pick up a numbered ticket.

SOS Avocats

(43.29.33.00). **Open** 7.30-11.30pm Mon-Fri.
Free legal advice over the telephone.

Town Halls also answer legal enquiries (free service). Phone for details and times; ask for 'Consultations juridiques'. *Mairies* are listed by arrondissement in the phone book, under 'Mairies'.

LODGING
Sous-direction du Logement

50 rue de Turbigo, 75003 Paris (42.74.21.21). Metro Arts et Métiers. **Open** 9am-5pm Mon-Thur; 9am-4.30pm Fri.
Free information on financial assistance, housing exchange, legislation on rents and so on.

SVP Logement

(42.71.31.31). **Open** 9am-5pm Mon-Thur; 9am-4.30pm Fri.
Free telephone advice and information service on housing benefits, rent legislation and other housing matters.

WOMEN
Maison des Femmes

8 Cité Prost, 75011 Paris (43.48.24.91). Metro Faidherbe-Chaligny. **Open** varies, phone for details.
Maison des Femmes organizes exhibitions, concerts, workshops, debates and self-defence classes. Will give details of the various feminist cultural organizations, as well as rape crisis/battered women's associations.

Flora Tristan Organisation

142 avenue Verdun, 92320 Chatillon (47.36.96.48). Metro Porte d'Orleans then bus 195. **Open** (office) 8am-7pm Mon-Fri.
Refuge centre for battered women.

HELP LINES

ALCOHOLICS
Alcoholics Anonymous in English

(46.34.59.65).
The 24-hour recorded message gives schedules of the AA meetings (take place at the American Church, 65 quai d'Orsay, 75007) and a list of members' telephone numbers for additional information.

CRISIS COUNSELLING
SOS Help

(47.23.80.80). **Open** 3-11pm daily.
English-language crisis hotline.

SOS Dépression

(42.22.20.00/45.44.04.05). **Open** 24 hours daily.
Here people not only listen but give advice and can even send a counsellor or psychiatrist to your home.

RACISM
SOS Racisme

64 rue de la Folie-Méricourt, 75011 Paris (48.06.40.00). Metro Oberkampf. **Open** 10am-7pm daily.
A non-profit making association defending the rights of ethnic minorities.

SEXUAL MINORITIES
SOS Homosexualité

(46.27.49.36). **Open** 10am-midnight daily.
Legal, medical and psychological assistance for all sexual minorities: gays, lesbians, transexuals, sado-masochists, paedophiles. Multi-lingual staff.

USEFUL NUMBERS

GAS & ELECTRICITY

Electricity in France runs on 220V. Visitors whose appliances run on 240V (such as British appliances) can simply change the plug or use a converter (available at most hardware shops); those whose appliances run on 120V (such as American ones) need to use a transformer, available from specialist hardware shops or department stores such as the BHV (*see chapter* **Shopping**).

Gas and electricity are supplied by the state-owned **EDF-GDF** (Electricité de France-Gaz de France). They are the ones to contact for queries concerning bills, or in case of black-outs or gas problems in the building. However, they are of no assistance in case of trouble in your flat, when you'll have to phone a plumber or electrician (*see below* **Emergency Repairs**). During the day it's best to phone a local repair service, which you'll find in the Yellow Pages under 'Plombiers' or 'Electricité'. If the problem's with a boiler, contact the manufacturing company.

EDF-GDF

(43.87.59.99). **Open** 8.30am-4pm Mon-Fri.
Contact for information on supply, bills and power failures or gas leaks in buildings.

EMERGENCY REPAIRS

There are many 24-hour emergency repair services dealing with plumbing, electricity, heating, locks, car repairs, carpentry and much more. They usually charge a minimum of 50F call-out charge and 100F per hour's labour, plus parts. Below we list the most reputable:

Allo Assistance Dépannage *(42.55.59.59).*
All Dépannage Express *(42.50.91.91).*
All Dépann '24 *(free phone 05.13.68.18).*
SOS Dépannage *(47.07.99.99):* the most publicized but also the most expensive of the lot.

LOCKSMITHS

For a local locksmith, look in the Yellow Pages under 'Serruriers'. If you're locked out in the middle of the night, *see above* **Emergency Repairs**.

TRAVEL

DISCOUNT AIR TRAVEL

The following reputable agencies specialize in discount charter flights. Phone them for details of current prices.

Don't count on the staff at the municipal lost property office (listed under **General Information/Lost Property**) *to find that bunch of keys you left on the café table. Once you've convinced them of your claim, you'll have to sift through the lot.*

Access Voyages
*6 rue Pierre Lescot, 75001 Paris
(40.13.02.02). Metro Châtelet.* **Open** 9am-7pm Mon-Fri. **Credit** AmEx, DC, MC, V.

Forum Voyages
*55 avenue Franklin Roosevelt, 75008 Paris
(42.89.07.07). Metro Franklin D Roosevelt.* **Open** 10am-7pm Mon-Fri; 10am-6pm Sat. **Credit** MC, V.

Nouvelles Frontières
many branches throughout Paris. Phone 42.73.10.64 for details of the one nearest you. **Open** 8.30am-8pm Mon-Sat. **Credit** MC, V.

Go Voyages
*98bis boulevard Latour-Maubourg, 75007
Paris (47.53.05.05). Metro Ecole
Militaire/22 rue Arcade, 75008 Paris
(42.66.18.18) Metro Madeleine.* **Open** 9am-6pm Mon-Fri; 10am-5pm Sat. **Credit** MC, V.

USIT
*12 rue Vivienne, 75002 Paris (42.96.15.88).
Metro Bourse.* **Open** 9.30am-6.30pm Mon-Fri. **No credit cards.**

TRAIN
For full details on travelling by train within France, *see chapter* **Trips Out of Paris**; below we list agencies that deal in discount train travel within France and Europe.

Transalpino
*137 rue de Rennes, 75006 Paris
(45.48.67.56). Metro Saint Placide.* **Open** 9.30am-6pm Tue-Sat.
Credit (over 300F only) MC, V.

Wasteels
*3 rue des Mathurins, 75009 Paris
(47.42.35.29). Metro Opéra.* **Open** 9am-6pm Mon-Fri; 9am-noon Sat. **Credit** MC, V.
This company specializes in reduced-price train and plane tickets for the under-26s.

COACH
L'Autobus
*4bis rue Saint Sauveur, 75002 Paris
(42.33.86.72). Metro Réaumur-Sébastopol.*
Open 9am-6.30pm Mon-Sat.
No credit cards.

Eurolines
*3 avenue Porte de la Villette, 75019 Paris
(40.38.93.93). Metro Porte de la Villette.*
Open information: 7am-11pm daily; tickets: 9am-8pm daily. **Credit** MC, V.

USIT
*12 rue Vivienne, 75002 Paris (42.96.15.88).
Metro Bourse.* **Open** 9.30am-6.30pm Mon-Fri. **No credit cards.**

HITCH-HIKING
As in all big cities, drivers are not used to seeing hitch-hikers in Paris and are not likely to pick them up. Should you be desperate enough to try it though, follow the obvious rules of safety: avoid hitching alone, don't get in the back of a two-door car, and so on. If you're planning a trip out of town, set yourself at the start of the highway by the RER or metro stop, or contact:

Allô Stop
*84 passage Brady, 75010 Paris (42.46.00.66;
from outside Paris 47.70.02.01). Metro
Strasbourg-Saint Denis.* **Open** 9am-7pm Mon-Fri; 9am-1pm, 2-6pm, Sat.
This organization matches hitchers and drivers for a reasonable introduction fee (20F-60F for a journey of less than 500km/310 miles) and petrol contribution (16 centimes per km).

MOTORCYCLE HIRE
Mondial Scooter Location
*20bis avenue Charles de Gaulle, 92200
Neuilly sur Seine (46.24.63.64). Metro Les
Sablons.* **Open** 9am-12.30pm, 1.30-6pm, Mon-Fri. **Rates** (scooters only) 150F-230F per day plus deposit; 840F-1,200F per week plus deposit. **Credit** MC, V.

Scoot'heure
*6 rue d'Arras, 75005 Paris (43.25.69.25).
Metro Cardinal Lemoine.* **Open** 9am-7pm Mon-Fri. **Rates** (scooters only) 135F-230F per day plus deposit; 850F-1,300F per week plus deposit; 280F-500F per weekend plus deposit. **Credit** MC, V.

Wills
*84 avenue de Versailles, 75016 Paris
(42.88.40.04). Metro Mirabeau.* **Open** 8.30am-7pm Mon-Sat. **Rates** *scooters*: from 200F per day, from 980F per week, plus deposit; *motorbikes*: from 800F per day, from 4,500F per week, plus deposit.
Credit AmEx, DC, MC, V.

CAR HIRE
Driving in Paris is absolutely unnecessary. If you don't lose your mind – and your way – in the traffic jams, you'll definitely go mad trying to find a parking space. For trips out of Paris, though, there is no better way to get around than driving. We list below some reputable car hire agencies. Most have branches throughout Paris; phone the numbers listed below for details of the one nearest you and rates. Expect to pay between 220F and 400F per day; between 2,000F and 3,000F per week, plus mileage and insurance. Most companies offer some sort of weekend deal.

Avis *5 rue Bixio, 75007 Paris (45.50.32.31).*
Credit AmEx, DC, MC, V.

Europcar *48 rue de Berri, 75008 Paris
(45.63.04.27/Reservations 30.43.82.82).*
Credit AmEx, DC, MC, V.

Hertz *92 rue St Lazare, 75009 Paris
(42.80.35.45).* **Credit** AmEx, DC, MC. V.

Inter Rent *42 avenue Saxe, 75007 Paris
(43.06.32.49).* **Credit** AmEx, DC, MC, V.

Thrifty *20 rue de la Folie Méricourt, 75011
Paris (43.55.13.00).* **Credit** MC, V.

Valem *41 boulevard Richard Lenoir, 75011
Paris (43.55.81.83).* **Credit** MC, V.

PARKING
There are very few free parking areas left in Paris, and those are usually always full when you do find them. If you park illegally (pedestrian crossing, loading zone, bus lane and so on), you risk getting your car clamped or

towed away (*see below*). Parking meters have been replaced by 'Eurodateurs', usually one for each block. Insert your coins (4F to 6F per hour, or more near train stations) and the machine will produce a ticket which must be displayed inside the windshield.
If you've come to Paris by car, it might be a good idea to park on the outskirts of the city and then use public transport, which is very efficient (*see chapter* **Travelling Around Paris**). The following car parks by the various main entrances into Paris are located near metro stations:

North
Porte de Saint Ouen *avenue de la Porte de
Saint Ouen, 75017 Paris (42.29.31.96).*
Open 24 hours daily; 10F per 24 hours.
Porte de Clignancourt *30 avenue de la Porte
de Clignancourt, 75018 Paris (42.64.03.82).*
Open 24 hours daily; 36F per 24 hours Tue-Fri; 50F per 24 hours Mon, Sat, Sun.

East
Porte de Banolet *rue Jean Jaurès (in front
of Hotel Ibis), Bagnolet (43.61.92.41).* Open 24 hours daily; 10F per 24 hours.

South
Porte d'Italie *176 avenue de la Porte
d'Italie, 75013 Paris (45.89.09.77).* Open 7am-8pm Mon-Sat; 30F per 24 hours.

West
Porte Maillot *place de la Porte Maillot,
75017 Paris (47.57.29.99).* Open 24 hours daily; 69F per 24 hours.

24-HOUR PARKING
If you must drive into Paris, you may need to use a car park. Michelin map No.11 includes underground car parks, symbolized by the international 'P' sign, which cost from 6F to 12F per hour. You can also get parking information by phoning 43.46.98.30 (9am-5pm Mon-Fri). The following, listed in order of *arrondissement*, are all open 24 hours:

1st: Parking Pont-Neuf *place Dauphine
(46.33.97.48)*; 10F per hour; 70F 24 hours. **Parking
des Pyramides** *opposite 15 rue des Pyramides
(42.60.53.21)*; 9F per hour; 70F 24 hours.

4th: Berri Washington *5 rue de Berri
(near the Champs-Elysées) (45.61.01.18)*;
10F per hour; 100F 24 hours.

9th: Chauchat-Drouot *12 rue Chauchat
(42.46.03.17))*; 10F per hour; 105F 24 hours.

12th: Paris-Gare de Lyon *193 rue de Bercy
(40.04.61.26)*; 9F per hour; 86F 24 hours.

15th: Tour Montparnasse *17 rue de
l'Arrivée/10 rue du départ (45.38.68.00)*;
10F per hour; 110F 24 hours.

18th: Place de Clichy/Montmartre *9 rue
de Caulaincourt (43.87.64.50)*; 9F per hour;
85F 24 hours.

CLAMPS & CAR POUNDS
If you've had the misfortune of getting your car clamped, contact the local police station (*see above* **Useful Numbers**). There are six car pounds in Paris, each covering several *arrondissements*. You'll have to pay a 450F removal fee plus 21F storage charge per day;

*A home away from home for lonely British visitors, the **British Council Library** (listed under **General Information/Libraries**) is also a good place to meet French students brushing up on English literature. Tea and toast is available from the British Institute café in the same building.*

add to that a parking fine ranging from 230F to 900F (for parking in a bus lane) and you'll regret you ever used your car.

1st, 2nd, 3rd, 4th, 8th, 9th: *Parking Saint Eustache, Forum des Halles, place Carrée entrance, level -5, 75001 Paris (42.21.44.63). Metro Les Halles.* **Open** 8am-8pm Mon-Sat.

5th, 12th, 13th: *18 boulevard Poniatowsky, 75012 Paris (43.46.69.38). Metro Porte de Charenton.* **Open** 6.30am-8.30pm Mon-Sat.

6th, 7th, 14th: *33 rue du Commandant Mouchotte, 75014 Paris (43.20.65.24). Metro Montparnasse-Bienvenue.* **Open** 8am-8.30pm Mon-Sat.

8th, 16th: *8 avenue Foch, underground parking level -2, 75016 Paris (45.01.80.13). Metro Charles de Gaulle-Etoile.* **Open** 8am-8.30pm Mon-Sat.

10th, 11th, 19th, 20th: *15 rue de la Marseillaise, 75019 Paris (42.00.76.99). Metro Porte de Pantin.* **Open** 6.30am-8.30pm Mon-Sat.

15th, 16th, 17th, 18th: *8 rue de Bois Leprêtre, 75017 Paris (42.63.37.58). Metro Porte de Saint Ouen.* **Open** 6.30am-7.45pm Mon-Sat.

24-HOUR PETROL

8th: *corner of avenue des Champs-Elysées and avenue Georges V.*
10th: *1 boulevard de la Chapelle.*
12th: *55 quai de la Rapée.*
13th: *2 place du Docteur Yersin.*
14th: *avenue de la Porte de Chatillon.*
17th: *31 boulevard Gouvion Saint-Cyr; 6*
avenue de la Porte de Clichy.
18th: *avenue de la Porte de Saint Ouen.*
20th: *217 boulevard Davout.*

CAR BREAKDOWN

Whether your car or motorcycle has broken down in the middle of the road or just makes worrying noises, the following garages offer 24-hour assistance:

Aleveque Daniel
116 rue de la Convention, 75015 Paris (48.28.12.00/42.50.48.49). **Credit** AmEx, MC, V.

Alfauto
69bis rue Briançon, 75015 Paris (45.31.61.18/48.56.29.38). **No credit cards.**

Aligre Dépannage
92 boulevard de Charonne, 75020 Paris (49.78.87.50). **No credit cards.**

Allô Bernard
92 rue Cartier Bresson, 93500 Pantin (48.34.24.34). **Credit** MC, V.

Assist-Auto
10 rue René Villerme, 75011 Paris (43.38.44.08). **No credit cards** but cash in any currency accepted.

EMBASSIES

When going to an embassy or consulate, it's advisable to phone and check opening hours; you may also need to make an appointment.

All are closed on French public holidays and those of their own country. We list below all the main European and other embassies and consulates; you will find a full list in the phone book (both the White and Yellow Pages) under 'Ambassades et Consulats'.

American Embassy
2 avenue Gabriel, 75008 Paris (42.96.12.02). Metro Champs Elysées-Clémenceau. **Open** 9am-5pm Mon-Fri. **Visa section** *2 rue Saint Florentin, 75001 (42.61.80.75). Metro Concorde.* **Open** 9am-noon Mon-Fri. **Tourist information** *(42.60.57.15).* **Open** 1-5pm Mon-Fri.

Australian Embassy
4 rue Jean Rey, 75015 Paris (40.59.33.00). Metro Bir Hakeim. **Open** 9.15am-1pm. **Visa section** *(40.59.33.07).* **Open** 9.15am-12.15pm Mon-Fri.

Austrian Consulate
12 rue Edmond Valentin, 75007 Paris (47.05.27.17). Metro Ecole Militaire. **Open** 9am-noon Mon-Fri.

Belgian Embassy
9 rue de Tilsitt, 75017 Paris (43.80.61.00). Metro Charles de Gaulle-Etoile. **Open** phone for details. **Visa section** *1 avenue MacMahon, 75017 Paris (42.27.45.35). Metro Charles de Gaulle-Etoile.* **Open** phone for details.

British Embassy
35 rue du Faubourg Saint Honoré, 75008 Paris (42.66.91.42). Metro Concorde. **Open** 9.30am-1pm, 2.30-6pm, Mon-Fri. **Consulate** *122 avenue des Champs-Elysées, 75008 Paris (43.59.52.20). Metro George V.* **Open** 10am-1pm, 2-4pm, Mon-Fri. **Visa section open** 10am-1pm Mon-Fri. *See also chapter **Study & Business**.*

Canadian Embassy
35 avenue Montaigne, 75008 Paris (47.23.01.01). Metro Franklin D Roosevelt. **Open** 9am-noon, 2-5pm, Mon-Fri. **Visa section** *(47.23.52.20).* **Open** 9-10am Mon, Tue, Thur, Fri.

Chinese Embassy
1 rue de Bassano, 75016 Paris (47.23.38.21). Metro George V. **Open** by appointment only. **Consulate** *9 avenue Victor Cresson, Issy les Moulineaux (47.36.77.90). Metro Maire d'Issy,* **visa section open** 9am-noon Mon-Fri.

Danish Embassy
77 avenue Marceau, 75016 Paris (47.23.54.20). Metro Alma Marceau. **Open** 9am-1pm, 2.30-5pm, Mon-Fri. **Visa section open** 9am-12.30pm Mon-Fri.

German Embassy
13 avenue Franklin D Roosevelt, 75008 Paris (42.99.78.00). Metro Franklin D Roosevelt. **Open** 9am-1pm, 2.30-5pm, Mon-Fri. **Consulate** *34 avenue d'Iéna, 75016 Paris (42.99.79.57). Metro Iéna.* **Open** 9am-noon Mon-Fri.

Greek Embassy
17 rue August Vacquerie, 75016 Paris (47.23.72.28). Metro Kléber. **Open** 9am-4.30pm Mon-Fri. **Consulate** *23 rue Galilée, 75016 Paris (47.20.40.64). Metro Boissière.* **Open** 9.30am-noon Mon-Fri.

Irish Embassy
4 rue Rude, 75016 Paris (45.00.20.87).
Metro Charles de Gaulle-Etoile.
Open 9.30am-noon Mon-Fri.

Italian Embassy
47 rue de Varenne, 75007 Paris
(45.44.38.90). Metro Varenne. **Open** 10am-
1pm, 2.30-5pm, Mon-Fri. **Consulate** *17 rue*
Conseiller Collignon, 75016 Paris
(45.20.78.22). Metro Muette.
Open 9am-noon Mon-Fri.

Japanese Embassy
7 avenue Hoche, 75008 Paris (47.66.02.22).
Metro Charles de Gaulle-Etoile.
Open 9.30am-noon Mon-Fri.

Luxembourg Embassy
33 avenue Rapp, 75007 Paris (45.55.13.37).
Metro Alma-Marceau.
Open 9am-noon Mon-Fri.

Netherlands Embassy
7 rue Eblé, 75007 Paris (43.06.61.88).
Metro Duroc. **Open** 9am-6pm Mon-Fri.
Consulate *9 rue Eblé (same phone number*
as embassy). Metro Duroc.
Open 9.30am-3pm Mon-Fri.

Norwegian Embassy
28 rue Bayard, 75008 Paris (47.23.72.78).
Metro Franklin D Roosevelt.
Open 9am-noon Mon-Fri.

Portuguese Embassy
187 rue Chevaleret, 75013 Paris
(45.85.03.60). Metro Chevaleret. **Open** 9am-
10.30am, 1-3.30pm, Mon-Fri.

Soviet Embassy
40 boulevard Lannes, 75016 Paris
(45.04.05.50). Metro Porte Dauphine. **Open**
9am-1pm, 2.30-7pm, Mon-Fri. **Visa section**
8 rue de Prony, 75017 Paris (47.63.45.47).
Metro Monceau.
Open 9am-noon Mon, Tue, Thur, Fri.

Spanish Embassy
13 avenue George V, 75008 Paris
(47.23.61.83). Metro Alma Marceau. **Open**
9am-1pm, 2-6pm, Mon-Fri. **Consulate** *165*
boulevard Malesherbes, 75017 Paris
(47.66.03.32). Metro Malesherbes.
Open 10am-noon Mon-Fri.

Swedish Embassy
17 rue Barbet de Jouy, 75007 Paris
(45.55.92.15). Metro Varenne.
Open 9am-1pm, 2.30-5pm, Mon-Fri.

Swiss Embassy
142 rue de Grenelle, 75007 Paris
(45.50.34.46). Metro Latour-Maubourg.
Open 9am-1pm Mon-Fri.

HYGIENE

Public Baths are mainly situated in the
more working class, north-east area of Paris.
Municipal baths are open from Thursday to
Sunday only: noon-7pm Thursday; 8am-7pm
Friday; 7am-7pm Saturday; and 8am-noon
Sunday. A shower costs 4.60F, and you'll be

charged extra for soap and towel. You'll find
a complete list of public baths in the phone
book under *Bains municipaux.* Listed below
are a few of the more central ones:

8 rue des Deux Ponts, 75004 Paris
(43.54.47.40). Metro Pont Marie.

18 rue du Renard, 75004 Paris
(42.77.71.90). Metro Hotel de Ville.
This establishment has recently been
entirely renovated, and is open noon to 7pm
Wednesdays, as well as the standard times
mentioned above.

188 rue Charenton, 75012 Paris
(43076487). Metro Bastille.

50 rue Lacepide, 75005 Paris (45.35.46.63).
Metro Monge.

2 rue Fillette, 75018 Paris (46076001)
Metro Marx Dormoy, Porte de la Chapelle.
A municipal pool with public showers. Opening
times are subject to change, especially during
school holidays, so phone to check.

DISABLED

The tourist office (*see chapter* **Essential
Information**) produces a free pamphlet,
Touristes Quand Même, giving details of facilities for the disabled at major tourist attractions. For further information, help and
advice, contact:

Comité National pour la Réadaptation des Handicapés
38 boulevard Raspail, 75007 Paris
(45.48.90.13). Metro Sèvres Babylone.
Open 9am-noon, 2pm-6pm, Mon-Fri.
This association gives out information
and advice for the handicapped, from
health and social provisions to social
clubs and travel facilities. Phone for an
appointment.

Airhop
7bis avenue de la République, 75010 Paris
(40.24.34.76). Metro République.
Open 9am-4pm Mon-Fri.
Arranges transportation for the disabled.
Charges within Paris average between 16F
and 40F; to Orly Airport 160F; to
Roissy/Charles de Gaulle Airport 220F.
Group discounts are available.

LOST PROPERTY
Bureau des Objets Trouvés
36 rue des Morillons, 75015 (45.31.14.80).
Metro Convention.
Open 8.30am-5pm Mon-Fri.
See **picture and caption.**

LIBRARIES
American Library
10 rue Général Camou, 75007 Paris
(45.51.46.82). Metro Alma Marceau. **Open**
2-7pm Tue, Thur, Fri; 10am-7pm Wed, Sat.

Bibliotheque Publique d'Information
Beaubourg Centre, entrance via rue du
Renard, 75004 Paris (42.77.12.33). Metro
Rambuteau. **Open** noon-10pm Mon-Fri;
10am-10pm Sat, Sun.

Paris's mega-library, with an average of
11,000 visitors per day. Extensive English-
language section.

British Council Library
9-11 rue de Constantine, 75007 Paris
(45.55.95.95). Metro Invalides.
Open 11am-6pm Mon-Fri.
See **picture and caption.**

Documentation Française
31 quai Voltaire, 75007 (40.15.70.00).
Metro Rue du Bac/bus 68, 69, 83. **Open**
10am-6pm Mon-Wed, Fri; 10am-1pm Thur.
This is the French government's central reference library. Here, you will find almost any
subject you wish to research documented in
detail. You'll need ID and must pay a small fee.

RELIGION

Churches and religious centres are
listed in the phone book (Yellow
Pages) under 'Eglises' and 'Culte'.

CIDR
8 rue Massillon, 75004 Paris
(46.33.01.01). Metro Cité.
Open 9.30am-noon, 2-6.30pm, Mon-Fri.
This information centre, although dealing
mostly with Christianity, can help put you in
touch with religious centres of every faith.

ANGLICAN
American Cathedral
23 avenue George V, 75008 Paris (47.20.17.92).
Metro George V. **Open** 9am-12.30pm, 2-5.30pm,
Mon-Fri; 9am-noon Sat; 9am-1pm Sun.
Services 9am, 11am (choir), Sun.

Saint George's English Church
7 rue Auguste Vacquerie, 75016 Paris
(47.20.22.51). Metro Etoile. **Open** 9am-11pm
daily. **Services** 8.30am, 10.30am (choir), Sun.
One of the best choirs of Paris.

Saint Michael's Church of England
5 rue d'Agusseau, 75008 Paris (47.42.70.88).
Metro Madeleine. **Open** 9.30am-12.30pm, 2-
5.30pm, Mon, Tue, Thur-Sun. **Services**
12.45pm Thur; 10.30am, 6.30pm, Sun.

BUDDHIST
Centre Buddhiste de Kagyu Dzong
40 routhe Circulaire du Lac Daumesmil,
75012 Paris (43.41.86.48). Metro Porte
Dorée. **Open** phone for details.

Institut National de Buddhisme
20 cité Moynet, 75012 Paris (43.40.91.61).
Metro Reuilly Diderot. **Open** phone for details.

CATHOLIC
Basilique du Sacré Coeur
35 rue du Chevalier de la Barre, 75018 Paris
(42.51.17.02). Metro Anvers. **Open** 7am-
11pm daily. **Services** 7am, 8am, 9am, 10am,
11am, 6.30pm (6pm Sat), 10.15pm Mon-Sat;
7am, 8am, 9am, 9.45am, 11am (sung mass),

11.30am, 12.30pm, 6pm, 10.15pm, Sun.
See chapter **Sightseeing** for more information.

Cathédrale de Nôtre Dame de Paris
place du Parvis Nôtre Dame, 75004 Paris (43.26.07.39). Metro Cité. **Open** 8am-7pm daily. **Services** 8am, 9am, noon, 6.10pm (6.30pm Sat), Mon-Sat; 8am, 8.45am, 10am (sung mass), 11.30am, 12.30pm, 6.30pm, Sun. **Concert** (free) 5.45pm Sun.
See chapters **Sightseeing; Middle Ages & Renaissance** for more information.

Saint Etienne du Mont
place Sainte Genevieve, 75005 Paris (43.54.11.79). Metro Cardinal Lemoine. **Open** phone for details.
Saint Étienne shelters the only remaining rood-loft in Paris. Beautifully ornamented seventeenth-century organ.

Saint Eustache
place du Jour, 75001 Paris (42.36.31.05). Metro Les Halles. **Open** 8.30am-7pm daily. **Services** 10am, 6pm, Mon-Sat; 8.30am, 9.45am, 11am, 6pm, Sun.
One of the most beautiful churches in Paris. Concerts are given, phone for details.

Saint Germain des Prés
3 place Saint Germain des Prés, 75006 Paris (43.25.41.71). Metro Saint Germain des Prés. **Open** 7.45am-7.45pm daily. **Services** 8am, 12.15pm, 7pm, Mon-Sat; 9am, 10am, 11am, 5pm (Spanish), 7pm, Sun.
Ancient Benedictine abbey in the heart of the students' quarter. Concerts are given; phone for details.

Saint Louis des Invalides
2 rue de Tourville, 75007 Paris (45.55.92.30). Metro Varenne. **Open** 10am-6pm (5pm Oct-March), daily; closed public holidays. **Services** 6.30pm Sat; 9.30am, 11am (sung mass), Sun.
Also called the 'soldiers' church'. Sober architecture decorated with old flags taken from the enemy. Beautiful seventeenth-century organ. Concerts are given; phone for details.

Saint Médard
141 rue Mouffetard, 75005 paris (43.36.14.92). Metro Censier-Daubenton. **Open** 9am-12.30pm, 2.30-7.30pm, Tue-Sun. **Services** noon, 7pm, Tue-Sat; 8.30am, 10am, 11.15am, 6pm, Sun.
Interesting paintings and a remarkable sixteenth-century triptych. In the early eighteenth century, miraculous healings were said to have been performed in the cemetery, until they were forbidden by Louis XV in 1732. Harpsichord concerts are given; phone for details.

Saint Merri
76 rue de la Verrerie, 75004 Paris (42.74.42.96). Metro Hôtel de Ville. **Open** 9am-9pm daily. **Services** 12.10pm Mon-Fri; 12.10pm, 6.30pm, Sat; 10am Sun.
Beautiful woodwork, sixteenth-century stained glass windows and a seventeenth-century organ chest. The fourteenth-century bell is probably the oldest one in Paris. Concerts are given; phone for details.

Saint Pierre de Montmartre
2 rue du Mont-Cenis, 75018 (46.06.57.63). Metro Abbesses. **Open** 8.30am-7pm daily. **Services** 8.45am, 5pm (Fri only), 7pm (except Fri), Mon-Fri; 8.45am, 6pm, Sat;

Built on the site of a sun temple – a metal band in the floor indicates where the mid-day sun falls at solstices and equinoxes – **Saint Sulpice** *(listed under* **Religion/Catholic***) has been much altered over the centuries. Mural paintings by Delacroix and the biggest organ in France can be seen here.*

9.30am, 11am (sung mass), Sun.
One of the oldest churches in Paris (twelfth century).

Saint Roch
296 rue Saint Honoré, 75001 Paris (42.60.81.69). Metro Pyramides. **Open** 8am-7.15pm daily. **Services** 11am, 12.15pm, 6.45pm, Mon-Fri; 11am, 6.30pm, Sat; 8.30am, 9.30am (in Latin), 11.45am, noon, 6.30pm, Sun.
This is the artists' (particularly musicians) church of Paris. The Sunday noon mass is held in their honour. Concerts are given; phone for details.

Saint Sulpice
place Saint Sulpice, 75006 Paris (46.33.21.78). Metro Saint Sulpice. **Open** 7.30am-7.30pm daily. **Services** 7am, 9am, 12.05pm, 6.45pm, Mon-Sat; 7am, 9am, 10.30am (sung mass), 12.05pm, 6.45pm, Sun.
See **picture and caption.**

CHRISTIAN SCIENTIST
First Christian Science Church Reading Room
36 boulevard Saint Jacques, 75014 Paris (47.07.26.60). Metro Saint Jacques. **Open** 12.30-6.30pm Mon-Sat; 3-6pm Sun.

JEWISH
Synagogue
15 rue Notre Dame de Nazareth, 75003 Paris (42.78.00.30). Metro République. **Open** phone for details.

Synagogue
44 rue de la Victoire, 75009 Paris (45.26.95.36). Metro Notre Dame de Lorette. **Open** phone for details.

MOSLEM
Grande Mosquée de Paris
Puits de l'Ermite, 75005 Paris (45.35.97.33). Metro Monge. **Open** for visits 9am-noon, 2-6pm, Mon-Thur, Sat, Sun. **Admission** 10F. **Service** Fri prayer 12.30pm (reserved to Moslems).

ORTHODOX
Saint Alexandre de la Néva (Russian Orthodox)
12 rue Daru, 75008 Paris (42.27.37.34). Metro Courcelles. **Open** 3-5pm Wed, Fri. **Services** 6pm Sat; 10.15am Sun.

Saint Etienne (Greek Orthodox)
7 rue Georges Bizet, 75016 Paris (47.20.82.35). Metro Alma Marceau. **Open** 8am-noon, 2.30-6.30pm, daily (Sat till 8pm). **Service** 9.45am Sun.

PROTESTANT
Amercian Church in Paris
65 quai d'Orsay, 75007 Paris (47.05.07.99). Metro Invalides. **Open** 9am-10.30pm Mon-Sat; 9am-8pm Sun. **Service** 11am Sun.

Church of Scotland
17 rue Bayard, 75008 Paris (47.20.90.49). Metro Franklin D Roosevelt. **Service** 10.30am Sun.

Swedish Church
9 rue Médéric, 75017 Paris (47.63.70.33). Metro Courcelles. **Open** 9am-10pm daily. **Service** 10.30am Sun.

WORKING IN PARIS

EEC nationals are entitled to live and work in France, the only formality being the *Carte de Séjour* (residency permit) if you want to stay longer than three months. All other nationalities will find it difficult to get a work permit. For information, contact:

Préfecture de Police (Police Headquarters)
7 boulevard du Palais, 75004 Paris (42.77.11.00, ext 5172). Metro Cité.
For information on residency and work permits. You will be directed to the appropriate service according to your nationality and status.

Don't fool yourself: finding employment in Paris is not easy. Consult the daily papers:

the *Figaro* has a free employment supplement on Monday (check the back pages of the second section for translations, teaching, waitressing and couriers jobs); the *International Herald Tribune* has a few more offers than usual on Thursday. The monthly English-language *Paris Passion* has a 'Jobs Offered' section in the classified pages. You should also check the notice boards at the British Council Library (*see above* **General Information**) and at the British and American churches (*see above* **Religion**).

Teaching English is an obvious solution, either through a language school (listed in the Yellow Pages under 'Enseignement Privé de Langues') or through private lessons by putting notices on bill-boards in schools, universities and local shops (laundromats, bakers and so on). You could also enquire in bars, restaurants and tea rooms, as such places are often on the look-out for waiters and dishwashers. Good luck.

ANIMALS

Bringing your dog with you on holiday to Paris is not a very good idea as there are few parks for it to romp freely in. But if you're planning a long stay and don't want to leave your pet behind, all you require to

pass French Customs is a medical certificate of good health from your vet, including up-to-date rabies vaccinations. Bear in mind you are subject to your own country's customs regulations on your return – six months' quarantine in the UK, anti-rabies certificate or no.

VETS

Assistance aux Animaux
90 rue Jean-Pierre Thimbaud, 75011 Paris (43.55.82.24). Metro Couronnes. **Open** 9am-noon, 1pm-6pm, Mon-Sat.
Check-ups, vaccinations, operations and castrations at a minimum charge. Phone for an appointment.

Dispensaire Populaire de Soins pour Animaux
8 rue Maître Albert, 75005 Paris (46.33.94.37) Metro Maubert Mutualité.
Open 9.30am-6.30pm Mon-Fri; 9am-11am Sat.
No vaccinations against rabies, but very small fees for check-ups and castrations. Phone for an appointment.

S.O.S. Vétérinaires
(47.54.18. 00). **Open** 24 hours daily.
A free referral service, giving details of local vets on duty.

Vétérinaires à domicile
(42.65.00.91). **Open** 24 hours daily.
If you're unable to transport your pet, these vets will come to your home (minimum charge 380F).

BOARDING

Pension A6
28 rue de Cherelles-Nonville, 77000 Nemours (64.29.01.26). Open 7am-9pm daily.
If you're planning a trip out of Paris and can't take your pet along, let it have a holiday as well, in this animal boarding house set in the middle of a huge park. Average prices: 35F per day for cats; 60F per day for dogs.

GROOMING

If your dog needs a trim or a new raincoat, treat it to an afternoon out at one of the following:

Au Chien Royal
109bis avenue Charles de Gaulle, 92000 Neuilly (46.24.17.37). Metro Sablons.
Open 9am-7pm Mon-Fri.
This shop has 40 years' experience in grooming.

Au Comfort du Chien
80 rue du Rendezvous, 75012 Paris (43.43.68.42). Metro Picpus.
Open 8.30am-noon, 2pm-7pm, Tue-Sat.
Specialists in grooming long-haired dogs.

LOST ANIMALS

If you've found an animal without identification, the best thing to do is take it to the nearest vet, where its owners will probably think of enquiring. If you have the time, inform local shopkeepers who will pass the word on. Likewise, if you have lost your pet, try the local vets or the **SPA** (Société Protectrice des Animaux) at *39 boulevard Berthier, 75017 Paris (43.80.40.66).*

The notice board at the American Church (listed under **Religion/Anglican***) is usually full of ads offering temporary or teaching work and rooms in exchange for work.*

Index

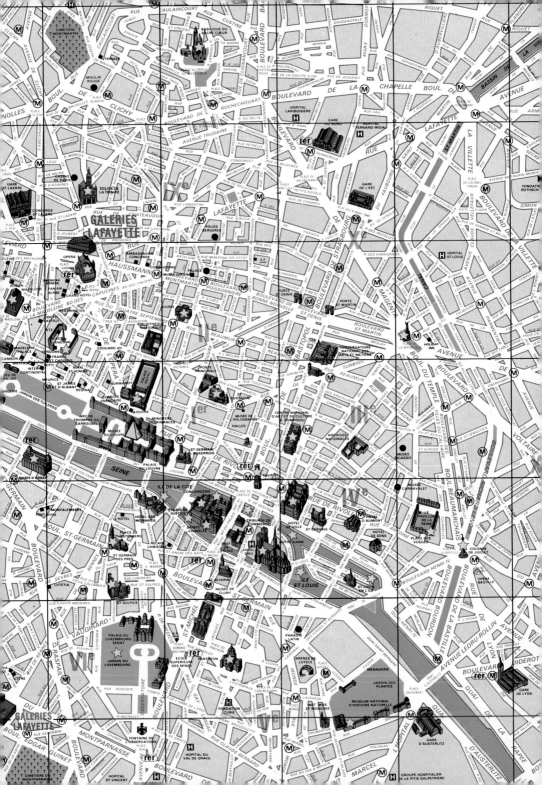

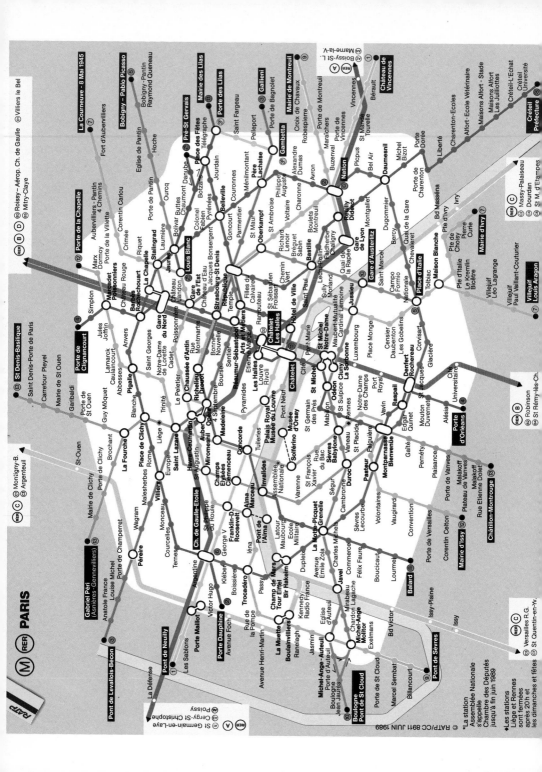

Written, edited and designed by Time Out
Publications Limited, Curtain House, 134-
146 Curtain Road, London EC2A 3AR
(071 729 5959/Fax 071 729 7266).

Editorial
Managing Editor Hayden Williams
Editor Katja Faber
Associate Editor Marion Moisy
Consultant Editor Robert Sarner
Assistant Editor Conor McCutcheon
Listings Editor Valerie Morris
Production Manager Su Small
Sub-Editor Caroline Taverne
Indexers Nick Rider, Edoardo Albert
Editorial Assistant Jo Berry
Listings Assistants Jo Reed, Amanda Isaac,
Simon Key

Design
Art Director Paul Carpenter
Art Editors Ashleigh Vinall, Annie Carpenter
Design Assistants Nancy Flint, Asim Syed,
David Pinto
Picture Editors Lynda Marshall,
Katherine Hoy

Advertising
Advertisement Sales co-ordinated by Time
Out Publications (London)
Sales Director Mark Phillips

In Paris
Advertisement Sales handled by Paris
Passion
Advertising Director André Goldstein
Ad Sales Nathalie Duran
Ad Assistant Isabelle Booth

Administration
Publisher Tony Elliott
Managing Director Adele Carmichael
Financial Director Kevin Ellis
Company Accountant Suzanne Doyle
Accounts Assistant Sonia Jackson

Cover Illustration Lo Cole

Features in this Guide were researched and written by:
Sightseeing Grant Palmer. Paris by Season Alice Brinton. Essential Information Celine Moisy. Travelling Around Paris Lucy Jones. Accommodation Corinne LaBalme. The Seine Alain Adijes. The Right Bank and The Left Bank Gail de Courcy-Ireland, Pierre-Georges Guille. Artistic Paris Gail de Courcy-Ireland. Village Paris Gail de Courcy-Ireland, Pierre-Georges Guille. Roman Paris Sheila Mooney. The Dark Ages Sheila Mooney. Middle Ages & Renaissance Sheila Mooney. Ancien Régime Sheila Mooney. The Revolution Sheila Mooney. Empires & Rebellions Sheila Mooney. The Third Republic Sheila Mooney. The War Alice Brinton. Post-War Paris Alice Brinton. De Gaulle to Mitterrand Alice Brinton. Paris Today Alice Brinton. A la Carte Paul Lyons. Restaurants Robert Noah. Bars Sheila Mooney. Cafés & Salons de Thé Sheila Mooney. Fashion Mary Gallagher. Food & Drink Shops Sheila Mooney. Specialist Shops Mary Gallagher. Services Mary Gallagher. Art Galleries and Museums Fiona Dunlop. Cabaret Babs Sutton. Children Babs Sutton. Dance Corinne LaBalme. Film Lisa Nesselson. Gay & Lesbian Joseph-Marie Hulewicz. Music: Classical & Opera Victoria Horbovetz. Music: Rock, Folk & Jazz Paul Wallfish. Nightlife Sophie de Santis. The Early Hours Sophie de Santis. Sport & Fitness Greg Rowe. Media: Newspapers & Magazines Alice Bidel. Media: TV Alice Bidel. Media: Radio Alice Bidel, Paul Wallfish. Theatre Victoria Horbovetz. Study & Business Gail de Courcy-Ireland. Trips Out of Town Corinne LaBalme, Greg Rowe. Survival Celine Moisy, Valerie Morris.

The Editors would like to thank the following people and organizations for help and information: The staff of Paris Passion, the staff of i-D magazine; also the Galeries Lafayette, and the RATP.

Picture credits: Sandra Allison/Susan Griggs Agency page 264; Elene Barrault/Musée Kwok On page 174; Patrick Bertrand/Bureau de Presse Carole Bracq page 262; C.L.Bricage/Maison de la Culture de Créteil page 191; John Bulmer/Susan Griggs Agency page 242; Willy Camden pages v, 1, 3, 4, 5, 6, 7, 9, 10, 11, 12, 13, 22, 24, 26, 27, 28, 29, 30, 37, 38, 41, 42, 43, 45, 47, 48, 49, 50, 51, 53, 54, 55, 57, 58, 59, 60, 61, 64, 65, 66, 67, 68, 69, 71, 72, 73, 75, 76, 77, 78, 80, 81, 82, 84, 85, 86, 88, 90, 91, 92, 94, 95, 96, 97, 99, 100, 102, 103, 105, 106, 107, 108, 109, 112, 114, 115, 116, 117, 119, 120, 121, 122, 123, 124, 125, 126, 128, 130, 131, 134, 135, 137, 138, 139, 141, 143, 144, 145, 146, 147, 148, 149, 151, 166, 167, 168, 169, 170, 171, 172, 173, 175, 176, 177, 180, 181, 182, 183, 185, 187, 188, 189, 190, 192, 194, 195, 196, 197, 199, 200, 201, 202, 204, 205, 207, 210, 212, 213, 215, 216, 218, 219, 221, 222, 224, 228, 232, 233, 234, 236, 237, 239, 241, 244, 268, 269, 270, 272, 274, 275; Cotton Coulson/Susan Griggs Agency page 265; Fiona Dunlop pages 104, 159, 161, 162; French Government Tourist Office pages 250, 251, 252, 259; Charles W Friend/Susan Griggs Agency page 266; Alison Harris pages 15, 17, 18, 19, 74, 246, 247, 248, 253, 256; Monique Jacot/Susan Griggs Agency page 257; Richard Laird/Susan Griggs Agency page 261; Barry Lewis/Network page 254; London Photo Library page 39; Christian Richard Photographies page 225; R de Seynes page 31; L Sylly-Jaulmes/Musée des arts décoratifs Paris page 165; P Terrasson page 211; Adam Woolfitt/Susan Griggs Agency pages 245, 255, 258.

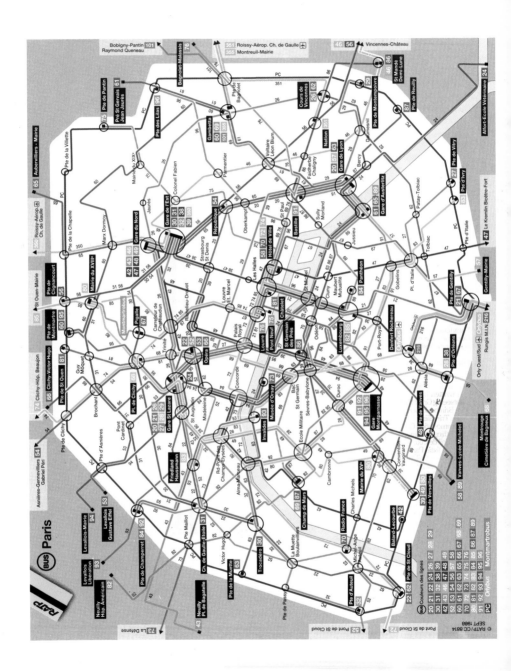

(bus) Paris

RATP

© RATP/CC 8814
SEPT 1966